A Dinner of Herbs

A Dinner of Herbs

a novel by
CATHERINE COOKSON

HEINEMANN : LONDON

William Heinemann Ltd
10 Upper Grosvenor Street, London WIX 9PA

LONDON MELBOURNE TORONTO
JOHANNESBURG AUCKLAND

First published 1985
© Catherine Cookson 1985

SBN 434 14257 3

Filmset in Monophoto Garamond by
Northumberland Press Ltd, Gateshead
Printed and bound in Great Britain by
Richard Clay (The Chaucer Press) Ltd,
Bungay, Suffolk

Better is a dinner of herbs
where love is, than a
stalled ox and hatred
therewith.

Proverbs XV.17

Contents

To Tommy Bates, whose Langley Dam inspired me to write this story, my warm thanks.

Acknowledgements

My thanks to Mrs Ida White of Langley and to Mr Jack Young, also of Langley, for providing me with supplementary information covering the area as it was in the early nineteenth century; not forgetting my debt to *Forster's Strata* for guidance on lead smelting.

PROLOGUE

1

Peter Greenbank threw back his head and sniffed; then, looking down at the small boy he was holding by the hand, he said, "There's the smell. God! yes. It's a stink. I smelt and tasted it as a boy. It's a different smell altogether from the coal dust; it chokes you does the smell of smeltin'. And they built a wall round the mill thinkin' to keep the smell in. Did you ever now know anything as daft as that?"

"Are we far from this place now, Da?"

"Far from it ... Langley? We're in it, boy, we're in it. You are standing now in the Barony of Langley, although I can see why you don't recognize it from my tales of it, for by! it has changed. Oh yes." He nodded his head now. "That was all open land there" – he pointed into the distance – "but now they've got it under trees. And it'll be pleasing to look upon when they reach their age, which won't be for a year or two yet I'm thinking."

"Is it far to this house, Da?"

"Why? Are you weary?"

"No, no," the boy lied valiantly as he looked up at the tall man, a mixture of awe and adoration showing on his face. This was his father who had come back into his life not three days ago and transported him into a wide new world. He was five years old when he had last seen him and he remembered him vividly: he had stood by the side of his mother on the Newcastle quay and waved frantically to him as his boat sailed down the river to Shields, from where it would go into the wide sea. Now he was seven and a half years old and the man looked the same to him exactly as on the day he had waved him goodbye: he was tall and strong and bright of countenance, with big dark brown eyes. His mother had always said he himself had his father's eyes and would one day be exactly like him. He wanted to be like his father. Oh yes, he did. So he added now, "I could walk ten miles ... more, twenty."

His father cuffed him gently on the head but in doing so knocked his cap off and when they both stooped to pick it up their brows touched for a second and they looked into each other's eyes and laughed. Then hand in hand again, they walked on over the narrow uneven path in silence for some way until the boy said, "The castle, Da, will I see the castle?"

"In two minutes you'll see the castle, boy."

And it was after exactly two minutes that Peter Greenbank brought his son to a halt and pointed, saying, "There it is, over there ... the castle."

The boy stared long and hard at the pile upon pile of stone, and when he made no comment his father said, "Well, what d'you think?"

"It's old."

"Aye, lad, it's old."

"And it wants mendin'."

The tall man burst out laughing as he said, "Right again, it wants mendin'."

"Does nobody live there?"

"Not any more. You're disappointed in the sight of your first castle?"

"It isn't me first castle, Da; there's a castle back in Newcastle, a fine one."

"Yes, you're right, you're right." Peter Greenbank cuffed his son's head again. This time the boy grabbed at his hat with both hands, and once more they were laughing together. "Well, come on," said his father; "it's evident you're not impressed. We'll have to see what you think of the smeltin' mills."

"That's where you said you used to work, Da."

"Aye, that's where I used to work." Peter Greenbank nodded his head and kept it nodding for the next ten paces the while his mind went back to his days in the smelting mill. He had gone there when he was sixteen after he had left the coal mine up on the hill, and it had been a case of from bad to worse. They had lived in Allendale at the time and he had walked the four miles every morning, hail, snow, or blow, and dragged himself back the four miles every night. For six days a week all he had seemed to do was work, eat and sleep. He hadn't, at that age, drunk heavily like the other workers, many of whom had further to walk, some living as far away as Hexham, but some of them never reaching home because there was an inn that acted as a half-way house, and a load of beer on top of their physical weariness would cut off their legs, and so they would sleep where they fell, perhaps in a barn, until the next day.

But he hadn't as far to walk as had his father, because he worked in the mines up towards Allenheads; at least he did, until the day they carried him in his box to the cemetery, another victim of the lead.

It was after his father died that his mother moved them near to Catton. This still left him two miles to walk, but that seemed nothing. Yet, he had never been settled in himself after his father went and he had become obsessed with an unusual craving, he wanted to go to sea. But he knew he couldn't do this because he was his mother's only support.

When he confided this niggling desire to Mr Makepeace, who was their nearest neighbour, the old man had said, "Thee must be mad, lad. You might think the lead and the coal mines an' the smeltin' mills bad, but the work in them is child's play, aye, child's play, compared with what you have to go through afore the mast." And he was speaking from experience, he'd said, for he had been at sea for ten years when he was young.

It had never been known for any man in his own family to take to the sea; his grandfather had often talked to him, not only of his own father but of his grandfather too. They had all been bred on the land and died on the land: first as farm workers on the big estates; then, wanting a more independent life but not an easier one, they took to the mines. So he did not know from where it came, this craving within himself for the sea. But not many days after his mother died, he packed his bundle and gave what pieces there were in the house to Kate Makepeace, who was by this time widowed, and the rest to Bill Lee who had just got married and had a one-room shanty round the other side of the quarry from Kate. Then he had made his way to Newcastle, thinking that all he had to do was to go to a shipping office and sign on; that was the procedure, so he understood.

However, it was nine months later before he got his first trip on a merchant boat for although he wanted the sea he didn't want to join the navy after having listened to what happened to press-ganged men, by which time he had married the daughter of the little house in which he was lodging. Now, more than eight years had passed, and during this time he had been only three times ashore in this country, when the time between trips had, on two occasions, been but a matter of days, not weeks, and a man who has been without a woman for years at a stretch does not waste time in longing to tramp the fells of his childhood. So this was the first time he had been this far since the day he left the place. But this trip was different. By God! yes, it was different.

"Da."

His thinking was brought back to the present and he looked down on the reason for his return, and absentmindedly he said, "Aye?"

"How far is it to the old woman's house?"

"You mustn't call her the old woman. Her name is Mrs Makepeace."

"But you call her old Kate."

"What I can do an' you can do are two different things. Now, you ask how far it is. Well, after we cut up here to the mills it won't be all that far."

In a matter of minutes they came to the first mill, then crossed a rough road and an open space and there ahead of them stood a great group of stone buildings, some with chimneys, some that looked like offices and stables, and all around there was activity with men and horses, and, filling the air, a clamour of voices and rumbling of carts and the clanking of harness.

When his father pulled at his arm, apparently intending to bypass all this, the boy said, "Aren't you going to show me the mill, Da, like you said?"

"That'll be another day. Come, the stink is enough; we must skirt it." And he held out his hand to help the boy over the iron tracks running into the distance, then past some scattered cottages, through a thicket and onto a path running by a stream, where the boy exclaimed, "Oh, Da, look! It's bonny, isn't it?"

"Yes, lad, it is bonny. It always was bonny. Beyond the mill there's a rill and a canny little waterfall. You'll see it some day, but now time's getting on, and it's shorter this way." He pointed uphill. "And so let's put our best foot forward, eh?"

By the time they reached the top of the long slope the boy's step was dragging and he looked with a sort of longing to where in the distance stood a group of houses and he said, "Is that where she, the old ... I mean, Mrs Makepeace lives?"

"No, no. That's Langley Top. You'll see that an' all, come another day. But now, here!" He lowered himself onto his hunkers, saying, "Get up." And the boy climbed onto his father's shoulders.

Some way past the houses he stopped and turned to look down the valley, only to stare at a stretch of water just below, and he muttered, "Why! I can't believe me eyes. They talked of it, but now they've actually done it." And he walked forward again to get a better view of the water, and looking from one end of it to the other, he muttered, "Must come from Stublick, and goes out down to the mill through that culvert." He nodded. Then humping the boy further up on his back, he stepped back onto the track again, only to stop abruptly and straighten his back so quickly that the boy had to cling on tightly to his neck. "Good lord! That must be the flue." He pointed to what looked like a stone-built chimney lying on the ground and his eyes followed its length back towards the smelting mill. "That's what it is. The wall was no good. This must take the gasses away. No wonder the trees and grass look fresher."

"Will I get down now, Da? Am I too heavy?"

"No, lad, you're like a feather."

But his son wasn't like a feather: his son was thin but, like himself, he was big-boned and bones weighed heavy. But he enjoyed the feel of him clinging to his back, for the aloneness went out of his body at the proximity of his own flesh. Strange, how lonely he had felt these last few days. In all those months at sea, in all those years at sea there had been periods of loneliness that almost made a man run amuck. Yet it was a different kind of loneliness from what he was experiencing now because then he had known he had a wife on shore waiting for him, and a son too. Well, he still had the son, but not for long.

They had now entered woodland again and because of the low branches crossing the hardly discernible path, the man stooped and let the boy slide from his back, saying as he did so, "Another half mile and we'll be there."

"Is this the wood you told me about, Da?"

"Aye, this is the wood above the quarry."

"What's a quarry like, Da?"

"You'll see it in just a tick through a break in the trees. It's just a big hole. Here we come to the first opening. There, look, but don't go too near the edge, it crumbles away." He himself stepped nearer the edge and looked over, saying as he did so, "Yes, there's been some landslides since I last ripped me backside sliding down there."

6

"You used to slide down there, Da?"

"As a lad, aye. It was a Sunday game. An' we used to make little caves to hide in. It was a grand place to play in. Now you can scarcely see the bottom of it for brushwood. Come, let's be going."

They continued their way, leaving the quarry behind them. At one point Peter Greenbank stopped and, looking down at the track, remarked, "Well, it's still used. In fact, by the look of it, more so than in my day."

The track led to a roadway, beyond which the land dropped into a small green valley, and there, sunk, as if in the bottom of it, was a cottage. It was square, having a small window at each side of a door, and underneath deep eaves another window that glinted brightly in the afternoon sun. The cottage was situated in what looked like an overgrown garden, and to the side ran a small burn that was little wider than a drain in parts.

"Is that it, Da, Mrs ... Mrs Makepeace's house?"

"Yes, that's it, and it's the one thing about here that hasn't changed with the years. But I hope we find. . . ." But he did not finish the thought in his mind which said, Old Kate still surviving there.

How old was she when he left? Well, nearing sixty he would say. But no one knew her real age, for unlike other women, as she was in all ways, she refused to wear a bonnet or a cape such as denoted age.

They went rapidly down the slope to where the land levelled out, then through a gate and up a rough uneven stone path and to the front door, which Peter had noted was closed when he had stood surveying the cottage from the hill, but was now open. Yet there seemed to be no one about, and so he put out his hand and, leaning forward, knocked twice on the weathered oak, and waited before poking his head forward and calling, "Anybody at home by the name of Mrs Kate Makepeace?"

Still there was no answer. But when he heard a door close, he spoke again, calling, "Hello, there!"

From out of the deep shadow at the far end of the room stepped a woman. She was of medium height with a thickset figure. She wore a skirt and a blouse of blue cotton, which was open low at the neck showing the skin at the top of her drooping breasts as having the same dried wrinkled appearance as that on her face. Her hair was thin and drawn tightly back over her scalp. It wasn't white, not even grey, but was as dark as the shadow from which she had stepped. And now, her eyes moving into slits, she peered towards the two figures standing in the doorway and her mouth dropped open into a gape and then closed again before she said, "In the name of God!" And Peter answered, "Aye, and He be blest that I find you well."

"Peter Greenbank."

"The same, Kate, the same."

She looked down. "What's this? Your boy?"

"Aye, my boy, my son, six months off being eight."

"Well, well. I knew it was a strange day, when I rose this mornin'. I knew it was to be a strange day, and it wasn't the heat. Come in, come in; what are you standin' there for? Surprises never surprise me, but this is different. I . . . I thought you must be dead; I'd heard no word of you. That you were married, aye, but that was a long time ago. Newcastle is a long way off and South Shields further. She was from there, the rumour said."

"Aye, she was from there."

"Where is she now?"

He bowed his head and sat down on the stiff wooden chair by the side of the open hearth in which a fire blazed, and this a very hot day, before he said, "I hope she's with those she believed in, her people, if not the angels."

After a pause, the old woman said, "God rest her soul. . . . When?"

"Oh, six months gone."

"Six months! And the laddie?"

"Left to God and good neighbours, and from what I saw of some of them, not so good. That's why I'm here."

"Oh, that's why you're here. Ah well, whatever's brought you I'm pleased to see you, Peter. I never thought though to see you again, for the sea's a treacherous mistress. But away with thoughts and down to the needs of the belly. Have you eaten?"

"We had a decent bite in Hexham, but that's some hours ago, and a nibble in Haydon Bridge, but it's a drink we're both needin', I think." He glanced at his son and added, "Eh?" And the boy said, "Yes, Da."

"Hip drink. He'd like my hip syrup."

"He couldn't but help."

"And you? I have a herb beer an' a ginger, but better still, a sloe wine. I keep that for best like, for an occasion, and I haven't had an occasion for a long, long time, so why not now. Sloe wine it'll be, Peter."

"Indeed, indeed, I can't wait."

She smiled, a skin-stretching smile; then her head lowering, she passed her glance over the boy before turning away and shambling up the room, which was much bigger than could be gauged from outside.

When she disappeared through a far door the boy looked up at his father, and he, pulling a face, whispered, "There now, that's Mrs Makepeace. What d'you think?"

"She's" – the boy hesitated – "all right . . . nice I think, but . . . but. . . ."

Peter's head came lower, until his eyes were looking into the boy's, and they were merry as he added, "Frightening, gives you a gliff." And to this the boy responded immediately, grinning now, saying, "Aye, Da, a gliff."

"She's a good woman, wise and brave." Peter's face was straight now, and the boy, sensing something behind the words, let the grin slide away and he nodded his head as if he understood.

Within a minute the old woman was back in the room carrying a mug in each hand, one smaller than the other, and it was the latter that she handed to Peter, saying, "A little of that, I tell you, will go a long way. It was put down well afore you left."

"Then it should have a kick in it."

"Aye, it has. It'll measure that of an unbroken pit pony any day. I can promise you."

The father and the son now sipped at their mugs. Then the boy, blinking, looked up at the strange woman and, smiling, said, "'Tis nice."

"Yes, 'tis nice," she repeated. "I've never heard different about that. And what d'you think?" She looked at Peter, and he, drawing a deep breath, said on a laugh, "If I'd had a drop of this when my fingers were stuck to the rails with ice, I'd have been free in a flash. 'Tis mighty powerful and almost as clear as water."

"Well now" – she sat down opposite to them – "tell me what's happened you this many a day, then I will get you something to eat. You're stayin', I hope?" There was a sharp enquiry in her voice, and he said, "Overnight, and perhaps for a day, if you'll have us."

"As short as that?"

He glanced at the boy, then said, "For me anyway. I want a crack with you, Kate." Again his eyes slanted towards the boy, and she nodded and said, "Aye, well, aye, but go on."

"Well, what is there to tell? Sweat and hard tack and" – he gritted his teeth for a moment – "cruelty, the like you never saw of."

"Well, I've seen a bit, you know that."

"Aye, I do. But this kind was different in some way, Kate: men reduced to janglin' pieces of raw flesh. Oh." He screwed up his eyes tight and jerked his head.

"Then why do you stay?" she said.

"Can't tell really, Kate."

"You wouldn't think about takin' up here again?"

"In the pit or the mill? No! No, never again. There's one thing you get on the sea if nothing else, fresh air, at least when you're up top, an' light. Two things I should have said. But . . . but life will be a little different from now on; I've left the old tub an' next week I'm joinin' a ship that does the Norwegian run. She'll only have another two or so to do afore storms and the ice shuts up the sea, and then for the winter I'll get a job on shore. In any case I've enough on me to see me through those months, work or no work; I've been sparing over the years with meself. So what I've come for, Kate" – he cast a glance towards the boy – "is this one here. You see, when I got back to me house, which was a decent enough place when I left, three rooms it had and away from the waterfront . . . but not far enough for the swabs to move in, once he was left on his own. A neighbour took care of him. That's how she put it. She moved her squad in, and he was running wild with them, hardly a rag to his back, an' lice-ridden. You never saw the like. I've never used me boot in me life afore. They won't come near that door for a time. It's me own house, you know, I own it. Well, through Betsy. It was there I went to

9

lodge with her mother after I left here. Her father had been captain of a coaster and buyin' the house had been the result of his labours. It's worth one hundred and twenty pounds, if a penny, that's when I get it cleaned up, and then I'll sell it or let it out for rent. It'll be according to what the solicitor man advises me, 'cos the deeds are with him. I saw him yesterday. Have you ever been in front of a lawyer, Kate? Stiff they are. He was polite enough, but stiff. But that's the way of 'em. Anyway, I told him I was comin' out here to you and gave him the address of the cottage."

"What if I'd been dead?"

"Huh! Well, Kate, I thought of that, but then I thought, well there's Bill Lee, he'll surely still be there, for he was just married when I left. And with his mother still in Allendale, he wouldn't want to move. And her, I mean Jane coming from Haydon Bridge, well, you know what families are when they think you are going to shift away. Anyway, I counted on that and I left Bill's cottage name with him an' all. But is he still there?"

"Oh yes, aye, he's still there. An' he's made a fine job of that shanty. Built on two rooms he has and a stable for the pony. And that not alone, he's been granted four stints."

"Four stints!"

"Aye. Oh, there's been lots of changes since you left, you wouldn't believe. You remember some of the types that worked alongside of you in the smelting mills? Aye, and the mine. Drunks, almost to a man. Well, that place called the Greenwich Hospital got an idea into their heads that would cut out on their drinkin', which drinkin' made them late for their work and their heads buzzing so much they weren't up to it when they got there. And so, what did they do? My, you wouldn't believe, they've built them fine cottages and allotted each of them so many stints, and with each stint they are allowed to keep a cow and chickens or a few pigs or sheep an' such like, according you know to the size."

"Well, well! that Greenwich Hospital lot have a head on their shoulders. I knew it when I was workin' there, the things they did. Mr Fawcett represented them then. He was the mill bailiff, a straight man, honest, as honest as any one in a high position can be. Is he still there?"

"Oh, William Fawcett is still there; but Mulcaster seems to be the man now, so I understand, and Mr Wardle bailiff to the mine. But tell me, I've never been able to get it into this stupid head of mine, is this hospital a real place for the sick or what?"

"No, no, Kate, it's a kind of . . . well, I'm not quite sure, but it's like a concern, a company, like a shipping company I should imagine or a coal owner, but bigger, aye, oh bigger, because they buy up estates. 'Twas they who bought up the whole Barony of Langley from one end to the other, you know. No, no, they are not that kind of a hospital, but what they really are I couldn't put me finger on except as to what I've said."

During all this talk the boy had sat gazing at them while sipping at his drink. Then after he had placed the mug down onto the floor to the side of him, he leant his head against the high wooden back of the chair and went peacefully to sleep.

They both became aware of this at the same time and they looked at him a moment or so before Kate said, "He's a bonny enough lad; takes after you when you were that age. What was his mother like? Has he any of her features?"

"She was a good lass, a bit on the religious side, but open like with it, not narrow. Took after her father in that way. And she was pure."

"Huh!" Kate gave a wheezy laugh. "Pure. You would go after a pure one, wouldn't you? Did you ever think of Nell Feeler?"

"No, no, I never did."

"Well, I thought it was as much to get rid of her as your hankerin' for the sea that took you off."

"Maybe, but there were t'other things, you know."

They looked at each other hard before she said softly, "Aye, I know." Then as if desiring to change the subject, she said, "I don't think she ever forgave you ... Nell. She had a bairn after."

"What?"

"I said ... well, you heard me, she had a bairn about eight months after you were gone."

"In the name of God! Kate, what are you sayin'?"

"I'm not sayin' anything, only stating a fact. She married Arthur Poulter, an' quick. He was another one of Bannaman's men. But the child came seven months after the wedding. Still, it might have been early."

"Aw, Kate."

"Don't keep sayin', Aw, Kate, like that as if you were a monk out of a monastery." She laughed now, and after a moment he said, "Bannaman. What's he doing now?"

At this the old woman got up and going to a black oak cupboard opposite the fireplace she took out a platter on which was bread and a cheese dish, and placed them on the bare wooden table that stood in the centre of the room. She then returned to the cupboard and brought out the remains of a chicken and a wooden bowl of green stuff before she spoke again, saying, "Things have been quiet for the last few years. Yet, when I say quiet, I don't know what I mean. Perhaps I mean he's left me alone. But things have happened. There was an outcry five years gone when the coach carryin' the wages to the mill was held up and the guard wounded. He didn't die, but he won't walk straight again. It was the Christmas pay out and the roads were frozen hard. The coach was carrying all of three hundred guineas, they said. The bank teller and Gabriel Roystan, the mill clerk, they were both knocked out."

"Did they find the culprits?"

"No, not really. It snowed heavily that night and went on for almost a week and later, when it thawed, they found Falsy Read. I don't know if you remember him. Nobody could say he had anything to do with the hold-up 'cos he hadn't a penny on him, and anyway he was found near the edge of the quarry, and that's some distance from the coach road. But now, the odd thing is, three days ago, Gabriel Roystan, the clerk, the very one who was in that particular hold-up, goes missing and apparently the wages with him.

"You see, they've devised different ways of bringing the wages in. They hired the militia for a time, but for the past year, I understand, one man alone has carried it on horseback but taken different roads. This has been ordered at the last minute as a precaution. Now you remember Gabriel Roystan, he had ideas above the station for a clerk, but after his wife died he seemed to go to pieces."

"And you say Roystan has disappeared?"

"Aye, that's what I said, it's my bet he's already on that sea you think so much about, 'cos where was his horse discovered? In Newcastle. I got it from Bill who got it from the carrier who came in from Hexham around noon. In Newcastle mind. And what goes out of Newcastle? Why, ships. Bill says some fellow found the animal tied up on the waterfront. But there's one thing I can't understand, he might have been a bit above himself, Gabriel Roystan, an' not the type I'd take to at all, but he was God-fearin', a hard worker, and loved his son. The lad is a year or so older than yours there." She pointed to where the boy was still sleeping, and then, as if on an afterthought, she asked, "What do you call him?"

"Roddy. Full name Rodney Percival Greenbank." He smiled. "After his grandfather. It's a mouthful that, Rodney Percival. It was his mother's wish."

She sighed. "'Tis a mouthful. Well now, getting back to the reason for your visit, Peter. What do you intend to do with the lad? 'cos that's why you're here I think. Am I right?"

"Yes, yes, you're right, Kate."

"Well, let me tell you afore you go on an' say another word, I'm past lookin' after bairns, and it would be no life for a bairn in this house, me with me funny ways, an' the only other child hereabouts is little Mary Ellen Lee and she but five. Although she's got a tongue that'll clip clouts an' you would swear that she was ten if a day. I don't know who she takes after, for neither of them are great talkers, or doers for that matter, plodders both of them, but not wee Mary Ellen. I said from she first gave a bawl that she had a part missing, that's the only thing that stops her from being a lad."

She laughed, showing her discoloured but whole mouthful of teeth, and he laughed with her. "You're a wise woman, Kate," he said, "and it's you I'd like to leave him with. But nevertheless, I understand how you feel. Still, if Bill and Jane will take him on for a time they won't be out of pocket, I promise them that. But I'd like you to keep an eye on him, Kate. There are things you can teach him that no one else can. You learned them to me, and that's all of thirty years ago an' you've gained, I know, in wisdom since. I'd hoped he'd benefit from it."

"Aye, well, I can promise you that I'll keep an eye on him an' tell him the paths that lead straight in his mind, and where health is to be got from the ground. But that's as much as I'll be able to do for him; like you, he'll go his own way. Now come on, wake him up, then sit up and have this bite. And let me say again, Peter, my eyes are glad to see you."

It was six o'clock when Peter said to Kate, "We'll take a dander over to Bill's and see if he's in favour of taking on another young 'un. I can't see that he wouldn't if he's only got the one. Can you?"

"It'll be up to them. If the lad there had been a girl now, they might have welcomed her straightaway as a companion for Mary Ellen, because to my mind she's too much amidst the grown-ups and is as old-fashioned as a maiden lady. Still, Bill might see it differently, bein' a lad." She looked down on Roddy, laughing as she did so, saying now, "That's one thing you can't change in life, laddie, the way you're made. Change your mind, aye, but that's about all with regard to yourself. You're quiet. You've had little to say for yourself." She now looked up at his father, saying, "Is he always as tongue-tied as this?"

"No, by gum, no. At least I haven't found him so. It's strange, all this is."

"Aye. Aye. Well, away so you can get yourself back afore dark, that is unless you want to take a lantern."

"Me take a lantern round the quarry, Kate! You jokin'?"

"No, I'm not jokin', but as you remember there were parts giving way in your day. Two years gone, after a heavy rainfall, there was a big bite taken out of the east side. You see, they took more stone out of the far side to build the flue. And even along this side the walls have broken away in different parts until the edge has almost reached the path. And there's water lies in the bottom as never before."

"I noted that the path is quite well worn. Do you get a lot of people coming to you now for your herbs an' such?"

"No, I don't. Nor do I want. If you had noted so much, you should have noted an' all, that the path turns away up the ride, the straight where they used to break in the galloways for the mine. They still fetch them there at times. Yet most of the farmers have got so rich doin' horse dealing on the side that they do the breakin' in their own fields. Even those with stints seem to manage it an' all. It's mostly gypsies that use it. But they don't last long around here. Anyway, if you're goin', get along with you. I'll have a shakedown ready for you both by the time you get back and a hot bite in the pan, because the nights are comin' in chilly now."

She stood at the door and looked up at the sky, saying, "There should be a moon later on. It was on its back all last week, and so we had rain for five days without let up. But for the last couple of nights it's steadied itself. So if you do lose your way after all this time you won't need a lantern." She smiled widely, and he, too, laughed before pausing on the pathway and looking first to one side and then to the other over her garden, saying, "'Tis still a tangle, Kate. And I see" – he pointed to the far end of the land where some chickens were scratching – "you still keep the bantams."

"Aye, and add to that six geese in the field beyond and two goats who make me never want for milk or cheese."

"You're a clever woman, Kate. I always said so." He jerked his chin at her before turning and holding out his hand to his son.

They went through the gate and across the hollow and up the rise that led to the quarry, neither of them speaking. It wasn't until they were walking in the shadow of the high brushwood that bordered the path that the boy said, quietly, "Da, I . . . I don't want to stay here. I . . . I want to go back with you."

Peter sighed. "Now, now, you don't know how lucky you are. Wait till you see where you'll likely be stayin'. They're fine people, and you heard what Kate . . . Mrs Makepeace said about little Mary Ellen. She could make a fine playmate for. . . ."

"I don't like girls, Da. When I went down to the quay it was always with the lads."

"Aye" – his voice was harsh now – "what kind of lads? Scum. Riff-raff. Where would you have been if I had left you with them, eh? Had I gone back to sea and left you there, where would you have landed? I can tell you where you would have landed, in the House of Correction, and you know what place that is, don't you?"

The boy swallowed deeply, then muttered, "I . . . I just want to be with you, Da."

Peter's voice was softer now. "I know that," he said, "and I want to be with you, but it isn't to be so. I've got to earn a livin' and I can't earn it on the land, such is me nature." Then he added more brightly, "But me trips will be shorter, some of them just a matter of weeks, both ways, no distance, and then come December when the rivers are covered with ice, I'll have to stay on shore, and I'll make me way out here every weekend."

"You'll come every weekend?"

"Aye, I will."

"When will that be, Da?"

"Oh, well now, not very long, just a matter of weeks. We'll soon be into October, then after November, well, no more sailing to Norway." He pressed the small hand within his own and they walked on silently now until Peter stopped abruptly and looked along the path branching off to where it curved away into high brushwood, and more to himself than to the boy he said, "Well, well, how trees can grow in eight years. I could still see through there afore I left, and walk through, but look at it now, it's thick with undergrowth. And the ride. . . ." He took some steps backwards and shielded his eyes against the setting sun. "The ride, as she said, may be used still but it doesn't look half the width it was in my

14

time, no, not half. Well" – again he sighed – "time doesn't stand still. It's an old sayin', but nevertheless true." He grinned down on his son as he said, "Me old captain always used to be saying that. 'Get on with it, lads. Get on with it. Time doesn't stand still, an' it's runnin' away from you. So put a move on and catch up with it. Up with you! Up you go! Reach it afore it passes the top of the mast.'" He shook his head slowly. "He was a man, a tartar, but a man. Still, thank God I won't be under him again." Then in a highly jocular mood he cried, "Come on, I'll race you to the top of the quarry. See yonder, that great pile of stones? That was once a barn. That marks the head of the quarry. One—" He took a stance and made the boy do the same. Then crying, "Two, three," they both ran along the uneven path, and Peter, seeing that the boy was running well away from the quarry edge, allowed him to outpace him.

At the ruined barn they both leaned against a crumbling wall and Peter, his chest heaving much more than was necessary, said, "By! you've got a pair of legs on you. 'Tis me that must be getting old. No one has ever beaten me afore."

"Never, Da?"

"Never. That's my word on it, honest."

It was ten minutes later when they reached the dip and Bill Lee's cottage. And again Peter stopped as he became aware of another change that had taken place during his absence, for what had been a tumble-down one-room shanty was now, what could be called, a smart little house with outbuildings attached, and as he gazed in admiration he thought, That's enterprise for you. What one could do another could, but had any of them before bothered to enlarge their cottages over the years? It wasn't for lack of material, for there were stones all around for the taking. Of course they had to be carried, and for that you needed a horse and cart. And to be fair, for many people years ago the only means for transporting anything had been their legs and a barrow.

Hurriedly now, he went towards the cottage door, and finding it closed, he knocked sharply on it, crying jovially, "Come out of that and show yourself, Bill Lee! Or you, Jane!"

He waited, a smile on his face, but when there was no response he turned to the boy, saying, "Well, well, they must be out."

He now tried the door, and when it did not move under his push, he said, "'Tis bolted. They definitely are out. It's something new, though, to find a door bolted in these parts. But then, going by the outside there must be something to steal on the inside."

Looking about him now, he said, "Well, well, they'll surely be back afore dark. Gone to visit her people likely. Must have been on early shift to be free at this time. Come on." He jerked his chin towards the boy. "We can have a walk round the fields in the meantime, but before that we'll see what he's got in his stint."

He found that Bill Lee had a dozen chickens, two pigs, one heavy with a coming litter which he pointed out to the boy, saying, "How many wee 'uns has she got inside her?"

"Two, Da."

"Two? Ten, twelve, perhaps."

"No, Da."

"Aye. Anyway, when you're livin' here you'll be able to see them born. It's a fine sight to see animals born. And over there, look, sheep. I can see four of them. My, my! He's done well for himself. And look at that patch there, gooseberry bushes if I'm not mistaken, and apple trees. Well! Well! Well!"

So they spent the next half-hour admiring the land and its occupants around the cottage, and when there was still no sign of the owners and the twilight was deepening fast, he said, "Could be they're away for the night, must be someone ill or dead. Anyway, there's always the morrow. Come on, we'll hie home. Did you hear what I said there, lad? I said we'd hie home. Funny that I should think of Kate's place as home. Yet not so; I spent many a day in that cottage or trailing after her skirts, picking herbs for her. Come on, come on." . . .

When they entered the wood leading to the long ride, the twilight turned to night and the boy walked closely against his father's side, his hand pressed tightly into the big fist; and the silence and the darkness contributed to a fear that made itself felt through his father's hand, and Peter, drawing him close to him, said, "Never be afraid of quietness, lad, learn to like it, nor be afeared of the dark because in the dark your wits become sharper. You understand?"

"Yes, Da." Yet he didn't know what he understood except that at the moment if he hadn't been with his father he would have taken to his heels and run out of this darkness into where there was more light.

"Look." Peter pointed upwards. "There she comes, as Kate prophesied. She was always a good one with the moon, was Kate. Do you know, they used to come and ask her what the weather would be like on Fair Day. And she's cured more with her medicines than I can count, both animal and human. Although at one time . . . well, people are more enlightened now, at least some, please God.

"Ah, look. Now isn't that a bonny sight!" They had come out of the wood and to a gap in the brushwood that bordered the quarry and, pointing downwards to where the reflection of the moon was just touching the edge of the water at the bottom of the quarry, he said, "'Tis a bonny sight to see the moon washing itself in the water. I've watched her riding alongside us many a night skipping over the waves. Aye. Aye, and the white clouds chasing her. But I must admit there were times when I didn't appreciate the sight like as now, for then, at those times, me belly would have been crying out for a decent meal, something not running with maggots; or I was so froze I longed to die. Aye." He looked down at the shadowy face of the boy now as he added, "Would you believe that, your da longed to die because he was so cold and hungry? I hope you never want to go to sea, lad. But come, look, the bank's clear, let's sit down here for a minute and enjoy that sight 'cos it won't last long; she'll be scudding away hiding herself behind black skirts in a minute or so. And the night is young yet, and—" His voice dropped to a soft whisper now as he lowered himself down onto the grassy verge of the quarry, saying, "I want to remember just this, you and me sittin' on the bank where I sat many a time as a lad looking down on the same scene. I never thought one day I would have a fine son of me own." He pulled the boy's head against his chest, and like this they sat quietly looking to where the moon appeared to be skipping along the edge of the water at the far side of the quarry.

It was Peter who heard the sound of horses' hooves first, and he gently pressed the boy's head away from him as he swivelled round on the grass, peering backwards into the dark towards the far end of the ride. After a second or so he got to his feet, saying as he did so, "There's a horse, or horses coming. You'd better look out in case we are trampled. Come on" – he pulled the boy up – "we'll keep close in until they pass."

He now pulled his son across the pathway and into the shrubbery opposite and waited for the rider to pass. The horse, he realized, was walking, and slowly, but his ear, which in his youth had been alerted to all sounds of the woodlands and the fells, realized there were footsteps accompanying the rider. He decided he wouldn't speak in case he should frighten both the rider and the horse, and part of his mind told him that the rider might have a gun: the man could be out poaching, and he didn't want to be taken for a keeper.

When the sound of the horse's hooves and the footsteps stopped some little way to the left of him, he warned the boy to silence by gripping his shoulder; and turning his own head to the side and his ear cocked, he listened to the low voices that he guessed weren't more than a dozen feet from him along the path. The sounds that came to him were, he recognized, from voices indulging in question and answer, but he couldn't make out the words until, his head poked further forward, he heard one say, "Are you sure of the place?"

And the answer came, "Of course I am. I should be; I spent three hours here last night digging it. It's just beyond that gap there. I covered it up."

Then came a low hiss-snapping rejoinder, "Don't use that tone to me."

There followed a pause and the mumbled reply was inaudible.

A voice came again, saying, "It's the wrong time."

"Not to my mind," was the answer. "Couldn't be better. Most of them are at the barn dance."

The barn dance. Peter nodded to himself. That's where Bill and Jane must be, and the child with them. The barn dance. Yes, of course. But why hadn't Kate known of their going? But then, why should she? She mightn't see them from one week's end to the other.

The words came as if from right beside him now. "'Tis in here to the left. I widened the gap meself, pulling some of the brushwood up so there would be a bit more light."

17

There was a pause now in the talking but a scuffling of feet and a movement as if something was being carried. And then quite suddenly Peter pulled the boy's face tight into his belly and turned his own head towards the thick undergrowth, oblivious that part of it was a holly bush, the leaves of which were pricking his cheek.

His body took on a ramrod stiffness as he felt the figures almost brush past him carrying a weight between them. Then the branches of the very bushes against which he was standing moved by the pressure of the bodies turning at right angles from the path.

There was an interval of about thirty seconds before he heard a voice saying, "Bring the pony in here," and another voice answer, "There'll be nobody along there the night. The late shift doesn't come up until ten."

"Bring it from the path." The words were low and gritted.

There was the sound of a grunt, then he was conscious of a figure passing close to him, but he didn't turn his head to look in its direction. But when the horse passed him its body sweat wafted over him, so close was it to him.

It wasn't until he heard what he realized was earth being shovelled that he moved cautiously onto the path. The boy was by his side now, his body shivering with fear of he knew not what, only that there was something disturbing his father. And when the hand came on his shoulder the pressure told him that he was to stay where he was. But no sooner had his father stepped into a gap in the brushwood than he almost leaped after him and the crack of landing on a small dead branch echoed like a revolver shot through the night.

Peter did not stop to chastise his son, it was too late. A lantern on the ground, though shaded, showed up the scene: he was in a small clearing, and there before him were two men, one on each side of a hole in the ground. The hole wasn't all that deep, for he could see that in it was a body, half of it covered with soil, but the face still exposed looked startlingly white yet at the same time had a hue.

"My God!" The words came out on a thin whisper, for he knew he was looking down on Mr Roystan the smelting mill clerk, the man who was supposed to have run off with the wages. As he made a dive for the man nearest to him he let out a yell, crying, "Feeler! You bloody swine, Feeler!"

As the shovel was raised to come down on his head his fist caught the man under the chin, and his boot in the lower part of his stomach, which sent him reeling. Then crouching like an animal now, he peered at the figure standing at the other side of the hole. He was in the shadow out of the light cast by the lantern and so he couldn't make out his face, at least not at the moment. But then the moon, coming from behind a scud of clouds, gave sufficient light for him to recognize the tall figure, and his mouth dropped open before snapping closed with his teeth grinding together.

"You! You murdering sod, you!"

The boy now watched his father step back in order to take a jump over the narrow grave, and he cried, "Da! Da! Oh, Da!" Then he screamed as he saw the shovel leave the tall man's hands and come right across the side of his father's neck. He now put the fingers of one hand right into his mouth and bit on them as he saw his father fall almost on top of the little man who was in the act of staggering to his feet.

Running to his father, he knelt by him, crying, "Da! Da!" but when a hand lifted him bodily upwards by the collar he turned, screaming and kicking at the tall figure until his mouth was clamped shut and his hands gripped tight. Then he heard a voice say, "Pull yourself together. Get him covered up and we'll deal with this one. My God! for this to happen. D'you hear? Pull yourself together! I'm talking to you. Get it into your head, if you don't want to hang at the end of a rope, finish the job."

"I ... I can't. He almost did for me."

"My God! I'll do for you. Look, take this one here, and hold his mouth tight. God! When all's said and done you're a soft-gutted swine." The pressure temporarily gone from his mouth, the boy once more attempted to yell, but before he could do so something was again clamped over his mouth; not a hand this time, yet it was a hand, but not an ordinary hand. His head was pressed back tightly and he was looking up into a thin face, the mouth of which was open and with blood pouring from one side of it. When it began to drop onto his own face he closed his eyes and once again kicked out with his feet. The groan from the man made him redouble his efforts, but the last thing he heard before a great blackness overtook him was the voice above him appealing to the other man by name, and the words were to the effect that he was feeling bad and couldn't hold the boy any longer. It was then the blow came on the side of his head.

The tall man stood panting as he looked down on the small limp figure while cursing his companion. His words punctuated with oaths, he said, "Of all the bungling buggers, I'd have to rely on you." And the other man muttered in defiance now that spoke of subservience mixed with suppressed retaliation, "You've been glad to rely on me afore. And I didn't bungle this, it was yourself. You said you knew the right road he was takin', but he diddled you. You seem to forget he didn't come the Newcastle road: that leaked out to put people off the scent. There's cleverer than you, it seems, mister. He came the open way across the moor, and it was me who caught sight of him else we wouldn't have had him at all. Remember that, mister."

"I'll remember that," the tall man growled. "And what have we got out of it so far, eh? Tell me that. Nothing, only a dead man."

The smaller man's voice trembled as he said, "He ... he wasn't all that dead, I ... I simply knocked him out." He looked towards the hole in the ground and the half-buried man and the soil that covered the body, and he gave a whimper like that which might have come from a child as he said, "Same as Hellier. You shouldn't go that far. No need."

"And who's to blame?" The voice came at him again. "He saw you, didn't he? You said he did, as plain as daylight. And what would have happened if he had come round? And, my faithful servant, let me ask you this: would you have kept your mouth shut? No, not you. So, he's dead enough now, and God knows if we'll live to see another day if that man's voice and his boy's screams have carried. So, put a move on and bring that brushwood. Get going, if you don't want my foot in your backside."

Both men now shovelled earth into the hole, then collected small pieces of brushwood which they stamped on the loose earth. They next gathered some stones and threw them haphazardly here and there over the brushwood. "What if the earth sinks in?" the small man said.

"Well, it'll be your job to come and put more stones on. Understand?"

"But what if I'm seen in these parts?" There was a tremble in the man's voice now. "I'm rarely over here. They'd want to know...."

"For God's sake, shut your weak-lipped mouth. And now look at those." He pointed to the two prone figures on the ground. "What d'you think you're going to do with those, eh? Bury 'em? You know who that is?"

"Aye. Aye, I recognized him, young Greenbank, that was."

"Aye, young Greenbank. Well it's a certainty he's got to be that was, as you say, else God help us both. Do you understand what I mean?" He had spoken much more quietly, and the smaller man peered at him through the dappled moonlight, but he gave no answer, he just drooped his chin onto his chest and listened as his companion said, "There's one thing we can thank God for: heavy rain often causes bits of landslides in this particular hole in the ground. Now, over with him."

"Wh ... what?"

"Well" – the voice was loud in its hissing – "what shall we do? Leave him here to recover, and the lad an' all? Get his legs!"

It took them all their time to lift the body from where it lay across the narrow path and to the edge of the quarry. Then with a heave they let go of it and waited, their own bodies bent forward as they peered downwards towards the water.

The sound that came to them now was of a soft thump, then the dislodging of rocks. But the rumbling lasted only a matter of seconds.

They had both turned from the edge of the quarry when the sound of the boy's choked cry and that of voices coming from the distance brought them crouching low. Quickly but quietly and still crouched, the big man moved towards the clearing, and seeing the boy about to scramble away grabbed him; then holding him as if cradling a baby, he kept his hand tightly over his mouth.

The voices came nearer but their words were indistinguishable, and became more so as they then moved further away.

The boy's eyes were wide and he was looking up into the face of the man who was holding him. It was a different face from the one he had seen before, the thin face. This was a big face with heavy black brows and a beard, and eyes which looked enormous. He had no hat on his head and his hair hung down over his ears. It too was black.

"Quick!" the man hissed back to his companion, and straightening himself up while still keeping his hand over the boy's mouth, he brought his other hand sideways on to the child's head just below his ear. The body went limp in his hands, and he carried it to the edge of the quarry and dropped it over. He did not wait to hear its fall but, taking two steps to the right of him, he pulled at a sapling that was growing out of the side of the quarry, heaving it backwards and forwards. At last he wrenched it from the ground, then jumped back to the safety of the path.

It wasn't until he felt the ground under him shudder that once more he sprang back, and only just in time, for within seconds the loosened earth and rocks were bounding their way down to the bottom of the quarry....

The passers-by, two miners on their way to High Stublick colliery, were on the track leading to Kate's cottage when they heard the distant rumbling, and they stopped for a moment and one said, "You listen to that. That's the quarry talkin' again. Good job it didn't speak when we were on its neck, eh?"

"Aye," said the other. "Could have been nasty. Safer in the pit." And they both laughed.

2

Kate was angry. She had made a pan of broth and mixed up some dumplings ready to drop into it the minute they entered the door, because although the days were warm, the nights could be biting. But the twilight passed into darkness and when they didn't put in an appearance, she imagined that Bill Lee had been brewing up his own beer again, and this had set their tongues wagging loosely, and there they were jabbering away recalling old times, older in Peter's case, but nevertheless recognizable to both of them. But when ten o'clock came, which was far past her bedtime because she went to bed with the fading light and rose with the dawning of it, she became vexed.

She had made up a bed for him on the floor near the fire: an old tick stuffed with straw could have the feeling of down when a man was tired, and a boy too, as they both must be after their day's tramping. But when it neared midnight and they still hadn't put in an appearance, her annoyance turned to anger; for although she reasoned that Peter had drunk so much that he had thought it better to bed down there than tackle the quarry road back, and the boy with him, nevertheless, he had put her out.

She lay on her bed awake for some time until her reason said she couldn't imagine the beer that Bill could brew would have the power to knock Peter out, for, him being a sailor, he was used to his rum and such.

She dozed at intervals, but before the dawn broke she was sitting on the edge of her bed, her thin lips munching backwards and forwards portraying her anxiety, and asking herself why that odd feeling of foreboding that she experienced in times of crisis should be on her. Could anything have happened to them both? But what could have happened around here? True, the men at times were rowdy, although not so bad nowadays since they were living in respectable cottages and each with his stint of land. 'Twas only on the pay-days, when they would go as far as Hexham one way or Allendale the other, that they got out of hand. And anyway, a man such as Peter could certainly take care of himself.

She rose from the bed and blew up the dying embers of the fire and heated some goat's milk into which she dropped some pieces of bread and goat's cheese. But before she was halfway through it she found she had no appetite for it, and so, getting into her clothes and taking her shawl from the back of the door, she put it over her head, strapped it under her flagging breasts and tied it in a knot in the middle of her back. Then picking up a wicker basket she went out. What she would do, she told herself, was to take a stroll towards Bill Lee's, but should she meet Peter and the boy coming back, she would show no anxiety, perhaps a little temper at their lack of consideration, but she would say she was out as usual gathering her herbs.

Of course there weren't many herbs to be got alongside the quarry track; nothing worthwhile grew in the brushwood that had sprung up over the years. Still, she was pleased that part was covered for it took the scars from the land. But over towards the spinney beyond which Bill Lee's cottage lay, there was a patch of meadow that on occasions seemed to give forth those herbs she needed, that is if once again they hadn't let the young horses play in it. Anyway, should she meet up with her visitors, she could offhandedly tell them she was making for there.

The morning light was bright and the sun was coming up over the hills when she reached a part of the quarry pathway that brought her to a standstill; for here she saw had been a fall and not the usual one. This then was what she had heard early on last evening, but she had taken little notice because there was always some noise from either the smelting mills or the mine. It was a joke that one day Stublick miners would come up out of the bottom of the quarry.

To get round it she had to make her way into the brushwood. As she did so she came to a part she decided had been flattened down by a number of feet. There were stones strewn about and fresh earth had been trampled here and there. It couldn't have been gypsies, she told herself, else there would have been a fire. Yet they wouldn't have been so silly as to make a fire here amidst all this kindling. She had to push her way through hawthorn and bramble to reach the path on the other side and she stood there looking down into the quarry. It had been a mighty big fall, bigger than usual. Well, that's what the rains did.

She was about to turn away when her eyes narrowed, and she moved a cautious step nearer the edge and looked down. There, to the left but not right at the bottom, what she thought her eyes saw brought her hand to her throat and she whispered, "No! God Almighty! No!" Then with the agility of someone half her age, she was running back the way she had come and to the head of the quarry, and there, slithering down the path that had been made by the countless tracks of the horses and waggons, she came to the edge of the water. Skirting it, she stumbled over the strewn boulders and earth towards the latest fall, and when she stopped, it was to gaze upwards to where she saw once again, but more clearly now, what she had viewed from the top pathway, a small hand dangling

23

from out of a black sleeve. But now she could make out the body which had been caught in the branches of a sturdy bush.

"'Tis the lad. Yes, 'tis the lad." She heard her own voice like a high cry, and as if in an unanswered prayer for help, her eyes now lifted to the top of the quarry to where two blackened faces were peering down at her.

Throwing the basket aside, she lifted up her arms and waved them frantically, at the same time crying, "Help! 'Tis a boy caught. Help!"

For answer it seemed that both of the men leapt over the top of the quarry edge. Bounding from stone to stone and causing minor falls here and there, they were within seconds standing at her side. And they too looked upwards, and one of them repeated her words, saying, "God Almighty! He must have been passing at the time. We heard the rumble on our way in last night."

"Can ... can you reach him?"

"Aye, yes, we'll reach him, Kate, we'll reach him."

She watched them clamber up to the bush and gently extricate the small body from the branches. Then one man held the limp form across his arms while the other man got behind him and gripped his belt, steadying him on his descent towards the bottom.

When they laid the boy at Kate's feet she knelt by his side and immediately her hand went into his jacket and stayed there. When she looked up to the men whose silent gaze was asking her the question, she answered, "'Tis tickin' slightly."

"Do you know him? Is he from round about?"

"No, no." She shook her head. "He came to visit me with his father ... yesterday."

"With his father?"

She nodded her head and looked to the side where the boulders were spread far into the water.

The two men exchanged glances before one of them, turning to her, said, "And you think he's ...?"

"No other place for him," she answered; "he wouldn't have left his boy, not like that he wouldn't. He brought him to me to look after. They were on their way to Bill Lee's to have a chat. Will ... will you carry him back for me?"

"Aye. Aye, Kate. But we'll have to have help; we can't move that lot ourselves."

The other man spoke now, saying, "The shift'll be spread out, they'll all be home by now."

"There's the top 'un and the pullers."

"Aye. But let's get the boy back first." And turning to Kate, he said, "We'll get him. If he's there, we'll get him." Then looking at his mate again, he said, "You get back and rake them up, Joe. I'll take the wee 'un along."

*

The sun was directly overhead when they carried Peter into the cottage. Bill Lee was one of the four men holding the canvas and his face was almost as ashen as that of the corpse, for although Peter's head was split open at the back, his face was as clean as if it had just been scrubbed with sea water.

After the men had left, voicing their sympathy with low mutters, there remained only Bill Lee and his wife Jane; and Bill, looking down on the man who although only four years older than himself, had been both his mate and mentor as a boy, he muttered, "I'm shaken. I'm real shaken. To think that this could have happened on his way to see us. And you ... you say he wanted us to take the boy, Kate?" He glanced to where the boy, who also looked dead, was lying on a hap on the wooden saddle.

"Aye. Aye, he did; but that was only after I felt I was too old to see to him. But now somehow ... well, we'll see. If the boy survives, we'll see."

"Aye, Kate, aye. But you know we'd be ready. Wouldn't we, Jane?"

"Oh, yes, Kate, we would be ready to take him anytime."

Again Kate said, "We'll see, we'll see." Then she added, "I expect Mr Mulcaster will be along directly, for the quarry, too, comes under him. They should have railed it off years ago. I've said that again and again, 'cos afore the enclosure the cows and the sheep went down there regular. But this is the first time it's taken human life. And likely, it won't be the last, the way it's droppin'."

"They'll bring the justice in it, too, I shouldn't wonder."

"Yes, probably. Anyway, I want to get him cleaned up afore they come."

"Will I help you, Kate?"

"No, lass, I can see to this meself. I would rather. Somehow—" She paused and looked at the earth-stained figure; then her voice low, she said, "'tis as if he were me son."

The young couple remained silent for a time; then Bill said, "We'll away then. But we'll be back in a short while."

"Yes, yes." She nodded, but didn't look towards them, and they went out, closing the door quietly after them.

She had stripped and washed Peter and covered him with a white sheet, and now she took all his clothes, with the exception of his belt, including his outer coat, and put them in the stone washhouse attached to the back of the cottage. She had taken the folder from his coat in which he kept his seafaring papers together with a silver chain on which was hung a wooden heart, the latter polished so much with handling that it was as smooth as glass; also a watch in a metal case, but the watch was broken. Back in the kitchen, she sat on the foot of the saddle and opened one of the two pockets in the belt and took out a small chamois leather bag. Tipping its contents onto her hand, there spilled over a small heap of sovereigns. Three had dropped onto the hap covering the boy, and these she picked up last, counting twenty-one, twenty-two, twenty-three.

Twenty-three golden sovereigns. "My! My! He must have saved and saved," she was muttering aloud.

In the other pocket of the belt was a quantity of silver amounting to three pounds. Now – she nodded to herself as she looked down on the hoard – were she to hand this over with the rest of his clothes to the authorities, what would happen to it? Would the boy get it if he survived? Likely a little of what was left when it went through them courts and lawyer men.... Well, they wouldn't get their hands on it. This was rightly the boy's. Yet – she looked around the room as if her decision had been questioned – they would know he'd have something in his wallet, wouldn't they? So she'd leave two sovereigns, which was a good amount, and a pound's worth of silver, the rest she would keep for the boy, should he survive. And if he didn't? Well, then it would be hers. Some day her own son might return – who knew? – and would be glad of twenty-one golden sovereigns and two pound's worth of silver, for she herself would not touch a penny of it.

Going now to the fireplace, to the side opposite the round bread oven, she put her hand upwards as if into the chimney and, gripping a stone, she gently moved it backwards and forwards before pulling it out.

The encrusted soot on it was proof that it was some long time since it had been removed. Now, putting her hand into a space which was larger than the stone she had extracted, she tipped up the handful of sovereigns and silver, then replaced the stone and, as of old practice, she rubbed her hands round its edges, spreading the disturbed soot so as not to show a definite line should anyone hold a candle to this wall.

Now shaking the soot from her hand and sleeve, she went once again into the washhouse and cleaned herself.

Returning to the kitchen, she bent over the boy. He had not moved or made any sign of life since the pitmen had lain him down there. Although her herbs were a cure for most things, they had to be drunk or chewed, and so, with some reluctance, she had followed the advice of Bill Lee and he had passed on the word to the carter going into Haydon Bridge to tell the doctor there that he was wanted this end, and soon.

She washed the boy's body, as she had washed the father's, and put ointment on his bruises. Although his face had been covered with blood there was no open wound on him to signify that he had bled, which was another strange thing. She was still troubled by one of her feelings, different from the premonition of last night, but nevertheless strong, which caused her to ask herself why there should have been such a distance between where the boy was hanging and where his father was found, all of twenty-five feet. Surely they would have been walking together hand in hand. Even if they hadn't and the boy had been running ahead, one or the other would have been warned by the fall. And too, there was the fact that the obvious fall in the top of the quarry measured only about five paces. One of the pitmen had pointed this out and his explanation was, the full force had taken the father with it, and the boy had tumbled to the side. But she couldn't see it like that, the distance was too great. Though what other explanation was there? She didn't know, only that she had this strange feeling on her. Yet again, if there had been evil deeds, and most evil deeds meant robbery, they would not have left him with his belt; most people knew what a sailor carried in his belt, little or much. . . . She was troubled.

The boy stirred and she quickly took his hand and said softly, "There now. There now." She felt his brow. It was hot and sweating as if he were in a fever. Well, exposed to the night air like that he would be in a fever, and if she could get some medicine down him she would soon cure that. He groaned and opened his eyes and stared at her, then closed them again and seemed to sleep.

The boy slept on and off for three days. On the third day, whilst awake, he looked at the men lifting a box from the table and carrying it away, but he showed no interest. This was caused, the doctor said, by something called concussion – it meant that it would take time for him to come round – and he had told Kate that none of her potions would quicken his recovery. She was just to let him lie quiet, and feed him milk and eggs, beaten up raw for preference, for the white of the egg would help tone his muscles and get him on his feet quicker.

She had never heard that before, but nevertheless she did it, beating up the raw eggs and spooning it into the boy.

Two things happened on the fourth day: the boy sat up, and Kate realized with a kind of horror that he had forgotten his past life.

When he had sat straight up for the first time and looked about the room, she had said, "There, there, me laddie, you're feeling better." And his lips had moved a number of times before he said, "What?" then "Where?" And she answered softly, "Well now, you remember me, Kate? That's what your da called me, but he made you call me Mrs Makepeace, you remember?" He made a slight movement with his head and his eyes blinked hard before he again looked round the room. And then she asked quietly, "Don't you remember what happened when the quarry edge gave way and you fell?"

"Fell?" he repeated. Again the slight shake of his head.

Then straightening her back, Kate pulled her chin into her wrinkled neck and, narrowing her eyes, she said, "What's your name?"

"Name?" He looked down on to the quilt. Then his fingers moving slowly to a loose thread, he pulled at it before lifting his eyes to hers once again, and his mouth fell agape.

"Your name's Roddy."

"Roddy? I don't know."

Very softly now she said, "Don't you remember your da?"

His eyelids flickered. It was as if he was trying hard to recall something. Then he said, "No." And his face puckered as if he was about to cry.

Patting him soothingly she hastened to reassure him. "There now. There now," she said. "It'll all come back. It's because you bumped your head." She stroked his dark hair. "Don't worry. Don't worry. It'll all come back to you as you get stonger."

She wondered for a moment whether, if she told him that his father was dead, the shock would revive his memory. But that might do more harm than good. Far better leave things as they were and to nature; nature cured all, given the time. . . .

It was later in the day when the doctor called and shocked her still further. Standing outside the cottage, he said, "He might never recover his memory. There are such cases. In his fall he must have hit himself on a vulnerable part of the head; it causes what we call amnesia."

"What?" Kate said.

"Amnesia," he repeated. "It's a kind of forgetfulness. It could cure itself tomorrow, or never. It's a thing like that."

"Dear God!" Kate had replied.

And the doctor, being a man who, like herself, had doubts about the Almighty, had answered jokingly, "Dear, indeed! The prices He causes one to pay at times."

He was an odd customer that doctor, but not unlikeable. No, not unlikeable.

But she couldn't say the same thing about her next visitor, for if she hated anybody in this world, it was Dan Bannaman.

Dan Bannaman was in his forty-fifth year. He was tall and handsome in a rugged kind of way. He was a farmer who had prospered in all years. When other farmers were suffering from drought, or floods, the sun seemed to shine on Dan Bannaman, for his herds grew and his house got larger. And his nine-year-old daughter was being educated like a lady, and his only son, who was eight years old, was boarded out at one of the fancy schools in Hexham. Everything had seemed to fall into Dan Bannaman's lap since he'd come as a young boy in his teens to his Uncle John, who was then running Rooklands Farm.

John Bannaman had been liked and respected, although everybody knew that he spent more time hunting and drinking than he did on his farm. And when he died childless and left his one thousand acres of land, mostly poor stuff, being on the hills, he also left innumerable debts to be settled by his nephew Dan. Yet, from the time Dan Bannaman came into possession of the estate he seemed to have, as it was said around, the touch, for he not only married Rosalie Fountain, who came of good family, but whereas most farmers took on the occasional buying and selling of horses for the mines and mills, he did so in a big way. It was thought that the dowry Rosalie Fountain had brought with her must have been scraped together by her family, for although they were of good class they weren't wealthy by any means. But a dowry she must have brought.

There were three people, four at the most, who knew that Dan Bannaman's rise to prosperity didn't originate from his wife's dowry. There had been six at one time in the know, but one was now dead, another was in America.

Kate held the door in her hand and stared at the man, and when he smiled at her and said, "Well, hello, Kate. Aren't you going to ask me in?" she said flatly, "No, no, I am not."

The smile slid from his face, "That's a pity then, Kate," he said.

To this she answered, "You can't frighten me, not any more."

"You'd be surprised, Kate."

"Aye, I would that."

"I have friends over there."

"You might have, or you might not have, but America's a very big place, and he's moved on."

"How do you know that? You have no way of telling."

"You'd be surprised." A thought coming into her head, she said, "We had a visit from a sailor, poor man, who died underneath the quarry fall the other night. Perhaps you heard of it?"

"Aye, I heard of it." His tone was stiff.

"Well, you might remember him, his name was Peter Greenbank. He was a lad who was born and bred here and worked here until about ten years or so ago. Well, since then, he's travelled the world, and America was one of his spots, and he brought me news, news I've been waiting to hear for a long time." She made herself smile a grim smile. "So it's my turn now to say, be careful, Mr Bannaman, be careful, for where it might take a lifetime to track down my son, it would take only an hour or so for the justice to come out from Newcastle."

They stared at each other for a matter of seconds before he said, "And what about your own skin, Kate? Harbouring's an offence."

"Oh, I'm past caring about that. Me time's almost on me; it wouldn't matter. But you, you're in your prime. With your fine house and your great farm and your standing in the county, oh, Mr Bannaman, you have a lot to lose, both you and your henchmen. And I'm warnin' you now, don't try anything on me like you did on Les Carter...."

"I had nothing to do with Les Carter." His voice was grim. "You know who was to blame there."

"Your word, that's all, your word. An' I've had me doubts about that this many a year."

"If it hadn't been for me, your lad would have swung."

"So you say, but I think different, and so did Pat. Anyway, I'll tell you this: I've left word that if I die in any other place but in me bed, then they'll have reason to question a couple of men. I've left this word in two places and they're both in sealed letters, sort of wills. My Pat, as you know, could read an' write. He was no thick-skinned smelter, or yet a drink-sodden lead or coal miner, he was a young fellow with brains. An' you used them, an' played on them. But one thing he did afore he got away was to tell me what to do just in case, and I did it. So, Mr Bannaman, I'm just tellin' you."

Dan Bannaman looked down at the ground now and, shaking his head slowly, he said, "You don't give me credit for one decent thing, do you, Kate?"

"I speak as I find and I see nothin' in you to give you credit for. I even suspect your every step you take, so I ask what you are doin' round here miles away from your mansion?"

"Something very suspicious, Kate, I've brought my man to gather young saplings of pine and fir. I'm starting a plantation, I've got permission from James Mulcaster. So what devilry can you pick out of that? Eh?"

"Firs and pine? Why have you to come this far? They're thin enough this end. They're just startin' to grow up on the top."

"Thin, you say, they're choking each other up there. They'll grow like spindles if they're left as they are. You with your plant wisdom, Kate, I would have thought you realized that these things have to be thinned out. Trees are like human beings, herd them together and they grow like weeds, crooked, spidery. Give them air and light and they expand."

She looked at him through narrowed eyes, saying, "Wise talk doesn't come smoothly from your tongue, Dan Bannaman. Stick to that you know best, it's recognizable, covert threats an' such."

A noise from inside the room now turned Kate's head towards the saddle to where the boy was sitting on the edge of it, swaying slightly, and at this she left loose of the door, calling, "Keep still, boy, I'll be with you in a minute."

"Is that the little fellow who fell down the quarry?"

She turned and caught hold of the door again, but it was wide now for he had pushed it open and he was looking towards the boy who was looking towards him. They stared at each other for fully a minute while Kate looked from one to the other, and when the boy stumbled to his feet Kate hurried forward and led him to a chair.

After a moment, while still looking at the boy, Dan Bannaman said, "Is he badly hurt?"

"Bruises mostly."

"Poor little fellow." He had advanced into the room and was now standing within a couple of feet looking down on the child and he said softly, "Hello there." And the boy looked up into the clean-shaven face but he did not speak or show any other sign but a vague blankness. And Bannaman, now turning to Kate, said, "Can't he speak?"

"Yes, but the doctor says he's" – some portion of her mind was asking her why she was hesitating to tell him what the doctor had said, but she had to go on and finish what she had begun and so ended – "he's lost his memory for a time, but ... but it could come back. That's what the doctor said, it could come back."

"Poor mite. And his father dead."

"Yes, his father dead."

"I was talking to Mr Mulcaster about the quarry. I think they'll do something at last. It's been crumbling away for years to my knowledge."

"It shouldn't trouble you, it's not on your doorstep."

"Oh, Kate, give me credit for a little human feeling, will you?" He now looked at the boy again, the while speaking to her, saying, "What's going to become of him?"

"I'm keeping him."

"You are?"

"Yes. He has no one else as far as I know."

"Well, well, at your age, taking on a child. Well, I suppose he could do worse than be brought up in your care. But ... but I tell you what." And now he wagged his finger at her. "Don't say, what's behind it? Do you hear? But if you want to give the lad a start.... How old is he?"

"Coming up eight I understand."

"Well, he'll soon be ready for work, or at best, part-time schooling. But if I can do anything in that line, I will. You could do worse than let him come to me on the farm. He'd learn a lot. And I mean it." He bent towards her now. "Give me credit for this one good thing, Kate."

She had been brought up to think that there was some good in everyone, that no one was totally bad, so on this she wanted to answer, "All right, I'll take you at your word," because if anybody could help a lad like this one without a father and without any good prospects but those of going into either the smelting mills or the coal mine, he could. But what she said was, "He'll not lack for education. I'll see to that and at the right time. As for work, that'll come at the right time an' all."

"You don't change, Kate."

"No, I don't change."

"'Tis a pity."

"For who?"

"Both of us."

"That remains to be seen. I wish you good-day, Mr Bannaman."

The man looked once more at the boy who was still looking at him, then turned and went out.

She paused a moment, then looked at the door before going and opening it and looking to where her visitor, now on horseback, was riding over the field. Presently, as if coming to a decision, she closed the door again and walked slowly to the boy and said, 'Do ... do you remember that man?"

He stared at her for a moment. "No," he said.

"You haven't seen him afore?"

"No."

She straightened herself; then with a smile she asked, "Do you feel better?"

For answer he put his hand to his head and she said, "Your head aches? Oh, I'll give you something that'll fix that."

But before doing so, she went once again to the door and, having opened it and satisfied herself that Bannaman had really gone, she stood thoughtfully looking into the distance. Why had he shaved off his beard? But then he'd only had a beard during the last three or four years; he'd always been clean-shaven before that. But why had he shaved it off now? And this talk of gathering up young trees.

Later on she would go up to the copse and look round.

Towards evening she went up on the top of the quarry and she stood on the part from which she had caught sight of the boy's hand four days ago, and she walked round the small clearing where the bushes had been trampled down. But there had been much more trampling about since then so that now there was nothing to see but stones scattered about. Men from the mine had been clearing a way to make a fresh path to get from one end of the quarry to the other.

She next walked further along the track, penetrating the growth here and there, and although she saw that there were holes where young trees had been dug out, there were not all that many, not enough to start a plantation, not more than a couple of dozen all told.

That weird feeling was still on her. If only the boy could remember what had actually happened. Well, all she could do was wait, and likely when he did remember she'd be able to say to herself, I hadn't me feeling for nothing.

PART ONE

❦

The Children

1

"Now I've told you, Mary Ellen, anyway you know as well as I do, your da doesn't like you changing your Sunday clothes and rampagin' around like a wild thing."

"'Tis the only day I've got to rampage around, Ma."

"Don't be cheeky."

"I'm not, Ma; but I don't see why I can't take me good boots and frock off and have a dander in the wood."

"Dander? You mean gallop." Jane Lee turned on her young daughter, half smiling now as she said, "I didn't give birth to a daughter but something atween a rabbit and a fox, I think, because I do believe if you could burrow into the earth you'd do so."

"Rabbits sit still, Ma, to wash their faces, and they sit stiller when a fox stares at them."

"Cheeky face!" Her mother's hand came out and slapped her gently on the cheek, at which Mary Ellen coaxed, "Aw, Ma, let me change me frock; me da won't be back from Haydon Bridge for another two hours. And look" – she went and put her arms around her mother's waist – "I'll be back long afore then and I'll do another quick change and I'll sit on the chair" – she nodded towards the seat she had just vacated – "and I'll put me hands on me lap and I'll cross me ankles and when he says, 'Well, what have you been up to, miss, since I've been away?' I'll say, 'Nothin', Da; I sat here waitin' for you.'"

A none too gentle push knocked her almost onto her back, but her mother was laughing as she said, "I know where you'll end up, in the House of Correction while you're alive and in hell when you're dead."

"Eeh! Ma."

"Never you mind, 'Eeh! Ma.' You're as wily as that fox you were talking about."

They stared at each other for a moment, and when Jane next spoke there was a serious note in her voice: "You know, Mary Ellen," she said, "you're ten and you're going out into the world next week and you'll have to stop your flighty ways."

"Oh, Ma." Mary Ellen moved her head from side to side now and it showed her impatience as she replied, "It's only Mr Davison's farm, and I've been goin' back and forwards there for years, and I know them all."

"Yes, miss, you might know them all, but you knew them when you

35

were fetchin' the milk, now you're going to work in the kitchen, and Mrs Davison will be giving you a wage and so she'll expect respect and no back answers."

"I don't back answer . . . well" – her lips were pursed now and a deep twinkle came into her eyes – "only you and—" she drew her lips into a tight line before she added softly, "me da."

"Your da." Jane jerked her chin upwards. "He's to blame really for the way you are, he's ruined you, broken your neck an' given you ideas above your station."

"Yes, Ma, yes, he has, like makin' me wear me Sunday clothes all day. Sarah and Mary Roberts don't have to."

"Sarah and Mary Roberts!" Her tone was scornful. "It's a wonder they've got a decent rag to their backs, the way their father goes on. And anyway, you know your da doesn't like you mixing with them. And another thing about mixin', now I've got to tell you this, and I'm serious" – Jane wagged her finger at her daughter – "you've got to stop this running wild with the lads."

"I don't, Ma." The small figure stretched, the ringlets of hair bobbed up and down, the chin was thrust out, and the brown eyes blazed with indignation. "I don't run wild with them, they always come after me."

"That isn't true and you know it. You're never away from Kate's when you think Roddy's there."

"Well, Roddy's different. I've always played with Roddy."

Jane's voice had a patient note to it now as she said, "Yes, you've always played with Roddy, that was when you were little, but now you're ten years old and he's a young lad. What is he? Coming up thirteen, and he could be taken for sixteen any day. Your playin' days are over, Mary Ellen. And it isn't only him, it's Hal Roystan, too. Now he is fourteen, although strangely he doesn't look it. It's the opposite way with him, not being of Roddy's height and build. Now I've always warned you against Hal, haven't I? He's a strange lad, bitter. Of course he's got something to be bitter about. It was all right when you were all little together, but now you're all growing an' there are things you should know. . . ."

"Ma, I don't want to know, I mean I don't want to know any more, please."

The appeal in the voice and small face silenced Jane and she stared down on her daughter's troubled countenance. At times, her child both amazed and frightened her with her understanding of things that she herself could not explain in words, nor yet conjure up in thought. And now she listened as Mary Ellen said, "I've told you, Ma, I don't like Hal, but in a way I'm sorry for him, and I get a bit pipped against him at times because he always wants to be with Roddy. I suppose it's because Roddy found him that time sleeping out in the woods and brought him to Kate. . . ."

At this point Jane put in, "Mrs Kate," and was immediately answered with, "Not any more, Ma. Kate herself said I needn't call her missis any more now I was goin' out to work. She said that only yesterday. But Hal, Ma, I've never run wild with him 'cos he doesn't like me any more than I like him. But where Roddy is, he's always there an' all. Just 'cos he works alongside of him he has to go rabbitin' and fishin' with him."

"And what about swimming?"

"Oh! Oh Ma" – again the small body bristled – "I never go near them when they're swimmin'. And anyway, the water in the dam would freeze you. It's bad enough if you plodge along the edge. Ma—" Once more the small arms were round Jane's waist and the face upturned to hers and the voice placating as it said, "Don't worry about me. I'll be good at Mrs Davison's an' do me work and I won't answer back, but Ma, don't stop me goin' to Kate's and ... an' seeing Roddy, 'cos ... 'cos, Ma, I like Roddy."

Jane closed her eyes. Then, her voice as soft but not as placating as her daughter's tone had been, she said, "Mary Ellen, don't let on to anybody, not anybody mind, that ... that you like Roddy. Lasses don't do that kind of thing. Well, not until they are fifteen or sixteen or so, and you've got a long way to go yet."

"But ... but I couldn't stop liking Roddy, Ma."

Jane sighed and, unloosening the hands from around her waist, she held them together in front of her as she said, "Nobody's asking you to stop liking Roddy, but you haven't got to say it out. You see what I mean? You don't go round saying, you like lads, this one or that one, not even one like Roddy.... You haven't said to him you like him, have you?"

"No, Ma."

"*You haven't?*"

"*No, Ma, I haven't.*"

"Well, don't ever."

"Not ever, Ma?"

"Oh! child. Well not until you're grown up, and by then you'll likely have your eye on somebody else and have even forgotten Roddy."

"I'll never forget about Roddy, Ma."

Jane had been in the act of turning away to attend to her baking, but now she looked at her daughter again and in the glance they exchanged there was certainty on the one side and fear on the other, and the fear almost caused Jane to shout now as she said, "What if he regains his memory and remembers that his da was a sailor and gets the urge to do what he did and go off? What about it then?" And her daughter's reply to this stilled any remark she would have made if she could have thought of one, for Mary Ellen said quite quietly, "We've talked about that, and he said it might happen and it might never happen, time will tell, it's all in the wind."

*

"What you want to draw my face for when there's better looking things even in the pigsty, I don't know."

"Keep yourself still, and stop twitching your nose."

"I'm sweatin', it's running out of me hair." Kate slanted her eyes to where the boy was sitting, a slate held on his knee, a chalk poised over it, and there was love and admiration in her glance, for if this lad had been born of her own flesh, she couldn't have loved him more dearly. Looking back now, she hardly remembered her own son; her life seemed to have begun the day she saw this boy's arm hanging from the quarry wall. And she had loved him from that moment. Sometimes she was surprised that she hadn't carried him in her womb, so deep was her feeling for him, and so close were they together in all ways. She only wished one thing, that fortunes were different, that he hadn't to work down in that stinking smelt mill, for God knew, even with their newfangled tunnels leading to chimneys on the hill to take away the gases, life was limited if you spent twelve hours a day, six days a week, over there.

Her eyes now slid to the other occupant of the room. She had feelings for him too, but they were mostly of pity for he'd had a hard life of it since his father, the big-headed clerk, had slunk off with the wages. The lad had been hard put to survive. Twice they had taken him to the poorhouse, and twice he had run away. And then had come the day that Roddy brought him to her, dirty, practically starving and more like a wild animal than a boy. It was she who had gone over the hill to Abel Hamilton, who was a widower with no chick or child of his own and a man who was against all order. He lived by what he made out of his stint and the few animals he kept on it, and she had persuaded him to give the lad shelter in return for which he would work for him. And Hal had worked for him till he was eleven, when he went, first, into the coal mine, and then, for bigger money, down to the smelt mill.

She sometimes thought that the lad had grown like the old man, wary, close, wasting no words on speech. The only time he had ever let his tongue loose was the day he came to her for a potion for his bruises, for he had been kicked black and blue by some louts from Haydon Bridge way. And on that occasion he had said to her, "I'll suffer to me dying day for what me dad did. Nobody'll ever let me forget it. But you know something, Mrs Kate, I've a feelin' in me that one day he'll come back. I get it strong at times." And then he had cried: his head in his folded arms, he had sobbed while she rubbed his discoloured body with a balm that never failed to give ease, for her mother had passed the recipe on to her before she had died, and over the years since she could have made a pretty penny, had she had enough to hand to satisfy all those who had offered to pay her for it, especially those who went hunting and could not keep their seats.

The next day the boy had brought her a sack of peat, saying her salve was magic. And she had agreed with him, saying, "Aye. Yes, it is," for so it had proved in many other cases. Always she kept her recipe to herself:

to enquirers she would say, "Oh, 'tis mainly oil of roses, and St John's wort." To others: "Pound up some baccy leaves in a mortar with some balsam." She never mentioned turpentine or masticke, or a drop of wax, or resin to give the whole a stiffness, or the quantities. And so the recipients of her information always came back to her, saying, "I did what you said, Kate, but it didn't work for me like yours does."

One thing that irritated her about Hal, but not to the extent it did Mary Ellen, was the fact, to put it in her own words, he hardly let Roddy breathe. But then he had no other friend to her knowledge, nor did he trouble the lasses.

Hal now caught her glance but there was no answering smile in his eyes, and her lips champed against each other before she spoke with an effort to keep her face straight, "Did he ever want to draw you, Hal?" And the answer she received was "No." And now, trying not to move, she turned her eyes in Roddy's direction and asked, "Why don't you draw Hal?" And the answer she was given this time was, "He's got a difficult face."

And now she did move: she put her head back and laughed, and Roddy cried, "Oh, that's done it! Well, I'll finish you later." And he stood up and turned the slate downwards, and when she said, "Let me have a look," he answered, "When it's finished and I've put it on paper."

"I'll likely be dead by then; that's the third go you've had on me."

"I shouldn't wonder, as I'm not very good at faces."

"You mean you're not very good at mine. Anyway, after that business of sittin' like a stook I've got a thirst on me. What about you two?"

Before they could answer she glanced through the open door, saying, "Ah now, here's one who never refuses a drink." And as Mary Ellen stepped into the room, Kate said to her, "I was just saying you'd like a drink."

"Aye. Yes, thanks, Kate, I would; it's hot." Mary Ellen pulled the top of her cotton dress away from her neck. Then looking towards where Roddy was putting his slate and chalk into what looked like a canvas bag, she added, "You been drawin' again?"

"No, he's been fishin'."

She turned a sharp glance on the boy sitting to the side of the fire, and she retorted immediately, "Yes, I can see that an' all, and you likely got the hook in your tongue, you're so sharp. You should have got the line round your neck——" She was about to add, "and swung from it", but she thought that nasty; instead, she continued to return the stare of the steel-grey eyes until Kate said, "Now, now, you two. And you, me lass, get yourself in the room afore you start."

"Well" – she tossed her head – "he started, not me."

"It doesn't matter who started, I'm stoppin' it. Do you want ginger or herb beer? But need I ask, it's ginger, isn't it?"

"Yes."

She ignored the abrupt reply, nor did she ask the boys what they wanted as she struggled to get up.

The room to themselves now, there was silence between the three of them for a moment before, looking at Roddy, Mary Ellen asked, "You goin' down the dam?"

"No" – Roddy shook his head – "I'm goin' over to the mill."

"The mill?" She looked him up and down. He was in his Sunday suit. And he explained briefly by muttering, "I'm drawin' it from the top of the bank."

"Drawing the mill? What do you want to draw the mill for?"

"Because he doesn't get enough of it while he's there, and he wants to remember it when he gets home."

Again she was staring at the older boy. "Clever clogs." She made a face at him, then added, "I bet you don't use a knife to spread your drippin', you do it with your tongue."

At this Roddy laughed and said, "Well, I bet I know who showed him how to do it." And he gave her a push in the shoulder; and now she laughed too, a gay high laugh, ending it with the question, "Can I come?"

"Eeh! no. Your da's forbidden you along there, hasn't he? And there'll be a shift goin' down about now."

"And they use naughty words."

She again looked towards Hal but ignored his remark. She knew, though, she had been silly to ask because it wasn't so long ago that she was given a skelping on her backside for going down to the mill.

She had protested strongly to her father that she'd only gone to meet him, but he had told her time and again he didn't want to be met. Yet she had noticed other children, not only meeting their fathers but working in the slag. She often wondered why her da insisted on her being different; there was no fun in being different. Even when they went to the barn dance he wouldn't let her romp with all the others. Her ma would have, but then her ma didn't have the final say in such matters. All her ma would say at such times was, "Behave yourself or you'll have his brows as black as drawn slag," whatever that meant. She had never seen drawn slag, she only knew it was something that came out of the kilns in the mill. She didn't like the mill and somehow she knew her father didn't either. One day she had dared to say to him, "Why don't you work on a farm, Da?" And he had answered her in a strange way, "Do you like to eat meat every Sunday?" he had said.

"Yes," she had answered.

"And you like to have boots on your feet an' not clogs?" he had said, and again she had answered, "Yes."

"And do you like a new frock come Easter?" he had said.

"Yes, Da, yes. I love a new frock come Easter."

And then he had said, "Well, all that takes money, more money than I would get workin' on a farm. But remember this, never crave for too much money, just enough to bring a little comfort to the inside and outside of your body, because with money often comes misery and a discontent with your lot. Learn to be satisfied with being well shod and well fed and a good bed and a hap over you to keep out the winter winds."

Her da was a funny man. That wasn't the right word, but she knew what it meant inside her head.

When they had finished their drinks, the two boys made for the door, and there Roddy turned and, looking towards her, said, "I'll be comin' over to your place the night. Your da's promised to tell me a thing or two because on the morrow's shift I go in on the floor." Then turning more fully to look at her, he said, "An' you start up Davison's, don't you?" She nodded, and he returned her nod with a smile before swinging round and running down the path to join his friend.

Mary Ellen stood in the doorway watching the two figures, one tall and straight, the other hardly coming up to his shoulder, but whose body seemed to be of twice the thickness, and she wondered if there would ever be a time again when she would have Roddy to herself; they had been together such a lot before he had gone to work at the mill.

"So you start work the morrow?"

She turned to Kate and half-heartedly she replied, "Yes. And . . . and I don't know whether I'm gona like it or not."

"Well, hinny, you can't stay tied to your mother's apron strings forever."

She took no umbrage at this because she knew she had been lucky to be at home all this time and not sent out tatie picking, or stone picking, or scarecrowing. She said now, "I'm gona miss poppin' in."

"Huh!" Kate laughed. "You won't be away forever. You're lucky, so your ma tells me, a half day every Sunday and a whole day once a month. My! It's usually a half day a month for them in service, leastwise in the big houses, and the half day starting in the middle of the afternoon an' all in many cases."

"Did you ever go into service, Kate?"

"No, I never did, lass, not in that way. I was free. I worked in me father's carpenter's shop until I was sixteen. Then it was burnt down and that finished him. I married Davey who had been apprenticed there and just out of his time, and with him and me mother I came here to this cottage, where she herself had been born and had left to get married, and here I've been ever since."

"Did your mother know about herbs and things?"

"Yes, and her mother, and her mother afore her. Which reminds me, higtaper will be out about now. You know the kind; you'll find it along the ditch yon side of the wood."

"Why do you always call longwort, higtaper, Kate?"

"Because I've always known it as higtaper. There's a male and a female, but as you know I prefer the female. An' you know what it's like, don't you? Well, you should so, you've picked it long enough."

"Well sometimes I get them mixed up 'cos they're nearly alike except one's white and one's yellow."

"So—" Kate laughed a deep throaty laugh that denied her years as she

41

went on, "Likely God made the female plant white to denote purity, although, as I often say, His eyesight must have been affected now and then. But anyway He made it for the lungs, especially those in cattle that get choked up. And when you're on, if you should happen to come across a cowslip ... but they're mostly over now. Still, here and there they persevere, and there's a dank place, you know, near the ride. I wouldn't tell you to go near it if it had been raining of late, but it should be dried up now, or nearly so. Still, there might be parts soggy enough to grow a cowslip. I wish I could get up there meself, but me legs are refusing to obey orders these days and I can only keep to the flats. There now, take this basket and, as I always tell you, don't pass any dead nettle. If you come back by Peter Stubbs's cottage you'll most likely come across a heap of it because if ever there was a lazy beggar in this world, it's him lettin' his ground go rank. Still, I shouldn't grumble about that, for he's given me the best supply of dead nettles from round about for many a year. It's a good job he's a good mill worker or else he would have been put out a time ago."

Mary Ellen, taking up the basket, grinned now as she said, "Oh, I'll collect the dead nettle for you if nothin' else, 'cos I love those sweets you make with the flowers, and me da loves the potion."

"He's not the only one. But I can tell you something for nothing, Mary Ellen, anybody who wants that this winter is gona pay for it. I'm givin' no more away, except to your ma and da of course. The neck of some people walking miles to ask me for a pick-me-up, and the most they leave'll be a penny, when the sugar syrup costs twice as much. Oh, away with you and let's stop yammerin' or else you'll never get back home in time for supper. And then what'll happen? Your da will be along here goin' for me, demanding to know why I've kept you."

"He'd never go for you, Kate. No, he wouldn't. And he knows I'm all right when I'm here. Anyway" – she sighed – "'tis me last day."

"Last day indeed! Go on, get yourself away. You talk like an ancient; your head's too old for your body. Always has been, miss. Go on with you." She shooed her out of the room as she did the chickens, wafting her apron at her, and Mary Ellen, joining in the charade, made cackling sounds as she ran down the garden and through the gate and into the field.

But her step had slowed to a walk before she reached the place where the ride divided, one twisting track rising towards the quarry, the other also going steeply uphill but skirting the wood that had thickened in all ways during the past five years; not only had the saplings grown but the brushwood had taken over densely in parts.

Knowing that she would take the bottom road back by Stubbs's cottage in order to gather the dead nettle, she decided to look at the bog first to see if there were any late cowslips still there. She dismissed the thought that her father had forbidden her to go near the bog ever again since that time she fell in and was stuck up to her knees. It was a good job, he had said as he lathered her ears, that she had stayed near the edge, for a foot further in she would likely have been sucked under. This had happened when she was seven years old. But at times he would still warn her, "If you are going up the ride, madam, keep clear of the bog." But that was whenever they'd had a wet summer. This summer had been scorching hot; the streams had dried up; even the dam down at Langley was well below its bank.

She now pushed her way through some low shrub, stepped over a fallen branch, then came onto a rough pathway that had at one time bordered the ride, and there to the left of her was the dried up bog, the whole of which was not more than twelve feet across. What vegetation grew about it was now shrivelled up; the mud was cracked in parts and to some depth, showing crevices inches across, and the whole expanse of mud had dropped to almost a foot below the rim, and in one glance she saw that there was no possibility of any cowslips being found there. But what did draw her attention was something that looked like a handle sticking out of a crevice in the mud just below where she was standing.

Being of a curious nature, she responded by immediately kneeling down on the hard crusty earth and, bending over, she touched the half circle. It felt hard like wood. In the ordinary way she would have taken it for a fallen branch, except that part of it was showing black where the dried mud had dropped from it and around this black part was a ring of brass or steel or some metal. Gripping the handle now, she went to pull it up because she guessed there was something attached to it. What her mind didn't say, only told her there was *something* below the mud.

Forgetting for the moment she was still in her Sunday clothes, she lay flat on the bank now and, extending her two hands and taking a firm grip on the handle, she endeavoured to move it backwards and forwards, with the pleasing result that the dried mud at each side gave way and there came to her ears a small sucking sound. Her efforts now became really vigorous, and when more of the dried mud fell away and exposed the thing that the handle was attached to, she stopped and gazed down in amazement at the top of a bag. Immediately, she recognized the type of bag because it was the same shape as the one old Doctor Cranwell carried when he went to the mine or the mill when there was an accident.

Frantically now, her grip tight on the handle, she again resumed a rocking motion. Of a sudden there was a sound like a cork leaving a bottle and her elbows gave way and her face almost hit the edge of the bank, and there at the end of her extended arms she saw she was holding what she imagined to be an exact replica of the doctor's bag, except perhaps it might be a little bigger.

Having pulled it onto the bank, she noticed that the bottom of the bag was covered with wet mud, and she thought, it must be still soggy underneath and you could still get stuck; me da was right. But what was in this bag?

She got to her feet, but when she went to lift it she found it was almost too heavy for her, being still caked with mud, she imagined, and so,

43

picking up some dried grass from nearby and a piece of wood, she proceeded to scrape the bag as clean as she could.

Her efforts showed that it was a leather bag which had become as hard as iron with being in the mud. She also saw that it had a lock going through the flap on one side of it. There was no key in the lock, so she couldn't find out what was inside. But there was something inside it and it was movable because when she pushed the bag onto its side she heard that something move, and when, with an effort, she turned it completely upside down, whatever was inside fell to the top which was now the bottom of the bag.

Still kneeling, she stared down at it as if waiting for some directions. At one point she thought, I'll go and tell Kate. But Kate couldn't come up here. And then, she couldn't go and tell her da because no matter what was in the bag he would skin her alive for having disobeyed him, especially for her daring to come near the bog, even if it was dried up. But of course he was right, it was never dried up at the bottom, as the bag had proved. And another thing, she was still in her Sunday clothes.

As she continued to stare at it her eyes narrowed as she imagined she saw a letter on the side of the bag. To prove whether it was imagination or not she spat two or three times on the spot, then rubbed it with some more dried grass, and her efforts proved that it wasn't her imagination because she was looking at the letter "B". Further spitting and further rubbing disclosed another three letters to make up the word, "Bank". And now as if a veil had been lifted from her eyes and a door opened in her mind, she saw her father standing in the kitchen after he had returned from a visit to Hexham market and he was saying to her mother, "That Hal will do someone a damage one of these days, for if I hadn't pulled him free, it would be him that would have got the damage the day, for he was tackling three of 'em. Apparently they had jibed at him about his father stealing the payroll and likely now living in luxury in a foreign country on the money. I brought him back on the cart with me and dropped him off near the road. And you know something, he's a strange lad, for he was about to walk away when he turned and, looking at me, he said in a voice like an old man instead of a lad, 'My dad never did that, he wouldn't.'"

She looked down at the bag, and now there was no doubt in her mind as to what was in the bag. But what would she do with it? Money always caused trouble. Her da was always saying that, money always caused trouble. If Roddy was here he would know what to do with it. But then, if Roddy was here, Hal would be with him, and if Hal got his hands on this bag she knew exactly what would happen: he wouldn't take it to the authorities like her da or Roddy might, for he would think it was his 'cos his da had suffered for it no matter where he was across the world, 'cos he had gone across the world. She had heard the tale so often about his horse having been found far away in Newcastle, which could only mean he had gone on a ship. Yet, why hadn't he taken the bag with him?

Her mind gave her no answer, except to ask what was she going to do with it. Throw it back into the mud? No, no. That idea was immediately rejected. Anyway it wouldn't sink now; and what was more she hadn't much time. Whatever she was going to do with it she must do it straightaway because she had to gather the herbs and then get home afore her da got back.

There was that hole on the other side of the quarry that she had discovered when she was blaeberrying last year. By, she had got a gliff that day. The blaeberry bushes were thick there and she had scrambled up a mound to get to the big berries, and her scrambling must have loosened something because she had suddenly to hang on and then the earth had given way beneath her. She didn't fall far, but her feet seemed to be entangled with large stones like in the quarry. Presently, she realized she had fallen into a kind of tunnel, and it wasn't a natural place, for it had been stone built. Perhaps, she thought, it was one of the tunnels the men had been making to take the gas from the smelt mill and hadn't gone on with it. Anyway, it was dry inside and she sat in the opening until she got her breath back and then she climbed up onto the bank and was surprised that she had really only slid a short distance because when her feet had given way she had imagined she had fallen from heaven.

So that was it. She could stick the bag in there for the time being until she could think what to do with it. But could she carry it?

Slinging the basket onto her shoulder, first she stood up, then bent and gripped the bag with both hands and found that yes, holding it like that, she could carry it. It was hard like a piece of wood. But she hadn't taken more than two or three steps when she asked herself what would happen if she met someone.

Well, she needn't meet anybody for she knew her way through the thicket and from where she was now it would only take her a few minutes to be at the end of the quarry....

Long before she reached the sloping bank where the blaeberries grew, she was panting. The way seemed longer than she had imagined. When she at last stopped she dropped the bag onto the ground, then took the basket from her shoulder and pushed it into the bushes. She took up the bag again and foraged forwards for the tunnel.

The bushes had grown amazingly and it was only her feet that told her she had reached the entrance, because now there was a bush hanging over it and as she bent down a twig caught her bonnet and pulled the straps tight around her chin and she whimpered aloud, "Oh, dear me. Oh, dear me."

Pushing the bush aside, she crawled into the aperture, the bag behind her. She had to blink a number of times to accustom herself to the dim light coming through the bush. Kneeling down, she crawled some little distance until she could see no further, and there she left the bag, but not before she had patted it and then asked herself why she had done so.

Outside and having retrieved her basket, she vigorously dusted her dress down, saying the while, "Eeh! it's a good job it's a fawny colour so the marks don't show." This done, she made her way back to the wood and towards the field where she would find longwort, all the time wondering to whom she could talk about the money. Kate seemed the safest person. But yet again a door opened in her mind and she recalled an incident that had happened a long, long time ago when she was small. She had seen a man in the wood picking herbs and she had talked to him because she liked talking to people, and when she told Kate about the man, Kate had looked at her and said, "Which man goes round here picking herbs? Did you know him?" And she had answered, "No, but he was a little man with a funny hand." And at this point Kate had become quite excited and she had put her shawl on and gone out, and had told her to go home. Later, Kate told her to look out for the man and to tell her when she saw him. But she hadn't seen him again.

Now why should she think of that? She didn't know, but somehow it prevented her from choosing Kate as the recipient of her secret. The only one she could really tell was Roddy, and she must get him by himself sometime tonight, and then she would know what to do with the bag.

Meanwhile Roddy and Hal were sitting on a bank above the smelt mill. Being Sunday, there was little activity around the works.

Hall, sitting slightly behind and to the left of Roddy, had watched him in silence for sometime before he said, "Why do you always keep drawing the outside?"

"To get the feel."

"The feel of what?"

The boy stopped drawing, straightened his back and looked down on the huddle of buildings. It was some seconds before he answered. "I don't rightly know, except when I get the chance to do inside I'll be able to fit things in better."

"You could get the chance to do inside any Sunday, if you so minded."

"Aye, and have me lugs scoffed off by Mr Holden or Coates or Lance Ritson."

"Why do you mind them?"

Roddy turned and looked at his mate now, saying, "Because they think it's daft, lasses' stuff."

"They don't think Will Campbell's daft and he carves wood into all kinds of things."

Roddy considered for a moment and then nodded as he said, "Aye, he does. He's clever at it an' all. Yet somehow, they always scoff at me."

"They're only pulling your leg. Anyway, Mr Mulcaster doesn't seem to think you're daft. He encourages you. Why don't you ask him to let you loose inside? You've just got to say the word, I should imagine."

"Aye, I've only got to say the word and he would let me have the run of the place, when everything's quiet. But I don't want that: I want to go in and stand around and watch the lead being run off; I want to see the flue glass come off and men chokin' with the dust like; I want to see them stuffin' the coal into the cupola; aye, an' I want to see them takin' the hatches off to let the air through into the furnace; I want to see the lead comin' out into the pan. Aw, you don't understand, man, I want to see everythin' as it happens like, you know, as it happens."

"Well, God above!" Hal had moved to his side now. "You can see that every day in the week."

It was some seconds before Roddy made a reply to this. He had dropped his slate onto the grass and his body had slumped and his voice had a weary note in it as he said, "Aye, as I'm runnin' backwards an' forwards like a scalded cat, wheelin' the dross, blinded with sweat, half choked."

"Well, wouldn't you be half choked if you were standin' there drawin', man?"

" 'Twould be different."

"You know what I think?"

"Aye, I've a good idea."

"Aye, well, I'll say it, you're barmy."

Roddy's back straightened. He swung round on his knees, grabbed up his slate and got to his feet, crying, "Then why the devil do you keep taggin' on to somebody that's barmy? 'Tis true what Mary Ellen says, I can't breathe without you."

This unexpected attack, the very first he had experienced, caused Hal's eyes to darken and the shape of the lips almost to disappear into a thin line. Then in a flash he was gone, and, almost as quickly, Roddy was running after him. But he didn't catch up with him until they were dropping down the bank opposite the dam. Gripping the smaller lad by the arm, he pulled him to a halt, only to have his hand shrugged away. And when, his voice contrite, he said, "I didn't mean that, Hal. I didn't. There's nobody I would have for a mate but you. You know that," Hal's lips parted but the teeth were still tightly together and his voice came through them, saying, "On top, aye, but underneath you're just like the rest."

"That's not fair." Roddy was shouting now. "I've stood by you through thick an' thin. And you're not the only one that's gone through the mill, we both lost our dads at the same time."

"Aye, we did." The boy's voice was quiet now. "But the cases were slightly different, weren't they?"

"Aye, they might have been, but then you have one advantage over me, you can remember what yours was like, I can't."

"Well, I would change places with you any day in the week, and I wouldn't feel sorry for meself."

"Who's feeling sorry for himsel'?"

"You are, and always have done, 'cos you've been brought up soft,

47

pampered by old Kate an' the Lees, an' nursed by that little tonguey bitch of theirs...."

At the same moment that Roddy threw his slate aside his other fist shot out and caught Hal on the cheekbone, and the next minute they were rolling on the ground, kicking and punching at each other.

What finally stopped them was a basket descending on both their heads spraying weeds over them. They rolled away from each other and lay for a moment, Roddy on his back, Hal leaning on his elbow, looking up at the red face staring down at them, and listening to her voice as high as a scream yelling, "What's up with yous? Have you both gone barmy? An' on a Sunday an' all."

"Shut up!" Roddy pulled himself to his feet and, glaring down into Mary Ellen's astonished countenance, continued to bawl, "As for you, you leave me alone, do you hear?" Then added, turning his head in Hal's direction, "Both of you. Get somebody else to trail." And with this he swiftly picked up his slate and marched away, leaving the two people who loved him staring after him.

Her eyes were moist and her lips were trembling when she turned towards Hal, demanding now, "What did you do to him?"

"Me do to him? It's what he did to me. Knocked me on me back afore I knew where I was."

"You must have said something."

"Aye, I did."

She waited.

Wiping the trickle of blood from his jaw, he poked his head towards her, saying slowly and in a tone that always had the power to enrage her, for it laid heavy emphasis on each word, "I told him that you were a tonguey bitch and followed him about like a cacklin' hen."

"*Oh you!*" Her mouth was thrust out, her small chest heaved and for a moment she seemed incapable of further words; but when she cried, "Talk of following anybody about, you don't let him breathe. He just puts up with you, 'cos nobody else will. Nobody likes you; as for lovin' you, nobody ever will," it was immediately evident she had struck home. The look on his face told her she had indeed hit him hard for his cheeks, usually red, were devoid of colour and the blood that was still running from the scratch looked scarlet.

She waited for the stinging retort. But none came; he just continued to stare at her for a moment before turning about and walking away. He did not rush as Roddy had done, but he went slowly like someone deep in thought, or sad.

She stood, her head drooped, looking down at the basket and the herbs scattered around it – and she wondered why she should feel so awful, not for the same reason which had brought the tears to her eyes a few minutes ago when Roddy had barked at her, but because of what she had said to Hal.

After picking up the best of the limp herbs and placing them in the basket again, she remained for a moment looking to where the stocky figure was disappearing round the bend in the path, and twice she said, "Well! Well!" before swinging round and making her way back towards Kate's.

And on the way she decided she wouldn't tell Roddy about the bag, she wouldn't tell anybody because she felt it would only open up trouble. What kind? She didn't know, except that it would be grievous trouble and she had enough to contend with, because once she got to Kate's she would have to explain why she had got so few herbs and that would bring out the row between Roddy and Hal. And having got that far, the cause would come to light, and then Kate might go for her for breaking up the friendship between the two lads, because Kate, in a way, had sympathy for Hal. And then if it came to the ears of her da there would be more explaining to do. And he would certainly go for her. By! he would that.

No, she would leave the bag where it was and let it rot there just as it had in the mire, 'cos she was in for enough trouble the night.

PART TWO

❧❧

Youth

1

"And you really think they'll like them, Mr Mulcaster?"

The overseer looked at the young man whom he had watched grow from a skinny youth at the age of ten into this upstanding figure that could be taken for a mature man in his middle years, not one who had just passed his twentieth birthday.

And it was odd about his birthday. It was one that old Kate had given him. He had come into her care on the last Saturday in September, eighteen hundred and seven, when she understood he was then seven and a half years old. And so when the boy never recovered his memory she added another six months on, so that he would have a birthday on the last Saturday of the next March, whichever date that happened to fall on.

"They are excellent drawings," Mr Mulcaster said, "and I'm sure Mr MacPherson will think the same. Now this could be a chance in a lifetime, Greenbank. Don't be afraid to speak up because remember, after all, we are merely human beings, each one of us."

Roddy smiled at the man as he thought, and you're the best of them. Yet there were folks who didn't like the agent. But then, there were folks who didn't like anybody in power, and these were the ones who wouldn't know what to do with it if they had it themselves. There were people who never saw two sides of a situation.

"What if I can't get back the same night, sir?" he said.

Mr Mulcaster smiled as he replied, "Well, find somewhere to stay. Tomorrow's Friday and the place won't drop down without you for one day . . . or two." And he gave one of his rare laughs, which caused Roddy to hang his head slightly. The sarcasm wasn't meant to be hurtful, but although he knew he was as good a worker as anyone else he wasn't a natural smelter, not like Hal, because his heart wasn't in it in the same way.

But in the technique that went into extraction of silver and lead from the ore, there he knew his interest lay. And there wasn't a piece of machinery that he hadn't drawn since first as a small boy he had raked out the bouse from the shoe and seen to it that the flow of water through the shoe kept the rollers cool.

As time went on he had drawn the waterwheel from all angles, every cog of it. As for the odds and ends such as the dolly tubs, he had dozens of drawings of these smaller items. In the smelting apparatus, he had done sketch after sketch of the ore hearth, the slag hearth, the assay furnace.

It wasn't what they looked like from the outside, it was what went on inside that had fascinated him. Whenever there was a furnace to be cleaned down he was there drawing sections and cross-sections. One day one of the men asked him the purpose he had in doing all these drawings because all the hearths had been working as they should for years. How did he expect to better them? And his answer had been that he didn't rightly know if he wanted to better them; he just wanted to draw the innards of things and satisfy himself why they worked as they did.

Most of the men laughed at him: even Mr Mulcaster hadn't at first been in favour of his drawing the machinery, saying that the company had all the mechanical men and architects they needed. Yet, as years went on and the boy still drew, even going further afield on Sunday tramping to the lead mines at Alston or Allendale, the man recognized that the boy had something that should be cultivated. But it wasn't until he had seen a drawing that he had done, not of a piece of machinery, or of the innards of a smelting hearth, but of the abbey in Hexham that his interest had really been aroused.

Eventually he had spoken to a friend of his in Newcastle about this young fellow who had a flare for drawing beyond the usual. And so it had come about that an appointment had been made for Roddy to meet Mr MacPherson, one of a select group of people in Newcastle at that time who were interested in the arts, as it was said.

"If Mr MacPherson so wishes he might invite you into the meeting," Mr Mulcaster was saying. "There you would make the acquaintance of Mr Richardson and Mr Parker, both fine artists in their own way. But now may I suggest something to you. Of course, it will depend on how much money you will have to spare. Have you got anything put by?"

"Yes, sir, a little bit."

"Enough to get a change of clothes and shoes? Now, now, not that I'm saying you aren't decently put on; in fact, I would say you are better put on than most of them around here, but your dress is typical of the country. Do you follow me?"

After a moment Roddy moved his head and said, "Yes sir, I follow you."

"I don't mean to suggest that you should get anything elaborate or expensive, but something a little different. I mean no offence. You understand me?"

"Yes, yes, I do perfectly, sir, and I'm of the same mind."

"Good, good. Well then, as you haven't to meet Mr MacPherson until three o'clock tomorrow afternoon you'll have plenty of time to get fixed up." He now held out his hand, saying, "I don't know what might come of this, Greenbank, but I hope it will open up a new way of life for you."

"Thank you, sir. Thank you very much indeed. I'll always be beholden to you."

They inclined their heads towards each other before Roddy turned away and went out of the office, down the stairs and across the yard, passing some men who, having withdrawn the dolly from the tub, were now beating the sides of it with hammers, a process that allowed the heavier ore to settle gradually at the bottom with the lighter refuse coming to rest upon it. And after they let the water out of the tub, they removed the dross to the dead heap, leaving the pure ore to be taken to the bingstead.

How many times he had trundled that dross to the dead heap during his early days, and in this moment he hoped he would never again hammer on a dolly.

The men chaffed him as he passed them, Paul and Johnny Fowler shouting after him, "Doubled your wages then, has he? By, we'll have your neck for that, Roddy boy." Will Campbell just straightened his back and stared after him: nobody had ever shown any interest in his own handicraft, and he could whittle wood into any shape. Favouritism, that's what it was, favouritism.

Roddy wasn't unaware of the mixed feelings towards him in the mill. Most men didn't like change, they feared change, and anyone who wanted change was to them a disturber of the peace. They had their pattern of life: they worked hard; the majority of them still drank hard, although now they didn't allow their drinking to interfere with their work; they kept it to a Saturday night and Fair days.

Roddy had come among them as an odd boy who couldn't remember his past, but now he was a young man who still couldn't remember his past but who lived very much in the present and thought of the future and was one of them who wanted change. Moreover, besides his drawing, working on the rudiments he must have picked up while a boy in Shields, he had taught himself to read and write. But he wasn't the only one who could do this, there was Hal Roystan. They said he had a shelf of books in old Abel Hamilton's cottage. Of course, this was only since the old fellow died for he'd no use for books, old Abel, a pick and shovel had been his tools.

Hal Roystan, they thought, was as opposite in temperament from Roddy Greenbank as chalk was from cheese; yet they were very close in a way, and both connected with old Kate.

Now there was a funny one for you: you had to keep on the right side of her or you found yourself with boils on your neck, and even on your nether regions an' all. See what happened to Ben Fowler that night he got blind drunk and took the wrong way home and kicked her mongrel dog while passing. He couldn't move the next morning, stiff as a ramrod. It took him weeks to get his back straight again. And then what about Jed Pierce? Just because he made up to Mary Ellen Lee on the road on her Sunday off while going home. He had wanted to court her, he said it openly. And he told Kate that, after the lass had run from him to the old woman's, and what had Kate said to him? "You wantin' Mary Ellen! You can't even keep your snotty nose clean. If you come within a

mile of her again you won't be able to sit down for a month, I'm tellin'
you." And begod! that's what had happened. He got a carbuncle, as big
as a double-yoked egg it was, and it nearly drove him mad, at least the
treatment did, for his brother Roger and his two sisters had held him
down while his elder brother Billy stuck a stone water bottle filled with
steam on the offending carbuncle in an effort to draw it to a head. Jed
had smashed half of the crockery in the kitchen before they got hold of
him again.

So she had powers, had Kate Makepeace, and it was as well to keep on
the right side of her, as those three certainly did, for they had all
prospered in different ways: Roddy Greenbank was well in with the boss
while Hal Roystan had risen to be one of the best paid men on the floor;
as for Mary Ellen Lee, Farmer Davison and his wife had almost adopted
her, treated her like one of their own, they did. Aye, it was well to keep in
with witches.

Roddy could almost hear their voices going through his head, and as
he made his way quickly home, striding out as if he were going to his
shift instead of just finishing the ten hour stretch in the sweltering heat
and dust, he wasn't only thinking of the meeting with the artists, there
was something else on his mind which was even more important than
the success of his drawings. Yet in a way they were linked; the happy
outcome of one might depend on the other.

Kate greeted him as usual. "Well," she said, "another one over?"

"Aye, Kate." He put his bait tin down on the table and stood looking
at her, a small shrunken figure with a face like a dried nut but with a
voice that still denied age.

"All set?" she said.

"Aye, Kate, all set. I go first thing in the mornin'. I've got a letter
here" – he tapped the inside of his coat – "and I'm likely to meet some
big names. Well, that's the impression I got from Mr Mulcaster. By the
way, Kate, could ... could I have a little money?"

"Could you have a little money? Why do you ask me, lad? What's
there" – she now turned and pointed with a crooked finger to the inside
of the chimney – "is yours."

"No, no. We've had that out a long time ago."

"Aye, I know you've said that afore but I'll say again, what's there's
yours. Anyway, if you don't have it now you would have it later. As you
know the money I took from your da's belt went in the lean years, but
the fifty-five pounds those thieving clerks sent for the sale of the house is
still there as it came. Fifty-five pounds! when it was sold for a hundred
an' ten. Eeh! Daylight robbers. Anyway lad, take it for whatever you
want to do with it."

"I don't want fifty-five pounds, Kate. Look, I've got two of me own."
He jerked his head now. "I know it should be twenty-two, and would be
if I didn't buy so much bloomin' paper and the like, but if I could sort of
take three. You see. . . . Well, he meant it kindly enough, but I really
don't see any need for it," he lied emphatically, accompanying his words

with a quick nodding of the head, "but Mr Mulcaster thought, seein' as I'm meetin' these upper type of people, I should have some different kind of clothes."

"Different from your Sunday ones?"

"Aye."

She seemed to consider for a moment, and then said, "Well, I suppose he's right. He knows what he's up to, he wouldn't want you to show up there with straw sticking from under your cap. But remember, lad, an' more so when you meet these other folk, it isn't what's underneath. They say if you look a man straight in the eye you can see right through him, but don't you believe it. Some eyes have had long practice in deceivin', and there's them that could smile while cuttin' your throat."

She turned from him now to lift a black pan from the fire, but paused while she held the handle, adding, "What if they take you up there? I mean, take to your drawin's an' want you to go further like, a sort of trainin'. What'll you do?"

"I don't know. I've thought about that. But anyway——" He paused, so stopping his tongue from saying, "If a miracle should happen;" instead, he said, "If anything like that came about and I had to work in Newcastle I could always be home at the week-ends."

She brought the pan to the table now and set the sooty bottom on a flat piece of stone, and as she took off the lid she said, "London town, I understand, is the place for artists and suchlike. What if they sent you ...?"

She didn't finish because in a voice that was deep now and firm he said, "Never! Never, Kate. I'd never go out of Newcastle. Not a step further. No."

She lifted her head and looked at him. "No?"

"No."

"You seem sure of that."

He looked at her, the while pulling the muffler from his neck; then took off his coat, crossed the room with it, and hung it on the back of the scullery door before turning and looking at her again.

"I should have told you," he said, "but there seemed nothing to tell. There still isn't anything really, but well, Kate, I've ... I've got me eye on a lass, and even if there wasn't you, she'd keep me here."

He had a half smile on his face, shy, diffident, and she answered it by saying, "Tell me something I don't know."

His eyes now screwed up, he took two steps towards her, saying, "You can't. Well, nobody ... I ... don't even know meself. As for her ... well." He put his head to one side now and peered at Kate. They said she was a witch, but this was impossible. He watched the look fade from her face as she said quietly, "Not Mary Ellen?"

His face stretched, and when he spoke there was a note of incredulity in it. "*Mary Ellen?*" he said. "Good God! Kate. *No, no, never* Mary Ellen. Why, she's like a sister...."

Her outburst cut him off. "Sister be damned! She's no sister, an' she's had you in her eye since you first lay on that saddle there." She stretched out her thin arm and pointed. "My God! man, you must be blind. And you've played up to her."

"Oh no, no, Kate. Now don't say that. I've been the same to Mary Ellen as I always have. I've argued and fought with her; even last Sunday we had an up-an'-downer. She's got a tongue that would clip clouts and she's got a head on her that would fit her granny, the things she comes out with."

He knew a deep concern now as he stared at the old woman whom he looked upon as a mother for he knew that she had taken him in and cared for him from he'd had the accident. And in that first year he must have been a handful, raving half the time, apparently. Recalling those early days, there also came into his head queer pictures, jumbled up incidents that had no relation to anything he could remember. And even now, the grown man that he was, they raised a fear in him, because when he tried to think back his head would swim and he would have the most odd feeling as if he was going to tumble down, faint, like some refined lady.

Softly now, he said, "I'm sorry. I'm sorry, Kate. I never thought you...."

She took a ladle and scooped some stew onto a plate and pushed it across the table, but he remained still, looking at her. The very fact that she had put out the meal without waiting for him to be washed told how upset she must be. He again said, "I'm sorry, Kate, but ... but I think you are wrong with regard to how Mary Ellen feels."

"*Shut up! Shut up!* man. Don't you know you're like a disease with her? Always have been, a skin rash that she can't get rid of, an' never will. Anyway, who's this other miss you've got in your mind? Someone from round about?"

He shook his head and it was some seconds before he said, "She's not from this part. Anyway, I ... well, you see, I hardly know her. We've only met three times."

"And you know she's the one you want to mate with for life?"

His chin came up, his face hardened, as did his voice as he said, "Yes, Kate, it's like that. I've never bothered with lasses. You know I haven't...."

"No, because you've had Mary Ellen to fall back on."

"I've never fallen back on Mary Ellen as you put it; she's been there, like you've been there, one of the family. I've never thought of her in that way, never. But ... but this other is different; as soon as I clapped eyes on her I knew."

Kate slowly lowered herself into a chair now and she drummed her fingers on the table as she said, "What's her name?"

"I ... I don't know."

"You don't know her name?"

He hung his head as if slightly ashamed. "No, I ... I don't know her name," he said.

"You don't know? You mean to stand there and tell me you've met her three times and you don't know what they call her?"

"Aye, that's it."

"They must have been brief meetings."

"They were. Yes, Kate, they were, just brief."

"How long have you known her?"

"Nine months."

"Nine months! and you've only seen her three times?"

"Yes; and the first twice we never spoke. Isn't that strange now?" He was mimicking her. "And I'll tell you something else that's strange, Kate. I saw her first through a window, sitting at a table in the tea house off the main street in Hexham, and I went in and had tea just to look at her. Now, isn't that strange? And the second time was in the market, and I was close to her and we looked at each other, we looked at each other long. The third time was just a week ago, in Haydon Bridge, and it was there we spoke, not for long, but long enough to know that she'll be in Newcastle the morrow." He didn't mention the times he had stood outside a particular house in Hexham where he had discovered she visited.

Kate stared at him in silence for some seconds before saying, "Was the drawing business just an excuse to meet her away in Newcastle?"

"No. That was all arranged a fortnight ago. You know that. This other just happened to fit in."

"And you still don't know her name or where she's from?"

"No, I still don't know her name. There wasn't time to ask as we were standing in the street, and the coach came. One thing I did learn was that she comes from over Catton way, towards Old Town."

"Oh, then when you know her name, we'll know all about her, because Catton isn't the back of beyond."

"It's far enough away from people to mind their own business."

He had never spoken to her like that before and they were both aware of it. And he turned from her and went into the scullery and, taking up a pail of water, he emptied half of it into a tin dish before dragging off his shirt and singlet. And he washed himself, thinking as he did so, I shouldn't have spoken to her like that. What's come over me? And somewhere in the back of his mind he got the answer. Love had come over him, and for the first time in his life he was finding it an overpowering emotion, and bewildering, because he had never imagined that a man could feel this way. Oh aye, want to take a woman. And he had; unknown to Kate, he'd had a go two or three times in Hexham. That's really where his money had gone, not on his drawing paper as he had made out. But what he was feeling now was different. Not that he didn't want to hold this perfect being that had come into his life and to love her in a way that a man loved a woman. But there was something more that he could not as yet understand. It was, in a way, he considered, a silly feeling, because he felt that it would be a kind of sacrilege to deface her virginity, she was so beautiful. Yet no, she wasn't beautiful, her features were too strong, too defined for beauty. But her eyes laughed, and she had a presence that one would consider only a princess or someone of high breeding could acquire. She was like someone from another world, in all ways from another world.

And of late, this had troubled his nights. So, in order to enter her world it was imperative that he succeed tomorrow in convincing those people in Newcastle that he was worth something more that a labourer in a smelt mill for the rest of his life.

And Mary Ellen? ... Mary Ellen in love with him? He scrubbed his face with the rough coarse towel. She was always going for him, arguing with him. Fancy being married to Mary Ellen. God in heaven! He wouldn't know a minute's peace. Talk about a fishwife. She would upbraid him more than any fishwife every day of his life. Marry Mary Ellen? Oh, really! Kate had got the wrong end of the stick there. Wishful thinking. It was laughable. And Mary Ellen would laugh at it too, he bet, if she knew. Anyway, he understood Lennie Davison, her master's grandson, was sweet on her. She had said as much herself, at least hinted in that way. Lennie was just turned twenty-one, there had been a great do for his birthday a short while ago – he had been there – and she had danced with Lennie more than once in the barn that night. In fact, who hadn't she danced with? Oh yes, she was bonny enough in a way, and sprightly. It was only her tongue that was wrong with her.

Aw, Kate had been imagining things. Anyway, he'd bring her something back from Newcastle and make his peace with her.

2

He had never paid more than four shillings for a pair of breeches and five
shillings and six pence for a coat, but here he was, dressed in clothes that
had cost him twenty-three shillings, and that wasn't taking into account
the cravat or the new boots, or the cloth bag he'd had to buy to put his
Sunday clothes in. He had never realized how ordinary his Sunday garb
was until that tailor had spread out his range of wares. It was after he had
made his choice that the man had brought out a full suit of clothing. It
had been ordered by somebody who had gone away, he said. Dead, he
meant, but it fitted him to a T, except that it might be just a little tight
under the oxters. But he could put up with that, for he had to admit that
in this rig-out he really did feel different. He likened it to a kind of
armour ready-made for his meeting this afternoon. But more so, it
would, he felt, impress her: she would see him differently from the
tongue-tied fellow he had presented to her in the market place. Clothes
like this did something for a fellow, for from the moment he had walked
out of that shop in the side street he realized there was a world awaiting
him which was strange and exciting.

He took out the silver-plated case from his pocket and looked at the
round watch lying in it. It was the one that Kate had taken from his
father's belt. It had lain glassless and broken for years. However, a short
time ago he had had it mended, and although it now told him he had
plenty of time before he should reach the Assembly Rooms, it also again
created in his mind that muzziness that disturbed him when handling it
and which he had experienced more than once of late.

Twenty minutes later he was standing on the pavement opposite the
Assembly Rooms in which a concert was to be held that afternoon. She
had hinted, no, more than hinted that she might be attending it. That
was when he had told her last week that he was to take his drawings to
show to people of importance in the city.

He recalled that she had smiled and raised her eyebrows and repeated
softly, "People of importance?" From another's lips it might have
appeared that she was scoffing, but he couldn't imagine her ever scoffing
anyone, she was so different. She seemed so alive. Perhaps vital was a
better word. Aye, vital. Yet what did he mean by that? He didn't know.
He only knew that he was in love for the first time, and he couldn't see it
ever fading.

He watched the carriages draw up and the people descending and going in to the concert hall. Would she arrive in a carriage? No – his head moved slightly at the thought – she wasn't a carriage type. Not that he didn't think of her as somebody superior, but she wasn't a lady, not in that sense, she wasn't prim. He could derive that from her speech. Again, not that she spoke in an ordinary voice, but she didn't talk like the lady of the manor, as Hal would have termed it.... How was he going to talk to Hal about the feeling he had for this lass, because Hal couldn't stand lasses. Look how he went for Mary Ellen. But then, when he came to think of it, he hadn't done that so much of late, he seemed to have eased off her.

Oh. Oh. There she was, crossing the road. But his heart sank; she wasn't alone, there was another woman with her. Well, what did he expect? That she would be walking the streets of Newcastle by herself? This was the city, not Hexham.

He saw that they were laughing together. They had their heads slightly down and their glances were slanted towards each other as they drew nearer to him.

"Good-afternoon, Mr.... Er...."

He took off his cap and nodded, first to her, then to her companion as he said, "Good-afternoon."

"This ... this is my friend, Miss Freeman."

"Pleased ... pleased to meet you."

Her friend was smiling but her lips were tight and her eyes were blinking.

"Are you going to attend the concert, Mr ... Mr Er?"

"Greenbank. Rodney Greenbank."

"Greenbank." She put her head to the side as if trying to recall something. Then in a polite tone she said, "You are taking your drawings for inspection today, I understand?"

"Yes." He nodded, smiling at her.

And in the ensuing silence it seemed to him that for the first time she noticed his change of dress, because she looked him up and down before remarking, "'Tis a pity you cannot attend the concert."

"Yes, yes, it is. But another day. Do ... do they have them every week?"

She was about to answer when her eyes moved swiftly from him and, looking across the road, she said, "There is my father. We must be going. Good-day, Mr Greenbank."

"Good-day." He nodded first to one and then the other. And as he watched them cross towards the man on the opposite pavement, he exclaimed to himself in a start of surprise, Why, that's Mr Bannaman. Good God! Her father, Mr Bannaman? God Almighty! This would set up complications. What would Kate say because she hated the very name of Bannaman? Wasn't he the man who had got her son sent away, supposedly helping him? He had never got to the bottom of that story. He had heard of the smuggling of spirits and things, but you didn't skip the country for that. But Bannaman!

Still, what had happened was all in the past, years gone. Odd, but he had been determined he would ask her her name just before they should part today, but now that he knew it, it made him uneasy.

He hadn't seen the man for some years. When he was younger, he had come across him and his woodman gathering young fir trees from the thicket above the quarry, and he had only twice seen him in Hexham in later years. But then he himself rarely got into Hexham early on a Saturday 'cos of his shifts, which was why he hadn't come across her either, he supposed. But one thing was clear now: she was the daughter of a farmer, but what was also clear, of no small farmer.

He watched her father talking to her, then press her and her friend towards the hall, but not before he had stopped and looked across the road at him, a hard scrutinizing look.

What would happen when he found out that he was a smelter? He was wise enough to know that smelters, like pitmen, weren't rated worthy of farmers' daughters. But let him wait, he wouldn't be a smelter much longer. He straightened his shoulders and walked away, but as he did so he wasn't unaware that the man had not yet entered the hall but was standing at the door looking towards him.

He went up the steps bordered by iron railings, and knocked on the plain mahogany door. It was opened by an equally plain looking maid. After allowing him in, she said, "What be your name, sir?" And when he told her, she went to a door across the small hall and, opening it, she said, "Mr Rodney Green . . . bank." She split his name as if it were two words.

All eight men in the room turned and looked towards him; then one of them stepped forward with outstretched hand, saying, "I'm Mr MacPherson. How do you do?" Then he looked at the two bags that Roddy had laid down on the carpet before extending his own and, with a broad smile on his face, he said, "Don't tell me both of those are full of drawings."

"Oh, no, no." Roddy said, smiling self-consciously; then stooping, he lifted a flat case from the cloth bag, muttering as he did so, "I've . . . I've been shopping. 'Tisn't often I'm in the city."

"Well, come along, and bring the important parcel with you." And Mr MacPherson now led him towards the other men, adding, "It's a pity Mr Mulcaster couldn't be here this afternoon. But some of us have got to work." He laughed now, and the other men joined in.

"Now this is Mr Richardson . . . and Mr Parker."

"Pleased to meet you. Pleased to meet you." On and on it went until the names merely buzzed through his head. The introductions finished, he undid the string round the case and slowly lifted one large drawing after another and placed them on the long table. Some he turned about

63

so that the men on the opposite side could see them. And then he stood back listening to the low exchanges.

When one man with his head bent low over a drawing said, "Promising. Very promising," another to his side growled, "Promising be damned, Willie."

At this he felt his face turning scarlet. It was like a dire condemnation. But then the man who had spoken these words looked up at him through narrowed eyes and said, "How long have you been on this, son?"

His first reaction to this was a slight bristling at having been called son – of course the man opposite was elderly, but he himself looked no boy – and he muttered in a stiff tone, "As . . . as long as I can remember . . . far back."

The man straightened his body, and now his next words brought a warmth flooding through Roddy that heightened the colour still further in his face. "Well," he said, "for my part, I would say you haven't wasted your time. You've got somewhere. This roasting furnace is good. Never missed a brick in it, did you?" But then he qualified all he had said by adding, "Not that you haven't got a lot to learn. You understand?"

"Yes, I understand, sir."

Then his bright thoughts of a rosy future were dampened yet again by a voice at the end of the table saying, "But all these have been done before, don't let us forget that."

"Nobody's forgetting that, Jim" – his champion was speaking again – "but there's additions here and initiative in the suggestions. I know damn fine constructive drawings have been done before and about smelting – I've seen dozens of them, hundreds in fact – but this applicant won't stick to smelting, will you, Mr Greenbank?"

He heard himself muttering, "No, sir," while wondering about the use of the word applicant. Then he was made to wonder still further when his champion went on, "Of the three of them, this lad's got my vote."

"Well, we'll see, we'll see." It was the quiet voice of Mr MacPherson coming in now, and he went on addressing Roddy pointedly, asking, "Have you done any other kind of art, live art, or landscape, or anything like that?"

Roddy paused, swallowed, then said, "Not much, sir, just a few sketches of the hills and things."

"No portraits?"

"No, no. Very few I'm . . . I'm not very good at that kind of thing."

"You never know. Art has many springs feeding the river so to speak. Anyway, gentlemen" – he looked around at the other members seated at the table – "we'll discuss this further after we have a cup of tea with the ladies."

A cup of tea with the ladies. He was hot under the collar.

But the cup of tea with the ladies turned out to be a very jolly affair, and very informative because he discovered that all of the six women present were artists in different ways; and further, that they were all people of means; and further still, to his surprise he learned that he was one of three applicants whose work they were considering for sponsorship, which meant that they would pay his board and lodgings for two years to study art either here or in London. It was a gesture to the unprivileged, as one less than tactful lady had pointed out to him; also, that they were aware that here and there among the working class were talents that should be furthered.

When an hour later he left the house he didn't know whether he was pleased or otherwise. The meeting had been an eye-opener for which Mr Mulcaster had not prepared him. He had thought he would be meeting two or three men who were interested in engineering drawings. Yet on the other hand the thought of being trained properly for two years was like the revelation of a dream that he had never really dreamed but which had lain deep in his mind since he had first taken up a pencil. Anyway, he wouldn't know the outcome for another month. One other thing that had disturbed him in the meeting was the knowledge that he was wearing the wrong-coloured suit. This had come from a very talkative lady who apparently did portraits and, after eyeing him for sometime, had said, "You would make good material: you have very good bones; but your clothes are wrong. You should never wear grey, not that shade anyway, it's much too light for your colouring; if I were to paint you, you would be in rough working clothes."

Was that how *she* had seen him, Miss Bannaman? Someone who looked like a workman in spite of his gentlemanly dress?

Oh, he'd get himself away back home. He didn't like Newcastle, well, not today he didn't. If he had to live in it he might get to know it better. But first of all he must go and buy something for Kate, a head shawl or something like that to placate her. But was she a person you could placate? No. He shook his head at the suggestion. And when she knew that the girl he was sweet on was Bannaman's daughter, then the upset he had already caused her by saying he had no feelings for Mary Ellen would be nothing to that news.

Why were things turning out like this?

It came to him as something of a surprise that he didn't like being disturbed, and that up till now his life had run smoothly; at least, until today, he had known where he stood. But now, be-damned if he did, in any way.

65

3

Mary Davison said, "Put a shawl over your bonnet, the wind's high.
And look, if you're going to get away, get away or else you'll not be back
afore dark. On the other hand, though, if you have a mind to wait,
Lennie should be back at any time now and he'll take you over in the
cart."

"Aw, ma'am, I know me way blindfold. And anyway I won't call
home because I'll see me da the morrow, but Jimmy said he found Kate
none too well, so I feel worried."

"Well, I can understand that. She shouldn't be there on her own at all.
She should have moved in with your father, it would have been company for him since your mother died."

Mary Ellen said nothing in answer to this, she only knotted the head
shawl tighter under her chin, thinking as she did so, What a daft thing to
say that old Kate should have moved in with her father. Kate would
never leave that cottage. And anyway, who'd have looked after Roddy?
As for moving in with her father, her father couldn't put up with
himself, so irritable he was these days, never mind putting up with Kate
and her set-in-ways. Oh, Mrs Davison was a good mistress but she did
say daft things, things without thinking. It was, she supposed, because
she liked company, the more the merrier. She should have had a great
big family whereas she'd only had Lennie's father. She was indeed a
loving kind of woman, but she didn't think.

"Now here's the basket. That piece of pork should grease her innards.
An' there's a loaf there, and half a dozen real eggs, not like those pips
from her bantams. And there's a bag of cheese bits and a sugar bun. That
should keep her going. Aye, it should."

Mary Ellen looked softly at the small tubby woman and she had the
desire to put her arms around her and kiss her. She often had this desire,
but you didn't give way to things like that with your mistress. So what
she said was, "Thanks. Ta, ma'am. Kate'll appreciate it, she will," at the
same time thinking what Kate would say which would likely be, "Does
she think we starve over here? You tell her I have plenty." Yet when
later it was time to leave, she would add, "And thank Mrs Davison for
me. She's a kind woman when all's said and done." But likely as not she
would add, "Although she hasn't enough up top to keep her bonnet
on."

Mary Ellen took up the basket and went out of the kitchen, across the

roughly paved farmyard and onto the puddled ground that led to the
gate. She didn't bother where she walked because she had already lifted
the waistband of her skirt high enough for the hem to come above her
boots, the tops of which reached the bottom of her calfs. Her legs were
thin; in fact, she was all thin. This troubled her. At eighteen years of age
other lasses had busts; some had showed from when they were fourteen,
but hers had never seemed to grow. Grow she did, but as she told
herself, instead of going a bit outwards, she went upwards. It wasn't
good for a lass to be too tall, not taller than a lad, the one you hoped to
marry. But she wasn't taller than Roddy, she was just about his height.
Of course, that was now. If she only stuck this way. Farmer Davison and
Mr Archie, his son, both said that she had talked herself skinny. They
laughed about her and teased her. But Lennie didn't. Lennie always took
her part, maintaining that she could beat them anyday, at least with her
tongue, and with most jobs on the farm, except the horse breaking, and
she was going to tackle that an' all.

Funny about the farm and the Davisons. They seemed more her
family than her father did. Even when her mother was alive, she hadn't
felt the same warmth from her as she did from her mistress. The farm
and all in it was home to her, and she loved them all.

When she said she loved them, she did, but not in the way Lennie
wanted her to love. Lennie was nice and he was kind, he was like his
grandmother in that way, but also like her, he said and did the daftest
things. Slap-happy, Kate called them both. But it was nice to be slap-
happy; she wished she could be slap-happy. She was now and again
when she could forget about the things she wanted most in life and
which now troubled her more and more in the night....

When she reached the cottage she found Kate lying on the bed and
asked anxiously of her, "You feeling bad, Kate?"

"No, I am not feeling bad. I can lie down, can't I, without feeling
bad?" Then the acid tone changing she said, "Why do you come, lass, it
isn't your time off?"

"Missis sent me with some odds and ends."

"Thinks I'm starvin' again? How does she imagine that I've kept alive
all these years and kept that big 'un. By the way, what time is it?"

Mary Ellen turned and looked at the wooden-faced clock on the
mantelshelf and she said, "Turned half-past six."

Kate now raised herself up on her elbow; then sliding her legs over
the edge of the bed, she stretched her gnarled arms slowly, saying,
"Well, now you're here, take your things off and sit yourself down."

"I won't be able to stay long, Kate. It'll get on dusk shortly." She
turned to the table and began to empty the basket, asking now in an offhand manner, "What time did Roddy say he'd be back?"

"He didn't say, lass, he didn't say."

Kate's tone made Mary Ellen turn and look towards her for a moment
before she walked back to the bed again and, sitting down beside Kate
and taking her hand, she said, "What's the matter? Something wrong?"

"Aye, you could say that, lass, something's wrong."

"You worried about ... about him going away if they like his drawings?"

"Well, a little bit I was, but ... but not so much. 'Tisn't that, 'tis about you I'm worried."

"*About me?*" Mary Ellen pulled herself up until she was looking down on the wizened form of her very dear and beloved friend and she said, "Worried about me, why Kate? I was never better. I have a job in a lifetime, and they couldn't be kinder to me if I was their own. You know that."

"I know, I know all that." Kate's head was nodding. "It isn't the present I'm thinking about, 'tis the future, your future and what goes on in that mind of yours. Well, you know me." She turned her head now and looked into Mary Ellen's questioning eyes and said, "Open and straightforward has always been me way of life, no beating about the bush, so I'm going to ask you now, do you like Lennie?"

"Lennie?" Mary Ellen screwed up her face. "Lennie Davison?"

"How many Lennies are there in this valley for God's sake? He's the only one I know of."

"Yes, you're right. Well, of course I like him. I've sort of ... well, seems to me I've been brought up with him."

"Now don't tell me—" Kate closed her eyes and wagged her hand before her face as she said, "That you like him as a brother, 'cos it's well known he doesn't like you as a sister, the way—" Here she paused and drew some spittle into her mouth; then opening her eyes, she turned her head sharply and again looking into Mary Ellen's face she ended, "Roddy does."

With pain evident in her eyes, Kate watched this dear, good lass, as she thought of her, sink slowly down onto the bed; she watched her pressing her joined hands between her knees and gaze at them as she muttered, "He ... he doesn't think of me as a sister, Kate."

"He does, lass."

Presently, Mary Ellen turned her head slowly but did not look fully at Kate as she said, "What makes you say that?"

"Because ... because, lass, he said as much in plain words. He said as much."

Mary Ellen rose from the bed and walked slowly to the table and began to rearrange the things on it: first, the meats she had brought with her; then, the two china mugs, the bread board and the cheese platter; she moved them round as if fitting them into a puzzle. And now her voice scarcely above a whisper, she said, "Why did you tell me this, Kate?"

"Because ... because I thought you should know, lass. You will sooner or later. He's got his eyes on somebody else."

Mary Ellen jerked round now and her voice small and almost like a whimper, she said, "No!"

"Yes, lass, aye."

"He said so?"

"Aye, afore he went yesterday. We had words, the first real words, aye, the first real words we've ever had."

The fire was burning low. Mary Ellen looked at it; then she picked up some turfs from a straw basket to the side of the open hearth and piled them onto the low embers. She did this swiftly as if she was following a routine that she carried out evey day. And now taking up two pieces of wood she knelt down and pressed them, one at each side of the fire as if to give support to the whole. Then dusting her hands, she got off her knees and, going to the table, she stood there for a moment before asking, "Who is she? Do I know her?"

"No. Nor me, lass. He doesn't himself, I think."

"What!" Mary Ellen's voice was sharp now and loud, and she repeated again, "What!"

"Somebody he's just caught a glimpse of. And that bein' the case, I tell meself it'll pass. I hope to God it does, anyway. But I know I'm right in forewarnin' you because if it had come from him and as a surprise it would have been worse. You're better to be fortified against it, especially you feeling the way you do, for the sun has shone out of him from the first day you saw him."

There was a lump the size of a green apple in her throat, yet her eyes were dry. She lifted up her head shawl and, putting it on, she walked towards the bed, her eyes blinking rapidly now as she said, "Will . . . will you be all right?"

Kate's hands came out towards her and caught hers, and she gripped them tight before she spoke. "There's an old sayin' about there being many more fish in the sea than the one that slipped the line, but it's always the one that slipped the line you think about, not about the rest, at least for a time. But then comes the day when your line goes out again and there's a different fish on it. And you've learned a lot in the waitin', and what you've learned is, you weren't meant to catch that first one, you had to have some practice."

"I—" Mary Ellen's voice was breaking now – "I don't want any practice, Kate. You know I don't. From I was little" – she put her hand out to measure the height – "I've known he was for me. And . . . and he has too, he's known it."

"No, lass, no." Her hands were being shaken up and down between the gnarled ones now. "Give him his due, he didn't. With him, you've been too close. If you had come on his horizon out of the blue like, it may have been different. But you've been too close, so close that he cannot see you, more fool him. Oh aye, more fool him."

The tears were starting, and she gasped, "I've . . . I've got to go, Kate. You'll . . . you'll be all right?"

"I'll be all right, lass. It's you I'll say it to now, you'll be all right. Time'll tell, but you'll be all right."

"I won't, Kate, I won't, ever."

She turned blindly away and groped for the basket; then she went out and closed the door quietly behind her. But once she had got down into the meadow she began to run, stumbling as she went. When she reached the fork she took the ride path, running now until she came to a thick belt of willow herb, and she pushed her way through this to where she knew there was a small open space. And here she threw herself down into the long grass and gave way to her grief, for it was grief, and as painful as if she had been suddenly told he was dead. And all the time she cried she asked herself the question: Who was she, this girl who had taken him from her? Because he was hers. Had he ever looked at any of the other lasses round about? No, never, not to her knowledge. He never bothered with any of them, even at the harvest suppers. He might dance with this or that one, but just one dance he would give them, a reel or a jig or the barn dance, but with her he would dance for most of the evening, which proved that he was for her and he was showing everybody she was for him.

Her face was buried in the grass, her two hands clutching at it. The ground was very damp after two days of rain, but she was aware only of the fact that she was experiencing misery and didn't know how she was going to go on bearing it. What was she going to do? What she was going to say if she saw him?

When a hand came on her shoulder she screamed and rolled onto her back, her hands now clutching her throat, and looked upwards into the concerned face of Hal on which was an expression she had never seen there before, and the tone of his voice was one she had never heard before as he said, "Mary Ellen, what is it? What's happened? Somebody done something?" He was on his hunkers now, kneeling by her side, his hands holding hers, and she was aware that this was the very first time there had been any personal contact between them, and that this was strange for she had known him as long as she had known Roddy.

For a moment she could only gasp, but then managed to say, "You . . . you gave me a fright."

"Aye, and you gave me a fright an' all. What's happened? What's upset you like this?"

Lowering her head, she shook it from side to side, saying, "Nothing. Nothing. Nothing."

"Aw, don't tell me that. For you of all people to bubble like a bairn, something must have happened and it cannot be light. Are you sure . . . sure somebody hasn't done something?"

She again shook her head; then pulling her hands from his, she swung round, got onto her knees and stood up.

She was slightly taller than him but he being of the breadth he was his head seemed to be on a level with hers, if not looking down on her. He said now, "Which way are you goin'? To Kate's or back to the farm?"

"Back to the farm."

"You've just come from Kate's?"

"Aye."

"Well, something must have happened there. Is Roddy back?"

At the sound of the name she turned her head away, then said, "No."

He looked down at the ground for a moment as if in bewilderment, then he said quietly, "Well, tell me what's upset you so?" And there was a half smile now on his face as he added, "You know me, I'll pry and pry till I get to the bottom of things."

"Yes, you would, wouldn't you?" For a moment she was her old self and he was Hal Roystan, someone she had never been able to stand. Yet a moment ago, he hadn't seemed sarcastic or sneering, but thoughtful and concerned, not like himself at all.

"That's better," he said, smiling widely now, "that's more like Miss Mary Ellen."

"Oh, you!" It was her favourite expression she used against him when she found that her tongue in no way could cap his remarks. And she turned to walk back along the ride.

As he walked beside her, she said, "I'm . . . I'm all right. I can find my way back; I know it, you know." Her head was nodding at him now, and when she sniffed away her last remaining tear and wiped her cheeks with the wet ball of a small handkerchief, he put his hand in the breast pocket of his rough coat and drew out a clean square and handed it to her.

The very fact that he should carry a clean handkerchief seemed to surprise her still further and for a moment she stared at the outstretched hand and the article in it. Then without a word, she took it from him and rubbed her face with it, and as she passed it back to him she said in a small voice, "Ta."

They had walked a considerable distance before he said, "Do you think anything will come of his lordship's visit to the high and mighty patrons in Newcastle?"

It was a moment before she answered, "I don't know, and I—" She stopped herself from saying childishly, "I don't care." But he put in now on a small mirthless laugh, "Don't tell me you were going to add, I don't care. Ah! Then I have got to the bottom of the trouble. 'Tis our noble friend, isn't it?"

"Oh, you!" She turned and confronted him. "You speak like that about Roddy as if at the back of you you didn't like him. Yet you never leave him alone, you're like his shadow. I know you, you're. . . ."

"You don't know me." His words were like a sting now. "You know nothin' about me. Do you hear? Listen to me for one moment, Mary Ellen Lee. You don't know me and, I repeat, you know nothing about me, what I think or what I do, or what I want to do, or what I mean to do, nothing, nothing at all. You never have. All you've ever wanted in your life has been to possess Roddy, mind, soul, and body. But you've gone the wrong way about it. I've watched you. I've watched you for years digging your own grave: that tongue of yours lashing at him about stupid little nothings, not letting him do what he wanted to do, grow; following him when he didn't want to be followed, pestering him. That's what you've done, and by! as I've said, you've dug your own grave, because you're not for him. And that's what it's all about, isn't it, the cryin'?"

Her teeth were clenched tightly together. She was gritting them backwards and forwards as she had never done before, and the spittle was on her lips as she blurted out, "I hate you! Do you hear, Hal Roystan? I hate you! I've always hated you and I always shall."

An expression passed over his face that she could not define in any way, and his tone, too, was different as he said, "I know that, I know that fine well, 'tis no news to me, but at this moment I'll tell you something: I'm sorry for you an' what you've got to go through because I know all about it, what you're going to go through." And on this, to her astonishment, he turned and left her.

He walked quietly, his arms swinging, his shoulders slightly forward as if on the point of a run. She watched him until he had disappeared back along the ride, then she turned and went on her way, her emotions so mixed that, as she said to herself, she didn't know which end of her was up.

Well, something had come into the open at last. She had told him how she felt about him, and always had. But there, it had been no news to him. Instead, what had he said? He knew what she was going to go through because he had experienced it.

4

"You're late."

"No, I'm not, Father."

"I say you are. You generally get here at two o'clock, and look at it, it's turned half past. You've been to Kate's again afore comin' home."

"I haven't. I haven't been near Kate's."

Bill Lee drew in a deep breath; but then asked more quietly, "What have you brought?"

"The usual."

He rose from his chair by the fire and came towards the table, and it was noticeable that he was finding it difficult to breathe. He was but forty-two years old, yet he looked a man of sixty, but unlike many of his mates who had started in the smelting mill when boys, he was still alive. But the gas and dust had taken toll on his lungs, although, as he would remind anyone who would listen, he had helped to build the tunnels to the chimneys, or the condenser as it was called, that was to perform miracles. Well, it might do for the coming generation, but it had happened too late for his.

It had seemed to Mary Ellen that the gas had affected not only her father's lungs, but his whole character. He had always been strict with her, but, as her mother had so frequently pointed out, it was because he loved her. However, since her mother's death from consumption six years ago, his attitude towards herself had changed, his strictness had turned into a domineering possessiveness in which there was no element of love.

"You've let your fire go low," she said.

"Aye, well, I've nobody to fetch and carry for me."

Rounding on him, she cried, "And neither have I, Da! I'm fetchin' and carryin' all day for somebody and if you cannot go out and bring the wood in after I've chopped it, then you'll have to go cold, won't you?"

He stared at her, surprised at this unusual bout of retaliation; then in a much quieter voice, he said, "What's ... what's come over you? What's the matter with you?"

"'Tisn't what's the matter with me, 'tis what's the matter with you, and is always the matter with you, Da. You're never satisfied: nothing that I do is right. I never get a minute to meself. I take me half leave day on a Sunday when I could take it on a Saturday and go into town, which I would like to do sometimes, but no, I take it on a Sunday so I can have two hours longer to see to you. But what do I get? Never a word of thanks. I'm tired. Do you hear? I'm tired."

He stared at her as if he were being confronted by a strange preacher. Presently, his voice low now and self-pitying, he said, "I'm sorry you find me a burden."

She turned her head away and stood leaning on the table for a moment. "I don't find you a burden, Da, but I get tired of not hearin' a civil word," she said.

At this, he turned from her and went towards the fire, and, sitting down, he said, "I'm sorry, lass. I'm embittered against life and everything. Why should I have this?" He thumped his chest. "And why should Jane have been taken from me? Your mother was a good woman, never did or said a wrong thing in her life. I could put up with anything when I had her. There's no sense or reason to life. Why should she be taken when there's women left who are bad to the core and acting like mongrels on heat. There's Maggie Oates, forty-five if a day, and still supplying men practically on me doorstep. They slink past here shame-facedly. I feel at times, if I had a gun I would shoot them, or her."

As she unpacked the things from the basket she thought of the change that had come over her da. When her mother was alive he used to laugh about Maggie Oates, joked about her, at least when she herself wasn't there. Many's the time she would hear him say to her mother, "I think I'll take a stroll along to Maggie Oates," and they would laugh together. And she wondered why her da had never gone to Maggie Oates's cottage. Of course it was a good distance down the valley, a mile or more. But she knew other people went to Maggie Oates, because she was a friendly creature. She herself had spoken to her a number of times. Once, when she had come across her sitting in a field, she had made her a daisy chain. Looking back, she thought it was from that very incident that her da had become strict with her, telling her what she must do and what she must not do, especially that she must not speak to Maggie Oates.

She said, "This pie's fresh, I baked it this mornin'. Will I cut you a shive?"

He nodded, and when she handed him a wedge of the meat and potato pie he looked up at her and said, "Thanks, lass." And on this she turned away and went into the scullery where she took an old coat from behind the door and after putting it on went out and into the woodshed. And there she began to chop wood, sufficient to keep the stock up and to help out with the peat.

After finishing this chore, she next started on the room. She changed his bed and put the two fresh twill sheets and a pillow case that she'd brought with her from the farm: Mrs Davison allowed her to do his heavy washing when she had the wash-house pot on on a Monday. Following this, she tidied up the kitchen and the little room that had once been her own, all the while thinking, He could keep it better than this, he's not all that bad. But then telling herself that men didn't do housework, considering it demeaning, and her father had never done any in his life, and that it was only hunger that had made him make meals for himself.

He had nothing further to say all afternoon, and it wasn't until she was almost on the point of leaving that he said, "What's the news? You've hardly opened your mouth."

"Well, I'm followin' your example. Anyway, I don't like talking to meself. As for news it's the same as last week: Monday, washing and cleaning; Tuesday, ironing and cleaning; Wednesday, in the dairy, cheese making, butter making; Thursday, the big baking day and cleaning; Friday, the same; Saturday, packing for market; and the day, scrambling through everything so I can get off on time. That's my news, as usual."

He looked at her from out of the corner of his eyes, saying, "I thought you liked it there?"

"Aye, I do. I've always liked it there. But first and foremost, I'm there to work. Well, you asked what me news was, and that's me news."

"What about Kate ... and him?"

"What about them?"

"Well, you're not stupid. Knowing you, I would have thought you would have been ready for the jump long afore now. He's the only one you've trailed so far."

"Da, I haven't trailed him. We were practically brought up together, always friendly."

"Well, all right, have it that way. But has he spoken?"

Her body was hot, she wanted to turn and run from the house, but she had to look down into his face and answer his question, and she did, saying flatly, "No, he hasn't, and never will, as far as I'm concerned. As I said" – she was finding it difficult to go on now – "we were brought up together like ... like brother and sister."

He cut her off now by saying, "Oh, be damned to that for a tale, he's a man and you're ready for marryin'. You've got a head on your shoulders about most things, why haven't you got him up to the scratch?"

She turned from him, went to the door and took her coat and bonnet off a peg and, with her back still turned to him, she put them on. When at last she looked at him her voice was steady and she said, "I'll marry when I think fit, Da, and who I think fit. And let me say this, it will be an unlucky day for you when I do marry, 'cos there's one thing I'm tellin' you, I'm not startin' me life in this place. Now" – she pointed to the hearth – "I've brought you enough wood and peat in to last for a couple of days, and while the weather's fine keep it stocked up. There's food enough in the pantry to see you through the week and there's still a half sack of taties left. If you can't wash them, peel them and boil them, then I'm afraid you'll just have to go without. As the weather's getting chilly I'll bring you some bones over next week for soup. Well, I'm off. Ta-ra." She stared at him; and he returned her look for a moment before he said flatly, "Ta-ra, Mary Ellen."

When she had closed the door behind her she did not immediately walk away but stood with her eyes tight closed for a moment. If only he was different, like he used to be when she was younger, for although she had been a little afraid of him, she could talk to him, tell him all that had happened to her during her rambles, or what had transpired at Kate's.

Drawing in a deep breath, she now walked slowly across the garden which had lost every vestige of its past neatness, and out onto the narrow path that led up to the quarry, and round it to Kate's.

It was as she neared the cottage that she saw Roddy leaving it, and they met at the gate.

He, holding it open for her, was the first to speak. "Hello," he said, and, she, looking up at him, answered, "Hello." His face looked drawn and tense and she forced herself to carry on speaking in an ordinary tone as she asked, "How did you get on then?"

"Oh" – he jerked his chin upwards – " 'Twas a strange experience, different from what I thought. Anyway, I won't know the result until a month's time."

"Didn't they like your drawings?"

"That's what I won't know until they make their choice. As I understand it, there are three of us."

"Three of you!" she repeated. "What for?"

"Well—" He now rubbed his hand up and down the side of his thigh as he went on, "The one they consider to have the best drawings or possibilities, they are going to offer him a two year course in . . . art." He hesitated on the word: it didn't sound right, too fanciful for his drawings, he thought, and he explained by adding, "It's to learn not only engineering drawing, but all kinds, landscape and portrait and things. Although they are not in my line the winner will have to study them, I suppose, if he wants to take advantage of the offer."

"And what is the offer?"

"As I said, two years learning and they'll pay for your board and such, either in Newcastle or" – again his chin jerked upwards – "London."

"London?" Her head came forward in enquiry. "You mean the London, where the King is?"

"Yes, that London."

"And would you go?"

He looked away from her now towards the hills before once more he turned his head in her direction and said, bluntly now, "Aye, yes, I'd go."

Her voice was small as she asked, "You wouldn't mind leaving here?"

Again his eyes roamed over the hills and again his voice was flat as he answered, "Just in a way."

When she repeated his words, "Just in a way?" there was that recognized sting to her tone which put him on the defensive, and he said, "Aye, that's what I said, just in a way. I'll miss Kate of course. But there's lots of other things I wouldn't miss, the mill for one. . . ."

"And me for another, I suppose. That's what you were going to say, wasn't it?"

76

"No, I wasn't. Don't be silly."

"I'm not silly, and I'm not blind or daft either. You've got somebody else, haven't you?" She watched the scarlet suffuse his face. But then, after a moment, when he spoke his words cut into her like a knife, for what he said was, "I've never had anybody else before her. Get that into your head, Mary Ellen. I'm fond of you, aye, I am, always have been and always will, but ... but not like ... well, let me put it bluntly, not like taking you for a lass. You understand?"

She understood, but could not voice a word, the pain in her chest seemed to be riving it apart. As she stared up into his face she thought, He's cruel. That's what he is, cruel. He needn't have put it like that.

His voice softening now, and his head moving from side to side, he said, "You always put people in the wrong, make folks say what they never intended. It's that tongue of yours. Ah." He stopped and bowed his head deeply onto his chest for a moment, then muttered, "Don't look like that, Mary Ellen, please. Look, I'm tellin' you now, there's nobody I like better or think more of in a brotherly kind of way than I do you, but ... but it isn't the way one feels when one thinks of marryin'."

Yes, she understood him. They were looking at each other, their eyes on a level, and when slowly she turned from him and walked towards the house, he took his doubled fist and beat it against his brow before continuing on his way.

When she entered the cottage Kate said, "I saw you talkin' to him. From the looks on your face, it wasn't pleasant ... What did he say?"

Before answering Kate, she put the basket down on the floor and sat down with a plop on a backless wooden stool and her voice was quiet as she said, "He gave it to me straight."

"Gave you what straight?"

"What he thought about me."

"Oh. And he didn't tell you about her?"

"No." She turned and looked at the old woman. "Who is she?"

"Well, seeing who she is, lass, it's a pity you made him give it to you straight, because I can see no furtherance in that link up. Do you know who she is?"

Mary Ellen shook her head.

"Dan Bannaman's daughter, his only daughter, and she's older than him by three or four years if not more from what I remember. Now Dan Bannaman is as likely to let his lass link up with Roddy Greenbank there" – she nodded towards the window – "as you would with the devil, because I know this much an' I've worked it out over the years, that whatever happened to Roddy's father when he fell, supposedly accidentally, down the quarry and brought on a landslide, that man had some doin' in it, because he came here shortly afterwards and his face was clean-shaven and for years before he had sported a beard. And I can see his face now when he saw that the lad lying on that bed there" – she thumbed towards her bed – "didn't recognize him. Then there was the day that you came in and told me that his henchman was up there

77

looking for something. Well, whatever it was, they didn't find it, because every now and again they've come back, up till these recent years. So perhaps they did find it. I don't know. But as I said, Roddy has as much chance to link himself up with Bannaman's girl as would the devil in hell, in fact he'd have a better chance I would imagine. So, 'tis a pity you brought whatever you did into the open, for this would have died its natural death, and then you could have brought your wiles to work on him, usin' it instead of being so careless of your tongue."

"It wouldn't have been any good, Kate. He doesn't love me and never will. I could see it in his face."

"Nonsense, nonsense. Men change. From one season to another, men change, even the best of them. By the way, have you seen Hal?"

She hesitated. "Not the day," she answered.

"When did you see him last?"

"Well, last evening."

"Well, he hasn't been here, and it must be the first Sunday he hasn't shown up. And it's troublin' his nibs, because he's gone out to look for him. Although he grumbles about him tackin' on to him so much, he's worried now because he's mssed a day."

She went towards the fire and, taking up a poker, she stirred the centre of the fire into a dull blaze as she said, "I wonder how he'll take to Roddy leavin' for good, 'cos that's what he's gona do, you know." She turned her head and looked towards Mary Ellen. "One way or another, he's leavin' us, lass, and we've got to face it. To me, it'll be like losin' a dear son, me second. To you, it's the man you've loved all your life. And for that I'm sorry, lass. And for Hal, what's it gona be like for him? One never knows how that lad feels and I doubt if one ever will, because he's got a strength there that outweighs the three of us. 'Tis a pity he can't put it to some use, because there's good in him. Aye, there's good in him." She nodded her head and turned again to the fire and began moving the peat gently around the flame as she added softly, "'Tis a pity you'll never be able to see it."

5

He was late getting into Hexham. He had missed the carrrier, but Bob Allen, the blacksmith, had given him and Hal a lift. It was now just on four o'clock. He hadn't found Hal last Sunday, and so it wasn't until the first shift on the Monday morning that he met with him. And when Hal offered no excuse for his absence on the Sunday, he had made up his mind not to ask him, telling himself that it was probably for the best: perhaps he would have a little time to himself in future and not have one or the other trailing after him. Yet some part of his mind was piqued that his mate hadn't offered a reason for his non-appearance: over the years, it had become an understood thing that they spend their Sundays together.

But today as they came off the shift, he could not help but ask, "Coming into town the day?" And Hal's unenthusiastic answer, "May as well," put things on a level footing again.

Bob Allen's last words to them were, "Mind, I'll be leaving for back around half-past six. If you're not in the market place here, I go. Mind, I'm tellin' you." And he had smiled broadly at them.

It was Roddy who answered, "I'll be here . . . we'll be here; I'm not up to trekking across the hills the night. So long."

"So long then," said Bob, and drove his cart away across the market and down the main street to the fields beyond where the pony could munch in the care of a ha'penny lad until he returned.

In the market place, Roddy, looking at Hal, said in a somewhat shamefaced way, "I'll see you in about half an hour then, or perhaps a little later. I'll meet you back here." He pointed to the fruit stall and was somewhat taken aback when Hal answered, "But I mayn't be ready to be back in half an hour or so, as you say."

"Well then, if you're not here I'll wait for you. How's that?"

"Fair enough."

They stared at each other for a moment longer before Roddy turned away.

Crossing the market place he made for the archway that was set in the high wall opposite the Abbey. Once through the archway, he hurried now down an incline until he came to a pair of iron gates, and taking up his stand at the other side of the narrow road and in the shelter of some shrubs he waited.

It seemed to be her habit now and again to visit someone in the house beyond the gates and she usually left around half-past four or thereabouts. That she was Bannaman's daughter he no longer saw as an obstacle, if he ever had. He knew what he intended to do: he would tell her of his prospects, and ask her to wait. He had not for a moment considered what her feelings might be towards him; if his mind had enquired along those lines, it was to reason that no one could love as he loved her and the feeling not be returned.

But when the clock in the Abbey struck five he made up his mind that he had missed her and he told himself he didn't know how he was going to get through another week without catching a glimpse of her; it was as if he had inhaled some strange potion mixed up by Kate, for he couldn't get the girl's face out of his mind. Yet she was no girl, she was a woman, a handsome attractive woman, and she had smiled on him, and her eyes had spoken to him. . . .

He felt his heart actually jerk against his ribs when the gate opened, and there she was. As if he had been shot from the bushes he was at her side, and no doubt he startled her, for she stammered as she said, "Mr . . . Mr . . . Greenbank, please!" And she pulled her arm from his grasp.

"Oh, I'm sorry. I'm sorry, miss. It was just that I . . . I thought you had gone, an' it was sort of impulse that caused me to make such haste." He watched her draw herself upwards. Now she was walking up the bank to the market place and he was keeping his step in line with hers, talking all the time. "I . . . I had to see you. Do you understand? What is your first name? I keep giving you names."

She paused for a moment and there was no laughter in her eyes or warmth in her voice as she said, "My name doesn't matter. And no, I don't understand what you want of me. Because I have allowed you to speak to me on two occasions I think you are taking advantage of the situation, Mr Greenbank."

He was utterly taken aback. Nevertheless, he still persisted, he felt he had to. "Taking advantage?" he repeated. "I understood you were interested in the fact that I was going into Newcastle to present my drawings to a company of gentlemen. I . . . I just wanted you to know the result, or at least what happened."

"I'm well acquainted with what happened, Mr Greenbank. My father is in a position to know Mr Mulcaster at the mill; you are, I understand, a workman there, a smelter, and might be given the opportunity to further the talent you have in drawing. My father. . . ."

They were nearing the arch now that led into the market proper and he pulled her to a halt by again gripping her arm and swinging her round to face him, saying now, "This is not you, this is not the young lady who has spoken to me afore. It's your father, isn't it? He has forbidden you to speak to me, that's it, isn't it? I'm below your station, that's what he says, isn't it? But let me tell you, I won't always be a smelter. Oh no. Oh no."

"Leave go of my arm, please."

"I will when I'm ready. You've got to listen to me. Do you hear?

Look, tell me, please" – his voice dropped to a pleading note – "what is your Christian name?"

"Mary!" The name came loud and clear, but not from her, and he turned to see Mr Bannaman standing in the shadow of the arch. Then the man was towering over him with a look on his face that could only be described as black rage, and his voice was coming hissing through his teeth like steam from an escaped pipe: "Don't you dare lay hands on my daughter! You approach her again, come within a mile of her, and I'll see you skinned alive." The words, although hissed, were so quietly spoken that even a passer-by couldn't have heard them. But they evoked an answering rage in Roddy, and in his turn it was so deep that it blocked out words; and yet it brought into focus that odd feeling he experienced at those times when his memory tried to drag itself back to his early years. Staring into the man's eyes there came a dizziness in his head, and he wasn't aware at first of the man walking from him, taking his daughter with him. Not until they were passing through the arch did he seem to come to himself, and then he sprang forward and yelled, "I'll see her when I like. You can't frighten me, nor her."

"Don't be such a fool!" He turned to the side to see Hal within an arm's length from him, and he glared at him as he went on, "So that's the piece. You must be up the pole. Apart from bein' Bannaman's daughter, if all tales are true, she's had more through her than the stamp mill. Why, her engagement to Mr Jimmy Leader from Newcastle was broken off last year, and why? 'cos she was found with one of her horse-riding mates up in the stables. It was common knowledge, and you, you idiot, would have heard it if you hadn't your head so far up in the air...."

He got no further before Roddy's fist caught him between the eyes and sent him reeling, and he hit the wall. And he stayed there for some seconds before, with shake of his head, he sprang on his lifelong friend and the man, you could say, he loved.

Immediately a small crowd gathered around them.

"Now would you believe that?" one man was saying. "I know those two, like twins they are."

"Must be drunk," another said. "It often happens that way. God! they are goin' at it."

Then part of the crowd had to disperse to let a high-stepping horse and a trap pass round them. And from his seat Dan Bannaman looked down on the squirming figures on the ground. And his bearded face quivered before he brought his whip so viciously around the horse's flank that it reared before it sprang forward, and for most of the long drive to his home, he kept the animal moving at a trot.

When he eventually arrived in the courtyard adjoining his farm he threw the reins to his daughter, barking, "See to it!" Then he made for his woodman's cottage, and there, calling Pat Feeler out, he spoke rapidly to him, finishing with, "If you want to save your neck as well as mine, move, because I saw it in his face. It could happen any minute, it nearly did then. Get Vesper and Prince out, they're fresh. Those two might return separately or both together. If they come by the Allendale cart it'll be around eight o'clock. Move man! Don't stand there like a petrified rabbit."

God! to think it's come to this after all this time. And all through that blasted bitch. By God! I'll horsewhip her, that's if I live to get the chance. The last words he spoke to himself for Pat Feeler was already running towards the stables as if being pursued by the devil himself.

At the crossroads, Roddy and Hal slid down from the back of the blacksmith's cart, and they both swayed slightly and came in contact with each other for the first time since they had taken their seats. The long twilight was dropping into dark and hid the fact that both their faces were bruised, Hal's showing discoloration that was spreading to both his eyes and Roddy's a cut and swollen lower lip that was still oozing blood.

They had to take the same road as far as the mine where Roddy would turn off to go to Kate's, leaving Hal to go on towards his cottage.

Roddy strode ahead, his anger still burning in him but mixed now with a great sense of humiliation. It had been bad enough, the confrontation with Bannaman, but the brawl in the market place would forever stamp him as a lout. Yet he had been the first to raise his hand. And rightly so, he told himself. To say things like that about her. For two pins he'd turn and start on him again. Only the fact that he would have had to take the long track back from Hexham on foot had got him onto the carrier's cart when he saw Hal already sitting there.

He stopped dead in his tracks as Hal's voice came to him now, saying in a tone between a mutter and a growl, "I'm sorry. That's all I can say, I'm sorry."

"Sorry!" He turned on him. "You say you're sorry after taking somebody's character away like that, and in the open for all to hear?"

"Nobody heard me; it was just for your ears."

"Well, I heard you and I think you're a bloody swine. Do you hear? A bloody swine."

"Aye, well, you can think what you like, but I know what I know, and I'll say this, you're a blasted fool and.... All right! All right! You start anything—" He held up his hand more from instinct than to combat any movement he had seen Roddy making as he went on, rapidly now, "You start anything again and I'll finish it this time, as I could have finished you back there in the market. Oh aye, I could. Oh aye, I could."

"You finish me?"

"Aye, me finish you. I could have kneed you or battered your face, but I let you off. Aye, I did, I let you off."

"You let me off? You're all talk, all blow."

"Huh! That's funny, when I'm mostly blamed for not openin' me mouth. But you know inside your head what I'm sayin' is true. Anyway, I say again, I'm sorry it happened."

There was silence between them; then Roddy swung round and marched on, and Hal kept in step just a stride behind him.

It happened just as they were approaching the path that would have separated their ways. For a moment each thought that the other had attacked him, until the next blows came out of the blackness and they both gasped and fell to their knees, and when they were struck for the third time they tumbled and lay side by side, both on their backs, their heads lolling towards each other.

"Go on in and sit down, Kate."

"I won't sit down, and I won't go in. What are you sayin'? I don't believe you." Kate held up the lantern and peered at the two black faces staring at her, and the pitmen exchanged glances before one said, "'Tis true, Kate, 'tis true. We're sorry to say but 'tis true. Come." He reached out and took the lamp from her while the other man pressed her gently backwards into the cottage where he again said, "Sit you down."

The first pitman put the lantern on the table as he said, "We were comin' off the shift, an' that was the road we usually take an' we nearly stumbled over them. I thought it was a trunk that had fallen across the way, and then we saw them. It's as I said, Kate, they had been fightin' and one has a knife in his ribs and they are both ... well, they're not pretty sights. They must have pummelled each other almost to the end before they finished it."

"He's ... he's not ... Roddy's not?"

"We don't know, Kate," the other man said a little comfortingly. "Hal Roystan had a knife in him but he was still breathin', but we don't know so much about Roddy."

"Where ... where are they now?" The words jerked from her trembling lips.

"Where we found them, Kate. We ... we covered them up, but 'tis a serious business and one of our mates went for the doctor and one for Mr Wardle, the bailiff. We thought he'd know what to do, because, I'm afraid, Kate, it looks like a case for the justice, besides which, as me mate here said, if we move that knife the wrong way it might do more harm than good."

Kate now pulled herself to her feet, saying, "Take me to them."

"No, no, Kate. The night's sharp, you'll get your death."

"I'm expectin' that, so it won't matter how it comes. Just take me up there."

The men exchanged glances; then one of them said, "Well, wrap up, wrap up well, because it could be a long night for you. Likely, they'll take them down to the doctor's room at the mill. Then where they go from there only God knows. I've come across many strange things in me time, but those two were like brothers, closer than many, and yet one has got to go and kill the other. 'Tis somethin' so unexpected it's affected us all. We've known them since they were lads. Good workers, both of them, both in the mine and at the mill, so we hear, and yours highly respected. We all know you've looked after him like a son."

Kate turned her dazed eyes on the men and she repeated, as if to herself, "Aye, I've looked after him like a son." Then she added, "And that's what he's been to me. Yes, that's what he's been to me."

6

The man leaning over the iron bed said, "Four days now. If he lasts the day, he'll make it, if not, he'll go." And his companion, from the other side of the bed, said, "Well, aye, he'll go in any case, once he recovers enough to move him to Newcastle or Durham. Durham it'll be likely, if the other bloke snuffs it."

"T'other one's in better shape than this. His was only a stab and a few bruises, but he must have battered this 'un silly afore he got the knife stuck in him. But how this one managed that in the state he was in, God knows. He's muttering again, the same as afore, callin' for his da. It's a bad sign. They always want their folks when they're just on goin'."

"Is the old 'un still outside?"

"No. A fellow on a farm cart came and took her an' the young lass back about an hour gone. Well, I'm off duty now, he's all yours. Funny—" He looked down on the bruised and swollen face and, shaking his head, said, "I wonder if he ever thought when he started that fight last Saturday night in the market he'd finish up back here."

"Seems to me," said the other man, "that for him it ended up over at Langley. By! they must have gone at it. Well, I'm away. See you in the mornin'."

The man walked from the room, leaving the other man to draw up a chair towards a small table which, except for the iron bed, was the only other article of furniture in the room. And after making himself as comfortable as he could in the chair, he lifted his feet and rested them on the edge of the table. Then taking a clay pipe and a pouch from his pocket, he took from the pouch a plug of tobacco which he shredded and packed into the pipe, and bending sideways, he picked up a stick from the hearth and, stretching out, stuck it into the small fire to the side of him. When it had caught alight, he brought it to his pipe, sucked on the stem, then threw the stick back into the grate. And now leaning his head back against the high back of the chair, he sat staring at the prone figure on the bed.

There would be no more visitors today, either official or unofficial. He was on duty until six o'clock in the morning and it was up to him to make the best of it. If the fellow remained as he was he himself could have a good sleep; perhaps when he woke up the other would be gone to the place from which there was no return. And to his mind, it would be the best thing for him, because although he mightn't swing, it was a long term that was facing him, or transportation.

Within half an hour he was sound asleep and snoring loudly.

It was around midnight when Roddy once again fought the blackness in an endeavour to come to the surface. His father was with him, he had him by the hand and he was telling him a story, but he didn't know what the story was about because his father kept coming and going, only his hand remained clutching his, and always outstretched pulling him upwards. He knew he was sad inside because he was going to lose his da, and he knew if he left loose of his hand he'd be gone from him and sail away in his ship and not come back for a long time. And there was the old woman, she was walking behind him, close, too close, pushing him upwards, and he wanted to go upwards. Yet there was the man with the beard and the cold eyes, and the man was holding him over a big hole and in the hole was another man and he was fast asleep. Then his da cried out and left hold of his hand. And he was now being smothered by another hand, which wasn't a hand; it was something, but it wasn't a hand. And because of the weird feeling created by this thing across his mouth, he screamed, he screamed at the top of his voice: he opened his mouth and screamed, yet the sound remained in his head; and he kept screaming as he saw his da jump into the air as if he was a bird, he saw him flying. And once again he was looking into the eyes of the man with the beard and the man's face swelled and swelled until it covered everything, all the dark land, and the big hole where they watched the moon shining on the water.

But his da had hold of his hand again and he was pulling him up through layers and layers of smothering, choking blackness. And when his head at last burst through it he saw the man again. He was standing under the arch and there, near him, stood a woman, and the man was talking to him, threatening him. He took his fist and struck out at the man, blow after blow. Yet the only actual movement he made was that of his fingers on top of the rough blanket that covered him. But his voice came out of his mouth, and he could hear it. He called for his father: "Da! Da! 'Tis him, Da. 'Tis him!" And his voice becoming stronger, he called again, "Da! Da! I know him, an' t'other. 'Tis him! 'Tis him! Don't go, Da. Stay with me. I tell you, 'tis him. 'Tis him!"

"Oh my God!" The man in the chair roused himself. "Going to be a night like that, is it?" And he lowered his feet from the table and stumbled towards the bed and, bending over the prisoner, he said, "Now, now. What is it? What is it?"

"Me da."

"Aye, lad, aye lad, you'll soon see your da."

There was silence for a time. The man on the bed lay quiet and the warder bent over him and stared down at him. The light from the candle lamp on the table seemed, he thought, to be playing tricks with him, so he turned and, picking it up, held it above his charge who was now looking at him with eyes that had a good semblance of life in them and

86

the voice that came in a small whisper supported this: "Where am I?" it said.

"Well, man, you're in bed." The warder's voice was kindly.

"Why?" The whisper came again.

"Oh, it's a long story, lad. How you feelin'?"

"Bad."

"Aye, well, yes, you're bound to."

"Where am I?"

"In bed, lad. Now just you rest. Would you like a drink of water?"

Roddy made no reply, and the man, returning to the table, picked up a jug and poured some water into a mug. Taking it to the bed, he raised his prisoner's head gently and let him sip at the water, saying as he did so, "Well, that looks promising, although if it's for the good I wouldn't know. Still, it doesn't look as if you're goin' to kick the bucket this time." When he let the head drop back on the pillow he added, "There now, I'd go to sleep. You'll feel better in the morning, I've no doubt."

Roddy lay looking up at the man. His mind was in a whirl. He was sure he had been with his da just a minute ago before ... before he was thrown over the cliff. Oh, God! God! God! Yes, that's what had happened. His da had been thrown over the cliff and they'd thrown him an' all. And the man in the grave, the man they were burying.

Bannaman. Yes, Bannaman, and the other little fellow with just a finger and thumb. That was the man, Feeler, Patrick Feeler, Bannaman's woodman. Oh, God! God! He was remembering. Kate! Kate! he tried to rise: he must tell Kate; she'd have to go to the justice.

"Now, now, calm down. You were all right a minute ago. Go to sleep now."

"I ... I want to see Kate."

"Kate? Is she the old 'un, like your mother?"

"Yes, aye."

"Well, she's been here every day since they brought you in. She'll likely be here the morrow. Now go to sleep and you'll be more fit to talk to her."

He lay, unaware of pain, unaware that his body was bruised from head to foot, unaware of the situation he was in; he knew only that he was remembering and that the past was clearer than the present and that what he had to reveal would explode the countryside. He must keep awake and think, think it all out. Yet even as he told himself this, his mind seemed to leave him and he sank back into sleep.

He was brought to himself again through experiencing sharp pain, intense enough to make him cry out. He was being rolled onto his side by the doctor and the warder so that the bruises and lacerations on his back could be attended to. He was sufficiently aware of things to note that the sun was well up and that the warder had been changed, and to ask the doctor how he could have come by his injuries.

"That's good, that is. What d'you say, doctor?" the warder immediately remarked.

And so he tried to tell the doctor what was in his mind. But, nodding, the doctor said soothingly, "Yes, yes. Well, you can tell all that later to the justices," and he glanced at the warder, tapping his forehead to indicate to him that the man was suffering from mental strain, as he went out.

7

"You're a silly girl . . . and ungrateful an' all."

"Oh, Mrs Davison, I'm not, I'm not. And I'll work late at night an' get up an hour earlier; I'll be in the dairy at four."

"I don't want you in the dairy at four. Do you think we can order the cows to change their time of milkin'?"

"Well, I could get it cleaned up. . . ."

"It's got to be cleaned up, as you know, after the day's work."

"I've got to go, Mrs Davison. I'm sorry, yes I am, but I've got to go and see him."

"You went three times into Hexham last week, and now it's New-castle you're aiming for. My goodness, girl! Apart from everything else, do you know what you're up to, goin' into Newcastle on your own?"

"It's in the daylight, Mrs Davison."

"Daylight or dark, there are a lot of rogues there. I've only been in there twice in me life and never again. They overcharge you, pester you. But anyway, what am I talkin' about? I'm talkin' about your wastin' time, girl, takin' advantage."

"Oh, Mrs Davison, I'm not, I'm not. I'm ever so grateful for all you've done, always. But he's got nobody, an' Kate can't go, not all the way. She managed it to Hexham but she could never stand the coach to Newcastle; it would shake her to bits. And she's dyin' to know what's happenin' to him, what they're goin' to do."

"Everybody knows fine well what they're goin' to do with him. Got too big for his boots, he did. He should have been content to work at the smelt mill, but no, he had to take up something fancy like drawing; and then to drink and fight."

Mary Ellen now reared up. "He doesn't drink," she said in a loud voice, and it became louder as she went on, "Not that kind of drink, a little ale, but he's never been drunk. And I know what he and Hal were fighting about in Hexham, 'cos Hal told me when I saw him last. But he swears they weren't fighting up on the hill, he says they were attacked. He says he had told Roddy he was sorry 'cos it was something he had said that started the fight."

"And what was that?"

"'Tisn't my business, Mrs Davison; I can't say."

"Well, well." The little woman flounced round, grabbed up a coarse square from the brass rod, lifted up the iron latch of the oven door, pulled out a big brown earthenware dish, and taking it to the table, she banged it down, and when the lid jerked and the liquid spurted onto the table and onto her hands, she cried out, "See what you've done! I'm burnin' meself now. That's never happened afore. Go on, get you out of my sight. And if you're not back here in this house by four this afternoon, don't come back at all."

"Oh, Mrs Davison, don't say that. Don't say that."

Now the little woman lowered her head while continuing to rub her scalded hands and, her voice quiet, even sad now, she said, "Girl, it worries me to be harsh with you and it worries me more to know how concerned you are for Rodney Greenbank, when our Lennie would give you his eyeballs."

There was quiet for a moment in the kitchen, then Mrs Davison lifted her head and said, "Why can't you like him?"

"Oh, but I do, Mrs Davison. I do like him. I think the world of Lennie. He's kind and good, but...."

"Aye, it's but. You don't like him that way and it grieves me, girl, it grieves me, 'cos you'll never get a chance like this again. Do you realize that? Although we've made you one of our own an' treated you like a daughter, you are still nothin' but a servant-maid, and here's me grandson been knockin' on for you since the day you came into the house. Aye, even afore that he had his eye on you. Although I say it meself, you couldn't get a better, 'cos he's a good-livin' lad. Doesn't drink, leastways only holidays and barn nights. You're a fool. Do you know that? You're a fool."

"Aye, Mrs Davison. Aye, yes, I know that, and it hurts me."

"Oh, get yourself away. Get yourself out of my sight."

Mary Ellen turned now and picked up the basket that her irritable but kind mistress had filled for her with odds and ends of food, and she went out of the farm kitchen and crossed the yard, her head down. She shouldn't have said she knew she was a fool for not takin' Lennie because she'd be worse than a knave if she took him, not lovin' him. Half the battle of life seemed to be sayin' things you didn't mean just to keep the peace.

Oh! She gave a start as the man in question came round from behind the byre wall, blocking her path. He did not speak to her immediately, but looked at her for some seconds before he said, "Aye, well, you're off then?"

"Yes, Lennie."

"You've never been to Newcastle afore, have you?"

"No."

"It could be frightening. You could get lost."

"I've got a tongue in me head."

He laughed gently now, saying, "Aye, sure you have, Mary Ellen; you never leave anybody in doubt about that."

"I'm sorry. I never mean to be curt."

"Oh; now, don't say you're sorry when you've got nothing to be sorry for. I love hearin' you." His voice had become lower; and his head was nodding gently now as he added, "You know that, don't you?"

"Oh, Lennie. I've told you."

"All right. All right." His voice rose again to its normal pitch. "We won't go into that; only I . . . I worry about you; I don't want you to do anything silly. An' to my mind, that fellow, he's not worth you; something about him. Anyway, you've been brought up like brother and sister, haven't you?"

"We're not brother and sister." Her tone was certainly curt now. "But no matter what we were, or are, we're not marrying. I'm marryin' nobody. So there! Do you hear, Lennie? I'm marryin' nobody."

"Aye, I heard, Mary Ellen. We'll let it pass for the time bein'. Look. If you could wait another half hour or so I'll be takin' the cart into. . . ."

"No, Lennie. No. Your grannie wouldn't like it."

"She needn't know."

She shook her head at him now. "That isn't right; I wouldn't do anything underhand."

"It isn't underhand. Only, I've got me own life to lead, Mary Ellen; me grannie's had hers. Me father and granda understand, where she doesn't, being a woman."

"Thank you."

"You know what I mean; don't pick me up wrong. Anyway, do you think you'll be able to catch the coach?"

"If I stand here much longer I won't."

She went to walk from him, but he accompanied her to the gate, saying now, "What if you can't get on? They like to know aforehand."

"I'm thin; I'll squeeze in somewhere. Anyway, if I miss that I can always get the cart."

"Don't be silly, Mary Ellen. The cart won't get into Newcastle until well after dinnertime, and won't pass this way again coming back until dark the night."

"Ta-ra! Lennie." She hurried away from him, and he called after her, "If you miss the coach at Haydon Bridge take the cart into Hexham; there's a later run there from The Angel."

She turned her head towards him, saying, "Thanks, Lennie. Thanks, I will."

He was nice, was Lennie; perhaps she was being a fool after all.

She reached Haydon Bridge only to see the coach disappearing in its own dust. And she was still watching the settling dust when she heard the quick trot of a horse's hooves. She turned quietly, and there, coming towards her, was a market cart, piled high with vegetables, and at the front, perched on the iron seat were a man and a woman.

She called to them as they were about to pass her, crying, "Are you makin' for Hexham?"

Pulling the horse to a standstill, the man said, "Aye, lass, that's where we're makin' for."

"Would you be so kind as to give me a lift?"

The man looked at his wife, and her answer was to move closer to him, saying with a smile, "Well, there's not much of you, broad on that is. Climb up."

And so she climbed up, and squeezed on to the end of the seat and thanked them as she did so.

They enquired where she was bound for, dressed up as she was in her Sunday best, and she told them, Newcastle. She had no need to explain why she was taking her journey for the woman became voluble: she had been born in Newcastle; she knew every street in Newcastle; and she chattered all the way.

It wasn't until Mary Ellen stepped down from the cart in Hexham market place that the woman thought to ask her whereabouts in Newcastle she was making for, and when, without thinking, she said, "The prison infirmary," the woman and man gazed at each other, and she left them speechless.

The coach was almost ready for the last section of its run into Newcastle, the driver about to mount the box, when she asked permission to board. "Well, we're full inside lass, and there's six fellows up there," the driver replied, jerking his head towards the back of the coach. "You could squeeze in atween them if you like. Cost you sixpence, seein' as you're a thin 'un."

She looked up to where on the end seat two young men were looking down on her, both smiling. They didn't look like working men, yet not like gentry either, and when she hesitated the driver said, "Well, take it or leave it, lass; we must be off."

She took it. Hands came out and lifted the basket from her outstretched arms; then with an "Up! you come, milady," the young men brought her, with a plop, on to the hard seat between them.

She had been in touch with men all her life: with Roddy and Hal, as a child, then as a young girl, and now as a young woman; she had chatted to the miners and the mill workers; but except when her father had lifted her up into his arms when she was small, she'd had no close body contact with any male – if Roddy's hand had touched hers it had been to give her a pull over a ditch or up a hill – but now here she was pressed close between two men, and they seemed to be making the most of it for, with the intention of keeping her steady, they both put their arms around her shoulders. And when she shivered at their touch the one on her left, who had a long thin face and a large mouth that was full of very white teeth, enquired, "You cold, hinny?"

Turning her full look on him, she shouted in a high voice to make herself heard, "No! I am not cold, sir."

"You're not?" he said. "Well, were I to leave go of you . . . were we to leave go of you" – he leaned over in front of her and appealed to his friend – "you would fall off. Wouldn't she, Harry?"

"She would that," said the other man.

When the coach went over a particularly rough piece of rock road their holds tightened about her, until she felt she was blushing down to her waist and beyond.

When the long-faced man's hand squeezed her breast she acted instinctively: her hand flying to her hat, she pulled out one of the two hatpins and drove it with some force into the gentleman's leg.

The yell he let out as he jerked himself sideways nearly unseated the three of them. What it did do positively was to stop the coach, and the coachman, swinging about, glared at them, shouting, "What's up, there! What's up."

She twisted round on the seat and, looking between the other outside passengers she gasped, "He started to handle me, an' I stuck him with me hatpin."

The coachman stared from one to the other, shouting now, "Begod! if it wasn't for losing time I'd come round there and help you do it again. Now, you two!" – he bounced his head from one to the other – "any more of that and I'll drop you on the road, young gentlemen or not. And it isn't the act of a gentleman, is it? Which one of you did it?"

"It was only a bit of fun," the man said, his face now grim.

"Well, we always pay for our fun, an' you've paid for yours. Anyway, miss, move to the side of the other fella. Go on now. You'll only have to defend yourself against one then."

As she stood up, the second man moved along the seat to take her place and she sat at the end of the narrow seat squeezing herself against the iron rail. And as soon as she was settled the driver gave a "Get up there!" and they were off once more.

They rode in silence for some miles before the man next to her spoke. But he didn't look at her as he said, "I'm sorry. I apologize. It was very bad of us."

She kept her gaze straight ahead. It wasn't he who should have said he was sorry because his hand hadn't strayed past her shoulder.

The man went on speaking. "My friend meant no harm, not really. We are . . . we are rather excited: we are going into Newcastle to take up new positions today. We are young doctors, you see."

Now she turned and looked at him. He had a pleasant face, a kindly face. "I'm not sorry I did it," she said.

"No, I don't suppose you are" – he gave a wry smile – "but I think he is, and his first patient will be himself when we get in."

After a short pause he asked, "Are you going to take up service?"

She made no reply, just stared at him. Was she going to take up service? That's what she must look like, a young girl going into place. And she had her best clothes on an' all. She had always considered them smart, a cut above the rest of the girls, because she made all her own clothes except the coats. He was waiting for an answer, and so she shook

93

her head before saying, "No, I am not goin' into place, I have one. I work with a farmin' family. I ... I'm going to see a friend. He's ill."

"In hospital?"

She swallowed deeply and looked ahead before she said, "Sort of."

"Sort of?" He bent slightly towards her and looked into her face.

"He's in the prison hospital."

"Good God! ... Oh, I am sorry. What has he done?"

"They said he stabbed a friend, but he didn't. I'm sure he didn't; he would never stab anybody. And he liked Hal, I mean his friend. He was very fond of him. Always has been. They were mates." She didn't know why she was telling him this. She had been mad at them, at the two of them not so long ago, and here she was telling him her private affairs. But he wasn't like the other one, sitting there with a face like thunder.

"Do you know Newcastle?"

"No. I've never been afore."

At this point the coach rocked and she was thrown against him, and he steadied her with his hand on her arm. But as soon as they were running smoothly again he left go of her; then asked, "How did you expect to find the hospital?"

"I thought I'd just have to ask."

"Dear, dear. I must say, and don't take umbrage at this, you are much too pretty to ask the way. But it is fortunate that I know the town well, and I'll show you how to get there."

"Thank you."

By the time the coach reached Newcastle she had learned that both he and his friend had done part of their training in the Newcastle Infirmary and had been in Edinburgh for only a year. And they were both now fully fledged doctors, and, what seemed very strange to her, to use his own words, very poor.

When finally he helped her down from the coach and handed her the basket she did not even thank him, for she was, in a way, speechless. The enormity of the city had overwhelmed her: the throngs of people, the carriages, the carts, the scramble of the vehicles to the side of the road to make way for the coach, and people as thick as flies on a midden had bereft her of speech. But not of hearing, for the man whom she had made acquainted with her hatpin was saying, "Don't be so damn silly; let her go. She'll find her way all right. She's quick on the uptake, is that one. My leg's paining like blazes."

"It served you right. You asked for it. Anyway, I'll see you in about half an hour."

"You won't. I'll not wait for you."

"Please yourself. But he's expecting us both together, and, if I remember rightly, you don't like him and he doesn't care all that much for you. So please yourself about not waiting."

When he returned to her side again he said, "Come along. It's about a ten minutes walk. Are they expecting you? I mean is it visiting time?"

"No; I just thought they would let me see him."

He stared at her for a moment; then bit on his lip before saying, "They don't do things like that, not in prisons. But fortunately I happen to know someone there, that is if he's still in charge of the sick bay. I did some of my training in there, you know." He nodded at her, smiling as he spoke, and she thought, He'll be a good doctor; he'll make people feel better just talking to them.

Mary Ellen didn't believe in angels, not even guardian angels. But, while waiting in the bare stone room for the return of this new friend, as she thought of him, she felt positive in herself that some power had arranged her meeting with this young doctor, for never, never could she have found this place on her own; and never, never could she have stopped anyone in the street and asked the way, not even the women, who to her had looked like foreign beings, and were loud-mouthed and yelling, some so poorly dressed that they appeared to be in rags. And yet there were carriages with fine ladies sitting in them. And what was absolutely certain, if she had, on her own, managed to find this place, they would never have let her in.

The young doctor returned, and with him a man in a thick serge uniform. He was a burly type, with a big head and his hair cut close.

The doctor spoke to him, saying, "This is the young woman, Pilling." Then turning to her, he said, "This is Sergeant Pilling. Now he is going to let you have a little time with the pri . . . your friend. Then he will tell you how to get a cab to take you to the Cloth Market, and this will put you off at The White Hart. That's from where The Doctor Syntax leaves around half-past three."

She looked at him; and now there were tears in her eyes and she held out her hand, saying, "Thank you. I . . . I don't know what else to say. But I can see now that it was stupid of me to come to this town alone; I . . . I would never have got here without your help. I'll . . . I'll always remember your kindness, sir."

He shook her hand warmly, saying, "I'm sorry we had to meet under such circumstances. It was a sharp introduction for us both, except that you didn't introduce me to your hatpin." He laughed now as she bowed her head; and turning from her, he looked at the warder again, saying, quietly, "Thank you, Pilling. I'll be seeing you."

"Very good, sir. Very good." The man jerked his head towards him, then said, "Well, come along, miss. Come along. Time's getting on."

"Goodbye, doctor." She turned towards him, and he said, "Goodbye," then went out of one door as she, following the warder, went out of the other.

When she entered the cell-like room and saw Roddy propped up in a narrow iron bed she wanted to groan aloud, such was the pain that the sight of him in this awful place caused her. Not only was the room stark, but it was the smell, the queer smell. It wasn't a midden smell or a dirty smell; she couldn't put a name to the smell, only that it frightened her.

When Roddy held out his hands towards her she dropped the basket and ran to him, and, grasping them, she muttered, "Oh, Roddy. Roddy."

"Ten minutes, miss. That's all. I'll be back in ten minutes."

Roddy opened his mouth wide, and three times he closed it before he brought out her name: "Oh, Mary Ellen."

"It's all right. It's all right, Roddy."

"I ... I never expected...." He was gasping for breath. "How ... how did you get here?"

"I came by coach. And I've brought you some things. Look, there." She turned round to where the basket was reposing on its side on the floor.

He shook his head; then his grip tightening on her hands, he pulled her down on to the side of the bed and, putting his face close to her, he said, "There's not much time. Listen, will you, Mary Ellen. Will you listen?"

"Yes, yes, of course, Roddy, yes."

"Well, it's like this. I've ... I've remembered."

"No!"

"Aye, yes. But not all. Things are mixed up, but two things are clear: the grave...."

"The grave?" Her eyebrows shot up.

"Aye. Aye, the grave. With a man in it. I can see his face. I've just got to close me eyes and I can see his face. And then, me da." He now lowered his head before muttering, "Mary Ellen ... they threw him over the cliff. I ... I saw him flying through the air."

"Who threw him over the cliff? Who? Who, Roddy?"

"Bannaman."

"Bannaman? ... Mr Bannaman?" She could hardly hear her own voice, it was so filled with awe.

"Aye. Bannaman and his woodman."

"No! No!" She shook her head. "He's ... he's a respected...."

"Mary Ellen." His manner and his voice changed: he appeared no longer a sick man, and, his hands going to her shoulders, he actually shook her as he said, "Listen! 'Tis important. 'Tis me life. Do you understand? 'Tis me life. Go to Mr Mulcaster. Tell him what I've told you. Tell him to bring in the justice, and dig up near the place where the fall was. They'll know it 'cos it's given way again of late and taken the path with it. It's just there, just round there. I know it. I know it."

"All right. All right." She loosened his hands from her shoulders, and now she held them, saying, "'Tis a big accusation to make, Roddy."

"'Tis the truth. That's why he tried to do me in and put the blame on me for what happened to Hal. By the way, how is he?"

"I don't know, except when I heard last he was all right."

"Will you be seeing him?"

"I don't know where he is, 'cos they moved him to a different place."

"Ask where he is, will you? Ask the warder. Go and see, will you? Go and see him, Mary Ellen. Tell him I never did it."

"He'll know that. He'll know that, Roddy. But about t'other."

"Aye, t'other. They tell me the case comes up in a fortnight. I'll be on me legs by then. If I thought I could get to that quarry I'd be on me legs now. Look ... look, Mary Ellen" – he shook his head – "I'm not ... I haven't gone mad or dreamin'. I tell you, when the sense was knocked out of me by them throwing me after me da, it must have been brought back when Bannaman tried to do me in again. But he left me in such a state that he never thought I'd survive. Nor yet Hal, by all accounts. 'Tis a miracle that I'm alive. The doctor said that. He said it again and again, 'tis a miracle that I'm alive. But I am alive, Mary Ellen, and that man is a murderer. He not only murdered me da, but whoever was put into that grave. And you know, I've got me thoughts on that, an' all."

"You have?"

"Aye. I have, 'cos you know, Hal has always maintained his da would come back and he'd see him again. Well, likely he will. If what I feel to be true, likely he will."

It was at this point that the door opened. Mary Ellen started up from the bed, only to have her hands gripped again; and Roddy, looking up at her and his expression one of anguished pleading, said, "You'll see to it, won't you, Mary Ellen? You'll see to it? And right away."

"Aye. Aye, Roddy, I will. I will. This very day, I will. Or as soon as I get back." She now pulled her hands from his grip and, rushing to the basket, she picked it up, took it back to the bed, on which she emptied its contents, while looking towards the warder and saying, "I'm comin'. I'm comin'."

"'Tis all right, lass. 'Tis all right." He too was looking at the food on the bed, and he smiled grimly at her now as he said, "That should keep him going for a time. With a load like that you'd be welcome every day." And he ran his lips one over the other.

She said nothing, but backing across the small room, her head nodding all the time, she stopped at the door held open by the warder and muttered, "Bye. Ta-ra, Roddy. I'll ... I'll be back. I'll be back."

He made no reply, but his whole expression spoke for him.

Once out in the corridor, she turned to the warder and said, "Is there another infirmary near here?"

"What kind of an infirmary are you lookin' for? This is a prison infirmary. The general one is some distance away."

"Would that ... would that be where the other man was taken?"

"You mean the one he tried to do for?"

Now she reared up, her voice even strident as she cried, "He never did! He never would; they were mates."

"All right. All right." He flapped a hand at her. "As you say, he never did. That's what he says, an' all. Well, the justices will work that one out. Anyway, if you're lookin' for that young fellow, he's not a stone's throw away along the road. Turn left out of the main gate. 'Tis a red building right opposite to you. You can't miss it. But the doctor asked me to see you to a cab. What about that?"

97

"I'll get one from the other place. And I'm ... I'm sorry I was hasty, but you know...."

"All right. All right, lass, I know." And he flapped a hand at her again. "'Tis the law of the land, a man is innocent until he's found guilty, But I wish him well 'cos he's decent enough spoken."

At the end of the corridor he passed her over to another warder who saw her out of the gates. On the cobbled road once more, she turned left and there at the end of the street was the red building....

After she had rung the bell, the heavy oak door was opened by a woman in a black dress and with a white cap and apron. "What's your business?" she demanded.

"Would ... would it be possible for me to see Mr Hal Roystan?"

"Are you his wife?"

Her eyebrows went up again. Did she look like a wife? What would the woman say if she said she was just a friend? Likely she wouldn't let her in.

"I'm ... I'm his sister."

"Oh. Oh well, seein' you're a relative, come in. Though it isn't the day for callers. Have you come far?"

"Yes, right from Langley."

"Langley? Where's that?"

She hesitated. Where was it? "Well, it's beyond Hexham, on the way up to Allendale."

"Oh. Oh, I know Hexham. I've been to Hexham. Went by coach once. Splendid place, Hexham."

They had walked across the wide hall; and now the woman pushed open a door and led the way into a long room which seemed to be packed with beds, and all occupied. Some men were sitting up, some were lying down; and two men were sitting on wooden stools to the side of their beds. And on the sight of Mary Ellen, one of these rose to his feet and appeared not to be believing what his eyes were seeing.

The woman did not immediately direct Mary Ellen towards the bed, but called up the ward to where another woman was sitting behind a small table: "Roystan's sister," she said. "Give her ten minutes. That's all, ten minutes." And as Mary Ellen walked towards the astonished man, part of her mind was saying, "Everything is timed to ten minutes."

"Hallo Hal."

He seemed unable to speak for a moment; but then said, "Hallo, Mary Ellen. How did you get here?"

Again she gave the same answer to the same question; "By coach."

He did not say he was glad to see her, but pointed to the stool, and she sat down, while he sat on the edge of the bed, but not before he had glanced down the ward towards the woman seated behind the table.

"How did you find out where I was?"

"I've been to see ... Roddy. He ... he wants me to tell you that he never did...."

"Oh, I know that. I know that. We were jumped. How is he?"

"He ... he doesn't look well. He was knocked about awful. They didn't expect him to live. Nobody did. But ... but listen, Hal. Listen! I've something to tell you."

She hitched herself towards the edge of the stool and as she leaned towards him he lowered his head down to hers as she whispered, "He's remembered. He's remembered what happened. I ... I can't believe it, but yet I know it's true. The night his father died there wasn't a landslide, he was thrown over, he says, after" – she gulped – "he saw a man in a grave ... two men were burying a man in a grave. And the men took his da and threw him over the cliff. They must have done the same with Roddy, and he remembers who the men were."

"No! No!"

"Aye. Yes. So listen, Hal." She went to grip his hands as she had done with Roddy, but then hesitated and withdrew them, and joined them lightly in her lap. Her voice dropping still further until she could hardly hear her own words, she said, "He says it was Mr Bannaman an' ... and his woodman. And you know who his woodman is, it's Mr Feeler. That's the man, you know, with only half a hand who at times would come to the woodland to gather fir trees. At least that's what he was supposed to be doin'. But thinkin' back now, I remember Kate dashing up there one time when I told her he was in the wood gathering fir trees."

"My God! Christ!" Hal wasn't looking at her, but over her head as if into the distance, down the years. She had to call his attention to her by saying, "He wants me to go and tell Mr Mulcaster and for him to go to the justice and get them to start digging to prove he's right."

He was looking into her eyes now. "Who do you think they were burying, Mary Ellen?" he said.

"I don't know," she answered, her gaze half shaded.

Again he looked away from her before he said, "You know my da disappeared around that time. Because they found the horse in Newcastle, they put two and two together and added it up that he had skipped with the money on a ship. Never—" His teeth were ground together before he said again, *"Never* have I believed it." His face now darkened and he actually glared at her as he repeated, *"Never for one moment have I believed it."*

He was gripping the round iron bed frame so that his knuckles were shining white as he muttered, with bent head, "God Almighty! If I can prove them wrong. Oh God, if only this proves them wrong." Then his head jerking up, he said, "I'll soon be out of here, the morrow or the next day. I'm healed, at least enough to get me on me legs. And you do what Roddy said. But mind, be prepared for stumbling blocks: Bannaman's a name in the county, at least he is now; they've forgotten to ask how he made so much money so quickly years gone by. But soon it'll be explained, please God."

He put his hand out now and gripped her arm. "Don't be put off, will you not? Don't be put off, because that's what they'll do, them up top. They all stick together, because if this is true, an' I know it is, aye, I know it is" – his head was bobbing now – "it'll raise such a stink that the smell from the mill will be like scent in their noses." He got up and pulled her to her feet, saying, "Go on. Get back as quick as you can." And his hand went out as if to push her to hasten her going; but then stopped midway and, his manner changing and his voice soft, he said, "Thanks, Mary Ellen. I'll ... I'll never be able to thank you enough for this day."

She smiled weakly at him now, saying, " 'Tis all right, Hal. 'Tis all right. And I'll do what you say." Then in apology for coming empty-handed, she added, "I'm sorry I haven't brought you anything."

"Aw, Mary Ellen, what you've brought me is pure gold dust. Go on now; and travel safely for so much rests on your shoulders. You know that?"

"Aye." She nodded at him, then said, "Ta-ra then, Hal." And he answered, "Ta-ra, Mary Ellen."

The woman had left the table and come down the room, and she opened the door, and pointing across the hall, said to Mary Ellen, "You can let yourself out. But be sure to close the door after you. We're short-handed."

Mary Ellen closed the door after her; but once outside on the cobbled road again, she did not hurry to where she hoped to find a coach or a carrier cart to take her home, but stood like a perplexed child nipping on the nail of her first finger as she thought, What if they don't believe me, 'cos he's a big man, is Mr Bannaman. He could easily have me locked up for carrying such a message 'cos the gentry are a law unto themselves. And Mr Bannaman although not quite gentry was known as a very worthy man.

There was trouble ahead. Whether they believed her or not, there was trouble ahead.

It was seven o'clock in the evening and she had run all the way from the coach road, past the castle and up through the woods to the mill, hoping to find Mr Mulcaster still there. She knew that they banked down some of the fires after six, but she had heard that Mr Mulcaster and the clerks were often in the offices till late on some nights. It was deep twilight when she surprised a number of men as she scrambled her way over the horse tracks and stumbled round the mounds of bouse before she asked one of them if the agent was still about or had yet gone to his house which was nearby. No, the man answered, he was still in his office; and he had pointed to the buildings across the yard. And there, on her reaching the end one, a door opened as if at her bidding and two clerks stepped out, staring at her in surprise. But she ignored them and looked at the man following behind them.

Gasping, she said, "Mr Mulcaster, please may I have a word with you?"

The three men stood looking at her for a moment before Mr Mulcaster, observing her agitated state, said, "Yes, if it's all that important."

"'Tis, sir. 'Tis."

The clerks seemed now reluctant to leave, until the agent said to them, "Well, get along." Then indicating that she should enter he picked up a lantern from a shelf just inside the doorway and went before her along a passage and up a flight of stairs and into a room. Then having closed the door behind her, he peered at her and said tersely, "What is it that's brought you here in such a flutter? You're Mary Ellen Lee, aren't you?"

"Yes, sir."

"Well, speak; tell me what you have to say because—" he took out his watch and, looking at it, he remarked, "I am due for my meal about this time, and ready for it." But he smiled kindly at her.

And now she began to gabble: first of all reminding him of what had taken place between his two workers; then of her visit to Roddy and of his disclosure.

He did not speak or interrupt her gabbled discourse in any way until she was finished and stood gazing at him through the hazy lantern light when, looking at her steadily, he said as if in astonishment at her request, "You're really asking me to inform the justices?"

"Yes, sir."

"But . . . but I can't do that. Well, not on such . . . slender evidence. Young Greenbank's mind could have been disturbed in another way by the treatment he had from his assailant, whether it was his friend or, as you maintain, some other."

"Mr Mulcaster, sir." She put out her joined hands as if in supplication towards him. "Believe me, please. He's in his right mind, he is. He described how he saw his father flying into the air. It was when they threw him over the cliff. And then they must have done the same to him. And what's more, he knows there was a man buried in a grave. Likely Roddy's father came on them—" She refrained from mentioning Mr Bannaman's name again, but said, "The men were burying somebody. That's why they turned on him. And . . . there's something more, sir."

"Something more?" His face stretched slightly, and she nodded as she went on, "I went to see Hal . . . Hal Roystan, an' I told him. And you know, sir, he's always been firm about the fact that his father never stole that money. And he didn't, sir. I . . . I know that." She now closed her eyes tightly. She had said too much. If she said she knew where the money was they would ask her why she had kept quiet about it all this time. Could she say what was absolutely true, that for years at a time she'd forgotten about it? And now that place was so overgrown she imagined it would be hard to get at it. Why, trees had sprouted up all around.

"Why are you so sure he didn't steal the money?"

She shook her head slightly as she said, "Well . . . I mean, from what Hal said his father would never have done a thing like that. And . . . and when I told him about the man being buried that Roddy saw I know he thinks it was his father. And another thing, sir."

"Yes? Yes? Go on."

"At odd times over the years, I've come across Mr Bannaman's man, that Mr Feeler, up in the wood on top of the quarry. He always said he was looking for young fir trees, but now I know he must have been looking for something else, searchin' like. And even Mr Bannaman's been up there at times, again supposedly gatherin' fir trees."

"Not supposedly gathering fir trees, but actually gathering fir trees, my dear girl. With my permission."

"Yes, but as Kate has often said, I mean Mrs Makepeace, why did they want to come this end to gather fir trees, young fir trees, when there's those plantations nearer them?"

Mr Mulcaster sat back in his chair as if pondering this point; and he remembered that he himself had sometimes wondered about it, yet recalling that he had felt a certain pride knowing the pines growing on the estate were of such a hardy type that they were coveted by others.

He pushed his hard hat gently back from his brow. He had not removed his hat; there had been no need as this female was of no importance. But he looked down at her, noting that she had grown into a very bonny girl; in fact, she did not look a girl but more like a young woman: her fair hair was lying in moist ringlets down each cheek; her hat was tilted to the back of her head; and in this light he did not know whether her eyes were green or hazel, but they were large and long-lashed and full of concern. She had a beautiful skin too, and a figure that many a fashionable lady would envy. He remembered her as a child running wild around the fells, very often accompanied by the two boys who were now men and the centre of this tragedy. Well, what was he going to do? He could not pass over this information, yet were he to investigate by having men dig in these places where one or two of the landslides had happened over the years, what would be the outcome? Well he'd have to wait and see, wouldn't he, and in the meantime think about it.

He said quietly now, "Leave this with me, and I'll think about it."

Then, to say that he was surprised was an understatement, astounded would have been a better description of his reaction when this young servant-maid, because that's all she was, confronted him boldly by saying, "There's no time to think about it, sir. If you don't go to the justice straightaway, and there's one lives on the Allendale road, in the Hall there, then I'll have to make me way there meself, because there's no time to lose, they'll be bringing Roddy up afore the justices any time now. And he could be sentenced and despatched any place. And to prove what I've said will take some diggin', so please, sir, there's no time to think. What I mean is. . . ."

He held up a hand to check her flow, and he said in an almost placating way, "It's on dark now. Anyway, Mr Morgan will undoubtedly be at his supper."

Ignoring that Mr Morgan might be dining, she persisted, "'Tisn't far, sir. Not more than ten minutes on your horse. And I can be there as soon as you because I'll cut across the fields."

She watched him bring his hat more forward on to his brow now, then place his hand tightly around his chin, while continuing to stare at her. Then in a voice that was almost a growl, he said, "Come along, girl."

She scurried after him, and into the yard, where a swaying lantern showed up a man standing at the head of a horse, and as Mr Mulcaster made his way towards them he said in an undertone, "Walk beside me."

And so that is what she did: she walked, stumbling by the side of the horse over the rough ground, until they came to the even pathway that led down to the road below the dam. And both seemed oblivious of the men they passed on the way and who must have wondered what a bonny lass like young Mary Ellen Lee was doing in the company of the agent and, too, making their way into the night.

8

"A nice hornets' nest you've stirred up, girl: half the countryside digging the quarry for a body that nobody can find! 'Tis the third day they've been at it, and people walkin' miles to see, all because that fellow thinks he remembers what he didn't see."

"He did see, mistress, he did see. And if they'd only fetch him he'd likely point out the place."

"Don't be stupid, girl. Thirteen years it'll be since it happened, whatever did . . . if it did. Anyway, it was the time Gabriel Roystan did off. . . ."

"Perhaps he never did off. That's what'll be proved. Hal's always said. . . ."

"Hal . . . Roddy . . . there's been too many men in your life, girl. You've been brought up along of 'em, granted, but as I said afore, you ran wild with them when you should have been put to work. 'Twas that father of yours thought you too good for service. I took Nell Bradley on when she was nine. She hadn't time to get flighty."

"Yes, and what did she do, mistress? She flighted off, didn't she? That's when you took me. . . ." Mary Ellen stayed her retort and bent her head, and in a whisper now she muttered, "I'm sorry, mistress. I am. I should have never spoken like that."

She raised her eyes slowly and looked at the small plump woman whose face was tight with her indignation, and some part of her mind scorned herself as she began to placate her now by saying, "She didn't know when she was well off; it was a good thing for me she went. I'm sorry, I am, mistress, but I'm all upset like."

"And right you have to be." The small body was bristling when the kitchen door opened and Farmer Davison entered, to be greeted by his wife pointing a short wagging finger at her maid, crying, "You won't believe this, Joe, you won't believe this, but she cheeked me, Mary Ellen cheeked me."

Joe Davison looked at his wife, raised his eyebrows and said, "Cannot believe that, wife. Mary Ellen has never cheeked you afore; thinks highly of you, I would say. Don't you, Mary Ellen?"

"Yes, master. Yes, I do. I do indeed."

"There now" – he looked at his wife as one might do at an erring child – "'tis mistaken you are."

"I am not mistaken, Mr Davison. I am not mistaken. She's gone clean lopsided, she has. All over this Roddy Greenbank imagining bodies."

He walked to the mantelpiece and took up a clay pipe from a wooden stand, and he bent and knocked out the doddle on the side of the stone fireplace before saying, "Natural like. Natural. She's only trying to save him from transportation, and Australia is sure where he's bound for if it's proved he stabbed young Roystan. Seven years at least, could be, if not life. It all depends who the justices are where he's tried. Now if it was in London, Ted Yarrow was saying last night down at the inn, because Ted, you know, was in the navy and many years he put in, as he said himself, in that hell-hole. Well, there, he said, they send off to Australia and Botany Bay ten times as many as we send sheep to market in a year in these parts."

"Shut up! will you, or she'll be on the floor in a minute." The woman bustled round the table and unceremoniously pushed Mary Ellen down on to the settle, saying, "Control yourself, girl! Don't you start no faintin' fits in this house. No time for such."

As Mrs Davison now took a wet cloth and none too gently began applying it in slaps around Mary Ellen's face the kitchen door once again opened, and there came into the room with a rush her son Archie, followed by her grandson Lennie. And speaking rapidly and his face alight with excitement, Archie cried, "They've found it! They've found it, da" – he nodded to the elder Davison – "the body. And it is Gabriel Roystan. He had a short leg, you know, an' wore a built-up shoe. Well, that's how young Hal recognized him. But it was Roddy Greenbank when they brought him from prison who pointed out where he remembered the grave was. And it was with the help of Kate Makepeace: she stood in the bottom of the quarry and pointed upwards; that's what they said. But 'twas all overgrown with trees. Yet Roddy measured the part from where he remembered he sat on the side of the quarry and kept on that they dig there. Trees had grown on top, but that's where they found the body. The place is alive. They've put it in one of the mill sheds, they say. And you'll never guess where they're off to now. Well, this much I saw meself on the road. You'll never guess."

"Well, go on then. Where? Where they off to? And who?"

Archie Davison pointed at his father as he said, "Bannaman's. Mr Bannaman's. They're after Pat Feeler."

"Pat Feeler? That little chap?"

"Aye, that little chap. And that's not all. There's other rumours goin' about: folks are hintin' and noddin' but not saying anything in case they get brought up. But I saw them meself. There was Mulcaster, the mill agent and two high-topped gentlemen in a coach leading the way. And behind it, in a market cart, was another two gentlemen ... well, ordinary looking men, constables I should think. But with them was Hal Roystan and Roddy Greenbank, at least what's left of him, because he was a robust lookin' young fellow last time I saw him, now you'd take him for a strip of lint, no flesh on his bones and his face as white as pig's fat." ...

"I told you. I told you."

105

"All right. All right. So you told us. And you've come round enough to chirp in again." Mrs Davison was nodding her head at Mary Ellen now. Then turning from her, she said, "Did they find the money in the grave?"

"Don't be daft, woman," her husband put in and puffed out a cloud of smoke from his clay pipe and watched it ascending to the black-beamed ceiling before adding, "You do say the daftest things, Mary. You do indeed. Whoever robbed him and buried him, they did it for the money, and it's been long spent now, I'd say."

"Perhaps well spent, perhaps to start a new herd or some such."

The father and son exchanged glances across the kitchen table as if they had at the same time revived buried thoughts. Then their attention was brought back to the mistress of the house because she was once more upbraiding her maid, saying, "Now don't you attempt to go off, miss. You got your tongue back a minute gone, so come on, up on your pins an' get to those pans for they won't scour themselves." And with this she hauled Mary Ellen to her feet. And as she pushed her towards the sink she said, "Were I to ask are you fit enough to go this minute an' see what's happenin' to that one you're so churned up about, you'd find your legs then, wouldn't you?"

To the surprise of her mistress and definitely to the astonishment of the three men, Mary Ellen turned about and, bouncing her head towards the little woman, she cried, "Yes, I would that. Yes, I would." Then turning her look on the only occupant of the room who hadn't as yet opened his mouth, she cried in no small voice, "Yes, I would. And run like a hare. So there you have it! All of you!" And having silenced them, she turned to the sink and, taking up the bowl of sand and salt, she began to scour the pan, while her master and mistress and their son and his son stared at her unbelieving.

But the maid's retort was causing the most indignant reaction in her mistress. This was the young lass they had treated as an equal, even allowing her to eat at the same table with them, going as far as to imagine they would welcome her as a permanent member of the household, and she, after all, but a servant. So generous had they been towards her that they hadn't bonded her these past two years. And on top of this, why! they kept her ailing father in food. And what was their reward? Insolence, the like they had never heard from any servant in the kitchen. What were things coming to? The world was in a dreadful state: people being murdered, graves being opened up, young men fighting and stabbing each other. But all this was nothing compared to the fact that her maid had dared to speak out of turn.

9

"Good day, Gentlemen. And to what do I owe the pleasure of your company?" Dan Bannaman's manner was jovial, as was his countenance. His cheeks were floridly red above his beard; he held his head high and his chin was thrust outwards. The only sign that could be taken for agitation might have been the movement of his jaw bones that put his sidewhiskers into constant motion.

Justice Craig's disposition seemed to be quite the reverse, for his countenance showed no joviality; his round clean-shaven face looked set, and his hands as he smoothed down the front of his long coat showed a nervousness. But his companion, whom he now introduced as Mr Saviour, attorney-at-law, showed no such nervousness.

Mr Saviour was a man of unusual height and was broad with it; his head was in proportion to his size; and his appearance was more that of a prize fighter than a man of law. But his voice held a cultured tone as he answered Dan Bannaman's greeting of, "If you have a mind to come inside I can offer you some refreshment," with, "Thank you. Thank you. That will indeed be acceptable for we've had a busy morning."

These words caused a startled glance from Justice Craig; then the attention of the three men was drawn to the arched entrance to the yard through which a market cart was now passing and, on the sight of at least two of its occupants, Dan Bannaman's manner underwent a lightning change.

"What is this?" he demanded. "Why is that man here?" He was pointing directly at Roddy who was now being helped down from the cart by the two officers.

It was the solicitor who answered, saying, "If we could follow your invitation and go inside, then all could be explained, sir."

"That man is not coming into...."

"Then I'm afraid, Mr Bannaman, we'll have to say what has to be said outside." It was the justice speaking, and as he stared Dan Bannaman straight in the eye he watched the man grind his teeth before swinging round and thrusting back the heavy oak door.

Slowly now the two men followed him, but not before beckoning towards Roddy, Hal and the officers.

As Roddy entered the house, preceding the other three, he saw the women. They were standing at the far end of the long hall; they were mother and daughter, and it was at the daughter he looked. His eyes rested on her only for a fleeting second, but they saw enough to convey her feelings of both fear and disdain. There was no such look on her mother's face, only one of perplexity, and it came to him in a fleeting thought that she might be unaware of why they were all here, although at the same time her daughter was not so ignorant of the matter.

They were now in the large room, evidently used as part library, part office, for the two side walls were lined with bookcases, while at the far end stood a large desk with various ledgers on it, one open.

Roddy did not take his eyes off the man as he strode towards the desk where he turned and with apparent righteous indignation demanded, "Well, gentlemen, out with it!"

The solicitor and the justice exchanged a questioning glance before the justice, turning his gaze on Bannaman, said, "First of all, I will say that a great deal of unpleasantness could be overcome if you would accompany us back to Newcastle, there to answer questions concerning a most grievous matter brought to light by this young man here."

"Grievous matter! What grievous matter could I be concerned with?"

"Will you accompany us there?"

"No, I certainly shall not. I haven't the slightest idea to what you are referring. Perhaps you will be kind enough to enlighten me."

The justice and the solicitor again looked at each other; then the justice, drawing in a deep breath, began: "On a certain night in September, 1807, when this young man was a boy of seven and a half years old, he was returning along the quarry track to the cottage of a woman called Kate Makepeace, and there something happened to him and his father. It was this woman, Kate Makepeace, who next morning found the boy hanging from between the branches of a bush whilst some distance away his father was found dead under what appeared to be a stone fall. The boy" – he inclined his head to the side indicating Roddy – "remembered nothing that happened that night. When he came to his senses he did not even know his own name; but during the years that followed he was troubled by vague impressions and dreams. It should happen, as he himself said, he unfortunately let his affections stray towards a young lady, not knowing who she was; and when one day, whilst he was speaking to her, you angrily came upon him, his latent memory stirred. Angered by your attitude towards him, and further angered by a comment his friend" – he again inclined his head but towards Hal now – "made disparaging the lady in question, he attacked him and, as many people witnessed, they fought in the market place at Hexham. Yet, later, they returned to their homes walking side by side. All they both remember of that evening's walk was they were attacked, bags having been thrust over their heads and arms before they were knocked senseless.

"It is now common knowledge that when they were found Mr Roystan had a knife in his ribs, placed there apparently by Mr Greenbank. Yet it was later discovered that Mr Greenbank had himself been so brutally treated that it would have been impossible for him to have inflicted the wound. Now say he had done so before he was given such rough treatment, then surely Mr Roystan could never with a knife in his ribs have beaten his friend into such a state that it was feared when they were both found that it would be he who would die first. However, and strangely, it was this very treatment that restored Mr Greenbank's memory, and he sent word through a friend who had visited him in hospital to Mr Mulcaster here saying that he remembered what had happened on that particular night. He recalled that he had seen his father murdered and thrown down into the quarry; he recalled having seen a man's face in a grave; but most of all he recalled the face of the perpetrator. And so," he paused here, "he accuses you, Mr Bannaman, of the murder of his father, and also that of the man in the grave, a man whose memory has been defiled for years, a man who supposedly stole his employer's money, then made off overseas, the man who was the father of Mr Roystan." And he now pointed to Hal whose face was grey, and whose lips were tight but whose eyes were wide and staring, giving the impression that at any moment he would spring on the man standing with his back to the desk.

"This is infamous!" Bannaman bellowed. "It is the result of sheer spite of that individual there" – his arm was thrust out, his finger pointing at Roddy – "who dared to made advances towards my daughter. This is all because I threatened what I'd do to him if he approached her again. You can't believe a word of this, surely. All right, a grave has been found with the clerk in it, but to say I had a hand in such a crime is outrageous. You'll pay for this, all of you who dare to suggest that I. . . ."

It was Mr Mulcaster who stopped his flow by holding up his hand and saying quietly, in an aside to the justice, "Patrick Feeler."

"Yes, yes." The justice nodded. Then turning to the two officers who were standing someway behind them, he said, "The man . . . the woodman. Bring him here."

"You will do no such thing. I don't have my woodman in my house. I. . . ."

"This is one time you must make an exception, Mr Bannaman." The solicitor's voice was cool.

"Don't you dictate to me, sir! You are in my house, I will have you understand. And you will all suffer for this accusation, let me tell you."

The justice now broke in: his hand held up in gentle remonstrance, he said, "Let me advise you before you go any further, sir, there is something else you should hear. The woman, Kate Makepeace, has made a statement. She has told how her son was a member of a company, which you headed, and whose purpose was smuggling. The statement goes on to say that when it was suggested your activities should stray from smuggling merchandise to the more human kind, her son remonstrated his disagreement, as did another of the group. This man was found dead, and Kate Makepeace's son was found near his body. All he could remember was that he had drunk heavily the previous night.

However, his mother's statement goes on to say you saw him safely shipped out of the country in order to evade a charge of murder, for it was known that Makepeace and the deceased man were drinking companions. The statement goes on to say that her son knew he was being got rid of but that he could do nothing about it; he felt that if he did not allow himself to be deported secretly he would end up like his friend, found dead in a ditch. Now what have you to say to that?"

"The same as I said to your previous accusations: that woman has hated me all my life. She is a wild creature, as her folks were before her. She is of witch stock; who would believe her? As for smuggling. Years ago, yes, I might have accepted a bottle of spirit or some tobacco, but I ask you, who in this county didn't, from parson to pauper. With the possible exception of a Quaker, there isn't one who could say they have never handled smuggled merchandise; and so I can laugh at anything Kate Makepeace could conjure up out of her twisted mind."

There was the sound of scuffling outside the door; then it burst open, and the two officers thrust a thin squirming man into the room.

Patrick Feeler was not yet sixty but he looked to be a man well into his seventies as he stood hunched and shaking staring at the faces turned towards him. His body was thin and his corduroy jacket and breeches hung on him as if on a fleshless frame, but his voice came out strident as he cried, "What's this, master? What's this?"

Dan Bannaman made no reply, but the justice, turning to Roddy, said, "Do you recall this man?"

Roddy looked at the thin quivering face and he answered truthfully, "No. No, I don't recall him, at least not his face. But the hand." When he pointed to the man's hand, Feeler pulled it up the sleeve of his jacket, only to have one of the officers step forward and grip it, then thrust it forward for closer examination by Roddy.

Roddy stared at the hand, which showed only the index finger and thumb beside the roughened stumps where the three fingers had once been, and he said in a voice that trembled, "I . . . I recall that. The feeling comes back of it across my mouth. It wasn't a hand, yet I didn't know what it was."

"'Twasn't me. 'Twasn't me. Anyway I just did what I was told."

"Feeler!" It was Bannaman barking now. "Control yourself. You're not being accused of anything."

"I'm not?"

"No, you're not."

"But you are." It was the justice speaking to him now. "You will be accused of being an accessory to the murder of Gabriel Roystan, clerk to the smelting works in the Barony of Langley."

"*Me? No! Look, I tell you*" – the man was yelling now – "I . . . I didn't. I just did what I was told. Always have. Always have."

"Were you told to waylay the clerk?"

"No, no." The man's head wagged from side to side as if in desperation. Then looking towards Dan Bannaman, he implored, "Tell them, will you, I didn't do it. A man couldn't do a thing like that on his own anyway. You . . . you said yourself." He gaped, his mouth wide open: the room had become still and all eyes were on him. But a movement at the top of the room brought attention from him to Dan Bannaman at the other side of his desk, and as he was about to pull open a drawer the justice called one word, "Constables!"

The two men sprang forward and the pistol was knocked out of Bannaman's hand.

In the ensuing struggle, Bannaman seemed to have the strength of four men. He threw one constable onto his back and was about to send the other following him when the solicitor sprang forward and, getting behind Bannaman, he put his arms tightly round him which forced him to loose his hold on the constable.

Then something strange happened that caused everyone in the room to become still. Even the first constable in the act of pulling himself up from the floor by gripping the edge of the desk held his position as he looked into the contorted face of the man he had been struggling with only moments earlier. Bannaman's whole body had gone into a spasm that left him contorted, his hands hanging like two big flippers in front of the solicitor's arms as if they had been frozen as they were about to break his opponent's hold. His head had dropped to the side, his mouth was wide open and his tongue was lolling from it.

"Dear God!" Mr Mulcaster had moved to the aid of the now amazed solicitor, murmuring, "Lay him down, it's a seizure. You must get a doctor. Dear, dear, dear. What now? What now?"

The justice, turning to one of the constables, said quietly, "Go and call the servant, or . . . or better still his wife." His voice had trailed away as his eyes darted around the room. Then looking at Hal, he said, "Where is he, the woodman?"

Hal himself now looked around; then glanced at Roddy whom he had placed in a chair, and Roddy answered simply, "He's gone. He must have slipped out. But he won't get far, he's too well known." And as Hal made hurriedly towards the door, he called weakly after him, "Where are you goin'?"

"To find him," Hal called back grimly. "He's one who's not gona get away, strokes genuine or faked." And with this he went out, leaving the door open. And again Roddy saw the two women still close but hurrying across the hall now, and when they entered the room the sight of the contorted figure on the floor brought them, aghast, to a momentary stop.

Mrs Bannaman moved first: she ran towards her husband; the daughter walked more slowly and she stopped half-way up the room where Roddy was now standing, supporting himself against the back of the chair. His gaze full on her held deep pity, but the embers of his love died as, standing so close to him that her breath wafted over his face, and each word a hiss, she said, "You're scum! You and your kind are scum. You know that? Scum! No matter what he did, you wouldn't be fit to be his lackey, and if my brother was here I'd have him kick you out of the house."

Each word of the onslaught was like a blow, not only to his mind but to his weakened physique, and he thought for one agonizing moment that he was about to have a recurrence of the sensations he'd had when he was recovering from the brutal assaults on his body, when he would scream out loud, then cry like a child.

As he watched her move further up the room, then kneel down on the floor by the side of her mother, he asked himself if he had ever loved her, the woman who now looked like a fiend, and the answer he got was, yes, he had. Oh, yes, he had loved her; been crazy just for the sight of her. But why? How had it come about that he had allowed himself to feel like that? Scum, she had called him. She was the daughter of a murderer, of a man who had murdered, not once, but apparently many times, and she had dared to call him scum and class her father above him. For a moment there arose in him a hate against her as great as hers was for himself. Oh God! He was going to give way. Please, please God, don't let him have a turn. Not here. Not here.

"Sit down. Sit down." It was Hal speaking to him and pressing him gently onto the chair again. "You've had enough," he said. "We had better get you back."

He looked up at Hal and it passed through his dizzying mind that they were like brothers who had lost their father one night. And it was true; at least, both their fathers had been buried the same night. Hal's bitterness was deeper than his own, perhaps because he had suffered more. Hal had said to him earlier that morning, "I want to see him hang. I'll never feel happy again until I see them both swing."

He now said meekly, "Did you find him?"

"No; he's skipped, took a horse and made off. But he won't get far. I'm not worryin'; I'll get him, and I hope afore they do." The tone of his voice made Roddy shiver: Hal was a strange fellow, deep in his loves and hates.

The justice was now saying, "When will your son be returning, Mrs Bannaman?" And the woman answered, "Sometime this afternoon."

"I'm sorry to have to press this matter further, the state your husband is in" – the justice's tone held concern for the woman – "but the excisemen will wish to search the house. I hope you understand."

"No. No, I don't." The reply was almost a tearful whimper, but was cut off by her daughter's voice, saying, "I do. I understand. You're quite at liberty to search where you like because you can't do anything further to him. Even if he lives, you couldn't charge him, so you can do nothing more, either to him or to us." And on this she added, "Come along, dear," and taking her mother by the arm, she led her from the room.

Looking after them, Hal thrust out his chin as he muttered through his clenched teeth, "There you're mistaken, miss; you'll find a lot more can be done, so much so, that you, me fine lady, will end up having your nose rubbed in the mud, and I'll be there to see it." And when he ended,

"Come the day, come the day soon," Roddy lowered his head and for a moment he wished from the bottom of his heart that his memory had stayed a blank.

10

Mary Ellen was seething inside with a mixture of impatience and anger. Her mistress had purposely found work for her to do well past her leaving time, and the basket she was carrying to her father was light compared to what it usually was on Sundays.

She had never imagined her kind, although scatterbrained, little mistress, could be spiteful, but since it had been decided that Roddy had not to return to prison, this term was the only one Mary Ellen could use to describe Mrs Davison's attitude towards her.

It was more than three weeks since the body of Hal's father had been found, and the district had still not settled down to normality. For days the place had swarmed with all kinds of men wanting to write about the affair. It was said some had come from as far away as London town. Mr Davison had said that this was rubbish; but it couldn't be said to be rubbish that they had all swarmed round Kate's cottage wanting to talk to Roddy.

The men from the newspapers had been after Hal too, but he wasn't as easy to get to as Roddy, for he was away scouring the hills and fells. So determined was he to find Patrick Feeler, he had even borrowed a horse, for nothing had been seen or heard of the man since he had escaped from the farm on the morning Mr Bannaman had been taken with a seizure. And with regard to him, everybody said it was just as well fate had dealt him that blow, if not, it would have been the rope for him. But as it was, he could neither speak nor move, and his end was expected any time.

And there were always sightseers, besides the newspaper-men hanging about the farm as if waiting for this to happen.

The latest rumour was that the mill owners were going to compensate Hal for the loss of his father. However true that was, Mary Ellen didn't know, and she wouldn't know until she reached Kate's. And no matter how her father would go on about her being late, she was going to Kate's first, not just to hear about Hal, rather she was more anxious to hear the result of Roddy's visit to Newcastle to those new friends of his, the painter people. Three of them had come out all this way to see him, and Kate hadn't been pleased, for she had said to her on the quiet, "They treated him as if he were family, and talked about his future. They even spoke about it to the newspaper-men."

For the past three weeks Mary Ellen had not walked along the track which would have taken her past the quarry, but had gone the longer way, keeping to the road, because she had been afraid to go past the scene where the body had been found. Today, however, she did not hesitate, for the immediacy of her desire to know about Roddy overcoming her fears, she stepped out onto the ride and wove her way over the torn ground circumventing the holes and piles of earth and uprooted trees that seemed never ending.

People had stopped coming to the quarry to gape; in fact, she saw no one except a solitary figure. He was standing still and looking down at the earth, and she wasn't surprised when, drawing nearer, to see that it was Hal; nor did he seem surprised to see her, for on her approach, he turned his head towards her and said quietly, "Hello, there." And she answered as quietly, "Hello, Hal." She felt kindly towards him these days.

He looked at the ground again, saying in the same quiet tone as before, "I'm going to have a stone put there."

"But ... but I thought he ... I mean your father, is in the cemetery now."

"Aye, yes, he is; but nevertheless I'm puttin' a stone there and I'm going to put one word on it ... injustice."

She stared at him, her eyes wide, and when he turned and looked at her he muttered thickly, "They should have known he wouldn't have done anything like that. That firm was his life; he lived for nothing else, except me. As I remember, he was as proud of it as if he owned it. And anyway, what was two hundred and seventy guineas compared with the sums he had carried afore that? He used to talk to me, you know," – he nodded at her now – "about the skills he used to dodge the footpads. And the footpads, he always said, were more dangerous than the highwaymen, because they would let you off with your life, but not the pads. No" – his voice rose – "not the pads, like Bannaman and Feeler. And if he'd carried a gun like he should have done he'd likely to be here the day, but he relied on his head to outwit them."

She continued to stare at him in silence wondering, as she watched the muscles of his face working, how strange it was that the name of footpad could be applied to Mr Bannaman. But that's what he had been in his early days, as the evidence showed when the customs and the constables searched the place. A store of all kinds of things had been found in a secret place going off the cellar. 'Twas said it was a tunnel like an air shaft and went right under the house.

More to break the black concentration on his face than anything else, she asked, "Have they found Feeler yet?"

He shook his head a little before saying, "Not yet, but they will ... or I will, because he's here, hereabouts." And he looked around as if expecting to see the man emerge from one of the heaps of rubble and twisted undergrowth. "I can smell him. A rat like him would be afraid to run far, thinking everybody would recognize him. And too he must know that his closest friend, if he had one, would turn him in on sight, 'cos it says on the notices that have gone out, anybody harbouring him is likely to the same or such. No, he's hiding hereabouts." And he nodded twice before turning away; and she moved off with him.

They walked in silence for some time, until she stumbled, when he put his hand out and steadied her, saying, "You shouldn't come along this way, it isn't healthy."

"It's a short cut, and I'm late. What I mean is, later than usual. Mistress kept me back."

Again there was silence between them, but at the roadway he stopped and said, "I'm not goin' in, in fact I've just recently left there. But I'd better warn you, there's bad news. Well" – he shrugged his shoulders – "that's how you'll view it."

"What do you mean? What's happened?"

"He's leavin'."

"What! Roddy? He's not fit."

"Oh, he's fit enough now."

"Where's he goin'?"

His lower jaw worked from side to side before he said, "Newcastle, for a start. His brand-new friends came during the week with what they call a career mapped out for him: lodgings at Newcastle, his dues paid for art lessons, an' then what?" Again he shrugged his shoulders. "London town, the world?" His tone changed and now there was real bitterness in it as he said, "They talk so big, act like gods, an' he laps it up. It's a chance in a lifetime, he says. He doesn't give a damn about leavin' Kate or" – he poked his face towards her – "you." Then he added bitterly, "As for me . . . well, I may never have existed; I might have lain with me da all these years an' just come on the scene now. I'll tell you this, Mary Ellen, one of the two things I've ever craved for in me life was to have me da's name cleared." He did not go on to mention the other thing, but said, "I tell you this, though, I wish to God he had never got his memory back, because he's changed he is."

After he had stopped speaking they continued to stare at each other. This news had caused her whole being to ache with the loss that was to come, yet so intense was this man's feelings that she could forget her own for a moment and say, "He thinks the world of you, Hal, always has, you know that, at least you should. He's . . . he's pushed me off time and again to go with you, walkin', fishin'."

"No, Mary Ellen, I pushed you off to go with him, and you know that's true. In our young days we are fools, eaten up with wants and fancies that have no place in real life . . . real livin'. It's that that's got to be faced, Mary Ellen, life. Once you've turned the twenty mark it's life you've got to face. You think you're a man when you start work at ten or so, and your thinking has taken on a surety when sixteen or seventeen, but nothing prepares you for the blows to come, an' I don't mean punches to the body, but things that happen to your thinkin'. You hate deeper and you love deeper and you learn that all the will in the world of mind and body won't bring about the things that you want. As I see it, Mary Ellen, life is a parcel tied up with twine. Some folks never have the guts to undo the twine, so they live in the parcel in which they were born to the day they die. Others have the parcel opened for them an' in it there's the contents of their life ahead. Like it or not, they're stuck with it. That's happened to me and Roddy. As for you, Mary Ellen, you haven't opened your parcel yet. And don't look at me like that. I'm not talkin' through me hat, and if you don't know what I'm gettin' at now you will someday. Anyway, let's hope." And with that, he inclined his head towards her in farewell, then turned abruptly and walked away.

She herself did not walk on; all the hurry seemed to have left her. She stood gazing after him. He was a queer individual, he really was, the way he talked, like a preacher. No, no, she contradicted her thinking; there was no preacher about him, for what he said went deeper than the preacher's talking. All that business about life being a parcel, well, she supposed, there was something in it, but she felt sure that very few people looked at it like that. He had said she hadn't opened her parcel of life yet. What could he mean by that? Except perhaps, that when she did she would be hurt. Well, she couldn't feel more hurt than she did at this minute.

She turned now and took the path leading to Kate's. She had somehow felt that what she had done for Roddy would make him feel differently about her. In fact, she felt sure he did feel differently about her. On the three occasions she had seen him since he had come home he had been nice to her, more than nice, and talked openly to her. He had even, in a roundabout way, remarked on his feelings for that girl, the Bannaman's girl, or woman, as she was. His words referring to her had been stilted: "Must have gone through a mad phase to let me feelings rampage as they did," he had said. "Anyway, it's over, thank God. Never again. Some lessons are hard to learn, but I've learnt." Well, if that wasn't sayin' plainly he no longer thought about the woman, she hadn't been hearing aright.

But now, what did it matter? He would go. Oh God! She couldn't bear the loss of him. His going would drain the blood from her heart, from her whole body. What would life be like if she wasn't to see him on a Sunday? She knew what it would be like, just days of toil and listening to the chattering voice of her mistress going on and on, jumping from one thing to another, hardly stopping to take a breath it would seem from she came down to the kitchen in the morning at six o'clock: expecting everything to be ready for the breakfast, the fat pork laid in strips, with the white pudding next to them, and the thick slices of greased bread ready for the frying-pan. And she would talk as she fingered each portion, then turn and examine the hearth to see if it had been bath-bricked properly. Oh yes, that would be her life.

There would be no need to open the parcel: she knew the routine that would be in it; it would be the same as it had been every morning since she had gone into the farm at ten years old and for the first time in her life had been roused from her bed in the attic at five o'clock in the morning, and on the stroke of nine at night had been pressed up to it again by the little woman. And so it had gone on, for never ever had she been allowed to remain in the kitchen after that hour at night with the menfolk. Her mistress went to bed at nine, so she must too.

And this was to be her life ahead. Even if she were to marry Lennie, which she wouldn't, the pattern would remain the same, except it would be he who would push her upstairs at nine o'clock in the evening. She shuddered at the thought and protested almost verbally, never, never, because if she couldn't have Roddy, then she'd remain alone and her nights would go on being filled with her imaginings, imagining what it would be like to be held close to him without the barrier of her frock, her petticoat, her habit-shirt and her corsets. Her thoughts at night were wicked. She was well aware of that, but she didn't care.

Her attendances at church, travelling there with Mrs Davison, were limited to Festival Days because as her mistress said, neither of them could be spared more often: God's work had to be done in the kitchen and the dairy and the byres, and He understood that even if parson didn't. Anyway, it was enough that Lennie should represent the family by calling in at Hexham Abbey should he be in the town.

One Sunday, after a visit to the House of God, she had caused consternation in the kitchen by asking a simple question of how long people were likely to last in the sizzling heat of hell, seeing that bacon could be kizzened up within a few minutes if the fire was hot enough....

When she pushed open the cottage door the scene that had become the usual over the past Sundays was not that which met her today: Roddy was not sitting in the big chair to the side of the fire with his feet on a cracket, and Kate was not seated at the table sorting out her herbs or pouring muddy-looking liquid from a jug into little bottles. She was sitting on a cracket, but her back was pressed against the stonework of the fireplace as she watched Roddy, at one end of the table, packing drawings into a folder, while on the floor to the side of the table stood a cloth travelling bag, full and strapped.

She became still, and they both looked towards her. It was Kate who spoke first. "Hello, girl," she said. The words were usual but not the tone of the voice which trembled slightly.

"Hello, Mary Ellen." Roddy's voice, too, was different.

She didn't answer him with, "Hello, Roddy," but as if she were unaware of his imminent departure she said, "What's all this?"

He spread his hands slowly over the table, saying sheepishly, "I'm . . . I'm going to school."

"School?" She had moved up the room and was standing opposite Kate now, and it was Kate who answered. Nodding her head, she said, "Aye school. We all have to live and learn."

"What kind of school?" She had turned to face Roddy, and he, his colour rising, hesitated before he said, "Well, 'tis not like a real school I suppose, 'tis learning about drawing and things."

"But you can draw." Her voice was stiff.

"Aye, so I thought, until I saw other people's work; now I know, well, I haven't even started yet. 'Tis amazing what people do, you know," he said nodding at her.

"Aye, yes, 'tis amazing." Her tone was tart and her inference clear. And he came back at her angrily now, saying, "Well, what would you have me do? Sit on me backside here, a burden on Kate?"

"Don't you say that, lad. You've never been a burden on me and never would, and you know it."

"Well, I'm not fit for the mill any more, so what would I have done, Kate?" He had placed his two hands on the table and was leaning across towards them now. "I've had the guts knocked out of me: I couldn't do a day's manual work to save me life, well, at least, not at present. Here" – he now patted the cardboard folder – "I'm being given a chance I never even dreamed of. It's one in a lifetime. And anyway" – he straightened his back and was now addressing Mary Ellen – "you would think I was set for the other end of the earth. I'm only goin' into Newcastle. I'll be back every other week-end at least. I'll ride up on the Friday night an' go back on the Sunday. I'll really have more week-end time here than if I was in the mill. So what's all the fuss about?"

"Who's making the fuss?" She reared up now, her head wagging. "Only you. Your conscience is prickin' you because you're goin'. And let me tell you somethin': if what has happened hadn't happened, you would have still gone. I know you, I know you. You would have still gone." And with this last statement she bent down and grabbed up the basket and, her face twisted and looking towards Kate, she said, "I'll call on me way back when the room's clear." And almost at a run, she went out.

Pulling herself to her feet, while steadying herself with the back of the chair, Kate looked at Roddy, saying sharply now, "Go on after her and make your peace."

"But ... but what have I said?"

"No matter what you've said, you've said too much. Go on. Do this for me."

Reluctantly it would seem, he went out, buttoning up his coat as he did so. He could see her in the distance hurrying, her head down, and he called to her.

When she didn't stop, he didn't attempt to run for he knew he wasn't up to running; but again he called, "Mary Ellen! Mary Ellen! Hold your hand a minute. Please. Please." And he watched her steps slow, then draw to a halt, and he was panting as he came abreast of her, saying, "You're the devil's own imp. You'll never change. Now why did you have to go off the handle like that?" He looked down on her bent head.

The rim of her bonnet was covering her face and he put his hand on her shoulder, saying, "Don't let's part in this way, Mary Ellen. You trouble me because I owe you so much. I'll never forget you're the only one besides Kate who put a finger out to help me, and if it hadn't been for you, God knows where I would have been at this minute, so I'm grateful to you, deep in me heart I'm grateful to you."

Her head slowly came up. Her expression had changed, her eyes were moist, her lips were trembling, as was her voice as she said, "I'm sorry, Roddy, but the place won't be the same when you're gone. You've always been there, sort of like a. . . ." She would not say like a brother. "I've never bothered with anybody else, only you. You know I haven't. I'll . . . I'll miss you."

He bent his face closer to hers now, saying softly, "But you only come home on a Sunday, Mary Ellen, and I'll be here when you come, at least, as I said, every other week-end. An' look, I'll tell you what. It won't be long until the fair and the in-between hirings, so you ask your missis for a Saturday off and I'll take you along. How's that?"

She smiled gently now. When a lad took a lass to a fair it signified something, it was a start to stronger ties to some. She said softly, "Aye, I'll do that now. I'll give her plenty of notice. I've never had a whole Saturday off."

"When is it? Three weeks or a month's time?"

"A month."

"Well that's a promise." He straightened up and nodded at her. "Anyway, like as not, I'll be sittin' in Kate's corner seven days from now as if I've never been away. And I'll have a lot to tell you. All right, Mary Ellen?"

She nodded at him brightly now, saying, "All right, Roddy, and I hope everything goes well for you. Are they nice people where you're stayin'?"

"Oh, aye, very nice. I have a room at the top of the house. It's a big attic and I can work there, and I have me bed and everything. And it overlooks the river. It's . . . it's a new world. What I mean is, to see the mass of shipping going up and down. And the people. You wonder where they all come from. 'Tis another world out there you know, Mary Ellen." He spread his arm wide. "We don't know we're alive really here."

She wanted to put in now and brusquely, "We do know we're alive, very much alive, if pain and worry is anything to go by. People here-abouts know they are alive all right." There was her da trying to keep alive, gasping at life with each breath he took; there was old Mr Holden – old she thought, and him only fortyish; and Lance Ritson, who had died last week leaving seven bairns and a sickly wife. Oh they knew they were alive all right. And they knew they were dying, some of them. But she managed to curb her tongue and smile when he put out his hand and took hers and said, "Now everything's all right, isn't it?"

"Aye, Roddy, aye."

"'Bye then."

"'Bye, Roddy. Take care."

"And you. And you."

They looked at each other for a moment longer; then she went on, and he turned and walked slowly back to the cottage. . . .

Her father greeted her with, "You'll land on a Monday morning one of these days. Where've you been?"

"I called at Kate's." She put the basket on the table.

"You generally leave that until after you've been here."

"Well, I didn't the day."

"No need to be snappy."

When the contents of the basket was on the table he poked his head forward from where he was sitting, then said, "That all she sent?"

"Aye, that's all she sent."

"Why?"

"I'm in her black books."

"Your tongue been waggin' again?"

"Yes, you could say that, me tongue's been waggin' again."

"It'll get you hung one of these days. Don't tell me you've cheeked her."

"Aye, I suppose you could say that an' all."

"My God! You don't know when you're well off. What if she sacked you?"

"She won't sack me."

"What makes you so sure of that?"

"'Cos I'm equal to three pit-ponies, the work I do, that's why."

As he shook his head she wondered if she saw a semblance of a smile on his face; but if she did it was gone with his next remark.

"You've always thought too much of yourself, girl. It'll get you nowhere, nowhere."

"Well, I won't mention who I take after for that. Now forget about me an' face up to the fact that my basket might get lighter with the months, because I can't promise to keep me tongue quiet, so you'll have to dip into your store, won't you, to buy yourself the necessities."

"I've got no store, or very little of it left." He lifted up the poker and raked at the bars of the fire.

"Well, you'll have to use it until it's gone then."

"What about your store?" He turned his head towards her. "You should be tippin' somethin' up. She gave you a rise last year."

"Yes, threepence a week. I'm now on one and ninepence." She leaned towards him. "Do you know, if I take it into me mind I'll up an' go down to Hexham; there's good jobs goin' there for three shillings a week, sometimes more, and everything found. Now don't aggravate me, Da, else I might just take me basket and walk that way instead of goin' back to the farm."

There was a half-smile on her face as she finished and he turned to poking the fire again, and after a while he remarked, "Well, has his lordship gone?"

She paused before she answered, "As far as I know, yes."

"Beggars on horseback ride to hell."

"What do you mean by that?"

"Oh, simply that you wouldn't think about invitin' an Irish pitman into the castle even if it was habitable."

"He's no Irish pitman."

"He'll be the equal and stick out, the folks he's goin' among. Them ridin' up in their carriage to meet him and takin' him to dine in an hotel."

"*When?* How do you know this?"

"Oh, I have a visitor now an' again. Didn't you know? Didn't he tell you? Anyway, how do you think he'll pass himself with people like that? Carriage folk don't take up with smelters without there's somethin' behind it."

"Aye, well, there is somethin' behind it. He's got talent. He's an artist."

"Artist be damned! Anybody could draw what he does, given a little time." He twisted his head towards her now, saying, "You'll never see him again, you know that, don't you? So if you're wise you'll leave your petticoat on the bed at the farm."

"I'll leave no petticoat on no bed at no farm. Now get that into your head, Da. If you think I'm gona provide for that basket" – she stabbed her finger towards the empty basket – "being filled for you for the rest of your life, then you're mistaken. Now, I see you're well stacked up with wood an' coal, so you can keep on stackin' it up for yourself, and also tidyin' the rooms, because for me, I've had enough for one day, so I'm goin'."

"But you've only come." He half rose from the chair.

"Aye, and I wish I hadn't passed through the door. I'm sick of everything. Do you hear that? Sick and tired." She grabbed up the basket, pulled the string of her bonnet tight under her chin, then marched to the door, and as she opened it he yelled at her, "You've seen the last of him. Make up your mind to it, or else you'll end up a kizzened old stick like Betty Fullman."

She had the door latch in her hand as she swung round, and she was even astonished at her own words as she cried back at him, "No, I won't end up like Betty Fullman, not if I have anything to do with it. More like Maggie Oates. And I could start the morrow. So think on that. And if I did you could be sure of your basket being full then." And with this she banged the door, then took to her heels and ran till she reached the copse where the trees had been cut down. And there she sank down on to the damp earth between the stumps and, kneeling over a gnarled root, gave vent to her pent up feelings.

When, after some minutes, she sat up and brought her knuckles across her streaming eyes, she thought to herself, fancy saying she would end up like Maggie Oates who, as everybody knew for miles around, was a real bad woman and shunned by all other women hereabouts because she was so sinful. And yet, she always seemed so cheery. She had never forgotten the times when she herself was a little girl, she'd always had a kind word for her. Her da had forbidden her ever to speak to the woman, so when Maggie Oates stopped her to chat, she never let on at home. Except once. She had asked her mother if sinning made people happy because Mrs Oates was always laughing. But for her to say to her da that she would become like Maggie Oates, well, what had come over her? It was this tongue of hers, it said things that were never intended.

As she rose to her feet and dusted the twigs from the bottom of her skirt, she asked herself, if she had the choice who would she rather be like, Betty Fullman, who lived in a cottage near the ruined castle and who was so proper that nearly all the workmen called her miss, or Maggie Oates, whom the workmen joked about and visited on the sly?

At this moment she couldn't give herself a truthful answer.

11

She had to hold her hat on with both hands as she struggled against the wind. It was a nice wind, fresh and lifting. The sun was shining, the sky was high. The hills as far as she could see appeared to be coated with carpets of yellow, red, and brown, mostly brown, but a bright warm brown. The blood in her veins seemed to be bubbling with life, good, happy, free life. And she felt free as she couldn't remember ever feeling before. But more so, she had a feeling of belonging, and to the only one she wanted to belong to in the whole world and who was now striding by her side, laughing at her.

Roddy had kept his word. Not having seen him for two week-ends, she had given up all hope that he would remember his promise to take her to the fair. But last night Kate had got word to her through Paul Fowler. He had come out of his way from his shift at the mill to give her the message, which just said she had to be there early if she wanted to catch the cart.

Early had meant leaving the farm at ten o'clock at the latest; and then, although her mistress had some weeks ago reluctantly agreed she could change her leave day from Sunday to Saturday – and yes, since she was so bent on it she could have the whole day – she had of a sudden changed her mind and said there was too much to do and that she couldn't let her go before twelve.

Mary Ellen had actually cried with vexation, but had kept a curb on her tongue. And this, it seemed had caused her mistress to relent, saying she could go at eleven, and yet, knowing full well that that would be too late to catch the cart into Hexham.

When she had left the farm wearing her first pair of white cotton gloves which she had bought from a pedlar the previous week, Mrs Davison sent her on her way with a prophecy: "No good will come of this, girl, flaunting yourself in the face of God and good neighbours. You'll get your name up, that you will."

Kate then had her say about the farmer's wife not letting her get away, but Roddy was unperturbed. "We'll go to Allendale," he said. "It'll be a fine walk on a day like this."

And so it was turning out to be. She much preferred this arrangement to going into Hexham, for from the moment they took their seats in the cart they would have been surrounded by people, whereas here in these wide open spaces that rolled away on all sides into the sky, there was not one person to be seen, except the man at her side, not even a house to be espied, only grey dots of sheep spotting the ground. And she felt this was as near heaven as she would ever get. She didn't even mind Roddy talking so much about Newcastle and his new friends, because he was talking, and talking to her as if he wanted her to know all about his life there and, as she imagined, to take away any fears that she might have that his interests were other than his drawing.

"I thought you liked living on the waterfront?" she shouted across at him.

"I do. Yes, I do. It's wonderful. But there's tremendous noise and bustle all the time, so when Mr Cottle offered me a room in their house I jumped at it. He's a portrait painter."

"But I thought you said it was a painter who lived in the house on the waterfront where you had the attic, the one who does the ships and things."

"Yes, yes, I did. That's Mr Beale. He's a professional man and he liked the bustle, but you want a bit of peace and quiet when you have to study, and there's none on the waterfront. Oh no."

"I'd like to see the waterfront."

"Well, all right, I'll take you one day."

"You will, Roddy?"

"Yes, yes, of course."

She had stopped. Her two hands going up to her hat again, her head back, she looked at him. His eyes were bright and shining; his straight brows were as black as the hair that was showing from under each side of his cap; his skin, that had always appeared as if it was tanned, had a slight flush to it around the high cheek-bones and it took on a blue hue of restricted hair towards his chin.

He was a pretty man. Oh, far beyond pretty, he was beautiful. Since that awful do he had lost flesh, but that only seemed to have made him taller. Altogether he was beautiful.

"When will you take me?"

"Oh." He opened his mouth and laughed. All his teeth were even and unbroken; she saw that his tongue was not furred like those of a lot of men whose open mouths created in her a feeling of revulsion. Farmer Davison's was like that.

"What did you say?"

"I said, whenever the dragon will let you have a full day off, so we can take the coach in."

"You'd take me in the coach?"

"Well, yes, unless you'd like to walk."

Her laughter joined his now. Then she turned from him and ran, skipping over the hummocks in the ground, and at one point when she left loose of her hat to lift up her skirt in order that she could run faster, her hatpins came loose and her hat took flight, and she turned to see Roddy retrieving it. And when he had brought it to her he stood looking at her, and the expression in his eyes was soft. She did not put out her hands to take the hat because she wanted him to put it on for her, but he didn't, he handed it to her, asking, "How many hatpins had you in it?"

"Two."

"Well, I should say you've lost one."

"Eeh!" – the smile went from her face – "the mistress gave them to me for a present last Christmas. She'll be vexed."

"Well, there's one thing certain, you'll never find it among that lot." He pointed to the grass and stubble. "Sometime, if somebody sits down, they might come across it."

Again they were laughing, loudly now, at the picture his remark had presented, and when he placed his two hands on his buttocks and gave a slight jump, crying, "Oops! a daisy," she told herself she would die with her laughing for she had never seen Roddy in this mood. This was a different Roddy. He had never been one for jokes, being of a sombre turn of mind, she thought, but he had changed. Everything about him was changed, including his manner towards her. Oh yes, that was warmer, different. And when presently walking on, he took her hand, she knew that this day was the beginning of something wonderful that would fill her lifetime right till the day she died. Oh yes; for she would go to her grave loving him.

And the feeling persisted until they entered Allendale.

The square was packed. There were carriages outside the inns. There were mingled sounds of laughter and quarrelling, because half the men there were the worse for drink.

"Oh Lord, I forgot about that," Roddy said; "yesterday would be the day of the pays. They're burning their money or washing it down. We'll have a job to get anything to eat here. It'll likely be a stand up pie and peas."

"That'll suit me. I'm so full up with food I could last for a week. I'll say that for the missis, she's never stingy on the table."

"You're lucky then." He took her arm and pushed her round the outskirts of a group of women, farmers' wives by the look of their dress and the baskets on their arms, and towards the far side of the square where the pies and peas stall stood. And they didn't go unnoticed, and she felt a burst of pride as different people called out to him, "How goes it, Roddy?"

"Back on your pins?"

"By! you're lookin' set up."

"How's life in the big city?"

And to all he answered merely with a laugh and a wave of his hand. That was, until they both came to a dead stop. Hal had turned from talking to two other men and he looked first from one to the other before saying, "Well, well! The people you meet in a foreign country. Come to spend your pay?" He was addressing Mary Ellen, but it was Roddy who answered and on a laugh, saying, "Aye, she's treatin' me: pies and peas and a pint of ale." Then he added on a more serious note, "I called round this mornin' but couldn't see hilt nor hair of you."

126

"No, you wouldn't, because as Parson Phillips-Brown would put it, I was about me father's business."

They had, the three of them, been making their way together towards the stall. But with Hal's words they turned as one and stood in the comparatively empty space near an archway that led into the back of a building.

"Oh! man," Roddy said, "he'll be gone miles away by now. Likely he's takin' the trip that they said your da took, across the water."

"No, not him." Hal's eyes were narrowed and he was looking away from them over the heads of the crowd milling about the square, and he repeated, "No, not him. He wouldn't have the guts. He's here, round about somewhere. It's as though I can smell him." He actually sniffed now. "He's undercover somewhere. Somebody's hiding him. It isn't his wife or his daughter, I made sure of that. By the way" – he turned and looked fully at Roddy now – "did you know they were turfed out yesterday, the Bannamans, lock, stock and barrel?"

"No." Roddy's voice was quiet.

"Aye." Hal was smiling now, a grim smile. "I changed me shift when I got wind of it so I could watch it. After the evidence they found in that cellar, the excisemen reckoned there was very little left for the family. The jewellery goes to Newcastle where it will likely be claimed. All their other stuff was taken into Newcastle to sell. The farm will go onto the market next week. But they left in a carriage. Oh aye, they had to leave in a carriage: the mother, the son and heir, and her, and you know, she spoke to me." He nodded at Roddy. "She lent out of the window and her voice was like that of a fishwife as she yelled at me, 'We'll be back. Remember that, we'll be back,' she said. And I answered her in a voice as loud as her own. 'I've no doubt,' I said; 'there's good pickin's on the Newcastle to Edinburgh road.'"

It was as if a blight had come on the day. Mary Ellen was standing with her head bowed, and the brightness had gone from Roddy's face and his voice was sullen as he said, "What's past is past. You cannot raise the dead. And you weren't the only one to lose a father. You want to remember that."

"Oh aye, I do." Hal pursed his lips and his head moved up and down before he repeated, "Aye, I do." Then his voice changing to a deep growl, he said, "But I was the only one made to feel like muck, I was the only one who had a mark on him. If me da had been caught stealing and hanged for it, I would have been the son of a kind of hero. But no, they said he had done off, taken money out of the country. That was unforgivable. But anyway, as you've heard, I'm to be compensated." His voice rose now to a mimicking cheeriness: "I'm to go before my lords and masters in the City of Newcastle come next Wednesday and, as I understand it from Mr Mulcaster, I'm gona be compensated for all the pain of me youth, for the stigma on me name, and that on me father. Now isn't that something? What do you think I'll get? Give a guess."

"Whatever it is, I hope it'll be enough to satisfy you."

The artificial smile on Hal's face was again replaced by grimness, and a suppressed anger sounded in his voice when he said, "You know something, Roddy? I don't think you give a tinker's curse about what happened to your father. All your remembering meant to you was saving your own skin, and you wouldn't have done that if it hadn't been for her." He made a sharp movement with his head towards Mary Ellen. "She ran here and there like a scalded cat to save you, and what's her reward, and Kate's too, come to that, and everybody else's? You jump at the chance to get away from us all and live in Newcastle among your new fine friends. But have you thought what might happen if you don't come up to their expectations? Because you know you're not all that God Almighty bright with your pencil; there's others about here, given a little time, could come up to you, and pass you."

"Yes, you're right, that might be so." Roddy's face was as dark as his accuser's now. "Everything you say could be right except your accusation that I don't think of my father. Let me tell you, I've thought as much of him as you ever could, only thing is I haven't opened me mouth so much about him. You know, I'll tell you this, in a way, I'm sorry I ever got me memory back, for then you would have gone on being yourself, only opening your mouth when you wanted to cut somebody to pieces. Now apparently you can't keep it shut. As for not being grateful to those who have helped me over the years, and to Mary Ellen here most of all" – he thumbed towards her now – "for what she did for me, you know nothing about it; only time will tell how much I appreciate it."

He stopped speaking and the two men glared at each other as if they had never known one day of friendship. Then Hal, letting out a long drawn sigh, seemed to slump before turning away, saying, "Aw! to hell. To hell with you! Do you hear? To hell with you!"

Mary Ellen stood and watched him pushing his way roughly past the people in the square. She dare not look at Roddy, although his last few words had seemed to put a stamp of certainty on her hopes, for there was in her a sadness that these two men who had been so close, closer than real brothers, should now be at each other's throats. Although she had always resented Hal's presence, she recognized now that he had needed someone, not only as a boy and a youth, but as a man. The clearing of his father's name hadn't seemed to expunge the stigma; he was still filled with bitterness, and that she couldn't understand. She doubted if she would ever understand him. But then, it didn't matter, the only person who mattered was the man now standing by her side, who had, in a way, made a public promise to repay her for all she had done for him. Not that she wanted any payment for being the means of saving him from deportation, but in a way she wanted payment for all the sleepless hours and the longing and desire that he evoked in her. Now that would come. He had as much as said it. That would come.

12

She was full of excitement the following Sunday as she hurried across the hills: it was as if she was going to her wedding. But like that of the bride who waited at the church in vain, so her heart sank with disappointment as she entered the cottage. Her first words to Kate were, "Is he out?"

Kate was seated at the table chopping up a root on a board, and she turned her head and smiled her skin-stretching smile, and as if she hadn't heard the question she said, "Blustery day an' cold enough to shrivel you."

Mary Ellen went and stood at the other side of the table. She hadn't put her basket down but was holding it stomach high with both hands. "Where is he?" she said, her tone almost a demand now.

Kate stopped chopping at the root and, pressing her bent back against the chair, she muttered, "Somewhere in London town, I imagine, at this moment."

"*London town?*" The words seemed to force their way out through the top of her bonnet and the woollen scarf that had been keeping it in place.

Kate sighed now as she looked at this girl who had been like a daughter to her, in a way more than Roddy had been a son, for she had talked more to her and been more open with her. She said gently, "Take off your things and sit down."

As if in a daze Mary Ellen did that; then slowly pulling a chair to the opposite side of the table, she looked across at Kate and asked quietly, "He's been then?"

"Aye, but not the day, or yesterday. He came on Tuesday and early on, for they left at six in the morning. They came by Mains Diligence. It sets off from the Rose and Crown in the Bigg Market at that hour. They got off at Hexham, and there they hired a trap from one of the carriers in Hexham, but not afore they had breakfast at the inn, she informed me."

"She?"

"Aye. His new godparents or such, or whatever you might call them, came with him." There was a touch of bitterness in her voice now. "Apparently the man, Cottle his name is, wanted to do some sketches hereabouts and it was a good opportunity, he said. And she an' all was at it. She drew the outside of the cottage."

"Is she old?"

Kate now attacked a bulbous corm as she said, "No, not old as age goes."

"How old?"

"Oh" – Kate seemed to consider – "thirty, perhaps. Aye, thirty. But he's a lot older, old enough to be her father."

Mary Ellen was silent for a moment. Thirty. Well, thirty was old. "What was she like?" she asked.

"Oh." With her knife whose end was sharpened to a point Kate attacked the white pulp of the bulb as if she had a grudge against it as she said, "Oh, I don't take that much notice of folk; I don't wear me eyesight out looking at things that don't matter."

But then she almost started in the chair as Mary Ellen's hand, thrusting out, gripped her wrist and she cried, "It does matter. You know it does matter to me, Kate."

"My God!" Kate looked at the knife that had dropped from her fingers onto the table. "You could have cut me finger ends off. Do you know that? That knife's like a lance. And then Farmer Yates would come bellowin' at me as loud as his bull because I couldn't make the cuckoo-pint powder to open up his beast's gut. I've got used to it making blisters on me fingers with its strength, but I want me fingers."

"I'm sorry. I'm sorry. But ... but you know what I mean."

Kate now scraped her chair back on the stone floor; then having pulled herself upwards, she shambled to the row of shelves that covered one third of the side wall, and, taking up a small jar, she returned to the table and began to spoon some white powder out of a mortar into it. And when the mortar was empty she replaced the pestle in it out of habit and pushed it to one side before placing the jar on the table. She put her hand on Mary Ellen's shoulder, saying, "You've got to accept things as they are, lass."

Mary Ellen slowly lifted her head that had been resting on her hand and, looking up at this old woman whom she could say she truly loved, she whimpered, "I can't, Kate. I can't. I've tried, but I can't. Tell me straight, this woman, what is she like?"

"All right, I'll tell you straight. She's a smart piece, as is her man. Not like artists that I had in me mind. I thought they mostly ran round in their bare pelts. She's good lookin', after a fashion, but pert. Well, that isn't the right word. Bossy. Aye, that's more like it. It's she who rules the roost. So there you have it, but don't get wrong ideas into your head: she's a married woman, and of the class, which is another thing that surprises me, her being the artist type. I always thought artists were lucky to have a crust. Anyway, not these two, nor their friends in London town where they're taking him, seemingly to extend his knowledge and to show him round the galleries, whatever that might mean. But there's one thing I'll tell you, an' I suppose I say it as shouldn't, but no matter how he's dressed his class'll stand out. Here, he always appeared to be a cut above the rest, for most are but rough working men, but in their presence he'll be the brisket end compared to the top cut, if you know what I mean."

She knew what Kate meant all right, but she still wasn't comforted.

"Did he leave any message for me?" she asked quietly.

"Aye, he did. He said to tell you he wouldn't be seeing you until come the New Year, but he'd write you a letter."

"He said he'd write me a letter?" Her eyes widened.

"Aye, that's what he said. And only last week he was tellin' me that his letter from Newcastle to here had cost sevenpence. He wasn't grumbling about it, it was me asking if he had money to throw away. So God above knows what his letter from London will cost – a shilling or more I wouldn't be surprised. Money thrown away. But then not in this case, if he sends you a letter. That'll be something, won't it?"

"Aye. Aye."

"I've just brewed some mint tea. Would you like a cup?"

"Yes, please, Kate." Her voice was quiet. Her whole body was quiet, sunk into momentary apathy, for there seemed nothing to look forward to, nothing to live for. She had been buoyed up with hope all the week: she had felt that if they could only be together once or twice more like they had been last Saturday, something would come of it, he would kiss her.

There had been times at night when her imagination had been so vivid she had felt his mouth on hers, and she had gone to sleep wrapped in happiness. Even this morning she had stilled her tongue when her mistress's voice had dinned continually in her ears extolling the virtues of her grandson and denouncing girls who were thankless and wayward. Even when Mrs Davison had said, "You needn't think you'll get anything from me towards your wedding chest," she had stopped herself from retorting that it wasn't the wedding chest that mattered, it was the man. And she cared for one man and one man only, and admitted guiltily to herself that she had long since ceased to care for her father.

The thought sent her hands to the basket, and she took out a slab of cheese and another of butter; then taking up the knife that Kate had been using, she cut them both in half. And Kate, seeing her doing this, said, "Oh, now don't do that; your da needs them to get him through the week."

"Not more than you he doesn't; he's got money in his tin that he can buy food with."

"So have I. So have I. It's in the wall there." She pointed to the chimney. "I told him to take it, but he wouldn't, except a few pounds to buy a gift or two, as he said."

To buy a gift or two. Mary Ellen's body stiffened. Who for? Not for her. Likely, if he'd had a gift for her, he would have left it here.

Kate broke in on her thoughts now, saying, "You'll be kept as busy as a bee up there next week, especially on Christmas Day, because they usually have a big table then, don't they?"

"Yes. Yes, they do." Her voice was flat.

"Well, I meself will be havin' a chicken, and Benny Fowler will be killin' one of his pigs. He always brings me some rib and chitterlings. And then there'll be the beast killin' up in Allendale. I never like that, you know, the beast killin'. They take so long over it. A feast they make of it. Drunk as noodles and battering the things slowly to death. I sometimes wonder why I've ever ate meat. We could all do without it, you know. But then, as I say to meself, I'm not averse to havin' a bit of pork or killin' a chicken on me own. We are full of contradictions, you know, Mary Ellen. Aye, we're full of contradictions. But what I was comin' to is this: your da's on his own. Now he's not a very sociable individual, as I know, but I hate to think of anybody on their own at Christmas. It will be the first one for many a long day that I've eaten at a solitary table, so would you like to ask him if he'd come and take a bite with me?"

"I will, I will, Kate. I can't promise that he'll come, because you know what he's like."

"Aye, I do, man and boy. And there wasn't a nicer young fellow walkin' than your da, let me tell you, Mary Ellen. Life's embittered him. When your mother went she drained his veins. There's no life in him now, except that what he rakes up to be miserable with. Still, you tell him I'd be pleased to see him, will you? And he'd be doin' me a favour. Tell him that."

"Yes, Kate, I will."

"Well now, drink up this tea. It'll taste a little different from usual for I've put a wee dollop of rosemary into it. Very precious that, the rosemary, for it's difficult to come by in these parts. Farmer Yates brought me some when he returned from his brother in August. He lives miles away down the country in Lancashire, his brother, an' the stuff grows like weeds there. So, knowing that he owes me a debt or two for what I've done for his animals, I told him what I would like if he ever came across such as rosemary, and he remembered and brought me a good stock of flowers, enough for me to distil a bottle or two from them. But God knows when I'll get the next, for now Farmer Yates's brother is dead. 'Twas to his funeral he went last time. Anyway, lass, you'll feel better after this for it's a great comfort to the mind and body is rosemary."

Mary Ellen drank the mint tea that today had an added scenty flavour, but there followed no miraculous feeling of well-being. And even half an hour later, when she wrapped up once again and said goodbye to Kate and went on her way to her father's, the rosemary's magic powers had still failed to lighten her heart.

Christmas came, and went, followed by the excessive eating and drinking on New Year's Day.

Then the year took on the appearance of any other year: it snowed, then thawed, then a frost took over and turned the roads into a sea of glass; then it thawed again.

She managed to get to Kate's on the second Sunday in January, but still no letter had come for her. Kate had little to say except that she didn't know how she was going to get through the winter as her flesh now didn't seem to hold any heat.

On the third Sunday, with warnings from her mistress that she shouldn't make the journey at all as the sky was laden with snow, she wrapped up and set out. Her basket was full today, as it had been last week. It was her mistress's way of telling her that she was forgiven, but more so it was showing her how bounteous life could be if she would come to her senses and have no more truck with that fellow who had caused all the trouble; she had been cute enough to realize from her handmaiden's manner that things weren't going as hoped in that direction.

Mary Ellen had no sooner left the farmhouse than her mistress's prediction showed signs of being fulfilled, for single large flakes began to fall, and before she reached the cottage they were coming down thick and fast.

Then behold, when she pushed open the cottage door, there he was. At least, at first sight she thought it was him, but then for a second not, because he looked so different. He had an overcoat in his hand and was standing, about to put it on. He was wearing trousers not breeches, the material being a sort of thick twill and of a salt and pepper colour. It was akin, she thought, to the clothes the gentry wore, and when, with a quick movement, he pulled on the overcoat which was of a deep fawn colour, she walked up the room gaping at him, and even when he said, "Hello, there. I thought I was going to miss you," she still offered no greeting.

"I'm having to look slippy." He thumbed towards the small window. "If this keeps up the roads will be blocked."

She said weakly, "You're going now?"

"Yes, I'll have to. If I'd taken Kate's advice——" He nodded towards the fire where Kate was sitting in the chair, her gaze concentrated on the big black iron pan set on the iron stand that was pushed half-way into the fire. "She told me it was coming, but I thought I'd hang on a bit in case you turned up early. What are you looking at? These?" He flicked his hand down the front of his open overcoat and laughed self-consciously as he said, "I haven't gone mad and spent all me money. These are Mr Cottle's cast-offs. He's fatter than me but Mrs Cottle had them altered. I've never worn anything so warm in all me life. An' they feel good." He now buttoned his coat. "I'm sorry, Mary Ellen, but I'll have to be on the move. Kate will give you all me news. Anyway, if this doesn't lie" – he again looked towards the window – "I'll be along next week-end."

He walked past her and went to Kate, and bending down to her, he said, "You heard what I said, didn't you?" He put his hand on the side of her head.

"Aye, I'm not deaf yet, lad." The words were like a rebuff, and he straightened up and rather sheepishly he turned to Mary Ellen and said, "Well, ta-ra. Take care of yourself. You're looking fresh."

This remark she ignored, and more to detain him than anything else, she said, "Have you seen Hal?"

He shook his head: "No. I only got here late yesterday afternoon. Apparently, he's still out on his hunt. I went along to his cottage but it's all locked up and there was no fire on that I could see. He'll drive himself mad. It's ridiculous; the whole thing's over and done with. He should have been satisfied when Bannaman died, but no, he's out for blood. That's Hal."

She made no answer to this, but when again he said, "Ta-ra," she answered, "Ta-ra."

When the door closed on him it was as if a stranger had walked out. There was silence in the room. The basket was on the table; her two mittened hands were gripping the handle; the melting snowflakes dropping off the head shawl round her bonnet were dropping onto them. It was Kate, turning from the fire, who spoke. "Sit yourself down, lass," she said. "You look buffered."

Mary Ellen loosened her hands from the basket now and stretched out her fingers as if they were cramped; then she went round the table and sat on the cracket opposite Kate. Her hands now joined tightly in her lap, she asked, "What's all his news that he's talked of?"

Kate bent down and, taking up a square of peat, she placed it behind the black pan and as she did so a waft of smoke came down the chimney and she turned her head away, coughing. After a moment she remarked, "I'll have to get a brush up there; it's tight at the top. . . . About his news. His friends are leaving Newcastle; they are going to London town. And they want to take him with them, so he came yesterday to ask my advice." There was an unusual bitter note in her voice as she uttered the words. Then looking fully at Mary Ellen, she said, "That was only a form; he'll do what he wants in the end. I've had to come to terms, sort of face up to the fact that he's a lad . . . no, no, not a lad any more, a man who'll go his own road. He'll do it quietly and without fuss if possible, but he'll go it. He doesn't mean to hurt anybody so he beats about the bush. And that's what he's doin' now, because, lass, let's face it, he's bound for London and all it proffers. Better instruction he says, wider outlook on art, whatever he means by that. Up there, there are people who can draw and paint, he says. I did say to him, I'd understood there was a lot of fine artist-like people in Newcastle. He agreed, but apparently the Cottles think there are better still up in the big town."

Mary Ellen's heart was like lead. It was as if she had just heard he had died; in fact, she was wishing she had heard that he had died, because then she could still think of him as hers. Her voice was like a thin whimper as she asked, "When is he going?"

"Oh" – Kate jerked her head – "apparently not until the spring, somewhere around April, because of what he calls the term ending. And the Cottle man is committed somewhere with his work until then. But truth to tell, I don't think it is the man who has so much to do with it as the woman."

Oh, Kate, shut up! Shut up! she only just stopped herself from shouting aloud, for Kate's words were like a knife being thrust into her. But then mustering what common sense she still had charge of, she decided she was silly to have any fears about the Cottle woman: Wasn't she old? Past thirty.

The silence fell between them again, and during it, staring at Kate, she realized she wasn't the only one who would suffer from his going. Here was someone who had looked after him all his life, at least since he was a young lad. And now she was a very old woman. She didn't know how old, because Kate would never talk about her age, but she was wizened like a nut and her back was bent and her fingers twisted. Had he thought that Kate might die, should he go to London town? If he was in Newcastle there would have been some chance of his coming home to see her during her last days, that's if she had any and didn't just pop off. But in London, which was another world away, how could he ever hope to see her again once he left for there? Kate was right about one thing among many others, he would always go his own road.

As she began to recall incidents from the past she checked herself saying, Stop it. Stop it. Everybody's got their own ways of doin' things, and 'tis only because he doesn't like to hurt people. But he was hurting Kate, and he was hurting her. Oh, dear Lord, how he was hurting her. If only she could get over this feeling for him; if only she could take a scrubbing brush and scrub herself all over, then sluice herself with a bucket of cold water, for then, when she was dried, she'd be rid of it, like when you had a rash or the itch. But hers was an itch that started in the core of her being and she couldn't get at it, and never would.

She rose from the chair, took some things out of the basket and put them on the table, then said, "I'll be off to me da's. I'll call on me way back. Bye-bye" She paused; then bending down, she kissed Kate softly on the cheek, and Kate reached up and gripped her arm with her gnarled fingers, saying brokenly, "Bye-bye, lass."

The first thing her father said when she entered the room was, "Hello. What's the matter with your face? Has it slipped?" Instead of retorting in her usual way she answered him, "Leave me alone, Da, please. I'm not feelin' too good."

After a pause he said, "Aye, well, there's two of us. Nearly broke me neck the other mornin' on the bloody ice outside the door. So get as much wood in as you can when you're here the day, 'cos by the look of it, we're in for another window-sill wiper."

As she took off her things and began to empty the basket, giving no answer to his comments on its contents, she wondered if there was one other person in the world besides Kate who did anything for anybody and didn't expect a return? He was her father, true, and she had a duty to him. Then there were the Davisons. She had a duty to them, too, and she certainly repaid it every hour of the day. She paused for a moment and looked at her hands. She had pulled her mittens off and the bare ends of her fingers looked swollen, and the rest of her hands were red and roughened and there were corns on the mounds between her fingers. She had the inclination to cry, but then she admonished herself: "Stop it! Stop it!" for she knew that the condition of her hands, or the attitude of the Davisons, or her father, or anyone else wouldn't have mattered a fig if the one person in her life was not going to vanish from it.

She stopped for a moment in the act of reaching upwards to a shelf in the pantry. What about the promise, or should she say the suggestion that he had voiced to Hal in the square at Allendale? Had he spoken like that just to show that he wasn't ungrateful to her? And that's all he had meant them to be, just words, no deeper meaning? And what about the letter he had promised to write to her?

Oh, why did she keep on; if Kate said he would go to London, he would go to London. Kate could see through people. She knew what they wanted even before they knew it themselves.

As if her father had picked up her thoughts, he called, "Her askin' me to go along there on Christmas Day. She's as able as me to get out."

Like a flash she called back, "Don't be silly, Da! She can hardly crawl about."

"That's put on half the time. She's as tough as cow's hide. She's been as old as she is now for as long as I can remember. She's got potions that keep her goin', and she won't peg out till they run out."

She was speechless. Kate had been so good to her father and mother, and at one time he had appreciated it. He had said she was the best and wisest woman that he had ever come across. She remembered he had gone to a revival once when the Evangelists were speaking in Allendale square, and when he came back he had said to her mother, "'Twas all hell fire and brimstone, same as the rest, only that one stoked his fire up the day with his best coal, because it was so red-hot he had women folk faintin'. No wonder some tried to break up the meetin'. But as I remarked to Benny Fowler on the way back, if old Kate had been on that box, she would have had their ears spread out and their mouths agape with her wisdom."

And that wasn't so long ago, well, seven years gone. But did it take seven years to change a man? Most of them could change overnight.

She stopped before shutting the pantry door and, looking inwards at the stone-slabbed shelves, she said to herself, "Kate says if you think of a thing first thing every morning afore you even open your eyes, it'll come to pass." She had said that to her as a child when she had wished for some toy or other. Well, she had said certain words to herself every morning now for years and what had they brought her? Nothing but pain. So she must change them. But what could she put in their place?

13

It was May. He was going to London. This was the last time she would see him.

It had been an unusually warm day. It had been a lovely spring altogether. Too dry, some people said, for there hadn't been a drop of rain for a fortnight and people were foolishly casting off the heavy clothes of the winter, while the wiser ones chanted, "You'll suffer for it. Ne'er cast a clout till may is out."

They had been walking side by side in silence for some time. It was Kate's suggestion, given in an aside to him, that he should see her back to the farm. They were on the quarry path now and she had the mad notion to turn to him and say, "If I was to show you where a bag of gold lies, would you stay?" But her heart knew the answer, because even if she were to claw her way into that old tunnel and show him the bag, his answer would be, "That's stolen money. It should go back to the firm."

It was strange, but long, long periods could go by without her ever giving the bag a thought, but during these last few heart-torn weeks her mind had dwelt on it. She could be rich. She could set up some place on her own, only how would she explain from where she had got the money.

She'd had the idea of setting up a little cake shop in the market place at Hexham, for she was a dab hand at cake making. But it was only an idea and vague, merely another wish that she knew could never come true.

He broke the silence by saying, "I'm not going to Australia, Mary Ellen, so don't look so glum, although I'll never forget, if it hadn't been for your good work on my behalf that's exactly where I might be at this minute." He put his hand on her arm, and she stopped and peered up at him in the deep twilight, and all she said was, "Oh, Roddy." And he, his voice tender now, said, "I ... I think the world of you, Mary Ellen, always have and always will. You must remember that. But ... but...."

When he shook his head she screwed up her eyes tightly. Then swinging round from him, she ran into some low thicket to the side of the path, and when he came after her, calling softly, "Mary Ellen! Mary Ellen! Look, don't be silly," she still kept on, until, coming to an open space, she flung herself down onto the moss and, burying her face in her hands, she began to cry unrestrainedly.

He knelt by her side and endeavoured to raise her up. But she remained stiff and lay there, her whole body racked with her sobbing, and all he could say was, "Oh, Mary Ellen. Mary Ellen."

When her crying subsided she pulled herself up and around, and as she groped at the bottom of her petticoat to find the pocket wherein lay her handkerchief he said, "Here. Here." And now he was wiping her face, one hand on the back of her head, the other moving the handkerchief around her eyes.

"You've got moss on your chin." He laughed, shakily. "It looks like a beard." And when he rubbed at her chin, she whimpered, "Oh, Roddy, don't go. Please, don't go."

"Now, Mary Ellen, you know I must."

"Roddy." Her voice was just a faint whisper.

"Yes, what is it?" he asked.

"I ... I love you."

"Oh, Mary Ellen. It's ... it's just because we've been brought up together."

"No, no, Roddy." She was staring into his face now, but in the dim light, and the tears still in her eyes, she saw it as through an enchanted glass. It was beautiful, so beautiful that she could not control her hands, and when they both went out and cupped it she was whispering again, "Roddy. Roddy. Will ... will you do something for me, just one thing, something ... something to remember you by?"

"Aye, yes, of course, Mary Ellen, anything. What is it?"

There was a long pause now as her hands slid round his shoulders, and she pressed herself against him before she said, "Love me."

Although she felt his body jerk away beneath her hold she did not relinquish it, but again she pleaded, "Just ... just once, Roddy. I ... I must have something of you to remember you by. Just once. Oh, Roddy."

"Mary Ellen, you don't know what you're sayin'."

"Yes, yes, I do, Roddy, I do. I know all about it. I know what I'm sayin'."

"But if ... if?"

"It won't. It won't. Nothing will happen, just ... just. ... Oh, Roddy, Roddy. Please, love me. Please, love me."

When she felt the trembling in her own body being answered in his, she lifted her face up until their lips were an inch apart. Then when she pressed hers to his she felt his body go rigid. But this did not deter her. And when they fell onto their sides they lay still, still and trembling.

"Mary Ellen! Mary Ellen! No, no. It ... it mustn't happen. Oh, Mary Ellen." As he repeated her name his hands began to move over her, and immediately the agitation inside her ceased and she lay perfectly still.

The daylight vanished. A night animal ran past them and gave an eerie squeaking cry at finding an obstacle in its path.

Roddy was the first to sit up, but he did not straighten himself: his body doubled, he held his head in his hands, muttering unintelligibly; whereas Mary Ellen all the while lay limp and relaxed, staring upwards to where in the far far distance a small star was appearing in the sky.

So this was it? This ecstasy that was nearly all pain; this transient thing that had changed, not only her body, but her mind, for her worrying had stopped. It was as if she had never known worry and would never know it again, for now she had an antidote against it in the knowledge that she was holding Roddy to her forever more: if she never saw him again he would be hers.

It was at the moment she was thinking, no matter what happened in her life again it wouldn't affect her, that Roddy's voice penetrated her euphoria and the sound told her he was speaking through his clenched teeth.

"You shouldn't have done it, Mary Ellen."

She felt him move then saw the dark outline of him rise to his feet. And she knew he was fumbling with his clothes. She hadn't bothered about hers; she hadn't even been aware of their disarray; but now her hands were quickly thrusting her skirt and petticoat into place. And she raised herself on her elbow as his voice came at her again, saying, "You shouldn't have made me, Mary Ellen. That's you, you must have all you want."

The euphoria slid away from her like a cloak falling from a greased body. She pulled herself to her feet now and muttered, "Roddy. Roddy."

"You know what you've done, Mary Ellen? You know what you've done?"

"Yes, Roddy, yes. I know what I've done."

"My God! What if there's consequences?"

She paused before answering. Previously she had thought of the consequences and it hadn't mattered, for deep down in her she had imagined that if there were consequences he would shoulder the responsibility, and they would be married, and perhaps she would go to Newcastle to live there with him. And she would have learned to pass herself among his fine friends, because she was quick to learn anything. But now as she listened to him, for he was still talking, another change was taking place in her mind and body. Her body had gone numb as if it hadn't experienced any sensation at all either of pain or pleasure. As to her mind, she was trying her best not to recognize what it was telling her, that this man who was talking at her was the real Roddy, not the one she had fostered in her mind all these years, for he was repeating in several different ways that it was she who was selfish, it was she who must always have everything she wanted and if she didn't get it she flared out with her tongue. And now look at what she had done, the hole she had put him in. He finished by saying, "Oh! God."

She stood peering up at him. What had she done? She had forced him to love her. But what she had experienced, was that love?

She could just see the outline of his face. It wasn't as she had imagined it just now, she was seeing him as Kate saw him. Kate loved him, but she wasn't deluded by her love, as she herself had been. She remembered something that Kate had said last week. She hadn't fully understood it then but she did now. When she herself had been going on about him not visiting and the weather fine, Kate had said, 'A slack string on a fiddle alters the whole tune. It's like human beings. We all have slack strings, weaknesses, selfish traits."

Well, now she recognized his slack string: he was selfish; in a big way he was selfish. He had been upbraiding her, and behind his words there was a suggestion that she had acted like a loose woman.

He was saying now, "I'm surprised, Mary Ellen, I am, but I'm not without blame, I blame meself."

"Thank you, Roddy."

"Oh, don't come back like that with your sarcastic clips. You know it would never have happened if. . . ."

Something snapped within her head and she was shouting at him now, "Yes, yes, I know."

Quickly he thrust out his hand as if to put it over her mouth, at the same time hissing, "My God! Do you know what you're doin'? Anybody could hear you on the path above."

"Well, I don't mind. I would have thought you wanted everybody to know that I'm a bad woman, because that's what you think, isn't it, I'm bad?"

"Don't be daft, no such thing. Silly, yes. And out to have your own way as always. . . ."

"Roddy." Her voice was now low and deep as if coming up from the pain-filled depth within her and with a tone of quiet recrimination in it as she said, "Think again. What have I had with regards to me own way, ever? I was subject to me da; and from then I've been subject to me mistress, and all the Davisons for that matter. The only person who's never made any demands on me has been Kate. Now it's my turn, Roddy, to say this, the one big mistake I've made, and I can say it now, is to think that you were different from what you are. And deep within me I'm sad as sad that I've found it out. Newcastle didn't change you, and not even your fine friends did, 'cos you've always been like that. Looking back, I've had the name of trailin' you since we were bairns. And I did. But just think, there were times when I didn't, and what happened? You came after me. Not many times. But when I went off somewhere on me own, there you were, demandin' why I hadn't turned up. You liked to be trailed, Roddy. It was the same with Hal. Hal trailed you. Hal thought the sun shone out of you, and now you couldn't care a tinker's curse about Hal or what effect your leavin' has on him. Not that that worries me because it's been only too plain to everybody that Hal and me spark off each other like tinder off flint. And I know this much an' all: you've altered since you got your memory back. As you said, you've become your real self. But the one afore that was pretty much the same. So I can say to you now, Roddy, go on your way, and don't let your conscience trouble you. Just keep tellin' yourself that all that happened was my fault."

As she turned about and almost stumbled over a fallen branch, he muttered, "Look, Mary Ellen. Look."

She did not turn to him, but groped her way back to the path. He followed her. And there she turned to him and said very gently, "Goodbye. And don't come any further, I know me way. I should do."

"Mary Ellen, please, look. Don't let us part like this."

She swung round now and she knew that his eyes were blazing, and her lips were squared back from her teeth as she ground out, "Roddy Greenbank, you go to London and to hell. To hell! Do you hear?"

And on this she swung round from him, knowing that she had silenced him, even stunned him. And she went blindly on her way, for once again the tears were streaming down her face and she had to keep one hand in front of her to push against the branches bordering the side of the path, because at times she staggered like someone drunk.

14

Mrs Davison was worried about her maid. For weeks now she hadn't been herself. It was all because that big lump of a smelter had gone off to London. Well, she thanked God for that. He was now out of the way and time altered everything, as she knew only too well, for didn't God send it to alter the seasons: nothing but time could melt the hard frozen earth and make the ground fertile for planting and bring forth the shoots, and nothing but time could lead to the harvest and the gathering in. Yes, time altered everything; so she believed it would alter Mary Ellen's outlook towards her grandson. Apart from providing Lennie with a wife to hand, because he wasn't of the nature to go searching, she could see before her in the young girl a lifetime of help, for she was as strong as a dray horse and as willing. Oh, just a little more time to make Lennie a little more pushing and everything would go as she had planned it in her mind for this long while.

Then one morning Mrs Davison began to worry still more. What was the matter with the girl? She looked as peaked as a hen with the croup, and she wasn't as perky as she had been. Not that she neglected her work in any way, no, but there was something not right with her. And these last two or three days she had been running back and forward to the midden. Well, what could you expect when she was eating green apples. Thinking to give her a change the other day, she had sent her into the orchard to pick up the windfalls. And when she herself, wanting a breath of air, had strolled down there, she saw her picking with one hand and stuffing herself with the other. "What's wrong with you, girl?" she had said. "They'll give you the gripe, eating green apples. Don't you get enough food that you must eat green apples?"

And all the reply she was given was, "I like green apples." Now that was odd.

The little woman sat down on the settle near the fire. When had Mary Ellen expressed the wish for green apples before? If there wasn't enough sugar in the apple pies, she had screwed up her face.

As a light penetrated her mind and illuminated a thought, she bobbed up from the seat and squealed aloud, '*No! No! It can't be. No! No! Never!*"

Now she looked about her kitchen, which had a place for everything and everything in its place, as if she were searching for an answer. But then, in a way, she had already got it; and she asked of the delph rack,

"What was the time he left? Early May, wasn't it?" And when the delph rack appeared to answer she nodded at it. Then counting on her fingers, she said, "Early May to early June one, to early July two, to early August three, early September four. . . ." She stopped and stared at her hand. Then gazing up at the ceiling, she said, "Holy God!" before bringing her gaze down to the delph rack again and denying her thoughts by slapping her thighs and crying, "No, no! 'Tis the apples and the belly-ache." And lifting her gaze once more to the ceiling, she concentrated it on three hams hanging there. They were dangling from the beam above the open fireplace where they would be tinged by the smoke before being cut into at Christmas. And the middle ham seemed to sway and say, Go and ask her. And she said aloud, "Where is she?" In the cowshed helping to muck. Aye. Hadn't she purposely sent her over there to give Lennie a hand? She knew herself that there was nothing like the smell of warm cows and the running of milk from swollen teats to put one's mind in the right frame for courting.

Her small body seemed to stot out of the room and across the yard, and there she was standing at the open byre door, calling now in a voice that seemed larger than herself, "You! Mary Ellen."

"Yes, ma'am?" Mary Ellen, wielding a large bass brush, was sweeping the cow dung from the far end of the byre.

"Put that down and come with me."

Mary Ellen hesitated for a moment. She turned her head and glanced at Lennie who was looking at her from where he was untethering a cow from its stall, and his look said, What's got into Gran?

Of a sudden Mary Ellen knew what had got into Gran. This was the moment for which she had been waiting, for some weeks now, and she wondered it hadn't come sooner. It must have been the green apples that had given the game away. But if it hadn't been them her stomach would have answered her mistress's question in a very short while, because, being well into the fourth month it was rising.

She went down the byre and rubbed her hands on a coarse towel that was hanging from a nail, before crossing the yard and going into the kitchen. She knew what her mistress would say, she knew what they would all say. But she felt she knew the outcome of it: they would take her on if she would marry Lennie. And she had decided that's what she would do, because there was no other way out, and he was a good fellow, was Lennie. That she would have to put up with his piousness for the rest of her life would be trying, and also pay his grandmother with her labour until one of them died. But as she saw it, it was the lesser of two evils; what kind of a life would she have if she went back to her father? And anyway, who would keep her and her child? In some way or another she would have to work. But where? And who would take her on? Except a poor farmer, who would work her as he would an old and decrepit horse, getting the last ounce out of it.

So she wasn't too afraid when she stood before her mistress and saw that the little woman was finding difficulty in speaking; in fact, when she did open her mouth she stammered, "Ma ... Ma ... Mary El ... El ... Ellen, I ... I want to ask you something, but if I'm wrong, I beg your pardon. But if I'm right. Oh, say I'm not right, Mary Ellen."

"I'm ... I'm sorry, ma'am, but you're right."

"Oh! Oh, my lord!"

Mary Ellen watched the little woman push her hands up both sides of her round face until her stubby fingers were lost under her starched cap. Then her fat body bending forward, she seemed to do a dance step, for she hopped completely round the large table before she stopped, and now banging her double fists onto it, she cried, "You mean to stand there, Mary Ellen, and tell me that you have—" She swallowed as if unable to voice her thoughts; then she actually said the words, "fallen with a bairn!"

Mary Ellen stood with her eyes downcast, and now she nodded her head slowly as she muttered, "I'm ... I'm sorry if it's upsetting you, ma'am."

"*Upsettin' me!*" Now the voice was almost a scream. "You say you're sorry at upsettin' me! You don't say you're sorry for your wickedness with that scoundrel who's gone off to London. Oh! and to think you've been working in this house all these months and covering up your sin."

"I don't look on it as a sin, ma'am."

The quietness of her maid's tone seemed to infuriate the woman, and now she screamed, "Wait until Mr Davison hears of this. He won't believe his ears." And she now rushed to the door and, her voice still pitched high, she yelled across the yard, "Mr Davison! Mr Davison! Come here this minute."

Instead of her husband, her son Archie and her grandson appeared in the yard, saying, "What is it?" And she yelled at her son, "Get your father! Get your father here this minute."

A few seconds later it wasn't only her husband who came into the kitchen, but also her son and grandson, and all in a rush, her husband demanding, "What is it? Chimney caught ablaze?"

Then he became silent, and the three men looked to where Mary Ellen was standing at the end of the table, her head bowed, her hands gripping the edge. Then their attention was turned on the mistress of the house as, her tone lower now but grim, she said, "Prepare yourself for a shock. This one" – she thumbed towards Mary Ellen – "has—" It appeared again that she couldn't voice the condition that her maid was in, and it was her son who said, "Aye, she's gona have a bairn."

Both his father and his son seemed to jump at once with the horrifying thought that flashed through their minds, but Archie quickly dispelled it, saying, "No, my God! No! 'tisn't me. Mary Ellen can tell you that. An' who it was an' all. But I noticed, like the cows when they drop, Mary Ellen's had her fancies. Apples it was in her case." He turned and looked kindly on her, and she gazed back at him in gratitude, until her master spoke.

"Well, I've had longer experience with cows than you, our Archie,"

he said, "but I never noticed. Now that I know, I'm amazed. I am that."
His voice rose. "I'm amazed, Mary Ellen. Do you hear me? I'm amazed.
And after your mistress has been so good to you all these years you could
go and do this on her."

It struck Mary Ellen at the moment that it was being implied that she
had become laden with a child just to spite her mistress. How silly some
people could be. She wished they would hurry up and get round to it.
She glanced towards Lennie. He was looking at her through narrowed
eyes and there was an expression on his face that she had never seen
before. She couldn't put the word disdain to it, but she said to herself in
something of surprise, He's not for me. And at this she became worried;
then comforted herself with, He'll do what his granny tells him, and his
father an' all, and his father thinks not too badly of me, I can see that.

Then her idea of the future in this house was shattered with her
mistress's next words. "You'll go, girl," she said. "You'll get out of this
house, for we are respectable people. Always have been and, as long as
I'm here, always will be. I'll give you to the week-end until I can find
somebody else to take your place, and many will jump at it. Oh aye, they
will, and call me a fool for pamperin' you all these years. To think——"
Now her lips trembled and tears came into her eyes as she looked at her
husband and said, "To think this is how I've been repaid. What do you
say to my decision, Mr Davison?"

He paused only a moment before he said quietly, "'Tis right. 'Tis
right."

"Oh, Dad." His son Archie turned to him, saying now, "I wouldn't
jump at it like that. She's made a mistake, aye, but she's not the first one,
and she won't be the last."

Again the family were looking at him with suspicion, and his mother
now attacked him in much the same voice as she had used on her servant,
crying, "You stand there, me own flesh and blood, and defend her, and
go against what I say, what I want? This house is clean and is not going
to be besmirched with the likes of her. What she can do now is follow the
man who has filled her belly, and get him to see to her, because 'twas
him, wasn't it? Open your mouth, girl. 'Twas him, wasn't it?"

Mary Ellen stared at the little woman, then at the three men, and
having got over the shock that she was to be thrown out, her old spirit
revived and she said, "Who's given me the bairn is my business, missis,
and I won't stay till the week-end, until you get fixed again. If I'm to go,
I'll go now this very day, this very minute. And I'll tell you something
afore I go. Aye, you've been kind to me, but I've repaid you for it, not
twice over or three times, but a hundred times, because you've worked
me like a slave. Inside and outside you've worked me like a slave from
the day I came into your shelter. One thing more I'll say." Now she
turned from the gaping dumbfounded woman to her son and what she
said was, "Thank you, Mr Archie, for having the heart to stick up for
me. I'll always remember you for that. But as for you, master——" she had
now turned her attention to the grizzly-haired man – "being so shocked

at the way I am, you haven't been above letting your hand stray over the years, have you?"

On the sight of her master's scarlet face and her mistress being on the point of a swoon, she turned about and marched up the kitchen and to her garret room. And there she whipped her Sunday clothes from the peg on the back of the door and threw them onto the pallet bed. Then going to the chest of drawers that stood in the corner, she pulled the top one open and took out her petticoats and stockings and three white handkerchiefs. After she had bundled them all into the patchwork spread on top of the bed, which was her own and had been given her by her mother, she tore off her starched bonnet and flung it onto the floor, and threw after it her coarse apron before sitting down on a wooden stool and pulling off the heavy boots that had belonged to Lennie when he was younger. Then she pulled on her own boots and buttoned them with trembling fingers, and when she was ready to go she stood for a moment looking round the room that had afforded her the only privacy she had known in what seemed long years going back to her childhood.

When she reached the kitchen she saw her mistress sitting on the settle being comforted by her son, and she flung the bundle on the table, undid the knots and said, "You'd better examine these, missis, to see that I haven't taken anything that doesn't belong to me."

" 'Tis all right. 'Tis all right, Mary Ellen." It was Archie's voice, still kind.

She knotted the bundle again; then, looking at him, she said, "I won't forget your kindness, Mr Archie." And on that she turned about and went out.

Lennie was standing in the middle of the yard. She expected him to say some word to her, but he didn't. He just stared at her with the same expression, and before she reached the gate, she was aware that his father had come out of the house and was speaking to him in harsh tones, but she couldn't make out what was being said. Then as she went to open the gate she heard the quick steps behind her and for a moment she thought it was Lennie, but turned to see his father. She had never been very fond of Mr Archie. He was a bit rough in his speech and came out with things that brought the colour to your face, but now he looked at her in the most kindly fashion as he said, " 'Tis sorry I am, Mary Ellen, and I'll tell you this afore you go and it may be of some comfort for you to know that everybody doesn't think the worst of you, and it's just this: if things were different, if it was me own farm, I'd marry you the morrow."

She bowed her head and could not restrain the tears that ran down her cheeks; then looking up at him again, she said, "I'll always remember that, Mr Archie, and thanks, thanks very much."

He opened the gate for her and she went through and down the road towards her father's house, where she knew she'd have to spend the rest of her life.

But here another surprise awaited her.

Bill Lee was amazed at the sight of her carrying her bundle and in her Sunday clothes. He was at the fire, about to lift some baked potatoes

146

from the ashes, and he tossed one from hand to hand before hurrying to the table and dropping it there; then staring at her, he said, "What's this?"

She placed her bundle on the floor, pulled off her hat, and sat down in a chair near the table, at the same time indicating another chair to the side of him and saying, "I think you'd better sit down, Da."

He sat down, his brows puckered, his mouth slightly open, waiting for her news.

"I've been given the sack."

"You've been given the ... you mean, from the Davisons'?"

"Aye."

"In the name of God why?"

She looked to the side as if searching for a respite, but then, her eyes on him again, she said, "I'd better give it to you straight. I'm with bairn."

She watched all the creases smooth out from his face as it stretched; she watched his mouth, that at one time she had thought kind because it rarely spoke badly of anyone, clamp shut; she saw the shape of it disappear as he sucked in his lips; she watched his hands come out and catch hold of the side of the table as he pulled himself upwards. Then he was leaning towards her, saying, "You mean to sit there and tell me that you're ...?" He gulped, unable to go on.

She stared, unblinking, back at him, saying softly, "Aye, I do. That's how it is."

He said again, "You mean to say?"

He straightened up. He seemed to have no trouble now with his breathing for it did not stop the flow of his words, as it usually did, as he cried at her, "You bloody brazen young bitch, you! You sit there as cool as they come an' tell me that you've been with a... God Almighty! I never thought to see the day. It's him, isn't it?"

"Doesn't matter who it is." She was on her feet too, now, her face and her body stiff. "That's how I am. It's done, it can't be undone. Anyway you'll have someone to run an' fetch an' carry for you an' do your biddin' now in return for a shelter."

"Ooh! ... No!" The first word was long-drawn-out. "*Oh, no* you don't, miss. If you think you're comin' here and flauntin' the result of your running the moors, you're mistaken. Bloody well mistaken. The only thing I'm surprised at now, when I come to think on it, is it didn't happen afore, for you've trailed him for as far back as I can remember. An' now he's skittered off to London, an' you're left with your belly full, an' now you're lookin' for some place to spill it out. But it won't be here, lass. Oh, no. I've always held me head up high; respectability's been me second name, as was me father's and his father's afore him. And the wives they took were clean women, as was your mother. And now you." He turned his head to the side and seemed to be resting his chin on his shoulder as he said, "Thank God she's not here to witness this. I never wished her dead afore but I'm glad she's gone now."

There was utter astonishment in her voice as she muttered, "You mean ... you mean you won't let me? I ... I can't stay here?"

Looking back at her and his eyes now blazing with anger, he cried, "So right you are! So right you are! Now you can take up your bundle and get out of that door an' make your way an' get him to pay for his pleasure, because bedamned! here's one who's not going to stand in for him." He made a sound like a groan, then went on, "Having you about me for the rest of me days, knowing what you did, and a brat, a bastard crawling about me house? No, no, never! Not in my house, the place I built up for your mother an' me. Never. Never.... So get you going. Yes, I know where you'll make for, an' no doubt she'll welcome you with open arms."

She ground her teeth together before she said, "What if I don't go to Kate's, eh? What if I don't go to Kate's, but I go along to Maggie Oates's? She'll give me a bed an' gladly, and I can earn me keep in more ways than one. What about that, Da? Eh? What'll happen to your respectability then?"

His face blanched, and for a moment she became terrified by the look in his eyes as he took a step around the table towards her, saying, "Do you know what would happen then? Do you? I'd come over there an' cut your throat. I would, I'd cut your throat."

She had lifted up her bundle now and she moved backwards towards the door as she tried to answer bravely, saying, "Well, you just might have to try that. But don't forget she has lots of friends, has Maggie, and I could get their protection, couldn't I? Couldn't I, Da? I could get their protection. An' you're not fit to stand up to anybody in the valley now, are you?"

"Get out! Get out! I don't want to set eyes on you, not till me dying day, and not then."

When she banged the door behind her all fight left her and she felt so faint that she thought she was going to drop to the ground. She couldn't believe this was happening to her. She had felt sure that Mrs Davison, after upbraiding her, would see her predicament as a way to getting her to marry Lennie. And when that didn't turn out, she had taken it for granted that her father, after the first shock, would look upon her return home as a godsend for he'd have someone to see to him in his declining years which, with the disease on his chest, wouldn't be all that many.

At the spinney she put down the bundle and leant against a tree, thinking to herself, What if Kate ... if Kate turns against me? But she knew Kate: Kate would never do anything like that. But hadn't she thought she knew her mistress? And hadn't she thought she knew her father? Oh God! Oh God! Don't let it be the poorhouse. She was running now. The bundle pulling her down sideways, she kept changing it from one hand to the other. And then there she was in the field opposite Kate's cottage.

She came to a stop when she saw Kate just within her gateway. She saw her straighten up and look towards her, then turn away, and such was her reaction that she had to put her hand over her mouth to stop herself from vomiting.

When she reached the gate, she called softly, "Kate. Kate." And the old woman turned and, coming towards her, said, "It was you, then? I thought I was dreamin', or it was somebody passin' by. What in the name of God! Aw——" She stopped, then said, "Come away in."

The relief almost bringing her to the verge of hysteria, she had the urge to laugh and cry at the same time. She stumbled into the cottage, dropped the bundle and, rushing to the cracket, she dropped on to it and, bending herself double, she laid her head on her folded arms and gave way to a bout of body-shaking emotion.

Kate did not go to her, or speak, but she went to the rack where her potions were and took down three bottles. From each she took a small measure and put it into a tin mug, stirred the liquid around, then went towards the fire, saying, "Lift your head, girl. Lift your head and drink this."

Mary Ellen lifted her head. Her face was awash, her breath was coming in small gasps, but she grabbed at the mug and went to swallow the draught in a gulp, only to choke and cough and spit half of it out.

"Careful. Careful. 'Tis too precious to be wasted. That lot would cost one of the gentry sixpence." Kate accompanied her last words with a tight smile; then she said, "Sip it slowly."

Mary Ellen sipped at the concoction. It had a bitter-sweet taste and it seemed to dry up her tongue as it passed over it, but when she had finished it she rose from the stool and sat on a chair and leant back. Of a sudden she felt quiet inside and she looked at Kate and said, "D'you know why I'm here?"

Kate herself sat on the cracket that Mary Ellen had just vacated, and folding her scraggy arms round her equally scraggy body, she rocked herself as she looked at the young girl before her, and she said, "I don't have to guess, or when it happened. I only wondered at the beginning when you would tumble to it, or when you would arrive home, because you've come to stay, haven't you?"

"Oh, Kate, Kate." Mary Ellen brought her body forward now, and her head drooped, only for it to be brought up sharply again by Kate's voice, always strong, always giving the lie to her old infirm body: "Don't bend your head, girl," she said. "Shame is a self-made thrashing stool. Have none of it. Look them straight in the eye, all who would scorn you. Did she turn you out?"

Mary Ellen leant against the back of the chair now before she said, "Yes, right off." Then she added, "No, not right off; she gave me to the end of the week, till she could find somebody else, but I told her what she could do."

"That's a good sign, you stood up to her. Were they all against you?"

"Not all. Mr Archie spoke for me."

"Archie? Well, well. But then he would. A bright lad he was in his youth. His wife was a whining whinney. He was glad when she died, and so became a regular visitor along at Maggie Oates."

"Our Mr Archie?"

"Aye. Aye, your Mr Archie."

"He said . . . if things had been different, he . . . he would have married me."

Kate let out a high hollow laugh. "Did he begod?" she said. "Did he? Well, you could have done worse. Yes, you could have done worse. But you'll do a damn sight better in the end, let me tell you. Now, your da?"

"That was quicker."

"I'm not surprised. He's turned into a right holy Joe, has your da. I'm well acquainted with human nature and at one time I never thought I could read wrong, but I did with him, for there wasn't a nicer or more straightforward lad in his youth, but now I know he was only that way because he had your mother. He went to pieces after, or perhaps he just became his real self, narrow, mean, because that's your da, Mary Ellen. Say what you will, that's your da. Anyway, lass, you're here to stay, aren't you?"

"Please, Kate."

"Aw, don't put thank into your tone because you've come to me. You've come as a gift, lass, as a gift. Tell you somethin', I've always wanted you. Oh, aye, I loved Roddy. I still do, but not with that intensity. You see, again I've got to admit I was slightly wrong in reading human nature there. But with you, from you were a nipper, I wished you were mine. And now you are."

She pulled her twisted body up from the cracket and, going over to Mary Ellen, she bent forward and, for the first time in their long acquaintance, she kissed her. It was a gentle kiss, yet the wrinkled lips seemed firm on Mary Ellen's cheek. But the kindness was too much and Mary Ellen started to cry again, only to have Kate bark at her now, "No more of that. That's one thing we're gona put a stop to, cryin'."

After a moment, Mary Ellen, wiping her face, said, "How long have you known, Kate?"

"Oh, as I said, since the night he left. You were ripe for it. It had to be."

"You must never blame him, Kate, 'cos . . . 'cos I made him."

"Doubtless. Doubtless. The way you were that night you could have stirred a dolly-tub from the mill to rise to you."

Mary Ellen was about to hang her head again when Kate laughed and said, "There's no lass worth her salt if she can't get a man to do what she wants when she wants."

Mary Ellen's head didn't droop now as she muttered, "But he didn't want to, Kate. And . . . and he went for me after. And that did something to me, it changed me somehow."

Kate was staring at her. Her hands hanging by her sides, she said, "He went for you after it happened?"

"Yes, aye."

"Blamed you?"

It was a moment before Mary Ellen admitted, "In a way, yes, yes."

"God in heaven! I never thought I'd say I was ashamed of him."

"Aw, please, please, Kate, he had a right to be."

"He had no right to be." The old woman's voice was loud. "I'd say this and I'd say it to his face if he was here. I'm disappointed in him right to the core. All right, he's given you a bairn, but he should have rejoiced in it. You untouched and offerin' yourself to him. I doubt if he's ever had a virgin in his life afore. Doubt, did I say? I know fine well he hadn't, the place he went for his amusement."

Mary Ellen's eyes were round now, and her eyebrows were pushing upwards towards her hair as she said, "He ... he had been with...?"

"Oh, aye, aye. Tell me of one who lives in the valley who hasn't."

"But who? Which lass?"

"Oh, no lass from here, the paid pieces from Hexham. He hadn't the nerve to go along to Maggie, because he would have his lugs pulled by the men. Oh, no. But there are plenty suppliers in the town."

Again Mary Ellen felt she wanted to vomit. She was a fool, she was ignorant. She wished she was dead.

As if she had read Mary Ellen's thoughts, Kate said, "Now don't sit there looking like that and wishin' your life away; he was a man, just like every other one. But by God! he should have appreciated you. If I hold nothin' else against him, I'll hold that. Now if it had been Hal."

"*What?*"

"I said, if it had been Hal."

"Hal?"

"Aye, Hal. Like many another, you don't see that fellow except from the outside."

"Well, that's been enough for me.... Oh Kate, what am I going to do?"

"What would you have done if that fat empty-headed little bitch hadn't turfed you out?"

Mary Ellen sat and thought for a moment, then said, "Likely married Lennie."

"And then what?"

"What d'you mean?"

"What would your life have been like? Work from Monday mornin' till Sunday night, never a let up, and never let you forget the reason why you were there. What I'm meanin' is, you'd have had to work. Well, we all have to work one way or another."

"But where'll I find work round here, except I do grubbin' at the mine?"

"You'll not go grubbin' at the mine; you'll find work. But I'm tellin' you this" – the gnarled finger wagged at her – "you'll have to learn. You can read and write your own name, but that's not goin' to help you much, an' what I've got in mind takes a good memory, a real good memory, or else you'll be in the soup." She smiled now and the flesh came up round her small bright eyes and almost closed them as she added, laughingly, "Oh aye, if you put some of my concoctions into the soup you would be in it. They'd likely hang you for poisoning, and they would have done not a hundred years gone in me grannie's time. Oh, the things she told me."

Mary Ellen cut the old woman's reminiscing short by saying, "What d'you mean, Kate, about me memory, havin' to be good for a job?"

In answer, Kate twisted her body round and looked towards the end of the room to the shelves holding bottles, jars and boxes, and she said, "There, that could be your new job."

"Do what you do?" Mary Ellen's voice was quiet but high. "Make up potions?"

"Aye, just that. But it isn't as easy as it sounds. As I told you, it all depends upon your memory. Now listen here. I've been silly all me life with regard to that treasure." She was now wagging her finger towards the shelves. "What I should have done many years ago was have a stall in the Hexham market on a Saturday. That would have kept me in clover. And when I saw what some of the fakers made out of bottles of coloured water, sugar, and salt, why, I knew I was a fool. But there, I was never one for bargainin' or askin' people for money, even if they were gettin' good value. So here I sat and let them come to me, and as you know they've come from far and near over the years. But what have they given me? D'you know that nobody has ever paid me more than sixpence a potion in me long lifetime. But then, if I'd got sixpence for every potion, I'd have been sittin' pretty. In fact the hole in the wall there" – she nodded towards the chimney piece – "wouldn't have held it, I would have had to take all the bricks out." She again gave her crinkled smile. "Well, things are goin' to change from now on. They have changed over the last weeks. I've been breakin' them in, those of me customers. 'No, Bob,' I said, only yesterday. You know, Bob Allen the blacksmith. Well, over the years he's come for a lotion for his back. 'Tis all right in the spring and summer, but with the fall of the leaf he gets his twinges. So there he was with a penny in his hand and I said, 'I'm sorry, Bob, but I've got a hard winter ahead of me, and your special potion will be threepence from now on, and that's cheap,' I said, 'because you go into Hexham market or up to Allendale and what'll you pay there to the apothecary for stuff that has no more in it than plain pig's fat? Ninepence you would pay. Well, not less than sixpence, nothing's less than sixpence in the apothecary's when you're askin' for potions. So it's threepence from now on. What d'you say, Bob?' And you know, after a minute he laughed and said, 'You're a marler, Kate.' But he put his threepence on the table there. And then there was Rosie Fowler. Carryin' again she is, and her oldest one twenty. She's as good as any sow for turnin' them out. Well, there she was last week complainin' again of giddiness and swimmy feelings and the panting of her heart, so could she have me lavender spike potion, and not only the potion but the conserve, and the water for dabbin' on her head. Now for years she's had the three at a penny a time, a penny mind for the three lots. You know, when I told her that in future she'd have to pay a penny for each lot, she got on her hind legs and said, 'You can pick lavender anywhere.' So I said, 'You can go and pick it, Rosie. You go and pick it.' And there she stood wavering. But in the end I got me threepence, for as you will learn, Mary Ellen, there's more to the lavender potion than lavender. There's cinnamon powder, crushed nutmegs, an' cloves, and they've all got to be worked at, whereas the conserve, as you know, is mainly sugar. But look at the price of sugar. And then there's the time that it takes if you want to make some oil from the flowers. Oil of roses, why they're nothin' to it."

"And ... and you've kept all these things in your head all these years?"

"Aye ... aye, I have. But I started early, much earlier than you. I was picking from I was five years old and I could tell every plant and weed for miles. And I'll tell you somethin', I wasn't half as good as me mother, for as a girl she had been away in the Midlands, and then in the south of the country in service, and like the different types of people you get in the different counties, so do you get the different growths of weeds and herbs."

Now she was laughing widely, her tongue flicking in and out of her mouth past the stumps of her front teeth as she said, "I laughed a bit gone. Doctor Cranwell, the head vicar you know who scatters his curates like dockheads flying in the wind, well, one of them came to the door there knocking and politely asked, 'Are you Mrs Makepeace?' 'I am,' I said. 'I was told to come to you, because I was bitten by a dog last week and the salve I applied hasn't seemed to heal the wound.' Did I think I could do anything? I could but try, I said, if he would sit down, and let me see his offended part. It was on the calf of his leg and it was nasty. So I bathed it with a solution made from wild thyme and gave him the same to drink in little quantities first thing in the morning. Then, who sent him? I asked. Oh, he was a bit chary in telling me until I laughingly said, ' 'Twouldn't be the vicar?' Then his face colourin', he said, 'No, no, it wasn't the vicar.' And he laughed with me. A nice young fellow he was. And he came back the next week for another supply because the wound had almost healed. And he said he felt much better in himself, and after a little more conversation we agreed that the vicar must never hear of his visits."

Mary Ellen was actually smiling now, a weak and watery smile, but nevertheless she was looking relaxed and she asked, "How much did you charge him?"

"Oh" – Kate turned her head away – "what could I charge him, the church mice could feed any curate with their left-overs? But not so the parsons and them they call the doctors of the church. Live like lords they do, in mansions. This one'll likely come to that later on and he'll forget he was ever hungry. Do you feel better, lass?" Kate's tone and manner changed now as she looked gently towards Mary Ellen, and Mary Ellen's response to the kindness emanating from her friend brought her to her knees and, with her arms about the thin, but clothes-padded body, she laid her head on Kate's lap and murmured, "Oh, Kate. Kate. What would I do without you?"

"I don't know. I just don't know." The answer was intended to bring a smile again to Mary Ellen's face but instead it brought another flood of tears. And now, the old woman's hands cupped the bright head and pressed it to her as she muttered, "There, there. Now this is the last burst of cryin' you're goin' to indulge in. Do you hear me? There's to be no more of it, 'cos it'll only harm what's inside you. Lift up your chin now." She pressed the head gently from her and, looking down into Mary Ellen's face, she wiped the tears from each cheek with her fingers, saying, "We're both sick at heart over one person, so we can comfort each other, but there's good days ahead. We'll make them so. You know" – she continued to stroke each cheek – "I've had a feelin' on me of late that something good was goin' to happen. I felt strongly that my Pat would walk in the door. Sometimes I imagined he was in the room. I began to be a bit uneasy at those times" – she nodded at Mary Ellen – "because I've always told meself, me body's old, ancient, but me mind is still young and active, but when you start thinking things like that, well. . . . But he seemed very close, so I thought, perhaps he's on his way. And he could be. Aye, he could be. But the other good thing that happened to me is you, lass. I've never been one for constant company except a selected few: my Davey, then Pat, then you from you were a baby in your mother's arms; then of course, Roddy. Only four people. Oh no, five. I'm forgettin' Hal. And recalling him, there's somethin' in the wind in that quarter, for there he was first thing this mornin' in his Sunday best. He said he was goin' into Hexham."

"What d'you mean, something in the wind?" asked Mary Ellen.

"Well, it could be that Florrie Pierce or her sister Fanny has hooked him."

"The Pierce girls after Hal?"

"Aye, the Pierce girls after Hal. They would have lain their blanket down for him any day. What you don't seem to recognize, Mary Ellen, and never have is, Hal is a very presentable man."

"Well, I must be blind, because I haven't seen it. All right, he's not bad looking and he's got a body on him, but it's his manner and his ways. Who's going to put up with them? All right, all right." She was nodding at Kate now, and they both said together, "Florrie or Fanny Pierce." Then they were laughing.

'And what's more, I'll tell you," said Kate now: "you know Peggy Fowler who was married a few weeks gone?"

"Aye, yes."

"Well, she was after him, an' all. She even got through the window once and tidied up his place. Not that it was ever untidy; he keeps it neat and clean. But there she was with a meal on the table for him, brazen as brass. And what he told her must have acted like a dose of gunpowder up her nether regions, because she ran from the house crying her eyes out. And her brothers Johnny and Frank came at him the next day. But just to talk, because before he had that knife in his ribs he was as good a wrestler as you'll find for many a mile."

"Hal, a wrestler?"

"Yes, lass, Hal a wrestler. The only thing you know about Hal is that on sight of you, he draws a sword and you reply with a sledge-hammer."

"Oh, Kate, Kate."

"Oh, thinkin' of Hal." Kate put her hand to her head now. "I wonder what he'll say when he comes back?"

"What about?"

"Oh, well, lass" – Kate rose from the cracket – "it should happen this mornin' first thing. You see, you comin' in like you did just now had taken it out of me head. But John Tollett an' Will Campbell were on their way to the mill. They came over the quarry, and there, not a couple of feet from where the grave was opened, on the only big tree standin', because they chopped and hoiked all the others up to find the place, well, on that one big tree, as I said, was Pat Feeler. He had hung himself. He was like a scarecrow, they said. He must have been livin' rough all this time an' things had got too bad for him, 'cos there he was, danglin'. Well, there's one good thing I can say for that, it'll stop Hal's roamin', because he hasn't had a good night's sleep since it all happened. I don't know how he's carried on."

"Hung himself? How awful!"

"No more awful, lass, than the one he buried. And there was the other one that sent my lad across the water. Oh no, not awful. A rightful end I would say. Justice will out. Aye, justice will out. But I wonder how Hal will take it? Because he himself wanted to finish him off and now he's been baulked. Aye well, we'll soon know, at least when he comes back from the town."

15

Mary Ellen had worked all day. She had cleaned up the room as it hadn't been cleaned for a long time. She had climbed the ladder and crawled under the rafters and stripped the bed on which Roddy had lain for years, and only with a stern admonition had she stopped herself from throwing herself down on to it and once again giving ease to the pain in her heart, which had been deepened by the treatment she had received from the Davisons and her father. But even feeling like this, there was, nevertheless, some small part of her that, in a strange way, was at peace for she felt she had found a real home and she was about to learn a business.

This proposition of Kate's had excited her. She knew she'd never be wise like Kate, but she also knew she had a good memory and was quick at picking things up, and, with more writing practice, she would be able to stick labels on the bottles, unlike Kate who recognized them only by their colour, taste, and smell.

That was what had always been nice and attractive about Kate's cottage, the smell. It was a soothing smell. Kate said it was mostly from the calf's snout that hung from the beams in the room. She herself had always thought it an awful name for such a nice plant; she liked its other name of snapdragon better. Yet, when you looked at the top of the flower, that's what it appeared like, a calf's snout. She had a lot to learn and she had begun already. She had wanted, late in the afternoon, to go out and start on the garden, but Kate said, "Are you daft, girl? You start tidyin' that place up at this time of the year and there goes our wages for the winter and a couple more to come." And she smiled and nodded at the old woman as she said, "Yes, of course, of course."

And so the day had passed, and now the fire was blazing in the hearth. Three tallow candles in their brass candlesticks stood in a row down the middle of the table and as Kate had said it was never too late to start, she had brought six jars from the shelves and had just placed them on the table when there was a rat-tat on the door and at the same time it was pushed open, and Hal entered. He was carrying a sack over his shoulder and in his other hand he held a parcel that looked like a long box. Mary Ellen moved from the table and went over to the fire while Kate rose from her chair, saying, "Well, well! What brings you at this time of night laden like a pack-horse? Robbed a coach?"

"Aye, in a way, yes, Kate, you could say that."

He walked slowly towards the table before dropping the sack from his back, and the sound it made as it hit the floor was like a jingle of tools. The long parcel he placed gently on the table, and then, leaning slightly forward, he peered to where Mary Ellen was sitting on the clippy mat, reaching out to retract something from the ashes. "What ... what are you doing here? It's Tuesday," he said.

When Mary Ellen made no reply he glanced at Kate, and she said, "Get yourself off your feet."

He didn't sit down but widened his eyes questioningly at her as he nodded towards Mary Ellen, who seemed to remain quite unaware of his presence, for she continued to poke at the ashes with a small rake.

That he was perplexed by Mary Ellen's presence was shown by the hunching of his shoulders before he gently pushed the long wrapped parcel along the table towards Kate, saying, " 'Tis for you."

"What is it?"

"Well, open it and see."

As she attempted to undo the cord she said, "Aw, you might as well tell me to unknot a ship's hawser. I can't get me fingers through those knots."

"Give it here." He undid the knots, pulled off the paper, opened the top of the box, then, placing it on the floor, he pointed into the box, saying, "Now do you think you can lift that out?" And Kate, bending over it, thrust her two hands into it, then paused and looked up at him before bringing into view a glass shade. But when her hands began to tremble, he said, "Here, give it to me, woman." And, taking it from her, he revealed a tall fancy lantern with rose-coloured glass sides.

After setting it on the table, he stood back and, looking at her, said, "There, that'll give you a bonny light, 'cos look, it has sockets for three candles." And he turned quickly towards the fire and, stripping a sliver of wood from one of the logs stacked to the side, he thrust it into the blazing embers, at the same time glancing towards Mary Ellen who still did not acknowledge his presence in any way.

A minute later the room was illuminated with a soft light that brought a low muttering sound of delight from Kate and caused Mary Ellen to turn towards the table.

"Ah, lad, what made you think of that?"

"Oh, I've thought of it for a long time, 'cos I knew you were lying when you said you didn't want a candle lamp and preferred those." He pointed to the fluttering tapers of the tallow candles. "Now," he said, "I'm hungry and starved inside and out. I've never had a bite since dinner-time, then not much. So I'm going to sit meself down opposite this young person here, who I've never seen in me life afore, and ask her her name and what she's doing here at this time of night!"

"Aye, sit down, Hal. Sit down." Kate said, and the tone of her voice silenced his jesting.

He sat down, after pulling a chair towards the fire opposite where Mary Ellen was once again poking at the ashes. And now, Kate, taking her seat to the side of Mary Ellen, put out her hand and placed it on the girl's head while she looked at Hal, saying, "The top and bottom of it is, she's in a bit of trouble, an' she was turned out of her job, and from her father's house, an' all."

There was silence in the room; then not only did Kate look at him, but Mary Ellen too, as he repeated quietly, "A bit of trouble . . . that kind of trouble?"

"Aye, Hal, that kind of trouble, as you say, that kind of trouble."

He did not speak as he rose to his feet, nor whilst he stood for a moment staring down into Mary Ellen's firelit face; but then, going to the table, he brought his fist so hard down on the edge of it that the candle lamp jumped and he had to thrust his hand out to steady it. And his voice a loud bark now, he said, "Damn him to hell's flames!" at the same time swinging round towards Mary Ellen who had pulled herself to her feet. "The rotten bugger!" he said. "And you're nothin' but a weak-minded silly little bitch to let him."

Now she was yelling back at him, "*Shut up! you. Shut up!* You know nothing about it. 'Twasn't his fault."

"*Oh, my God!*" He put his two hands up to his head and ran his fingers through his hair, making it seem to stand on end as he spoke now directly to Kate, crying, "Did you hear what she said? Even the simplest of them, that dotty one who goes round the market place laughing, if it had happened to her even she wouldn't have said it wasn't the man's fault. God Almighty!" He now swung himself round to face Mary Ellen again. "Have you been knocked silly, stupid or somethin'? You're standin' there tellin' me that it was you who took him down? You got him into the grass and had your way with him? He hadn't a chance. *Oh, you. You.*"

She had promised herself her crying was over, but once again the tears were running down her face, and the sight of them brought his head deep on to his chest and his voice muttering low now: "I'm sorry," he said; "I'm sorry. But, oh God, Mary Ellen, to let that happen to you. He wasn't worth it." And he turned from her now, beating one fist into the palm of the other hand. "If I had him here this minute I'd do for him. I would. I swear on it, I'd do for him."

These words seemed to be a cue for Kate to take over once again, and she said, "Well now, he's not here, so you can't do for him. But I've some news for you. Talking of doing for anybody, they found Feeler hanging on the quarry top this mornin'. You had gone to the town afore the news got about."

She watched him straighten his back and take a deep breath; then turning fully to face her, he said, "I could have told you that, Kate, and around towards dawn."

"What d'you mean?"

"Just that I hung him there, or at least I saw that he did it himself. I gave him two choices: either I do it and I'd do it slow, or he could do it himself and make a quick job of it."

When Mary Ellen made a sound as if she was going to be sick, they both turned towards her, and Kate, going quickly to her, pressed her down into a chair, saying, "Now, now. Now, now. He had it comin' to him." But Mary Ellen didn't answer; she turned her gaze on to Hal and for a moment she didn't see him as he was, but his body seemed to fill the room, his eyes to look like pieces of glinting coal; and when he took a step in her direction she shrank back against the chair.

"What are you cringing for? I only did what the authorities would have done if they had got him. But I promised meself this right from the start, this was my due. Now I can breathe again." He bent towards her now, his face almost on a level with hers as he asked her, "Do you think he had any pity on me father when he killed him and buried him? All right, it could have been on Bannaman's orders, but he did it. And how many others, God alone knows, because, besides Les Carter, how many others had they done for? Likely they didn't stick to these parts, but roamed wide. So don't become weak bellied because I've done a justice." He straightened up now and turned to Kate, saying, "They never found the money my da was supposed to steal, did they Kate?'

"No, never a penny."

"Well" – his voice had a light note to it now – "there's some justice left in the world, because I found it, at least Feeler did. He must have come upon it looking for a hide-out, because if he'd known of it afore it wouldn't have been there now. And 'tis strange how it came about. Do you know he was on our doorstep all along, all these months. He's been not five minutes walk from here. And there was me ridin' miles away lookin' for him. But the night afore last I was takin' a short cut with me pony across the moor, because I was due to go into me shift, an' there, in the distance, I saw what was like a whiff of mist risin' out of the ground. I went over to have a closer look. It was just on dark and I found I was standing near the end of the blocked up tunnel. You know, you told me they came up against a snag with one of the first tunnels they made to take away the smell, and in later times they cut through it when they dug the quarry out. Anyway, I traced the mound back right to the top of the quarry where I guessed the entrance was. And I was about to make me way down the bank when I saw a parcel hidden in the scrub. Somebody was supplying him with food, likely his wife or daughter. So, I gave meself the pleasure of takin' it to him. Being crafty, he had lit his fire at the far end of the tunnel, a good fifty yards in, but his stores and this—" He now darted round the table and, lifting up the sack, dropped it at Kate's feet, and repeating, "And this was just inside." He now tipped the sack upside down, and there spewed on to the floor small clinking bags and the big black bag which was now in two pieces. And pointing a trembling finger downwards, he said, "He had each of those bags of sovereigns arrayed like soldiers, spaced along the wall. They had all been opened and counted and tied up again except one, and it had four sovereigns less than the others in it . . . Well, he must have seen the light of me lantern, and I had to go in and drag him forward. But even until his last breath he kept denying that he had known where the money was.

He must have had it stacked away all these years but dipped into it lately."

"*He hadn't. He hadn't.*"

They both looked to where Mary Ellen was standing, gasping as if she had just come running into the house. And she gabbled now, "He knew nothin' about it. Not . . . not where it was. I . . . I put it there."

"You put it there?" Hal was standing in front of her, close to her, and when he went to put his hand on her arm, she thrust him from her. And now flopping back into the chair, she said, "I found the bag in the bog the dry summer. Your father must have thrown it into the bushes when they chased him. That's how I've worked it out since. And it fell into the bog and sank, and when it dried up, the bog, I saw the handle sticking out. 'Twas" – she gave her head a shake before going on – " 'twas on the Sunday you and Roddy had your first row and rolled fighting on the grass. I . . . I had come across the tunnel when I was blaeberrying, and so I . . . I put it in there, and I was going to tell Roddy, but I got vexed with him. I was afraid to tell me da because he had forbidden me to go near the bog. Anyway, in a short time I forgot about it. But I've thought about it now and again over the years. It got more difficult to tell because they would ask . . . the authorities, why I hadn't brought it to light afore now."

Her head now drooped onto her chest, and when she raised it again, both Kate and Hal were seated opposite to her, staring at her in amazement. And it was Kate who said, "All these years, girl, you've kept this to yourself. Don't . . . don't you realize it would have cleared Hal's father if you had brought it out into the open?"

"I . . . I didn't link it up with your father." She was looking straight at Hal. "Only in after years did I realize what that little man was looking for." She stopped now and closed her eyes for a moment while she recalled what had happened to the little man, and who had caused it to happen, and she seemed to have difficulty in going on, for her voice was low and her words disjointed as she said, "It went out . . . out of my mind for years. Me . . . me da always said money caused trouble; I didn't want to cause trouble. And then when I began to put two and two together, I was too frightened to mention it. Anyway, the damage was done. Both you and Roddy, I thought, had got over losing your fathers. And you, Kate" – she was nodding wildly now at Kate – "you were always saying, let the dead bury the dead. So I didn't bring it up. Anyway I wonder somebody didn't come across it afore now. 'Twas likely 'cos of the falls the bairns didn't go there."

"Oh, Mary Ellen." Hal's tone was quiet and soft and the fact that he wasn't going to go for her made her see him in a different light. But only for a moment, for he said now, "Well, you did one good thing anyway: keeping your tongue quiet, you've given me a little fortune to start a new life."

"*You're not goin' to keep it?*"

"I'm not goin' to keep it? What do you think I'm gona do with it?"

"Well" – she looked from him to Kate, then back to him again – "give it to the owners. It was the money for the pay."

"Look, Mary Ellen" – his tone was recognizable again – "what would happen if the morrow mornin' I went down to that office and said, there's the money that you accused me da of takin' over thirteen years since. You know what would happen? They would say, thank you very much, Mr Roystan, and that would be that. It would go into the company and would be swallowed up like a drop in the ocean. Do you know what that company's worth, The Greenwich Hospital lot? Millions. Millions and millions, to the guess; they don't know the extent of their own wealth, they've got their fingers in so many pies. You must think me a dud, Mary Ellen."

" 'Tisn't your money."

" 'Tis my money." He was standing over her now. "Every rotten sovereign of it is my money: I starved as a lad; I was hounded; Kate here was my only friend; some of them would have lynched me at that time, because they had to wait for their pay till another assignment was sent through. I tell you, I've earned every penny of that two hundred and twenty-one sovereigns. No, Mary Ellen, that money is gona get me out of that hell hole. I'm no longer goin' to be a smelter." Now he thumbed his chest as he added, "Already I can feel a tightening here; it's been worse since I got the knife in me ribs. Oh, no, no, it's not gona get me; I've had enough. There's a little farm I've got me eye on. I think I've had me eye on it for years. Like one does on seeing a mirage down the pit: if something drops on your head an' you're not completely knocked out you see things. Twice it happened to me as a lad and twice I saw the same thing, a great open sky with a house in the middle of it. Well, there's open land enough there and a little well-built house in the middle of it. And the old Douglas couple are on their last legs. It hasn't come up on the market yet, an' of course it's rented, but the way things are at the moment on the land, I don't think there'll be many after it when they go...."

"But lad," Kate interrupted his flow, "won't they wonder where you got the money?"

"No, Kate, no. I'm a wily one at bottom. I've thought everything out and it's fitted in beautifully. Remember when I had to go to the company to be compensated, you remember? You were the only one I told what I got, twenty-one pounds, two shillings, equal to me da's full year's pay. And you would have thought they were giving me silver nuggets from a year's lead draining. Well, when I got back, as you can imagine, there was a lot of the men chippin' me. No one asks you outright, you know, Kate, just hints, and so I hinted back and helped them with their guessing. In the end they were guessing into hundreds and I've let them go on guessing. I must have been forearmed in a way."

"But the company'll know what they gave you, lad, and that that amount wouldn't set you up on your feet and stock a farm."

"I'm away ahead of you, Kate, I'm away ahead of you. I've got it all worked out. I have always saved up and with the help of the seven pounds that old Abel left me, and not having a wife" – he slanted his eyes towards Mary Ellen – "nor chick nor child on the side to support, I can go to the bank an' say, 'There's forty pounds; I want to rent a farm. Would you let me have a loan to add to it to buy stock?' And they will. They will. And they'll charge me interest, they always do, but within two years, I'll have supposedly made enough profit – whether I do or not – to pay them back. And within another two years me stock will have improved and from then on I'll gallop ahead, much as Bannaman did on stolen money. Funny, isn't it, Kate? Funny."

"You think you're clever, don't you?" The whispered hiss came from the area of the fireplace, and immediately he rounded on Mary Ellen, crying, "Aye, I do, cleverer than the next, because I use me head, not like some bloody fools." He was glaring at her now. Then as if there had been no talk about hanging, or money, or farms, he demanded, "Does he know?"

"No, and he's not going to."

"We'll see about that. Oh, we'll see about that."

She sprang from the seat and actually gripped his hand in both of hers, pleading with him now, "Hal. Oh, please, please. No, I don't want that. You mustn't. Oh, don't don't, Hal. I've . . . I've never asked anything of you 'cos we're" – she gulped – "well, do this for me, will you? Don't, don't tell him."

As he looked at her face in the lamplight the expression on his own softened, and he said in a more moderate tone, "What if somebody else tells him?"

"Oh, that's a slim chance." They both turned and glanced at Kate, and she nodded as she added, "All those hundreds of miles away. Do as she asks. 'Tis better so. There's no happiness comes out of a trap whether it's on man or beast."

He turned away from them both, muttering now, "He should be made to face it, not leave her on her own like this."

"She's not on her own, Hal. She has me . . . and she has you, hasn't she?'

His head jerked, and he looked at her hard before emitting a mirthless "Huh!" Then turning slowly, he looked at Mary Ellen again and said, "She would rather have the devil on her side than me. Isn't that so, Mary Ellen?"

She didn't answer, but her lips quivered and moved over each other. Her head sank on to her chest; then she slid from the chair onto the rug and took up the hook and began scraping the nuts towards the end of the hearth. But when one that had been in the flames burst its shell and shot out with a crack on to the mat beside her, Hal laughed and said, "That's her answer, Kate, isn't it Mary Ellen? The nut's spoken for her. She would rather be shot than have me on her side. . . . So be it."

16

The winter started hard. The light of the day was short and the darkness
of night long. For the first few weeks lying on the attic bed sleep would
evade her, but now the heaviness of her body and the work of the day
began to tell, and she soon had no trouble in falling asleep.

There was no more rising at five o'clock. She climbed down the ladder
at seven, stirred up the fire, heated up one of Kate's winter concoctions
and took a mug full of it to the bed for her, and a smaller portion for
herself.

Kate was very rarely asleep, and so she would sit on the edge of the
bed but would say nothing until Kate had drained her mug. Then she
would enquire how she felt and after would listen to her planning out the
day for them both, saying perhaps, " 'Tis Sunday, so Will Campbell will
be here afore his clothes are on like as not. Now his potion is the
groundsel. You know, you learned last week its two different uses: if it's
boiled with ale and vinegar and a drop of honey in it, it'll bring up the
vomit in the case of children havin' chewed the wrong berries an'
poisoned their stomachs; but the leaves now, as you will remember,
boiled in a drop of water ... or wine, parsnip or tatie I usually have
plenty of, but the fruit ones I'm sparin' of. I've told Will for a long time
that he wouldn't have such a sour stomach if he went straight home on a
Saturday an' didn't sit in the inn swilling; his innards are not made for
what he puts into them."

Or perhaps she would say, " 'Tis Friday. Jane Stubbs will be passing
on her way to Haydon Bridge for her flour and grains and such. Now
she'll want the same as usual, colewort. I've never seen such a family for
carbuncles. As I've told her afore, it's too much fat. They have three
stints and are overrun with pigs. They live on pork the lot of them, an'
fat's got to erupt somewhere, and it does, mostly on one end or the
other, the neck or the backside."

The first time Kate talked of Jane Stubbs and the carbuncles, she
laughed and said, "But by! she's gona get a shock when she next puts her
nose in that door. A penny? I'll say. Oh no, Jane, a penny's no good. If
you want this salve that'll draw nails out of the walls, an' takes me a full
day to gather and make, it's threepence you'll have to pay in the future.
I've got to live."

And so it would go on.

When the prices for the potions and salves went up, Kate's clientele thinned to a mere trickle. But that didn't disturb her. They'll be back, she would say; they'll be back. And she was right. For now with the winter on them and people coughing and sneezing and pains in backs and arms increasing, never a day went by but that there was somebody at the door. And one notable Saturday they had as many as ten visitors and their takings for the one day were four and threepence. As Kate said, she had never made as much as that in a week as far as she could remember.

During Mary Ellen's first weeks in the house the number of male customers seemed to increase, and eventually led to Hal's coming to blows with one of them. This upset Mary Ellen but brought only a cynical comment from Kate.

This particular young fellow was a well-known patron of Maggie Oates, and Hal, coming on him standing in the kitchen grinning, asked him what he was after.

"Same as you, a potion," the young fellow had replied. "Aye well," Hal had answered, "you're a mile or so out for the potion you're after." And the fellow, on a laugh, said, "Aye well, that be as it may; I mightn't have to travel so far in the future."

In a lightning jump Hal had him by the collar and through the door and into the garden. And just as quickly the implication of the man's words struck Mary Ellen and made her turn and climb the ladder and hide herself under the eaves.

"Come down here this minute, girl!" Kate yelled. "You'll have to put up with worse than that afore you're much older." And when she had descended the ladder and stood, her head bowed before Kate, the old woman had put her hand kindly on her shoulder saying, "We won't be troubled with that kind again; Hal's put a stop to it. But he'll likely have to stand the racket for doing so."

And this further implication was not lost on Mary Ellen, who couldn't bear to look at Hal when he returned to the room with a split lip and said on a shaky laugh, "Can I have a potion for a busted mouth, Mrs Makepeace?"

But now it was December and the child was seven months heavy within her. She was carrying high and her whole appearance had altered; she no longer looked a young girl, but a woman. Her prettiness had vanished, her face, at times appeared plain; and there was always a sadness in the back of her eyes, which even her laughter didn't dispel. What was more, as her time approached, she felt less well. The chores of the day became much harder to get through, although all the heavy ones had been taken from her, because Hal now came at least two or three times a week and chopped wood and dug peat and brought in whatever they needed from the town.

Hal's life had altered out of all proportion even to his dreams. He hadn't got the Douglas's plot, but had rented, through the courtesy of his employer, Barley Moor Farm. It was situated two miles to the west of Kate's cottage. It had eighteen acres of land and four stints.

Attached to the land was a brick and tile works, and he had been very tempted to rent this too. But the rent would have been forty-eight pounds and four pence a year, and had he succumbed to the desire to take it on it would undoubtedly have caused comment, not only among the neighbours but more so in the firm. However, he kept the idea in the back of his mind, and was happy, more than happy to be a tenant in a house that had a parlour, a kitchen with a stone-flagged cupboard and two real bedrooms up above. Outside was a cow-byre that would hold seven head of cattle with a fine hayloft, a piggery, and a coal-house; and lastly a privy. There was also a vegetable garden.

The furniture he had brought from Abel Hamilton's cottage was scanty, but he had added to it over the past months by attending house sales. Moreover, he had three cows in the byre, a pony in the stable, a pig lying with litter, a dozen hens, and four ducks. At times, as he made his way in the evening to Kate's cottage he would strut over the moor, so good did he feel. But always on approaching the cottage he would put on the cloak of casualness, and when relating his progress to Kate's willing ears, he'd be offhand: Oh, yes, things were going fine, slowly, but fine. Well, wasn't the milk in the can proof that his cows weren't dry.

So altered was his life that often he found it difficult to recall that it had ever been otherwise; except when he looked across to the hill rising above Carts Bog, beyond which was Bannaman's farm. That house seemed to stand out as the only connection with the years behind him.

Both Kate and Mary Ellen showed no surprise when the door was pushed open early on a Tuesday morning and he came in as usual carrying something. He put the lidded can of milk on the table; then dropping a sack onto the stone floor, he said, "Them's turnips. Farmer Gordon kindly dropped me in a load yesterday. Oh, the goodness of people." There was a mocking tone in his voice now. "He only wanted a couple of days work out of me in payment, put over nicely of course, Neighbourly help, he called it, neighbourly help. I could have bought the load for a shilling. Anyway, what d'you want in the town, I'm on me way? There's a sale on and I'm goin' after a young bull."

"Bull?" Mary Ellen and Kate exclaimed simultaneously.

"Aye, a bull. You know, a bull." He demonstrated as if he were charging, and they both laughed and Kate said, "All right, all right. You've explained what a bull is." Then she added, "What d'you think we need, Mary Ellen?"

And Mary Ellen, looking at Hal, said, "We've got a stock of flour and sugar, but I think we should add to it just in case. And if you should come across a bit of live yeast, I'd be grateful. And a bit of barley to make some white puddin'."

"Do you want anything fancy for Christmas?" His voice sounded quiet; and Kate came back, laughing: "Aye, get me a new pair of legs, will you?"

"I'll do that," he nodded seriously at her; "what size? Had I better measure them?" And he made to lift her skirt.

165

"Go on with you!" She flapped her hand at him.

Mary Ellen now said, "You can get me some wool if you wouldn't mind going for it?"

"No, I don't mind going for it. I told them last time I'd taken up knittin'."

Again they were laughing; and Kate said, "I've known stranger things. Why, there's Ben Holt – he works in the mines at Allenheads – they tell me he sews. Aye, and better than most women, smocking and the like, and makes banners with silk threads. So you needn't be ashamed to tell them you're knittin', lad. And you might make a name for yourself by it, quicker than at farmin'."

"Now, what d'you mean by that? I'm not doin' badly, although I say it meself." '

"No, no, you're not. I'll give you that. What you killin' for Christmas, a pig?"

"Aye, a pig." He pulled his coat round him, then buttoning up the top button tight under his chin, he asked casually, "Any news?"

Neither Kate nor Mary Ellen answered, and he turned for the door, saying, "Well, there's still plenty of time, I suppose. Be seeing you."

It was some seconds after the door had closed on him that Kate said, "It doesn't mean that if we've had no word that he isn't comin'; he could just pop in the door any time next week."

Mary Ellen rolled up her sleeves, at the same time kicking a felt pad towards the bucket of steaming water, then knelt on the pad, saying, "I've told you, Kate, but you won't believe me, that I hope he doesn't come. I . . . I don't want to see him. Not like this, Kate, not like this. I'm not goin' to hold this over him now or ever. Funny." She knelt back on her heel, hands on the rim of the bucket, and she looked into the distance as she went on, "I would have sold me soul, as the sayin' goes, to get him to marry me afore this happened, and the possibility of him asking me seemed to be forever wavering between us. But now, if he asked me, well, I wouldn't do it . . . marry him, 'cos then it would be like a gun at his head and forever after."

"You would change your tune if he asked you. And ask you he will when he sees the pickle he left you in, or its result."

"You think I'm that weak, Kate?"

"No, lass, I don't think you're weak at all, far from it, but strength of will has no chance against the business the heart gets up to. And if you're that strong, you can ask your heart what it feels, and how it'll feel when you clap eyes on him. And I know what the answer'll be. So get on with the floor, lass."

And Mary Ellen got on with the floor; and while she scrubbed at the stone slabs, she thought, She's right, she's right. How many times of late had she imagined him walking through the door there, then coming to a dead stop at the sight of her, knowing without a fraction of a doubt that he was the cause of this great ugly bulge in her body. But she did not think of the life under the bulge as ugly; her thoughts for it were tender, full of longing to see it, to hold it.

When Kate gave a slight groan, she stopped her scrubbing and looked up; then drying her hands quickly on her coarse apron, she rose and went to the old woman who had now seated herself in the chair to the side of the fire, and bending over she said, "That pain again?"

"Aye."

"Will I give you the usual ... marjoram?"

"Aye, I suppose so. No; I tell you what, I'll have a drop of groundsel."

"Groundsel? But I thought that was for making you vomit after poison and stuff."

"Aye, it does; but a wee drop is good for stomach pain, especially the choler. Bring the jar."

After Kate had poured herself out a small potion from the jar and had drunk it, she grimaced and said, "Well, if that doesn't work, nothing will." Then she went on. "Hand me me tin from the box."

Mary Ellen dutifully brought the tin from a large black box that stood under the shelves that held the bottles and jars and, when Kate opened it Mary Ellen looked down on what looked like the thin slivers of sweets that could be bought in the candy shop in the market. And she said just that: "They look like candy sweets, Kate."

"Aye, but with a difference. Eat a fistful of these and you'd be as merry as a monk after a fast. There's great comfort in this rosemary sugar, and we'll have some come Christmas. I made these at the beginning of the year for a special occasion. Tell you the truth" – she looked away and across the room – "it was when I had that feelin' on me that I told you of that my lad would walk in the door. Still" – she smiled now – "we'll leave some just in case. Oh, there are lots of things in the big box you've got to learn, Mary Ellen. But then you haven't done too badly. No, not at all. And they're beginning to respect you, the men, I can see that."

"When they're not leerin'?"

"Oh, take no notice of that. Anyway, 'tis but one or two of the dimwits an' them without a wife."

"What about the wives? You said yourself, you've never had so many women since your son was born."

"Aye, 'tis true. But they got short shrift, and it's only me regulars show their faces now. Anyway, human beings are like cattle. Oh! no, they're not. I always question that sayin' an' chide meself for it, because some cattle are more sensible and cleaner than some folks that I could name, an' not a mile away at that. Still, everybody must live their own life, as I keep tellin' you, girl. So finish your floor, then get the peat in, and I'll tell you what" – she smiled conspiratorially – "then we'll settle down and I'll take you through the big box."

So Mary Ellen finished scrubbing the stone floor, then laid sacks over the front part to take the tread of dirty feet, after which she brought in armful after armful of peat and stacked it up at each side of the fireplace. When this was done, she sat down on the bench by Kate's side, the box between them, and so learned more about the mystery and use of herbs and potions. And yet all the while she was asking herself what she would say or do should Roddy come in that door.

She need not have worried herself on this score, for when Hal returned that evening he brought them a letter. It had been delivered by the coach to the office in Hexham, together with the mail for the agent at the mill, and it was picked up by a clerk who, knowing Hal, said, "Would you like to take a letter I have here for Mrs Makepeace?"

On entering the room he didn't hand the letter to Kate but held it in his hand and said, "I've got a letter here for you."

"Aye, you have. Well, where's it from?"

"London."

"Oh, London." Her voice was flat as she said, "Well, get on with it."

He opened it; then looking at Mary Ellen who was sitting at the table rubbing brittle leaves between her fingers, he asked quietly, "Would you like to read it?"

"No." She shook her head, but she stopped what she was doing and stared at him and waited. And he began,

"Dear Kate,
    'Tis sorry I am to have to write these few lines, and disappointed I am too, but I will not be able to manage the journey home for Christmas. Perhaps it is selfish of me but I'm sure you will understand when I tell you that I have been invited to accompany Mr Cottle over to Paris in France to see an exhibition of paintings.
    It is a chance that I never dreamed of, and if I had been with you, you would have said, take it, 'cos chances like that won't come very often in your lifetime. So I know you will understand, Kate. I shall miss seeing you, but come the Spring I will be home. I send you my warm affection.

As always,
Roddy."

When Hal finished reading he looked towards Kate and repeated, "I send you my warm affection. As always, Roddy. No: Give my regards to Hal, and of course he wouldn't think of Mary Ellen. No, of course not." And saying this, he turned to look at her. But she was already rising from the chair, and as she hurried up the room towards the ladder, his voice came at her, crying, "Don't be so thin-skinned and daft. I knew he wouldn't turn up. And you in your heart knew it. He's gone. He's gone for good. Kate here knows it. So you make your mind up to it an' all."

"I'll make me mind up to whatever I think fit. And I won't ask your opinion of it. You never change: you keep on and on, nigglin', nigglin'. Oh, you!" And she began to climb the ladder, lumbering, and when her legs disappeared through the hatchway he walked quietly to the settle and, sitting down beside Kate, he said, "We don't change, do we?"

"You ask for what you get, lad. You should leave her alone on that quarter."

"He's a swine, a selfish swine. I've said it afore, and I'll say it again." His voice was low but his words were thick and deep. "He's already grown too big for his boots. If we ever see him again I'll be surprised. And you know it in your heart, don't you?" He pushed her arm gently, and she answered quietly, "He'll be back, sometime he'll be back, if not out of affection, out of pride, because he'll want to show all around how he's got on. And he'll get on." She now turned and looked fully at Hal. "He'll rise. He means to. And he must be fittin' in with his new friends or they wouldn't have put up with him this long."

"Perhaps it isn't the male but the female friend that is puttin' up with him."

"You think that?"

"Aye, I do, not only think it, but I'm sure of it. That madam that came along here with him that day, she might have considered herself too young for her husband but not too old for him. Women of that age like them young, especially if they're tied to a fading man, and from what you've told me he must have been sixty if he was a day. Oh aye, our Roddy will get on, but he'll have to pay for it, 'cos a woman like that will demand the last ounce of him."

Kate stared at him through her narrowed bloodshot eyes for some seconds before she said, "You seem to have learned a lot about women, Hal."

"Enough, enough." He nodded at her before picking up the poker and stirring the fire into a blaze.

"Then why don't you use different tactics on...?" She jerked her head towards the ceiling.

"Why should I? It wouldn't make any difference." He stabbed the poker into the heart of the fire now and stirred it round. "She'll come to like me when the devil likes holy water. Oh, there's no hope in that quarter."

"But you'd like hope in that quarter, wouldn't you, Hal?"

"Me" – he screwed up his face at her – "and Mary Ellen?" He now jerked his head towards the ceiling. "You must be daft, Kate. Now, if you had said Maggie Oates, there might be some chance."

He laughed, and she joined in with a croak, adding now, "Aw, there's too much competition in that quarter; you'd be just as unlucky there."

"Well, there's one place I'm not unlucky and that's on the farm. Aw, Kate, I wish you could see it. Look, I'm going to bring the cart over some day if we have a break in the weather and I'll take you across. You won't believe how I've got that little house now."

"What for? To live there on your own?"

"Suits me."

"Don't be silly, man. If you can't go one road, go the other. Take a lass, take a wife. There's plenty that will be willin'."

"Oh aye. They're fallin' over their feet to get at me, I'm havin' to dodge 'em."

"Go on, get yourself off home."

"Yes, that's where I'm goin', home. 'Tis the first real home I've had, Kate. Do you realize that? Abel's place wasn't a home, merely a shelter. Ah, well, good-night. I'll pop over the morrow, or soon anyway."

"Wait a minute. Did you get your bull?"

"No, I didn't get me bull."

"Why not? Weren't there any there?"

"Aye, there were three, but even a lonely cow wouldn't have looked at the side they were on. Fit for the hammer, poor devils, that's all they were. But I'll get me bull and one me lasses will trip over to get at. I usually get what I want in the end. Good-night, Kate."

"Good-night, Hal."

Kate screwed her body round and stared into the fire, muttering aloud, "I wonder. I wonder if you'll always get what you want."

17

The weather was changeable: there were no heavy falls of snow, only hail, sleet, rain and wind; then days when the whole world seemed to be covered with glass.

Mary Ellen had prepared for such emergencies. Both sides of the cottage door she had piled high with wood and peat, and she had a good stock of pulses in and flour and fat.

The child was not due until early February, but just before Christmas the feeling of dragging tiredness turned to a feeling of illness. This seemed to have started after she had experienced that unpleasant incident.

It had been raining without let up for three days and nights. Every place seemed to be awash with mud. Kate, who had taken to her bed a week before, unable to go about any longer because of the pain in her stomach and refusing to let Hal fetch a doctor, said to Mary Ellen on this particular morning, "I've never seen rain keep up like this for years. What does it look like at the bottom of the garden?"

"I can't see much down there for water," Mary Ellen told her.

"Well, if that's the case, the ditch is stopped up. One year we had it coming into the kitchen here and my Davey made a drain down there. It's never been blocked up for years, but if it's blocked now it needs clearin'. How far is the flooding from the front step?"

"Oh, not half-way up the garden."

"'Tis more than enough. Another day of this and, I tell you, we'll have it inside. When Hal comes, get him to clear it."

"That won't be till later on," said Mary Ellen; "he said he was going to Allendale the day. I'll go down and have a look at it meself."

Kate made no protest at this, but said, "There's a long rake in the wood house. Take that and poke it to the right of the gate, you know, where the drain is. There's likely stuff stuck on the grid."

Mary Ellen had already pulled on an old coat and tied a shawl around her head; now she got into a pair of working boots that were much too big for her, for they had once belonged to Roddy, and then went out.

It was the middle of the afternoon, but she could hardly see through the rain. Having found the rake she made her way down to the gate and began thrusting through the swirling water in an effort to find the drain. Within a few minutes the iron head of the rake struck the metal of the grid, but scrape as she might she couldn't dislodge it. And so, with an

171

impatient movement, she pulled up her sleeve and, bending awkwardly to the side, she thrust her hand down into the icy water, groped for the grid, then with a tug she cleared the obstruction, almost falling on her back as she did so.

Whilst standing looking down to where the flood water was now being sucked in a spiral down the drain, she was aware of figures approaching over the rise that connected with the road to Haydon Bridge. It wasn't anything unusual for people to take this short cut when making for the mill cottages, but because of the rain she hadn't been able to distinguish who they were. But now, as they came upon her, she saw that there were four men, two of whom she recognized, for they had been temporary visitors to Kate when she herself had first come to live here. And it was one of these, a thin faced, smallish man, who greeted her loudly, saying, "Why! hello there, Mary Ellen."

From the tone of his voice and the look on his face she recognized he had been drinking liberally of ale, as had the others, because they were all standing grinning at her now.

"How's it goin', Mary Ellen?" said one of the other men.

She didn't answer, but made to go past them to the gate. However, the man who had first spoken to her stopped her by thrusting out his arm and gripping the gate post and saying now, "On your time, aren't you, Mary Ellen."

"Let me past, Mr Smith," she said.

"Oh, what's your hurry, Mary Ellen? Eh, fellows, what's her hurry? Like to take a bet? Will it come out a big 'un with black hair, or a broad 'un with brown hair, eh? Like to take a bet?"

One of the men now said, "Come on, Nick, come on. Enough's enough."

"Enough? Couldn't get enough of Mary Ellen. Tried, didn't I? Tried. An' you know what? When this's over I hear she's settin' up house against Maggie. Well, she's got a better chance than Maggie of makin' a fortune, hasn't she? An' you know summat? I'm booked up to be her first customer. Aye, aren't I, Mary...?"

The rake in the left hand and the grid in the right, she'd had the greatest desire to swing the grid into the man's face, but instinct told her she might do him a great injury. Yet the insult wasn't to be borne, and so, flinging the rake and the grid to one side, she stooped and gathered up two handfuls of the clarts and swung them with force into her tormentor's face.

There were gasps from the other three men and a spluttering yell from the man Smith, for he'd had his mouth open and the mud had gone into it and down his throat. But it had covered only one eye, and now, like an infuriated beast, he came at her. His arm swung out and sent her flying, and she fell back on top of the drain that she had just cleared, her fall spraying more clarts over the man and bringing cries of, "God damn! you shouldn't have done that," from the others.

"Bloody bitch! Well, she asked for it," yelled Smith.

Two of the men heaved Mary Ellen to her feet. Her head was swimming; she was gasping for breath; her back was weighed down with the mud and water on her coat and shawl.

Thrusting off the men's hands she had staggered up the garden path, and once inside the cottage she stood leaning against the door aware that she would have to scrub it down afterwards to get the mud off.

Kate was resting on her elbow. She had pulled herself to the end of the bed. "What was all that out there?" she said. Age had taken toll of every part of her body except her ears, for her hearing was as keen as ever.

Mary Ellen did not reply because she couldn't, she was divesting herself of her mud-clotted clothes; and when she stood in her dress and her stockinged feet she still gave Kate no answer, but went into the scullery and washed the mud off her hands, then her face. And after doing this she stood, one hand gripping the shallow stone sink, the other tight across her open mouth, her head turned to the side as if away from the sight of something repulsive. When eventually her mouth closed she dropped her hands on to the mound of her stomach and there dizzied round in her mind the words: "Big 'un with black hair or a broad 'un with brown hair?"

That's what they were saying about her. And that man . . . those men, all of them, the village, the cottages all around, the farms, saying she would go like Maggie Oates.

Kate's voice, harsh, had brought her back into the kitchen, and she moved slowly towards her, and when Kate's bony hand clutched at her hand, pulling her down on to the side of the bed, she did not wait for Kate to ask for further explanations but said, "He . . . that Nick Smith, he named Hal or Roddy for givin' it me and he said, I'm . . . I'm goin' to be like Maggie . . . Maggie Oates, and he was goin' to . . . to be me first. . . ." Her head bowed on to her chest and the tears streamed down her face. And now Kate's arms came out and pulled her forward, holding her tightly but saying nothing for some minutes. Then patting her back, she remarked, "Why, you're wet, lass. Your frock's wet."

"He . . . he knocked me over."

"He *what?*"

"Well, because of what he said, I . . . I threw some clarts at him."

"You did right an' all. I would have choked him with them. And he knocked you down?"

"Yes, aye."

"Do you feel hurt?" The hands were moving over her now, and she replied, "Shaken like, shaken. I'll . . . I'll go upstairs and change me frock."

"Do that, lass. And look, I'm all right for the next hour or so. Lie on the bed and rest. After a fall like that you don't know what happens. So do what I tell you now, lie on the bed and rest."

Mary Ellen made no answer but rose from the bed and went up the ladder. Once under the roof she pulled off her dress; then dropping onto the pallet bed she pulled the cover over her and, turning lumberingly on to her side, she buried her face in the pillow to smother her sobs.

It was about an hour later when Hal came in. When he pushed open the door it stuck, and after having entered the room he looked down at the obstacle, the mud-covered coat and shawl, before hurrying to the bedside where Kate had propped herself upright in the bed, and demanding, "What's this? Why that lot there?"

"Sit yourself down."

"What is it? Where is she?"

"Be quiet. Don't raise your voice. She's upstairs and likely sound asleep. Pull up a chair."

When he was seated by the bedside she related to him what had happened and she ended, "Why, in the name of God, they should name you, I don't know."

He said nothing; nor did he when he rose from the chair, which caused her to ask anxiously, "Where you goin'?"

He still did not answer, until, her voice harsh and loud, she called, "Hal! Make no do about this."

He turned now and demanded, "Why did you tell me then, if you didn't want me to make a do about it?"

"I told you because you wanted an explanation, but not to stir up more trouble. Let it die its natural death."

"Aye, he will when I've finished with him."

"Hal!" She had pulled her legs over the side of the bed, but he was gone. And after resting a moment, she lay back, saying, "Oh my God! What now?"

He was back much sooner than she expected. In the dim light of the room he looked just the same; that was until he lit the lamp, when she could see that he, too, was bespattered with mud and that there was blood on his cheek. When she asked, "What happened?" he answered in exasperation, "What d'you mean, what happened?" And when she cried at him, "Don't be such a bull-headed bugger," he went up to the bed and, leaning over her, he said, "I called him out. He was sleeping it off, him and his brother. It was a good job there were two of them for I might have done for him on his own. I left them both something to remember, and I can promise you she'll have no trouble from that quarter again."

"Don't be so bloody soft, man. They'll have it in for her all the more now, and for you."

"Well, let them. There's decent fellas in the mill, an' friends of mine, they know the rights of the case, her case. They mightn't say much, but they feel for her. John Tollet and Will Campbell came out of their cottages and witnessed the whole thing, and I made no small mouth of what it was about. So they know what to expect if anybody gets fresh. But there's always a rotten apple in the barrel, you know, and the Smiths are it around here. Anyway, when did you eat last?"

"I'm not hungry, lad."

"Hungry or not, you want somethin'. Will I do you some gruel?"

"Aye, that would be nice, and for her an' all."

He made a pot of gruel and divided it in two bowls, and having put each on a wooden platter together with a spoon, he gave one to Kate before mounting the steep ladder, balancing the other wooden platter on one hand, conscious as he did so of this being the first time he had been up here.

From the glimmer in the room below he could just make out the huddled form lying on the plank bed. Slowly now, he made his way on his knees towards her. Then placing the platter on the floor, he tentatively put out his hand and touched her shoulder.

She did not respond immediately; and so he shook her gently, and then she gave a great start and a gasp and he said quickly, " 'Tis all right. 'Tis all right. I've brought you something hot."

"Ho . . . t?" She pulled the cover up under her chin, and he said, "Sit up and get this gruel."

"Gruel?"

"You haven't gone deaf, have you? That's what I said."

She blinked, then slowly turned on to her back, saying, "I . . . I must have fallen asleep."

"Aye, you did. Get this into you. It'll do you good."

"What time is it?"

"Oh, I don't know. Gettin' on four I think. But in no time this gruel will turn solid. Come on, sit up."

He watched her pulling herself upwards until she realized she had nothing on but her petticoat, when quickly she pulled the cover further up around her. And he made her more self-conscious of her action by turning on his knees and saying, " 'Tis all right, I'm on me way down. It's on the floor at your side there."

His body was half through the hatchway when she said quietly, "Hal."

"Aye?"

"Did Kate tell you?"

"Aye, she told me."

"She . . . she shouldn't have. . . . Hal."

"Aye, what is it?" Only his head was above the floor now.

"Don't do anything, will you?"

"Not any more. 'Tis done."

As he disappeared from her view she gasped and clutched her throat, then made to scramble from the bed, but checked herself. 'Tis done, he had said, and what was done was done and he had likely done it with his fists.

175

Slowly she leant over and picked up the platter, and, gratefully now, she drank the gruel from the bowl; and when it was empty, she lay back on the pillow and there came into her mind a thought: Would Roddy have gone after that man if he had been there? And the answer came: But if he had been there things would have been different, they would have been married.

It was after this that the feeling of illness came on her and she felt the child could be born any day. There was a pressure towards the bottom of her stomach and a nagging pain in her side, and overall she felt, as she put it, not right. There was also another worry in her mind, and it induced her to pay a visit in an effort to erase it.

On Christmas Eve, after talking it over with Kate, she made the journey to her father's cottage. There had been a light fall of snow but nothing to impede her walking. And as she approached she saw the smoke rising from the chimney, and there was evidence that he had been out for wood because of the churned snow outside the door. She had knocked twice and, having received no answer, she now called softly, "Da. Open the door. Please open the door. 'Tis me." When she still received no reply she took her fist and banged hard on the wood and shouted, "I've got some things here for you; I'm not here to ask anything of you, I'm well settled. Just open the door. 'Tis Christmas."

She waited. A gust of icy wind crept round her and she pulled her shawl tighter over her chest and shivered. The pain had started in her side again. She pressed her hand on it. Then, as she was about to turn away, his voice came muffled through the door, saying, "Get yourself away to where you came from. You know what I think. I don't want to see your face."

She had stood with her head buried deep on her chest for a moment, but she did not cry; instead, her teeth gritted against each other, and with an angry gesture she picked up the basket she had laid on the step and turned away.

Could that voice belong to her da? Was that the man who had loved her as a child? Yes, yes, it was one and the same, because he had been rigid in his rules even then.

Her feet were trailing when she entered the cottage, and Kate greeted her with, "It's no more than I expected. I'm sorry I advised you to go."

"I would have gone in any case," she said.

"He's a pig-headed swine of a man. Well, you've done your duty, lass. He'll be the one that suffers, not you. You need have nothing on your mind any more concerning him. Sit yourself down. There's nothing more to do; everything's ready for the morrow. You know, I thank God every day for Hal."

Mary Ellen went to the fire and held her hands out to the blaze, thinking, yes, she too should thank God for Hal. But somehow he still got her goat. It was his offhand manner, she supposed; and the way he ridiculed most things and capped everything she said either with something funny or sarcastic. She could never sit at peace in his company. Yet, what would they have done without him these past months; and more so at this time? Yes, she wished she could see him as Kate did.

Christmas Day, it rained but everything was warm and cosy in the cottage. Kate, miraculously was on her feet again, the pain in her stomach had seemed to ease. They had a good meal and they exchanged presents: socks and a muffler for Hal, a pound box of china tea for Kate, and a soft Shetland shawl for Mary Ellen. His gift had touched her greatly and she was warm in her thanks to him. Later, they sat round the fire and he even made her laugh spontaneously about his neighbour Farmer Gordon and his wife and three unmarried daughters, the latter all well into their thirties. He imitated the farmer's voice shouting for them, demonstrating by standing up, his stomach thrust out, and yelling, "You A! . . . B! and C!" and the women hastening to do his bidding. Apparently the eldest was called Annie, the second Bella, and the third Carrie. He said he had wanted ten of a family and he would name them after the alphabet; however, they stopped at three. And Hal said he treated them as he would a small squad of soldiers. His wife never spoke except with her thumb. Again he demonstrated, pointing his thumb to different corners of the room and ending, "I bet her thumb speaks in five different languages. It's bent right back like this . . . and it wobbles."

When Kate was able to get her breath again, she said, "There's a slate loose there. There was in his father afore him. He came down from Scotland and he wore a skirt, kilt they called it, and he used to march around Hexham market on fair days, his bum swinging like two pig's bladders. And the women used to go into fits. But his slate wasn't completely loose for he was a good farmer, at least when it came to bargaining. And this one is much the same I should say."

The darkness had set in when Hal made a move to go to see to his cattle, and Mary Ellen went to open the door for him in order to let him out quickly because a high wind was blowing. She stood with the sneck in her hand for a moment and looked at him through the candle-light, saying, "Thanks, Hal. 'Tis been a grand day."

His voice serious for once, he said, "It has that. I've enjoyed it. It's the best Christmas I've had for a long time, in fact, ever." Then he became silent for a moment while he stared at her before asking, "You all right?"

Her lips parted twice before she admitted, "Not so good at times."

"Do you know exactly?"

"Aye. It should be towards the end of January or early February. Kate says you never can be clear cut with . . . with a first." Her voice trailed off.

It was the first time they had discussed the matter openly; and now he said, "Take care. Have you seen about a midwife?"

"Mrs Patterson's comin' in from the mill cottages."

"Aye, well, she's a sensible woman and has a squad of her own. Anyway, I'll be over every day."

"Thanks, Hal."

"You're welcome. You're welcome." His tone had returned to the one she recognized and she opened the door and he bent his head against the blast and went out.

After closing and bolting the door she stood for a moment drawing in gasps of air. She had said she would go to the end of the month. Would she have to suffer this pain in her side and this awful feeling till then? Yes, she supposed so. This was what carrying a child meant. But how did some women carry on till the last minute? All she really wanted to do now was lie down and not get up again. Oh – she moved from the door and shook her head impatiently – she mustn't think like that. She mustn't, she mustn't; she had some weeks to go yet.

18

It was the second week in January and it had snowed for a full day and a night, thawed a little, then a frost had turned the slush into ice. On top of this there had been another heavy fall; and Hal told of roads blocked and horses in drifts, of the coaches being delayed and no hope of some of them getting through for days. Each time he came he would observe Mary Ellen anxiously, and once he said, "Do you think you'll travel the time?" in answer to which she could only shake her head.

During each visit he would stack plenty of wood and peat by the door and fill two buckets of water from the well, together with the same number of jugs. His usual time of arriving was late in the afternoon, and sometimes he had to light his lantern to get here.

On this particular day she had just got back into the cottage from emptying the slops when she heard him kick his feet against the wood pile. And when he came in he stood on the mat inside the door and shook himself free from the fresh falling snow.

"You're early," she said in surprise.

"Aye. I thought it best. It's been comin' down steady for hours now an' the sky's low. It could go on all day and I mightn't be able to make me way across later on, so, look, I've brought you extra milk and a cut of bacon. Now if anything should happen that I can't get across in the morning, don't worry, I'll make it later somehow. They're out cutting through the drifts now on the main road. It isn't the bloomin' snow, it's where it drifts to. If only the wind would go down.... How are you?"

She drew in a long shuddering breath before she said, "I ... I've got to admit, Hal, I'm not feelin' too good."

"Should I go and tell Mrs Patterson?"

"No, I saw her yesterday. She knows."

"How is she?" He nodded towards the bed.

"She's not well at all. Her chest's bad. She can hardly speak this mornin' and she's got this pain in her stomach. She's asleep now."

"Her potions no good?"

"No, they don't seem to answer."

"Funny" – he shook his head – "she can ease other people's pains but not her own. She should see a doctor. If I happen to come across him I'll tell him to call in. But there again, there's small chance of him gettin' here at the moment. Look" – he moved nearer to her – "I would stay, only ... well" – he gave a little smile and he wagged his head from side to side, "it's funny in a way. Well, not funny, I didn't mean it like that, but

I've got a cow comin' on to calf any minute an' you know I'm new at the game. Although I saw Farmer Gordon bringing one through recently I get a sort of scared feeling in case anything should go wrong with her. She's a nice old cow."

His voice was soft, the look in his eyes warm. She had never seen that expression on his face before, and her voice, too, was soft as she replied, "Oh, you must go, Hal, and see to her. It will be wonderful to have a calf. But you know, you needn't worry, they see to everything themselves, unless something goes radically wrong."

"You've seen them born?" His face stretched slightly, then he added, "Oh, well, aye you would on the farm."

"I've helped sometimes." Her voice was low.

"You have? Aw, well, you'll know all about it then. I wish you could come along and give me a hand." They exchanged smiles now, then she said, "It'll be all right. But I always think it's amazing they can stand on their legs after about an hour, after their mothers have cleaned them, an' the mothers always look so pleased. I . . . I've always liked cows. They're so sensible, at least most of them are, but you can get some that can be naggy and bad-tempered. One used to kick the bucket over every time she got a chance. Oh!" She brought her jaws tightly together and put her hand on her side, which brought him closer to her, saying, "Starting?"

"No, no." She lied with a grin. "He . . . it kicks."

"Oh." He pursed his lips, wagged his head in an embarrassed movement, then said, "Well, you'll be all right then for a time?"

"Yes, yes, I'll be all right, Hal. I hope it's another little cow for you."

"Oh, I wouldn't mind what it is as long as she gets it over. Well, I'll be off. Now take care, won't you? I'll be back the day if I can, later, if it eases off. But in any case I'll be over tomorrow, sometime or other, hail, rain, or snow. Huh!" He laughed. "Or snow, I said."

She smiled at him, pulled open the door; he nodded at her, then he was gone.

Slowly now she made her way towards the table and sat down and, leaning her forearms on it, she muttered, "Oh, if only he could have stayed." Then bending her head lower still, she muttered, "Oh dear God! What am I going to do if it should come afore time?"

A croak from the bed brought her slowly to her feet, and she went over to it. Kate was lying on the far side near the wall but her face was turned towards her, and in a cracked voice she asked, "That Hal?"

"Yes. He came early, 'cos the roads are blocked here and there, but he's comin' back later. If he can see the doctor he's gona tell him to call for you."

"Useless. Useless. I want no doctor. 'Tis you who wants a doctor. Rest, girl; lie yourself down here."

"I . . . I will in a minute, I've one or two things to see to."

The one or two things to see to included tearing up a flannelette sheet into squares, carrying the water from the scullery and putting the pails to the side of the fireplace, trimming the candles, and lastly, putting some oats in a big black pan and pressing this into the ashes.

This done, she went to the bed and, pulling off her boots, she got under the top cover. Kate made no sound: she had been chewing on whole marigold leaves which must have eased her pain and put her to sleep.

Kate had been very reluctant about discussing the uses of the marigold: she had warned her only of the dangers of the African marigold, which, if eaten, could make you swell up like a balloon. But even the leaves of the ordinary marigold she never gave whole to anyone who called. She might sprinkle a little in with a mixture of other herbs to perfect a cure, yet she herself would chew on the dried whole leaves.

She, too, at this moment felt in need of whatever solace the leaves could give her. But she resisted the urge to lean over Kate and help herself, and slowly the pain eased and she dropped into a sleep.

When she awoke, the candles had guttered and there was a chill on the room. She sat up slowly, asking herself how long she had been asleep. There was still no movement from Kate.

Shuddering, she put her feet on the floor and went to the fire. It had burnt low. Lifting the lid of the pan, she saw that the oats had swollen and absorbed all of the water. She raised her eyes to the clock and couldn't believe what she saw. It was three o'clock in the afternoon. She looked towards the window but could see nothing. The room seemed to be holding a great silence.

As she bent to reach out to pick up some wood to put on the fire, she was attacked by a pain that brought a cry from her. And the next minute she was kneeling on the mat, her head towards her knees, her arms hugging at herself and the sweat pouring from her.

This was it. This was surely it. When the pain eased she dropped onto her side and laid her arm on the settle and dropped her head onto it. After a moment she got onto her knees and hastily banked up the fire; then pulling herself upwards, she went towards the window, and when she rubbed at the pane she could see nothing but a great white blur. Cautiously now, she opened the door and her face stretched at the sight of the barrier of snow three feet high. A gust of wind took the top off it and drove it into her face and into the room, and she banged the door closed and, leaning against it, stood gasping as she thought: He'll never get through in this. Neither will Mrs Patterson.

When the pain seized her again she cried out against it. Then struggling to the bed, she shook Kate on the shoulder. "Kate! Kate! Wake up! I ... I think it's comin', and Mrs Patterson, she won't be able to get through. The snow's nearly up to the latch outside and it's still coming down. What am I goin' to do, Kate?"

"Lie down. Lie down. If it comes, it comes, an' come it will. Lie down. I ... I can't do anything for you, girl, but it will be all right. When did the pain start?"

"Just a little while ago, and bad."

"Oh, that could go on for a day or more, two in fact. Don't worry. There's more to come. All you've got to do is hold your breath, grip onto something an' push. It'll come when it's ready." Her voice trailed away and she turned her head into the pillow.

Mary Ellen sat on the edge of the bed, panic filling her. And now she began to whimper, "Oh, Ma. Ma." Oh, if she was only back at Mrs Davison's. Or if Hal was here. Oh no, not Hal, not when she was havin' the child. Not Hal. That would be too much, Roddy's child comin' into the world and Hal seein' it. Oh no, no. She started to wag her head from side to side until a stern voice from within her commanded, Stop it! Stop it. Pull yourself together. Get things ready. The wash-basket from the scullery. Put a blanket and a sheet in it. Yes, yes. She nodded at herself as if the advice were coming from someone else.

She was only half-way down the room when the pain struck her again, and once more she was kneeling, but on the stone floor now. After a moment, she told herself it was no use, she must go back and lie down on the bed. As Kate said, if it came it came. But oh dear Lord, she wished there was somebody here who could help her.

How many times she had cried out she didn't know; what time of the day or night it was she didn't know. The room was in darkness and it was cold and silent. Whenever she broke the silence with an agonized groan or open-mouthed cry, Kate at times would mutter, "That's it. That's it. 'Tis comin' strong." But most of the time Kate slept as if she was already dead.

At times, she felt that she herself was already dead, for her mind was playing strange tricks on her. She imagined that the house was floating in snow and she opened the door and swam into it, and she swam as well as the boys had done in the dam. Then again she knew she wasn't quite dead when the pain screwed her inside into knots and brought her knees upwards.

When she heard the scraping on the door she thought it, too, part of her imagination, and even when it grew louder and the noise turned into bangs, she did not fully comprehend what was happening. Not until she saw the weird snow-clad figure bending over her did she realize that help had come. But then once more pain gripped her and she was yelling aloud.

Hal tore off the muffler that was holding his cap in place and threw off an outer coat before at the same time looking wildly round the room. Then running to the fireplace, he got on to his knees and blew the dying embers into a small flame. Within minutes he had piled on wood and had a blaze going. He was about to rise from his knees when he heard her scream again, and he screwed up his face against the sound. He had left the door open to let a little light in, but all it showed of the outside world was a narrow way cut through a six-foot drift of snow.

Before closing the door, he lit a candle; then, hurrying to the bed, he caught hold of her hands, saying, "How long have you been like this?"

She made no answer, only tossed her head from side to side. Her stockinged feet were sticking out from the bottom of the coverlet, but when he felt them they were cold. Yet her face was running with sweat.

He looked around him for a moment in bewilderment. This end of the room was dim. There was no table on which to stand the candlestick and he couldn't get round the other side of the bed because it was against the wall and Kate was lying there. He did not enquire after her, because he had guessed she had drugged herself to sleep to get rid of her pain.

Springing now towards the ladder, he went up it and under the eaves, and there he pulled the clothes off the pallet bed and dropped them through the hatchway. Then he tugged the biscuit mattress from the wooden base and did the same with this.

When once again he was in the kitchen he dragged the pallet to the fireplace and laid it lengthwise to the side of the fire, and he put the bedclothes on it, but before returning to Mary Ellen he thrust the porridge pan into one side of the fire and the water pan into the other. Then going to her, he said gently, "Do ... do you think you can get to your feet?"

All she could reply was, "Oh, Hal!" and these two words came out on a groan.

"You've got to get to the fire, Mary Ellen. Do you hear me? Look, swing your legs over."

When again all she answered was, "Oh, Hal!" he pulled the rumpled cover from her and threw it over Kate. Then, thrusting one arm underneath her shoulder and the other below her bent legs, he heaved her upwards and staggered drunkenly to the hearth. There in an effort, he went down on one knee before letting her slide on to the pallet.

He now brought two pillows from the bed and put them under her. She was lying with her feet towards the flames and he pulled off her stockings and chafed the soles of her feet between his rough hands for a moment before looking at her again and saying softly, " 'Tis gona be all right. 'Tis gona be all right. Can you undo your skirt?"

Her mouth was open, her eyes wide as she muttered now, "The pain, Hal. Oh, the pain."

"It'll soon be over, Mary Ellen. It'll soon be over. Can you undo your skirt?"

When she made no effort to do so his hand went to the band of her skirt. The buttons were at the side and they were undone, but there was no way he could get the skirt off her, and the top of it was taut across the big mound of her stomach, as were her petticoats beneath. He paused for only a moment before running up the room and taking a clasp knife from the pocket of his outer coat, and in a minute he had split the skirt down. But there were the petticoats. One of the tapes was undone, but the bottom one was still fastened and, to his mind, was no doubt restricting her breathing. So he slit the two of them, and when they fell aside there was the mound of her body as he never expected to see it. And when her legs jerked upwards and she let out another piercing scream, he gritted his teeth and closed his eyes for a moment. Then gripping her hands again, he entreated, "Press down all you can. Press down. . . ."

If he said these words once, he said them fifty times during the next hour. He wrung out hot cloths from the boiling water and laid them across her stomach, and she didn't flinch at the heat because now she was only semi-conscious and growing weaker. Once she looked at him and muttered, "Mrs Patterson."

And he said, "She could never get through. But don't worry, I know what to do." He nodded at her; and then he smiled as he said, "I've had practice. I must have known what was goin' to happen. I brought a calf into the world yesterday, at least the mother did." He kept talking to her now; "You should see her, she's beautiful. Just try to let go, don't be stiff. Come on now, come on. Mary Ellen" – he moved her face from side to side – "listen. Listen. You're gona be all right. Yes, you are, you're gona be all right. I'll see to it. D'you hear? D'you hear? You know me, don't you? Stiff neck, that's me. Whatever I say I don't budge from and so you're gona be all right. D'you hear? I've said it, you're gona be all right."

Yet when another hour passed he began to have doubts, grave doubts, and once or twice he let them escape, saying, "Oh, my God! Mary Ellen, no! don't give up. Come on. Come on, lass. You've got to live. Even if it doesn't, you've got to live. D'you hear me?"

When an even greater yell than usual rent the room, he saw the child coming into life; but it was himself who groaned when, not the head, but the feet appeared. He talked rapidly now as the nails of her two hands pierced the flesh of one of his, and with the other he reached out and held the little feet, crying excitedly, "That's it! That's it! Another heave. Come on, another heave."

She seemed to answer his bidding and the child slid out up to its shoulders, and there it stopped. And now, "Oh no!" he muttered aloud, "God Almighty! No!" He knew what he might have to do and the thought of it was terrifying him. He had seen Farmer Gordon do it to a cow. But this was no cow.

She was gasping now but not crying out. He put his hands between her breasts. Her heart was racing like a millstream. "Can you push a little more, Mary Ellen," he pleaded, "just a little more?"

When she made no response he looked around him as if for help. Then pulling his hand from hers, he let go of the child and, picking up the knife, he plunged it into the boiling water.

Then it was done, but on a scream that tore at his ear drums. And the next instant, there, on both his hands, lay a child, and it, too, screamed.

The sweat was pouring down his face. He bowed his head over the child and his blood covered hands; then swinging round on his knees, he placed it in the clothes basket that had stood ready to the side of the fireplace before turning back to Mary Ellen.

Gripping her face in his hands and in a voice that was shaking, he said, "It's all right, lass. It's all right, she's here. You've got a daughter. Listen to her! Listen to her! D'you hear, Mary Ellen?"

She opened her eyes and looked at him, yet didn't seem to recognize him for a moment, then she said, as she had said often during the last hours, "Oh, Hal." And he answered, " 'Tis all over. 'Tis all over. We'll get you cleaned up. She'll need a wash an' all." He swallowed deeply. "Soon you'll have some gruel and you'll be yourself again in no time."

An hour later the child was washed and wrapped in a blanket and sleeping peacefully. He thought it should be put to her breast but she seemed in no state as yet to feed it. Well, there was plenty of time for that: another hour or so and she'd be ready for it. . . .

Three hours later she still wasn't ready for it. Her heart was racing, the sweat was pouring from her and she was wandering in her mind. And he was in a state of fear that he had never experienced before. The child had to be fed, and Mary Ellen needed medicine of some kind. But what? There was old Kate over there who had never moved an inch during all this screaming and yelling. For a moment he felt like shaking her awake. Yet he knew that such was her state that she might have already awakened on that distant shore that preachers were always yapping about, from where, once you landed, there was no return.

When the child's cry turned to a whimper, he tore some linen into strips, rolled one piece round his finger, then tied the end of it into a blob and after dipping it into warm milk pushed it gently into the child's mouth. And when it sucked hungrily at it he knew some measure of relief. After repeating the process a number of times, it lay quiet again.

He turned to Mary Ellen, saying, "Well, I've got over that difficulty. . . . Mary Ellen!" He shook her gently. "Mary Ellen! Come on. Come on. Open your eyes. Come on, open your eyes."

When obediently she opened her eyes, there was a faint recognition in them and she tried to speak, and he whispered, "What is it? What is it?"

"Look . . . look after her. Look after her, will you? Look after her?"

"Mary Ellen. Listen." He put his arms about her now, holding her up from the pillows. "You're goin' to be all right. Listen. Don't let go. D'you hear? For God's sake! don't let go. Mary Ellen! look at me. You haven't got to go. D'you hear me? Because I can't go on without you. There it is. I can't go on without you. I've said it, Mary Ellen, you're all I have, or ever wanted. *Listen. Listen.* You've got to hang on. D'you hear? Oh, my God! Don't go. *Mary Ellen. Mary Ellen.*"

He put his lips on hers now; then moved them round her face, in desperation muttering all the while, "Mary Ellen. Mary Ellen. I'll stand anything, even you marrying him, only you've got to be there. I've got to see you. D'you hear? I've got to see you. Oh, love, love. Come on, come on, you've got this far."

When a hand came on his shoulder he himself let out a cry now and, his head dropping back, he gazed up at the weird figure of Kate tottering above him. Her straggling white hair was loose about her face; her eyes were bleared; her lips looked cracked and her voice was a mere croak as she said, "Afterbirth."

"What?" He moved to the side.

"Afterbirth. Has it come?"

He shook his head in answer but more to himself than to her. That was it. The afterbirth hadn't come. He had thought he knew all about these things.

He watched the old woman now crumple up on to the settle, then point towards the far wall, saying, "Bring the tin box."

Scrambling from his knees, he did as she had bidden him, and when he placed the box at her feet, she indicated that he should open it. And her hand went straight to a brown bag. Lifting it out, she extracted some leaves, saying, "Burn them on the shovel."

"Burn them?"

She moved her head and he did what she bade him. Once he had put a light to the leaves, the room became filled with the smell that was like an evil stink. Kate herself now slid on to her knees, and when she was kneeling by Mary Ellen's head she reached up and took the shovel from him and placed it as close to Mary Ellen's chin as it would go. Then jerking her head around, she said, "Dip your arm up to the elbow in the hot water there, then you know what you've got to do."

He felt stunned for a moment. To bring the bairn was one thing, but that. Well!

As he thrust his arm into the hot water he knew that whatever happened in the future, whether she be alive or dead, or whoever she took, she would be his.

19

For five days Mary Ellen hovered on the brink of death. On the third day Mrs Patterson had got through from the village, and her pronouncement made Hal yell at her, "Don't say that, woman! She's got this far."

Kate kept doping her with her potions, having to drop them drip by drip down her throat. It seemed that the emergency had enabled Kate to throw off her own illness and weakness, for when Hal wasn't there she scurried backwards and forwards attending to the child. But Hal seemed to be always there. He would disappear for an hour or two, but back he would come, his face rimmed with frost or snow.

When the thaw set in on the fourth day he made his way into Haydon Bridge and brought back the doctor, not the old doctor, but a new one who, after staring at Mary Ellen, said to her, "Why, we have met before haven't we?" And from the great blackness she had been swimming in, she seemed to come to the surface for a moment and, peering at the face hanging over her, she recognized the man who had sat to one side of her on the top of the coach, the same that had paved her way to see Roddy. And the strange face kept her on the surface of the blackness for a time, until he said, "That's it. Go to sleep. Go to sleep."

The young doctor straightened his back and looked at the old crone standing to his side. She was a weird apparition, like a skeleton hung round with old clothes. And she was as strange as was this room, for there, along one wall, were shelves filled with bottles and jars, and bunches of herbs were hanging from every beam in the ceiling. He had heard about people like her, country crones, but she was the first one he had himself come across. Not so many years ago, she would have been one of those that were burnt. He had never seen anyone who looked so old. Yet her voice was strong and her words sensible. "She's been worse, much worse. She's over it," she had said as a consequence of his remarks.

Perhaps she was right, but the girl had a long way to go, she was still very ill.

When she had told him earlier what had happened at the birth, he had thought he had better examine the girl in case she was festering. And having done so and found the cuts clean and healthy, he had thought he couldn't have done a better job himself. Perhaps he mightn't have made the incisions so big, but nevertheless, they had evidently been done in time, and had certainly helped to save the girl's life, as had the removal of the afterbirth.

It was amazing the things that happened in the country. He had thought when he came here a few months ago that he would be bored with the sameness of the life, but hardly a day passed without something unusual happening. Funny incidents, tragic incidents. All around he felt there was tragedy, especially in the coughs of the men working in the lead and smelt mills and coal mines. Some of them would never see middle years. Yet, the poor here were different to the poor in the town, for they were better housed. Oh, yes, indeed, especially around the mill. And they had their good plots of land with animals and vegetables. They wouldn't go hungry, as did so many in the cities.

One thing he was learning: most of these people were born into a set pattern of life, but those of a strong mind and will could alter it. And in here, in this strange room, there must have certainly been a battle of wills a few days ago, for this girl should surely have died if a stronger will than hers hadn't taken over. And it belonged to that fellow who had asked him to call. No, not asked him, demanded him. He had left him at the door here, saying he had to go and see to his beasts but he would be back. There was one thing certain, if that man had been responsible for the girl's condition, she would have been married by now. What had happened to the other man, the one who created all that fuss when there were graves opened and a rich farmer was accused of murder?

He said to the old woman, "Where is the other young man, the one she came to see in prison?"

The reply was brief: "Away, in London."

"London?"

"Aye, that's what I said, London."

He wanted to say: Is he responsible, does he know about the child? But the look in the bleared eyes told him he had asked enough questions, for the present at any rate. And so he left, saying he would call the next day and bring some medicine. And the answer he was given was, "Bring some medicine? She has all the medicine she needs." But he countered her words and tone with those of authority, saying, "Nevertheless, I shall bring her medicine, and you will see that she takes it." And her last words to him as he made towards the door were, "How d'you think she's got this far?" Then she added, "Pull the door tight shut, there's a wind." . . .

When Hal returned, she told him what had transpired with the young doctor, and he said, "I hear he's good and knows what he's about. If he brings her medicine, she'll have to take it. Understand, Kate?"

And Kate's voice had the same implication in it as she had given to the young doctor. "I'll do as I think fit an' best for her," she said. Then pointing to an animal that had followed on Hal's heels, she said, "Whose is that?"

Hal turned, a half smile on his face as he looked down on the dog, saying, " 'Tis mine."

"Since when did you have a dog?"

"Since yesterday. I bought him from an Irish tinker. He was camped out near the old barn. He had his horse in there and three dogs. He'd asked me the previous day if I had any turnips, so I dropped him a few by. And there was Boyo." He nodded towards the dog. "He looked at me, and if ever a dog spoke, he did. 'Take me,' he said, because, as you can see, like the tinker's horse he had been fed on gypsies' hay, which, as you know, is the whip. He was the smallest of the three dogs and likely, if there was anything going at all, he came out the worst. So I did a deal, I bought him. Sixpence I paid for him."

"You were robbed, by the look of him."

"He'll be all right. He's big boned, let him get some flesh on him. Anyway, I've been thinkin' about a dog for some time: the passing gypsies are not above comin' in and helpin' themselves, especially to chickens an' hay. He'll be all right. Won't you, Boyo?" He stooped down and patted the dog's head, and the animal pressed itself against his leg and looked up at him, then turned and went towards the clothes basket where the baby was lying, and after sniffing two or three times he lay down by the side of it, his head on the rim of the basket.

"Well, what d'you think about that?"

"I think he knows when he's on a good thing. He looks a mixture."

"He's young, part sheepdog, part hound, I'd say. Anyway, enough." He turned from her and went towards the bed and looked down on the white thin face and, softly now, he said, "Mary Ellen. Mary Ellen."

Slowly she opened her eyes, then blinked her lids as she tried to get him into focus. And when she did, she lifted her hand slowly and put it out towards him, and as he gripped it, he brought his lips tight together to stop their trembling, for the gesture was as if she had bestowed on him the gift of herself, for never before had she put her hand out willingly to him.

As day followed day, she became stronger, but it was no thanks to the doctor's medicine, for as soon as he had left the room, Kate made it her business to pour it into the swill bucket and fill the bottle up with her own concoction, which happened to be much the same colour.

The snow slowly disappeared and by the beginning of February the earth was showing itself again, except higher up on the hills, and these would keep their white caps for some time yet.

The first time Mary Ellen brought her feet over the side of the bed she felt as if she was about to float away, her body seemed so light, but her mind was clear. She sat with a hap over her legs looking down the room to where the fire glowed and the child lay in the basket to the side of it.

"Could I have her?" she said softly to Mrs Patterson. And Mrs Patterson, a slight figure of a woman with a melancholy face, said, "Aye, lass, aye, if you think you're up to it."

"I'm up to it."

Mrs Patterson brought the child to her and laid it in her arms. It was not the first time she had held the baby; but she had not then taken its weight, for it had lain across her arm on the bed; now she was holding it, supporting it, and she looked down on to its face. Its eyes were round and looked deep blue, but then as Kate had said, most babies' eyes were blue to begin with, as they grew older they could turn to black, brown, green or hazel. The cheeks were round, the mouth like an open flower, and the skin like velvet. She was a bonny baby.

"What are you going to call her?" asked Mrs Patterson.

"Kate."

"Kate? Oh, well, aye, I suppose . . . yes you should, 'cos she's brought you through, has Kate. Not forgetting Hal. My God! no. Say what you like about him, and he's not the easiest to get on with, takin' man or woman, but he's worked like a Trojan these past weeks. How he got through to you that mornin', nobody knows. Must have taken him hours, half the night I think, because nobody could move for two days. Do you know, there were four horses lost in the drifts below the mill. And John Tollett was found almost frozen to death. Trying to get home he was. His son found him not twenty yards from their door. How long he'd been lying they didn't know. But his feet are not right yet, they're swollen up like balloons. Eeh! It was a dreadful time. I remember me ma sayin' there was a like fall in 1802, or was it three? But anyway, it was round that time and they found Jimmy Crawford, the journeyman, dead in a ditch. Frozen as stiff as a seven-day corpse. And there's never been a fall like it since. And they say there's more to come."

Mary Ellen listened to Mrs Patterson's voice droning on. It was known all round the village she was a harbinger of bad news: she was happy when she was foretelling disasters. She wished she would go and Hal would come.

Hal. There was a mist in her mind covering the past weeks, yet through it she knew he had been there all the time, and she knew she owed her life, not to Kate's potions, but to him. Vaguely she could recall the agonizing hours before the birth. But the memory that surpassed that agony was the one when his knife went into her flesh. The mist thickened after that but Kate had cleared some of it away since, and she knew if he hadn't done what he did, she wouldn't be here now. There returned to her mind again and again the faint memory of the time she knew she was going to die, and his face on hers. She could not remember what he said, only the essence of it through the tone in his voice. She knew he had begged her not to go, and the intensity of his plea had awakened something in her that lay in the depths beyond the pain. Yet, as she became stronger, it seemed to sink deeper and deeper to where lay another pain, and its name was Roddy.

Roddy. If she had known what she had to go through, would she have forced herself on him, as her honesty told her she had done? And the answer she got was, yes, because at that time she had no knowledge of childbirth, all that mattered then was the easing of her desire.

She had lain here for days now asking herself odd questions such as, Why had God put this craving into girls who were not yet women? It was a craving that defied understanding or explanation. And as one grew up it became stronger, especially when it was centred on one person. God was funny, not really sensible because He told you to be good yet put into your being something that made you do bad, bad, that was, unless you were married.

And then there were her mixed feelings about Hal, for her mind was presenting her with a picture of him that she had never seen before, having never associated him with tenderness. Even during the past months before the child came, he had been kind, but never tender, never. Then there was something else, something she couldn't define. She only knew that if he stopped coming she'd miss him as much as she had missed Roddy. And now what she could not understand and what was troubling her for it didn't seem reasonable, was that she had to add the word, more, to that....

It was a month before she started pottering round the kitchen again. The doctor's visits had ceased. He had been six times in all and each time she had reminded herself how strange it was that he of all people should have come doctoring in this part of the world. He was a nice young man. She liked him. Not so Kate. Kate was rude to him. In fact, she had told him yesterday that she could buy him at one end of the street and sell him at the other. And he had been so nice to her: he had laughed and said he had no doubt in his mind at all that she could do just that. And not at the end of the street, he had said, but half-way down it.

Even that hadn't placated her. To her, the word doctor was just another name for butcher. Apparently one such had amputated her father's foot when it had gangrene, and hadn't even knocked him drunk before doing so.

She walked to the window and looked out. The sun was shining. There was a wind blowing. The earth looked fresh, bare but fresh.

As she stood, she saw a figure dropping down from the slope. The dog was running round it in circles. She smiled to herself. That dog was a funny creature. She had never seen one act like it did. There had been dogs on the farm: you only had to tell them to lie down, but this one, if you said lie down, it came and licked your hand. The only time it lay down was by the child's basket. It seemed to love the child. At least, next to its master, it did, for if Hal went out of the door to bring some wood or peat in, it was at his heels, or whining until he came back.

She saw that Hal was carrying something as usual. He had kept them going with both milk and food for weeks. She must ask him about this woman who cooked such good pastry.

She moved from the window and when Hal entered the room she was sitting at the table chopping some onions on a board.

"Hello, there," he said. "How's things?"

"As you left them," she answered; then turned her head slowly to where Kate was nodding in a chair by the fire. When the dog came up and nuzzled her she patted its head, saying, "He's turning into a fine beast." And he answered, "He should do; he eats like a horse." And to this she said, "You didn't ride over this mornin'?"

"No. I felt like a walk. And anyway, I can leave her out in the field now. She's had enough of late and her coat is lookin' shaggy. We all need a rest now and again. And having said that, what time did you get up?"

"Oh, not long ago." She looked now at the parcel on the table. From its shape she guessed what it was: "Another pie?" she said.

"Aye. Annie brought it over last night, two of them in fact."

Annie, he had said; before, it had always been, one of the farm lasses.

"Which one is she?" she asked.

"Oh, the youngest. I say the youngest, she must be kicking forty. But you can't help feeling sorry for her. She's glad to escape, I think, and open her mouth, because she daren't do it in the house. And she chatters away like a magpie; used to talking to herself most of the time by the sound of it, because I leave her at it."

"Does she do for you?"

He turned and glanced at her, a twinkle in his eye now as he said, "Aye, for most things."

And when she lowered her head and went on with her chopping, his voice altered slightly and he said, "She's a canny soul. I give her two shillings a week, and by! you would think I was giving her gold dust. I don't think she tells the others what she gets, for her father sends her over in payment for the odd jobs I do for him now and again. Payment in kind, so to speak, 'cos he won't part with a ha'penny. He must have a tidy packet put by. I wondered the other day what would happen when he kicks the bucket. I'd like to bet they'll all go stark starin' mad with spending. I'd like to see it. In fact I'd take them all into Hexham in the cart."

She looked at him now. He was pouring the milk from the can into the jug, and he was smiling broadly. He looked nice. She didn't say attractive. She could imagine this Annie liking to work for him. That was another facet of his, kindness. Why hadn't she recognized before that he was kind underneath?

He took off his outer coat and hung it on the nail behind the door, then came back and sat at the table opposite to her, saying but not smiling now, "You know who I saw on me way over here? They were on the Allendale road, going towards Rooklands. The two Bannamans, the son and her, the daughter. And that's the second time I've seen them within the last few weeks. They're after somethin', I'd bet me life. The place has been up for sale for months now but there's been few takers, so I understand. I wonder what they're lookin' for? They're not makin' that journey from right beyond Corbridge for nothin'. Perhaps they're lookin' for something that the excisemen couldn't find. Yet, they found enough in that tunnel that was under the cellar. Anyway, I'll keep me eyes open. If I see them on that way again I'll know it isn't sentiment that's bringin' them, although, as I remember, she did say she'd go back."

"I'd leave them alone, Hal, if I were you. It's all over and done with." Her voice was quiet.

"Aye, it might be on the surface, but not in that one's mind. Nor yet in me own, to tell you the truth."

As she raised her eyes to his she saw that his face had that tight look about it. And she recalled that this man had hanged someone, or at least, as he said, seen that he hanged himself. For a moment she forgot the kindness he had shown of late, and even his thoughtfulness for this Annie woman, whom she was beginning to feel curious about, and there returned to her the old feeling she'd had for him, for underneath he was still the old Hal with a bitterness still in him that would never be erased.

He startled her somewhat by saying, "Why are you lookin' at me like that?"

"Like what?"

"Well" – he pursed his lips – "like you used to do at one time."

She looked away from him for a moment before facing him again and saying, "Well, truthfully, for a moment you did look as you used to do, full of resentment, ready to hit out."

He stared at her for a second or so; then leaning across the table he brought his face down to hers, saying softly, "We are what we are, Mary Ellen, and nobody knows what goes on inside deep under the skin. After all, we only see what we want to see in each other." He paused before straightening himself, then adding, "People judge you by the look on your face or what rolls off your tongue; they don't want to look deeper and see why you look like that. An' why should they? Anyway" – he drew in a sharp breath – "there's no use me standing here, I've got to go into the town. I still haven't got me bull, not the one I want." He laughed now, saying, "A funny thing happened the other day. I called in at old Frankland's, you know beyond Catton. I understood he had a young bull for sale. Well, there was something about it that just didn't take me fancy and when I said so, but not in so many words, he said, 'What you lookin' for, a close relation, somebody like yourself?' Then he bellowed like his bull, and I joined him and said, 'That's it, I shouldn't wonder.'"

"What are you lookin' for in an animal then?"

"Oh, I couldn't put me finger on it. A quiet fellow, I'd say though. A quiet fellow."

"Huh!" She laughed. "Then it certainly won't be like you."

Like lightning now he turned on her, saying, "There you're wrong,

Mary Ellen, there you're wrong, as you've always been about me." And on this he went down the room, muttering, "I'll get the wood in and see to the water."

He was in the scullery before she rose, calling to him in a conciliatory tone, "I can manage, Hal."

"One day I'll take you at your word," he answered. Then the door banged, and she sat down again. And she wasn't surprised when Kate's voice came from behind her, saying, "And he could well do that one day. Think on it, lass. Think on it."

20

❧❧

It was towards the middle of April. Hal had got his bull. He had ridden over to another farm over towards Whitfield and as he stroked the ringed nose he had said in an aside to it, "I've had to pay through that for you, remember that me young buck." And the farmer had countered, "I could have got more for him in the market. If you don't want him it's all the same to me."

"Let's stop this sparrin'," Hall had said; "we're both satisfied, and we know it. I'll collect him the morrow, and on foot, because as you see me pony's nervous at the sight of him."

He was aware that the farmer knew all about him and considered him too cocky, too big for his boots, just as a number of others did. Well, people would think what they wanted to think, it didn't upset him. But there were two things that were upsetting him at the moment: Kate was near her end definitely this time; and last week there had come a letter from the big fellow to her, saying that he hoped to come through soon to see her. The first worry had a sure end. The second, he wasn't so sure of at all. What would happen when he walked in that door and saw the result of his fling, and looked on Mary Ellen as she was now? For the girl had gone and in her place was a comely young woman, a very comely young woman.

They had got on fine together these past few months. Once or twice they had scratched the surface and gone back into the old ways, their tongues thrusting at each other. But it had been over and done with in a minute.

What if the other one saw her differently now and wanted to take her back with him?

He had come up from the steep valley bank and had reached the Allendale road, but then decided to divert and take a short cut home. With this in mind he turned his pony into a narrow path in a thicket until they came on to open country. And there he put it into a trot. But he hadn't gone very far, when he drew it to a walk again. He had come to a broad track and along it in the far distance and disappearing into a patch of woodland, he saw a horse and trap with two figures sitting in it. Although he couldn't recognize them or the trap, he felt instinctively they were the Bannamans on their way again to Rooklands.

Now why? He looked first one way and then the other. His desire a moment ago was to get back, not only to home, but to go later to the cottage to see how Kate was faring and, naturally, to see Mary Ellen, because he was never at peace with himself unless he was in her presence. Yet, what were those two going along there for? How many times had they been there when he hadn't seen them? But this was the third time he had come across them.

He did not pause to think any more but now he himself took the track that led to the Bannamans' farm.

The farmhouse was an imposing building. It was stone built, two-storied with attics above. But what were more imposing still were the outhouses. There was a fine range of them: stables, a big tack-room, a fine barn, a granary store, and a set of dairy buildings that would take some beating. He had been round the place a number of times, but had never encountered anyone. He had peered in the windows and seen the high-ceilinged well-shaped rooms, and the mice scurrying round them. He had been down in the cellar and seen the tunnel that the authorities had unearthed. And so again he wondered if those two were looking for something that the authorities had missed.

He left his pony tethered to a tree some distance down the road from the main opening to the farmyard. There was a high wall bordering the yard and he walked along under cover of it, then he paused before stepping round it and into the yard, and looked towards the arch.

The trap was standing in the yard, but there was no sign of anyone. He walked towards the trap, not stealthily, but openly. The horse turned its head and looked at him, and the wind lifting its long mane, brought it over its eyes. It tossed its head now and Hal laid his hand on its neck and stroked it to quieten it. Then he walked on, asking himself the while why he was doing this. But the answer he got was, he didn't really know. Perhaps it was to gain a little more satisfaction from their downfall.

The last time he had seen her face to face she had looked like the devil, and it was then, as he had recalled earlier, that she prophesied she would be back. But she hadn't meant flying visits just to look round; no, she had meant she'd come back here to live. Well, that would need money, wouldn't it? And it must be money or valuables she was after now. He'd stake his life on it.

He did not ask himself what would happen when they should come face to face again for he considered he had just as much right being here as anyone else: the place was up for sale. Anyway, sightseers still came and looked round it. It was the objective of a good Sunday walk.

He walked along by the front of the house and peered in the window of the room in which he had stood on that fatal day, at least fatal for Bannaman.

He made himself turn slowly when a voice came from behind him saying, "What are you looking for?"

They were standing some feet from him, the brother and sister. There was no resemblance between them; in fact, he could have been the woman and she the man, for he had a thin refined look, whereas her face was strong. And her expression was dark and grim now. "Just lookin' round like yourselves," he answered quietly.

"You have no right here."

"Don't be stupid, woman." His tone was suddenly scathing. "Everybody has a right here now, everybody. What's the matter with you? Have you lost your mind? Can't you recall what's happened to you, the lot of you? It was a long time in comin' but justice will out. He got off too lightly, your father. He should have swung, like the other one."

He hadn't meant to say any of this, but there it was, out. And her face was livid as she cried at him, "The other one you referred to didn't swing, not by his own hand, he didn't. Did he?"

"Well, whose hand did you imagine did it?"

"He hadn't the guts to take his own life. If he had he would have done it straightaway. He was made to do it, wasn't he?"

"If you say so, miss, if you say so." The sneer in his voice also became apparent on his face. "Now I'll ask you a question," he said. "What are you doin' here? Saying a last farewell? No; for if that's the case, you've said it two or three times already lately, haven't you? Anyway, I don't know how you've got the nerve to come back, knowing what your evil devil of a father did. If I had my way I'd burn the whole place down to get rid of the stench. Aye" – he nodded at her now – "that's an idea. In a short while, that's what I'll do, buy it and burn it, wipe it off the face of the earth."

He watched them turn and look at each other. Then pulling up the front of her long skirt with one hand, she ran down the yard to the trap, round to the back of it, picked something up, and then there she was standing, a gun held at shoulder level and aimed straight at him.

He watched her walk slowly towards him and when she said, "Turn round," he muttered, "Like hell I will." The next instant he had his hand over his eyes and a spray of shots went over his head and one pellet penetrated his hand. My God! She was mad, and bad, as bad as her father. A thought flashed through his mind: What in the name of God had Roddy seen to love a woman like this?

The brother now spoke to him, saying quickly, "Do as she says. She means it."

He turned round, and now her voice came at her brother, saying, "Open the barn door." And as the man ran across the yard she pushed Hal in the back with the barrel of the gun, saying curtly, "Move!"

He moved.

When he entered the barn he saw it was empty except for a platform up above with odd broken bundles of hay on it here and there. And when she ordered her brother up on to the platform, he watched her gaze towards the great beams supporting the old part of the barn, and he thought, My God! She means to hang me. And for the first time he knew real fear. Swinging round on her now, he cried, "What d'you think you're up to, woman?"

"Time will tell," she said. "Get up the ladder."

"I'll be damned if I will."

"Well, if you're blind or not, you'll go up the ladder. I will count five and I'll discharge this full into your face. What about it?"

He climbed the ladder to the platform, and there stared at the white face of the young man who was staring back at him, and he was about to appeal to him when her voice came again, commanding, "Lie down, face down." She herself must already have climbed the ladder.

He hesitated for a moment, thinking she couldn't mean to hang him, then he lay down.

"Put your hands behind your back." And he did as he was bid. Then her voice came again: "Catch this," it cried, and when a coil of rope fell to his side a tremor went through him again.

She was kneeling by him now, the gun pressed to his head, and she said to her brother, "Tie his hands!"

As his wrists were being tied he wanted to cry out, for the rope seered his flesh as if he were being burnt.

"Get him to his feet!" He was tugged upright by the young man. But now it was she who pushed him forward to the far end of the platform where the beams criss-crossed down to the floor level.

"What are you doing to do?" It was the brother's anxious-sounding enquiry. And she said, "You'll see. Lie down, you!" Her foot caught him in the back of the knees and sent him sprawling. His head hit a beam and he fell on to his knees now, then forward on to the hay-strewn floor.

What happened next actually made him scream, for she wrenched his legs back up to his hands until his whole body was arched, and there she strung them together. Then with her foot she pushed him on to his side, and saying to her brother, "Give me your scarf," she pulled it from his neck. And now bending slowly, she said, "Open your mouth." And when he didn't she took her fist and brought it under his chin, and his mouth sprang open, she rammed the silken scarf across it, pulled it round the back of his head, brought it forward again and knotted it across his mouth.

Rising, she looked down on him and said, "Now you know what it feels like to lie speechless and not able to use any part of your body. My father lay like that for weeks. There's only one thing I'm sorry for, the other one isn't here to join you. But you're a good substitute. You're afraid, aren't you? That's what Feeler must have experienced before you made him string himself up. Because that's what you did, wasn't it? Wasn't it? Nod your head."

When he didn't obey her, she said, "Well, it doesn't matter. I know what I know." Now she turned to her brother, saying, "Push him over to the beam."

Every fibre of his body screamed in agony as he was dragged towards the beam at the end of the barn. And when her brother said, "What are you going to do?" she said, "Make sure he can't wriggle. Here, take the end of that," and she threw him the loose end of the rope. "Put it round that beam there, and pass it to me." When she had the end of the rope in her hand again, she jerked it hard, and continued to do so until his legs and arms were pressed against the beam, and as the agony of his limbs brought the sweat pouring from him, he watched her pull the loose straw towards him and he heard her brother whisper, "Look, Mary, that's enough. What do you mean to do?"

"Oh, just build a barrier round him so that anyone putting their head over the top of the platform won't see the ... poor ... creature." She drew out the last words. Then kicking some straw near to his face, she added, "And by God! you'll be a poor creature when they find you. And you won't be able to give any evidence of all this happening to you. That's for sure. But even if you could, we'll be where no one will find us. So, Mr Roystan, your retaliation is at an end. And one more thing I'm going to tell you." She bent down until her face, like that of an insane devil, hovered above him as she ground out, "I said to the other one and I say it to you, no matter what my father was, he was worth a thousand of you and your kin, because you're nothing but trash, the lot of you. Now" – she straightened up – "you'll have plenty of time to think in the days ahead. And I'm being merciful, because I could set all this damn lot afire and let you roast slowly, because nobody would bother hurrying out to an empty barn. Would they?" She now took her foot and gave him a vicious kick in the lower part of the stomach. And he closed his eyes and his head drooped forward.

When some minutes later, he opened his eyes again he was alone, and he told himself that this was the end and the quicker it came the better, for the agony that was tearing at him couldn't be endured for long before his mind snapped.

21

Mary Ellen wiped the cold sweat from Kate's brow. The old woman was conscious and clear-minded but very weak, and she surprised Mary Ellen by saying now, "The doctor fellow. Get him."

"You want the doctor?"

"Aye."

"I'll send for him."

"Hal, late."

"Yes, he is. He was going after a bull. Perhaps he's had trouble bringing it home."

It was four o'clock in the afternoon and Hal hadn't put in an appearance. It was the only day she could remember his being so late. But, as she had said, he had gone after a bull. He was so keen on getting a good bull; he saw himself starting a great herd of cattle. He had big ideas, had Hal, and being him he would likely see them come true.

She went to the door. Some of the miners passed by at the bottom of the field around this hour. She waited a few minutes, then saw a group of them in the distance and she ran over the field and called to them, and when they stopped she said, "Do you think you could get a message to the doctor in Haydon Bridge if there's any one riding that way?" They looked at each other and one said, "Well, aye, lass, the cart should be passing in half an hour's time. We'll give him a message. Is it for the bairn?" he asked kindly.

"No, for Kate."

"Huh!" They all seemed to laugh together. "Kate wanting a doctor? I understand she practically chased him out the last time he was in the house."

"Well, she's asked for him now."

Again they looked at each other and one said, "That's bad. Well, she's nearly as old as the hills around here. How old d'you think she is?"

"I don't really know. She's never said. But I guess she must be well into her eighties."

"Aye, and a bit more if I can reckon," put in another man. "Well, lass, we'll get him here as soon as possible. Likely be the morrow mornin' though."

"Thank you, thank you very much." She turned from them and ran back up the field to the cottage.

When the evening wore on and Hal did not put in an appearance, she became worried. This had never happened before and if he had been bad he would have sent his young helper over here to tell her. Little Terry Foster was only ten but he was very sensible. If anything had happened, surely he would have come over with a message.

She lit the candles; she fed the child; she saw to Kate; she set the pan of porridge near the ashes ready for tomorrow morning; she washed out some of the child's clothes. She did everything to fill up the time until eleven o'clock at night and still he hadn't come. She lay down, not by Kate, but on the pallet bed she had rolled up at the end of the room and which she brought out each night and laid by the fire so she could be near the child. What was more, there was a smell coming from Kate that no amount of washing seemed to erase and she found it nauseating.

Most of the night she just dozed, and at five the next morning she rose and built up the fire. Kate was asleep, her breathing short and heavy. At six o'clock she opened the curtains and then the door and let the clean air come into the room. And she stood on the step and looked to where the hills were rising through the morning mist. What if he didn't come this morning, what could she do? She must go over and see what had happened to him. And as the disturbing thought came to her, she muttered aloud, "No, no, I wouldn't believe that." Yet why not? This Annie he talked about seemed to be a very capable person and he was sorry for her. And why shouldn't he marry, even if she was older than him. Look at Roddy and that woman. Well, she didn't really know anything definite about those two, she only knew how Kate had described the woman.

Hal should be married. Kate was always saying so. But he would have told her, given her some hint. Well, hadn't he given her plenty of hints about this woman being a wonderful cook and how she had no home life. Pity could make a man do lots of things – it didn't matter about age – especially if ... well, he needed a.... She couldn't go on and say, a woman. But what she did say to herself was, as soon as that doctor comes I'll get Mrs Patterson to stay with them, then I'll go across there. That's if he doesn't come. But he surely will.

The doctor came at eleven o'clock and he must have thought it was she who needed attention, for he said, "You look anxious, peaky. What is it?"

"Nothing, nothing, only Kate wanted to see you."

"She asked to see me?" His eyebrows went upwards.

"Yes." She gave him a smile. "Wonders'll never cease."

He went to the bed, leant over and looked into the wrinkled face, saying, "How do you feel this morning, Kate?"

"I feel me end is on me. I wish it would hurry up," she said.

"You wanted to see me. You want some medicine?"

"No, you know I don't want ... medicine. I want you to write a paper."

"A paper?"

"Yes. I could have got the parson, but I don't like parson. Just write a paper."

He turned and looked at Mary Ellen, then said softly, "She wants me to make a statement of some kind."

He went to his bag and brought out a notebook; then returning to the bed, he said, "I'm ready. What do you want to say?"

"Not much. Only that what I have, all my potions and herbs, me bits and pieces, and the money behind the stone in the fireplace goes . . . goes to her." She made a motion with her head towards Mary Ellen. And Mary Ellen, biting on her lip, shook her head and said, "Oh, Kate, Kate, no."

When he had finished writing the doctor said, "Can you sign your name, do you think?"

"Can't write."

"Well, make a cross there."

He put the pen into her hand and guided it at the bottom of the page; then he signed his name and wrote something else. Then softly he said, "I have stated that this is your wish and that you are of sound mind, and that I have witnessed this, your hand. Is that what you want, Kate?"

"Aye, that's . . . that's what I want. She'll" – again she nodded towards Mary Ellen – "pay you for your visit."

"I want no payment, Kate."

She blinked up at him, then said, "Thank you. Thank you, sir."

"And thank you, Kate. It's an honour to be of help to you." She closed her eyes and both he and Mary Ellen turned away from the bed. And Mary Ellen trying hard to restrain her tears, said, "Fancy that. That's what she wanted you for. She was thinkin' of me."

"She's a fine old woman, 'tis a pity she's going. And from what I understand you've been like a daughter to her. You're going to miss her."

"Yes, yes, I am."

"You'll be here on your own?"

"Well, yes, but . . . but Hal . . . you know Hal, he pops over every day, but . . . but I'm worried."

"About Hal?"

"Yes, yesterday was the first day he never came and . . . and here it is nearing twelve o'clock and he still hasn't been, and he brings milk every morning."

"Perhaps he's gone into town?"

"He always calls."

"Well then, you must go and see what is wrong. Perhaps he's ill."

"Yes, yes, I mean to do that. I'm goin' to get Mrs Patterson in from the village." She pointed towards the door. "She'll look after them until I come back."

"I'm on my way there," he said, "at least to the mill. I'll be passing the cottages. Will I give Mrs Patterson a message?"

"Oh, if you would, please. I'd be very grateful." And as she saw him to the door she asked, "How ... how long do you think she'll last, doctor?"

"Oh, if she had her own way she'd go now, but she's got a strong constitution that's fighting the disease in her stomach. She could last a week or more."

"Is that all?"

"Yes, I'm afraid so." He put his hand on her arm now, saying gently, "Don't worry for her. She seems to have had a good life, and apparently she's lived it as she wanted to live it, independently. It's very good for a person to be independent as she has been. If you follow her pattern you won't go far wrong, Mary Ellen."

"No, I won't. No, I won't, doctor."

"Goodbye."

"Goodbye, doctor, and thank you."

Mrs Patterson did not arrive until an hour later and Mary Ellen was standing ready to go, her coat on and a shawl over her head.

"Where are you off to, lass?" Mrs Patterson enquired.

"I'm goin' over to Hal's place, Mrs Patterson. You see, he didn't call yesterday, nor yet today. I think he must be bad or something."

"Never came yesterday, nor today? That's not like him, he's never off your doorstep. Caused a lot of comment that, you know, lass. Aye, it has. But there are people who always find something to talk about. And as I said to Jennie Pratt when she came tattling in not long ago, it wouldn't be him you'd take as you were waitin' for the other one comin' back. That's right, isn't it?"

Mary Ellen's face was flushed and she said, "No, it isn't, Mrs Patterson. And you can tell Jennie Pratt to mind her own business."

"Oh, well, people will talk, lass, you can't tie tongues." The older woman had seemingly taken no offence at Mary Ellen's tone, and she added, "I can stay only an hour, mind, so don't be all that long."

"I won't. And thank you."

She hurried out, indignation now mixed with concern for Hal. Waitin' for the other one comin' back. Well, wasn't she?

No. No. The voice was loud in her head. No, no, she wasn't waitin' for him, not any more. Nor had she been for a long time.

She began to run. It was only two miles to the farm but she thought she would never get there, the paths seemed endless. And when she entered the yard, there was Terry Foster standing talking to a tall gaunt-looking woman, and they both turned at her approach.

"Where's Hal ... Mr Roystan?" She addressed the boy now, and he, looking at the woman, said, "Eeh! that's what we were just sayin'. We thought he must be over at your place, Mary Ellen."

She now looked hard at the woman who said, "I'm Annie Gordon. I ... I come and tidy up for him and do a bit of cooking. I haven't seen him since yesterday morning when he left to go over to Whitfield way to see about a bull."

They looked from one to the other now; then in a very small voice,

Mary Ellen said, "Not since yesterday morning? Anything could have happened him. He could have been knocked off his horse and lying somewhere."

"That's what I thought, Mary Ellen. I've just said that to Miss Gordon. Didn't I, Miss Gordon?"

"Yes, yes, you did, Terry."

"What shall we do?" Mary Ellen asked the question more to herself than of them; then she answered it by adding, "I . . . I'd better go down to the mill and . . . and see the men, and perhaps Mr Mulcaster will do something."

The sound of barking had been going on in the background all the while, and Mary Ellen said, "Boyo. Did he come back alone?"

"No." The young boy shook his head. "Mr Roystan never took him along with him 'cos he didn't know whether he was bringing the bull or not. But Boyo's been cryin' an' yellin' his head off ever since. I'm frightened to let him out in case he runs off."

"Who's seeing to the cattle?"

"I am." The woman nodded at Mary Ellen. "They're all right. I often see to them when Hal is not here. He's . . . he's been away a lot of late." She narrowed her eyes and said, "Well, of course you know that; you're the young person from over Kate Makepeace's place, aren't you?"

There was no need for Mary Ellen to confirm this, but she stared back at the woman wondering if she detected resentment in the look. She also wondered if the woman had had ideas about Hal. But then she dismissed them. What ideas she would have would be motherly 'cos she was gettin' on. You could see that, although she wasn't as old as Hal had made her out to be, middle thirties, she'd say.

She said to the boy, "Have you thought about looking over the moor?"

"No, miss; I've just been waitin' for him comin' back."

Quickly now she said, "I'll away to the mill. The men'll know what to do." And with that she turned and ran out of the yard, and down the hill. There was no one about the inn, nor at Nillston Rigg. She hurried along the lane, skirted the dam, went up the steep hill and along the waggon track. She could see a group of men crossing the yard. Stumbling over the rails and the debris, she came up to them gasping, and as she could not speak for a moment, they all stopped and gazed at her. Then one said, "What's the trouble, lass?"

"Have . . . have any of you see Hal?"

"Hal?" They looked at one another. Then one of the men, with a slight leer on his face, said, "Hal Roystan? Why, lass, don't you know he's no longer a common workin' man? Farmer he is now. Landed gentry is goin' to be his next step. Why, I thought you would have known."

Her body was already hot with running and there was colour in her cheeks, but now her whole face became suffused with a blush and in a manner very nearly her old self, she retorted smartly, "Yes, and what you say could just come true, Mr Conway. Then, instead of spittin' your spite you'd be raisin' your cap."

There were three Conway men in the group. The man who had spoken was a leading smelter in the mill and with his brothers John and Frank working alongside him, and his younger brother, Herman, mining at Stublick, he was known to think that his family ran the whole show, for he had a sister, too, who was married to a smelter, and experienced smelter men were the cream of the mill.

"What is it, lass? What d'you want?" It was the quiet voice of Ben Fowler. He was standing next to his son Paul, who, before she could answer, stepped forward and said quietly, "Kate gone? Is that why you're lookin' for Hal?"

"No, no." She shook her head quickly. "Hal's gone missin'. He went over to Whitfield yesterday to see about a bull and no one seems to have seen hilt nor hair of him since. I've been over to the farm. He didn't turn up last night, nor today either."

The men looked from one to the other and one said, "Perhaps he's gone off jauntin' to town."

"No. He . . . he went after the bull. Anyway, he always brings me milk every mornin'." She paused now and met the glance of Peter Conway and she repeated, "Aye, he brings me milk every mornin'. And just by the way, Mr Conway, I can tell you, he saved me life when the bairn came because nobody else tried to get through to me in the snow."

There was the sound of scraping of hobnailed boots on the stones, and one man muttered, "Lass, you should understand we couldn't move up here. Nobody could. Anyway" – the man was looking round the group now saying, "this needs lookin' into. What d'you think? He's not goin' to stop bringin' the milk and that without sayin' somethin'." He turned his head towards Mary Ellen again and said quietly, "He would likely have told you, lass, if he had been goin' away, wouldn't he?"

"Yes, Mr Fowler, yes, he would."

"And you say nobody's seen him since yesterday mornin'?"

"Yes, that's right."

"Well now" – he nodded his head – "that's comin' up close on two days. Look" – he half turned now and glanced towards the offices – "don't you think she could go and see the boss? Because somethin' should be organized."

"Aye, yes." They all agreed quickly to this. Then the old man said, "Come on, lass. Come on and see Mr Mulcaster."

Mr Mulcaster came to the office door and gazed down on Mary Ellen and the men behind her. And she told him why she was there.

At first he smiled at her tolerantly, no doubt thinking back to the last time she had approached him, concerning another man who had later thanked her for saving him from transportation by taking her down, then leaving her. Now here she was concerned about that same man's friend, and if all tales were true, hers also, for Hal Roystan was known to visit her pretty frequently. But she was showing real concern and it was true what one of the men had just stated, you wouldn't go away from around here for nearly two days without saying where you were going. Well, he supposed something must be done. But then, the young fellow could have taken it into his head to go jaunting. He was a young man and young men often went jaunting when the need was on them. And he said as much but he put it in a different way: Looking down at her, he said, "Now you don't think he just could have gone off on some business or other?"

She looked up into his face, saying quietly now, "He's got a farm. He loves animals. When he left he told the boy he'd be back around dinner time; it all depended if he brought the bull back with him."

"Where was he goin' for the bull?"

"A farm near Whitfield."

"That'll be Johnson's farm, sir, if it's over by Whitfield," one of the men spoke up now. "Or Plummer's," said another man.

"Oh, Plummer's is only a small place; he wouldn't have any bulls for sale."

"Oh, I don't know about that."

Mr Mulcaster held up his hand, saying now, "Well, it'll be one or the other. I think" – he paused a moment – "what must be done first is to organize someone to go across there and find out if Hal was there at all. What about you, Frank. You like riding a horse?"

Frank Conway didn't show any enthusiasm, until Paul Fowler said, "Well, if you don't want to do it, I'll go."

"Who said I didn't want to do it. I'll go. Can I take a horse from the stables?" Frank Conway was looking at Mr Mulcaster and the agent nodded at him, saying, "Yes, yes, of course. How long will it likely take you?" He paused and, reckoning in his own mind, he said, "You could be back here within an hour and a half, couldn't you?"

"'Tis over four miles each way."

"Yes, well, take a fresh pony, he'll skip the miles for you."

Ben Fowler turned to the others, saying quietly, "We'd better get cleaned up. Whatever message he brings back will determine what we've got to do." Then turning again to Mary Ellen, he said, "That's all we can do for the present, lass. The only thing I can add is, if he's not found by the morrow mornin' we'll have to call in the constable."

A shudder went through her as she thought of Hal lying out somewhere injured, especially on the moor. Another night could do for him, especially if a mist came down, because it sank into your bones even if you were scurrying through it.

Detecting her anxiety, Mr Mulcaster said, "Now stop worrying and go home. The men will call and give you their news as soon as possible."

She swallowed deeply, then said, "Thank you."

The men made way for her, and as she passed through them she moved her head from one side to the other, saying, "Thanks. Thanks."

"Don't worry, lass, he'll turn up. Knowing Hal, he'll be there in the mornin' like a bad penny."

Paul Fowler patted her arm and she inclined her head towards him, then hurried away.

Hal did not turn up like a bad penny the next morning. One of the men had called last evening to say that Farmer Johnson had said Hal had called at the farm but that he hadn't taken the bull with him because the pony had shied away from the animal. He had expected him back but he hadn't yet turned up. Farmer Johnson had related that the young fellow had been in high spirits and very pleased with his purchase. He had also warned Hal to beware his pony didn't throw him for it seemed very high-spirited.

The warning seemed to have been justified when, later that day, a pony was found nibbling quietly on the moor.

One thing puzzled the searchers who found it: it had a hole in its rump, as if it had been jabbed with an instrument of some kind.

All around were now deeply concerned. Hal Roystan had been well known, even before the business of the discovery of his father's grave and the downfall of the Bannamans. But now, at the mention of his name, be it in Allendale, Haydon Bridge or even Hexham, people would nod their heads to acknowledge their acquaintance with him.

On the afternoon of the fourth day, Mary Ellen stood in the kitchen of Hal's little farmhouse and with the tears running down her face looked about her. Everything was neat and orderly. The woman Annie had just gone after tidying up where there was nothing to tidy. She too had been crying, and her last words as she went out of the door were, "He was a lovely man, a lovely man, and kind. There'll not be another like him. No, there won't. No, there won't." And in her mind Mary Ellen endorsed this, for she knew now there would never be another like him. And she asked herself why she hadn't found it out long ago. She must have been blind, or just young and silly. She was about to sit down when she stopped herself, muttering aloud, "You'll have to get back. You'll have to get back." Kate was in a very low state, and Mrs Patterson could only stay with the child for an hour or so at a time.

She was a depressing woman, was Mrs Patterson. Before she had got through the door this morning she was saying, "It's hopeless. Four days now. They should give up. Some of the men are dead on their feet: they do a shift, then wander the moors, then back to their shift again. It can't go on." And then she had nodded at her, saying finally, "Make up your mind, lass, make up your mind. Wherever he is, there's no comin' back, not after four days out there. And they've been over the place with a small tooth-comb. 'Tis another mystery that'll not be solved for years, just like that of his father afore him. And they're sayin' now, and it's quite true, and it's strange, that when his father disappeared he was ridin' a pony. And where was that found? Right down the river in Newcastle. And now his pony's been found. I tell you, it's uncanny. History repeats itself in cases like this, always did and always will. Her lying there" – she had pointed to the bed – "she could tell you that." ...

Mary Ellen went into the farm sitting-room and stood there gazing around the room. No wonder he had been proud of his home. And he had picked up nice odd pieces of furniture. It was a lovely little house. It had everything. Oh, Hal, Hal.

The whining of the dog penetrated her mind, and she went out and stood in the yard looking towards the shed where the animal was, and she thought, Poor thing; it's as lost as I am. Going to the shed, she lifted up the heavy latch and pulled the door open a little way, and the dog thrust its head through and licked at her hand. She peered into the dimness and said, "Oh, you haven't got any water. Just a minute." And as she went to close the door again she felt the animal thrust itself against it, and then he was out in the yard dancing round her. And she called to it, "Boyo! Boyo! Stay! Stay, Boyo. Here! Boyo."

It stood still, but as she came towards it to grip its collar, it again darted from her; then it ran to the house door and, reaching up, scratched at the nob. And when once again she made to grab at it, it darted from her, then turning, fled from the yard. And she cupped her face in her hands, saying, "Oh now, where will they find him? If he roams he'll be picked up by the gypsies again or shot by a gamekeeper if he gets into someone's land." But what did it matter? She let out a long shuddering breath. If Hal was gone, and Hal must be gone by this time, the dog would pine; if not, he would certainly be unmanageable, because he obeyed nobody but Hal.

Her step was slow and weary as she made her way back to the cottage. ...

Mrs Patterson greeted her with, "I'm not gona ask if there's any news because I know there couldn't be, that's unless they find him. But anyway, the men are calling it off the night and leaving it to the constables. It's their job anyway, although what that handful will do will make no difference one way or the other."

"Thank you, Mrs Patterson. I'll manage now."

The woman put on her shawl; but before opening the door she said, "Me chest's not so good. I could do with a drop of that cough mixture. And our Mary isn't sleeping. Kate often used to give me a powder for her."

Everything must be paid for. The words echoed through her mind as she measured out the cough mixture and spooned some white powder on to a piece of paper. Kate was always saying that, everything must be paid for, even the help given by a neighbour in a kind of crisis. This was the third time this week she had made up potions for Mrs Patterson.

After the woman had gone she went to the basket and picked up the child. It was sucking on a pap bag, but it was empty. So she made up another one, dipped it in the milk and placed it in the child's mouth. The baby's face was very red, and she lifted up its dress and saw that once again Mrs Patterson had tightened its binder. Almost angrily now she undid the length of linen that was wound round the child's middle, and the baby let out something of a sigh. And she muttered aloud, "Why must it be made so tight? They can't breathe." But even Kate said the binder must be tight or the child's stomach would blow out like a balloon. There was moderation, though, there must be. The child was always happier and didn't winge when it lay in a slack binder.

She replaced the baby in the basket, then patted its cheek before going to the bed. Kate was lying with her eyes open and her mouth moved into the word, "Well?" but made very little sound. She didn't answer her but just shook her head.

When Kate tried to speak again Mary Ellen bent down and put her ear towards the thin blue lips and the word she heard was, "Ban . . . na . . . man." It sounded as if it had been split into three. She looked at Kate and said, "But they've gone. There's no one there. The house is empty."

Kate's lips moved again and once more Mary Ellen put her ear down.

"Ban . . . na . . . man."

Mary Ellen looked down into the eyes that still showed conscious intelligence and she shook her head and said, "They can do nothing, Kate. They've gone. The place is empty. The men were all round there yesterday, both those from the mill and the constables."

"Find out." The words were low and clear now. "Enemy. Hal's enemy. Find out."

More to soothe her than anything else, Mary Ellen said, "All right, Kate, all right. I'll tell them to find out where they are, the Bannamans. Yes, I'll tell them."

She watched the old woman's eyes close, and only the slight rise and fall of the hap indicated that she was still breathing. . . .

It was late afternoon when the scratching came on the door. She opened it, and in amazement saw the dog standing there. And she looked down on it, saying, "Why! Boyo. Oh, Boyo, you've come back. Come away, come on, that's a good dog."

But the dog did not come into the room, it turned round and walked half-way down towards the gate before stopping and looking back at her, as if trying to tell her something. And she knew it was trying to tell her something: it wanted her to follow him. In an agony of mind, she looked back up the room to the bed and then to the child. Then grabbing up the big shawl that used almost to envelop Kate, she put it over her head and tied it round her waist in a tight knot; then lifting the child up, she put her into the folds of the shawl between her breasts, and hurried out, closing the door behind her. And when the dog saw her he moved on, running now straight across the field towards the quarry top. When she reached the top of the bank she was gasping for breath. But the dog was only a few yards in front of her, and she thought for a moment, He's going to the tunnel. But that was silly. She had been there. The first thing she had done after she finally realized he was missing was to make herself go there, while trying to forget it was from there he must have dragged Feeler and made him hang himself.

But the dog turned down the road. She thought it might be making for the mine, but no, it went straight on. But with the mine in sight she saw two miners looking up towards her and she beckoned them while she still kept walking following the dog. She saw them hesitate and she called to them, "Here a minute! Here a minute!"

One of them hurried towards her, saying, "What is it, lass?"

"The dog." She pointed to the dog. "It got out early this morning, but it's come to the cottage and it wouldn't come in. It wanted me to follow it. I ... I think it must have ... well" – she shook her head – "it could have found him, or ... or something."

The man shouted back to his mate, "Here a minute. Come on," and began to walk by Mary Ellen's side.

When the other man joined them, he said, "Look there, the animal knows something. It came down to Mary Ellen's place. Got out this mornin', she said. Looks as if it's going straight on for Whitfield."

But the dog wasn't making for Whitfield. Where the three paths joined, it turned off left and one of the men said, "Wild goose chase, if you ask me anything. That road leads to Bannaman's place, a good mile and a half along there. And they've been over that with a riddle."

"It ... it mightn't be there, it might be somewhere around."

Both men looked at her; then one said, "The country's as flat as a pancake for some distance there. It doesn't start dropping until you get near Whitfield down to the river, the same as here." He was making a sweeping movement with his right hand.

The men had slowed their pace to accommodate Mary Ellen's for with the weight of the child she was finding difficulty in hurrying. And once when she stopped to ease the stitch in her side, the dog, some yards ahead, stopped too. And one of the men remarked, "That beast knows where he's goin' all right, and he wants us to go along of him."

"My God!" A few minutes later the man was pointing. "The animal's turned off to the farm. Look, there it is ahead. And it's runnin' now."

When they reached the opening to the yard they could not see the dog, but they could hear him barking, and when they went through the arch there was the dog, clawing at the barn door.

"I've been in there." The man's voice was very low. "There's nothin' but a bit of straw above. I even went up the ladder, so what's he after?"

The other man had hurried forward and had pulled the door open, and the dog rushed in and began sniffing around the bottom of the barn. Then he stopped at the foot of the ladder and, looking upwards, started to bark, loudly, harshly.

"There's nowt up there." The other man shook his head.

When the dog attempted to climb the ladder, Mary Ellen said, quietly, "Lift him up." And one of the men did this. He put his arm round the animal and hoisted him up the rungs, and once on the platform the dog seemed to go mad.

The other man had begun to climb the ladder when Mary Ellen called to him, "Will . . . will you take her?" And she stood on the bottom rung and held the child up to him, and the man, bending down, took the child from her arms and slowly ascended, with Mary Ellen following. At the top, taking the baby from the man, she stood watching the dog clawing at the hay.

"There's something in there, at the back, there must be," she said.

Both men now started pulling the loose hay aside, and then of a sudden they stopped and gazed at the dog that was pawing at the huddled figure tied to the beam.

"*Christ Almighty!*"

"*In the name of God!*"

"*Oh! Hal. Hal.*" It was an agonized cry wrenched up from the depth of her, and thrusting the child down on to the straw she flung herself forward and she pulled the scarf from around his face and closed her eyes for a moment to shut out the grotesque sight of the stiff gaping mouth. The men were now loosening the ropes that tied him to the beam; but once they had undone them the huddled form just toppled on to its side, and one of the men muttered, "He's a gonner."

"No, no." She looked up at him. "Do something. Get the doctor. Get the doctor. Go on, go for the doctor." The two men looked at each other for a moment, and one of them said, "Aye. aye. Go on, Bill. And bring the constables an' all."

As Bill scampered away, she looked at the other man and said, "Can . . . can you untie him?"

When the man attempted to unloosen the knots, he muttered, "My God! Whoever did this knew how to tie a knot."

The dog now was lying to the side of Hal's head, licking his forehead and making a sound like a child softly crying, and Mary Ellen, putting her hand on the animal said, "Oh! Boyo. Oh! Boyo. If I'd only let you out before. If only. If only."

Still struggling with the knots, the man muttered, "Aye, it might have saved him, but God, whoever did this wants stringing up, and I would do it meself if I could find them."

"He's not, is he? He's not?"

"I'm afraid so, lass. I'm afraid so. 'Tis four days, remember, and strung up like this is more than human flesh could stand."

Tentatively now she opened the top button of Hal's coat and put her hand onto his shirt, but she could feel no movement. And she closed her eyes and bent over him, her whole being crying, "Oh! Hal. Hal. Oh! my dear. Why? Why?" Then straightening up, she said to the man, "Kate was right. She . . . she said the Bannamans. She kept saying 'Bannaman'. She must have known it would be one of them."

"But they live miles away now, lass."

"Well, Hal said he had seen them over here two or three times."

"He had?"

"Yes. Aye."

"Well, if that's the case, they'll be in for it this time and won't get off by havin' a stroke."

As he unloosened the last of the ropes, the man said, "We'd better not try to unbend him, not till the doctor gets here. Think 'tis better he sees him like this, he'll know what to do. And the authorities an' all. Nobody would believe it, they'd have to see it."

"Oh! Hal. Hal." Her tears were dropping on to his face now. And the man put his hand on her shoulder and said, "Don't take on, lass. Don't take on. Rest assured somebody'll pay for this, 'cos I've seen some things in me life but never anything so cruel. A slow death."

"If . . . if we rubbed his legs or hands?"

"Can't see it's much use, lass. You've got to admit he looks a gonner."

"But . . . but couldn't we try? Just . . . just rub them gently."

"Well, if it would give you any satisfaction, lass, all right, all right, we'll do that."

She started on a hand. Taking the stiff fingers in hers, she massaged them one by one, while the man, taking up the other hand, did the same. But so rough were his hands she could hear the chafing of the skin as if a grater were being passed over the bloodless flesh.

"Knead his arms next, from the shoulder."

"I can't get at his shoulder at this side, lass, and I don't think we'd better disturb him. But you do it from where you are and I'll work on his legs. I'm more used to working on the legs." He gave a small smile now. "We often get the cramp you know, in the pit. Sittin' in one position too long, you get all knotted up. I'll be all right on the legs." And his hands began to move expertly up and down Hal's legs.

And so they went on for almost an hour, but there was no response from the twisted limbs.

When they heard the commotion in the yard the man rose to his feet and ran towards the end of the platform, then beckoned four men up the ladder. And when the leading constable looked down on the twisted form and the ropes lying to its side he remained silent, until the miner said, "You should have seen him trussed up there" – he pointed to the beam – "as tight as a vice. As I said, whoever tied these knots meant them never to be undone."

"Is he gone?"

"Aye, I should say so. We've been rubbin' him but there's been no effect."

One of the constables said quietly, "What's to be done with him?"

And it was Mary Ellen who put in quickly, "Wait for the doctor, please, wait for the doctor. He'll know what to do. He . . . he might still be alive."

"Well, we can easily find that out." The constable now knelt down on the hay. Then gently opening the jacket further and the shirt and the vest, he put his head on to the cold flesh, and it seemed an interminable time before he raised it and, his eyes blinking quickly, he said, "I think I can hear his heart still goin'. Could be, faint like."

"You sure?" The miner's voice was eager.

"Well, I'm not too sure but I'll try again." Once more he laid his head on Hal's chest; then he muttered, "Ease him over just a little bit."

Ready hands now turned the stiff huddled limbs gently to the side and the constable laid his head once more close to the flesh. Presently, sitting back quickly, he nodded and said, "Aye, I feel sure. I do, aye, I do, I feel sure. Now now, lass" – he put his hand out – "steady on. Look, you have the bairn to see to, so don't you go and pass out on us. Here, sit over here." He pulled her to the side. "Lean your back against the wall, put your head down."

She put her head down, all the while crying inside herself, "Come back, Hal. Come back, Hal. Oh, God, let him come back." She felt on the verge of a faint and heard one of the men say, "Here, take hold of the bairn. That'll pull you round. Come on now, take her." She took the child and her arms instinctively went round it and she began to rock her gently, all the while staring at the dead white face with the wide open mouth on the straw some feet away.

The further commotion in the yard brought her fully to her senses, and when she saw the doctor coming over the top of the ladder she turned on her knees and, with the help of one of the men got to her feet.

And she watched as the doctor, just as the constables had done, stood staring down at Hal in absolute amazement for a moment before dropping to his knees.

His actions, too, were much the same as the constables' had been, but his voice wasn't as enthusiastic as he said, "Yes, he could be, but it's a slim chance. We'll have to have a door. We must get him somewhere where I can apply hot water and oil."

"Bring him home to ... to Kate's."

He turned and looked at her. "Too far," he said; "his farm is nearer."

"Please, please. I ... I can see to him there, and ... and she has the salve and things."

"There's a cart in the yard," said one of the men. "There are enough of us to pull him on that."

Minutes later she watched them gently lifting Hal on to the cart in which the men had laid their outer coats to soften the contact with the wood. There were now at least twenty people in the yard, for such news spread quickly, and they formed a procession as they left the farm: two men at each shaft, two men pushing at the back, the doctor riding to one side on his horse, and Mary Ellen, the child once more tucked in the shawl between her breasts, walking at the other, the rest trailing behind. There was no chatter, it was like a funeral procession.

At the cottage the doctor spoke to the constables, and as if they were still attending a funeral quietly and without any fuss they asked the followers to disperse. And most of them, nodding, moved away.

Once inside and the child in the basket, Mary Ellen sprang to life. She pulled her mattress from the corner of the room, laid it by the fire, and the men gently laid Hal on it. Then thrusting a pail into the hands of a constable, she said, "Fetch some water." Then she went to the shelf and took down a large jar of goose fat.

The doctor now had his coat off and was kneeling by the mattress. Looking up at her, he said, "Get me a knife." And when she had fetched it, he systematically split the arm of the coat and then the trousers. These he gently eased off the twisted limbs; then did the same with the shirt, and then the long clothes. And when the body was lying bare he covered the middle with a sheet and said to Mary Ellen, "Keep the cloths coming."

And she did this. Just as Hal had done for her, she thrust her hands into almost boiling water and wrung out pieces of sheeting and handed them to the doctor who applied them to Hal's arms and legs, while the four constables stood around in awe-filled silence, at times shaking their heads at what they imagined to be the futility of it all.

Following the application of the hot cloths, the doctor now scooped handfuls of the goose grease and began to massage the stiff and seemingly frozen shoulders. And when at last he brought one arm gently forward, Mary Ellen imagined that there was a slight twitching in the muscles of the dead white face. But she said nothing, and the doctor continued massaging the other shoulder. Meanwhile she had been working on Hal's knees as the doctor had instructed her. It was exhausting work for both of them but eventually they had Hal stretched out on his back with a hot brick wrapped up in flannel at his feet and similar ones at each side of him.

When at last the doctor rose to his feet he asked, "Have you any spirits in the house?" And for a moment Mary Ellen thought it was for himself and she answered, "A wee drop of brandy. It was a present to Kate at Christmas."

"Fetch it, and a spoon."

A moment later she watched him pouring the brandy drop by drop into Hal's open mouth. And it was when the second spoonful had gone down his throat that there came a twitching of his face muscles. And Mary Ellen, who was again kneeling by his side, put her hand over her lips and looked up at the doctor, and he gave a small smile and a quick nod of his head before he poured out another spoonful, saying as he did so now, "That's it. Come along, come along." And as if answering a call, Hal's jawbones moved in an effort to close his mouth. And the men round about, as if suddenly becoming alive themselves, began to talk to each other.

"Eeh, my God! Did you see that?"

"Never thought it possible."

"Talk about comin' back from the dead."

"I'll believe anything now."

"Eeh! by doctor, you've done a job there. An' you an' all, lass. By! my, you have. Well, if any of us owes anybody else their lives, he does. Another day and he would have been a gonner sure. What d'you say, doctor?"

"Indeed, indeed, yes."

" 'Twas his dog." Mary Ellen pointed to where the dog was lying by the baby's basket, and they looked at it and then at her, and no one spoke for a moment until the doctor said, "His dog found him?"

"Yes." She nodded at him. "I kept him tied up but he got out. And then he came back and . . . well" – she moved her head in wonderment – "he practically spoke to me. Then I met Mr Boston and Mr York, and they came along of me."

The doctor now rolled down his sleeves, saying, "Miracles do happen, not very often, but they do. Now" – he looked down on Mary Ellen – "it may be some time before he comes round. Have some hot broth ready. Don't let him talk. Keep him quiet. I've got to go now but I'll be back later in the evening. I don't know at what time, but I'll be back."

When he went to pick his coat from the chair, the men made way for him. But he did not go immediately towards the door; instead he went up to the bed in the far corner of the room and stood looking down on Kate for a moment.

She was lying with her eyes open. She made no attempt to speak, nor did he, but he put his hand gently on her brow for a moment before turning away.

Mary Ellen went with him to the door and outside he stood looking up into the sky taking in deep breaths of air; and she stood for a moment, too, looking upwards. The stars were coming out, the sky was high. When he brought his gaze down to her he said quietly, "You're forming a knack of saving men's lives, Mary Ellen."

" 'Twas the dog," she said again.

"Well, we'll give credit to the dog, but you certainly have a hand in these things. Now the next move is to find out who attempted this act of slow murder."

"You won't have to look far, doctor. It was one of the Bannamans."

"That'll have to be proved."

"The scarf round his mouth has two initials on it: there's B.B. woven in with silk thread, and they call the son Benjamin."

"Well, it's in the hands of the authorities now. Whoever did it, it was an act of evil revenge." He smiled wanly at her now, saying, "I used to think nothing ever happened in the country, it was a dead place. Sometimes I think I'd like to go back into the town for a rest."

She answered his smile, saying quietly, "You'd be sorely missed if you did, doctor, indeed you would."

"Bye-bye, Mary Ellen, for the present."

"Goodbye, doctor." She stood for another moment watching him going down to the gate where his horse was tethered and where lanterns were swinging showing up the outlines of people still waiting for news.

As she went back into the room one of the constables said, "Two of us'll be away, lass. The others" – he jerked his head backwards – "they are stayin', they want to hear what he says when he comes round."

*

It was ten o'clock the following morning before Hal returned to full consciousness. At two o'clock in the morning he had opened his eyes and looked to where Mary Ellen was sitting by the fire, her head drooped on her chest in weariness. It was one of the constables who spoke to him, saying, "How you feelin', lad?" But he had made no answer, just closed his eyes and gone to sleep again. But at the moment he became fully conscious, Mary Ellen was kneeling by his side, and he blinked his eyes a number of times before endeavouring to speak. His voice a croak, he said, "I'm ... I'm alive."

She had the desire to gather him up in her arms and press his head tightly to her and say, "Yes, my love, you're alive." But what she did was to take one of his hands between her own and hold it to her, saying gently, "Yes, Hal, you're alive. You're going to be all right."

"Me legs."

"They're all right."

"I ... I don't feel they're there."

"Oh, they're there all right." She smiled at him while endeavouring to hold back her tears of relief.

"Demon."

"What did you say?"

"Her. She's a demon."

"Who, Hal? Who?"

"Bannaman."

At the sound of his voice, the other constable who had come on duty came to his side and, bending down, he said, "You know who did this to you?"

"Bannaman." The name was stronger now. "The daughter and ... and son."

"My God! A woman? She strung you up?"

"She ... she strung me up." He closed his eyes as he muttered, "Sent me ... into ... the next world."

"You're back, Hal, you're back." Mary Ellen was patting his cheek gently and she signalled to the constable not to say any more.

As the constable moved back to the table, Hal opened his eyes and, gazing at Mary Ellen, he said, "You found me?"

"No ... the dog."

"Boyo?"

At the sound of his name, the dog came from where it had been lying near the child's basket and, stretching across the mattress, he licked Hal's face. And Hal, putting his hand on its head, a little of his old manner returning, said, "Irish tinker. I'll ... I'll pay him double when ... when I next see him."

22

It was three days before Hal was sufficiently recovered to get on his feet; and then, as he said, he felt like a child taking its first steps, and the effort was painful, especially round the knee joints.

Mary Ellen had fed him with broth and whatever he could eat of the dishes that Annie had brought over from the farm. The big woman's first visit had been a painful scene, for she had stood over him and cried unashamedly. And Mary Ellen had felt deep sorrow for her and for a moment she had thought, Oh, 'tis a pity you're not younger; then had asked herself why on earth she should think that the way she herself felt. But nevertheless, she could gauge the loneliness and want in this big woman.

Her face awash with tears, Annie had assured Hal that his animals were all right, his house was all right, and Terry was doing fine. He had nothing whatever to worry about, but ... would he please come back soon.

When she had left, Hal had sighed and said, "She's a good lass. She's wasted."

The first walk Hal took was up the room to the bed where Mary Ellen placed a chair for him, and there he sat and held Kate's hand. And as she looked at him she said again the one word, "Bannaman." And he nodded at her and said, "Aye, Kate, aye, Bannaman." Then smiling faintly, he said, "They meant to wipe all the Roystans off the map, but they slipped up this time."

"Have ... have they found them?"

"No, not yet, Kate, but they're lookin'."

The fingers within his scratched gently on his flesh as she said, "Time's nearly up, Hal. I can go now ... any time now ... Hal."

"Yes, Kate?" He bent over her, the muscles of his face twitching.

"Mary Ellen. See to Mary Ellen."

"Don't worry, Kate. Don't worry. Mary Ellen will be all right."

"Hal."

"Yes, Kate?"

"See to Mary Ellen."

He drew in a long breath, then said, "I know what you mean, Kate. I know what you mean. I'll try."

"Don't ... don't wait for him ... Roddy. He's ... he's past."

"Would you like to see him, Kate?"

She did not answer for a time, but closed her eyes, then muttered, "'Tis no matter, 'tis no matter. Pat is here. Came yesterday." She smiled wanly, and he left loose of her hand and laid it gently on the counterpane. Then rising stiffly, he walked slowly down the room and, dropping onto the form by the fire, he looked towards Mary Ellen's back. She was standing at the table cutting up some meat and he said quietly, "I think we'd better send for him."

Her hands became still before she said, "I suppose so."

"I think it had better be an express letter."

"I'll get somebody to take it into Hexham to meet the coach going into Newcastle. It'll go quickly from there."

He continued to stare at her back as he muttered, "Aye, it'll go quickly from there. He could be here if he liked in four days or so."

When she made no answer but went on with her work, he said, "She thinks her son is here, Pat, and likely he is.

"Could you get word to him an' all after she goes?"

"'Twould be a hard job, he died last year. The letter came to her. I picked it up from the carrier. It was in a different hand, proper writing. I opened it. It was from a preacher. Reading atween the lines Pat had died in a fight. Well, the other one had just gone and I felt she'd had enough for the time being, so tore the thing up."

She gazed at him. What would he do next? He was a law unto himself; yet that action had been thoughtful.

He was saying now, "I'll have to be making me way back," causing her to turn towards him and say sharply, "You'll do no such thing; you can hardly stand on your legs yet. You'll stay where you are for the next couple of days."

He kept his eyes on her as he said, "That's all very well; but you can't expect that little lad to carry on on his own."

"He's not carryin' on on his own, he's got Annie there an' all."

"Oh, aye, Annie." He smiled wanly now. "A treasure is Annie. I don't know what I'd do without Annie." A teasing note had come into his voice.

She did not respond in like manner but, her face serious, she said, "That's true. I don't know what you'd do without her, nor me for that matter; she's kept us goin' in milk and food for the past days; so sit yourself still." ...

Sometime later, having attended to Kate, washed the breakfast crocks, done the hearth, brought in more wood and water, and fed the child, she took out a square of paper from a drawer, and a pencil and, sitting down at the table, chewed on the end of the pencil for a moment, then started to write. She did not begin, "Dear Roddy," but said simply,

"Kate is nearing her end, I think you should come."

She did not even sign her name. Her sprawled writing covered a third of the page. Then folding it up she wrote the address on one side of it, before going to the fire, where she lit a taper, took a piece of wax from the box on the mantelpiece and sealed the letter, then returned the wax to the box, knowing all the while her actions were being watched by Hal. But he made no comment on what she was doing until, a shawl about her, she went towards the door, saying, "Give an eye to her. I won't be long," when he asked quietly, "Have you got the money on you to send it?"

Her lips fell into a tight line. She hadn't thought about the money. She went back to the mantelpiece, lifted the lid of another small box and took out two shillings; then holding it in the palm of her hand, she asked quietly, "Will that be enough?"

"More I should say; a shilling'll be enough."

"To send it quickly?"

"Oh, aye. Anyway, ask the carter. And if it's Beardy Smith, give him a penny for himself, 'cos he'll have to go out of his way to get it to the coach."

She nodded at him her agreement, then went out.

Once the door had closed on her, Hal bent forward and put his elbows on his knees and dropped his face onto his hands. He felt sick, not from the pain that was still in his limbs, nor from the feeling of fear that he seemed unable to get rid of, for it had buried itself too deep, so deep in those first two days of agony that he felt he would have to live a number of lifetimes to be the same man again, one who hadn't been afraid of anything or anyone; no, this particular sickness was centred in his chest, for he knew that once Roddy stepped into this room life as he had known it during these past months would never be the same again. Her feelings towards himself had changed, they certainly weren't as they had been, he knew that, but she would only have to see *him* and she would be back where she was, at his feet.

He dropped his hands from his face, and they hung limply down between his knees, and he stared at the child lying gurgling in the basket. What would be his reactions when he saw her? Feel it his duty to marry Mary Ellen and take her back with him? He doubted it. There was a draw up in London town that had held him close for the past year. His last letter had spoken of how hard he was working towards some kind of test; the previous one had spoken of an exhibition his tutor said he must attend. All excuses, excuses. He was a skunk, a selfish self-preserving skunk.

He pulled himself to his feet and glanced up the room to the still form on the bed. That woman up there, too, had loved him, like perhaps she had never loved her own son. And what must her thoughts have been this past year? By God! No matter what happened, should he ever enter that door, or wherever he came across him, he would give him the length of his tongue. It was a pity he wasn't feeling fit, or he would give him the length of his arm and his fist into his good-looking face.

His thoughts now made him wonder what he had seen in him all those years; why he had trailed him as he had done. Oh, he knew why he had done since he was eighteen or so, but not before that. Likely, as he had already told himself a number of times, out of gratitude for being offered his friendship when he was being shunned by everybody else. Yet, he knew that Roddy had been as lonely as he had been, and more mixed up, if the truth was told, for he hadn't known who he was or where he had come from. And so in that case there should have been gratitude on both sides. But it had all come from him.

The child made a slight whining noise, and he went over to the basket and gently picked her up and cradled her in his arms. It was strange, he felt no resentment about the child; it was as if she belonged to him as well as to Mary Ellen. What would happen to him if they both disappeared from his life? He knew what would happen, he'd rot slowly. But he wouldn't die . . . huh! he might even take Annie in for comfort.

The latter had come into his mind as a form of joke, and as he sat rocking the child gently, he thought, Perhaps not so much of a joke either; man was so made he needed a mother in some form or other until the day he died.

Kate died in her sleep that night. At what hour they didn't know. Mary Ellen came down from the loft around five o'clock where she had been sleeping on a makeshift straw-filled pallet. She had the child tight pressed to her by one arm and she was surprised to find the lamp lit, the fire going, and Hal sitting on the settle fully dressed.

She did not go to bed but towards him and her first words were, "You feelin' bad?"

"No, no." He got to his feet and then, inclining his head towards the bed, he said, softly, "She's gone."

"*Aw! Aw!*" She quickly put the child into the basket, then hurried up the room, and there by the side of the bed she stood and with her hand over her mouth, a gesture which always indicated her intense feeling of the moment, the tears ran down her cheeks and she muttered thickly, "Aw, Kate, Kate." And looking to where Hal stood at the foot of the bed, she said, "I . . . I don't know what I'm goin' to do without her. She . . . she was more than a mother to me."

"Aye. And to more than you."

She glanced towards him. Yes, he was right, and to more than her, for in a way Kate had been the only mother he had known.

He said now, quietly, "She understood me when no one else did," then added on a different note, "She . . . she must have been really bonny when she was young. Look. Look at her face now. Most of the lines have gone."

Yes – Mary Ellen nodded to herself – it was strange, most of the lines had gone. She looked happy. Death was a funny thing. No, not funny, that was the wrong word, odd, frightening. And yet there was nothing to be frightened about, looking at Kate now. It was the first time she had actually seen a dead person. She had seen numbers of dead cattle and had never got used to the sight, especially when it was an animal she had talked to.

She felt Hal's hand on her arm. He was saying, "Come away now, come away. She wouldn't want you to cry for her. She thought the world of you, you know that. Come on." He led her down the room again to the fire and pressed her gently on to the settle, saying, "I've made some porridge."

When he handed her the bowl of porridge and laid a jug of milk to the side of her on the settle, she wanted to say, I can't eat it. But he was being thoughtful, so she must try.

She had eaten half the porridge when he said, "She'll have to be laid out. Can you do it?"

"*No, no,*" she spluttered on a mouthful of the oats. "I couldn't do that. I'll have to get Mrs Patterson."

"Yes, well, that's all right. Don't distress yourself. I'll go along to the village and tell her as soon as it breaks light."

"Are you up to it?"

"I've got to go out into the wide world sometime, Mary Ellen. Another couple of nights here and you won't get rid of me." He was staring at her. The firelight was playing on her face, bringing out highlights where her cheeks were still wet. And he wondered how he was going to face the wide world after these few days spent with her in this room. But face it he must, and gather up strength for what was to come when *he* arrived.

"It's a good job you got the letter off yesterday," he said. "It would leave on the mail coach from Newcastle round half-past nine. I think that's the time it goes. Something more than a day and a half I reckon it takes. He could be here within four days."

The spoon half-way to her mouth, she stopped her hand, saying, "That's if he leaves right away."

"Aye, yes, as you say, if he leaves right away."

He could not prevent himself now from asking the question that was rampant in his mind: "What's goin' to happen when you do see him?"

She put the spoon of porridge twice more into her mouth before laying the plate aside on the settle, and then she said quietly, "That remains to be seen."

After Mrs Patterson had finished laying out Kate she took a seat by the fire and in a tone that held some reprimand, she said, "It's usual to have a drop of somethin' in at a time like this, a drop of spirit; if not, ale of some kind. As I said, 'tis usual. But then you're young and not as yet used to death. That'll come though with time. Still, I thought Kate, even with her potions, would have held a little bit aside. She wasn't above a drop years ago when it flowed freely. I know that."

Apologetically, Mary Ellen said, "There . . . there was some brandy, but we had to give it to Hal."

"Oh, aye, aye. That's another thing: he's on his feet now and able to move; I think it would be wise if he got himself away back to his farm, 'cos people talk you know. Oh aye, people talk. He could have been near dead when they brought him in, but that was some days ago. You don't want to get a name like another Maggie Oates, now do you?"

Mary Ellen swung round ready to yell her protest at this gossiping old woman, but knowing that she was under an obligation to her, all she could say was, "Oh, Mrs Patterson."

"Aye, well, lass, I'm only speakin' for your own good; you can't stop people's tongues. And you've got to admit, since Kate put you on to this potion and herb business there's been more men here than there's been at Maggie's."

"Mrs Patterson, what you hintin' at? You know it isn't true, none of it."

"Oh, lass, you needn't start an' bubble. As I say, I'm only speakin' for your own good. 'Cos you got your name up with one, you don't want to have it with another. And he's got his name up already, has Hal, encouragin' that Annie Gordon to make a fool of herself. Comin' over here every day with food for him. They say she's never off his doorstep and her with whiskers on her chin. Eeh! What some women will do for a man. If they only knew what it was all about afore they started, they'd run the other way. By God! they would. Anyway, I'm off now and perhaps you don't know it but . . . well, I charge a shillin' for layin' and gettin' rid of the muck."

Mary Ellen closed her eyes for a moment before going to the mantelpiece, from where she took down the box and, taking out a shilling, she handed it to the older woman.

Looking at it in the palm of her hand, Mrs Patterson said, "Aye, well, nothing under, nothing over, I suppose," and without further words picked up her shawl from the back of the chair and went out.

Mary Ellen lowered herself slowly down on to the settle and she folded her arms tightly across her breasts and leant her head back against the wooden support as if she was resisting some force, which indeed she was, for she wanted to shout out her protests against the gossiping tongues. Even when she told herself to remember that everybody wasn't like Mrs Patterson, that there were kindly women hereabouts and that many of them had come to the door to enquire after both Kate and her, she still knew it just needed a woman like Mrs Patterson to start a rumour and even the nice ones would say: Well, there's never smoke without fire.

What was she going to do now? Kate gone and she here on her own. And every time Hal entered the door she'd be conscious that someone had seen him, and that they were all putting two and two together. And there would be no doubt that after a while other men would come knocking at the door supposedly for potions, and definitely after dark.

There was a way out, but she couldn't bring herself to take it: that kind of thing had to come from the man, because men being what they were, even the best of them, if you made the first step they would hold it against you forever after. Look what had happened with Roddy. She had made the first step there all right, hadn't she? Rushed in with both feet, and arms outstretched, and he had flown. 'Twas no use telling herself that he had been on the point of flying in any case. What had happened that night had scared him so much that he had made every excuse not to come back. So that's what would happen, she supposed, even in a minor way to any woman who made the first move. No, whatever was to happen between her and Hal had to come from him; she couldn't make herself cheap again.

She had opened the doors and windows to let the air sweep out the smell of death. There had been many visitors during the day, both men and women. They had stood by the bed looking down on the face that had already changed colour and was in sharp contrast with the white linen rag strapped underneath the chin and around the head.

The doctor, too, had called, and he had spoken so kindly of the woman who had seemingly not had a good word for him. "She was clever," he had said; "in her own way she was a very clever woman." Then he had sniffed as he walked down the room, saying now, "She'll have to be boxed and buried as soon as possible. You'd do well to leave the doors open during the day while the weather's fine. But a couple of nights closed up . . . well" – he spread out his hands – "the smell would get worse. Have you instructed the carpenter?"

"Yes, yes. Hal's seen to it."

"Amazing fella that." He had shaken his head. "I never expected to hear him breathe again. Did you?"

"No, no, I didn't, but I hoped."

As he went out of the cottage he turned and said to her, "There's a rumour going around that the Bannamans have flown. They were living in a house outside Corbridge and the last that was heard of them was they had taken a coach southwards."

"Well, as long as they have gone, that's all that matters I think. Although I feel they should be brought to justice."

"You're not the only one who feels that. And it could come about yet. Goodbye, Mary Ellen."

"Goodbye, doctor," she said. "And thank you." . . .

Hal had left about noon for the farm and he did not return until it was nearly dark.

"How are you?" he said.

"I'm all right. How are you?"

He pressed his lips tight for a moment while shaking his head; then he said, "I'm mad about the latest news."

"You mean about the Bannamans leavin'?"

"Oh, I knew about them leavin' days ago, but it's just been discovered they've taken a boat to America."

"No!"

"Aye. Her and her mother and her brother, goin' to the mother's cousin or somebody out there."

"Can the justices not do anything now?"

"I . . . I don't think they'll bother. If I had died, aye, perhaps; but, as the constable who brought me the news said this mornin', I'm on me pins and as good as ever I was – that's all he knows – so I don't think they'll take any further steps. But oh, by God!" – he ground his teeth together and thumped one fist into the palm of the other – "I would just like to come face to face with that one just once more. You know" – he turned and looked at her – "I never believed in devils, or heaven or hell afore, but now I believe in both devils and hell, because she's a devil an' she put me through hell. Heaven? Well, I won't know anythin' about that, I don't think ever. But the other two, aye. Oh aye." He stopped now and looked up towards the bed, saying, "I saw Bill Powell on me way here. He's had a word with the doctor. He's boxing her in the mornin'. The doctor thinks she should be buried the morrow or the next day at the latest. 'Cos you can't stand this." His nose wrinkled.

"It isn't so bad when I'm upstairs," she said.

"No, but it is when I'm down here."

She stared at him. "But . . . but you're goin' home."

"No, I'm not, I'm not leavin' you with that; she's not Kate any more. Kate's gone wherever good people like Kate go to. But what's left, that's somethin' else."

"Hal" – her voice was low – "you'd better not stay. I'll . . . I'll be all right. I'll be quite all right. I'd . . . I'd rather you went."

"Oh aye. Mrs Patterson been here? Of course she has. Oh, Mary Ellen, don't worry your head. I know what they're sayin' and you know what they're sayin'. Well, let them say. When they're talkin' about us they're givin' somebody else a rest, eh? Now, I don't like eating in here; let's go in the scullery. And bring the bairn. Oh, and of course" – he nodded down to the dog – "you go without sayin', don't you, old fellow?" He patted the animal's head, then pressed it against his knee for a moment.

The act of affection made Mary Ellen blink her eyelids and say, " 'Tis a pity he can't speak, isn't it?"

"Oh, I don't know so much about that. He's got a language all his own and it's very understandable. Haven't you, old boy?" He again patted the dog's head, then said, "Well, come on, let's get movin'. I'm hungry, and Annie's made a nice pie. Oh, by the way" – he chuckled now – "you'll never believe this, but I had a visit from her father this afternoon. You know what he asked me?"

They were in the scullery now standing one each side of the small table set against the wall opposite the stone sink. And now there was a rumble in his stomach and his head moved from side to side before he added, "He wanted to know what my intentions were towards his daughter. He's barmy, quite barmy. No wonder the lasses are odd and his wife scared out of her wits. He talked of recompense. Did you ever hear anything like it? Recompense! He said he'd be losing a good worker. He said she was as good as a right-hand man."

His shoulders were shaking when she asked, "What did you say to him?"

"I told him to get the hell out of it, but that if Annie wanted to come and work for me she was welcome, and that I'd take her on me payroll. Me payroll!" He snorted: "One ten-year-old and Boyo here, me payroll. But I was so bloody wild I told him some home-truths: I told him he was an old fellow and he would soon kick the bucket, but his daughters and his wife weren't half his age, and when he went, just think of what they'd do with that farm. And if I could advise them, I'd tell them to sell up the damn lot and give themselves the time of their lives. You know, I thought he was gona have a seizure on the spot. But he never said another word an' off he went. But did you ever?" – he brought his head forward towards her – "Annie and me! Seriously, Annie and me."

She stared at him, saying quietly, "You could do worse, I suppose."

"Aye." He stared back at her. "Aye, you're right. I could do much worse, and I could do better, much better. But there——" He turned to the table and unwrapped the pie, saying finally, "But you can't have all you want in life. The quicker you learn that, the easier life will be. Aye, the easier it'll be."

23

❦❦

They had to bury Kate on the Monday. Those men not on their shift attended the funeral, and others whose pains she had alleviated over the years came too, and the women from the surrounding cottages followed the cart carrying the plain coffin on which were small bunches of late primroses, cowslips and bluebells.

Hal walked alongside Mary Ellen, behind the cart, which provided food for comment later in the inn. He should have walked with the men, it was said, or she with the women.

It was a long walk into Haydon Bridge, but the day was bright, even warm. And after the coffin had been laid in the waiting grave most of the mourners turned away, leaving only Hal and Mary Ellen and the doctor who had joined the cortège at the cemetery gate.

The three stood until the grave-diggers had finished their work; then Mary Ellen placed the flowers in a row down the mound. Her face was twitching as she turned away and joined Hal, who walked stiffly with his head bent. At the gate Mary Ellen said goodbye to the doctor and thanked him for all his attention; then she paid the carter who was still waiting, and her eyes travelled to the group of men standing to one side of the road and the group of women at the other; and she looked at Hal enquiringly and he said, "I'll take the men for a drink, you go along with the women. Annie will have got the table ready."

Without further words they moved away from each other and she joined the women. There were eight of them, mostly from the cottages, and their talk on the road back was kindly. It wasn't until they were seated at the table eating with some gusto the pies and the spice cakes Annie had provided that one of them, who seemed spokeswoman for the rest, said, "Roddy. I would have thought he would have been here out of respect if nothin' else."

Mary Ellen looked across the table at the woman, saying, "He wouldn't have had time, tomorrow is the earliest we could expect him."

"Aye, well, the coaches run every day, so I'm told, from London. Travel overnight an' all. As for them from Newcastle, our Rob says they fly off like flies to every part of this county and Durham. To my mind, if he's comin' he should have been here by now." She looked round the table and the other women, some with eyes downcast, nodded their heads, and one murmured, "She brought him up, spoilt him, an' that's what you get."

"What'll you do if he doesn't show his face, Mary Ellen?" This from a woman who had been too occupied in eating to have opened her mouth to speak so far.

Being unable to curb her tongue any longer, Mary Ellen rose from the table saying, "The same as I've always done, Mrs Pratt: go on livin' and mindin' me own business. That was one thing Kate taught me, to mind me own business, an' you don't need to take any potions for that."

"Well! Well! To talk like that on a day like this an' all, and her still warm in the ground. Doesn't show much respect."

"As much as you're showin', Mrs Pratt. As much as you're showin'."

She looked round the table and, her mouth tight, she said, "Now if you're all finished I'd thank you to leave me."

"Well! Well I never!"

"Oh, Mary Ellen. Fancy you talkin' like that." This was from a quiet little woman and she sounded shocked as she sidled up, dusting the crumbs from her skirt.

One after the other they got to their feet, picked up their shawls and, after exchanging glances and muttered remarks, they made for the door, where one of them said, "We'll know what to do when you next shout for help."

"Well, it won't be you I'll call on, Mrs Taggart, so don't worry. I've never troubled you so far and I won't start now."

That all the women were amazed showed on their faces, and they filed out now, leaving the door open behind them. And she stood watching them walking down the pathway, their heads bobbing. She was clutching the front of her black blouse, and her throat was full and her eyes smarting, when she rushed forward and banged the door, then stood with her back tight against it, and she wished from deep in her heart and for the first time that she was miles away from this place. She felt alone as she had never been before: she had a father not a mile away, but it didn't matter to him if she lived or died; nor did it apparently matter to the father of her child; there was only Hal and he wouldn't speak, because he would never believe that she had got over her feelings for Roddy.

She moved from the door and went towards the fire where the child was sleeping peacefully in the basket. And she asked herself if, when he saw her and recognized she was his, would he offer to take her back with him to London? That would mean marrying her. What would she say? Oh, she knew what she would say all right. She knew what she would say. Closing her eyes now, she again gripped the front of her blouse and, as if it were a prayer, she muttered, "Hurry up and come. Hurry up and come, so I can say it and take what comes after."

24

She slept in the cottage alone, and she was up at five o'clock on the Tuesday morning. She was glad the day was fine for she meant to take outside every movable piece of furniture and wash it. She was going to strip the bed and air the mattress and wash all the linen. After this, she intended to whitewash the walls. It was going to be a long day's work.

By nine o'clock she had dragged most of the furniture outside. All that remained in the room now was the bed-frame, the table, the press that held the herbs and potions, and the settle that was fixed to the wall. So when Hal arrived, he stood gaping, saying, "What are you at? Goin' to start a bonfire?"

"I want to get rid of the stench."

"Aye." He nodded at her. "Well, I suppose it's the right way to go about it. But you should have waited and I'd have given you a hand to move the things."

"Don't be silly," she said, and she turned her back on him and walked into the cottage, adding, "You can hardly carry yourself along yet, never mind giving anybody a hand."

As he put the can of milk on the table he said, "Where's the bairn?"

"I've left her upstairs. It's too early in the morning to bring her outside, the air's too fresh."

"No trouble last night?" he asked now.

"No. I had no trouble."

He was really asking if she'd had any callers after dark. And she had worried after he had left last night that she might just have a visitor or two, supposedly for a cure for this, that, or the other. And if they'd come in the dark, they'd surely have been men.

Having stood for a while looking round the room, he said, as if it were a matter of little importance, "I'm havin' to make me way into Haydon Bridge now. There's some odds and ends I want for the cattle, and that old horse out there thinks I'm made of bran. And one or other of the carriers may have brought some letters in from the mail coach. If there's anything I'll call back."

She made no answer but just inclined her head towards him.

As he walked towards the door he said, "You've set yourself a job." And she answered, "It has to be done."

As she followed him outside he turned to her and, looking straight into her face, he asked quietly, "How are you feeling?"

"All sixes and sevens."

"What does that mean?"

"I'm sure I couldn't tell you. If I could I would have given you a better answer."

"Aye. Aye, I suppose you would." He turned and mounted his horse and, looking down on her, he said, "Perhaps by the end of the week you'll know?"

She didn't answer but stood watching him ride off. Yes, by the end of the week she should know. And the sooner the better.

It was sooner.

She had pulled the posstub outside the washhouse and brought pan after pan of hot water from the fire to half fill it. She had put a scoopful of soda into it and now she was sossing two unbleached sheets up and down in the steaming water. Her back was bent over the tub. Her face was covered with steam and she was intent on her work, so she didn't hear the trap's approach; not until it stopped at the gate, did she raise her head, then the sheet dropped from her hands into the water. Picking up the corner of her coarse apron, she began slowly to wipe her fore-arms.

She watched him come through the gate and walk towards her. And then there he was, this man whom she had loved from a child, this Roddy Greenbank who no longer looked like Roddy Greenbank, for he had put on weight, and his whole attire was such as that of a gentleman. He even had gloves on his hands. But it was his face that was different: it was clean-shaven to the point of pinkness, there wasn't a hair to be seen on it, except where two panels of dark hair came down from under his hat and finished at the lobe of his ears.

He spoke first. "Hello," he said.

She did not even recognize his voice. She answered simply, "Hello."

He looked about him at the scattered furniture, asking now, "What's happening?"

"I'm . . . I'm having a clean out." Her voice sounded like a thin croak.

"Kate?"

"Oh" – her head wagged just the slightest – "you're too late."

"What do you mean?"

"She was buried yesterday."

She watched him lower his head slightly and look towards the ground, then mutter, "I got here as soon as I could."

"Been a long journey for you, taken nearly a year."

His head jerked upwards now and he said, "I explained all that to her. She understood."

"She understood nothing of the kind." She walked from him now into the cottage, still rubbing at her arms, and, having followed her, he stood looking round him as if he had never seen the place before. Then the whole situation seeming to strike him, he said, "But why are you here? Why aren't you at the farm?"

"I left the farm many months ago."

"To look after Kate?"

"No. No." Her voice was loud now. "For her to look after me."

She went and sat at the end of the settle because of a sudden her legs felt weak. And he stood near the corner of the table looking towards her, saying tersely now, "There seems to be explaining to do."

"Oh, you've said that right." She nodded at him. "You've said that right. There's a lot of explaining to do."

His face took on a puzzled expression; then he said on a sarcastic note, "Do you mind if I bring a chair in?"

"No, if you can manage to carry it."

He stopped in the act of moving towards the door and, turning his head to look at her, he said, "You haven't changed, have you? The same old Mary Ellen."

"There you're mistaken."

He said nothing, but went out. And she looked towards the end of the settle. There was plenty of room there for him to sit, but it was evident he wasn't going to get too close to her.

When he brought the chair back into the room he placed it to the side of the table, and there was now some six feet between them. But she continued to look towards the fire at the one side of which a large pan of water was bubbling and at the other a small pan holding the porridge which occasionally gave off lazy little blurps of steam. And it was likely the sight of the food that made her ask, "Have you eaten?"

"Oh, yes. I had breakfast in Hexham as soon as we arrived, around nine."

She looked at him in surprise now, saying, "You didn't come in last night then?"

"No, no. I arrived in Newcastle last night; I got Adam Mains Diligence from there at six this morning. They have you up before your clothes are on round there. Then I hired the trap" – he motioned towards the door with his head – "from Hexham. And" – he spread out his hands – "here I am, and too late."

Yes, here he was, and too late. And perhaps by the look and sound of him, it was just as well, because Kate wouldn't have recognized him, talking of breakfasting and Diligences and hiring traps. The cart was no longer good enough for him. Dear God! Could a man alter all this much in a year? And as if Kate's voice was speaking in her mind it said, But he had been ready for it. There was something in him that had been working up to it, and he would have changed in one way or another wherever he was.

"How is Hal?"

"What?"

"I said, how is Hal?"

"Oh, he's recovering."

"What do you mean, recovering? Has he been ill?"

"Aye, I would say he's been ill, just on dead."

"What happened? An accident at the mill?"

"Oh, he's at the mill no longer, but that's another story. As to what happened, he seemingly took your place."

He leaned towards her, his eyes screwed up, and she nodded at him, saying, "Your lady love tried to do him in. She couldn't get at you, so she got at the next best thing."

"You mean?"

"Aye, I mean, Miss Bannaman. She came across him looking round the house and her and her brother strung him up. Not by the neck, but they bent his body into half and fastened it to a beam and gagged his mouth, and there he lay for four days covered with hay up in the barn. It was his dog that found him, to all purposes dead."

"When was this?" His voice was quiet.

"Oh, not two weeks gone."

"Where is he now?"

"Oh, on his farm."

"His farm?"

"Oh, yes, things have moved here an' all, you know. We may be in the country but we don't stand still."

"*Mary Ellen.*"

"And don't Mary Ellen me like that." She rose to her feet, but he remained seated.

"Well, keep your tongue-cutting down for the time I'm here; at least, let us be civil."

"Oh aye, we can be civil. And you say for the time you're here. You've got no intention of stayin' then, have you?" She knew he had none, but she had to say it.

"My work is in London."

"Aye, and your fancy friends an' all."

"They are good friends."

"No doubt. No doubt." She moved her head slowly. "But what if you had something to take back to London with you?"

Now he, too, rose to his feet, saying, "I don't know what you're getting at."

"Just a minute and I'll show you."

As she went past the scullery towards the steps leading to the attic she glimpsed Hal standing near the outer door. How long he had been there she didn't know, but it was obvious he had no intention of making his presence known: he had seen the trap outside and had guessed who the visitor was. She went on as if she hadn't seen him, mounted the ladder, picked up the basket in which the child lay, then bumping it on to her hip, she slowly let herself through the hatch and descended into the room again. And the motion, having roused the child, caused it to whimper.

Going to the table she placed the basket on it and not a couple of feet from Roddy, and she watched him stare down at it with a look that was a mixture of amazement and something else, and the only name she could put to it was horror.

"There you are then. How would you like to take it and its mother back to town with you and introduce them to your fine friends?"

"*Mary Ellen.*" The sound of his voice was like a growl. It was evident he could find no words to say, but she could find plenty, for now she said, "Be sure your sins will find you out. That's why you haven't put in an appearance, isn't it? You were afraid in the back of your mind what you would find."

Now he did speak. His voice raised, he cried at her. "And who's fault was it? I'll ask you that. You were like a crazed thing."

They stood glaring at each other, both their faces scarlet. She saw him now as the old Roddy: the gentleman facade had dropped away, his voice and manner was recognizable as those of the boy and the man she had loved, and she was back on the quarry top, his voice growling at her, "You shouldn't have made me do it."

All of a sudden she felt utterly deflated, all the fight went out of her and in its place she experienced a wave of humiliation.

At the drooping of her head, he too felt ashamed, and he muttered, "I'm sorry. But you make me say these things. Anyway, you needn't worry, I'll support it. As soon as I've finished this course I'm being offered a position."

She raised her head and looked at him again. He'd support the child. No talk of marrying her and taking her back. And this exclusion of herself from his life brought her tongue snapping again: "Thank you, but she doesn't need your support. We have managed so far, we'll manage the rest of the way. . . . You said you would support her, what about me? I don't come into it, I suppose. You didn't say, 'Oh Mary Ellen, I must take you back with me to live among my fine friends and show you a new way of life.' I wouldn't fit in, I suppose, for they wouldn't be able to mould me like they have you."

Now he came back at her, saying quietly but pointedly, "You're quite right, Mary Ellen, for once you've said the right thing, because you wouldn't conform, no matter where you were. You've got to say what you think without stopping to think. It's always been the same with you."

"All right. That's how I am, and that's how I'll go on being. But I'm going to tell you something. I'm going to tell you what you are, what I was too blind to see for years. You're the biggest upstart that I'll ever come across, no matter how long I live; you're like the devil on horseback ridin' to hell, an' mark my words, you'll reach it one day. That's what I prophesy for you, you'll reach it one day. And let me tell you something else. Had you come here this morning and, havin' seen her" – she thrust her finger towards the child – "then asked me to marry you, you know what I would have said, in what you call this coarse blunt way of mine? I would have said, thank you very much, but you are months too late, a year too late. And I say to you now, thank God you are, because I've realized since the very night she was conceived that what I felt for you was a silly childish emotion, the payment that all

232

young girls have to go through. But from that night I knew I had been a fool and from the day she was born I knew who I loved, and who I'm goin' to marry. Aye, widen your eyes, who I'm goin' to marry. And that's Hal."

Her eyes flicked from his face towards the scullery door; then back to him again, to see that he was on the point of a great laugh, and the laughter was in his voice as he said, "*Hal? You and Hal?* My God! Never. You've torn at each other's throats since I can remember. *You and Hal?*"

"Yes, me and Hal. And you're right, we did go for each other, but we didn't realize it was a cover up, at least I didn't, until he saved me life when she was born." She pointed to the child. "But for him I wouldn't be here, nor would she, because he brought your daughter into life and fought to keep me alive for days after. And after coming through snowdrifts that nobody else would tackle."

"My! My! Very heroic of him."

"Don't you sneer, Roddy Greenbank, for he was a good mate to you for years. Aye, like me, he was foolish enough to trail you, 'cos you had a bonny face. Aye." She nodded as if to herself now. "Aye, I suppose that was the attraction, your bonny face. But look at it now. Have you seen yourself of late? You're bloated."

"Shut up!"

"Don't you tell me to shut up."

"Well, keep that tongue of yours under control. Anyway, I came here to see Kate and settle her affairs."

"Settle her affairs! What affairs?"

"Her personal affairs. I was nearest to her."

"Oh! Oh!" She moved her head slowly up and down. "You're talkin' about the money behind the brick."

"Yes, I suppose, that an' all. It happened to be mine."

"It happened to be hers, and you told her that more than a few times."

"Yes, when she was alive she could have used it."

"Well, she took it as hers alive or dead, because she made out a sort of will."

"A will?"

"Aye, that's what I said, a will." She walked now across the room and from a drawer in the press she took out a sheet of paper, and as she handed it to him she said, "She got the doctor to do it for her so it would be legal like, because there wasn't only what you consider to be your money behind the brick, but the bits and pieces she had made over the years and more so during these last months when she was training me in the use of the herbs so as I could make it into a business and support meself. Well, she started the business, you could say, right away for from then all her callers had to pay for their potions. So the money behind the brick mounted and what she left was seventy-eight pounds and nine pence ha'penny. She left it to me, as she did the furniture" – she spread out her hand – "but more so, and above everything else, she gave me her love, because when it was known I was carrying a bairn, I was turned out of me job at the farm and even me da closed the door on me. But Kate's door was always open, as was her heart. So I'm afraid, Roddy" – she made slow motions with her head now – "you're goin' back to London empty-handed. But then I shouldn't imagine that you need any money: you're got up like a gentleman; you can order a trap now whereas once the cart was all you could rise to."

She watched his face turning to almost a purple hue, but she went on undaunted, saying more quietly now, "But are all these outward trappings just somethin' for show, cast-offs from Mr Cottle?"

She stopped and watched him pull at his breath and she heard it hiss through his teeth. Then he said grimly, "Mr Cottle died nine months ago. And now for your information, I can tell you that I am marrying Mary ... Mrs Cottle at the end of the year." And bending slightly towards her, he continued, "I shall tell her of this." He extended a flat hand towards the child lying in the basket. "She is a very understanding person and will likely offer to adopt it."

"*What!* You dare, you dare suggest such a thing!"

"Well, if she's mine it would only be the right thing to do, wouldn't it?"

She glared at him, fear in her eyes for a moment, before she said, "But you can't prove she's yours, can you? I could have been with Hal, or half a dozen, because let me tell you, it isn't for the want of chances. They're around me like flies; I'm practically vying with Maggie Oates."

He was gaping at her in amazement now. When he had last seen her she had been a very young girl, pouring her love over him, determined to tie him to her with it; here was no girl, but a woman, a bonny woman, even more, a beautiful woman; she had a figure now where she'd had none before. Some buried part of him stirred and he knew a moment of regret and longing, together with envy of his one-time friend: London, Mary Cottle, the art galleries, the high-flown conversations, the select little dinners, prospect of what he might in the future achieve in the art world, were all arrayed at one side of the table and at the other was this woman. Had he been a fool? Was he being a fool? No, no. Looks or no looks, she was still Mary Ellen with a tongue that could clip clouts. Yet, in town she would have been considered witty. Well, if not witty, quick on the uptake, especially for a woman. Yet, as she had said, she could never have been moulded, she would have always remained what she was, a country maid, capable of handling any domestic chore that a farm required. No, you could never alter a vixen, and she was a vixen. And he said as much now. "You know what you are Mary Ellen, and always will be? A vixen."

"Aye, well, it will be good for you to keep remembering that. Let you or your fancy lady lay any claim to her and you won't know what's hit you. Hal'll see to that."

"Oh, Hal! Hal! You know" – he gave a sarcastic laugh – "that amazes me, you and Hal. Huh! You and Hal. Anyway, I wish you luck, both of you. You'll need it, because, you see, I know you, both him and you."

"Aye, you do, or you did. You knew us for two soppy fools trailin' after you. Anyway, when we're givin' out luck, I'll give you mine an' all, with your old woman."

She thought for a moment he was going to raise his hand, and she narrowed her eyes at him and turned her head slightly to the side as if in warning. She watched him grind his teeth and saw the muscles of his jaw moving against his skin. But he did not come back at her; instead, he snatched his hat from the table and made towards the door; and as he did so, a wave of remorse came over her, and she wanted to rush to him and say, I'm sorry. I'm sorry. Don't let us part like this. I don't wish you any harm. But as she reached the door and saw him mount the trap, the look on his face stilled her tongue, and the thought came to her: He hasn't even asked what I've called her.

After he had turned the trap around she took three steps towards it, calling in an ordinary voice now, "Are you goin' to the cemetery? She's buried on the left-hand side." And for a moment it seemed he was about to answer her, but he whipped up the horse and it went into a trot.

She stood watching it; then suddenly she turned about and ran round the side of the cottage and there, putting her head out against the wall, she bent over and vomited.

When she felt the touch on her shoulder she become still, and when she turned around she kept her head bent deeply on her chest.

Hal now slid his arm about her and walked her along the side of the cottage and into the scullery, and there, she drew herself from him and, going to the sink, she took a mug from the side bench and dipped it into a bucket of clean water, and swilled her mouth; then taking the corner of her apron, she ran it round her face. But she didn't move from the sink until his arm came about her shoulder again.

Once more he was leading her, and into the room now, and to the settle. And after lowering her on to it, he dropped to his knees in front of her and, lifting her chin up, he looked into her face and muttered, "Mary Ellen. Oh! Mary Ellen." And with a swift movement now he thrust his arms around her waist and buried his head in her lap, and so strong was the trembling of his body that it came through into hers, and she placed her hands on his head and stroked his hair.

When, still holding her, he turned his face to the side and said, "I love you. I love you. I do. I do. Oh! Mary Ellen," she put her hands on his face and raised it upwards and, bending down towards him, she whispered now, "I love you, an' all, Hal." Then with a gulp in her throat, she said, "You heard it all?"

"Aye. Aye, I heard it all, and I've never been so happy in me life afore. Chalk and cheese, we might be, but you're for me. I've known that for years. But that you should care for me, ever . . . that's something I faced up to a long time ago an' all, 'cos I never thought it would come about, never, never. Yet I started to hope a little bit after the child was born. That was when you changed towards me, wasn't it?"

"No, no, Hal." She shook her head. "It was from——" Now she looked to the side, slightly ashamed of what she was about to say, "It was from nine months afore that, from the night she came into being. Something happened to me then, although I wouldn't face up to it. I thought, you can't stop lovin' somebody just like that, you've got to go on lovin' them, if you've always loved them, you can't change. And then, as the months grew and she became heavier inside me, I realized there is love an' love, different kinds. What I had for him was ... was like the mania that attacks all young lasses: they think they'll die if they don't get what they want. I ... I thought it was love, but it was just the pains of growing. I knew what love really meant when I saw you comin' through that door rimed with frost and snow day after day, bringing us the milk and things, caring for us. I knew then I was learning what real love meant. And you'll never know how ashamed I felt of the way I used to go at you, cuttin' you with me tongue."

He smiled broadly into her face now, saying, "You only came off second-best in that way. Now you must admit that. I was a master of it." Then the smile disappearing from his face, he said, "It was a cloak that I donned early on. I think you were about fifteen when I had to face up to what had hit me. Mary Ellen, I've loved you for a long time, and I'll love you to the day I die." Slowly now he rose and drew her to her feet. Then he kissed her, not gently, nor tenderly, but with a fierceness that, after a moment of shock, found a response in herself, and they clung together for long seconds. And when at last they stood apart, they looked at each other shyly, their hands gripped tightly now. Then slowly and simultaneously their faces moved into laughter, and they fell against each other, hugging each other like two children.

When they were once more seated on the settle he said, "We'll have to see the parson. He's a nice fellow."

She could only nod at him because there was a lump in her throat and a smarting in her eyes.

"And ... and about this?" He now moved his hand round the room. "It's rented, isn't it? A shilling a week. But it doesn't come under the mill so they can't claim it for a worker once you move out. I've been thinking about it. Well, sort of planning, wishful thinkin', you could say. It belongs to the Ribbons, doesn't it? And he won't mind who has it as long as the rent's paid. So I've thought about letting Annie have it."

"Annie? Comin' to live here on her own?"

"Aye. Poor old Annie, she'd give her eye-teeth to get away from her father and the farm. She's nothing but an unpaid slave there like the rest of them. She even asked me some time ago if I'd take her on full time and she would sleep in the loft." He pulled a face at her now. "Imagine ... imagine the oil that would have provided for the tongues. Yes, yes, indeed."

She pulled a similar face; then they both laughed again, and he drew her close once more and began to kiss her, until she pressed him away, saying, "Listen. Listen. You were talkin' about Annie."

"Oh, Annie, aye. Well, now, she's as good a worker as any man, and if she could just step into here with it all set up with its bits and pieces, it would be like heaven to her. If I give her four shillings a week and her keep, my! she won't know she's born. And there's your father. She might even soften him up, you never can tell. What d'you say?"

"I'd be only too pleased. But how'll she take me?"

"Oh, she'll take you all right. She knows how I feel about you; she's known for a long time. And only yesterday she said, 'She's a nice lass,' and that's a compliment from her."

She stared at him, her head slightly to the side now. Two men in her life and so different: one who thought of nobody but himself, and that was the one she had wasted so many years of feeling on, for, call it young love or what you will, it had been real and a torment; and now here was this man who had none of the outward attributes of the other, because he wasn't pretty, his face was too rugged for that, but unlike the other one, he was kind and thoughtful, just as he had said in his wishful thinking, he had thought of Annie . . . and her father. Oh! her father. She would be a miracle worker if she got through to him. Yet miracles did happen . . . one was happening to her now.

Putting her arms around his neck, she looked into his face and said, "I'll be a good wife to you, Hal. God willing, I'll bear you children that you'll be proud of. And no matter how our fortune goes, I'll be there beside you. As Kate was apt to say, better is a dinner of herbs where love is than a stalled ox and hatred therewith."

"Aye, she did. I've heard her say it many a time. But let me tell you, Mary Ellen, and this is a promise, there'll be no dinner of herbs for us, for I mean to rise, and one day I'll put you in a house worthy of you. All your young life you slaved for others. Aye, the Davisons might have been kind, but they were only so because they got their pound of flesh. But come one day, you'll have a servant or two of your own; what's more, you'll know how to treat them. That, Mary Ellen my love, is a promise."

PART THREE

❧❧

The Stalled Ox

1

❧❧

It was a Sunday evening in early November in the year eighteen forty-six. A high wind was blowing across the moor and bringing with it a heavy rain mixed with sleet that beat against the walls of the long stone farmhouse, diffusing the light streaming from the four long windows to one side of the front door. Two at the other side were also showing some light; and with the dim lighting coming from the windows on the first floor, altogether the farmyard seemed to be enveloped with a feeling of comfort and security. There was no sound from the animals in their stalls and outbuildings, which were ranged around two sides of the yard, which really had very little appearance of an ordinary farmyard, but looked like a courtyard attached to a small manor house. But when the animals were let out and the milk churns were rolled across the yard, with the clanking of harness and the bustle of workers, then it would come to life and be a farm, and a very busy one at that.

But on this Sunday the busyness was all inside the house, and particularly so in the dining-room, for the whole family had gathered to join in a special supper, special because it was the last the eldest daughter Kate would partake of as a single woman, for on the morrow she was to be married.

The dining-room was a large well-appointed room, the ceiling high with a deep cornice; the walls were half panelled and, standing against them was an array of very good furniture, one piece being a magnificent nine-foot-long sideboard on which was laid out a large quantity of glass and silver. Eighteen people could be seated at the dining-table in comfort. The dining-chairs were upholstered in hide, and a suite covered in the same material was positioned at one end of the room. There were several small cabinets and two corner cabinets filled with china. The fireplace was stone, not rude stone but sculptured, and in a way looked too ornate and slightly out of place in the room, as well it might, for it had once graced the drawing-room of a castle. The carpet in a deep red patterned design did not cover the whole floor but showed a good expanse of nine-inch-wide polished boards all around it.

Towards each end of the dining-table which was covered with a linen cloth, stood a four branch candelabrum, and round about them such an assortment of foods that there was hardly room for the diners' plates.

There were twelve chairs around the table, but only nine people were seated. Two empty chairs were tilted forward, their high backs leaning against the table, the tops of them protruding somewhat over it. To the left of these at the bottom of the table sat the mistress of the house, and next to her was another empty chair. This was usually occupied by Annie, who at the moment was in bed trying to ward off a cold so that she'd be fit for the celebrations on the morrow.

Mary Ellen was now forty-three years old, and for a woman who had borne ten children, she carried her age as might another who had known far less emotional stress. There was no grey in her hair, her face was unlined and her big rounded figure trim and straight.

At the other end of the table sat Hal. He was now turned forty-seven, but unlike Mary Ellen, he was showing the marks left on him by the years: his hair was grizzled, and there were two deep furrow lines running from the end of his nose down to his chin; his face looked weathered and his body, which had always been broad, had thickened still further, but it was a hard thickness, there was no flab about him.

Looking at him through the candlelight and amid the laughter and bantering chatter at the table, Mary Ellen thought, as she had done for many years now, If he'd only let up. If he'd only be satisfied, and know that I have all I want, and all I'll ever want, as long as I have him. If only I could make him believe that.

Hardly a day had passed in their twenty-four years of marriage that she hadn't, in some way, expressed her love for him. Yet, he was never certain of it, for always in his mind there was the memory of her first love, that all-consuming girlish passion that had given birth to her daughter Kate, whom she was losing on the morrow. Oh, how she would miss Kate. Of the nine children she had borne Hal, two had died with the typhus that had swept through Allendale and the surrounding district in forty-one. They had been her youngest, Peg and Walter, and they had been so beautiful, so full of life. Every Sunday night for years they had sat in those chairs now tilted to the side of her. And she could see their faces now, laughing and merry. They had been close, those two, and their natures had been sunny, like the twins John and Tom there, at the top of the table. They too had sunny natures. But not so their sister Maggie who came next to them. She didn't know who Maggie took after; she was, though, somewhat like herself as she had been years ago, free with her tongue. Maggie was twenty-two and there was no sign of her marrying, although it wasn't for the chance; she was a bit of a flibbertigibbet was Maggie.

Florrie came next. There was always a year between them. She had been regular in that way, except once, when it had come too early and she had miscarried. Florrie was quiet, not like any of the others at all, certainly not like Hugh, and Gabriel who followed him. These two were tough 'uns, hell raisers, as their father said, but laughing hell raisers. All her children laughed a great deal, except perhaps Kate.

With Walter her breeding had stopped. It was as if her nature had said, You promised to give him ten children and you have done that; enough is enough. And she could say she had given him ten because he loved

242

Kate as his own, yes, as his very own. And this worried her at times.

They had both been well satisfied, until their nine of a family had been depleted by death. Then a blight had fallen on them, and only now did they seem to be rising through it, for she couldn't remember such a merry night as this since before the youngsters went.

Up till a year ago not one of her family had shown the slightest sign of getting married; in fact, they had laughed about it. It was as Hal said, they were too well got at home to take on the responsibility of a wife or of a husband. But she knew that had suited him, for he loved them about him, inside and outside the house. And now here was Kate, although the eldest, the most unlikely one to have made the first breakaway; quite candidly, she had thought that Kate would always be with her, for as Maggie with her slack tongue had said, but on the quiet, well, their Kate wasn't everybody's cup of tea.

No, perhaps she wasn't, but how had it come about? Her father had been handsome, and she herself had been bonny. And when Kate was born she'd been bonny too. When had she changed? When had she first noticed her prettiness slipping? She could have said fancifully that it was from the day she married Hal, and the child not yet a year old. But certainly from she was two, because from then she noticed a plainness creeping over the child's face. Her skin thickened a little, but that was nothing. Then at five years old, she was as tall as a child of seven or eight, and she never seemed to stop growing. She was bigger than anyone in the family, being all of five feet eight inches tall, and big-boned with it. But it wasn't only her height or her shape, which you could say really gave her a fine figure, it was her plainness; but she was saved, God help her, from being ugly only by her eyes. They were fine eyes, finer than those possessed by any of her other children, being large and of a soft brown colour and which at times held an awareness that hurt one to see, as it had on that day she had said to her, "Why haven't I taken after you, Mam ... and him?"

She had told her that Hal wasn't her father when she was quite young in case it should be thrown in her face by other children, or whispered in her presence by other women. And on that particular day she had said, "You did tell me he was a fine-looking man."

Yes, she had told her that, but she knew now that that young girl had held that knowledge to her, not as a comfort, but as a big question mark in her mind: why she should look as she did if her father had been good-looking and her mother pretty.

Yet how was she to convince her daughter that she had qualities that outshone those in her other children. She was kind – not that the others weren't – and good-natured. If she had expressed her thoughts by saying, she's lovable, she knew that every other member of her family would have shown surprise, even John who was very fond of her would undoubtedly have been amused by such a term being applied to his big sister.

Moreover, Kate had a fine speaking voice, and she could relate a story.

When anyone heard Kate talk, really talk, they forgot what she looked like. And this must have happened to Harry Baker, for he had seen Kate for years and had taken no notice of her. That was until he had called to see Hal to ask for help: he and his folks among many had been hit by the poor crop; his farm, being not much bigger than a smallholding and on hilly land where the grazing was poor, had yielded not even enough to pay his debts, let alone survive another year. And it was when she herself had invited him to a meal that he had first heard Kate talking. She was relating an incident she had heard in Hexham market that brought them all to laughter, and his the loudest: she was adopting the tones of various voices engaged in argument.

She herself hadn't taken to him very much at first, having thought he was only after a free meal, but from the beginning she had realized that he was impressed by their way of living, for they always ate their main meal in the dining-room. She didn't know what kind of a cook his mother was, but on that first visit he had eaten twice as much as any of hers.

As it was quite a ride to his place, yon side of Haydon Bridge, which was a good six miles away, she had been to his place only the once, to meet his mother and father. But that didn't seem to prevent him from visiting weekly, when he didn't come on horseback but always brought his flat cart. One day, seeing Hal once again loading it up with hay and corn, she had said to him, "He's not daft, that one." And Hal had answered, "I know that. I know that, but me generosity isn't stretching to him so much as to Kate. She's going to need quite a bit of help in that direction. And he's no fool, he knows it'll come through her."

That night in bed she had said to him, the worry deep in her voice, "Hal, you ... you don't think that's the reason he's taking her?"

And she had become more worried by his reply: "Hard to say. He's handicapped because his father's a bit shiftless and his mother not much better. I should say, by the inside of the house, Kate's going to have her work cut out there. But the fellow himself, well, he seems he wants to get on. And let's face up to it, lass, he's about the only chance Kate'll have. There's been no one in the running afore, has there? They must all be bloody well blind, because she's a fine lass, is Kate. None better."

"Do you think she cares for him?"

And to this he had answered, "I was going to ask you the same question because she talks to you."

Yes, she did talk to her, but not on the subject of her feelings for Harry Baker. Perhaps later tonight, when she was saying good-night to her for the last time in this house, she would open up.

She looked down the table towards her daughter. She was seated to Hal's left. Even the two sons she had given him at one and the same time, when they had become old enough to sit at the kitchen table in his first little farmhouse, he hadn't had one on each side of him, Kate had always sat next to him, and to his left hand, for it was easier, she saw, for him to pass titbits to her with his right. And that's how it had been through all the years. None of the children she had given him had supplanted Kate. And Kate loved him in return. She couldn't have loved her own father dearer.

There were times when she thought of Roddy Greenbank, as he was when he worked in the smelting mill and roamed the hills in his spare time with his slate and pencil. And her thoughts would be soft on him then. However, when she thought of the man that both Newcastle and London town had produced, she would be filled with a bitterness, but mostly against herself for being a besotted fat-headed girl, she who was supposed by everyone to be full of common sense, but as dear old Kate Makepeace, her friend and benefactor, that wise old woman had said, "Sense came from the head, trouble from the heart."

Was it the head or the heart that was leading Kate to the altar tomorrow? She hoped it was the heart. Oh yes, she did, she did, because sense, although it might make you count your chickens after they were hatched, did little to help you while sitting on the eggs, and so, as she saw it, if the heart hadn't led you to the altar it was a sure thing you wouldn't look forward to going to bed that night.

She was recalled from her twisted metaphors by a great burst of laughter and seeing Tom thumping John on the back, causing him to splutter into his pudding, and she leant towards Gabriel who was sitting to her left and, smiling, she asked, "What was that?" And Gabriel, wiping his eyes, said, "They were talking about what happened on *Windy Monday*, the day they were burying Maggie Oates, remember? And the one woman who had braved the walk to the cemetery, and the wind blew her skirts and petticoats over her head, and she nearly fell in the grave. And there were only two men there besides the parson, and he only buried her because she confessed her sins before she went. And those two fellows had some nerve an' all, and brave, 'cos if all her customers had followed her, half the county would have been empty of men, so it was said."

"Oh, be quiet." Laughing, she thrust her hand out towards Gabriel, saying, "What d'you know about it?"

"Enough, Mam, enough. I saw her once. I was only about eleven, and she smiled at me. Didn't she, Hugh?" He looked up the table to his brother. "And she patted your head, didn't she?"

"Shut up! Shut up!"

Again there were gales of laughter.

Mary Ellen recalled Maggie Oates vividly, and the day she was buried too, because that was the day of the hurricane in January, thirty-nine. It tore up half of the countryside and played havoc in Allendale. And after it was all over people remembered that Maggie Oates had been buried on that day. And some wit in a bar had said she had gone out on a blast and not only with one devil and a gale of wind, but with all of them she had served over the years. So the story went around, and whenever Windy Monday was remembered so also was Maggie Oates's funeral.

She had once likened herself to Maggie Oates, that was after she had forced Roddy Greenbank into giving her the child, and she admitted, even now, that it was she who had done the running, and because of it she had been turned out of her post at Davison's farm, her father's door had been locked against her, and the only friend she had in the world had been Kate Makepeace. It was then that certain men had come to old Kate's door presumably for potions and herbs for their ailments, but really to look her over to see if she was a younger up-and-coming Maggie Oates. And, too, they had coupled her name with Hal when there was nothing between them but their own secret thoughts, which had risen to the surface the day he had fought through the great drifts of snow and found her in the agony of labour and with his own hands had then delivered the child, and afterwards saved her life by bringing away the afterbirth.

It was on the night they were married that she thanked him for being so good to Kate. And he had said to her, "She was mine afore you were, for I brought her into the world, and I feel that I'm her father as he never was." And that feeling had continued between her daughter and her stepfather, for strangely she was closer to him than were his own.

Hal was speaking now, and she smiled at him down the length of the table from where he was looking at her, for he was saying, "Come on, let's drink to our Kate and her happiness, and I wish that with all me heart, as I know you all do. And Kate——" Hal looked into the brown eyes of the big young woman sitting to his side, and he said softly, "Your chair may be empty the morrow but you'll still be in all our hearts."

"Oh! Dad." She leant forward and kissed him on the lips, and his hand trembled and the wine spilled from his glass, and Maggie cried, "Look out! Dad. I've got to get that stain out the morrow."

"There's no washing the morrow." This came from Florrie, her voice quiet, a soft smile on her face.

"Then Tuesday or whatever."

"Be quiet, tousle-head." Hal looked down the table towards his eldest daughter; then shifting his gaze on to Mary Ellen, he said, "To Kate, lass, to Kate."

They all stood up and raised their glasses and they drank while Kate's head lowered and her lids closed and the tears pressed from beneath them, and Maggie cried, "Oh, our Kate, don't start to bubble. It's unlucky if you bubble."

"No, no, it isn't; it's only unlucky if you don't."

They all looked towards Mary Ellen now, and she went on, "Have you ever known of a bride who doesn't cry? It would be like an Irish wake without a pig on the spit and whisky in the teapot."

"Oh! Mam." They were all laughing again. "The things that you come out with."

"Well, let's go into the sitting-room and have a sing-song." Hal was already on his feet, and he walked down the length of the table, but before he reached Mary Ellen, his hands came to rest gently, one on the back of each tilted chair. Then taking Mary Ellen's arm, he led her from the room; and the family followed, but only after each of them had made his way to the two chairs and laid his or her hands gently on the backs. It was a ceremony that had been enacted ever since they had lost their brother and sister, and it was one that had caused not a little talk in those who had been guests and had witnessed it.

It was said round about that it was a strange and unhealthy thing to do to keep the dead alive in a dining-room. But then Hal Roystan was a very strange man, a man who had spent his earlier working years since he was a young lad in the smelting mill, and then, starting with the few pounds the owners had given him in compensation following the murder of his father while in their employ, he had built up the most thriving farming business for miles around. Moor Vale was his fourth place in twenty-five years, and it was said he now lived like a lord, and had educated his children as if they were class. But be that as it may, he was still not accepted by the real people of the county and never would be, for his wife had had a bastard before he married her; and she was odd, too, in her own way, for she could make up potions and pills for man and beast that benefited both better than any doctor's medicine. Yet she only did it when she thought fit and for those whom she liked; others got short shrift should they go to her door.

No, the Roystans might live like lords and copy the gentry inside the house in the way they ate and outside in the way they rode for their horses were all good breeds, and they ran a trap, a dog cart and a brake, besides all the farm carts, but people had long memories and, given the chance, didn't let them forget from where they had come.

And many prophesied that the Roystans had gone up as far as they could, and that now the road would be downhill. And who would be to blame but themselves for getting too big for their boots. However, it had to be admitted he paid more than a fair wage to his one hired man, although he expected him to sweat for it, as he did three of his sons who worked on the farm. The latest news was that the second youngest one, Hugh, was going in for law. Now would you believe that? If it had been one of the twins, people might have understood it, because they, if you could put the word to them, appeared more refined, whereas the last two of the brood, Hugh and Gabriel, had been known to be tough since they were lads, and they were already in and out of scrapes. They were likeable enough, but rough. Yet, here was one of them going in for law.

Hal Roystan had seen to it that each one of his family had been given the chance of an education. The girls had gone to a dame school in Hexham, and the twins had gone to school until they were fifteen. But the last two, they had been sent into Newcastle. It had been expected that Gabriel would go into shipping, but no, he brings his fine education back and says he wants to work on the farm, at least for a time. And so Roystan had bought more land; and it had prospered.

But it was also said around that Hal Roystan's interest didn't lie only in farming, he had his fingers in other pies, and when Langley Smelting

Mills were rented by the Greenwich Hospital to Messrs. Wilson, Lee and Company, in eighteen and thirty-three, it was rumoured he had tried to get a share in there. Some said that tale was but a joke because his wife's name had been Lee before he married her. But it was no rumour that he had been after a brick works which was close to the farm he had at the time, but had been outbidded there.

Oh, he was a deep one was Roystan. Everyone knew. But wouldn't you have thought he would have got somebody better than Harry Baker for his ugly duckling. It was common knowledge why Harry was taking her: he had his eye open to the main chance, had Harry; although the lass wasn't Roystan's own, it was known he was very fond of her, and would see her all right. And that meant Harry would be all right, for his father would neither work nor want, and Harry himself wasn't all that eager; if he could take the easy way out, he did. And that's what he was doing by marrying Roystan's big 'un. And by! she was a big piece, and as plain as they came. She was credited with having a nice enough nature, but it wasn't the nature you looked across the table at in the long years of marriage, it was a face, and the nicest nature in the world couldn't do much to improve what God had given you. . . .

So it was said. And Kate Roystan having inherited the sensibility of her mother wasn't unaware of the gossip and chatter that her forthcoming marriage had evoked. And now, in a room at the end of the long corridor which had been added to the house a few years back, she looked about her at the familiar and loved objects she had grown up with, and she opened her mouth wide in order to take in a great gasp of air in an endeavour to settle the turmoil that was churning up her stomach. Slowly she began to undress, and when she was in her nightgown she went to the seat that was placed before the mahogany dressing-table that stood crosswise in the corner of the room, and she sat down so sharply on the seat that the springs creaked. Then pushing towards the mirror a china tray that held some trinkets, she put her forearms on the polished wood and laid her head on them.

Should she do it?

She was sick of the sound of these words in her mind. She had got this far so she must do it. That's if she wanted a family so badly. And how other would she ever be able to have a family? This was the one and only chance that would ever come her way. She had faced up to that. As also she had faced up to the reason why Harry Baker had chosen her. More rightly it could be said he had chosen her father, or the man she thought of as her father, and the prosperity that was his.

She raised her head, at the same time pulling towards her the candle-stick that was standing near the end of the dressing-table, and now, leaning her face closer towards the mirror, she asked another question of it, one she had asked again and again over the years but had never received an answer: Why did she look like this? She recalled the day she first asked herself this question through this mirror. She had never really seen herself till then. But her father had been to a sale in a big house on the outskirts of Haydon Bridge, and there had bought two full bedroom suites, both solid mahogany, and one had a full length mirror. She was fifteen at the time and she had looked at herself from head to foot. It had been in broad daylight and the sun was on her, and moving ever closer to the mirror she had picked out her features one by one. Why should her mouth be so wide and full-lipped when her sister Maggie's was like a rosebud? Why was her nose so big, bigger than those of the twins? Why was her hair straight with no kink in it, not like Maggie's soft waves, and Florrie's that was all curls? Why was her skin blotchy?

She had asked this particular question of her mother before. Because she drank too much cream, and that all young people had blotchy skins, had been the answer. From that day she had never touched cream, and she still disliked it, and yet her skin now, if not blotchy, had a thick texture.

When she reached her eyes, she knew they were all right. Her father had said she had beautiful eyes and a nice voice, but she knew she would gladly exchange these two attributes to look like Maggie or Florrie.

Peg had once said to her, "You've got what none of the rest of us have, Kate, that's a sort of—" She had stopped and fumbled for a word, then said, "Appeal," and went on to say, "Perhaps character would be a better word. People listen to you when you talk, they never do to me." Dear Peg. Sweet Peg. She had loved Peg. The house had never been the same since Peg and Walter had gone.

Tonight at the table she had thought, and with sadness, that her going was the reason for the first jolly meal they had had in years. There had been times when the table had witnessed the most uproarious meals, for her father didn't believe in "speak when you're spoken to"; instead he encouraged them all to talk. But tonight they had given her a grand send-off, for it was the last meal she would share with them. Oh, there'd be the wedding feast, and that would be a feast indeed, for her mother and the girls had worked like Trojans for the past week, baking and decorating meats and pies ... and the cake. It was a sight to behold, white, no colour at all, virgin white.

The thought brought her to her feet and she stood for a moment, her arms folded about her as if hugging herself. There was one thing to be thankful for, she had no need to be ashamed of her body. It was big but it was well formed and firm. But what did that matter after all? Your body was always wrapped up from your toes to your neck. It never saw the light of day, except with one person. The thought brought her head to the side and her teeth clenching. She didn't know how she was going to stand that. It wasn't that she wasn't fond of Harry and grateful to him, but that wasn't love: it wasn't the thing that existed between her mother and father, the thing that they couldn't hide whenever they looked at each other, the thing that had brought nine children into the world.

No, no – she swung round now and walked to the bed and sat on the edge of it, her big firm hands pressing her nightgown down between her knees – children could come without love. Oh yes, yes. You had only to look round the cottages swarming with bairns. It didn't seem to matter if they died young, there were always more to take their places, and while the women mourned, the men had a solace, they could drink themselves silly and probably get rid of their frustration afterwards in brawling. Oh yes, it didn't need love to bring a child into the world. So she could be sure of one thing, she would have a family; and another thing, she'd make Harry work in order to get a decent farm. And from the beginning she would tell him that they weren't going to rely on her father's kindness. No doubt that would shock him, for she knew he had been receiving liberally of late.

In a few minutes time her mother and the girls would be coming in for a last chat. And that, she didn't think she could stand without breaking down. There must be no more talk from now on; from now on words would only induce tears and through tears her true feelings might be brought to the surface.

Quickly she got up from the bed and extinguished the candle; then getting between the sheets, she turned on her side and buried her face in the pillow, and as she had done as a child she put the end of her thumb in her mouth and began biting on it.

At the other end of the corridor Mary Ellen climbed into the big four-poster and laid her head on the arm that was waiting for her, and Hal said, "Now stop worrying; everything's going to be all right. As you said yourself, it's her only chance. The only thing I wish is, it was somebody different who was giving it to her. But still, she seems to get on with him."

"She doesn't, else she would be willing to talk; she pretended to be asleep. And . . . and Hal, I hope you realize you'll have him on your back for a long time."

"Oh, no, I won't."

"What makes you say that?"

"I gave it to him plain this afternoon when I gave him. . . ."

"What did you give him?"

"Oh. A few bob to get him set up."

"You've been settin' him up for months now. What did you give him?"

"Well, I gave him a hundred pounds."

"A hundred pounds!"

"Aye, yes, and keep your voice down, I gave him a hundred pounds. But I told him that was the last and he had to build on that, and it was a damn sight more than I ever had to build on."

She did not remind him: "You're wrong there, my dear. Don't forget you built on the two hundred odd guineas stolen money that I found."

The few pounds he had got from the mill company for the loss of his father and the stigma he had endured for years would have hardly started him keeping chickens. But no, he liked to think he started from scratch. And after all perhaps he had, because he had always been of a determined nature. Even as a young lad, during the years they had fought like cat and dog, he seemed to have one purpose in mind and that was to show them, which meant, getting on.

"I wouldn't have given him anything like that until after the morrow," she said.

"Don't worry, everything will go all right. Anyway" – his voice rose – "we are talkin' as if he was doing us a bloody favour. In getting her, he's damned lucky. Now I'm telling you. If the fellows around here had had any sense at all, she would have been snapped up long afore this. I'm going to say this to you, Mary Ellen" – his voice dropped now – "I've never said it afore, but it's just this, and it's a funny thing for me to say, but she's worth more to me than all me own. Aye, I suppose it was because how she came into the world. I was the first to hold her. I was the first to feed her. I was the first to wipe her clean. So she's always meant a lot to me, has Kate, and always will."

"Oh, Hal, Hal." Her arms were around him and they were pressed close together. "My dear, dear, Hal. I love you, as much now as the day when I first said it."

"Well" – his voice was gentle now – "that's all I want to hear, lass, ever in me life.... Ever in me life."

2

She stood in the middle of the room dressed in a gown of white satin which brought out the curves in the figure as never before. Her long straight hair was wound in tight coils above the ears. She stood perfectly still while Maggie lifted up the short veil and placed it on her head, saying, "Nobody'll have seen headgear like this afore in the church; it's what the grand ladies wear. Bend your head so I can stick the pins in, you don't want it to fly off. But listen to that wind, we could all fly off the day."

Florrie, standing in front of Kate, said quietly, "Oh, you look bonny, Kate."

"Don't." The word was sharp and held a touch of bitterness, and before Florrie could make any further comment, Maggie moved to her side and, pushing the half veil back on to the front of Kate's head, said somewhat begrudgingly, "Well, you do, the day. And neither of us has got a figure like yours so just think on that. Here's me like a yard of pipe water; when I look at me bust I envy the cows."

At this Florrie nearly choked, and Kate, giving a shaky laugh, said, "I'm sorry. I'm ... I'm all worked up, and nervous."

"Well, who wouldn't be on their wedding day. If ever I get married I think they'll have to carry me there on a door. And now you've set the ball rolling, it mightn't be all that long before that happens."

Maggie nodded towards Florrie and she, chuckling, said, "Which one of them will be the unlucky fellow? Or will you get them all to the church and take your pick?"

"Aw, you." Maggie laughingly pushed her younger sister to the side, and as she did so the door opened and Mary Ellen entered the room. She was dressed in a wine-coloured corduroy suit with a small matching hat and over her arm she carried a white lace shawl.

"Aren't you two ready yet?" She looked from one to the other of the girls, and Maggie, who definitely had inherited her mother's ready tongue, replied, "We've only got our bonnets to put on. But we couldn't afford two hours titivating ourselves like somebody we know." She glanced at Florrie, laughter in her eyes, and Florrie, going up to her mother said, "You look lovely, Mam, and that colour suits you. I knew it would when I saw it in the shop."

"Well, I've had me doubts, 'cos I don't hold with shop-bought things. Go on, get yourselves off, both of you."

They were about to scurry away when Florrie turned and, going back to Kate, she kissed her warmly while muttering, "Be happy, Kate. Be happy."

When the door had closed on them, Mary Ellen went to her daughter and there was a tremor in her voice as she asked, "Ready?"

"Yes, Mam, as much as ever I'll be."

"You'll be all right, you'll be all right." Simultaneously their arms went out and they held each other for a moment; then Mary Ellen, pressing herself away and aiming to be matter of fact, said, "I'm crushing your frock. And look at the shawl," moving now behind her daughter and shaking out the very fine white lace shawl that she had spent many months making. She placed it round Kate's shoulders and as she did so she closed her eyes tightly and bit on her lower lip to stop the tears flowing. Then without once more looking at Kate she held out her hand, saying huskily, "Come, they're all waitin'."

Before descending the shallow oak stairs, Kate stood for a while gathering up the front of her gown; then she was walking down towards her family. There they all were: John and Tom, standing together as they nearly always did, two fine looking men, fair- haired and fresh complexioned and of their father's build, of medium height and broad with it; at the foot of the stairs, Hugh, tall and thin, with hair and eyes so dark as to appear almost black, and looking older than his elder brothers; next to him, Gabriel, who looked like his mother and had her colouring of skin, which the girls were constantly pointing out to him was wasted on a fellow; then directly at the foot of the stairs stood Maggie and Florrie, both with their father's colouring, Maggie as tall as her mother, but Florrie small made, her frame seeming to match her voice which was quiet and rarely raised. But standing behind them all was the man she thought of as her father. And it was to him she looked as she descended the stairs.

Amid the chatter and murmurs of approval from the men, she moved towards him; and silently he held out a cloak and put it around her, then ceremoniously drew her arm through his, and with her was making for the door when suddenly he stopped and, looking down the hall, said, "Where's Annie?"

It was Maggie who answered: "Likely finishing her crying in the kitchen and saying it's only her sniffles," she said on a laugh.

"Go and fetch her, the silly bitch."

"I've no need to be fetched." Annie came through the far door and into the hall. Although she had thickened out with the years her build in her younger days had been much the same as was the bride's now; in fact, many a time she had been taken for Kate's mother, so similar were they. And also over the years, she had been of invaluable help and even comfort to Mary Ellen; in fact, she'd had as much to do with the bringing up of the family as had Mary Ellen herself, and more so with Kate. At times, Mary Ellen had become a little mystified and more than a little troubled as she'd seen her daughter develop into almost a replica of

Annie, and Annie's devotion to the child had at times irritated her, for she would act as though Kate were really hers. Even when the others came along she never gave them the attention she gave to Kate.

"My! that's a new bonnet." Hugh flipped the velvet strings hanging from the brown straw bonnet with his finger and thumb. And Annie's tone was one of assumed grievance when she answered, "Give over, you! I can have a new bonnet, surely."

"I don't know so much about that. I don't think you've worked for it of late. Taking to your bed because your nose runs."

On this the whole party went out laughing, some more heartily than others, but all, to Kate's ears, forced.

The church was almost full. There were smelting families from Langley with whom Hal had kept in touch over the years; there were farmers and their wives from round about; there was Doctor Brunton and his wife and two daughters from Haydon Bridge, who over the years had been close friends to the family; but there was no relative of Mary Ellen's or yet of Hal's present, for they had none that they knew of. But, as yet, the bridegroom and his best man had not appeared, nor yet any member of his family; there were, though, a number of his friends, mostly men, seated awkwardly at the left-hand side of the aisle towards the back of the church.

The bride's company arrived at the church five minutes late, but as Hal went to help Kate down from the brake, the Reverend Scott came towards them from around the side of the church, passing through scattered onlookers, and in a hushed tone he said to Hal, "The groom hasn't arrived yet. He must have been held up on the way."

Kate, about to step down on to the grass verge, seemed to hang in mid air, her face looking down questioningly into Hal's, until he said, "Sit yourself down a minute. I don't suppose he'll be long."

As Kate sat back on the seat next to Mary Ellen she shivered, and Mary Ellen said, "Nice thing. And it isn't very warm out here; this wind goes right through you. Put the rug round your legs."

"No." Kate put out her hand and stopped Mary Ellen from taking the rug from under the seat, saying, "I'm all right. I'm all right."

The family had now gathered round the brake.

Mary Ellen sat back in her seat and drew in a long breath before casting a glance towards her other daughters, and it was Florrie who spoke, saying, "'Tis a good distance he has to come;" but then Maggie asked bluntly, "Is there anyone inside belonging to him?"

The men standing on the road looked at one another; then Hal said to John, "Go on and enquire, quietly like."

They waited in silence but with evident impatience till he returned,

254

which was a good five minutes later.

"Well?"

John looked at his father. "There's no one of his family there," he said, and turned his back on the brake and walked slowly along the grass verge, and the men followed him; and when at some little distance he stopped, they went into a huddle and he said quietly, "I had a word with two of his cronies. Apparently they were on a drinking spree last night in Allendale, finished up in some house or other, paralytic by what they said. They drove him home towards midnight."

"God in heaven!" Hal was beating on his mouth with his closed fist. It was as if his hand was cold and he was blowing into it, for his breath was making hissing sounds.

Tom said, "He could be sleeping it off."

" 'Tis turned twelve in the day. He had animals to see to. He wouldn't be sleeping it off till this time. My God! If he's let her down I'll slit his throat. I will, I swear on it."

"Be quiet!" Hal turned on Hugh now. "It's as Tom says, he's likely sleeping it off. And what cattle there is to see to, his father could have done that. There must be an explanation." He jerked his head to the side as if rejecting other thoughts. "I talked to him only yesterday afternoon. We had an understanding."

"What kind of understanding, Dad?" It was John asking the question.

"Oh." Now Hal flung himself round and looked towards where his womenfolk were sitting in the brake and, staring at them, he muttered, "I set him up, with a promise of more if he made good on it."

"How much?" Sounding already like a man of the law Hugh repeated, "How much?"

Hal turned towards him saying, "A hundred."

All the men seemed to toss their heads at once, very like the horses were doing, impatient with standing. But it was Gabriel who said, "What did you say, Dad? A hundred pounds? You must have been mad. By! I bet there was a hole made in that last night when he entertained his friends in Allendale."

" 'Tis usual to have a do before a wedding."

"Yes, on somebody else's money?"

Hal now turned to John, saying quietly, "She wanted to be settled. It seemed her only chance. Although why? In the name of God! why? I don't know, for she's worth all the bloody women in the county: she's got a head on her shoulders and common sense enough for ten; there's nothing she can't do inside or outside the house; and she's got a nature that's pure gold. . . ."

"Then why did you sell her to him?"

Almost as if he was going to strike Hugh, Hal now turned on him, grinding the words from between his teeth, "Because I understood her, Mr Big-mouth. She's a woman, not a lass any more, and she has her needs, of which you'll learn, I hope, some day. She wanted children. He was the only one that had offered. She's twenty-four years old, by which time your mother had almost all of you lot." He cast his eyes angrily round them, and when a voice came from the brake calling, "Hal! Hal!" he marched away and towards Mary Ellen.

"What's the matter? What's up?"

"Nothin'. Nothin'." His voice was light. "Just saying, the groom must have made merry last night and has slept in." He smiled at Kate, but there was no answering smile on her face. And now they all looked towards where Mr Scott was hurrying through the chattering on-lookers, and, having reached them, he said, "Would you like to come and wait in the vestry? The wind is rather cutting."

"Yes. Yes, thank you." Mary Ellen nodded to him. Then for the first time they all got down from the brake, and followed the parson through the gaping and now very interested spectators around to the back of the church and into the small bare-looking room that was furnished with only a table, six chairs and a book-case.

In a few minutes they were joined by the men, and now the room was crowded, and the parson, addressing Hal, said, "What do you think could have happened, Mr Roystan?"

"I don't know, Reverend. But he'll likely come galloping up at any minute. And believe me, he'll get the length of me tongue afore he gets into your church."

The Reverend Scott emitted a slight titter at this, but there was no echo from the others present in the room. . . .

When half an hour passed and Harry Baker had not come galloping up on his horse, Kate said quietly, "I want to go home, Mam."

"Hold your hand a minute." Hal bent over her and, looking into her face, said quietly, "There could be an explanation. As I've told you, they had a little do last night and likely he had one over many and, not being used to it—" He had no knowledge whether that fellow was used to drink or not but he went on, "It takes you that way. After the first real booze-up I ever had I slept for twenty-four hours, missed me shift." He straightened himself and, smiling now, nodded to his sons. "It's a fact. Weird feeling to miss a whole day. But worse at the end of the week when me pay packet was light. . . ."

At one o'clock the family mounted the brake and the trap under the eyes now of the whole church company, some of the faces showing their deep concern and pity, while others grinned and were impatient to be away to spread the news that Hal Roystan's big lass had been left at the church door. Others, more piously spiteful, would say, "Well, it was God's will and God's way of punishing Mary Ellen Lee for her sin in begetting a child outside of marriage. Anyone responsible for giving life to a bastard couldn't expect to get off scot-free. They might prosper, as she had, but God was not mocked, He had His way in the end." ...

When the party arrived back at the farm Terry Foster, who had worked for Hal since he was ten years old and, still unmarried, lived in a comfortable room above the stables, gaped in astonishment at the bride being helped down from the brake and then, surrounded by her family, all looking grim, making for the house. It was to Annie coming in the rear he said, "What's happened? What's up?"

Annie stopped and, taking him by the shoulder, twisted him around before she whispered, "He didn't turn up. And you know something? I'm glad, because she was throwing herself away. I'm glad, I tell you." And with this, she gave him a slight push before turning and following the family into the house.

The women went into the sitting-room with Kate, the men remained in the hall, and it was Hal who said, "Get the horses saddled."

"Aye, we'll get the horses saddled. By God! we will." It was Hugh who was speaking. "But let's get this damn finery off first, because I won't want these togs splattered with blood, and by God! ..."

"Hugh" – Hal's voice was low and grim – "leave this to me. You can come along of me, and you an' all, John, but you two" – he glanced at Tom and Gabriel – "get the horses ready, then stay around in case he should turn up here."

They set about obeying his commands without further murmur, and he turned and walked slowly towards the sitting-room.

Kate was sitting without her veil and shawl, her hands were lying limp on her lap, her head was bent slightly; her sisters, one at each side of her, were commiserating the only way they knew how, saying words to the effect that it would be all right, that there must be some explanation, he'd likely fallen off his horse and was hurt. It was when Florrie said, "You'll find you'll have to go through all this tomorrow again," that Kate raised her head slowly and, looking first from Florrie to Maggie, then to her mother, and after holding her sad gaze for a moment, she finally lifted her eyes to Hal standing now to the side of Mary Ellen, his hand gripping his wife's shoulder, and she said gently, "There'll be no tomorrow for me. Perhaps it's just as well. It was never meant to be."

"The bloody swine!"

" 'Tis all right, Dad," she said, and now with a swift movement she got to her feet, saying, "I'll get out of these things."

"I'll help you."

She put her hand out towards Florrie in a firm movement, saying, "No, no; thanks, dear. I'll see to meself." Then she went swiftly from the room, leaving the others silent, heads hanging as if the shame lay on their shoulders.

After a moment Hal looked at Mary Ellen and said, "I'm off to change; then we're riding over to get at the facts. But there's one thing I hope" – he moved his head slowly up and down – "and that is, that he's done a bunk, because otherwise there'll be bloodshed. I know that."

As he went to leave her side, Mary Ellen grabbed at his hand saying, "'Tisn't worth it. Let him go."

"But he may have had an accident." Florrie's quiet voice had a reprimand in it. And the three of them looked at her as if in pity, and it was Hal who answered her simply with, "Aw, lass," before going from them, and those two words conveyed how far-fetched and even silly he thought her statement had been.

It was almost an hour and a half later when Hal and the two young men entered the mud yard of the Bakers' small farm. There was no one to be seen. But when Hal thumped on the low back door it was opened by a woman in her fifties. Her face was red and her lids were blinking. She did not address Hal, but turned her head, saying to someone in the room, "They've come." The next minute a man with stooped shoulders and grizzled hair stood by her side, and he looked defiantly up at Hal, saying, "We expected you. Aye, aye, we expected you. And 'tis no good puttin' the blame on us. 'Tisn't our fault."

Hal stared from one to the other of them, then said slowly, "Where is he?"

"How do I know?" The man's head bobbed. "Left on the doorstep last night as drunk as a noodle. But at six this mornin' he was off bag and baggage."

"Where's he gone?" This was a demand from Hugh, and the man replied in a similar tone, "How do I know? I only know he's left me in a bloody mess. How am I gona manage here on me own with me back the way it is, and the missis here not worth two pennorth of copper." He nudged his wife with his elbow. "Anyway, you've got yourself to blame" – he nodded at Hal – "you gave him a few bob yesterday. He could never rest when he had a penny in his hand."

"A few bob? A penny?" Hal's voice was grim. "I gave him a hundred pounds."

He watched both the man and woman now turn and stare at each other in amazement, and it was the woman who muttered, "What did you say? A hundred pounds?"

"That's what I said."

"Huh!" The man laughed now but mirthlessly. "And you expected him to stay put, with a hundred pounds in his pocket? God Almighty! He's always wanted to see the world an' now you've made it possible for him."

"We'll find him. Sometime or other, we'll find him."

"I doubt it. But good luck to you, an' if I had him here meself this minute God knows what I'd do to him, leavin' me in a hole like this."

Hal stared at the man and woman. These were the people whom Kate would have had to live with. He had only met them three times before and he had judged them to be a pleasant couple: not very intelligent but homely and pleasant; and he could see Kate getting on with them and altering the little farmhouse, because she had a way with furniture and such like. She was like her mother. But now he wondered if his judgement of human nature was slipping, for why hadn't he gauged the type of man he'd been dealing with. For a moment he was thanking God what had happened had happened; then he was thinking of Kate and the effect this business was going to have on her for the rest of her life. Things like this had the power to turn a woman's mind, even a big sensible one, as Kate was.

Without further words he turned abruptly away and made for his horse, and after a second his sons followed him.

They had gone some distance along the road before Hugh said, "What now, Dad?"

"What d'you mean, what now?"

"Well, do you think it's any use going into Hexham or some place?"

"No, I don't. He'll be further afield than Hexham by now. What's done's done."

"And a good thing to my mind." John jerked the reins, causing his horse to alter its stride and to side-step for a moment, and when it was walking straight again he looked at his father and brother and added, "Kate would have withered in that hole, living with that pair ... apart from Baker, who I couldn't stand right from the beginning. But you were so bent on it; it looked as if you couldn't get rid of her quick enough." Again he jerked the reins, and now the horse went into a gallop.

Hal looked at Hugh. He was dumbfounded. If that speech had come from this one at his side he could have understood it; but John, like Tom, was a mild-mannered man. They had very little to say at any time, happy go lucky the pair of them, with, he had imagined, no strong emotions and therefore no strong vices. He muttered aloud, "Wanted to get rid of her? Well, I'll be damned! I'll let him know something." And he went to jerk his horse forward when Hugh said, "Hold your hand a minute, Dad, 'cos ... well, he's only saying what we all thought. I mean, the lads anyway."

"Sayin' what you all thought?" Hal's mouth tightened for a moment. "Then all I can say is I've got four bloody fools for sons, and four males that will never know what goes on in a woman. Kate, let me tell you, was" – he gulped in his throat – "was starved inside, she was ready for marriage, for bairns. 'Twasn't so much the man, but bairns. Women are like that. And apparently I've bred four bloody numskulls who look at the busts and bums and ignore the head. And I suppose you all knowing I wasn't her real father imagined that as another reason for me wantin' to get rid of her. Eh?"

When Hugh didn't answer but stared straight ahead, Hal jerked his chin upwards, exclaiming loudly, "My God! Where've I been all these years, asleep, not to know what was goin' on in the minds around me? Look" – he twisted in the saddle – "let me tell you this: I love, and have loved that girl from I brought her into the world, and like her own father would never have done. He saw her when she was just a few months old and here she is on twenty-four, and nobody's seen hilt nor hair of him since. Skited off to France was the last thing I heard of him. But never a word to the mother of his child, nor to that child. Any man worth his salt would have put in an appearance just to see how she had grown. Anyway, he could be dead now, and I hope he is. But for you lot to think that I wanted rid of Kate ... well, I'll tell you something, lad, and you can pass it on around the others, I think more of Kate than I do of any of you. Now there it is, and that's the truth."

"Thank you very much."

"You're welcome, lad, you're welcome." And with this Hal too spurred his horse on. But Hugh did not join him; he stared after his father, shaking his head. He wouldn't tell the others what his father had said; it would hurt them, because he knew it was true. Like them, he too had thought that the extra attention his father gave to Kate was to make her feel one of them all. But no, apparently it was the other way about: he had acted as he did out of love for her. He had always known his father was a man of very strong emotions. He had felt he took after him in a way; but now it could only be in a way, for he could never see himself loving a woman as his father did his mother, nor yet, as he had just confessed, the stepdaughter begot by a man who had been his one time friend, and whom he now wished dead.

He quickened the trot but did not ride to catch up with his father. The episode was apparently closed. Life would go on as usual, except, he supposed, that Kate would become a sort of recluse and would hide herself from everyone except the family.

3

But Hugh was wrong with regard to Kate hiding herself, and she surprised, astonished, and even shocked her family when, on the following Saturday morning, she got ready to accompany the cart into Hexham.

It wasn't an accepted rule that any particular one or other of them should go into Hexham or Haltwhistle or Allendale on Saturdays. Sometimes Mary Ellen went, taking Florrie with her, or Maggie; sometimes Maggie and Annie went; the only rule that existed was that they never all went for one of them would have to stay behind to see to the meal.

There were no servants at Moor Vale Farm. Mary Ellen and her three daughters and Annie ran the inside of the house and the dairies, Hal and three of his sons ran the farm, with help from Terry. Both inside and out one person was always left in charge. And it was automatically assumed that Kate would be that person on this particular Saturday morning.

But no, Kate was down in the kitchen at six o'clock as was usual. It was her week for seeing to the breakfast, the frying of long thick slices of bacon together with eggs and white pudding, and they all, including Terry, sat around the kitchen table and ate at seven o'clock in the morning. John, Tom, and Gabriel, as well as Hal, had been up since five. Hugh had returned to his studies in Newcastle yesterday, so there had been one less this morning for breakfast.

When the dishes were washed and the kitchen tidied and Maggie and Florrie had scrambled upstairs to get ready for the market, Kate said quietly, "I'll go and get changed then." And at this, Mary Ellen and Annie looked at each other and at Kate as she disappeared into the hall, and Mary Ellen muttered, "Surely she's not thinkin' of goin' in the day?"

"It looks like it, and perhaps 'tis for the best," said Annie.

"They'll cut her to pieces with their tongues."

"Aye, likely," Annie nodded. "But she's not your daughter for nothin', she'll put up with that and go back for more."

Mary Ellen made no reply, the words had taken her thoughts back to when she married Hal and went into the market for the first time. Tongues had certainly tried to cut her up: hadn't she been living with the man for months afore they got married; he was never off her doorstep.

And she hadn't had a midwife but had let him deliver her child. Now what would you think of a lass like that, and her not twenty?

"She knows what she's doing."

Mary Ellen turned to Annie, saying, "What?"

"I said, she knows what she's doing, and 'tis the right thing. Why should they put shame on the woman who's been left behind when it's no fault of her own? Yet they do, and expect you to go and hide in the attic for the rest of your life. If I was in her place I'd do exactly as she's goin' to do."

Mary Ellen nodded. Yes, that's exactly what Annie would have done. What a pity a woman like Annie had never married. And what a greater, greater pity that her own daughter, her own dear Kate would never now marry, for no matter how brave a face one put on a situation like this, it changed you. And she knew it had already changed Kate, for in the six days since she had been humiliated she had refused to discuss the matter in any way; in fact, she had acted as if nothing had happened. It wasn't normal. She herself had risen earlier than usual this morning and had prepared a breakfast tray to take up to her, but she had been astounded when Kate had walked into the kitchen, saying, "You're up early, Mam."

She had found it impossible to give her daughter any answer, but had watched her look down on the tray, then slowly take the things off and put them back into her place on the table. . . .

When Kate returned to the kitchen dressed for the town, Maggie and Florrie were already there, their bonnets and capes on. Mary Ellen was out in the yard supervising the last of the loading. It was Tom's turn to stay on the farm. John was already mounted. Terry was driving one cart and Gabriel the other, and Hal stood at the head of the brake adjusting the harness of the horse. Then turning, he looked towards the kitchen door, shouting, "You ready?"

The girls, in a flurry now, made for the door, but Kate did not immediately follow them. Looking at Annie, she said, "You don't mind managing alone, Annie?"

"No, lass, no." Annie came to her and put her arm around her shoulders and pressed her tightly for a moment, saying, "You know I don't, and 'tis the right thing you're doin'. Go on in there, look them straight in the eye an' smile. That'll baffle a lot of the bitches." And with this, she leant forward quickly and placed a shy kiss on Kate's cheek, and Kate, turning to her, kissed her back.

Annie was almost as dear to her as was her mother, for she had nursed her and carried her about as a child; she had played with her and romped with her on the quiet, and had her to stay when she had for a time lived in

Kate Makepeace's old cottage. She loved Annie. Perhaps it was because in a way they were alike, at least in build, and almost in features too, although she would have changed her own face any day for Annie's, even as it was now in age.

She went quickly out, and when she reached the brake Hal extended his hand towards her to help her up, but he could not resist muttering, "You all right?"

"Yes, yes, I'm all right." She smiled at him, but it was a strange smile, a smile that made him uneasy. . . .

They had no stall in the market. Hal had given it up on the last farm when he had started to sell his produce in bulk to other stall-holders. And now, nearly an hour and a half later nearing the market proper, Hal stopped the brake and helped his womenfolk down from it, saying as he held out his hand to Mary Ellen, "Twelve o'clock mind at the hotel. No dawdling."

At this she smiled at him, saying pertly, "If we should be late you can wait."

"I'm not waitin'." He looked from one to the other. Maggie and Florrie were laughing at him, but Kate's face was straight. And so, addressing her, he said, "You round them up. Do you hear? Once they get amongst ribbons and threads they tie themselves in knots."

The girls laughed aloud now and Mary Ellen pushed him gently with one hand while with the other she took Kate's arm. She knew it was all a play on his part; he was as worried over Kate as she was, for her attitude was more than puzzling to him. She knew that if Kate had cried and wanted to hide herself away he could have understood it, and the word he would have applied to anyone else taking up this stance would have been 'brazen'. But her Kate could never be brazen, she had always been more of a retiring nature, yet here she was, braving the town, when the scandal was still hot on everybody's lips.

"Mam."

"Yes, dear?"

Kate disengaged herself from her mother's arm, saying now, "You and the girls go and do your shopping. I'm going to the bookshop."

"Well, I'll come with you."

"No . . . no thanks, dear. I'd rather go on my own. Well, I mean, there isn't all that much time, and you know what Dad is like if he has to wait for his dinner, although," she added smilingly now, "he'll find fault with every item on his plate. I'll see you there around twelve. All right?" And she looked at the sisters standing silent and slightly open-mouthed, and then at her mother before turning from them and going through an arch and down a narrow side street to where, at the end, was Mr Ramshaw's bookshop.

She was breathing heavily when she stopped and looked in the window of the shop. Well, now she was on her own and about to face the ladies, because this is where some of them congregated on a Saturday morning, those who wanted to appear a cut above their neighbours, especially the Watfords and the MacNultys, who sent their daughters to The Dame School.

As she pushed open the door of the shop her entry stopped a customer being served.

Mrs Bitten was in the act of paying for a book which the assistant was handing to her wrapped up neatly in a little parcel, and both their hands became still and their eyes widened just the slightest. And Susan Bitten who was standing to the side of her mother, her hands in a muff, slowly brought the article up to her face as if she was going to bite on it.

"Good-morning, Mrs Knowles." Kate's voice was quiet as she inclined her head towards the assistant, and it was a second or two before the reply came, "Good-morning, Miss Roystan."

The Bittens and the Roystans were not on visiting terms. The men could speak and haggle over cattle in the market, but that was as far as it went, for the Bittens did not socially recognize the upstart smelting mill worker who had clawed himself up into a position where now he had one of the best farms for miles around, and was running a herd of fifty cows, the latest news of him being that he was going in for breeding. Of course, as was said, he could do this because he hadn't to pay a staff to carry on the work, for this was done by his family, though why they should want to labour on a farm after the education he had given them was a question they all asked themselves. There was only one who was seemingly taking advantage of it, the son who was going in for law. That was another thing, one of his tribe being clever enough to take up such a profession, which up till now, as everyone knew, was the prerogative of gentlemen's sons.

Then there was his womenfolk: dressed like ladies they were; and aping those above their station, too, so it was understood, by the way they ate in the house, dining-room meals every day in the week. Whoever heard of a farmer using his dining-room except for special occasions. Some people had accepted invitations but not the Bittens, probably because, as it was widely known, the Bittens were distantly connected with Beaumont who, everyone knew, owned the lead mines and smelting mills around Allendale, and, as Mrs Bitten would bring out now and again, who was so rich that his election expenses alone in eighteen and twenty-six had come to over forty thousand pounds. She didn't go on to state that less than two hundred pounds had been spent in the town where his money had been made which was Allendale, and where his workers lived and where many of them died an early death.

Mrs Bitten was a great source of information. She had also made herself the leader of the farming society in that part of the country. That wasn't to say, she was accepted by the real county families, except on the face of it when she and her husband, and son, and daughter, rode with the hounds. Then, as some said, even stray dogs joined in the hunt and servants were spoken to as if they were human beings. Now you couldn't ask for more, could you?

What Mrs Bitten now said and in an undertone to the assistant, and to her daughter, was, "That for nerve." And both her daughter and the assistant nodded in agreement.

Eighteen-year-old Susan Bitten looked to where Kate was now walking slowly alongside a bookcase, and she marvelled how a woman could be left at the altar on Monday, then walk into the town on Saturday as if nothing had happened; she herself would have died. Yes, yes, indeed she would, she would have killed herself, because of the shame. No proper woman could stand the shame of such rejection. But then, Kate Roystan wasn't a real woman, not a feminine woman, she was too big. And look at her face, more like a man's. She could understand how the man had run away, but she could never understand how the woman had the nerve to walk abroad as if nothing had happened.

Kate opened the pages of a book and looked at the frontispiece but without seeing it. She knew exactly what was being said, as if she was standing next to them. And she knew that round the corner at the reading table she would be confronted by several pairs of eyes, because it was at this table that certain ladies met, not to discuss reading matter, but to exchange the gossip of the week, while at the same time taking on literary prestige.

She replaced the book and walked round the end of the bookcase, and there they were: Mrs Watford and her daughters Marie and Eva, Mrs MacNulty and her daughter Sheena.

It was Mrs Watford, a farmer's wife, who after a slight gape spoke first, saying, "Why, Kate! Why, Kate!" And she made to rise, then changed her mind. She couldn't get over what she was seeing, for, only days ago she had sat in the church and waited and waited for the marriage service to begin, and only this very minute she had been relating to Mrs MacNulty all the narration that had been caused when the Reverend had come out and explained to them that no marriage was to take place. She herself had seen the bride drive off, her head almost on her knees in shame, and yet here she was as brazen as brass. She couldn't believe it.

"How are you, Kate?" Her voice was high, sounding almost like a squeak.

"Very well, Mrs Watford, very well, thank you. And you? And Marie and Eva?" She turned to the two girls who were sitting looking at her with looks almost of stupefaction on their faces.

Mrs MacNulty now spoke, using, as Dad would laughingly say, her day-off voice which she was wont to adopt in an endeavour to cover her broad Irish accent, for the Irish round about weren't held in any good esteem, a brawling and fighting lot, admittedly only when they were drunk, but, as Dad himself would admit, not a happier or pleasanter people you could wish to meet in their sober state. But then they weren't very often sober, for the men would sell their wives and grannies for a drink.

"Oh, Kate," she said. "And are you bearin' up, me dear?"

"Bearing up?" Kate raised her eyebrows. "I haven't been ill, Mrs MacNulty."

"No, no. I understand. Well, there's nothin' like puttin' a brave face on it. As I always say, face trouble and it splatters ... I mean, it disappears, and MacNulty always says, as long as you've got a back on you why face the wind."

"I like facing the wind, Mrs MacNulty." The words were quiet, the tone pleasant.

What could you do with a creature like this? Nothing. She was brazen. She wouldn't have believed it. Mrs MacNulty glanced at her daughter Sheena and was surprised to see her smiling broadly up at the big barefaced woman. And Kate Roystan was smiling down on her. Wait till she got her outside, she'd say something to that girl, she would that. She had been worried about her of late: too ready to talk back she was, and having opinions that weren't proper at her age, and she not yet seventeen.

"Goodbye, Mrs MacNulty." Kate moved on, only to encounter three more ladies, two of whom she wasn't acquainted with, but the third, after the usual gape, patted her arm kindly, saying in an undertone, "I understand. I understand."

Kate didn't question the lady's understanding but picked up a book from the shelf, went to the counter and paid Mrs Knowles for it, and the assistant said not a word to her, not even, thank you; then she left the shop, and deliberately now she walked back up the street and into the market.

It was there Hal came across her, and in a low tone and harshly, he said, "What you doin' parading around here on your own for? What's the matter with you, Kate? You asking for more trouble?"

"What more trouble could I have, Dad?"

"Aw, Kate, Kate. Don't take it so much to heart."

"I'm not. I'm not. Believe me, I'm not. Not that way. I'm glad. Yes, I am." She nodded at him and put her hand on his arm. "Believe me, I'm glad it happened as it did, for I know now I wouldn't have been able to put up with him, or his people." Her fingers pressed his coat as her voice dropped and she said gently, "You brought me up too well, made me soft in a way. And now you have me for life; you've made a rod for your own back." She smiled gently at him, and he lowered his head, saying, "Aw, lass, lass. Anyway, let's get out of this, they're looking at us as if they're expecting us to perform. Come on. Where are the others?"

"Shopping as usual."

"I could do with a drink before me meal. Come on. Let's get inside, it's enough to freeze you."

They walked now side by side, past the nodding stall-holders, some of whom even stopped weighing their goods to look at Hal Roystan's lass. The Baker fellow had left her in the lurch and gone off with a good pile of her money, it was now being said, after treating his cronies to free drinks in Allendale. But there she was putting a face on it. A bit brazen, they considered really. She could have kept low for a few weeks before showing her face; people would have had sympathy for her then. But as it was, she was making people think she was a bit of a queer fish.

In the hotel, Hal took off his coat and hat, then made for the settle by the fire. And when the waiter greeted him with, "Good-morning, Mr Roystan. What can I get you?" he said briefly, "Two hot toddies."

"No Dad, not for me."

"Two hot toddies, I said." Hal nodded at the man who smiled and repeated, "Two hot toddies. Very good, sir."

"You're going to drink this so that when the gang turns up you'll have some colour in your cheeks. You look like a corpse, girl."

"I feel like a corpse, Dad."

"Then why did you do it? I mean, show your face so early?"

"I . . . I don't know, at least I can't explain. It's a kind of defiance. I don't want to be pitied or hidden away."

"Nobody would have hidden you away, lass."

"No." She shook her head and smiled wanly. "No, but I would have been kindly guarded by you, and Mother, and the rest. Then in time, like a sick staggering colt, I'd have been led into the open. Well, I didn't see myself living like that. It's a long time, Dad, since I faced what I am, too ugly for a woman. . . ."

"Shut up! Shut up this minute afore I let me hands loose an' belt you. You're the finest woman that I know bar one, and you came out of her. And I know this, I feel this, being a man, I know somewhere there's one for you, one who'll see the whole of you. I know it. I made a mistake with the other one, I must have been. . . ."

"Oh, Dad." She smiled at him now, a warm endearing smile. "I only know one thing, I've been a very lucky person to have been brought up by you."

"Huh!" He threw up his head. "That's as maybe. Ah, here's the drink. Now get it down you and then we'll eat, if and when that lot turn up."

She drank the hot rum and did not shudder at the first taste, as a lady would have done or even any of the farmers' wives she had encountered that morning. But after draining the mug she gave a small laugh, saying, "Where's the fight?"

"That's me girl." Hal rose and, pulling her to her feet, laughed too, saying, "Come on, let's look for one."

They were still smiling when, further along the passage, they entered the dining-room. There, they saw enacted a little scene. His wife and two daughters had apparently just preceded them into the room and were weaving their way towards the far end to a table that had a view of the garden when a man, one of two sitting at another table, rose and pushed his chair back without looking behind him, and in doing so almost overbalanced Florrie. At this the man turned quickly and caught her by the arm, and when Hal and Kate reached them he was saying, "My apologies. I'm sorry. It was so clumsy of me. Are you all right?"

Florrie, smiling now, and in her quiet way said, "Just a few bones broken, that's all," whereupon the young man let go of her arm and laughed, retorting as quickly, "Dear, dear, that will make me liable for compensation."

He turned his head and looked at his companion, who had also risen to his feet, and now, when this man spoke, everyone looked at him for his voice was different altogether from that heard in these parts, either of gentry, farmer, or miner. In a slow, drawling tone, he said, "And I'll stand as your witness, ma ... am. And you could claim a mighty fine sum."

The man spoke English all right, but it was a foreign English, American English.

Hal cut in now saying, "What's all this? Murder on the king's highway?"

Then looking at the young man who had caused the slight affray, he said, "Good-day, Mr Bentley."

"Good-day, Mr Roystan." Both men inclined their heads towards each other.

"Trying to kill one of me family, are you?"

"No, sir, never that. Just merely attempting to knock her down." There was laughter now and blushes from Florrie, and Hal put his hand on her shoulder saying, "Well, away with you, miss, out of harm's way." And the party proceeded to make for the far table.

Kate, coming up last, had to pass round the other man and skirt the chair he was holding by the back, and when he quickly whipped it under the table and stood aside for her to pass, they stood eye to eye for a moment, and she looked into his face which was thin and tanned. His eyes looked almost black, like his hair, and this was thick and straight and came down almost to the collar of his coat. He had a thin figure dressed in good quality cloth and he was taller than herself.

The conversation as they settled at the table was purposely general until they saw the two men leave the room. And then Florrie enquired quietly, "You know him, Dad?"

"Yes, I know him. He's Mr Charles Bentley. He farms over the hills on the outskirts of Lord Redman's estate. Well, he's Redman's nephew."

"Lord Redman's nephew?" It was Maggie, wide-eyed now, repeating the statement.

"What have I just said. Aye, he's Lord Redman's nephew, but he's no better off for that, 'cos he works for his living. They laugh at him." He nodded towards Mary Ellen now. "Aye they do, a lot of them around here, the would be clever-Jacks. They think they're God's appointed where farming's concerned but I think that fellow could teach them a thing or two. I've only seen his place once. 'Tis small, called Little Manor Farm, and it's not much bigger than me first place." He looked at Mary Ellen. "A couple of cottages knocked into one." He nudged her, "Those were the days."

She smiled at him tenderly, saying, "Yes, those were the days. Frozen stiff in winter and the well dried up in summer."

They both laughed now. Then Maggie drew their attention by asking, "Do you know the other one, too?"

"No, I don't, miss, but by the sound of him I should imagine he's just off a boat somewhere. From the Americas would be me guess."

"He's handsome."

"Aye, he might be. Handsome is as handsome does. And get that starry look out of your eye. I'm havin' no foreigners in the family."

"Oh, Dad!" At Maggie's indignant tone they all laughed. And when he said, "Well, now, what about ordering?" Mary Ellen put in, "Aren't you going to wait for the lads?"

"No, I'm not going to wait for the lads. They could have been here by now if they'd liked, it wouldn't take all this time to unload. Anyway, I'd like to bet I know where one is. Master Tom will be hanging over Cissy Ludley's stall."

"Poor Cissy."

"What do you mean by that?" Hal looked at Maggie. "Do you mean that you're sorry for her 'cos our Tom's got his eye on her?"

"Don't be daft, Dad; you know what I mean. Them having the farm and the brick concern too, and she having to serve on the stall."

He leant across the table towards Maggie now. "And what disgrace is there in serving on the stall? Your mother served on a stall for years." He nodded towards Mary Ellen.

"Oh, well" – Maggie shook her head – "that was different ... well, you were struggling."

"And so are the Ludleys."

"Not to that extent, Dad. You know well what I mean. You said yourself, her father would sell his grandmother for a decent ewe."

"I might have, but after seeing his grandmother I knew he'd never be able to bring it off because she wouldn't be worth a decent ewe."

The laughter this evoked brought heads turning from all the tables in the long room, and some smiled. But others were wont to remark that the Roystan family were the queerest for miles around. The daughter left standing at the altar just a few days ago. And wasn't that her there with the rest of them, laughing her head off? You couldn't somehow place the Roystans. Starting from the bottom, they didn't fall into the category of fish, fowl, or good red meat. Oh, certainly not good red meat.

4

Christmas came. The family, as always, ate well, and they made merry, but it was, in a way, a forced merriment, especially when there were callers. And on New Year's Eve, as they all sat round the fire waiting for another year to come in, there wasn't the usual going over of events of the past twelve months. This they had all agreed was to save Kate's feelings. The only thing mentioned was the new road from Guidepost near Catton to Allendale that had recently been started, and which was to lead straight into the market place. And what advantages was it going to provide? Only to a few, Hugh had said, for coaches and the mail, perhaps, and those with their open carriages. He had, too, regaled them with the business his office had dealt with during the past year, such as that of the good people of Newcastle who were trying to get prison reform. So many tales did he tell of the hardships of prisoners and transportees that his father had laughingly asked whose side he was going to represent once he had served his articles, only to become more serious for a moment and to enquire quietly on what side of the law would he be on if a man was transported for seven years for stealing a poker from an inn.

At this the girls had exclaimed, "Never! Never! Dad. Don't be silly, that couldn't happen." And he answered, "Oh, yes, it did, in South Shields, and many more cases like it." But he did add that they had to be grateful because things at this end of the country weren't as bad as those in the south. Did they know that a little girl of twelve had been hanged in Newgate for stealing? Oh, yes! Yes! And it was on this sombre note the New Year was brought in, and with it came the atrocious weather.

January, February, and March provided great falls of snow, frozen roads, thaws, and rain. So it was on one comparatively warm and sunny day in April that Kate saddled her horse and said she was going for a ride. It was two o'clock in the afternoon, the time when the womenfolk usually adjourned to the sewing-room, there to work on their dresses or household linen, to hem with minute stitches pieces of lawn to make handkerchiefs, which, later, they would embroider with an initial in the corner.

Mary Ellen looked at her daughter, thinking, That's going to start again, for right up till Christmas, unless the weather was very bad, Kate had taken to riding out on her own, pointedly refusing company of any kind. So today, neither Florrie nor Maggie offered to ride with her.

It was agreed amongst the rest of the family, but in private, that Kate was changed: no matter what face she showed to the outside world she was no longer the Kate they all knew. She could sit in the sewing-room the whole afternoon and not utter one sentence, unless it was briefly to answer some question. And when the nights were long, after the evening meal was over and the dishes washed and the table set for the following morning's breakfast, they would gather in the sitting-room, and Maggie would play the spinet. But seldom now could they get Kate to sing. What spare time she had she would spend with a book in her hand. She and Gabriel were the great readers in the family, the rest were more for doing practical things. Hugh, of course, read quite a lot, but it was mostly to do with his legal work.

Mary Ellen was disappointed that none of the girls had shown interest in the making of potions or satchets of herbs. She herself still continued to go to her cupboard, as they called the little room where she kept her jars and bottles, and mix up winter medicines for coughs and colds, and salves and purges for the cattle.

But whatever pastimes the girls took up after their day's work, they seemed to do it with a relish. And, until late, Kate had been the most enthusiastic of them: her embroidery was so fine that on two occasions it had taken first prize at the Hexham Fair.

Ever anxious that her daughter should not isolate herself from them, Mary Ellen said, "Your father's going into Allendale, why don't you ride with him? You'll never guess what he's going to do?"

"No? What is he about to take on?" Kate asked flatly.

"Oh." Mary Ellen forced a jocular note into her voice. "He's going to honour them by at last changing his bank. As I've said to him for ages, the bank is well established now and you couldn't get more honest men than Mr Arnison and the Reverend Walton from Allenheads, and the town auditors. But no, you know what he's been like, saying that, as they couldn't see to the removal of the town dirt, they couldn't see to his money. But now things are changing." Her jocular manner faded as she ended seriously, "This'll make some of them in different quarters sit up and take notice when they see what he's got to put into their care. By! it will. Anyway, he'll be glad of your company."

"Mam." Kate's voice was quiet. "I know what you're thinking. I know what you're trying to do. But believe me, I'm all right. It's all over. It's as if it had never happened. And I'm glad. You won't believe me when I say again I'm glad it turned out as it did; but then . . . well, one changes. You know what I mean."

Yes, in a way, Mary Ellen did know what her daughter meant, for she herself had been forced to change. She sighed and said, "All right, dear. Go on, and enjoy your ride. Only be careful. I wish you wouldn't take Ranger, though; he's hard to handle."

"I can manage him. We understand each other." Kate made to go out,

271

then turned and there was a mischievous glint in her eye that hadn't been there for some long time as she said, "You know what I'm going to do, Mam?"

"No, Kate, no." Mary Ellen only too gladly capped her daughter's mood.

"I'm going to get some knickerbockers made."

Mary Ellen's chin dropped, her mouth fell into a gape then snapped closed before she said, "No! No! Kate, you wouldn't?"

"I would, and I am. Remember when I was little, I used to ride astride, and barebacked at that. So why not?"

"It ... it...." Mary Ellen stopped: she had been about to say, "It could get your name up." And it certainly would, a woman the size of Kate, in fact, any woman, straddling a horse like a man! She said quietly, "Don't do it, Kate. Anyway" – she gave a shaky laugh – "you're not serious?"

"I am, Mam. And why not? It's a simple thing after all. Don't worry." She put her hand out and patted Mary Ellen's arm. "When I wear them I'll not ride into Hexham or Allendale, I'll keep to the hills." And with this she went out.

The sky was high. There was only a slight breeze, just enough to cool the sweat on both her and the horse when, half an hour later, she drew the animal to a halt.

She leant forward now and patted the animal's neck, saying, "That was good, wasn't it, Ranger? All the cobwebs gone? That's it, breathe deep." This was when the horse put his head up and neighed.

For the next ten minutes or so, she walked the animal over land that dropped quite steeply into a wooded valley through the bottom of which ran a burn, spanned by a small stone bridge. And now, crossing it and approaching her, was a man on horseback, whom she recognized immediately as Mr Bentley. Since their meeting last November in the hotel dining-room, he had visited the farm three times, supposedly to discuss cattle with her father. But on two occasions he had stayed to have a hot drink and had partaken of it in the kitchen, the last time only a month ago, when Florrie, in large bibbed white apron, had been making pastry at the kitchen table, and he had pointedly talked to her, which, afterwards, had caused the boys to chip her and her to retaliate by saying, "Don't be silly. He is Lord Redman's nephew." Whereupon her father had got on his hind legs and said, "And what was Lord Redman, anyway, two generations ago?" And then they had listened to the early beginnings of the man who now owned a very large estate on the borders of Northumberland.

"Good-day, Miss Roystan."

"Good-day, Mr Bentley."

"Isn't it a beautiful day?"

"Indeed, yes, and it hasn't come too soon. It's been an awful winter." She dismounted from her horse now, saying, "He loves to drink here."

"Yes, they do, don't they? But I've just come down from my friend's cottage" – he pointed over his shoulder towards the far hills – "and her ladyship here" – he patted the horse's neck – "had her fill up there. At least as much as I would allow her, because if she had her own way, she'd take on so much I wouldn't even get a trot out of her. Strangely," he now added, "I was going to call on your father today. I want a little more advice. Picking his brains again. By the way, how is your family?"

"Oh, very well, very well, thank you."

"That is good to hear. No one suffered from the cold?"

"No, not really. A few sniffs and sneezes." She smiled at him and he laughed, repeating "A few sniffs and sneezes."

"Are you going on, or is this your limit?"

"I had intended to go on,"

"Are you making for the peak?" He turned his head and looked back towards the hill in the distance.

"Perhaps, yes."

"It's lovely up there today, a grand sight, although I don't know how my friend has stood the winter, his first in England. You ... you may remember, he was with me on that memorable day in the hotel in Hexham."

"Oh, yes, yes." She nodded at him. "The ... the ..." She could not say foreigner. "American, isn't he? American?"

"Yes, indeed, an American, and a very interesting one too. He rented the shepherd's cottage from me in the autumn last year, supposedly for two months. Of all things, he was writing the history of the villages, and the customs hereabouts. Apparently, his far forebears came from these parts, although he doesn't seem to know much about them, as far as I can gather. He's a great listener, but not all that much of a talker, which is something of a diversity from his fellow-countrymen, and I've met one or two of them. I have tried to get him to come down and meet your family, knowing that he would find you all most interesting, and no doubt you would find him that way too. But to no avail, he seems disinclined to make close contacts, although he walks the villages to gather all the data he can for his book or whatever he intends to write. At present, he's engrossed with Langley: the mill, the mine, and its surrounding land." He shook his head for a moment, saying, "He's a most interesting man. And besides writing, he's a very clever hand with a pencil. He's done some wonderful little sketches of the Abbey in Hexham and the old houses in Allendale. But, strangely, he never seems to complete anything. Part of a roof and a door, or a branch of a tree, and all on the bottom of the page on which he is writing. I think he's very skilful, though he firmly denies being either an artist or a writer. Well" – he jerked his horse's reins – "I'll get him down to be viewed by your family one day, I hope, because I cannot help but think he's rather lonely up there, and I can't manage to ride over as often as I'd wish."

There was nothing she could say to this unusual discourse, she could only nod her head. As he raised his hat with a "Goodbye, Miss Roystan, enjoy your ride," he put his horse into a gallop to take the first part of the hill.

Alone again, she led Ranger to the burn, then sat on the parapet looking down at the reflection of the sun dancing like stars on the water as it gurgled over the stones. He was a nice man was Mr Charles Bentley. Wouldn't it be lovely for Florrie if something happened between them. She felt no jealousy at the thought. Florrie was her favourite sister. She was sweet and gentle, yet had a mind of her own, and she'd be able to adapt to any company. Not so Maggie. Maggie was turbulent, and her tongue could have a flashing sting to it at times.

Ranger, unlike Mr Bentley's mount, knew when he had had enough and, tossing his head, he came up the bank and towards her, and she, taking up the reins, stroked his nose as she said to him, "There's no grass here for you to nibble; further up there will be." And with this she stepped onto the low parapet, then mounted the horse again.

There was no vestige of a road now, only sheep tracks. The land, open and bare, was patterned with the dull purply brown of dead heather and the burnt brown of crumpled bracken fronds, until once again, descending, she came upon an isolated piece of woodland, and when she emerged from it and rounded the bottom of a hill there, in the distance, she saw a cottage, so small it looked no bigger than the piggery sheds at home.

She drew the horse to a stop, wondering how the American could possibly exist there all the winter. Of course, there was plenty of wood from the thicket behind her, and there, not ten yards away, she could see the glint of water tumbling down over an outcrop of stone. But you couldn't live on wood and water. He'd have to carry all his essential foods up here. And at times he must have been snowed in for days on end. . . . Strange man.

She avoided going nearer the cottage, and drove her horse towards the base of the hill beyond the outcrop of rocks over which the spring tumbled. The hill curved sharply to the right and as she rounded it the horse gave a loud neigh of fright and she a startled gasp for there, lying stretched across the path, his head resting on a small mound, was the man she had been thinking about.

The horse's neigh not only brought him out of sleep, but scrambling to his feet. Blinking, he looked up at her, and she down at him.

She was the first to speak, saying, "I'm sorry. He was startled, the horse. He . . . he might have trodden on you. I'm . . . I'm so sorry."

"My fault." He smiled quietly at her. "Silly place to lie anyway. But the view's good." He thumbed over his shoulder, but didn't look away from her. "We've . . . we've met before," he said.

"Yes." She swallowed deeply. "In the hotel dining-room."

"Yes, in the hotel dining-room. The day my friend almost knocked over your sister."

Lost for the moment for something to say, she said quietly, "I . . . I have just seen Mr Bentley down by the burn."

"Oh, yes, yes. He left me right here not long ago." He too now seemed lost for further words, then found a subject in the view. Turning from her, he stretched out his arm, saying, "Look at that. People travel across continents and don't see anything finer. All those hills springing up from the valley and rolling on and on." He glanced over his shoulder now, his arm still out-stretched as he said, "Do you know that eternity is just beyond that last hill?"

She smiled faintly now as she said, "No, I didn't."

"Well, it is. I've tried to reach it. I walked a full day and a night and I might as well have just stood here."

She stared down at him. What a strange man he was, but nicely strange, and disturbingly strange. It was his eyes. She could well imagine them looking into eternity. She moved in the saddle and the horse, restless, took a quick step forward and his fore-paw rested on an open book. Pulling him up, she bent over, crying, "Oh! dear me. I'm sorry. I seem to be...." She didn't finish but, sliding from the saddle, she pulled the animal backwards and watched the man lift the book, saying, on a laugh, "It'll be worth more now than the author ever dreamed of, it isn't often a horse puts its signature to a page."

"Has he torn it?"

"No, no. Anyway, if it had, it would be of little loss. Horace Walpole stretches imagination a little too far, I think.... Do you read? Have you read this?" He lifted up the book: *The Castle of Otranto*.

"No, I haven't. I... I haven't read anything by that author, but I have read Sir Walter Scott."

She made the announcement as if with pride, and he nodded, "Oh, yes, your Sir Walter Scott. Yes, he is a good writer, but I find he drags things out. I suppose it goes without saying that you have also read Miss Austen's work?"

"Oh, yes, yes." She smiled frankly at him. "It goes without saying."

"De-light-ful woman."

She noticed how he drew out the word delightful, as he did most of his words, even the ordinary words sounded different on his tongue. She found she wanted him to go on talking. And remembering the advice Miss Pritchard had given to all her pupils should they be in a drawing-room and were called upon to keep the conversation going, either to ask a question delicately, or bring in tactfully some interest of your own, so now she said, "Referring to Scott, have you read *Quentin Durward?*"

"No, no, I haven't read that one."

"I... I should imagine that you might like it. It is full of foreign adventures."

"And you think I might like foreign adventures?"

She felt colour rising to her face, but said, "Well, seeing as you're not English, I... I imagined... well, perhaps, you might recognize some of the places."

"You give me credit of being a great traveller, which I'm sorry I cannot claim, for, apart from comparatively speaking short journeys I have made in my own country, England is the first foreign place I have visited."

"Do ... do you like it?"

"Very much. But I have one grievance." He inclined his head towards her and smiled. "Your cold is much too cold."

"Oh, yes, yes" – she returned his smile now – "especially up here." As she spoke, a quick gust of wind came up the valley and caused her to shiver slightly, and he was quick to say, "You see, even on a day like this, when the sun is warm, the wind reminds you that this is a cold climate."

"Yes, indeed." Again she felt at a loss for something to say. And so she turned to the horse and started to walk it back round the hill. He walked with her, and when they came in sight of the cottage he said, "It would be both American and English courtesy to offer you some refreshment, but I have no tea, I only drink coffee."

"I like coffee."

Now why had she said that? Miss Pritchard would not have approved. She would have put it under the heading of unladylike behaviour, angling for an invitation. Even her mother would have exclaimed, "Oh, Kate!"

He stopped and she drew the horse to a standstill, and once again they were looking at each other straight in the eyes, and of a sudden she felt embarrassed and deeply ashamed as she acknowledged that she had for a moment hoped that he would offer her coffee.

She gripped the pummel of the saddle, saying, "I must get home. Goodbye, Mr ... Mr...."

"Please." His hand was extended towards her. "I always have a pot on the side of the fire; I'd be happy if you would join me."

She turned her head and looked from his outstretched hand to his face again, then formally she said, "You're sure it will not be interrupting your work?"

His head went up and he laughed outright, saying, "I don't work. I haven't any work."

"Oh." Slowly she turned the horse in the direction of the cottage, and they were walking side by side when she put in quietly, "I understood from Mr Bentley that you are writing about the history of the county."

"Oh, that. Well, if that's work, then I work."

As they neared the cottage she realized that it wasn't so minute as she had first imagined. It had a low door, with two small windows to the right of it and one to the left, and there was a kind of byre attached.

When she drew the horse to a stop on the edge of the rough slabs laid in front of the cottage, he said, "You can tie him to the post there, or let him into the field with Daisy. Oh, Daisy would like that." He smiled at her and looked towards the dry-stone wall running parallel to the side of the cottage, and she smiled in answer, saying, "Oh, I'm sure he would like to meet Daisy." And on this she walked the animal towards a rough gate set in the wall.

There was no sign of another horse until he put his fingers to his mouth and whistled, then said, "She'll be away down the hill having a talk with Biddy."

"Biddy?" She looked her enquiry, and he nodded at her, saying, "Yes. I have a goat, and she gives me milk when I can catch her. See yonder" – he pointed – "at the bottom of the hill, you see a black dot?"

She saw what he termed a black dot.

"That was a shepherd's shelter, a very rude hut, and apparently Biddy was brought up there and her owner didn't tell me she had a preference for her own house when I bought her. So every time I bring her across the field and tie her up here to the wall or post, she is gone by morning. How she does it, I don't know, but once back near her own house she will give me her milk. But it's quite a tramp down there, especially if a gale is blowing. She's like her namesake. I christened her Biddy after a remarkable old Irish lady I met on the ship coming across to England: she'd walk the deck in storms, and had the captain worried to death; he could do nothing with her, she was so stubborn. . . . Mrs Biddy O'Leary, they called her." He laughed. "We became good friends. . . . But not so the goat."

"Have you thought of putting her on a chain?"

She was amazed at the expression on his face now. Gone was the laughter and his voice seemed to lose its drawl as he put in quickly, "Never a chain! No, never a chain. I'm against chains. Man or beast should never be chained."

"No." Her voice was small. "No, you're right, quite right. Neither should be chained. I'm sorry I suggested it."

His expression lightened a little. "No, no. Your suggestion was understandable, and no doubt many would follow it." He turned from her and pointed now to the pony galloping over the hill, saying, "If only she would show the same speed when I'm on her back, we'd get some place. . . . Oh! Oh!" He had opened the gate and had to step quickly aside as Ranger made eagerly to get into the field, and Kate cried, "Steady! Ranger. Steady! Let me slip the reins. There. There. Go on!" And Ranger went on.

They watched the two animals come to an abrupt stop, and their noses tentatively touched before they were away again galloping like the wind, the smaller horse leading.

"Wonderful. Wonderful."

Kate glanced at her companion. It was as if he had never seen horses cavorting before.

Then turning abruptly from the wall, he said simply, "Coffee."

He stood aside and she bent her head and entered the cottage. The room looked almost starkly bare. It was about twelve feet square and one wall was almost entirely taken up by the open fireplace, with a bricked-in part to the side piled high with logs. There was a small wooden table and a single chair in the middle of the room, and on the wall to the left of the wood store was a row of three shelves holding two pans and odd pieces of rude crockery. And under the shelves and just about a foot from the floor was a slatted rack on which were a number of books, about thirty in all, and writing materials. The wall to the right had a door in it which she guessed must lead into the byre.

He made no apology for the state of the dwelling, but said politely, "Please be seated."

She noticed that his manner at times was most formal, by which she gauged that whatever part of America he had come from, he must have been brought up in cultured surroundings, which in a way was surprising to her, for the impression that she held of the Americas was one of people living rough, mostly pioneers harassed by Indian tribes.

She sat down on the wooden chair and watched him now bring two mugs from the shelf, then go to the fire where a black coffee pot was standing in the hot ashes. She watched him pour out the liquid. It looked deadly black. Then as he handed her the mug he said, "Would you like some sugar?"

"If ... if you please."

He now left the room and went into the byre; then he was back again proffering her a bowl of brown sugar, saying, "I rarely use it myself."

She put a spoonful of the sugar into the coffee, stirred it before sipping at it, then knew a moment of panic when she almost spat the contents out of her mouth. It was with one great effort that she swallowed the liquid, but she could not stop herself from choking and coughing, so much so that she splattered. When she felt his hand patting her on the back, she thought in despair, Dear, dear; it would happen to me, wouldn't it? She groped for a handkerchief to wipe her mouth. Then still coughing, but less now, she gasped, "I'm sorry. Oh, I am sorry. I ... I seem to be saying that all the ... the time."

"Please, please, it was me. I'm a fool; no one but a madman would drink coffee like this. Here, give it to me." He grabbed the mug from the table and, going to the open door, he threw the contents out; then came back to her, saying, "A drink of milk, goat's milk? It will soothe your throat."

When he offered her another mug, holding some milk this time, she drank it gratefully, while at the same time telling herself that she had never been able to stand goat's milk. There was always that smell about it. Yet, it did ease her throat. And now she smiled at him weakly, saying, "You must have a very strong stomach."

"Yes, I must have." He was laughing nervously now. "A doctor once told me that such strong coffee is much more harmful than either whisky or rum, or moonshine ... home-brewed stuff, you know."

"I've no doubt about it."

"I'll promise you on your next visit I shall make you coffee fit for a lady." His voice trailed away and again they were staring silently at each other. On her next visit, he had said.

She noticed, too, the effect of his own words on himself, and now he murmured, "That is if you are this way again. I mean, should you care to call in. I ... I don't see many visitors, in fact, no one except

Charles. Of course" – his head wagged a little now – "I'm out a great deal."

"Yes, yes," she said; "I understand from Charles that you have been studying the history of Langley, its mill and its mine.... Have you seen the castle?"

"Oh, yes. What is left of it, of course. What a pity it's in ruins, although the original towers still stand, which is amazing when you think how old it is. But ... everything here is so old, isn't it? Everything has its feet deep in the ground going down to solid rock. You can stretch the imagination but never see it changing. So different from my country."

"Do you miss your country?"

He seemed to consider for a moment, then said, "I'll know when I get back later in the summer."

Why should she experience an immediate sense of loss. It was ridiculous. It was some seconds before she said, "You are returning home this year then?"

"Yes. Oh ... yes ... well" – he jerked his head to the side – "I say I am, but it all depends." His voice faded away like the echo of a note and for a moment she thought that she had detected a lost lonely quality in his expression. On an impulse she said, "Would you like to come down and meet my family sometime? They would be delighted to have you. My brothers particularly would like to hear about America. And you would find my father a source of information about this part of the world. You see, he once worked in the smelting mills."

To her surprise he now turned from her and walked to the open door and stood looking out for some seconds before he said, "I'm ... I'm not a very good mixer. I don't seek company as a rule."

She stared at him. His back looked long and thin and his black hair appeared like a large fur cap on his head. He had said he wasn't a very good mixer. She'd imagined he would be just the opposite, for his way of talking and his manner were both free and easy.

He surprised her further now by going to the side of the fire and rolling a large round log towards the table, seating himself on it, then looking up at her and saying, "Tell me about your family. I'd like to hear about them."

There was a long pause before she answered, and then her voice was tentative as she said, "Well, there is my mother and father, and I have six brothers and sisters. The twins are the eldest, John and Tom, then comes Maggie. She was the one in the hotel dining-room that day." She nodded at him, and he inclined his head in understanding. "Then there is Florrie, the one that caused the rumpus." Again she smiled at him and he answered her in the same way. "After Florrie comes Hugh. He is training to be a lawyer. He spends most of his time in Newcastle. He has rooms there. Gabriel is the youngest. He is eighteen. There were two others, Peg and Walter." Her voice dropped. "They died with the typhus, in forty-one."

"Oh, I'm sorry. I am, I am sorry."

279

"Well" – she lifted her shoulders – "that's the family. I mustn't forget Annie Gordon. She has lived with us at least all my life. She is like one of the family. We have no servants as we girls and my mother run the house and the dairy, and at times help outside, but most of the work outdoors is done by my father and three of my brothers. I said we had no servants, but Terry is a farm worker. He's been with us for years too, in fact since he was ten."

"Have ... have you always lived on that farm?"

"Oh, no, no. As I said, my father first of all worked in the smelt mills; then he had a little money left him and he bought a small farm. That was the beginning. He moved to two others after that, until ten years ago we came to Moor Vale."

"Life sounds very smooth and uneventful for all the family."

His eyes were hard on her now as if there were a question in his words and he was anxious to know the answer. And she gave it to him, saying, "Oh, there you are wrong. There have been many tragedies in the family, some that have made local history. Perhaps in your journeying you have heard of them."

There seemed another long pause before he answered her. "Yes, yes, one or two things," he said. "Some men were murdered and ... and the culprit hanged himself, or some such tale."

"He was only one of the culprits."

"But it was a grim business and such are best forgotten."

"Unless" – she smiled – "it is going to add flavour to your story."

"I ... I'm not writing a story. I am not an author."

"No?" There was a note of surprise in her voice.

"No. I ... I came over to England on a sightseeing tour and was rather ... well, the word is fascinated by your part of the country, and there is so much folklore here that I decided to make notes on it. If Sir Walter Scott were alive he would have nothing to fear from me, nor would Mr Walpole or Miss Maria Edgeworth. Have you read any of her tales of Irish life?"

"No, I'm afraid I haven't."

"They are well worth reading. Her descriptions are very poignant and clear."

"I must look out for her work when I next go into Hexham. There is a good bookshop there, you know."

"Oh, you needn't go that far; I can lend you the very one." He went to the rack and, taking from it a book, he handed it to her, saying, "You don't even need to return it, I'm finished with it."

She took these words not only as a prelude to dismissal but also as an indication that he did not wish his peace to be disturbed again; but such thoughts were scattered by his adding, "If you're riding this way again, you'll be able to give me your opinion of the work. It's good to hear other people's opinions. One gets very biased about one's likes and dislikes. Don't you find it so?"

"Yes, yes, especially in the country. An idea, however wrong, is often passed down from family to family. Father has found that out in the treatment of cattle, and Mother too."

"Your mother deals with the cattle?"

"Yes, in a way, because she is very good with herbal remedies for animal ills, and for humans too." She smiled broadly now. "People come from far and near at times for her poultices and potions."

"How interesting."

She said no more, but as she looked at him she became disconcerted by the expression in his eyes, for they did not so much seem to be looking at her as through her. Nevertheless, she found that she liked looking at him, he had such an interesting face. His skin was not ruddy like those of the boys; in fact, there was no colour in it, being of an overall matt brownish tinge, the same as covered one's arms in the summer.

She wondered what age he could be. Twenty-five? Twenty-six? But he could be older, for he gave off an air of maturity. She wondered too about his own people, but didn't like to enquire. She rose from the chair, saying, "Well, I must not intrude on your hospitality any longer."

She was surprised now to see his head go back and his mouth open wide as he laughed a deep hearty laugh. She didn't think she had said anything amusing, but he explained his reaction to her words when, bringing his head down slightly towards her, he said, "Forgive me, but you sounded as if you had been entertained in a drawing-room."

"Did I?" She tried to suppress a smile, for she felt she should appear ... what, a little grieved?

"Yes" – he nodded at her – "your tone was so polite, so gracious, and all wasted on a place like this." He wagged his hand from side to side. Then becoming serious, he looked round the room as if never having seen it before and he said, "It is sparse, isn't it? Almost a hovel."

"No, I wouldn't say that. Sparse, yes, but clean and warm. I always think there is too much stress placed on possessions. They don't bring happiness, not even comfort. Some of the most contented people I know live in cottages no bigger than this. But they keep a good table and a glowing hearth; they have a good quantity of bedding and crockery, a patch of vegetable garden and a few hens, and it is as if they owned the earth; they seem to want for nothing more. Once you start acquiring, the impulse becomes a habit. I should know" – she smiled broadly – "my father's got the habit. Each year he increases his herd, lengthens his stable, takes on a bit more land. I tell him it's a good job other people have boundaries. Do you find it the same in your country?"

"No, not the same, because outside the towns it would be difficult to encompass the land, it stretches endlessly away. Yet" – he pursed his lips – "when I come to think of it, there are constant battles going on between the Indians and the settlers to possess land, or for Indians to repossess it."

As she walked to the door she made herself probe by asking, "Are you from a large family?"

"No. I was the only child."

His tone was flat and sharp and brooked no further investigation. In fact, once more she felt embarrassed.

They walked to the stone wall in silence and there he whistled again, and after a moment the two horses came galloping towards them. . . .

When she was mounted, the pony put its head over the wall and let out a loud neigh, and on a lighter note now he said, "She's going to miss her companion."

"Yes, yes," she nodded. Then added, "Goodbye." There was nothing more she could say, she did not know his name. But he knew hers, for he answered, "Goodbye, Miss Roystan." And with that she left him.

For quite some distance she sat straight in the saddle, not trotting the horse but walking it. And it wasn't until she had left the hills and almost reached the valley bottom that she drew it to a stop near a group of trees, and tried to sort out her emotions. She knew she was disturbed as never before and she asked herself why this should be. It was only the second time she had encountered the man, and on this occasion he appeared an interesting and likeable young man. Then she questioned the likeable, because in a way he was strange. It wasn't natural, she thought, for a man of his appearance and evident education to live alone and in a place like that. Terry's quarters above the stables were a palace compared to it. At one time during their meeting, she had felt strongly that he wanted rid of her, she was intruding. That was when he had given her the book. But then he had said he would like to know what she thought of it.

Before spurring her horse into a trot, she told herself she wouldn't tell them at home about the meeting because Maggie would surely demand to accompany her on her next ride out, and she felt that he wouldn't thank her for bringing him more company.

5

The family were in conclave. Kate had just ridden out again. This was the fifth week in succession that she had taken a satchel with her, holding books.

"And there's a different one every week." Maggie said. "I went into her room and saw it last week, it was one by a Mrs Radcliffe, and before that it was by Mr Walpole, and this week it was another by Jane Austen. It must be someone of education she's exchanging books with. Why doesn't she say?"

Yes, why didn't she say? Mary Ellen nipped at her bottom lip. And it wasn't only the books that she put into her satchel. It had been Kate's turn to do the cooking last week and, as was the rule, she made the ten hand-sized meat pies and the same of fruit, but, to her knowledge, she also made a meat turnover, which did not appear on the table. Now if, whoever she was visiting, was a cultured person, they wouldn't be in need of extra food, would they now? Last week she had gone as far as to try to probe, but had been baulked before she had hardly opened her mouth by Kate smiling quietly and saying to her, "Let me have my half-day out a week, Mam."

Indignant and hurt, she had answered her, "That isn't fair, Kate, for you to say such a thing. You know that your time's your own, any time you want it." And Kate had hung her head and muttered, "Sometime I'll tell you, perhaps soon. You see, I have a little friendship with someone; I don't want it spoilt by the wrong construction being put on it."

Mary Ellen looked at her family and listened now to John going for Maggie who had suggested that one of them follow her. And she found herself searching in her mind to pin down someone she knew, some male whom Kate was seeing on these weekly visits. But she could think of no one. All the people she knew for miles around, those families with sons, would not be taken up with reading, other than newspapers. Yet this friend of Kate's was someone who lived in the vicinity, at least within an afternoon's ride to and from him.

"Perhaps she's come across an old teacher."

They all looked at Tom and nodded, and Florrie said, "Yes, that could be possible, Tom, for there are some learned men in Allendale. There's Mr Carrick, and Mr Dickinson, and Mr Arnison. Then there's the clever parson who's a great mathematician."

"Don't be silly. They are all old men." John dug Florrie gently in the

283

shoulder. Then Maggie had their attention, saying, "Well, it isn't so silly. Perhaps it is some learned old fellow she goes to see, it certainly wouldn't be any young learned fellow, would it now?"

"Maggie!" The word came harshly from Mary Ellen, and Maggie, tossing her head, said, "Aw, Mam. Well, you know what I mean."

"Yes, I know what you mean, an' it's very unkind of you." Mary Ellen rose to her feet and marched from the room, and Tom, looking at Maggie, said, "Your big mouth, sister, will swallow you one of these days." And on this he too left the room. And Maggie, indignant now, turned to John, saying, "It's only what we all think. Anyway, look what happened with Harry Baker."

"Harry Baker was a fool, and she was well rid of him; if I was a man on the outside and I had to pick and choose for a lifetime ahead, I know where I'd toss me cap."

As the door closed on John, Maggie turned to Florrie, saying, "Well, now you have a go at me."

"I agree with John," said Florrie. "If I were a man and sensible, I would pick someone like Kate to spend my life with."

"Oh, don't be so silly. If you were a man. How do you know how a man feels? Put a pretty face and a good figure before them and do you think they look for brains and a nice disposition? No, their thoughts are on the bedroom. And anyway, it's always Kate, Kate, Kate." And now it was her turn to stamp from the room, leaving Florrie with her lids blinking rapidly over her grey eyes and her fingers pressed tight on her lips.

She had been brought up on a farm. She knew how foals, calves, and lambs came into being, and she also knew how human beings came into being. And the latter had its place in life she knew, because she had thought about it, but never, never had it been openly alluded to as Maggie had just done. There was something happening in the house. It had begun the Monday Kate was left at the church.

When the typhus had taken Peg and Walter the house was weighed down with sadness for a long while, but they had all seemed very close; yet, since Kate's tragedy, and she thought of her desertion as such, there had been an uneasiness in the place. The harmony was gone. And now a strange thought occurred to her: It had gone because Kate herself had been the pivot around which that harmony had revolved.

The sun was hot on her face. Her body seemed to be sweltering under her riding jacket and skirt. Ranger's skin was shining with sweat and she hadn't galloped him at all, simply let him trot most of the way. She looked, first to the right and then to the left of her. The land looked parched. They had been without rain for some weeks now. The crops would be very poor, and already they were having a hard job to find grass for the herd. If the weather didn't change soon it would lead to a very hard winter for many people. So much depended upon the weather. She narrowed her eyes and looked up into the sky. It was cloudless, blue and high. She wished, like everyone else, to see it almost touching the far hills and the rain being driven horizontally by the wind across the moor. Yet, it was only because it had been so dry these past weeks that she had been able to make her weekly journey to the far hills, because once it should rain heavily, the path would become bog-like.

He had said he had been cottage-bound for five days earlier in the year just through the rain. . . . He had said. . . . He had said. She was always thinking of things he had said. Why was she going on, because this association, she knew, would only lead to heartbreak. Harry Baker's desertion had upset her, but the main feeling there had been one of humiliation, because she hadn't known then what it was to love. Now she did, and it was a torture, becoming ever constant, sleeping or waking, because she knew that the future was black. When he left to go back to America, which could be any time now, the dazzling light would go out of her life.

Why had this to happen to her? If she had been petite and pretty, she could have fostered hope. But as it was, she knew that there was not the slightest hope he would ever see her as other than the big-framed, more-than-plain-faced woman. He might think she was quite good company, as he surely did, for now he always welcomed her warmly, but she felt that he also looked upon her as being a sensible woman without any romantic or silly ideas in her head.

That seemed to be the curse of her life: everyone took her to be steady and sensible, a mature woman. Was she not? Yes, outside she looked her age, and her appearance pointed to sensibility, but inside, she felt like a young girl, and had only recently checked the desire she often had to pick up her skirts and run across this very moor and to stand on the summit of one of the hills and fill her lungs with air and then yell out her hidden joy. These were times when she seemed blind to the externals of her being, when her inner self took over and she was young, and beautiful, and attractive to men. Yes, to men . . . one man. She had once been gullible enough to imagine that somewhere there would be one man who would like a young woman with a big frame and a plain face because he would like the sound of her voice and admire the way she sang, not forgetting how she could cook and look after a house.

But those dreams were dead and buried. Yet the *one man* had come into her life the very week another had deserted her, and when he walked out of her life she would feel deserted again. But this desertion would cause her agony.

She bent over and patted the horse's neck, saying, "Not far now, and you'll see Daisy."

As if he understood her, Ranger answered immediately her signal to trot and in a very short time they were rounding the hill and in sight of the cottage; and on this she began to pray that he would be there today, for last week he had been nowhere about.

Now her heart seemed to bounce off her ribs for there he was coming out of the door and down the slope towards her. "Hello, there," he said.

"Hello. Isn't it hot?"

"Lovely. I can't get too much of this weather. But I seem to be the only one that is pleased with it, for all about, they are moaning."

"Yes, the crops are suffering."

"Of course, of course. I'm very selfish." He helped her down from the horse, then patted its neck, saying, "Daisy's been enquiring for you, old fellow." And turning his head towards her, he remarked, "I'm sorry I missed you last week. You must have just gone when I got back. I was held up in a place over there" – he thumbed over his shoulder – "called Haltwhistle. Got talking to two old fellows in an inn and the time passed so quickly and the ale was so heady that I overlooked the urgency to get back. But I must not forget to thank you for the pies. They were delicious. You are an excellent cook."

"I cannot take the credit for those pies," she said smiling at him. "My sister, Florrie, made them. You see we take turn and turn about to do the cooking, and my turn comes every fifth week."

"But I thought you only had two...." He stopped and laughed. "Of course, there is your mother, and ... Annie. I feel I know Annie."

"Well—" Her face was straight now as she said, "you would certainly recognize her. She is like me or, at least they say, I take after her."

"Really?" He stared at her, and she inclined her head towards him.

"And there is no relationship between you?"

"None whatever."

"Ah, here comes Daisy. I keep saying I wish she would move like that when I'm on her back."

Ranger neighed loudly as they let him through the gate. Then the horses were once again prancing away together.

He did not walk towards the cottage but stood with his back against the wall now, looking at her, and when he said, "I have news for you," she checked her breathing before she forced herself to say, "Yes?"

"I don't know whether you'll be vexed or pleased ... but I think Daisy is in foal."

She felt the smile pass over her entire body. "How wonderful! Why did you think I'd be vexed?"

"I don't know." He shook his head. "Silly thing to say, I suppose. Yes, indeed, it was a silly thing to say. And, of course, I forgot you are a farmer's daughter and will be quite used to such events."

"Yes, yes, I'm quite used to them, but, nevertheless, each birth or calving gives me a thrill. To see those thin beautiful straggling legs finding their way upright within minutes almost never palls; it's like a miracle each time it happens."

His face was straight, his eyes had that piercing look about them again and were tight on her. She blinked and, looking down at the satchel she had taken from the pummel of the saddle, she said, "I . . . I've brought Mr Richardson's novel back."

"Well?"

She pursed her lips, "I'm . . . I'm afraid I . . . I didn't enjoy it as much as others. Although, as you said, his books were written mostly for lady readers, I must confess not to be in that category. The characters, I found . . . well, rather unreal."

"I'm glad."

"You are?"

"Yes, yes, I am. I told you how I came across it with some others in the bookshop in Newcastle, and what interested me at first, it had been very much thumbed, and so I thought, well, there must be some good reading here. But I agree with you. I have one for you this week, though, that perhaps might be better to your taste. It's another of those I picked up. It's by Laurence Sterne, called *The Life and Opinions of Tristram Shandy*. It's a very odd book and rather difficult to get into, and surprising reading in parts, but his characters are real. Anyway, come along in. I have a cool drink ready; I have kept the two bottles in the spring since yesterday. It's what you call ginger beer. I suppose you'll know all about it."

"Oh, ginger beer, yes." She laughed now.

"I was visiting a house yesterday and they kindly gave me these bottles."

He was visiting a house yesterday. Where did he get to the rest of the week when she didn't see him? He had never expressed any desire to visit her people. In fact, he rarely referred to them. But whenever she spoke of them, he became attentive.

The ginger beer came out sparkling, and she was grateful for it, saying, "Oh, this is good."

"It is something that most people make around here, I understand."

"Oh, yes, a lot of people make their own beers. The herb beer, though, is more popular with the menfolk, its bitterness tending to be more like ale, I suppose."

They were seated at each side of the little table now. There was no fire in the grate today, and, by the look of the ash, none had been for some time. And she noted this and said, "What are you doing for your meals? How are you managing without the fire?"

"Oh, I don't mind drinking cold milk, and I go into an inn most days and have something. They do very good meals in most of them. And I'm quite used now to English cooking; I particularly like the enormous puddings, especially the suet ones. I'm going into Newcastle tomorrow. Is there any book that you would like me to get for you?"

She considered for a moment, then said, "No. I'm very satisfied with your choice, and very pleased that you loan them to me."

"Oh that." He made a face, then with a deprecating movement he added, "What is that, loaning a book." He leant towards her now, his eyes again tight on her face as he said, "I would like to buy you a book, two books, three books, as a present."

A sudden coolness came into her body. "You're leaving?"

"No, no." He straightened up. "Well" – he looked towards the door – "that's a question that's hanging in the air."

"Why, may I ask?"

He still concentrated his gaze on the open door as he said, "You'd be surprised if I were to tell you. But tell you I will one day." He swivelled slowly round in the chair and gazed at her, saying now very quietly, "It could depend a great deal on you."

She knew that her face had turned scarlet. She wasn't given to blushing, except when greatly disturbed, and now she was definitely greatly disturbed, because she thought that if she had been other than she was, his words could have meant but one thing. What did they mean? She had no idea. Her voice was small when she said, "How can your departure depend upon me?"

"Give me a fortnight, perhaps three weeks, and then I'll tell you."

Her elbows were resting on the table, her hands joined together, and when his hands suddenly dropped on them, the breath caught in her throat and her eyes misted as she listened to him saying, "I have never met anyone that I could talk to like you, Kate. Right from our first meeting, we were compatible. Don't you think?"

She made no answer, and the pressure of his hands tightened as he went on, "This kind of thing happens. I've read about it but never believed it, but now I do. Your friendship has come to mean something very important to me."

The heat slowly seeped from her body and a heaviness came into her breast. Friendship. Of course, yes. She had been mad to think it could have meant anything else. She must respond as he expected. So she forced herself to say, "I . . . I too value our friendship, more so than you can imagine, because of . . . of something that happened to me, the very week that I first saw you."

"What was that?"

She looked down towards their joined hands and it was some seconds before she said, "I was left at the church."

"Left at the church?"

It was as if he didn't understand the meaning of her words, and she looked up at him and explained, "I was to be married. He . . . he didn't come."

He held her gaze now as he said, "Oh, that. I knew about that. Charles told me. And I'm glad, because if he had come you wouldn't be sitting here now."

Again her face was suffused with colour and her emotions were mixed, because she could see that his friendship towards her had sprung out of pity. Yet, he said he was glad.

"Whoever he was, he was a fool, and someone always profits by a fool's doings, and it's myself in this case."

She gazed at him. He was so good to look upon, not handsome as one thought of a pretty man, but there was an appeal about him that went beyond his features. The way he carried himself, his voice, his understanding of things which, she judged, came through his constant reading. He was so different from the men in her own family and from any of the others she had ever met. And she had his friendship. Well, wasn't that something? More than she really should have expected, but not more than her heart cried out for, and for which she must take great pains to still its cry and the knowledge that when he eventually left she would know the devastation as never before. Yet, he had said his leaving depended on her. Why? But she must not probe. She must not act like some silly woman who would go on probing until he gave her the reason, for apparently he did not see her as a silly woman, perhaps not as a woman at all, just as a friend, a dear friend.

Slowly she withdrew her hands from his and rose to her feet, saying, "I must be away." But as she went towards the door he checked her, saying, "Kate." And she turned to him to find him still standing by the side of the table.

"Yes?"

"You remember when I asked you your name some time ago?"

"Yes, of course."

"And later I told you mine. Do you remember it?"

She smiled now, saying, "Yes ... Mr Benedict Fraser Hamilton."

He laughed gently now as he said, "Sounds nice when you say it like that. Well, I told you I was generally referred to as Ben. And you know something?" He waited a moment before ending, "You have never called me Ben."

Oh, that silly flushing of her face. It was bad enough to look as she did, but when her skin was so suffused with colour she dreaded to think what her appearance might be to the onlooker. She forced herself to say somewhat coolly, "The occasion hasn't arisen to make use of it. I suppose that's the reason."

He came up to her now and once more she was being forced to look into his eyes as he said, "Well, I think the occasion is now. You could say, I hope, Ben, you have a nice day in Newcastle tomorrow."

She began to laugh gently. At times he was so boyish in his ways that he appeared to be no older than Gabriel, whereas, when discussing books, he appeared a very mature man.

They were both laughing when she repeated his words, "I hope, Ben," and she emphasized his name, "you have a nice day in Newcastle tomorrow."

"That's better. And it won't hurt so much with use."

Now she laughed aloud, and he joined her, and they were still laughing when they reached the stone wall, and he called the horses to him.

When she was mounted he again put his hand on hers, saying, "Do you only ride out once a week?"

"No, I sometimes only ride out once a fortnight."

He slapped her hand, "That wasn't what I meant," he said.

And she answered quietly, "I ... I have my duties in the house. And towards the end of the week everybody is very busy getting ready for the market. But I sometimes go out on a Sunday, that is if we don't have visitors."

"Well, in future, I shall be in on a Sunday to receive visitors."

She made no reply, she did not even smile at him but jerked the reins and rode off ...

If this was his manner when dealing with friendship, what must it be like when dealing with love?

As she entered the yard she saw Charles Bentley about to mount his horse. Standing near him were her mother and Maggie, Florrie, and John. But when he saw her approaching he hesitated and waited for her to dismount when he greeted her airily with, "Have you been to visit our mutual friend? I ... I was just telling your family about him. At least" – he pulled a face – "the little I know. He's a very reticent fellow. I suppose you, too, have found that out."

She couldn't answer him, for she was answering the looks on the faces of her family. Charles Bentley did not appear to notice anything unusual in her manner, for he turned to Florrie, saying, "Until a week come Saturday then, Miss Roystan?" Whereupon Florrie inclined her head towards him and smiled. And now he mounted his horse, turned it about, and with a wave of his hand, he left them. And there they all stood looking at her.

"Well" – her chin went up – "so now you know. No more mysteries."

They followed at her heels as she marched into the kitchen, and there Mary Ellen said, "Well, why did you make a mystery of it in the first place, girl? You could have said, couldn't you?"

"Yes, I could have said." She nodded her head from one to the other. "Then what would have been the reaction? Another man to bring into the net. Fetch him home. Let us have a look at him. See if anything can be done about it."

"Oh, Kate." John's voice was soft. "It wouldn't have been like that."

"It would, and you know it, John. What's the good of beating about the bush?"

"Is he starving that you've got to take him pies?" Maggie's voice was tart.

"No, he is not starving, miss. And the next time I wish to make anyone a gift I'll buy some pastries in the town on Saturday. Will that satisfy you?"

"Now, now." Mary Ellen's voice was soothing. "There is no need for this."

"Well, if there's no need for this, why am I being made to look like a criminal?"

"Oh, don't exaggerate. And you've brought this on yourself anyway. To my mind it was sly."

"Don't you dare talk to me like that, Maggie." Kate glared at Maggie now. In different ways she loved each member of the family, but if she was honest with herself she knew that Maggie was at the bottom of the list, for there were selfish traits in her, and she was very vain about her looks. She recalled now that she had talked a lot about the American the day they had met in the hotel and wondered who he was. Well, now she knew. She swung round and went up the kitchen and closed the door none too gently behind her, and when she reached her room, she pulled off her hat and threw it onto the bed, then dropped into a chair. And leaning her head back, she covered her eyes with her hand.

When presently there was a knock on the door she knew it to be her mother.

Mary Ellen did not at first speak, but sat on the edge of the bed and, picking up Kate's riding hat, she moved it round between her hands; then she said, "I'm sorry, lass, but it was unintentional. He came, Charles Bentley, to ask your dad if he could take Florrie to a ball in Hexham. It's for some charity. And as your dad wasn't in, and Tom away with him, I told him to ask John. Florrie was over the moon. He's definitely got his eye on her, and it would be such a good match. Oh, a very good match. You know that yourself, Kate. And he's a very nice fellow."

"Who's saying he's not, Mam? Get to the point."

Mary Ellen had never had occasion to chastise her daughter for being sharp-tongued; Kate had always been so amenable, even as a child. But of late, since the church business, Kate had altered, which was to be expected she supposed. So she kept her tone level as she said, "Well, the point is, lass, he sat chatting over a cup of tea in the sitting-room, and he happened to say if he could persuade his American friend to come to the ball, it would be nice. He meant for him. Well, you know Maggie. She immediately started to ask questions about the man. And at that he said, 'Oh, well, your sister could tell you more than I can, because from what I gather they are great friends.' That's what he said. Well, you can imagine, it was only natural, we were all surprised." And Mary Ellen remarked to herself, That was putting it mildly. Amazed would have been a better description for their reactions. And now she went on, "Well, he seemed to think we knew about it, so nobody said anything, and the conversation went on to something else. Well, and then you came into the yard. So, if you're fair, you can't blame us altogether, lass, for being surprised."

"No, I suppose not, Mam, but you can't blame me either for acting as I did, knowing what reactions would be if I brought him home: What were his intentions? Was he going to marry me? Oh, I know, I know what it would have been. After his first visit he would have been scared to come back." She stopped herself from adding, "Unless it was to see

Maggie," because Maggie would have undoubtedly used her wiles on him. Oh yes, she knew Maggie.

"Don't you think he might have thought it odd that you haven't asked him to come home?"

"No, I don't. He's not one for company."

"Oh." Mary Ellen got up quickly from the bed. "From what we learned from Mr Bentley he's very much at home with company. Goes round all the villages chatting to this one and that, gathering information, and keeps some people amused in the inns with his tales of his country. So I wouldn't say that he doesn't get about. He's not a man of mystery. Perhaps you never asked him."

"That's right, Mam, perhaps I never asked him."

He's not a man of mystery, caused a barrage of questions to attack her mind, all leading to one thought. What did she really know about him? He had never mentioned his family to her. The one time she had tried to open up that subject he had adroitly closed it. He was very skilful at that kind of thing, answering a question by asking another. And hadn't he said that his staying or going would largely depend upon her? What facets of friendship were strong enough to hold a man or send him on his way? She didn't know, nor had she the vaguest idea of what would shed light on the matter.

Mary Ellen said now, "Your dad will have something to say about this, you know."

"Doubtless."

Mary Ellen drew in a sharp breath and hurried from the room. Doubtless, she had said, doubtless. And in that tone of voice. Oh, Kate had changed, and out of all recognition.

At the evening meal Kate knew that her father had already been put in the picture. The conversation would have been strained had he not taken it upon himself to regale them with the impending doom of the crops should this dry weather continue: Flour was now at three shillings a stone and he could see it jumping by sixpence towards the end of the year; in fact, the miller had said it could reach four shillings. And potatoes, why, some were already charging one and a penny a stone. Beef and mutton were still sixpence a pound, but couldn't stay at that. He looked at his sons and said, "It'll pay us to stock barley because the price it will bring later on will be hair-raisin'. It's sixteen shillings a boll now, but I'd like to bet by the turn of the year it'll go up to eighteen or twenty. Yes, we'll stock every grain of it." Then he had looked round the table with a grin on his face, adding, "And when things get really tight, you'll all have to pull your belts in, two notches at least, because I'll cut down on your oats then."

They all laughed or smiled with the exception of Maggie who had been sullen all throughout the meal. Then just before they rose from the table he looked at Florrie, saying, "And what's this I hear, consent being given to your gallivantin', without my knowledge? Going to the balls now, is it? Oh, we'll have to nip that in the bud."

Florrie smiled tenderly at him now, saying dutifully, "Yes, Dad, I think you'd better. But before you do it I'd like to have a suitable cloak to wear a week come Saturday."

Again there was laughter, the twins saying almost simultaneously as was usual, "Good for you, Florrie. That's it, get something out of him. We can't."

Hal now rose from the table, shaking his head and saying, "My God! Get something out of him. That's what you get for bringin' a family up. Well, you two, let me get somethin' out of you. Come on with you! There's a heifer we've got to get something out of the night, and if we're not careful an' she gets no better, she'll never live to be a cow."

All now left the dining room except Kate and Florrie; it was their turn to clear the dishes. But Hal had not been gone more than a few minutes before he returned and, without saying a word, he took Kate by the arm, led her down the room, through a door at the far end, along the corridor and into his office, and there, pushing her into a chair, he bent towards her, saying, "Now come on, open up to the old man."

She watched him perch himself on the edge of his desk before she said, "There's nothing to open up about. You'll have heard it all."

"What I've heard is you've been seein' this American fellow on the quiet, and I'd like to know why, I mean, keepin' your meetings quiet."

"I told Mam why, and she's already likely told you. The answer is evident: I did it just to prevent what is happening now. Questions. Questions. And then ideas: Was there anything in it? What were his intentions? And I ask you, you've seen him, what would a man as presentable as he is want with me other than as a friend, one who is interested in reading?"

"Aye, what?" He poked his face towards her. "He might want to marry you."

"*Oh, Dad.*"

He thrust out his hand and none too gently pushed her back into the chair as she had made to rise, saying, "Keep your seat a minute. As I told you afore, you've got the wrong idea about yourself, and naturally you're thinking as a woman all the time, you can't think otherwise. I remember saying this to you a few months gone. A man doesn't always go for someone who looks like Maggie, or then again Florrie. He's attracted by something else, as I was to your mother: a bit of fire in the guts, a partner, a mate, someone who could rough it with him an' doesn't want to be dollied up all the time. We leave that for the gentry and so-called ladies with their fancy men on the side. No, what an honest man wants is something in a woman that can't be put into words. But he recognizes it when he sees it, in her manner, in her eyes, in her tongue.

Oh aye, in her tongue. Like I did with your mother. It's something, if you like, that isn't in the flesh, yet is. Oh, I'm not a man with words. I stopped readin' books years ago, the only readin' I do now, as you know, is cattle pamphlets or the newspapers, an' generally only the headin's. But in here" – he thumped his chest – "I've got a knowledge that no words can put a name to. I've sometimes thought about it and likened it to what cattle must feel. They go mostly by the smell. And you know, 'tis the same with human beings, we've each got our different smells. Don't screw your face up like that." He smiled at her now. "What I'm sayin' is true. I sometimes think that a man unknown to himself, is attracted to a woman by what she gives off in her sweat. Oh no" – he now pulled a long face – "women don't sweat, do they? they perspire."

"Oh, Dad." She closed her eyes and lowered her head while she smiled and said softly, "Perhaps you're right. But ... but in this case your ... well, your instincts don't apply. And I can say this, I think he's got as much idea of marrying me as he would have of marrying one of the Indian natives called squaws he has spoken about in his own country."

Hal now slid off the end of the table and, taking his doubled fist, he rubbed it from one side to the other of his jaw, and when it came to rest under his lower lip, he held it there for a moment, saying, "Do one thing for me, will you, lass?"

"If I can, Dad."

"Invite him down to a meal. By what I hear he's not above eating in inns, and we can provide as good a table as an inn, can't we now?"

She turned her head away and thought for a moment. She couldn't say she'd already asked him and he'd refused because that would certainly raise a barrage of questions: aren't we good enough? And so on. So she said, "All right. Yes, all right."

Hal now put his arm round her shoulder and drew her to her feet, saying gently, "You know how I feel about you, Kate, don't you?" And she answered as gently, "Yes, I know, Dad, and I feel the same way about you."

"Well, I'm going to say something to you now, which I suppose I shouldn't. I fathered t'other two females and if they're happy, or not so happy, it doesn't seem to bother me. God forgive me, I shouldn't say that. But what happens to you, Kate, does. *Now, now, now.* I didn't say that to make you cry. Come on, come on, wipe your eyes." He took a handkerchief from his pocket and dabbed clumsily at her face, the while saying, "You go in there bubbling and she'll think I've been gettin' at you, an' then she'll get at me, and I've had a very tirin' day and a more tirin' night ahead of me if that silly little bitch doesn't calve. Come on. Come on."

She blinked her eyes and, smiling at him now, she said, "To the byres with you, Mr Roystan." And as if they were sharing a joke, he pulled at his thinning forelock, saying, "Yes, ma'am. Yes, ma'am. Indeed ma'am, that's where I should be. And I'll be away now, ma'am. Right now, ma'am, as I know me place." And on this he pushed her playfully before turning from her and going from the room.

She bit tightly down on her lip to stop the tears starting once more, blew her nose, and sniffed, then stood with her eyes closed in an endeavour to compose herself before making her way to the kitchen, there to do her part in the evening chores of washing up and setting the table for the morrow's breakfast, but mostly to prepare herself against the spate of questioning looks that would be directed against her.

6

The following week, she knew they were all waiting for her to ride out, so she didn't. On the morning of the day she could have done so, she offered to join her mother and Florrie on the long journey to Hexham in order to help choose a cloak for Florrie to wear at the coming ball. Whatever each member of the family thought of this, no one said anything.

It wasn't until the following Monday when the mail van stopped at the farm gate and the driver handed a letter to Hal, and he, bringing it into the house exclaimed, "I have a letter here, and would you believe it, by the postmark it was posted in Newcastle on Thursday afternoon, and here's almost five days gone. That's the newfangled penny post for you. A few years ago that would have been in Hexham the next morning and you could have gone to the office and picked it up. But now, will they hand over your own property to you at the office? No, it's got to be delivered to the house stated on the envelope.... 'Tis for you, Kate."

She had been about to go out of the far door and into the hall, and she turned and said, "For me?" then advanced towards him, took the letter from him, looked at the envelope and said, "Thanks."

"See what I mean about the date?"

She again looked at the envelope and said, "Yes. Yes, I do." But she didn't attempt to open the letter, but again said, "Thanks," and turned away.

She had been on her way to the dining-room to do some polishing, as it was Monday and her turn to help indoors this particular day while Annie, Maggie, and Florrie were at the washing, and her mother was doing the cooking.

She had no sooner closed the dining-room door behind her than she once again looked at the envelope. She wasn't in the habit of getting letters, and this certainly wasn't from Harry Baker, because he had been no hand at writing. Whoever had written the address had studied penmanship. She held the envelope tightly between her two hands before opening it. Then she unfolded a single sheet of paper and looked at the one line written there. It said, very simply,

I have missed you.
Ben.

She put her hand to her throat; her mind was again in a turmoil trying to understand how a man would act in the name of friendship.

"I have missed you. Ben." Of course, that could be said from one friend to another, but ... but did you write it?

What should she do? Her father had said the letter had been posted on Thursday. Were she to ask her mother if she could spare her this afternoon, and galloped over the hills to him, what would he think?

Well, what had he thought when she hadn't put in an appearance last week, after never missing one week during the past months? No, she couldn't go today ... she wouldn't go today; one didn't pick up one's skirts and fly to a friend as they would to a lover. She would go tomorrow.

She did not vouchsafe them the information they were all waiting to hear and by the time it came to their evening meal there was a further feeling of constraint in the house.

Later that night, when in bed and lying in Hal's arms, Mary Ellen said, "I'm worried about her. And that letter could have been from nobody but him. Why has she turned so secretive? She was never like this."

"Likely because we're a nosey lot. And it's partly my fault, because in my anxiety for her future I grabbed at the first fellow who showed any interest in her, and she's frightened it happens again. You know what Annie said to me the day? She said, 'You lot press her the way you're doin' and she'll walk out one of these days, just like I did to get rid of me da.'"

"Oh! Fancy comparing you or any one of us with her da, that man!"

"Well, she's right in a way. We've got to let up, and treat her for what she is, a fully grown sensible woman, not a daft lass who doesn't know her own mind."

"She couldn't have known her own mind when she promised to marry Harry Baker, a fellow like that."

"Oh, she knew her own mind all right. What she wanted was a family of her own, I've told you that afore, and she would have taken a clothes-prop with trousers on at the time to get it."

"Oh, you!" she pushed him. "A clothes-prop with trousers on."

He pulled her tighter and kissed her and for the time being they both forgot about the daughter she had had before she had married him, but whom, she knew yet couldn't understand, he loved better than those from his own loins.

The sun wasn't shining when she rode out the next afternoon. The sky was low and everyone on the farm and roundabout was saying, "It's a sign of rain, and thank God."

She did not know what she was going to say to him about her non-appearance last week. She was bad at lying. She could of course say that she hadn't been well, but that, she considered, would be tempting providence, because when other people were affected by sniffles and colds, and sore throats and aches and pains, she herself never experienced them. She was very healthy. Yet, she suffered pain, a strange pain underneath her breastbone. It had been there since she first saw her reflection in the mirror, and it had grown in intensity with the years.

About half a mile from the fork in the track which would lead to the cottage, she was approaching the bridle-way which she knew led down to and crossed the river when he suddenly emerged from it. She saw him pull his horse in for a moment, then set it into a gallop. And when he drew it to a skidding stop abreast of her, he said, "Hello there."

"Hello."

"It looks as if it's going to rain," he said, putting his head back on his shoulders and looking up into the sky.

"Yes, it does, and it will be welcome."

He turned his horse and came alongside of her, saying, "You got my letter?"

"Yes, yes, I got it."

"When?"

"Yesterday."

"Not until yesterday?"

"No. As my father says, the post delivery is much worse now than when one had to collect one's mail."

"Why didn't you come last week?"

"I ... I" – she blinked – "I was busy."

"Is that the truth?"

"No."

"What is?"

She let out one long breath before saying, "I'm sorry, I can't explain."

"I can. Charles told me he thought he had dropped a bombshell when he spoke of us as mutual friends."

They now rode slowly on, but at the turning into the bridle path he put out his hand and caught at her reins and said, "You remember, last time we met, I told you my departure depended quite a bit on yourself, and that in two or three weeks I should be able to tell you why? Well, since your family now know of our acquaintance the decision could be made earlier. Will you ride with me along here?"

"Where to?"

"A building, a house I would like you to see."

She nodded, the while questioning: Which house, which building lay along here that could be of interest to her? There were a number of reasonable farms, but he had said a building, a house. And a strange uneasy feeling entered into her, and it grew as they rode on and he became singularly quiet. And so she wasn't all that surprised when, a mile and a half further on, having crossed the river, they were riding by the broken walls of Rooklands Farm.

She knew all about Rooklands Farm. It had been like the ogre fairy tale during her childhood, as it had been too, for all the others.

When they stopped at the entrance where once had been a gate, he said, "The house is empty." And she answered, "Yes, I know. It has had a number of tenants, but they don't stay long. Have you been inside?"

"Yes. Come."

She hesitated and he said again, "Come."

"I'd rather not."

"Please." There was an appeal in his eyes.

Slowly she followed him through an archway into the yard. The once well-scrubbed stone slabs were grass-covered, the doors of the horse boxes were hanging loose, an upper window was open and an old curtain was trailing out of it.

He helped her to dismount, then tied the horses to a rusting iron post that supported a dry horse trough. Thrusting out his hand now, he caught hers, saying, "Come this way; there's a window open in the kitchen quarters. We can get over the sill."

"But ... but...."

"Please, do this for me."

Oh, dear God! She knew what he had brought her here for. He wanted her opinion of the place with a view to buying it. If that was the case, it would be goodbye friendship, for her father over the years would not even do business with anyone who had taken on Bannaman's farm. The very name of the place had the power to incense him or make him distraught. The years had not obliterated what both his father and himself had suffered at their hands.

But she was being drawn towards the side of the house, and now he was helping her over the sill and into, what must have been, a large store room. Still holding her hand, he led her along a passage where the paper was peeling from the walls. Then he opened a thick oak door and they were in a hall twice the size of the one at home, and off it, a broad shallow oak staircase rose to a half gallery.

"This must have been a sort of drawing-room."

She was now standing in the room which she knew, from what she had heard, was where Mr Bannaman had faced the constables, and her father, and her stepfather.

Strange thought that, that she had a father who might still be alive. She had ceased many years ago to ask questions about him, because she knew it would not only hurt her mother, it would also hurt the man she thought of as her father.

"Look at that ceiling, isn't it beautiful?"

Yes, the ceiling was beautiful. The centrepiece was beautifully painted like a star with spines of light stretching from it towards each corner of the room, and inset were painted panels.

"This couldn't always have been a farm, could it? It must have been part of a grand house at one time."

"Yes," she nodded, "it was a sort of manor-house."

"And look at the dining-room." He was beckoning to her now, and she followed him back into the hall and through another door, and now he was pointing to the floorboards, saying, "They must be all of twelve or fourteen inches wide. There were some old Colonial houses back home with floors like this. And aren't the windows nice? Long and wide. That must have been a beautiful garden out there at one time."

She now silently followed him into a library, then in and out of several other small rooms, and upstairs through the bedrooms. He never allowed her to miss even a cupboard. Lastly, he ended his tour by opening the kitchen door and saying, "Isn't it a shame that a house like this has been let go to rack and ruin?"

"It isn't a good house." She turned and faced him. And he, looking at her, said quietly, "No, the house isn't bad, it's the people who were in it sometime back."

"Well, that's what I mean. A family lived here who were evil. You see ... I know all about this house. The man who once owned it was a murderer. What you don't know is that the man I call my father, Hal Roystan, is not my father. My father's name was Greenbank, and Mr Roystan is my stepfather. My mother was not married when I was born."

"I know of that."

Her eyes widened. "You do?"

"Yes."

"Then you might also know that the man who owned this house by the name of Bannaman killed my grandfather, that is my real father's father, and attempted to do the same with him. But that's not all. He also murdered my stepfather's father, who was a clerk at the smelting mills. He was returning with the workmen's pay and he was struck down, then buried by this man and his servant. And that still is not all. He had a daughter who was even more wicked than him, for one day at gun-point, she and her brother forced my stepfather up into the barn." She pointed through the smeared kitchen window towards the outbuildings. "They tied him up in such a way that is really indescribable: his ankles to his hands at the back; they gagged him, then strung him to a beam so that he couldn't move. After that, they packed straw round him. The only thing they didn't do was set it alight. But this evil woman wanted him to die slowly, and he almost did. He was left like that for four days and was only saved by his dog. I think she must have been the most evil woman in this world."

She watched his face quiver, his eyes darken to a blackness that was like jet, but there was no hardness in their expression, only a look of pain and a great sadness, and the pain now came over in his voice as he said, "She was the most evil woman in the world. Yes, yes, she was."

She stared at him. Slowly her mouth fell agape. There was a truth dawning on her too great to grasp, but when he thrust it into her hold she felt she was going to faint.

"I know that for sure," he said now, "for she was my mother."

When she fell back from him he pleaded, "Please. Please. Don't turn from me, not like that. Please. Hear my side. Let me tell you why I am here. Come, sit down, you are faint." He looked round the kitchen, then pointed to the settle that was attached to the side of the great rusting fireplace, and hurrying to it, he took out his handkerchief and laid it on the seat, then waited for her to move towards him. But she still stood where he had left her. And now, going to her, he pleaded, "Kate. Please, Kate. Come and listen to me. There is so much to be said between us."

She resisted his outstretched hand but went towards the seat and sat down. With her head bent she waited.

From her lowered gaze she watched him pacing up and down in front of her; and then he stopped and said, "I will start at the beginning."

But it was some seconds before he did begin: "When my mother and her brother and my grandmother sailed from this country in eighteen hundred and twenty-two, they were bound for my grandmother's cousin in America. The journey had apparently been arranged sometime before, and by the boat sailing when it did my mother and uncle escaped being brought to trial for the attempted murder of your stepfather. It should happen on the boat a gentleman befriended them, his name Roger Fraser Hamilton, and he fell in love with my mother. Such was his passionate attachment to her, I understand, they were married shortly after the boat landed. Within the allotted time I was the result of their union. The passion, I should imagine, was all on my father's side, for my mother had no love in her to give to anyone. She was a being consumed by hate. I say she had no love to give to anyone. I think she had given it all to the man from whom she had inherited her evil traits, her father. Yet he had been known to horsewhip her for her slack, I could say immoral, adventures.

"It wasn't very long before my father discovered he had married a very strange individual, a mother who didn't care for her child. If it hadn't been for my grandmother I think I should have come off much worse than I did. But nevertheless, I was subjected to unmerciful thrashings. My father was in business which forced him to do a great deal of travelling. It was his father's firm, they were coachbuilders on a big scale. While he was at home my life was easier, but when he was away, neither my uncle nor my grandmother could save me from thrashings.

"I understood that from the second year of their marriage they ceased to live as man and wife. Yet, she was known to give her attention generously to other men. At times she became mad. I think that she was insane, that she had been insane all her life. Anyway, both my grandmother and my uncle were afraid of her, but like a lot of insane people she was very clever and wily. And when my father, at one stage, tried to get her confined to a clinic, she spoke to the doctors so reasonably that they could not agree on her mental state.

"My father wanted to send me away to school but she was against it. I was her whipping stool. It was nothing for me to be locked in a cupboard for twenty-four hours at a time. My father died when I was twelve, and the day after he was buried she gave a party to people from the lowest part of the town. What happened at the end of the party is still a mystery. It is known my grandfather Hamilton appeared on the scene, as did my Uncle Benjamin, who by this time was living his own life away from her. There was a fracas as they tried to turn out the motley crew, and in it, my mother was struck with a poker. It was whispered it was my grandfather who did it; then again, that it was her brother, my uncle; but of course the blame was put on one of the visitors who had disappeared back into their holes. Whatever the truth of that, she was dead.

"It was the happiest day of my life so far when I joined her funeral cortège. And after that life became so wonderful that I imagined that I, too, might die before I had had enough of it. My grandmother Banna-man is a very gentle woman, and as she grew older she talked more and more of her life spent in this country, mostly of her happy childhood and girlhood before she married."

He stopped talking and put his hands over his eyes, and she saw that beads of sweat were running down his face. And now she wanted to put her hands out to him and bring him down beside her, but he began to pace the floor again and talk as he did so, saying, "I forgot to mention that my grandmother's cousin didn't find her relatives from England very compatible. And if my mother hadn't married quickly, that association would have been broken up in any case. I understand she died when I was quite young. But—" He stopped in his pacing and, looking at her, he said, "As time went on and I listened to my grandmother reminiscing, I knew that there was something she was holding back, something she wanted to tell me but was fearful of doing so. Incident-ally, I was seventeen when Grandfather Hamilton took me into the business, but he was failing in health and three years later he sold the entire company. His retirement didn't last long and he died a year later. He had been a widower for many years, and but for a few bequests he left his entire fortune to me."

Her mouth fell open at this stage. He had said he had been left a fortune, yet had been living in that one-roomed hovel all the winter. What was the matter with him?

"You seem surprised, and I know what you're thinking. Why haven't I lived differently? I will tell you. Last year, my grandmother became ill, and fearing that her time might be running out, it was then that she told me the whole grizzly story of her husband's life, which she had had no inkling of until the constables came to the house, although apparently my mother had gleaned some knowledge of his doings earlier on. There was a store under the cellar." He turned his head and nodded towards the far wall of the kitchen. "I have been in it. She must have discovered it at some time. Anyway, she knew what my grandmother didn't know, and what my grandmother also didn't know until she had been some time in America, and she only learned of it from her son when he had drunk more than usual one day, for he became a heavy drinker, was that they had left a man trussed up in the barn of the house and that there was no possibility of his ever being found alive. My grandfather had apparently killed this particular man's father."

He now brought up his shoulders tight around his neck as if to shrug off some burden he was carrying, then ended, "You know all about it. And now, about me. When happily my grandmother recovered, I resigned from the old firm at which I was still working and came here, because I was haunted by the story. I could not believe that these things had happened until I remembered what my mother was like, and then I had to admit the truth of them to myself. Yet, I had to come.

"At first I stayed at an inn in Allendale and from there went out walking. And one day I saw that little hut of a cottage. There was a man on horseback outside it. He turned out to be Charles. He said at one time it had been a shepherd's cottage, and it happened to be on his land. I apologized for trespassing. He was very kind. We rode back together and adjourned to the inn, and as we talked the idea came to me to live in that place, to experience life at its lowest, and also to give a reason for my presence. I said I was a kind of writer, more of a journalist, and wanted to record this part of the country, for some of my forebears had come from here. I gave their name as Hamilton. He knew no one in the vicinity by that name. As he said, they must have lived here a long time ago. So there it is, Kate. Now you know why I'm here, and who I am. But there are two things you don't know as yet. The first is that I own this house and the land surrounding. I bought it last week. I have no need to come through the pantry window, I have a key to the front door. And the other thing that you don't know, Kate, or perhaps you do. I hope you do." He now moved slowly towards her and sat down on the edge of the settle and, taking her limp hand, he said, "I love you, Kate."

The room was spinning around her. Outside the smeared window the land was lifting from its base, the whole world was whirling. Something was happening inside her head. She was going to faint. No, she wasn't. She had never fainted in her life and she had very little use for women who used this as a last resort, mostly to achieve what they wanted. Isabel Younger over at Bretton House, could faint to order, and always succeeded, to bring her husband to his knees. No, she wasn't going to faint. But something was happening to her: her heart seemed to have stopped beating. Yet again, that was wrong, for it was thumping against her ribs so forcefully that she felt it would break through.

"Kate. Kate. Look at me."

She did not know that she had turned her head away, and now when she looked back at him, she heard in surprise her own voice saying, "You can't mean that. How can you?"

"I can, because I think you're the finest creature I've ever come across."

"Oh—" She turned her head away again, then muttered, "Don't make fun."

His hands were on her shoulders now and she was actually being shaken. "I was never more serious, Kate. Don't accuse me of making fun. Listen to me. I've loved you from our first meeting on the hills, perhaps even before that, when we looked at each other in that hotel dining-room. The spark was kindled then. These things happen."

"Oh, Ben, please" – her voice was soft – "don't make me say it."

"Say what?"

"Well—" She tossed her head now from side to side. "Look at me. I'm an outsize in women, but that wouldn't matter so much except I am beyond plain. Let me put it starkly. I have seared in my mind a remark made by a friend of ours. He did not mean me to overhear it, but what he said was, I wouldn't be everybody's taste in ale, but then the man could always close his eyes when he put the mug to his mouth."

"God Almighty! And you've stored things like that in your mind? Kate, you have never looked at yourself squarely. You've got a body on you like a Venus, and eyes the like I've never looked into before, and a voice that sounds like music. And in addition, you have a mind. And again, what is more, you are kind, your character oozes kindness. Kate, to me, you are a lovely creature. Oh, my dearest, my dear. Please, please, don't cry."

Now he had pulled her to her feet and, his arms about her, he was holding her tight, and as she leant against him she shivered from head to foot as if with cold. After a moment he pressed her head upwards and said firmly, "We shall be married, Kate, you and I, and we shall cleanse this house of all its past memories."

"Oh! Oh!" She pushed herself from him. "Ben, no, no." She turned away, her hands clasped tightly under her chin now. The situation had raced out of all control: her, living in this house; her, marrying a man, the son of the woman who had tried to kill her father, and in such a terribly cruel way, not forgetting how his grandfather had murdered both her father's and her step-father's fathers. The obstacles against their ever coming together were so gigantic that she groaned aloud. Shaking her head, she said, "It's impossible. It could never come about."

"It must." He was holding her by the shoulders again. "Because I know now, I hadn't to leave the comforts of my home in America, the friends I had made, the business I had been thinking of investing in, and undertake a damnable crossing just to find out where my terrible forebears had begun. No, they were best lain hidden, not unearthed. There had to be something else, and that something else was you. Then what stopped me marrying two years ago? I was on the point of proposing to the daughter of a friend of ours, but then I almost took to my heels and ran. I went off on a shooting expedition. Upset the girl greatly. But . . . but suddenly I knew I couldn't ask her to be my wife. Yet from the moment I looked up at you on your horse from where I lay dozing on the path, I knew the reason for it all: I had found the one that was for me. Don't shake your head in such a way, Kate, I'm no silly boy experiencing a calf love."

He was no silly boy. The statement brought forward the matter of age. He must be younger than her, quite a bit, but he looked older. Yet after all what did that matter? It would make no difference one way or the other. Yet she said, "You must be younger than me. That's another thing."

"Yes, I should imagine nearly eighteen months. But that's utterly irrelevant. Age does not come into this, but love does. You are for me, Kate, and . . . and I know now I am for you, because you do care for me, don't you?"

She closed her eyes tightly and put her hand across them, only to have it pulled away, and, his arms about her once more, he said, "Tell me. Just let me hear you say it."

Her mind was winging away from her, seeming to lift her big body from the ground. She felt light and for the first time in her life she knew it didn't matter what her appearance was like for she was being loved. Not that she hadn't known love. But that was family love, and that kept you solid and protected on the ground. This love bore upwards, made you feel beautiful inside and created in you a power that you imagined could conquer all obstacles, and brought to your lips words that you never imagined you would have the chance to say to any man. "I love you, Ben. Oh, yes, yes, I love you. But I can't believe. . . ."

Her breathing was checked by his mouth on hers and she knew that never in her life would she know a moment that would exceed the happiness that was in her now.

She was brought back to reality when he said, "You will tell them, your people? I particularly would like to talk with your father, not only about us, but to tell him how I feel. . . ."

As if a pain had now shot through her body, she drew in a sharp breath. And so evident was her distress he said, "Kate! Kate! What is it? Are you feeling ill?"

"No, no." She pressed herself gently from him, then slowly sat down on the settle again and, looking up at him, she said, "You . . . you don't know the . . . the feeling of bitterness and recrimination that is still alive in my father against all the Bannamans. Even the name is enough at times to set the muscles of his face working."

"But I am not a Bannaman."

She dropped her gaze from his, bit on her lip, and said, "She was your mother, and . . . and no matter what you felt about her, I . . . I can never see you bringing Father round to your side."

"But I must." He was on his knees before her now. "Kate, I must. We must. Either that or just go off together. I'll take you back home."

"Oh! no. That's impossible." She put her hands out and touched his face. "As much as I would like to see America, I . . . I could never just go off and leave them. My real father went off and left my mother. I couldn't repeat the pattern. It would be too cruel."

"The reverse would be too cruel as well, Kate. If they tried to part us, what then?"

Yes, if they tried to part them, what then? It was unthinkable. That must never happen. Yet what was to be done? The only solution that appeared to her mind was a slow breaking down of her father's prejudices, and it wasn't just the prejudices, it was the deep hate. Her mother had once told her that her father had periods when he would wake up in the night groaning and trying to speak. He would be reliving in nightmares the period when he was strung to the beam and knew he would suffer in agony till he died.

"I . . . I will come across with you and. . . ."

She almost toppled him onto his back, so quickly did she rise to her feet. But then, her hand going out to him, she pulled him upwards, and she said, "Leave it for a while, please. Let me see what can be done. I shall try to pave the way somehow. But, Ben" – her voice dropped to a murmur – "however I go about it I . . . I know there will be trouble."

"I can face trouble, any kind of trouble, as long as I know in the end we shall be together, and for good, whether it is here or across the water."

Quietly now he gripped her hand and they walked from the kitchen and into the hall, and there, taking a key from his pocket, he opened the oak door, and when they had passed through he locked it again. He untethered the horses, and before helping her to mount he went to take her in his arms. When she glanced around somewhat apprehensively he laughed gently and said, "No one ever comes here, at least I haven't seen anyone. But at the moment I wish there was a crowd standing at the gate, and then they could spread the news."

When she shuddered the jollity went from his voice and he said, "Everything will turn out all right. You'll see."

The answer that was on the tip of her tongue was, "You don't know. You have no idea of the strength of feeling that you'll have to combat before everything is all right," assuming that it ever could be combated, in which case it would mean they would never come together, no, no, this wondrous thing that had come into the wilderness that was her inner life would be lost. She must fight for it as he was prepared to.

After they had kissed, not once, not twice, but three times, she had to draw herself from him. And now he helped her up into the saddle, and when she leant forward and, taking his hand, laid it tenderly against her cheek, the softness in his dark eyes deepened and he murmured, "My Kate. My Kate."

They rode out of the gate side by side, and had little to say except in their exchanged glances until they came to where the paths divided and she would not let him come any further. His last words to her were, "Will you come tomorrow?" And she answered after a moment's thought, "I couldn't tomorrow." And when she added, "It's my turn for the ironing," he put his head back and laughed as he said, "Oh, Kate, Kate, it's your turn for the ironing. Oh, that is lovely, lovely. . . . When then? The following day?"

"Yes."

"So be it. I'll be waiting here at the same time. Bring me news that you have broken the ice."

She made no reply to this, but, turning her horse sharply, she rode off, without looking back.

In the yard John helped her down from her horse, saying, "Had a nice ride?" There was a big question mark in his words, and she answered, "Yes, John. I've had a very nice ride."

"I'm glad, Kate." He smiled at her. "Charles thinks he's a fine fellow."

"He is, John."

"Why don't you fetch him home?" He nodded towards the house.

"I . . . I will, one of these days."

"Do. Do, Kate. It would probably ease things. You see, something else seems to have got into Dad now; he's come back from Newcastle in a tear."

She left him with a puzzled look on his face and went into the kitchen. There, Maggie and Florrie were talking to Gabriel, and they turned and looked at her in such a way that she was forced to ask, "Is anything the matter?"

"We don't know," Gabriel answered; "but, as you know, Father went early into Newcastle this morning to see the solicitor about buying Morgan's piece of land. He said if things held him up he would stay overnight. Well, he couldn't have been there more than a couple of hours, and he's come back, and in a bit of a rage if his face is anything to go by."

Kate felt a fluttering in her throat. Could he have heard about Ben's true identity? But then no one except herself knew. Then what could have caused him to come racing back like this? He enjoyed his visits to Newcastle, and if he couldn't pick up a coach that would stop at Haydon Bridge or Haltwhistle, from where he could hire a horse, he often stayed in Newcastle overnight. Her voice was small as she asked, "Where is he?"

"Closeted with Mother in the office. They've been there this past half-hour or more. Something's up." Maggie was nodding her head. She looked at Kate as much as to say: Your business has hardly cooled down and now there's something else afoot.

"Would you like a cup of tea, Kate?" Florrie went towards the big brown teapot resting on the hob, and Kate answered, "Yes. I'll come back for it; I want to get my things off."

She went swiftly up the kitchen and was crossing the hall to the stairs when, along the corridor that went off to the right, the door opened and her mother appeared. She stood staring at her for a moment, then said quietly, "Will you come in here a minute, Kate?"

Dear God! They had found out. Some way or other they had found out. And what now? Well, she would make a stand. It was either them or Ben, and it would always be Ben. Always. She couldn't lose this precious thing that had seemingly been sent straight from heaven into her life.

When she entered the room her father was standing and she was surprised to see that his face was not grim and that he wasn't in a raging temper. She was puzzled, even by the sound of his voice as he said, "Hello, lass."

"Hello, Dad."

"Come and sit down."

She sat down, and when her mother sat near her and took hold of her hand, she looked at her and said, "What is it? Something happened?"

"You could say that." Mary Ellen nodded. "Aye, you could say that. I'll ... I'll let your dad explain."

Kate now watched Hal rub one lip over the other two or three times as though preparing to speak. But even before doing so he placed his hands on his knees and bent slightly forward and concentrated his gaze on the carpet; then abruptly he said, "I was a bit late in getting into the city, there was a hold-up with the coach at one of the toll-gates. A carrier waggon had capsized right across the road. Truth was, one of the horses had given up. Anyway, it delayed us for a while. But you know" – he gave a forced smile now – "I only need a bit of an excuse to lengthen me stay in Newcastle, 'cos I like a look round. Anyway, I went as usual to the Queen's Head in Pilgrim Street, left me bag, and sauntered about. My meeting with the solicitor fellow was not till half past one. So I dandered a bit and ended up in the Eldon Coffee Rooms in Blackett Street." Again he gave a thin smile as he said, "You can't only get coffee there now, you know, but a drop of the hard an' all. And being Tuesday, I managed to get the *Tyne Mercury* an' the *Northumberland and Durham Gazette*, hot, as you could say, from the press, otherwise I've got to wait days for them, that's if there's any left." His tone now changed and, looking at Mary Ellen who had closed her eyes for a moment, he said, "All right, all right, I'm getting to it. Going the long way around I suppose, but I'll come to it soon enough. You know I will."

Kate looked from one to the other. What was this? She was sure now it had nothing to do with her and Ben, for this tentative lead up to what he had to tell her would certainly not have been his reaction in that case.

"Anyway, there I was sitting looking at it and I saw an advert. It was for a coming exhibition opening on Friday to be exact. A man—" Kate watched him gulp at this point, and he repeated, "A man from these parts was putting on a show of his pictures." He stopped and straightened himself and looked straight at her, and now she knew what was to come. His voice low, he said, " 'Twas a big advert, praising this fellow's work and saying that he had lived in France for more than half his life and he'd just had a successful exhibition in London, and he was now in the city, prepared to open his latest on Friday. Well" – he drew in a long breath – "I didn't stay long in the coffee-house, but I walked along to the Assembly Rooms. That's where the exhibition was to take place. There was quite a bit of activity outside and as I stood a man and woman came out of the door. I couldn't recognize the woman and I barely recognized the man. But I couldn't have changed as much as him, for he recognized me.... 'Twas your father, Kate, and his wife."

They were both looking at her. Her face, she knew, had gone scarlet again. It was no use telling herself that the news didn't affect her. Since she had known she had another father she had often wondered what he was like. But the love showered on her by Hal had diluted the desire to meet him. She had only once spoken of him to her mother and that was during her teens, when she said, "I'm no good at drawing and that's funny, because you said my father was an artist." And she had added, "Was he a good artist?" And her mother had replied, "Yes, they said so." And then after a long moment she had put the question, "Has he ever seen me?" And Mary Ellen said, "When you were a little baby."

And the subject had seemed closed when she had said, "Then he wouldn't know me if he was to come upon me now, would he?"

At this moment Kate was recalling those words: He wouldn't know me if he was to come upon me now, would he? This man, who was an artist and who would, undoubtedly, like beauty, had been the begetter of something that was far from beautiful. Yet Ben had said.... Ben. For these two things to have happened in the one day. It was too much.

As she laid her head back against the chair Mary Ellen said anxiously, " 'Tis all right, dear, 'tis all right. You needn't see him if you don't want to." She didn't turn to her mother but looked at Hal, saying now, "Did he ask to see me?"

"Yes ... aye, he did. And being me, I told him he had left it a bit late. And being him, he made excuses, saying he had only been in England twice in the past twenty years."

"What is he like?" Her voice was low.

Hal moved uneasily in his chair. What could he say to her about this man, his one-time friend who had brought her into being, and whom he himself had followed for years, not only because he wanted his companionship but also he was something good to look upon? The successful artist he had seen outside the Assembly Rooms certainly wasn't that man. The slightly out-landishly dressed painter was big and blowzy like a woman gone to seed, with a belly on him like a poisoned pup, so much so that as he looked at him he had for the first time in his life felt physically superior to him: there was no surplus fat on him; his stomach was as flat as it had been in his youth; there were streaks of grey in his hair, and his face was ruddied by the weather; he had no begs under his eyes, just two deep lines running from the corners of his nose down almost to his chin. He had often wondered what his reaction would be if confronted with Mary Ellen's first love. And what her reaction would be too. Now he had no fear in that quarter. His fear was for this girl ... this young woman sitting opposite, this being that he loved almost as much as he did her mother. There was no length he wouldn't go to to save her being hurt, because he was well aware that if she was to be surprised at the sight of her father, he would certainly be surprised when he saw his daughter.

Kate now said quietly, "Do you want me to go to the exhibition?" She looked from one to the other. And it was Hal who answered again, saying, "He asked me to bring you. But I said no, if he wanted to see you, he had to come here. I suppose it was a kind of conceit on my part, for I want to show him how you've been brought up, not in a cottage where he last saw you, but in a home fit for a young lady. An' that's what you are, Kate, a young lady. And never forget it."

"Oh, Dad." Impulsively she got up now and, going to him, she put her arms around his neck and kissed him. And he blinked his eyes a number of times and rubbed his hand roughly across his lips before he said, "That's the worst thing about it: I'm not, am I, your dad."

"You will always be my dad and I want no other. I . . . I don't want to see him."

"You'll have to now, lass; I've invited him, and he's comin' the morrow. I suppose—" He nodded towards Mary Ellen now, saying, "I should have asked that one there before I scattered me invitations, but I also wanted him to see her as mistress of a fine house and a thriving farm, and a mother of a grand family. I wanted him to see what he had missed." He turned now to Mary Ellen, putting out his hand and catching at hers, saying, "You understand, lass, don't you?"

Mary Ellen didn't speak, she merely nodded her head. Oh, she understood, and she was with him every step of the way. She too wanted to show that big upstart what they had achieved, and by tomorrow this time she'd have every bit of silver out on the table; she'd have flowers in vases; she'd have fresh curtains in the sitting-room. If she had to stay up all night, she'd have everything spruce for the morrow.

Hal rose now and, as if picking up her thoughts, he said, "I'd better get out of these togs, because by this time the morrow anybody will be able to eat their meat off that yard outside. I'll work those three beggars until the fat drops off them."

Mary Ellen's voice was quiet now as she said, "I think we'd better tell them what it's all about first. What d'you say, Kate?"

"Yes, Mam, yes."

Mary Ellen was surprised at the way her daughter had taken the news. It was if there was nothing untoward, no red-letter day in her life the day she was to meet her real father. She couldn't know that there was nothing but relief in Kate's whole being, for now she had time to think, time to plan, time to enjoy this love that had come into her life, before Ben's identity should be revealed.

7

There had been no mention of Roddy's wife accompanying him. It had been taken for granted that she would come. In speaking of her later that night in the bedroom, Hal had described her as a well-dressed snipe who should have been wearing the trousers, because he had gauged within minutes who ruled the roost in that set-up. To Mary Ellen's enquiry, he had answered that she looked nearly as old as old Kate had done. He had admitted that this was an exaggeration but stated firmly that she looked old enough to be Roddy's mother, and that for the short time he had been with them she had acted as if she was, using words of endearment that had made him uneasy, like one would use to a bairn: darling this, and my love that. When Mary Ellen had asked if he looked happy, Hal had paused a long while before answering, "I'll leave you to make up your own mind about that when you see him." ...

And now the house and all of them were ready. Despite herself, Mary Ellen was experiencing a fluttering behind her breast bone.

Hal had taken the trap to meet the train at Hexham. That was two hours or more ago, so he should be here any minute.

It was a lovely day. They'd had a little rain in the night, nothing that would do much good, but it had laid the dust and freshened the air. The long windows in the sitting-room were wide open, looking on to the newly cut stretch of grass, and the white lace curtains were fluttering gently in the breeze. In the dining-room the table was laid for high tea and Annie, looking for a space to put down one last dish of small pies, remarked caustically, "Think the Queen was dropping in. If I'd had my way he would have got short shrift. By! he would that. You're daft. You know that, Mary Ellen, you're daft, laying on all this. If he's as big a noise as you make out this won't impress him. Likely been wined and dined like royalty afore now. To my mind he's got a damn nerve to show his face." She lifted her head and stared at Mary Ellen who was standing looking out of the window, from where she could see the drive that led round to the front door. But then, her voice dropping, she ended, "How are you feeling about it?"

Mary Ellen turned to her and pulled a slight face before answering: "I'm looking forward to it in a way."

"Hal not troubled?"

"About me? Huh!" She gave a laugh. "No, Hal's got me where he wants me, has had for years and he knows that."

"Aye, yes, you've had a good life together, you two. Rough passage afore, but you've made up for it."

"And you've helped, Annie." Mary Ellen's voice was soft, and she went on, "I couldn't have done without you in those early days. Although he was all in all to me, I needed someone, a mother, and you were better than most I've come across."

She watched Annie wag her head now, purse her lips, take up the end of her long white apron and blow her nose on it. Then almost on a bark, she turned on Mary Ellen, crying, "This is a time to tell me, isn't it? You know how me nose goes whenever I bubble." Her eyes blinking and her face crumpled, she stared across at Mary Ellen. Then her voice low, she muttered, "I'll have to put some flour on it," and turning, she hurried out of the room. And Mary Ellen, drooping her head, smiled to herself as she muttered, "Oh, Annie. Annie."

What she had said was true: she had been lucky to have Annie in those struggling years when she was starting on a new life. Now the old life was about to reappear, and she wasn't afraid for herself, but she was for Kate. Yet she had been amazed at the way Kate had taken the news, showing no great excitement. It was as if she was to meet up with an everyday event: there was a calmness about her that was puzzling. But then she had been puzzled in other ways a great deal of late. But where was she now? She must go and fetch her. Or should she wait to have a talk with him first?

She swung round as she heard the wheels of the trap on the drive. There was no time now to go and search for her. She hurried out of the room, across the hall to the open front door, and there she stood, watching Hal bring the trap to a standstill. Then he got down and was followed by another man. There was no woman with them.

Her mouth fell into a slight gape as the man walked slowly towards her. Hal had prepared her, in a way, for what to expect, but in her mind's eye she was still seeing the young virile looking Roddy Greenbank. But this big hulk of a man was no Roddy Greenbank. There was nothing recognizable about him, not even his eyes. He was indeed like a man gone to seed.

"Hello, Mary Ellen." The voice too was different. It had a foreign sound to it, as if English was his second language. "Good gracious, you've hardly altered." His look of appraisal covered her from head to foot, and the tone of his voice touched on surprise – and was it slight pique? – at how kindly the years had dealt with her.

"Come in," she said. "Come in." And he followed her into the hall, but immediately stopped and gazed around him, and after a second or so he said, "My! My!" And Hal coming behind him said, "What d'you mean? My! My!" as if he didn't know what the exclamation meant.

"Well, its em ... a ... a very nice hall. That's what I mean."

He was about to go towards the open door Mary Ellen was now holding open, when two figures appeared at the top of the shallow stairs, and he stopped again and looked at them descending. And Hal, going towards them, said, "These are my daughters" – he pointed – "Maggie and Florrie."

The two girls stood staring for a moment at this man who was Kate's real father before giving the smallest of curtseys and saying, one after the other, "Good-day, sir."

"Good-day. Good-day. My! aren't we pretty." He glanced at Hal while still addressing them, saying, "You certainly don't take after this old codger." His manner was hearty, friendly.

Mary Ellen's voice now came from the doorway: "Take the tea into the dining-room, Maggie," she called, and on this the girls, still smiling, turned away and hurried towards the kitchen, their best dresses making a frou-frou sound.

He was now in the middle of the sitting-room, and once again looking around him, and when he said, "Very nice room, very nice," there was definitely a note of condescension now in his voice. And when he added, "It's almost as big as my salon at home," Hal could hold his tongue no longer, and in his roughest voice he said, "Sit down, man, and drop your cloak off. Remember that we know each other of old. Whoever you're out to impress, it isn't us."

The man's face was red now. His already full cheeks puffed out a little more and his voice held a trace of its original tone as he now came back, saying, "Well, there's certainly one thing, the years haven't altered you."

"I never intended them to, but I've listened to your bragging since we left Hexham and I've had enough of it. Now let's be ourselves, shall we? You know what you've come for, well...."

"Hal." Mary Ellen's voice was quiet. "Stop that. Enough is enough." Now she turned to Roddy and said, "Sit yourself down. I'm sorry about this."

Roddy sat down, and his attitude now was recognizable to them both when, bending forward, he placed his elbows on his knees and joined his hands together and quietly he said, "I'm sorry too. As you so rightly said, it's a cloak." He now raised his eyes and looked towards Mary Ellen, saying, "Life's a funny thing. If we could think at twenty as we do at forty, how different things would be."

Hal had always told himself there was one thing he was sure of, and that was Mary Ellen's feelings for him. The love she had once given to this fellow was dead as any corpse in the cemetery. But there she was, looking at him tenderly, pity in her glance. "Be damned!" he muttered to himself, then broke in, "Will I tell Kate?"

Mary Ellen turned her gaze from Roddy, saying quietly now, "Fetch the lads in."

"The lads afore Kate? No." He stared at her hard before marching from the room, and she turned and looked at Roddy again, but did not speak for a moment. Presently, she said, "Kate doesn't look like me . . . she has your height, but that is all."

He did not answer but continued to stare at her, and now she smiled at him, saying, "I'm glad to hear you are so successful, Roddy. It must be a great feeling to have achieved all that, I mean, having exhibitions of your work."

"Yes, yes." His reply sounded dull, and there followed another silence before she asked very quietly, "Are you happy?"

"Happy?" He repeated the word; then on a louder note he said, "Oh, yes. Yes, I'm happy." And having made the declaration almost vehemently he became quiet while staring at her. And now he asked in a tone that she had never heard even the Roddy Greenbank that she remembered use because in it there was a well of sadness. He muttered, "If I can speak the truth for once in my life, I can say now, Mary Ellen, I've never known a day's real happiness from the time that I last saw you. You were washing, I remember, your arms all soapy suds, and you had turned all the stuff out of the cottage, and you brought the child down from the attic. That was the morning you told me you loved Hal and that you were going to marry him, and that what you'd had for me was a girlish fancy, like one of the pains of growing up. I think it was from that morning that I realized what I'd lost."

She got to her feet, saying, "Now, Roddy, the past's past, we can't go back. And I must tell you straight that what I said that morning, I still say: there's nobody in the world for me but Hal."

He was on his feet too now, his voice low, his words quick. "Yes, yes, I know, but you asked and I had to tell you. I'll just say this and no more, I envy him. I suppose that's why I've played the big fellow ever since I've met him. Understand?"

"Yes." She nodded at him. "Yes, Roddy, I understand. But your wife, don't you get on?"

"Oh . . . oh." He threw back his head now. "Oh, yes we get on. She's the world's organizer. I'm where I am today because of her; without her I'd still be doing some hack work in a back room in somebody's office. Oh, I've got a lot to thank her for." His tone was becoming light again and with it he was choosing his words as he went on, "There's different aspects to life. If one market closes on you, don't worry, try another. That's what Mary says. And she's right, it works."

He turned now as the door opened. He watched Hal push it wide. Then there came into the room a tall big-made woman. She was wearing a grey taffeta silk skirt and matching blouse. Her hair was black and straight and dressed in coils on each side of her head. But his eyes were riveted on her face. Mary Ellen had said their daughter wasn't like her and that she took after him only in height. And she was right. My God! he said to himself, she was right. This woman was plain. Yet . . . yet. . . . The artist in him searched for a word to fit her. The bone structure of her face was prominent, the cheek bones high, the jaws squarish. On a man he could have depicted a god with the same features. But here was a woman. She was standing but two yards from him now and he was looking into her eyes. Now here was something, here was something. They were beautiful eyes, her one good feature. But her lips were well-formed too.

"How do you do."

He was amazed at the sound of her voice: it was like a soft musical note coming out of a large unwieldy instrument. Yet no, she wasn't unwieldy, her body was magnificent from an artist's point of view. Put her on a dais in Paris and they would go mad about her. But here she was, his daughter. He had expected someone pretty, slim like Mary Ellen had been, pert like Mary Ellen had been, uneducated and somewhat raw as Mary Ellen had been. But here was this large cool creature who was speaking again. "I hope you had a good journey."

The ordinariness of the words and tone not only surprised the man who was her father, but definitely, too, Hal and Mary Ellen alike. They had both fully expected some emotional response, but it looked, as Mary Ellen thought, that Kate was standing summing up this man as if he was a visitor they all had some doubts about. Yet she was being confronted by her father.

"Hello, Kate." He could find nothing else to say. His voice sounded ordinary, no twang to it now. After a moment of most uneasy silence in the room, he added, "How are you?"

"Oh, I'm very well. And you?"

"Yes, I'm very well too."

"Oh, for God's sake, let's sit down." Another time Mary Ellen would have thought, Oh! Hal, there you go again, but now she smiled and said, "A better idea would be to let us have some tea. Come on." And she put out her hand towards Hal. "Let's see if the girls have got everything ready."

Hal paused for a moment as if reluctant to leave the room, but an extra tight pressure on his hand brought him forward. And when Mary Ellen pulled the sitting-room door closed behind them he hissed at her, "What did you have to do that for?"

"'Tis best to leave them alone for a few minutes, thick-head."

"Thick-head am I?" They were walking along the passage towards the dining-room now. "Aye, I might be, but I'm not blind. You're sorry for him, aren't you?"

"Yes, I am."

"My God! I never thought to hear that."

"Well, you're hearing it now."

She made a face, then smiled at him; then leaning her head impulsively against his shoulder, she muttered, "Oh, Hal, Hal. We're lucky."

He pulled her round and, staring into her face, he demanded, "No regrets?"

"Aw! man" – she shook her head at him – "don't be so damned silly. No regrets, you say. Twenty-four years working on you, having to put up with you! Of course I've got regrets." She watched him pull his chin into his neck before she added, "I'm only sorry it hasn't been forty-two." Swiftly he put his arms about her and kissed her hard on the lips, only to spring apart from her as John and Tom entered the passage and simultaneously turned away, their hands over their eyes, as Tom cried,

"In the daytime at that, John!" and John replied, "Shameless! Absolutely shameless."

"You two want me toe in your backsides?"

"You'll have to do a standing jump to achieve that all in one go, Dad." John's face was solemn, and Tom added, "Bet you the cream heifer, Dad, you can't do it." And at this, Hal's two fists swung out and the young men, dodging them, hurried ahead of their parents into the dining-room to find Gabriel already there with the girls. But once in the room and the door closed, their manner changed and Tom asked, "How's she taking it?"

Mary Ellen looked at Hal, and Hal looked at his family and said after a moment's thought, "You know, I couldn't really tell you. Polite, wasn't she?" He glanced at Mary Ellen and she nodded. "Yes, coolly polite."

"Coolly?"

"Aye" – Hal nodded now from one to the other – "that's the word, coolly. As cool as spring water I would say. I was worried – I thought on the sight of him we would have lost her – but I'm not any more."

"She wouldn't go away with him, would she?" They all turned and looked at Florrie, and after the mutterings of: "Of course not. Don't be silly. Whoever put that idea into your head?" Mary Ellen said quietly, "It's just possible, at least for a time. He's . . . he's a very famous man and he could show her a different part of the world."

Hal came at her now, saying, "What are you talkin' about? You never said anything like that to me."

"Oh, didn't I? I must have forgotten."

"Forgotten? Don't be aggravating, woman, and startin' me worryin', 'cos once she went away on a trip like that she wouldn't come back, would she? This life would be very tame after seeing France, Paris, and places like that." Then his voice dropping and his face becoming very serious, he said, "She wouldn't, would she? I mean, go off with him?"

"I couldn't say what she would do if he made the offer."

"Gabriel. No . . . you John and Tom, go and make yourself known to him and bring them into tea."

"You'll do nothing of the sort. They'll come when they're ready. Now sit yourselves down, all of you, and show a little patience and good manners." Then, her lips slightly trembling, Mary Ellen said, "I . . . I want him to see the bunch I'm proud of. . . ."

Back in the sitting-room Kate and her father were seated now opposite to each other, and he, leaning towards her, was repeating the invitation that Hal was dreading. "It would be an experience," he said. "You could just come for a month and I can assure you that you would enjoy it. The only thing is you wouldn't have a moment's peace: I . . . I have a number of friends who would want to paint you."

"Paint me?"

"Yes, yes."

She rose to her feet now, saying quietly, "And what would they see in me to paint?"

316

He did not get to his feet but, lifting his head, he let his gaze travel over her before he said, "So much."

"It certainly wouldn't be my beauty."

His mouth opened then closed: her frankness seemed to have non-plussed him for a moment. Then he said, "From an artist's point of view, they would find something more than beauty. Pretty faces and pretty figures you can engage for a few francs. Then ... then there is your voice. You have an unusual voice. You must know that. And besides everything else in our short acquaintance, I realize you've got a mind of your own. Oh, our friends would certainly enjoy you, artists or no artists. What do you say?"

"How would your wife take this?"

Now he did rise to his feet and he walked from her and put his hand on the high mantelpiece and looked down into the empty grate where the half-burnt logs were arranged tidily across the bars, and he said, "As an artist she would welcome you."

"But as a stepmother?"

He turned and looked at her, saying quietly now, "You have your mother's mind and her frankness. Perhaps you are right. But I had to ask you."

"Thank you. Now may I ask you a question?"

"Certainly."

"Why has it taken all these years for you to come and see me?"

He looked down into the grate again, placing his other hand also on the mantelpiece, and as she watched him droop his head forward she had the desire to go to him and say, It's all right, it doesn't matter. I don't want an answer. But he gave her the answer, saying, "I ... was afraid."

"Afraid to come and see me?"

Slowly he turned round towards her, his hands hanging limply by his side now. "No. This is between you and me.... Afraid to see your mother."

"Oh."

"Do you understand?"

"Yes, yes, I understand."

"We all make mistakes, even the strongest of us, and I've got to admit I'm not a strong-willed person. So when a different way of life was offered me I grabbed at it with both hands. Your namesake, old Kate, whom I'm sure your mother has told you of many times, she used always to say, everything in life must be paid for, and there was never a truer saying. And I have paid for it, and I'm still paying for it in an over-fed pampered body, hundreds of acquaintances but hardly one true friend, and a way of life that is ordered from the time I get up in the morning till I go to bed at night. It did not take me over long to realize where my real life lay, but as I say, I'm a weak-minded man." He now spread out his hands. "I must admit though I was surprised to see you as my daughter, so different from what I expected, but so much better. And undoubtedly

317

you are surprised to find that the great man you've heard about, billed and fêted, is just a shallow manoeuvred individual."

She looked at him. Yes, he was all he was saying. But what he wasn't saying was, he was clever in his own interests, for in a way he was playing on her sympathy, hoping that now she would succumb and say she would accept his offer of a holiday in France. For a moment a touch of bitterness entered her thinking as she imagined how he would present her. His daughter undoubtedly, but how would she be named by his many acquaintances? Oh, she knew how she'd be named: Greenbank's bastard.

He said now, "It's been a strange meeting, don't you think? I never intended to say any of this. It's the atmosphere of this place, not only the house" – he wagged his hand towards the ceiling – "the whole area." He walked from her now towards the window. "It's in the very air. Everybody speaks their mind, no reticence. If you had used tact, diplomacy, or polish, you would have been known as a nowt, an upstart. Even the upper class here washed their linen in public. Now that's funny." He swung round and looked at her. His manner had changed entirely now. It was as if he recognized his pleading had failed and was using one of his many fronts. "You know, the Hall and the many big houses around here, well at one time, I wouldn't have even been allowed into their stables, whereas now, believe it or not, I've had two invitations to dine, and with the best of them."

"Are you going to accept?"

"Perhaps. Perhaps not. We are only here for a week. There may be no time, there's a lot of functions to be got through in Newcastle."

He stopped a few feet from her and again they surveyed each other, and it was she who spoke next, saying, "Well, I think all that has had to be said has been said. Don't you? Shall we go into tea?"

He now gave a soft chuckling laugh; then with exaggerated courtesy, he held out his crooked arm and she placed the tips of her fingers on it, and like this they left the room and entered the dining-room, to the surprise, and not to say amazement, of all the members of her family.

The reaction of the family to Kate's almost forgotten father was varied. Gabriel's version of him when with his brothers was: "He talked too much." And both John and Tom rounded on him and said, "Well, you gave him plenty of leads, it was you who asked the questions," for Gabriel to come back with, "Yes, well, if I hadn't, the meal would have been dead, because you all sat there like stooks."

"I must say, though, I found him interesting."

John looked at Tom scornfully. "Only because he mentioned all the places he had been to in Paris."

"Aye, perhaps. Anyway, he made me feel I'd like to take a trip over there. And perhaps I will."

At this he received a none too gentle dig in the back from John who said, "Well, it won't be the Opera House you'll find yourself in, but that place called the Conciergerie or the House of Justice or some such."

"Anyway, he's given me an invite over and I might take it."

"What you'll take," said John, "is a journey to the byres. You can go by horseback, coach, mail van, or pack horse or just carrier cart . . . or on the tip of me boot."

As they were about to disperse laughing, Gabriel said, "I can't understand our Kate, she wasn't a bit ruffled, was she? You would have thought she met her father every week. She's changing is Kate, isn't she?"

His two brothers looked at him, and it was John who said quietly, "Yes, she's changing. . . ."

"That's what Maggie said to Florrie. As cool as the dairy slab she said she was. And I could have fallen through the floor when they came in arm in arm. I didn't like him. I felt he was acting all the time, and bragging."

"He was only telling us about his home and the way they live over there."

"Did you see how he looked at Mam when he left her? For a moment, I thought he was going to kiss her. Dad was glad to see the back of him, I know that, one-time friend or not. . . . No, I didn't like him. And Kate's been funny enough of late, and now she'll be funnier still after this."

During this conversation in the kitchen Annie had been standing at the table shredding up a cabbage, and for the first time she spoke, quietly saying, "And she's had plenty to make her funny, if you ask me. And whether you like him or you dislike him, I'd keep your tongues quiet about it when you are within earshot of her. You hear?"

"Yes, Annie," was the quick concerted reply.

They did not think it strange that they never retaliated when Annie chastised them, whereas, had it been their mother, Maggie at least might have put up a show of defiance. But in Annie's case it was different. She was family, yet not family, and in a sort of dependant position, so you did not take advantage. Moreover, she had been like a second mother to Kate. Moreover still, their father thought a great deal of Annie. . . .

Their father at this moment was discussing the very same subject. He was in the office reckoning up his outlay and income for the month and Mary Ellen was sitting opposite to him at the other side of the desk. She had her arms folded tightly across her breasts, and her lips, too, were tight. She determined to let him go on and get out of his system a suspicion that had come into his mind when he had brought Roddy home yesterday. He was on now about Kate's reaction, but she knew that any minute now he would hark back to the main subject that was troubling him.

"It amazed me that she should like him. He's a big-head. I would have thought with her common sense she would be able to see through him. My God! To think that we worked side by side in the mill, tramped the hills together; and it was me who used to go gathering charcoal so he could do his damned drawings. And another thing I'll tell you, he's not as well off as he makes out to be. Anybody can go round visiting fancy places if they live in a city. If I was going over to France I could brag about all the fine buildings in Newcastle. Anyway, people know that artists are ten a penny and that they don't make all that money unless they're right at the top of the tree."

She couldn't keep her tongue still any longer, for she now snapped at him, "He appears to have got there, doesn't he?"

"Aye, appears, appears. You're taken in by his fancy clothes and his pot belly. By God! I've never seen anybody so bloated. Look at his face. Where's your bonny boy now? But even so, you were sorry for him, weren't you? He got back at you, didn't he? Pushed you to where you used to be, goggle-eyed gazing at him, wishing now that he had taken you to London with him the last time you saw him. . . ."

He was startled as she jumped up, her face aflame now, and crying at him, but in a low voice, "I've heard enough. After all these years, I still haven't been able to convince you. Deep in you, you're still holding it against me that I had her. Well, I'll say what I said to you years ago, it was my fault that I had her, not his. He wasn't to blame. I made him. And don't say a woman can't make a man do what she wants. Some don't need much coaxing, but let me tell you what I've never told you afore, he needed a lot of coaxing. So there you have it, Hal Roystan. And you've spoilt something that was . . . was—" she choked and now stammered through spurting tears, "bea . . . beautiful."

He was round the desk and holding her straining body to him, pleading with her now, "Mary Ellen. Mary Ellen. I'm sorry. I am. But I was scared, scared daft. I was, I was. I'd always thought that there could be twenty Roddys come back to see you and I wouldn't turn a hair. But from the minute I saw him looking at you, I knew that he was regretting letting you go, and you recognizing this. Why, lass, I nearly went mad. 'Twas a wonder I didn't hit him, especially at the last when I thought he was going to kiss you. I would, I would, I would have hit him. Aw, Mary Ellen, don't, don't cry, please. It's 'cos I love you. I still feel like a young lad inside about you. I've been so sure of me damn self all these years, and now I'm not and never will be again." As his arm slackened about her she looked up at him, and now, slowly taking his face between her two hands, she muttered, "Oh, Hal, Hal, if you don't know now, there's no way I can make you believe it. And yes, I was sorry for him. I pitied him, and at the same time I was thanking God things happened as they did, for I know now I'd never have been able to put up with him. Underneath, he's still Roddy Greenbank, out for number one. To use old Kate's words, I'd sooner have a dinner of herbs with you than a fat ox with him."

"Ah, lass." He held her close, and after a moment he said, "Another thing that had me sick, I thought Kate would go off with him."

"Never."

"You didn't think so?"

"No, it never crossed my mind. Anyway, if it had, I would have put it aside, knowing that Kate would never do anything to hurt us, and that certainly would."

"No." He nodded his head. "You're right there."

Kate knew that her attitude towards her father during his long overdue visit was being discussed throughout the family, but John was the only one who had put a pointed question to her. "Did you like him, Kate?" he had said. And the telling pause that preceded her answer was, in a way, as explanatory to him as it was to her, "Yes and no." To which he had said, "Well, you should know if you do or you don't."

Yes, she supposed she should have been able to say precisely what her impression of the man was. Yet, wasn't it asking something of oneself to be able to define a character after such a short acquaintance? One thing, though, she did know: if she hadn't been so inwardly happy, she might have succumbed to the offer to visit him in France. And that, she knew, would have been looked upon, at least by her mother and father, as something of a betrayal. As it was now, her whole reaction to the man was tinged with pity, for his life, so successful on the surface, was barren underneath, and this she considered to be a dear price to pay for his fame.

Altogether, his visit had disturbed her less than it had other members of the family because all the while she had been holding close to her heart the thought of Ben. And at this moment, all she wanted was to get on a horse and race across those moors and feel his arms holding her.

Last night, it had not been her father's visit that had troubled her dreams; but three times she had woken up and questioned if it could be true that the man who had come out of nowhere and who, she imagined, could have the choice of any girl he set his mind to, could he really love her? Was there not some catch in it somewhere? At one period she had lain awake thinking, There must be. There must be. This kind of thing doesn't happen. In the fairy tales of the Brothers Grimm there was always an ogre. Who could represent the ogre in her life?

Her dad, Hal?

Sitting up in bed at this thought, she had whispered to herself, "No, no." But her common sense had protested, "Yes, yes." Her dad was the ogre and he had to be overcome. But how? If Ben talked to him, would he listen to reason? She had lain back and dropped off to sleep, and this morning she had forgotten the answer she had given to herself....

At the breakfast table the conversation was general, purposely so it appeared to Kate. Tom was saying, "Terry's taking the sheep into

Allendale this morning." He was looking at Gabriel, and Gabriel answered, "Well good Lord, there's only a handful, he can manage those."

"'Tisn't the sheep I'm thinking about," Tom said, "it's the return journey, him coming straight back or winding his way into one of the inns. You know what happened a week gone."

"Funny that." They were all looking at their father now, and he chewed on a piece of bacon before saying with a smile, "You would say that Terry was the quietest fellow in the valley, yet put a couple of pints of small ale into him and what have you? A rip-roaring wrecker."

There were smiles all round the table now, and Gabriel said almost on a splutter, "I'll never forget that day when they tried to put him into the stocks."

"Aye." Tom laughed now. "And you nearly went with him. You were hanging onto his coat tails, and I had to pick you up and whack you."

"I hear they're going to take the stocks down...." Before Maggie could go on any further, Tom interrupted her: "Well, as long as they don't do away with the ducking stool, I'll be quite happy." And he grinned at Maggie as she tossed her head, saying, "Oh, you!"

"Why are you sending the sheep in today?" This was from Mary Ellen and she was looking at Hal now, and after another bite and a large swallow of bacon, he answered her: "Well, if you want the truth on the subject: as in the past it'll upset your delicate stomachs" – he glanced now at his daughters – "there's a crowdy main on the morrow, and you know what Terry is for cockfighting. His pay will drop like bolts of lightning down into the cockpit."

"I think it's terrible. It should be stopped." Florrie was not given to airing opinions and she had all their attention now as she went on, "A cockfight is bad enough, two birds, but all those birds thrown into the hole and people joying in their dying. I think it's awful. And you, our Tom, should be ashamed of yourself for...."

"Now, now, hold your hand a minute." Tom was wagging his finger at her. "I'm not the only one in this household that likes a bit of sport."

"No, but you should have more sense."

"Why should I have more sense than the others?" They were all laughing now at Tom's stretched face. "Neither of them" – he glanced at his mother and father – "had any wits to pass on, they had hardly enough to keep themselves going."

When the laughing uproar had subsided, Florrie, looking across at Kate and as if giving the final word on the subject, said, "And Kate can't abide cockfighting. Can you, Kate?"

And Kate, being now the focus of attention, her eyes bright, she said, "No, you're right, Florrie. I can't abide it, and I've thought of a way of putting a stop to it." And she nodded at her sister as if there was no one else but themselves at the table; the rest of them waited, some of them even stopped eating, and after a moment she said, "Well, the remedy is, for all like-minded women to get together and to dig a hole big enough to take the stocks, and there, one by one, place in them those lovers of cockfighting, and turn it into a real crowdy main by putting down some of the best fighters. Oh, I forgot to mention the important thing, I would plaster the gentlemen with honey then sprinkle on it plenty of wheat, of a good quality you know...."

Somebody choked. It was Annie. Mary Ellen had to thump her on the back with one hand while still holding her side with the other, the tears of laughter running down her cheeks. After a moment it was John who said, "I believe you meant that, Kate."

"Oh, yes, yes, I did, and if I could get a few others of like mind, I would do it."

They were all on their feet now, the girls clearing the table and still laughing. The men were laughing too, theirs more subdued and touched not a little with surprise. And it was Gabriel who spoke, saying, "You know, you sound quite bloodthirsty, Kate."

And she nodded at him, saying, "Does that surprise you? All females are bloodthirsty."

"Where did you get the idea, lass?" There was a slight reprimand in Hal's voice now. And Kate, looking at him fully in the face, said, "I don't know, I must have inherited it. It is old as birth. I only know that where the female of the animals are concerned, they are more fierce than the male. It's the protective instinct in them, I think." And with this she unbuttoned the cuffs of her long sleeves and, rolling them up to the elbow and casting a glance at her mother, she said quietly, "I'll make a start," and she went out to the side door that led into the dairy, leaving Mary Ellen and Hal exchanging glances. It was in both their minds that Kate was trying to tell them something. But what?

Maggie's voice turned their attention from each other saying, "That comes from her high-falutin reading. It was bad enough before when she used to go to the bookshop, but since she's got her American friend...."

"Maggie!" Mary Ellen's voice was sharp, but Maggie came back at her mother, saying, "All right, all right, Mam. I can open my mouth surely. She's allowed to say what she likes, why not me?"

"*Margaret Roystan!*"

She swung round and looked at her father who was holding the latch of the door in his hand, and he said quietly but grimly, "Don't go too far," and with that he went out. And Maggie, glaring at her mother and Annie who were standing together, said angrily, "That's what I mean. You see, that's what I mean. Things are changing here now, you can't open your mouth before there's a clamp put on it." And she scraped the last of the fat and bacon rind from a plate, scattering it over the wooden table, banged the plate down on top of the stack of others and, lifting them up, marched into the scullery, leaving Florrie with her head bowed, a cloth in her hand wiping up the mess, and Mary Ellen and Annie looking at each other, their thoughts needing no expression....

A few minutes later Mary Ellen went into the dairy. She stood at one end of the stone slab, took a round of butter and put it under a press that left it engraved with a leaf; then pushing it to where there were a number of similar ones arranged in rows, she said, "If this heat keeps up, we'll have to float these on the burn, or it'll be oil we'll be cartin' to market the morrow. Anyway, it'll be a nice day for a walk over to the little manor. . . . What embroidery are you taking?"

There was a moment of silence before Kate turned from the churn into which she had just poured a basin of cream and said quietly, "I won't be going over the day."

There was another pause before Mary Ellen said, "Oh, Kate, Mrs Boston will be so disappointed. You know how she looks forward to your going."

"There are three of us go, Mam, not only me, and Mrs Boston would miss Maggie much more than me, because, as you know, Maggie is as good as the newspaper for news and titbits."

Yes, Mary Ellen knew that Maggie's tongue wagged incessantly when she had an audience such as Mrs Boston, but it wasn't like Kate to put it that way. She trimmed another round of butter before she said as casually as she could, "What do you intend to do with yourself then?"

It was a stupid question for she was asking the road she knew, and she knew it deserved the answer she got, but she was nevertheless hurt when Kate replied, "Mam, you know what I'm going to do. I'm going to take the horse and ride out. I'm going to meet my . . . my friend." Kate now closed her eyes tightly for a moment. She had almost said, love, because her heart was overflowing with the word, and beneath her calm exterior there was an urgency that was constantly sending her body racing over the hill. He had said she was like a goddess, and, as one, she saw herself taking the hills in leaps outdoing the deer. In fact, her new mind was presenting her with a picture of herself that she had never seen before, for the simple reason that no one had ever seen her as he had done. Her bigness, her plainness, had been looked upon as a drawback, even by the members of her family who, in their different ways, loved her. At least they all had till recently, but of late Maggie had turned spiteful.

Her mother was coming towards her, drying her hands on a piece of muslin, and when she reached her she said quietly, "What's happening, Kate? This isn't like you. We're mother and daughter, but we've been friends an' all for years. As you know, I love the others, but I've never been able to talk to them as I have to you. That's until recently. In a way, Dad feels the same about you, you're very special to him. He's worried, too, about the change in you."

"I'm sorry, Mam." Kate now hung her head. "Believe me, I wouldn't hurt either of you for the world. That is my worry, that I should ever hurt you."

"Why should you worry about that, lass? Nothing you could ever do would upset us. All we want is your happiness."

"Are you sure of that?"

"Why, of course." Mary Ellen put out her hands and placed them on her daughter's shoulders, saying now, "I can't understand why you should think otherwise."

"Mam."

"Yes, lass?"

There was a pause before Kate said, "There might come a testing time later on. Will you remember what you've said?"

Mary Ellen put her head to one side now and asked, "What are you trying to tell me, lass?"

"Nothing at the moment, Mam. I only want you to remember that I love you both dearly."

Mary Ellen now drew her hands from Kate's shoulders and as they hung limply by her sides she said, "You're thinking of leaving, aren't you? You're going to your father?"

"*No! No! Never! Never!*"

"No?" Mary Ellen's face relaxed; then she asked, "Well, what can it be?"

"Mam" Now it was Kate's turn to put out her hands and, gripping her mother's, she said, "Be patient. Say nothing, please. Do this for me: say nothing, not even to Dad."

"Eh? Oh, Kate, I. . . ."

"Mam, I ask you to do this for me. Just forget for the time being this conversation, will you?"

"If you want it that way, lass, all right." Mary Ellen inclined her head forward before withdrawing her hands from Kate's and walking out of the dairy.

Kate, now turning and gripping the handle of the churn, murmured, "Oh, God, let things come right," while at the same time knowing in her heart that she couldn't have it both ways: she loved two men and sooner or later she'd have to make her choice.

8

"Darling mine, all right, all right, don't get upset. I can play any game you want. The only thing, sooner or later it's bound to come out that I've bought the farm. Anyway, forget about that for the moment. Tell me more about your father." They were sitting close together by the side of the little table in the cottage, and she said, "I've told you all I know" – she put her hand up and touched his cheek – "except" – she smiled now – "when I looked at his big stomach, I thought, Ben must never grow like that."

"Oh, my dear." He laughed, lowered his head and bobbed hers gently with it; and now, their arms about each other, they kissed once more. And after a moment, looking into her face, he said, "You know, it would have been a solution if you had gone with him, I could have then sailed over to France and there our courting could have been open for all the world to witness, except that your father would likely have had you posing for his artist friends."

"Oh, Ben."

"Don't say 'Oh, Ben' in that deprecating way. You've got to change your way of thinking about Miss Kate Roystan, and if you don't, you're going to be in for a hard time when you become Mrs Fraser Hamilton, for then I shall dress you as you should be dressed."

"Indeed! Is my dress so frumpish now that it offends your eye, sir?" She assumed an indignant pose, and he answering in the same vein said, "I would not say frumpish, madam. The cloth" – he fingered the sleeve of her print dress – "is good honest homespun, but it lacks colour, and texture. You should always be dressed in velvet or cords in the daytime, silk or satin in the evening, never taffeta."

Looking at him critically now, she said quietly, "You seem to have had a lot of experience."

"Well, let's say I've never refused an invitation to a ball." Then his face sobering, he said, "There was a period when I felt I had just been released from prison and was tasting life for the first time: I rode, I danced, I drank, until" – he shrugged his shoulders – "they all became stale. But nevertheless, I enjoyed that period while it lasted. And so, madam——" He again assumed a haughty manner as he ended, "I am, in a way, a connoisseur of fashion both American and English, for I spent a month in London before coming here and attended the theatres almost nightly."

"And so, sir, you would like me to dress like an actress?"

"Not necessarily, madam. No, not necessarily."

"May I enlighten you on one point, sir?"

"You may, madam."

"It is just this: I shall dress the way I like, in what colour I like, in what material I care to choose. If my attire doesn't suit you, then I'm afraid, sir, our acquaintance is at an end." Even as she said the last words she shuddered inwardly that she should even joke about such a possibility.

She was again in his arms, and now he was laughing into her face, saying, "Woman of strong will, when I get you into my tepee, I shall skin your hide for you."

Laughing she said, "What is a tepee?"

"An Indian tent."

"I should like to see America."

"You could come any time, madam, any time. We could leave this very night."

"And what about the house you have bought?"

"Oh, that could be sold again."

"Oh, Ben. Ben." Her voice was low, her face sad now as she said, "There are mountains of obstacles between us and. . . ."

"There may be mountains and there are obstacles, but they are not between us. Nothing is between us. We're together on one side, your family on the other. But, remember this, my dear, there is nothing between us."

"Ben. Ben. I can hardly believe this is true. When I ride away I feel that it is for the last time, or when I am coming over here, I dread that you will have gone."

"Don't be silly. That is foolish talk. I'll never go anywhere without you. During all my life I've had to do a lot of thinking and I know now I am much older than my years and so I can say assuredly. . . ."

"That is another thing. I . . . I am older than you . . . fifteen months."

"Terrible! isn't it?"

"Some people would say so."

"Some people, some people. You know, that is something I must tell you: I never take much notice of what people say; I've got to see a thing happening before I can believe it. That's why when I read history I always question it, because it's been written by somebody who wasn't there, who has taken the facts from somebody else who has read about it and who wasn't there, and you know there's no one in the world who can repeat with their lips the story that they've heard through their ears. Because once it gets into here" – he tapped his forehead – "one's particular train of thought which depends much on one's upbringing takes hold of what it hears and presents it through the lips as the eyes of your particular type of imagination see it."

Her face was serious now as she said quietly, "Perhaps so. But do you believe what your grandmother told you happened at Rooklands Farm?"

He dropped his arms from her now and rose from the chair, saying slowly, "Yes, yes, I do believe that, every word, and that fact worries me and makes nonsense, I suppose, of what I've just said, at least in part." He came back quietly with the last four words, repeating, "At least in part, because there is so much mischief caused in the world by one person transposing another's thoughts through their own individual channels." He spread out his hands now and on a lighter tone said, "I had the idea a few years ago when I was nineteen that the world needed changing, and that I could do it by starting a kind of school and calling it The Academy of Reason and in it teaching nothing that couldn't be proved. But after talking it over with an old scholar, who laughingly said, 'Do that, it'll get rid of God,' I recognized my thinking was merely part of the growing pains of youth. Yet there are always germs left over from the thoughts of youth, good germs.... Why are you smiling like that?"

"I like to hear you talk. It's so different from what I've been used to: Was there too much cinnamon in the cake? Next week all the downstairs curtains must be washed. I must hurry up and finish the tapestry for that chair, it's almost threadbare. That's inside the house, and much much more. Outside: The number of sheep going to market. Should they send them into Hexham or Newcastle? Weighing up the cost of paying a drover to drive them into the city against taking them in themselves to Hexham. That problem comes up every year. Should they extend the herd? It would mean buying more land. And the latest excitement is starting a turkey farm. Strangely, I haven't minded it up till now, although I did look forward to Hugh coming home and hearing his tales of the city and its doings. And now, having said all that, I ... I feel ashamed, because we've all been brought up in a wonderful home life, and I'm ashamed that I should now look upon it as tedium. Yet, since the day I first stepped into this cottage my way of thinking and looking at things has changed."

"Mine too. But do you know what you have just described appears to me as the ideal life, and a pattern I'd like to follow from now on. And I'd like nothing better at this moment than to ride back with you and talk about the everyday things that you've just described with your menfolk." He paused; then, his voice low, he said, "It's got to come. Sooner or later, it's got to come."

"But not yet, not yet. You have no idea of the feeling."

"I have. I can imagine it."

She screwed up her eyes for a moment and brought her teeth tight down on her lower lip in a voiceless denial of his statement, and he persisted, "Believe me, Kate, I know exactly how your father will react."

"You don't!" Her voice was loud now. "You don't, Ben. His hate of the Bannamans does not lie under the surface, it's there on top for all to see. The whole countryside knows how he feels, and he still talks about it to anyone who will listen. The agony of the four days in that barn seared...."

"Don't. Don't." He had placed his hand gently over her mouth. "It's a kind of torture to me to think about that. Anyway, for the time being, they need know nothing about my identity. I am that fella from the Americas." He smiled. "That's how one gentleman in the Allendale Hotel addressed me the other day. 'You the fella from the Americas?' he said. Well, that's all I am for the time being, so take me down soon to meet them ... please Kate."

"Give me another week or so."

"But why, my dear? What do you hope to accomplish in that time? My name will still be Hamilton then."

"I'll ... I'll break the ice. I'll start talking about you, singing your praises, expounding your virtues."

"Oh, my! Then we are doomed to failure. Anyway, you've got to take into account their reaction when they find out I've bought this house."

"Yes, I've thought of that. Have you told Charles?"

"Only yesterday."

"What was his reaction?"

"Amazement. He said it's a bad house and he only wished I had consulted him before taking the step."

"And he's right."

"Well, I'll promise you one thing. If I ever feel I can't cleanse it, I'll burn it down. But in the back of my mind I can see it as a thriving farm once more, something like your father's. I passed your home yesterday."

"You did?"

"Yes."

"Oh, you shouldn't."

"Why? Everybody knows I am gathering details of the villages and hamlets around here. Look." He pointed to the shelf. One part held what looked like a ledger and a small stack of papers, and he said, "I'm putting it all together, it makes quite a history."

"You're writing about the Bannamans?"

"Yes, all about the Bannamans. And the Fountains. You see, my grandmother's name was Fountain. I took a coach ride last week to her birthplace, almost on the borders of Scotland. I found the house where she was born, but there was no living relation left. Another family had apparently lived there for thirty years. Anyway—" He now took her face between his hands and ended softly, "It'll be something to pass down to our children."

He was greatly perturbed when he saw the tears spurt from her eyes as she made a sound that was almost a groan before falling against him.

When she returned the yard was empty, and as she led her horse to the stables, she noticed there was no one in the byres either. It wasn't until she had unsaddled the animal and rubbed him down that the unusual quiet of the yard caught her attention, for there was always one or the other of the men to be seen somewhere about. It was as she was going to the grain store for feed that she saw Terry. He was coming from the barn, and she said, "Where's everyone?"

He thumbed towards the house, saying, "Indoors. Lads have got their boots off."

The lads had their boots off. That meant, for some reason or other, there was a meeting other than in the kitchen, because none of them was allowed through into the house with his working boots on, except her father.

She looked towards the kitchen door. And yes, there they were, three pairs of boots lying haphazardly near the foot-scraper.

What now? It couldn't be a visitor, for there was no sign of a horse or carriage. Had they found out? She felt a cold sweat on her brow as Terry said, "Mr Bentley come. His horse was in a lather. I put it in the bottom stable." He thumbed again. And she smiled at him now in relief, saying, "Oh, I must go and see what it's all about then."

"I could tell you from here."

"You could?"

There was a broad grin on Terry's face as he emitted one word, "Courtin'."

She flicked her hand at him, returned his smile, then saying, "See to Ranger's feed, will you?" she walked quickly across the yard. Courting? That meant he had come to see her father to ask for Florrie's hand. Oh, she was pleased, pleased for Florrie.

As she entered the kitchen she heard the hubbub in the hall, and when she went to open the far door she paused at the sound of high laughter and the chatter of voices.

The family were all gathered in the hall and they did not notice her entry, for they were looking through the open door. But when Mary Ellen caught sight of her, she cried, "Oh! here's Kate. Kate, come and hear the good news."

She was at the front door now looking with the rest of them to where Florrie and Charles Bentley were walking sedately side by side across the gravelled drive, making their way to the yard and the stables.

It was Hal who turned to her, saying, "Well, what do you think of that? He came and asked me for her hand." He put his head back and laughed. "All right and proper. Well, she's set, and well at that. 'Twill be you next," he said, bringing Maggie a wallop on the buttocks. "But who'll come for your hand, Richard Taggart or Barney Pilkton?"

Before Maggie could answer, Gabriel said, "No, Dad; it'll be Daffy Tull, and his twelve cats. It's said he's looking for a wife. The fourth is it, or the fifth?"

He turned and ran as Maggie made a dive for him. And in the hubbub as they made their way towards the kitchen, Hal's voice rose above the rest, saying, "Engagement party in the barn? We're having no such do in the barn, 'tis here in the house it'll be held. Do you hear what I say, Mrs Roystan?"

"I heard, Mr Roystan, and I'll remind you that we can get twice as many in the barn as in the sitting-room, dining-room, and hall combined."

"Who wants twice as many? ... Hello, there, lass." It was as if he had just noticed Kate, but his next words, as he held open the door for her, denied the assumption, for with an enquiry in his voice he said, "Enjoy your ride, lass?"

"Yes, Dad, I enjoyed it very much."

He let the door swing behind him before continuing, "Aye, well, that's what rides are for I suppose. Well now, let's all get back to work, for if I've got to pay for a wedding, it's got to be earned somehow."

"Oh, Hal." Mary Ellen shook her head at him, and he, shaking his head back at her and mimicking her voice, said, "Oh Mary Ellen." Then he went out, accompanied by his sons, and they were all laughing.

Mary Ellen now placed her hands on the table and let out a long drawn sigh and, looking towards the delph rack, as if into space, she said softly, "Isn't it lovely for her, to get a man like Charles?"

"Because he's related to Lord Redman?"

"No, miss, not because of that." She had turned sharply on Maggie now. "But at the same time it's nothing to be despised or sneered about."

"I wasn't sneering."

"But you were pretty near it. Anyway, when we're on, it's about time you were making your mind up who you're going to settle with. I hope it isn't Barney Pilkton, 'cos his mouth will swallow his head one of these days."

"Perhaps you would have me marry Daffy Tull just to get rid of me?"

"Don't be silly, girl."

"I'm not being silly, Mam. But I feel the odd man out hereabouts." She now turned her infuriated gaze on Kate. "I'm apparently of no interest to anybody. I haven't been discovered by a famous father, nor do I possess a secret friend up in the hills."

"*Maggie!*" Mary Ellen's voice was a yell, but Kate put in quietly, "It's all right. It's all right." And returning Maggie's look now, she said, "We can't all be blessed with good looks, so whoever doles out the compensations has had me in mind lately." And with this she left the kitchen, closing the door none too gently behind her.

Mary Ellen, leaning across the table, now cried at her daughter, "She wasn't blessed with good looks, but you are. But what you're not blessed with, Maggie Roystan, is a kindly disposition, and I'm tellin' you, it'll bring you no good. And when I'm on, I'll tell you this, that neither of those fellows you're tipping the wink at will provide you with much more than shoe leather. Have sense, girl. If you're going to cock your hat, cock it at somebody worthwhile. There, that's out. I should have made it plain to you afore."

"Yes, you should, Mam, and I would have known where I stood. But I know now. You never have cared for me like you have for the others. It's been Kate this, Kate that, or dear Florrie, gentle Florrie. But I've never heard you say a word in my praise."

"No, because you were too keen to praise yourself."

"You don't like me, do you?"

"Oh, girl, girl." Mary Ellen's voice softened and, now going swiftly round the table, she held out her arms. But Maggie would have none of it. She almost slapped her mother's hands away saying, "I don't want any of your left-overs, Mam. I can take care of meself. You see to your dear Kate and give her your blessing when she trots over the hills to her fancy man."

The slap that caught her fully across the face almost knocked her back towards the settle, and there was a dead silence between them for a moment, until Maggie, holding her head to the side, one hand covering her cheek and the tears now running down her face, turned and fled from the kitchen, leaving Mary Ellen, her arms tight about herself, her fingers clawing at her oxters, muttering, "My God! My God!"

She did not recognize that she was suffering no recrimination for striking her daughter but was agonizing over the fact that anyone should think Kate had a fancy man. But if Maggie could say this, others would think it, because her regular journeys up into the hills wouldn't have gone unnoticed: there were eyes behind hedges and drystone walls. She would have to speak to Kate. Yes, she would, and firmly.

9

But before Mary Ellen spoke to Kate, she spoke to Hal. "I'm worried," she said. "Our Kate'll get her name up if she's not careful."

"Get her name up? What about?"

"I had words with our Maggie this afternoon. She's turned against Kate of late. I don't know why. Well, yes, I do. 'Tis this American fellow. I saw she had her eye on him that first day in the hotel dining-room, and now she's calling him Kate's fancy man."

"*What?*"

"That's what she's saying. That's what she said, Kate's going over the hills to see her fancy man. Now if she's saying that, there'll be others who'll have seen her out on her rides and going in the same direction. 'Tisn't right that she should go off visiting him. He should be coming here and visiting her if he thinks so much of their friendship, as she calls it."

Hal stared at her now, saying, "Do you think it's something more?"

"Could well be. 'Cos any man with a spark of intelligence would find Kate good company. And that would be the least of her attractions, because once she starts talking you forget about her plainness. In fact...."

"Aye, in fact what?"

"Well, sometimes she doesn't appear plain at all."

"You're learning, woman, you're learning. Anyway, there's got to be change one way or t'other. She's got to stop her traipsing for her own sake, or he's got to take on the journey this way. Why he hasn't done it afore has puzzled me, I might as well tell you. So now you go on along to her room there and sort things out." ...

A few minutes later Mary Ellen knocked gently on Kate's door. She had done this for some time now, yet she never knocked on Maggie's or Florrie's door, nor yet on her sons'. However, she always made herself known with her voice before she entered their rooms, that was, since the day a few years ago when she had left Tom and John's room with a red face, when John had cried at her, "Aw, look Mam, I'm out of nappies, and I feel bare even in me long clothes."

When Kate said, "Come in," she entered, saying, "Not in bed yet?"

"No, I was reading a bit."

"You won't do your eyes any good reading in a single candle light."

They looked at each other. Kate had on a long grey wollen gown over a blue cotton nightdress. Her straight black hair was hanging in two long plaits over her shoulders, the tapered ends reaching her waist. Her face in the candlelight looked warm and soft, and the sight of her thus made Mary Ellen think, She's worth any man's love.

"Something wrong, Mam?"

"It's how you look at it, lass." Mary Ellen sat down on the edge of the bed and with the first finger of her right hand she began to scrape the inside of the thumb nail on her left hand, while concentrating her gaze on it; the action had become a habit over the years and portrayed an inner anxiety. After losing her two youngest children, she had sat doing this for hours on end.

Looking at the picking finger, Kate said quietly, "What is it, Mam?"

"'Tis about your rides out, lass. You're going to get yourself talked about."

"How?" The syllable was sharp and brought Mary Ellen's attention from her fingers to Kate's face, and now her voice low and her words rapid, she said, "People have tongues and eyes. They're linking your name with this fellow." She had no proof of this, but she knew it could happen, so she felt no compunction in enlarging on it, saying, "You'll soon be the talk of the place. Every week, regular as clockwork, going across there. Why can't he come across here?"

"Because I wouldn't let him, because you would have all put two and two together and made half a dozen out of it. Mam" – she put her hand out and gripped Mary Ellen's knee – "I asked you a little while ago to have patience."

"I've had patience, lass, and so has your dad, but it's running out. We were worried sick inside ourselves, about . . . about him . . . Roddy, your father coming. Then we knew relief after how you took him. But now, the night with Maggie. . . ." She bowed her head, and Kate came back quickly, "Oh, Maggie. Maggie's tongue."

"Aw, lass, I don't want you to be hurt again."

"I won't be, Mam. There's only two people in the world can hurt me now and they are you and Dad."

Mary Ellen screwed up her face and stared at her daughter before she said, "What about him, your friend?"

"He'll never hurt me."

"You seem very sure of that."

"I am, very sure."

Mary Ellen got to her feet, saying warily now, "Aye, well, the world's changin'. In my time there was no such thing as a friendship with a man. It was either one or the other, something or nothing."

"Good-night, Mam." Kate leaned forward and kissed her mother, but Mary Ellen did not return the kiss. Turning away slowly, she said dully, "Good-night, lass."

Kate now went to the door and gently slid in the bolt. The only one who was likely to visit her at this hour would be Florrie. She didn't want to talk to Florrie tonight. Returning to the bed, she dropped on to her knees and, burying her face in her hands, she prayed: Show me what to do. And in the silence that seemed to envelop her she waited, and after some minutes, when the answer came into her mind, she rose from her knees, snuffed out the candle and got into bed.

The answer had been simple: there was no need for them to know who he was. His name was Benedict Fraser Hamilton. She could marry him tomorrow and be Mrs Fraser Hamilton. The Bannamans were all dead and gone, all of them that is except the grandmother. She was in America and a very old lady and no threat. She had been silly to worry. The day after tomorrow she would go up there and fetch him home.

She rode out on the Thursday and was late coming back. They were finishing the meal when she walked into the dining room, and they all turned and looked towards her. Her face was flushed, her eyes were bright. She had taken off her hat and her hair looked tousled. Going up to the table, she looked at her mother and said, "I'm ... I'm sorry I'm late." And Mary Ellen, looking up into her face, said quietly, "I put the pie back into the oven."

"I'm ... I'm not hungry. I'll just have some bread and cheese.... Mam."

"Yes, lass?"

"Would ... would it be all right if my friend came to tea on Sunday?"

The room was enveloped in silence, until Mary Ellen said, "Certainly, lass, certainly. He'll be welcome."

She now looked towards Hal and she said, one word, "Dad?"

Hal, swallowing the remnants of a mouthful of food, covered his surprise by being jovial. "Well, I don't know. Will he bring his own bait?"

The men all laughed, and Florrie laughed, only Maggie's face was straight. Then Hal said, "Whoever you bring here, lass, is welcome."

"Thanks, Dad." She sat down now at her place at the table, and when John handed her the platter with the remains of a crusty loaf on it, he looked into her eyes and smiled.

It was Maggie who next spoke, "I can't wait," she said flatly. And Florrie ever quick to pour oil on troubled waters piped in brightly, "Nor can I, Kate. Charles says he's a splendid fellow and very intelligent, being widely travelled."

"Oh, my godfathers!" Gabriel now was pretending to choke, and he said, "I'll stay in the cow byres, and you two better keep me company" – he nodded at his elder brothers – "because we'd never be able to pass ourselves."

He was smiling at Kate as he finished, and she, coming back at him said, "Oh, don't worry, Gabriel, he's met a lot of idiots in his time. He'll understand that you're not responsible for your low mentality. One cannot help how one is born."

This retort brought laughter again, yet it wasn't whole-hearted. Their Kate was different somehow. No one of them could put his finger on it. Perhaps John came nearer to it as he looked at her, thinking, She's not aware of herself any more. It's as if her looks and size no longer matter to her. Or perhaps she's put a true value on them. Whatever it is, she's changed and is happier. That's all that matters.

10

Kate did not ride out to meet her friend on the Sunday afternoon. He was to arrive at three o'clock and the house had been agog since early morning; in fact, it could be said it had been agog for the past two days, because Mary Ellen had made as much preparation for Kate's friend's visit as she had for Kate's father.

The chores in the farmyard had been got through early and the men were in their Sunday best, as were Mary Ellen and the girls. But Maggie had added an extra touch: she was wearing a brown velvet band around her neck with a tiny locket dangling from the middle of it, and in her hair, which had been arranged in loose rolls on the top of her head, she had inserted a matching bow, and she brought with her a strong aroma of lavender water. Kate's attire in comparison looked utterly plain, yet her grey poplin sat on her figure as if moulded to it. And evidently she had been conscious of this, for she placed a pale blue sash high up on her waist below her breasts.

The men were in the sitting-room, all definitely ill at ease. Even Gabriel was finding nothing funny to say at the moment. And when, just on three o'clock, Mary Ellen, Florrie, and Maggie entered the room, Hal stopped his pacing up and down between the windows and, turning to Mary Ellen, said, "Three o'clock, she said, didn't she? Well, where is he?"

"It's only ten to."

"Where's she?"

"She's in the hall. And sit yourself down and try to act as if it was an everyday occasion."

"Huh!" The quiet exclamation from Maggie brought her mother's eyes sharply on her, but she said nothing. And now, turning her attention to her eldest sons, she said, "You two are sitting there like stuffed dummies. Why can't you read the newspaper?"

"You forget they don't know how to read, Mam." Gabriel's revival to lightness caused a little titter.

Then a flurry of movement affected everybody in the room as Hal jerked himself round from the windows, saying, "Here he comes." ...

Kate walked out of the front door and across the gravel to where Ben was dismounting, and, as if it hadn't been arranged, Terry ambled up and took the visitor's horse, saying, "I'll see to him, sir."

As Terry led the horse away, Kate and Ben faced each other for a moment; then in an undertone, he said, "How's things going?"

"All very stiff and proper. They're sitting in there as if for a church meeting. Now Ben" – her voice changed, dropping low – "you'll be careful, won't you?"

"I'll be careful. I am one Benedict Fraser Hamilton. I had forebears by the name of Fountain, which," he added, "is perfectly true. I shall not mention having bought Rooklands Farm. But what I shall do before I leave is to ask your father for your hand in marriage."

"Oh, Ben. I'm ... I'm quaking inside."

Ben bent his head towards her, saying in an undertone now, "That is a very good lead up to a conversation. I understand there's a sect in Allendale who go under that name."

"Don't joke."

They were walking towards the front door now, as he said, "I'm as nervous as you."

She cast a quick glance at him, saying, "Really?"

"Yes" – his voice was serious now – "because I feel I'm here under false pretences. If I had my way I would...."

"*Please, please, Ben.*"

"All right, all right, as we arranged." He smiled at her now. And then they in the hall, and there were Mary Ellen and Hal coming towards them, and Kate found herself chattering, as Maggie or any self-conscious girl would have done, saying, "You've already met my mother and father, but ... but this is Mr Hamilton."

"Mr Hamilton, is it?" Hal's hand was extended, and Ben shook it, saying, "I'm very pleased to make your better acquaintance, Mr Roystan. And ... and yours too, Mrs Roystan." He was now shaking hands with Mary Ellen who didn't speak, merely inclined her head and watched as he looked about him and then won her over immediately by saying, "What a fine hall."

Now she said, "Yes, yes, it is a nice hall. Will ... will you come and meet my family?"

"It will be a pleasure."

The men were standing when they entered the drawing-room, only Maggie and Florrie remained seated, as they had been taught to do by the dame at the school. Ladies never rise at the entry of gentlemen, had been her advice.

It was Mary Ellen who was making the introductions: "These are my eldest sons, John and Tom," she said.

"How do you do?" Ben held out his hand, and it was shaken vigorously by the twins.

"And this is my youngest son, Gabriel." And then she made a joke that broke the formality. "He was named after an angel," she said, "but I felt it was a mistake from the beginning, and time and again I've been proved right."

"Aw, Mam. Mam." Gabriel was laughing at the visitor, and Ben was laughing at him as he said, "Well, the fallen angel often comes out on top. But you know what they say, God is good with advice but the devil pays in cash."

Amid the laughter, Hal said, "Well, I've never heard that afore. Anyway, say hello to my two girls here, and you've seen them afore an' all, then settle down and make yourself at home."

As Ben bowed, first towards Florrie, and then towards Maggie, saying each time, "My pleasure. My pleasure," they inclined their head towards him, and Maggie's smile was sweet and her eyes lingered on him, and he appraised her for a moment before turning to Hal and saying, "You have a very fine family."

"Aye, well, they're not bad. Are you from a big family?"

"No, unfortunately...." He had only just stopped himself from saying, "fortunately", and went on, "I was the only one."

"They tell me you are doing a kind of book on this part of the country. Were your forebears from here?"

"Yes, hereabouts."

"What name?"

"By the name of Fountain."

"Fountain." Hal screwed up his eyes as if trying to recollect the name, and he said, "I seemed to remember that name, but there's no Fountains hereabouts. Horse troughs but no fountains."

There were a number of groans and "Oh, Dad," from around the room. And now he cried at them, "Well, I'm allowed to have a joke. And I've got Mr Hamilton laughing, if not you lot. By the way, have we got to call you Mr Hamilton?"

"I'd rather you called me Ben."

"Short for what?"

"Benjamin."

"I'm in good company." They turned and looked at Gabriel now, and he, grinning, said, "Another one from the Bible."

During all this time, Kate had been sitting opposite to Maggie and Florrie. She had her hands folded on her lap and it wasn't evident that her nails were pressing into her flesh. She kept telling herself that nothing could happen, he would make no slips. The name Bannaman would not be mentioned, at least not by him. Yet, she could not help but feel uneasy, and she kept looking at Hal. If he only knew who the visitor really was, his anger could be such that he would do something terrible, were her thoughts.

"What is your line of business?" It was Tom speaking now, and Ben said, "My father's business was coach-building, a firm owned by his father. My father died before my grandfather, who eventually sold out. I stayed on for a time with the company, but my heart wasn't in it. I . . . I decided to travel a bit before settling down to another occupation."

"What kind of occupation?"

He turned to Hal and shrugged his shoulder before he said, "Quite candidly, I haven't as yet made up my mind. It would be very nice to say farming, but I know nothing whatever about farming. It may be writing, I don't know yet."

"Well—" Hal now hunched his shoulders, saying, "if you're in a position to keep yourself without working, well and good. Of course, it won't cost you much up there in the wilds, in that but and ben. How did you last out the winter?"

"I really don't know. Sometimes I didn't think I would make it."

"Then why did you stay?" asked Hal bluntly.

Ben glanced towards Kate. Her face looked anxious. Then he lowered his head before he said, "It's a long story, but I went through a very traumatic experience some time ago, and I needed a period of recuperation, to be on my own and . . . well, work things out. Do you know what I mean?"

Hal didn't really know what the fellow meant. One thing he did know, he was puzzled why this man who talked and acted like an educated gentleman was living under conditions that a drover would scorn. There was something here that wanted sorting out. It was just as well that Kate and he were merely friends, for a bloke with no livelihood would be no good to her. And here they had been for the past two days, skiting from one end of the house and the land to the other, as if getting ready for a visit from the lord of the manor. And here was a fellow without a job, living practically rough, yet. . . . Wait a minute. He had said, living practically rough. Look how he was dressed. You didn't buy that kind of suit in Allendale or Hexham. And he had a gold chain hanging across his waistcoat, likely a similar quality watch on the end of it. And his boots, they were spanking leather. There was something fishy here. He was a good-looking bloke altogether. He was the kind of fellow, he imagined, that could get any woman he set his mind to. So why this friendship talk with their Kate? Not that Kate wasn't worth the best. He'd have to get to the bottom of it or he wouldn't be able to sleep the night.

He got to the bottom of it sooner than he expected.

When Annie unceremoniously pushed open the sitting-room door and said in no small voice, "The tea's ready," Mary Ellen, rising quickly to her feet, said, "Well, that's something we're all ready for and I'm sure you could do with a cup, Mr Hamilton."

"He said to call him Ben." Hal was getting to his feet, and he cast a sidelong glance at Kate saying, "That's right, isn't it? We are to call him Ben?"

When she returned his glance but said nothing, he thought to himself, She's worried, she's on edge.

On entering the dining-room, Ben once again paused and looked around him, saying now, "I suppose it's very bad manners of me, but these are such lovely rooms, and so tastefully furnished."

Hal drew in a long breath. The fellow was a little too polite for his fancy, but, making light of it, he looked at Mary Ellen, saying, "Be on your guard, lass, he's after something." Whereupon Ben, looking at

340

Mary Ellen, answered quietly, "He's quite right, ma'am, I am. And I'll come to that shortly."

The whole family paused and turned their full attention on him and he let his gaze slip over them, and when it came to rest once again on Mary Ellen, he said, still quietly, "But what I would like now is that promised cup of tea and some of the delectable eatables." And he indicated the table with the movement of his hand. Then a moment later, seeing that Kate was about to sit next to him, he held the chair out for her, and when she was seated, she lowered her gaze for a moment, thinking. They won't understand him. He doesn't speak their language ... delectable eatables. And his courtesy will be foreign to them. Even this part of it is not going to work out.

But as the meal progressed it seemed that she could be wrong, for he caught their attention with his description of the vast areas outside the towns of Houston and Galveston. Even as she listened to him she could see the vast stretches of country, much of it inhabited by Indian tribes with names like Comanches, Kiowas, Apaches, Cheyennes, and Arapahoes. And when Gabriel asked if it was true that the Indians painted themselves and raided homesteads and villages, he touched on it lightly, out of consideration, she thought, for the women present, saying now, "The Rangers have things pretty much under control." Then on Gabriel's further enquiry he described the type of men who became Rangers.

"Have you ever ridden out after Indians?" Tom was smiling at him, and he returned his smile with a grimace as he said, "Me ride out after Indians! More like running the other way. I'm a peaceful man, which is only another name for a coward." The men laughed. All except Hal, who, looking down the table from under his brows, thought again, he's too smooth. He's too clever, making out he takes to his heels when faced with danger. He didn't have that impression at all of the fellow, not with that shaped jaw and eyes as black as chiselled coal....

The meal lasted for nearly an hour. Three times Annie rose from the table and refilled the big brown teapot and the silver hot water jug. The plates that had held slices of pork and ham, meat pies, fruit pies, conserve tarts, seed cake, rice loaf, and an outsize loaf, were almost denuded now. And the atmosphere was relaxed: even Maggie was showing her better side, and had been for some time now, putting quite intelligent questions to the guest, and listening most attentively to his answers, her long lashed lids flapping, as Annie said later, like aspens in the wind.

Maggie's play was not lost on Kate, and she guessed what was in her mind, that if she herself was merely a friend of Ben's, there was every chance of someone else becoming closer to him, and why not her? Indeed, why not her? For was she not pretty and vivacious? And she wondered what Maggie's reaction would be when Ben stated the reason for his visit here today. And she hadn't to wait much longer.

It began with Hal saying, "Well, now, here's one who must get out of his Sunday togs and continue the business of the day. And that goes for you three weaklings an' all." He nodded towards his sons. "And what about you, eh?" He was now addressing Ben. "Would you like to come along with us, and see how things are run on a farm?"

"I should indeed. Thank you very much."

Hal made as if to rise, then sat back, saying, "But before we go about our several businesses, there was something you were going to ask of us. Well, would you like to ask it now; or is it a private matter?"

Ben did not answer for a moment, but, turning towards Kate, he took her hand and, lifting it up onto the white table cloth, he held it there, saying quietly now, "It was to be a private matter, yet it concerns all your family, because I hope to take Kate" – he glanced at Kate's almost white face now – "away from you all. I've asked her to marry me, and she has done me the honour of accepting. Now all I want is your blessing." He had not said, consent.

There was not a murmur or a movement around the table, for nothing he could have said would have surprised them more. Here was this fellow, a foreigner plainly from the way he talked, and a bit dandified into the bargain, but it came over more in his manner, like the way he was holding Kate's hand now in front of them all, not on the table any more, but against his chest. Then look at the difference between him and her. All right, Kate was a fine woman, none better, but sitting there, they looked like chalk and cheese: him as flat and as lean as a stripped willow, and Kate . . . well, she was a big wench, there was no doubt about it, she was a fine big wench.

It was Hal who seemingly got his breath back first, for now getting to his feet and thrusting the armchair aside, he said, "Aye, I think it should have been done in private. There are things to say, young fellow, things I want made clear, and now."

"Just as you say." Ben got to his feet. He still had hold of Kate's hand and he embarrassed the company still further by bringing it up to his cheek, the while looking down at her and saying, "Don't worry, my dear, don't worry. It's going to be all right." Then he followed Hal out of the room.

In the hall, he stood for a moment looking first one way, then the other, and saw that his host was standing outside a door at the end of a small corridor. When he joined him, Hal thrust open the door of his office and went in. He did not take a seat but, standing with his back to the desk, he began immediately, saying, "Now, mister, let's get this thing clear. You spring this thing on us, saying you are going to take Kate away. Where to, may I ask? Up into that shepherd's hut in the wilds? Kate's been used to a good home, a good upbringing. And anyway, nobody knows nowt about you. Who are you anyway?"

This, in a way, would have been the opportunity for Ben to say quietly who he was, trusting that this man would be sensible enough to let the past bury itself, and let him expiate, as it were, any residue that was left. Yet he had promised Kate, and he saw now, as she had indicated, that this man was of a fiery disposition; it would be best to tread warily with him, so he answered him quietly, saying, "I've told you who I am, sir. And as for taking Kate to the shepherd's hut, that was never my intention, even if she had consented. I happen, sir, for your information, to be a man of means. In this country I am banking with Lloyds. They have offices in London, and also in Newcastle. I give you leave to enquire into the finances I have had transferred from my home. There, I still hold shares in the coach business. I am the owner of a house of considerable style and value. My grandmother is there at the moment. I have enough money to keep myself and Kate in idleness for the rest of our lives if I so wished. But I had considered taking up residence in this country."

His manner had become stiff and formal, and it was certainly having an effect on Hal, for now, flopping down into his desk chair, he said, "If all this is true as you say, why are you living like you do? Why haven't you shown your face here afore, if you felt that way about Kate and it was not just a booky friendship, as she said?"

"To answer your latter question, Kate wished it that way. She's had an unfortunate experience as you so well know, and she was fearful of what significance you would place on our association, and she was content to let it be one of friendship. But for my part, from our first meeting, my feelings for her went beyond friendship."

"Aye, well." Hal took up a feathered pen and started stabbing the quill end into the back of a brown ledger, and he seemed at a loss for words until, his chin jerking up, he said, "But that doesn't account for a man of means, as you say you are, living rough."

"I wouldn't call it living rough! It's a sparsely furnished, but comfortable little room. It met the needs of the time, because I had come to England in ... well, I can only say, a disturbed emotional state."

"What do you exactly mean by that? I would rather you spoke plain. You been married afore?"

Ben now smiled and shook his head. "No, I can honestly say I have never been married before, nor yet have I proposed marriage to any woman until I met Kate. No, my emotional state was caused through ... well, you could say, family problems, things that had happened in the past having left repercussions."

"Aye, well, what I say is, a man can't be responsible for his people. If he's upright in himself, that's all that matters."

"I'm very pleased to hear you say that, sir, very pleased indeed."

"Aye, well, if we had to be responsible for our forebears' doings, half of us would die of shame."

Ben stared at the man. Here was another opening. If he were to say who his forebears were now, surely this man would have to eat his own words if he didn't accept him for what he was. If only he hadn't promised Kate. Almost immediately, however, he knew how right Kate had been when the man before him, his voice and mood changing, said, "Of course, like everything else there's exceptions, and bad blood can be passed down, and not only through the male as some would hold, but through the females an' all. Aye, by God! through the females an' all."

It seemed to Ben that the man must have forgotten his presence, for he sat staring down on the brown ledger. The pen had fallen from his fingers and they were spread out as if about to clutch at something. Then he sighed and lifted his head and once more they were looking at each other.

"Aye, well," Hal said, getting to his feet, "we'd better get back and put her out of her misery, although mind, I'll have something to say to her about her underhandedness in all this. By! I will. And so will her mother. But just one more thing." He stabbed his finger into Ben's shoulder. "About this taking her away: you're not thinkin' about America, are you?"

"No, not at the moment; in fact, not at all. That, I suppose, was an unfortunate phrase. Anyway, I know I could never take her away, not in one sense, for she has such deep feelings for you all, exceptionally so I would say for yourself and her mother. Her one aim in life seems never to bring you hurt."

"Aye, well, she never has. She's been a grand lass and I think of her as if she was me own. But I suppose you know she isn't. You heard about her father comin', I'll bet."

"Yes, yes I did. But strangely that incident seems only to have deepened her affection for you."

"Yes, well." He wagged his head in embarrassment, then said abruptly but with something of a grin on his face, "Come on, I've listened to your chit-chat long enough, let the others put up with it." And Ben grinned back at him, at the same time thinking, What a character. He'd fit beautifully into Galveston, especially the business side. There'd be no pulling the wool over this man's eyes.

But the mental picture created another disturbing thought: What would really be this man's reaction when he later discovered that Kate had literally pulled the wool over his eyes where he himself was concerned?

A sudden shudder passed over his lean body and there returned to him a feeling of fear such as he hadn't experienced since he was a boy: there was the overpowering figure of his mother advancing towards him, her hands outstretched as if she were about to choke him. And so strong was the feeling that it took all his will power to enable him to resume his usual poise before entering the sitting-room to face the waiting family.

11

Hal hadn't been well for the past week. The inheritance of the smelter's disease had, over the years, made itself evident, particularly during the autumn and early winter. But it hadn't until now made him take to his bed. For two full days, Mary Ellen had cosseted him with potions similar to those which old Kate would have used on this complaint. She had also rubbed his chest with goose fat and kept a hot iron oven plate at his feet. And although he wasn't much improved after the two days, he insisted on getting about and had, up till now, spent most of his time in the office which, Mary Ellen had said, could have been a smelting mill itself, so hot was the room.

All this morning he had sat pondering over his ledgers. The harvest had been anything but good – it was more than a quarter down all round on last year – so when he got his meal back from the miller he had to charge around eighteen shillings per boll for it, which worked out at almost three and six a stone in the market. And he'd had to charge as much as one and six a stone for his potatoes, which made it difficult to sell them. Everything else in proportion was up in price. What the fowl would bring today he didn't know. But as was usual, he had instructed the boys to wait and see the state of the market before pricing the butter and eggs.

Gabriel and Tom had driven the goods into market this morning, and only Kate and Florrie had gone with them. Florrie was to meet Charles in Hexham and ride back with him; he had been invited to supper. Kate was to see Ben, also in Hexham, so she had said, and she was to invite him, too, back to supper. However, Mary Ellen was doubtful of his accepting the invitation: to her mind, there was something strange about this match, because for the last fortnight he hadn't called at the house; instead, Kate had ridden out to him. Now that wasn't right, that a woman should ride out to a man as often as she did. There was something about the whole affair she couldn't put her finger on.

She looked towards Hal. He was sitting happed up with a big shawl to the side of the fire; she herself, was sitting as far from it as she could get. The room wasn't all that big and the fire was enormous. She was sweating and her fingers were sticking to her work. She was in the process of embroidering a sun bonnet; she was sewing a small frill round the edge of the neck flap. It was a special bonnet, for it was to go into Florrie's trunk. Not that she would be in need of many bonnets when she married Charles. But nevertheless, he was a farmer and she might sometime want to go out into the fields and help with the hay. She was happy for Florrie. That was a good match, she would never want. . . . Nor would Kate either by the sound of it. A man of means, Hal said he was, big means. So she wouldn't need a sun bonnet, nor a shawl spun from their own wheel.

"What about Maggie?"

The question came at her and brought with it a feeling of irritation. Oh, Maggie was likely to fall between two, three, or four stools. Maggie was a flibbertigibbet at heart, she was sorry to say. Not content with two on her tail now, she had plumped for taking the victuals over to the Bostons this morning, because John had said Andrew was home.

Andrew Boston, like Hugh, was going in for law. Hugh had been home last week-end, and while teasing Maggie and saying that all the lads in Newcastle knew of her, he happened to mention that Andrew Boston had been asking after her. This had been in the way of a joke, because Andrew had been courting Lily Quale on and off since they were children, at least it had seemed like courting, but she had never got him up to the scratch of an engagement. And so it was a family joke: they would say, "As long as Andrew Boston's courtship." But there, this morning hadn't Maggie proffered to take the weekly victuals to the little manor? Killing two birds with one stone, as she put it, because she wanted to take Betty some embroidery threads. So keen had she been to go that she herself had harnessed up the horse and trap, which had almost elicited a sarcastic quip from Gabriel – a look from her having warned him just in time – for it was well-known in the family that Maggie didn't like outside work at all, although she was quite good in the house.

"What did you say?" Mary Ellen leant forward, and Hal, his voice almost a croak, said, "I . . . I said, the house won't be the same with only Maggie left in it."

"Oh, there's almost a year to go, at least for Florrie. But if Maggie makes up her mind, it could be the morrow. You know Maggie."

They had both refrained from mentioning Kate's future, yet they each knew that it was in the forefront of the other's mind.

When he coughed a harsh chest-racking cough, she said, "I'll get you something hot." And he protested, waving his hand at her until he got his breath back and then he said, "I'm sick of hot drinks. I'll have some small beer."

"Not a drop of rum?"

"Woman, I said small beer. I want something thin to run down me gullet."

"All right. All right" – she nodded – "you'll get something thin to run down your gullet, but it's hot stuff you want inside of you, not cold. Being you, though, you know best, don't you?"

"Aye, I do. And get on with it."

After she had left the room, he sat grinning quietly to himself for a moment. Then his face took on a sober expression mirroring his thoughts: he had never been frightened about himself before, but this last was a bad dose. He had seen men die of the smelter's disease and in their young days, too. So he had considered he had been lucky to have got out of the mill when he did. But apparently it hadn't been soon enough. Then of course, the stab wound he'd had in his ribs from either Bannaman or his thug hadn't helped. From time to time he had a pain there that he didn't let on about.

Deep inside, he was angry at his state of health. Here he was, not yet fifty, and not looking anywhere near that age and most of the time able to work like a man still in his twenties, yet inside, there was this rotting. But anyway, he comforted himself now, he had got this far over the hump: if the smelt was going to kill you, it usually did so in your thirties; once you got over that it became more like a yearly visitation and an irritation. Look at Bob Hancock, turned eighty. He had been coughing for the last forty years. And Peter McIllroy. He was well into his sixties, and he had only been left the mine these ten years or so, and he was still going strong.

He sat dwelling on the survivors, willing himself not to recall the names of those who hadn't survived when the door opened and John came in in his stockinged feet, hunching his shoulders, saying, "By! this is where I'd like to be the day. How are you feeling?"

"All right. If it wasn't for your damn mother, I'd be outside. Coddling, coddling, she never stops."

"Yes, that's where you should be." John stood nodding down at him. "Swinging the lead, that's all you're doing. Anything for an easy life. Cough, hawk, and spit, just to show you're bad."

"Look out, you, I've still got enough strength in me hand to land you one."

"Aye. Well" – John's voice became serious now – "you want to hang on to it, your strength, and not be so damned stubborn. And get it into your head that the place is not going to drop to bits if you don't show your face in the yard every morning at five o'clock. There's four of us out there, and if we can't manage now, we never will."

"Oh, you think you can manage on your own, do you? You want me stuck in the corner with a pipe in me mouth, jabbering?"

"Oh, I can see the day. Yes, I can see it coming." John was smiling now. And when Mary Ellen entered the room he turned to her and said, "You know what he's telling me here?"

"No, what now?"

"He says he's fed up with work outside and he's going to sit in the corner with a pipe in his mouth."

They exchanged glances, then laughed; but Hal said nothing, just jerked his chin upwards and extended his hands for the mug of beer, and he was just about to take a drink of it when a voice was heard calling, "Mam! Mam!" And he looked at Mary Ellen and she at him, saying, "That's our Maggie. She's back early."

At this John said, "Likely she's raced home to tell us she's hooked Andrew."

"Don't be silly." Mary Ellen went to open the door, but it was almost pulled out of her hand, and there stood Maggie, her face red, her eyes bright, her breath coming quickly.

"What's the matter? What's happened?"

"Come here a minute, I want to tell you something."

"If you've anything to tell, lass, I'm here an' all. What is it?"

Maggie moved a step until she could see her father, and her mouth opened twice before she said, "I'd better tell Mam first."

"Come in here." His voice sounded like a rusty bark, and almost apprehensively now, Maggie glanced at her mother, then sidled into the room.

"Well, what news have you got that's of such importance it's made you red in the gills? And you've likely driven the trap as if the highway-men were after you. Well, speak out, girl."

Now Maggie glanced from her father to her mother, then to John, who, aiming to help things out, said, "Well, perhaps it's woman's talk. Is it?"

She shook her head.

"What is it, girl?"

Maggie now turned to her mother and, her voice low and as if there were no one else present in the room, she said, "It's . . . it's about him."

"Him?"

"Yes, him. Kate's supposed friend, her intended." There was a bite to the last word.

"What about him?"

Maggie now turned and looked at her father, saying, "You're . . . you're not going to like this, Dad."

"Well, whatever I'm not gona like, girl, you've broken your neck to get here to tell us, so out with it."

"He's . . . well, he's not what he seems, 'cos . . . and she's . . . she's sly, she must have known."

"In the name of God! girl, spit it out." Hal had pulled himself to his feet, and now Maggie, stepping back towards her mother, muttered, "He's . . . he's bought the . . . the Bannamans' farm."

They all stared at her in disbelief.

"'Tisn't true." Mary Ellen's voice came out on a hissing whisper.

"It is, Mam, it is. Andrew heard it in Newcastle. His father had heard it had been sold but didn't know who to. Then yesterday when passing he saw a lot of workmen and enquired. But the gaffer said they had been engaged by an agent. Then when Andrew came home he said it was in a roundabout way he got to know, 'cos the agent's son is in rooms next to his and studying for the same thing. And he got on talking about the American for whom his father was doing business and had bought a house out Andrew's way. That's how it came about."

When Hal yelled, "God's truth!" and ending on an oath that caused

348

Mary Ellen to screw up her face and Maggie to step back against the bookcase in fright, they all thought for a moment that he was going to throw the glass paperweight that he was gripping in his hand at one of them. And he might have done this, except that John's voice, quick and calm now, said, "Look Dad. Look, hold your hand a minute. He could have done it blindly. He may not have known."

Hal gripped the shawl tight around his throat and for a moment it looked as if he was about to choke. But when Mary Ellen, full of concern now, went to his side, he thrust her off and, dropping down into his chair, he now beat his closed first on the leather-topped desk, muttering thickly, "She must have known. All the time she must have known." Then looking up at Mary Ellen, he said, "Can you believe it? Kate, she must have known."

"There must be some other explanation," John's voice broke in quietly again. But once more Hal went into a fury, crying now, "Explanation! Never off his doorstep, then bringing him here. And he sat at our table and hoodwinked the lot of us with the American jabber. Explanation! You don't buy a house overnight. It takes time, meetings, deeds. Don't I know. But this explains it, her worried look of late, guilty look I should say. I would never have believed it of her. *Never! Never! Never!*" He banged his fist on the table, emphasizing each word. "I would have staked me life on her uprighteousness. As for you, girl" – he now turned his full attention on Maggie – "you were glad to bring this news, weren't you? Oh yes, you were. Yes, you were. Broke your neck to get back here and drop 'em. You're another one that's devious. Get out of me sight. *Get out!*"

So great was his anger that Mary Ellen turned hastily and took Maggie, who was now shivering with fear, from the room. And John, with difficulty keeping his voice low, said, "Why take it out on her?"

"'Cos she's being spiteful."

"Well, you'd rather that one of us brought the news than hear it from outside, wouldn't you? Because then you wouldn't have been able to fly your kite."

"Now don't you start on me. God! in heaven, don't you start."

"I'm not starting, Dad" – John's voice was stiff – "only I'm going to say this. If Kate's kept quiet about it, him buying the Bannamans' place, there's a good reason, and the first that springs to mind is she was afraid of your getting to know."

Hal now slumped in his chair, muttering, "She can't live there. I won't let her. No, I won't let her."

"I can't see what you can do about it if she's already made up her mind."

"She'll unmake it. She'll have to. She owes me that. Why?" He moved his head slowly from one side to the other. "I've looked after her from the day she was born. Why, I brought her into the world. She was something special to me...."

"Yes, we all know that." John's tone brought his father's eyes towards him, and he demanded of his son, "What do you mean by that? I've never neglected any of you."

"No, you haven't neglected any of us, but Kate's been first with you, and we've all been made aware of it, one way or another."

"That's a bloody lie. I've never shown preference."

"Oh, Dad, Dad, you couldn't help yourself. We were the eldest, Tom and me, we were lads and we didn't mind so much. But Maggie did. And so did Florrie, in her own kindly way. When the topic once came up she explained it like this. She said you were trying to make up to Kate for not being her father, for after all she was only half related to us being step-like. And that's why, as Maggie more strongly put it, it's been Kate this, Kate that, and Kate the tother. So I for one can understand Maggie's attitude the day: in a way she was hitting back, not only at Kate, but at you."

"My God!" Hal now drew on a long gasping breath before he said, "It's like a day of revelation, I'm being shown up for what I am."

"Don't be daft, Dad. You know what I'm saying is true. And if you take my advice you'll calm down before Kate comes in, because no good will come of your raging at her; she could up and walk out, you know."

"She never would. She never would."

"But she would. In a way I know Kate better than you, because I don't view her like you do, like a possession, she's just me sister. And what's more, she's a woman. She's not a girl any longer, and there's nothing to stop her going to him, and him being a man of means." John paused here, then wagged his finger at his father, saying, "That's it. You see, there could be an explanation. Not knowing anything about the Bannamans or the farm, he wanted to surprise her and bought the place and is getting it ready as a sort of . . . well, it could be a wedding present."

There was a long pause before Hal said, "I wish I could think that, then I would only have him to deal with."

"Well, think on it until she comes in, and then you'll know for sure. Now settle yourself down and calm yourself down. I've got to get back to the yard." With this John turned and walked out of the room, there to meet Mary Ellen hurrying across the hall. Stopping for a moment, he said to her, "You better pray, Mam, that Kate knew nothing about this, else there's going to be hell to pay."

Mary Ellen said nothing but went towards the office, thinking, There'll be hell to pay anyway, for there's something not right with Kate. Ever since she's got to know that fellow, she's become a different person. . . . There was something strange about that fellow. She couldn't put her finger on it. Only one thing she was sure of, he wasn't all he appeared to be.

*

John met Kate in the yard and he breathed a sigh of relief when he saw she was riding alone. She had ridden in ahead of the cart, and Charles and Florrie were riding behind more leisurely. And so he had time to say to her, "You better prepare yourself. You're in for a blow up. Have you any idea what it's about?"

He stared at her for a moment, and when she didn't answer he said, "Well he knows about the house ... your Ben buying the house." He watched her draw in a long shuddering breath and when all she said was, "Oh?" he came back quickly at her with, "You can say 'Oh?' like that. Don't you know what you've done?"

"I've done nothing, John."

"Well, I mean what you know and haven't let on?"

"There was a reason, a good reason, and likely you've experienced some of it already. He'd go mad when he heard."

"Mad's the word. You'd better go in and get it over with afore the others come."

As she handed the horse's reins to him he said, "How did the market go, by the way? He'll want to know that when he calms down."

"Not in the way that will please him. Prices being up, folks aren't spending, so the stall-holders say. Some of them can afford to wait. We brought four dozen eggs back and ten pounds of butter."

"Lordy, lordy. It's going to be that kind of a day."

In the kitchen Kate was confronted by Annie. Maggie was there too, but she was sitting on the settle, her face towards the fire and she didn't turn and look at Kate. And Annie said quietly, "I saw John talking to you: you'll be prepared for the hot blast awaiting you in the office. Go on in now, lass. And speak the truth and shame the devil. 'Tis the best way in the end."

Kate did not immediately move away but, looking at Annie, she said quietly, "If it was only as simple as that, Annie, I would have no fear." Then she walked up the room leaving the elderly woman staring after her, her head moving in small jerks, her teeth nipping at her lower lip.

Kate paused outside the office door; then turning the handle, she walked briskly in to see her mother and Hal sitting side by side, their eyes staring at her.

Getting to her feet, Mary Ellen said quietly, "We've been waiting for you, lass."

"So I understand." Kate nodded at her. Then looking at Hal, she said, "Before you start on me, let me have my say. It won't all be the truth, I'll tell you that at the start, because you wouldn't be able to take it. But this much I will tell you. I knew nothing about him buying that house until it was done; I was as shocked as you are. If I hadn't loved him so much I would have flown from him; in fact, I made an effort, but it was no good; I care for him in a way that I never imagined possible to care for anybody. So whatever he does is right with me, because——" She held up her hand silencing Hal, saying, "Just another minute, Dad. I repeat, whatever he does is right with me, because he's a good man. And I'll say this, too, you think that you had one hell of a life when you were young, but let me tell you, it was nothing compared with his. He's fighting his way back, I could almost say to sanity. Now that's as much as you need to know of his life at the moment. But with regard to the house, he bought it for a purpose."

"You could have told us."

She walked nearer to him and, looking down on him, she said, "How could I? How could I have come in here and said cheerfully, Ben has bought the Bannamans' farm, knowing how the very name upsets you and that you couldn't bear the thought of me living there?"

"*My God! You're not going to live there?* Oh, no. I couldn't have that." He pulled himself to his feet now and stood glaring at her. "No, Kate, you wouldn't do that to me, go and live in that place."

"He cannot see why not."

"Well, I'll bloody well tell him why not. You bring him over and I'll give him the history."

"He already knows the history."

"My God! He knows the history and yet he buys the place and wants to take you there. He's a swine of the first water."

"Hal! Hal!" Mary Ellen was gripping his arm now. "Stop it. It's not going to do any good. Sit yourself down." She pushed him back into the chair, and he yelled at her, "Did you hear what she said? He knew about it, knew the history."

Mary Ellen now looked sadly at Kate, and Kate, looking back at her, said quietly, "He imagines he can purge evil. As you know, it's a fine house, and all that happened in it is past and gone these twenty odd years."

Hal was now holding his head, muttering, "I can't believe this. I just can't believe this." He glanced at Kate, asking now, "Is he getting over mental trouble or something? By what you said earlier, has he had mental trouble?"

"No, not in the way you mean, but he suffered from someone who had."

"I give up. I give up." His hand on his brow, he stared towards the fire, and Kate, her voice soft now, said, "I wouldn't hurt you for the world, Dad. He knows that. But I can't help my feelings. And you should understand this part of it anyway: your feelings for Mam" – she glanced at Mary Ellen – "and hers for you; well, in a way, I feel I'm lucky, not only to have found someone to love, but to be loved by a man like him. And he does love me, this I know, and would lay my life on. I can't understand it, why he should do, me looking like I do, and knowing that I've been overlooked by all the men in the district, except that Harry Baker, which was no more than a beggar's choice. You thought so yourself, beggars can't be choosers. I was in that category. But along comes a man of class who says he loves me, and did from the moment he saw me, and I him. To my mind, it was like a miracle, and you don't ignore miracles, you grasp them with both hands and hold them tight." And she joined her hands, giving emphasis to her words, and pressed them hard between her breasts.

Hal and Mary Ellen stared at her. It was as if they had been mesmerized by her words. Then as if protesting against the intrusion of reason, Hal flung his head to the side and, once more banging his fist on the desk, he cried, "Aye, well, when all that's said and done, there's still the house. You can't go and live there, you know you can't."

"Why not?" The question was quiet.

And now he almost screamed at her, his voice cracking with the hoarseness, "You know what happened there. You know who lived there. The man who owned that place murdered your own grandfather and my father, and his daughter crucified me. That's the word, crucified. I have nightmares still. She can tell you." He jerked his thumb in Mary Ellen's direction but kept his eyes tight on Kate the while. "I wake up groaning, never yelling, because she stilled my voice, that devil, that demon who was born in that house, brought up in that house. Even to this day I feel the screws in my joints from the way she left me. And you, knowing this, would go and live there. . . . Does he know that it has been taken four times over the past years and the longest stay was five years? Two of them only stayed a matter of eighteen months and every crop they put in failed for the lot of them. The place is accursed. Why, nobody will ride that way after dark, even today." He paused, then, his voice dropping, he said, "There's other farms to let off or for sale within a few miles, why did he pick on that one? Like one or two of the others that took it, he had heard that there still might be some loot hidden away somewhere. And that was what that devil and her brother were after the day they cornered me. Has he heard that?"

"No, I don't think so." Her voice was quiet, dull sounding now. "Anyway, as far as I can gather he has no need of money."

"No, no? That's another thing I'd like you to explain to me, why a man of means should shut himself away in a place hardly bigger than a pig-pen, up in the wilds. Nobody's lived up there for the last ten years. Joe Stollard was the last and he was a lone man and wrong in the head. And—" His voice rising now, he ended, "You must be an' all. There's something fishy. And it's my belief, as you've kept close about this business, you're keeping close about other things."

"Let up. Let up." Mary Ellen pushed her hand towards him; then she turned and, walking quickly towards Kate said, "Sit down, lass, sit down," and pressed her into a chair. And when Kate was seated with her head bowed, Mary Ellen turned and looked at Hal and screwed her face up at him to silence any further protest.

A tap came on the door now and Florrie entered and, looking anxiously from one to the other, she said, "We're back. I mean, Charles is here."

"Charles? Tell him I want a word with him. Aye, he's another that wants sorting out."

"Stop it!" Mary Ellen turned harshly on him now. "You've said

353

enough for once," and taking hold of Kate's arm and saying, "Come on, lass," she pulled her up from the chair and led her from the room. And as Florrie went to follow them her father's voice came at her, saying, "Do what I tell you. Send him in."

A minute later Charles entered the room and he began courteously by saying, "Good day, Mr Roystan, although from what Florrie tells me it wasn't such a good day at the market, but...."

"Cut the cackle about the market, I'll hear about that later. Answer me truthfully, did you know that Kate's fellow had bought Rooklands, the Bannamans' place?"

"Yes, I did, but only after the business had been settled. If I'd known his intentions beforehand I should have persuaded him against it, knowing he was fond of Kate, and also how you felt about that place."

"Why didn't you let me know after he'd done it then?"

Charles looked down to the side as if he was examining his leather gaiters and paused a moment before he said, "Well, I suppose I sensed what would happen, what apparently has happened today. You've been very upset by the knowledge. Anyway, it was Kate and Ben's business, not mine; what had to come should have come from them."

"Right you are there. Right you are: what had to come should have come from them. But God's sake! man, I ask you, our Kate goin' to live in that house. Why? The whole countryside will be asking the question: why, of all places should she take that as her home? Because it isn't like if what happened there happened in the last century, it happened in the lifetime of all of us around here. True, you were but a lad yourself, little, admitted; and like to many another bairn the story was given to you as a fairy tale no doubt. Now am I right?"

"Well ... er, yes, you are, because I remember it being told to us in that way. And I was a good age before I realized that it was true, even though my father had stated from the beginning that it was true; but at Christmas time he would always regale us with tales of horror and ghosts, which he also maintained were true."

"Well, there was no fairy tale about Bannaman's business, you know that. Anyway, I'm goin' to ask you a straight question, and I want a straight answer. There's nobody here" – he waved his hand backward and forward – "to witness what you'll say. But now, tell me, give me your honest opinion of that fellow."

Again Charles hesitated for a moment before answering. "My honest opinion of Benedict Hamilton," he said, "is that, as far as I know, he is an honest young man; he is definitely an educated and travelled one; but having said that, I think there is something in his past that has been a great source of trouble to him. It may not have affected himself, by that I mean he is not the culprit so to speak, but in a way—" He now turned and looked out of the window and jerked his chin upwards before looking at Hal again and continuing, "I don't know how to put this. I mean, I don't know how to simplify my own thoughts on the subject. But I may be wrong, yet it seems to me he's expunging someone else's guilt. That might be fanciful, yet, I don't see him as a person who himself has committed any crime. I'm . . . I'm putting it badly."

"No, no, you're not, lad. No, you're not. You're explainin' things that's in me own mind, that's what you're doing. Aye, well, he needn't have committed any crime in that sense, but——" He leant forward towards Charles now and, pointing his finger at him, he said, "there's kind of crimes that are not crimes, such as he could have been married afore, or could still be married. What d'you think on that?"

"I haven't thought along those lines, but as you say, that could be."

"Aye, aye, that could be. America's a long way away, nobody knows what he did there, but whatever it was, it drove him to go and live by himself and put up with weather up there that we shy from."

"Yes, yes, you're right. Once or twice I was very anxious about him. But when I rode over I found that he was quite comfortable . . . well, as comfortable as he could be in that little place."

"He's a man of means. Well, he must be to have bought that place. He's told me all about that and the business that his people were in in America. He's talked about his father and his grandfather. The only one he hasn't mentioned is his mother. A man usually mentions his mother, doesn't he? Has he mentioned his mother to you?"

"No, no, he hasn't. His grandmother. . . . Oh yes . . . yes he did. He said that his mother died when he was, I think when he was twelve, and he had lived with his grandmother. He seems very fond of his grandmother."

"Then why did he leave her across all that water?"

"I don't know. I only know this, Mr Roystan, that I feel there is good in him, and speaking for oneself, I must say the more one gets to know him the more one likes him."

"Aye, well" – Hal sat back in his chair – "I'm no forrader. There's only one thing I do know, she's not goin' to live in that blasted place. Where is he the day?"

"He . . . he went into Newcastle early this morning. He left a message with me for Kate. He'll be returning by coach tomorrow I understand."

"Aye, well, the quicker the better, so I can get me tongue round him. We've got to know where we stand, him and me. By! aye, we have that." He began to cough now and to press his chest with the hub of his hand, and when Charles said, "Can I get you something, sir?" he gasped, then muttered, "No, just send the missis in. But thanks, lad, for being honest. Aye, thanks for being honest."

At this he sat back in his chair and closed his eyes while still pressing on his chest, and Charles left the room quickly to call Mary Ellen.

*

355

Hal did not have a meeting with Ben on the Sunday evening as he had anticipated, he had another attack and his breathing became so difficult that Mary Ellen sent Gabriel posthaste for the doctor, who said that the patient must stay in bed for at least a week and be kept quiet: Hal's chest was in a very bad state and the only way it would improve would be through rest, breathing air of a moderate temperature and the application of mustard poultices applied to the skin, and hot linctus taken inwardly.

So it was a fortnight before Hal came downstairs again. The whole family had been concerned for him, Kate equally as much as Mary Ellen. But it was almost another week later before she said to him, "Dad, Ben would like to come over tomorrow to have a talk with you. It's ... it's about the house."

"Oh, aye." He was in the sitting-room now. He had a ledger on his knee and had been going through the week's output of milk which had fallen for the obvious reason that two cows had gone dry. But the market prices of the meat and butter and potatoes had stabilized, and so last week there had been no goods brought back unsold.

He continued to look at the ledger as he said, "Aye, well, he'll be welcome."

"Dad."

"Yes, lass?" Now he did look up. "We ... we want to do what is right and what is going to be least hurtful to you."

"I ... I thought you'd see it that way, lass. Aye, I thought you'd see it that way. Thank you."

"Oh, Dad." With a quick movement she came and sat down beside him and, taking his hand, she said, "I could never be really happy if I hurt you."

He looked at her lovingly as he said softly now, "And you'd never hurt me on your own, through your own will, lass, I know that. I also understand how you feel about him, and when all's said and done, he's a good match. But having said that, lass, you know so little about him. That's ... that's what I'm afraid of."

"You needn't be afraid, Dad. I ... I know everything about him."

"You do?" He drew back his head from her.

"Yes, yes, everything."

"And you still think he's somebody you should marry?"

"Yes. Oh yes, definitely."

"Well, if you can say that, lass, with truth in your eyes as I see them now, then that's good enough for me." He leant towards her and kissed her gently on the cheek, and she bowed her head, and as the tears squeezed from her closed lids he said, "Aw, lass, lass, come on now. Come on. It just wants your mother to see you cryin' and I'll get it again. My God! I've gone through it enough up in that room from her. Come on. Come on. Here, don't use your pinny." He pulled out a handkerchief from the pocket of his soft house coat and handed it to her, adding now on a light note, "I've never been so long in bed in all me life. At times

I've thought to meself, this is what it must feel like to be dead."

"Oh, Dad." She was smiling at him, and he nodded at her, saying, "Aye, aye, I did. Your mother's a tartar you know. She always was and always will be, and she's got hands as gentle as muck shovels."

"Oh!" Kate now got to her feet. "You'd better not let her hear you say that."

"What had I better not hear?" Mary Ellen was coming up the room and she rounded the back of the tall chair and, facing Hal, she demanded, "What have you been saying about me now?"

"I was just sayin' to Kate how gentle your hands were, nearly as gentle as a couple of muck shovels, the long-handled ones, you know."

Mary Ellen turned her head to the side while still keeping her eyes on him and, matching his jocular tone, she said, "Very well, very well. Wait till that next mustard plaster goes on, I'll know what to do with the muck shovels. By! lad, I will."

"Oh, away with you! woman, and get in the kitchen and do some cookin'." But then, jerking his head towards Kate, he added, "She tells me that Ben's comin' over the morrow." And looking down at the ledger again, he finished on a mutter, "He's comin' to talk about the house."

Mary Ellen and Kate exchanged glances, and Mary Ellen let out a deep sigh, and, in an even more jovial tone now said, "Well, he won't be the only one comin' the morrow. There's Florrie's Charles. And what d'you think? Our Maggie's just told me she met Andrew Boston in the market and he asked her if he could call the morrow an' all."

Hal looked up at her, laughing now and saying, "Well, now she's doing something sensible at last that one. Andrew Boston. He's in for law like our Hugh, but I wonder who really did the askin'. Well, well. Has our John or Tom said they're bringin' anybody?"

"No, not yet anyway; but May Turner has been trotting her horse along this road quite a bit of late, and our Tom always seems to know the time she'll be passin'. I've noted that."

"May Turner?" He pulled a face. "Oh, well, he could do worse, couldn't he? Her dad, so I understand, tried to get his foot in the Coultas Dodsworth Company when they opened at Haydon Bridge Iron Works in forty-three. And his brother's got one of those nice little villas up on the hill above the village. He's in good company there with Mr Bewick, who's now got a lease on the Langley Barony Lead Mines. Oh, my! yes, our Tom's goin' to be in good company if he captures May or May captures him. Well, whichever way it goes he could get his saddles free an' all, because hasn't one of her uncle's got that fine saddler's place in Hexham? and he's got neither kith nor kin as I understand it, and she being the only child an' all."

"By! you know your history, Hal Roystan." Mary Ellen stood looking down at him, her arms folded across her waist. "You wouldn't care who any of them married as long as there was money in it, would you?"

"Oh, no." He nodded at her. "You're right there: I don't care a damn for any of them, it's the dowries I'm after an' the discount I could get off wares if me son marries into families that make saddles an' the like."

"Aw! You." Mary Ellen turned away, and Hal, laughing now, said, "What about our John? Isn't he set?"

"Yes, he's thinking of joining the ministry; they're looking for lay preachers for the Nonconformists' Chapel. He could rise to be a circuit minister. You never know."

At this, both Kate and Hal burst out laughing, for not one of them, nothing, could get John to church or chapel under any pretext. But as Mary Ellen walked down the room, Hal called after her, between short coughs, "Stranger things have happened. Conversion ... fear of hell ... or seeing the light." And Mary Ellen's voice came back at him saying, "True, true."

When the door closed on her, he looked at Kate and said, quietly now, "We said all that in a joke, but as I see it, anything could happen in this life. Like your miracle you spoke of a few weeks ago."

"Yes." She nodded at him. "Yes, like my miracle. Well, when he comes tomorrow, listen to him, will you, Dad?"

"Aye, I will. As long as what he says tends to your happiness, I'll listen to him. Aye, I'll listen to him."

12

The weather had changed: there had been high winds and rain squalls all night and for most of the morning; the rain had now ceased, but the wind was still high. And Kate, walking along the road to meet Ben, had to hold down her skirt with one hand, while holding her bonnet on with the other.

No one had passed any remark when she dressed for outdoors and stated her intention of meeting Ben on the road, however much her riding across the moors to meet a man was hitting convention with a hammer. Had either Maggie or Florrie suggested doing something similar, Mary Ellen would have said, "Oh, no you don't. And a day like this! Let them come to you. Men don't appreciate such eagerness." With Kate it had been different from the beginning. And yet she would have agreed with her mother's view that nothing about this courtship was conventional.

She was about a third of a mile along the road when she espied Ben, and, so it seemed, he her, for at that moment from a trot he put his horse into a gallop. But as he drew his horse to a skidding stop she moved quickly across the road and jumped the ditch on the far side, and laughing, she cried, "I'll send a complaint to the justice about your riding; 'tis a danger to man and beast."

He dismounted, then held out his hands to help her back across the ditch, and having done so, he put his arms about her, and she hers about him, and they kissed passionately. Then, his arm still about her shoulder, he took the horse's bridle, saying, "Court-room all ready?"

"Yes; and judge in the chair." Then looking up into his face she said, "Thank you, Ben."

"Oh, my dear." He lowered his head towards her again and, pushing his face under the rim of her bonnet, he kissed her temple, saying now, "Never thank me for anything, my dear. Leave that to me, because I shall never cease to thank you for just being you."

She remained silent. What could she say? Because at times she could hardly believe him when he talked like this. And more often than not he talked like this, telling her how wonderful she was, when all the while inside herself she still felt inadequate, plain, and ungainly. But perhaps not quite so much now. In order to come up to what she imagined was his idea, and ideal of her, she had of late practised the spinet a little every day, and had read more, even to the extent of taking less sleep in order to do so. And now she could discuss with him not only her hearsay knowledge of the authors of books, but the substance of what they were writing. The conversation she held with him would, she knew, sound as foreign to her family as he himself already did to them: not one of them accepted him as one of themselves, not even John, and John liked him, and this fact pained her. Charles was the only person who seemed to understand him and the whole situation. But then, Charles had been brought up in an atmosphere different from that surrounding the members of her family. Not that they hadn't all been brought up well: they all had their wits about them, and they could read and write, which wasn't usual with all farmers' families. Yet still, their outlook was limited, as hers had been, too, until she met up with this man.

They were nearing the gate when Ben, looking ahead, said quietly, "I never enter this place but I feel I'm here under false pretences, and every time your father looks me straight in the eye I want to tell him the truth and damn the consequences because, whatever the consequences, you are with me." He pressed her arm hard against his side, saying reassuringly now, "Yes, I know, I know, we've agreed. And this new plan ... well, if it is at all possible, will put some distance between us and him. And we've agreed on that too, haven't we?"

She nodded, murmuring, "Yes, yes."

"Well, into battle!"

They were now walking across the farmyard, and Hugh was coming to meet them. "Hello there," he said. "Weather's changing. How are you?" And he held out his hand to Ben who, taking it, answered, "Fine, thank you. And you?"

"Never better."

Hugh had met Kate's intended only once before, but Kate felt she could leave them together and make her way towards the kitchen.

Taking the reins from Ben, Hugh said, "Give him here, I'll see to him," then leaned towards Ben and muttered, "I hear you are to go before the judge, the court's in session." And Ben burst out laughing saying, "That's funny. I was saying something similar to Kate as we came along."

"Hope you've got your case all worked out. Don't worry; his bark's worse than his bite, only ... you know." His face lost its smile and became serious. "We all love Kate, but he most of all. And ... and he's only thinking of her. 'Twas unfortunate you picked on that neck of the woods as a habitation to set up in. Still, you weren't to know. Anyway, I'll be with you in a minute, I'll just take him along to Terry."

Consciously now, Ben squared his shoulders as he too walked towards the door that was now being held open for him by Maggie.

Before crossing the threshold he took off his hat and he was stroking his hair back from his forehead as he passed her. Unsmiling, she looked up into his face as he said, "Good-day, Maggie."

He hardly heard her response but he heard her close the door with a bang. Maggie didn't like him, and being a man he knew the reason: to use an expression he had heard used in the inn, she would have set her cap at him without any encouragement, and with just a little of it she would have fallen into his arms. He had summed up Maggie's nature from the first: she was vain and could be spiteful, but being very pretty, as she undoubtedly was, she imagined that covered all her defects. She could be a hussy, could Maggie.

After he had greeted Annie, whose manner as always was welcoming, she said, "Go on through, they're all in the sitting-room. Kate's taking off her things. Why she wanted to go out in a wind like this I don't know. Blow the hairs off a pig's back, it would."

He smiled at her, then went up the kitchen and into the hall, where he was met by Mary Ellen.

Holding out her hand, she said, "Glad to see you again, Ben," and he, taking her hand, said, "And I, you, Mrs Roystan. Definitely I, you."

That was one thing, Mary Ellen told herself, she couldn't get used to about him: when he paid a compliment, he nearly always stressed it by repeating it. Fanciful, she termed it. "The others are in the sitting-room," she said, "but Hal is in the office. Would you like to go and have a natter with him?"

"Yes, yes, of course."

She led the way across the hall, along the passage towards the study door, which she opened, saying loudly, "Here's Ben, Hal. Thought he would just have a natter afore tea. All right?"

"Yes, all right, all right. Come in. Come along in." Although still croaky, Hal's voice was hearty, and Ben went in and, extending his hand towards Hal who was sitting to the side of the fireplace, said, "How do I find you today, sir?"

"Better. Oh, much better. Back in the yard the morrow, even if I've got to shoot me way out."

He laughed, and Ben laughed with him.

"Sit yourself down, lad. Sit yourself down."

Ben sat down in the chair Hal indicated, which was directly opposite to his own, and Hal began by saying, "Weather's changing. Blowin' a gale all night. How's it up your way?"

"It was pretty bad during the night, brought a slate off. And" – he smiled –"that's the first one that's moved since I've been here."

Hal turned his head away and sighed as he now said, "Can't understand you, lad, can't understand you. But then.... Well now" – he looked at Ben again – "since we're on about houses, I might as well tell you, it was a mighty shock to me when I heard you had bought that place."

"So I understand, sir."

"You know what happened to me there. Kate has told you all about it – so you can guess within a little how I feel about letting her go to live there. All right, all right" – he put up his hand as if Ben had made some protest – "it's a fine enough place, none better for miles, for it wasn't ʋilt as a farmhouse but as a gentleman's residence. And that's what it was for years until the devil took a hand in picking who should go in. Anyway, you understand my feelings?"

"I do, indeed. I do, indeed. And therefore, Kate and I have decided to look for another house, but as I'm committed to this with the builders, I shall see it renovated and the land around cleaned up so it will be more attractive for a sale."

"Aye, well, I can see your point there, but you'll get no one to stay there long, lad. There's a curse on the place, and it will never be lifted, for those that wrought it were evil." He leant towards Ben now, saying, "You look peaky the day, a bit white about the gills, and winter'll soon be on us; you want to get yourself down from there afore the frosts come. Have you seen any place you fancy?"

"No, not yet. Well, not quite. But I have seen a little house to rent beyond Langley, in the direction of Bardon Mill. Although it, too, is somewhat isolated, it is in a sheltered spot."

"On the way to Bardon Mill, you say, sheltered? I know the very place. Butterfield Cottage is the name of it, isn't it?"

"Yes, yes, that's it."

"Well now, you're being sensible, 'tis a nice little place. I know who owned it at one time, 'twas sister of Mr Ellison, and he was undersheriff of the county just a year gone. Oh, you can't go wrong there. Anyway, I'm glad that's settled." He rose to his feet now, as, too, did Ben, and extending his arm, Hal placed his hand on Ben's shoulder, saying, "You've eased me mind, lad, because it was Kate I was thinkin' about. She's very dear to me, is that lass, and I couldn't bear to think of her startin' life in a place so tainted with badness. Why, I wouldn't be able to sleep, man. It would be as if the Bannamans themselves had come back. But come on now, they'll be waitin', and you look as if you could do with something inside you."

It was later remarked among the family that Kate's man had had little to say all evening, not like the first time he had sat at the table, and the change was put down to the fact that likely their father had lathered into him, and, as they all too well knew, that could be a numbing experience.

13

It was the middle of December and already there had been two falls of snow, bringing forth predictions from old hands of a very bad winter. And when the wild duck settled early on Langley dam and on the pool above the smelting mill, the bleak outlook seemed assured.

The early fall of snow had worried Kate a little for Ben was still living up in the shepherd's hut. He had been just too late to secure the cottage, for the owner, who now resided in Corbridge, had let it to a local Haydon Bridge family.

Her mother and Hal too were concerned that Ben should still be living up in the wilds, but she knew that he spent many a night at Rooklands now that the builders and decorators had gone. There was one room in the house that he had really made comfortable with the furniture that they had stored there. This had been another bone of contention between her father and Ben, the storing of the furniture.

They had made several trips into Newcastle and to house sales, and had secured some very good pieces of furniture. When she had first intimated to Hal that Ben was going to store them at the farm, he had again become irate, saying he would clear the loft. But, as they all knew, the loft was already stacked with the residue of his own visits to sales over the years, and so, reluctantly, he had to realize the inevitability of this, at least until they were able to decide on the house in which they would be going to live.

A dispute, too, about their future home had arisen. There had been a farmhouse and land going quite near, which Hal had been wholeheartedly for their taking, but Kate had had to point out to him it wasn't exactly what Ben wanted. And when he had demanded, "What does he want, I'd like to know?" for the first time she had snapped back at him, "Not a little farmhouse on your doorstep," which had silenced them both and caused a rift between them for days.

Her marriage, as was Florrie's, was set for the spring of the following year, and so over the past weeks every spare minute of the day and the long evenings was taken up with the sewing of bedding and gowns to fill each of their several chests.

It became an added irritation to Kate that every time she went out to meet Ben, Hal would say to her, "You're not going near that house now, are you?" And she would promise him that she wasn't going there, at the same time knowing that that was where she would find Ben.

The same would happen when Ben came to call to take her out. "You're not taking her near that house now, are you?" Hal would say, and Ben always had to swallow deeply before answering. Once, when all he answered was, "Don't worry, sir," Hal came back at him, yelling, "I do worry. She's not to go there. Do you hear?" and when Ben, not only to Hal's but also to the surprise of the other members of the family, had replied in much the same manner, "I hear, sir; as yet I am not deaf," before walking out, there was revealed to them that the American was not all soft-spoken geniality, and that he was perhaps becoming a little tired of being dictated to.

It was noted, too, that Kate was losing weight. Hal put it down to too much horse riding. "Gallivanting around the countryside would shake the flesh off anybody," he said. But Mary Ellen had different ideas. As she herself knew only too well, it was worry that stripped the flesh off your bones. And her Kate was worried; all the time she was worried. It seemed that since she had met this American she had never stopped worrying. But what about? Bannaman's farm had been sorted out; they were going to get another place. And that was something else. There must be dozens of houses round about that would or should have suited him, but he always found something wrong with them. She wished she could get to the bottom of it . . . the bottom of him. She still wasn't sure about him, although she wouldn't voice her thoughts to Hal because he was on constant edge as it was about Kate's going.

Kate was standing now in her bedroom tying a long scarf around her bonnet. It had been freezing hard for the past week, but yesterday a slight thaw had set in, and although today wasn't so cold there was a high wind blowing. She picked up her gloves from the dressing-table, then went out and down the shallow stairs to the hall. Tom was crossing it, and he said, "There's a smell of snow in the wind, you might get caught."

"It won't be the first time." And she smiled at him.

"Brr!" He pursed his lips. "Me for the fire. We've got the last of the sheep down. Aye" – he paused – "that fellow of yours must be tough. Up on those hills would freeze the backside off a bull. I don't know how he stands it; he doesn't seem the rough type."

"Never judge the man by the suit, Tom."

"Aye, there's something in that," he laughed, and went on towards the sitting-room.

In the kitchen she was surprised to see Maggie also ready for the road, and she looked at her. But Maggie did not give any explanation, it was Mary Ellen who said, "She's taking some patterns for embroidery to Betty Boston, and carrying some butter and cheese from me. They appreciate home stuff." It was as if she was apologizing for Maggie going visiting. Then she added, "Lass, you'll be blown away up on those hills."

"I'm well wrapped up."

"Does he know you're coming?"

Kate hesitated for a moment before she said, "Yes, in a way, it being Wednesday."

"But what if he's not there? He could be in the town seeing about a house again."

"Well, if that's the case, I'll only have to come back."

Mary Ellen stared at her for a moment, then said, "Well, time yourself. You don't want to be caught up there in the dark, and there's snow in the air."

"I'll be back before dark, Mam." She nodded towards Mary Ellen, then went out.

And Mary Ellen, looking at Maggie, said, "That goes for you too, mind. Don't get chattin' too long. And take the trap gently, we don't want an axle broken. Go on now, and give Mrs Boston my regards."

Maggie said nothing, but lifted the parcel from the table and went out.

Terry already had the trap into the yard and as he gave her a hand on to the seat he said, "Go careful, Miss Maggie, and don't rush him; he's been out once the day and he's a bit fractious."

Again Maggie said nothing, but she cast a disdainful glance down on the man as he handed her the reins, which she jerked and put the pony into a trot whilst still in the farmyard, all the time asking herself why it was that everybody was getting at her, hiding the fact from herself that for the past five days she had been in a state of irritation. And the knowledge that the whole family knew the reason didn't help.

A month ago when Andrew Boston had been home for the week-end and hadn't called on her, she accepted the excuse from his mother that he had only been able to stay overnight and had to leave early the next morning because of pressure of work in the office. Then on Saturday, on the road into Hexham, they had passed him on the brake accompanied by his father; she had waved to him and he had answered her salute. And after returning home she had waited for his visit, and again all day on the Sunday. But he hadn't come, and she had been filled with indignation that touched on rage. She had felt humiliated.

When on Monday, her mother had taken her aside and asked if he had spoken in any way and she'd had to admit truthfully that he hadn't, Mary Ellen had said, "Well, as I see it, it's your own fault. You act too bold, it puts them off." And this had caused her to retort angrily, "Me! act too bold. You don't say that to our Kate, who's the talk of the place running over the hills to that fellow every minute of the day. How often does he come here, I ask you? Too bold? My goodness me, Mam. It's well seen who you are for and who you are against." And her mother had become angry and retorted that she'd never made flesh of one and fish of another, and that she should be glad Kate was going to find a little happiness.

Kate! Kate! Kate! It was all Kate. Even Florrie and Charles were thrust into the background. Not that it seemed to affect Florrie, she was too slow to take in anything. Sweet natured, they called it. She jerked hard on the reins, but the pony did not respond and she cried at it, "Get up! there."

At the crossroads, she turned her head and looked into the distance to where she could see the hills mounting upwards, but she caught no sight of Kate, and she thought, Terry would not tell her not to gallop Ranger because he had been out already today. Oh no, she could fly to her beloved. And she almost spat out the last word. She was a disgrace. Now, if it had been herself doing that, even attempting to do it, her father would have locked her up. But not so his Kate.

The horse slowed down at the steep hill at the top of which the Bostons' house was situated behind a barrier of trees, planted to shelter both house and garden from the winds that swept down over the hills beyond. It was as the horse slowly reached the top that she happened to glance to her left and was about to look ahead again when her head jerked round and she pulled the horse to a standstill. There, where the land sloped away to a valley bottom before rising again to the hills, was a treeless road, and on it was a figure on a horse, and unmistakably she recognized Kate. She's not going up into the hills, she thought; she's going to that house. And she said she never went. The big sly two-faced thing. *Well!* . . .

It had been her intention to stay at the Bostons' and enquire delicately when Andrew would be coming home again. But once more things did not go as she had intended, for Mrs Boston received her in a manner that held some reserve: she seemed surprised to see her, but thanked her most warmly for the gifts she had brought from her mother, while stating that Betty had gone to spend the day with friends in Haydon Bridge. Then without any prompting, she gave Maggie the information for which she had come: she did not know when Andrew would be next home, because he was spending most of his spare time now at the Quigleys'.

Mr Quigley happened to be a dear friend of Mr Boston. She was so glad that Andrew was going there, it saved him the long journey home, and at the same time provided him with a family atmosphere, for they had three sons and a daughter, and Andrew had known them since they were all children together. And, she had ended, she would be pleased to see Maggie on the usual day for their sewing hour.

She had been snubbed! Her teeth were clenched and her anger and humiliation were such that she wanted to lash out, and literally she did when she turned the horse in the direction of home.

But it was when she again reached the crossroads that she drew the horse to a standstill and sat thinking for a moment before, with a "Get up! there," she turned it on to the narrow path along which she had seen Kate riding a little over half an hour ago.

There was only one thing clear in her mind, she wanted to confront Kate and tell her to her face that she was a liar and was deceiving them at home.

She did not drive the trap right up to the gate of the farm but led the horse on to the wide grass verge and linked the reins over a low branch of tree. Then cautiously she moved alongside the wall and to the gate, which she noted was a new double one, half of which was open. She noted, too, that all the yard was paved, whereas their own was only half done in this way; also that all the outhouses looked spruce with new stone tiles on the roof here and there.

And in the row of horse boxes one half-door was open and she saw Ranger. She was actually amazed at the size of the house. It was the first time she had seen it, for since she was first allowed to go out on her own she had been told never to go near it; and in consequence it always appeared like the ogre's castle. But now she could not help the materialistic side of her being impressed. She looked along to where the front of the house showed the door sheltered by a stone-pillared porch, but she did not go towards it. Going quietly, she went further into the yard and, keeping close to the wall, she passed two windows with iron bars across them, then a closed door, then two more windows, one of them looking into what appeared to be a large pantry, and the other just a small bare room. There was another door ahead, but before that there was a window, and standing to the side of it, she slowly turned her head and looked in. It was a kitchen, but it was empty even of furniture.

She moved on to the door which was ajar. She pushed it open, her head making small wagging movements the while as she thought of the shock her sister would get, that's if she was alone. She had caught sight only of Ranger, which would suggest that she was alone, and, also, that she had access to the house by a key. Oh, the sly individual. Just wait till she got home and told them.

Almost boldly now she walked up the room towards a far door. But here she paused before opening it quietly. And now she was looking into a hall, the size and decoration of which amazed her. Slowly and still quietly she went in and she had almost reached the middle of it when the sound of voices brought her to a frozen stop; only her eyes moved and took in the number of doors going off the hall. Then her ears seemed to widen as she recognized Ben's voice, and the tone with which he was speaking his endearments brought her eyelids blinking and her mouth into a gape, for they were words that she had dreamed someone would whisper to her. But as yet, no one had. These words, though, weren't being whispered: "My dearest one. My beloved," were being said aloud, and to, of all people, their Kate, a great big ungainly individual. If she had been wealthy or very accomplished she could have understood it, but in her opinion, the only word for her half-sister was homely, and she considered she was being kindly at that.

Then her body bent slightly forward in the direction of the half-open doors across the hall to the right of her as his voice ended, saying, "All right, all right, my dearest. I promise you on my word of honour, I will this time settle a deal on the house, the one that lies beyond Corbridge, for neither of us would have any peace were I to insist that we live here. And it has been borne in on me more every time that I see him, how right you are that he must never know the truth. The whole business seems as alive to him now as it was when it happened all those years ago. He seems to become infuriated by the very name Bannaman, and as you say, darling, God knows what his reaction would be if he found out I was her son. But there, it will be as you wish. You will be Mrs Benedict Fraser Hamilton, of Briars Mount, in the County of Northumberland."

There followed a pause which Maggie filled in with her imagination, and then Kate's voice came, saying, "And you won't tell him about our proposed trip to America, till after the wedding, will you?"

"Not if you don't wish it, darling."

There was another pause during which Maggie should have turned and fled, but the identity of Kate's man and of Kate's knowledge of his identity had filled her with such a feeling of amazement and even horror that she found it impossible to move.

Then there they were, standing, arms about each other in the open doorway, staring at her, as amazed and even as horrified as she herself was.

"*Oh, dear Lord!*" Kate dropped her head back on her shoulders, closed her eyes and bit tightly on her lip. Then, bringing her head forward, she opened her mouth to speak, but in the effort it took Ben's voice cut in coldly, "You were looking for someone, Maggie?"

"Oh, you! You two. Imposter! That's what you are, an imposter. And you" – she was spluttering as she glared at Kate – "knowing who he was. Oh, you sly, sneaking dirty...."

"Shut up!" Kate pulled herself away from Ben's hold and, advancing on Maggie, she said, "Well, now you know, and you're happy, aren't you? So get back home, fly, and tell them all, you mean-minded little brat, you. Go on!" She half lifted her hand, then clenched her fist, and Maggie, stepping back from her, swallowed deeply before she cried, "Yes, yes, I will. I'm going, and just see what'll happen to you then ... and your friend. Friend, you used to say he was. You deceived everybody then, but to think you knew he was a Bannaman. Dad will kill him. Yes" – now she turned and glared at Ben – "he's capable of it. So look out, the both of you." And with this she turned and ran down the hall and through the kitchen, out into the yard, onto the road and along to the trap. And as she did so the first large flakes of snow began to fall. Once she had taken her seat, she whipped up the horse until the animal went into a gallop. It was almost as Kate had said, she was flying home with the news....

Back in the hall Ben, holding Kate in his arms, said, "Don't tremble so, darling. Strange, but I knew all along it would have to come into the open, and perhaps it's for the best."

"No! No!" Her whole body moved in protest. "You don't know him. The very name rouses him to anger. As she said, he would be capable of killing. Oh, Ben, Ben, I'm afraid."

"Well, he's a sensible man, he should know what would happen if he started shooting."

"He wouldn't care. Oh, Ben, you don't know him, not like I do. I ... I think he would have got over his father being murdered, but ... but not what she did to him."

368

"Perhaps if I explained to him what she did to me, do you think it would help?"

"No. No. Yet, it might, if you didn't want to marry me."

"But I do want to marry you, and I'm going to marry you."

"Oh, Ben."

"Don't say, oh Ben, like that. You love me, don't you?"

"With all my heart, dear, with all my heart. You know that."

"Yes, yes I do, and so we will be married. . . . Shall I come back with you now and get it over. . . ."

"No, no!" She raised her hand as if warding off an invisible blow. "No, she will have had her say by the time I reach home, and then I shall have mine."

"And what will be your say?"

"Just as you said, dear, that we shall be married. Sooner or later we shall be married. We will be married."

He said no more, but, putting his arms around her shoulders, he led her across the hall and into the kitchen and there, at the door, he said gently, "It's snowing." Then taking her hands, he held them tightly to his chest as he said, "In a way, I'm glad it's happened. It's a weight off my mind. And now I needn't sleep up in the shack any more." He gave a wry smile. "I'll stay here tonight, but first I'll bring Daisy down and tomorrow morning I'll go up and bring the goat down and the rest of my books and papers. The odds and ends of furniture can be left for the next tenant." And he ended by saying, "Shall I come over tomorrow?"

"No. No, please, Ben. Wait here. I'll come to you as soon as I can."

He now lifted the scarf from her shoulders and, putting it over her bonnet, he tied it under her chin; then with an almost rough movement, he pulled her to him and kissed her hard on the lips before pressing her out of the door and across the yard to the stable in which the horse was tethered.

When she was mounted, she put out her hand to him and quietly she said, "Do you pray at all?" And he pursed his lips before he answered, "It isn't a habit of mine." And to this she said, "Well, I think now would be a good time to adopt the habit. Goodbye, my love."

He kissed her hand and answered, "Goodbye, my Kate."

Out on the road, she did not gallop her horse towards home, but trotted it gently. The snow was coming down thickly now, and when she passed three miners coming from their shift, one of them hailed her with, "Looks as if we're in for another blanket, miss." And she nodded at him and rode on, for she found that she was unable to speak, her throat was so tight with unshed tears, while her mind was crying, "Oh, dear God, make him understand," while at the same time knowing that if God Himself should appear before him and put Ben's case to him, he still wouldn't understand why she had deceived him, or forgive Ben for being who he was.

She had just entered the yard when John came out of the kitchen doorway. It was as if he had been awaiting her arrival. And as he made

369

his way towards her, he called to Terry, "Come and take him, will you?"

As he helped her down from the horse, he said quietly, "Kate. Kate." And she, standing still for a moment, looked at him and said, "Oh, John. You don't condemn me, do you?"

"Aw, lass, no." He gripped her arm. "The past is past. It happened in another lifetime, but would you be able to get him to understand that?"

"How is he?"

"He doesn't know yet."

"What!" Her eyes sprang wide.

"His cough was bad again and Mam gave him a dose and he fell asleep in the big chair. He's still there."

"Mam?"

"Oh, yes. The rest of us got the full blast. She couldn't wait. She's a bitch, you know, our Maggie. She's a bitch. Always has been, from the day she was born. It's jealousy. But God, she's stirred up a right hornet's nest the day."

"Where are they all?"

"In the kitchen. Mam's kept her there. It should happen that she'd called us in for a mug of tea and there we were, Tom and me standing at the table, and Mam and Annie baking, and Florrie had just come into the room when in she burst . . . Maggie. Honest to God! I've never seen fury like it. It could match Dad's any day. Oh, she's a damn little bitch that. Come on. Come away in, lass. You're getting wet."

As they kicked the snow from their boots and shook it from their clothes at the kitchen door, John said in a low voice, "I'll tell you one thing, not that it will be much comfort to you, Tom and me like him, and Gabriel an' all, and we think he's right for you."

"Thanks John, thanks." She drew in a long breath now and, putting out her hand, opened the kitchen door and went inside.

Mary Ellen and Annie were sitting one each side of the table. Florrie was lighting the candles and Maggie was sitting on the settle and, except for her hat, she was still in her outdoor clothes. At the sight of Kate, she rose to her feet, but Mary Ellen and Annie remained seated. No one spoke until Tom, coming out of the scullery, said quietly, "Hello, Kate." And she turned and looked at him but didn't answer. When she spoke, it was to her mother. Standing at the end of the table she said quietly, "Well, now you know."

"Lass! Lass! 'Tis true then?" Mary Ellen's voice was a mere whisper, and Kate replied, "Yes, 'tis true. Although I don't know exactly what my dear kind sister has told you."

"And don't call me your dear sister. I'm not your full sister. I wouldn't own you. . . ."

Now as if a bombshell had exploded in the kitchen Mary Ellen sprang up and rounded on her daughter, hissing at her, "Shut up! you. You mischief-making little slut, you!"

"Slut. You call me a slut when she's been roaming the hills with that thing! And . . . and whatever I am, I'm not a bastard."

The blow from Mary Ellen's hand knocked Maggie backwards and she fell onto the settle, crying out as she did so, and before either Tom or John could reach their mother, Mary Ellen had again raised her hand and had brought it across Maggie's face once more before they managed to pull her away, Tom crying, "Mam! Mam! What's come over you?"

When, in front of the fireplace, Mary Ellen had shrugged them off, she stood gasping for a moment before she cried, "Something that should have come over me long ago. She's been asking for it. I've never in me life seen anybody bring bad news quicker, and with such glee. And to call Kate that name. There's different meanings to that word and, my lady, let me tell you this" – she was now thrusting her finger towards Maggie who was crying loudly while holding her face – "if anyone's a bastard in this house, it's you."

So engrossed had they been they hadn't become aware that the door from the hall had opened and there stood Hal, his face screwed up as if he couldn't believe his ears. And now they all turned their attention on him, with the exception of Maggie who, still holding her head, was rocking herself.

Moving slowly forward, he looked down on Maggie for a moment before casting his glance around his family. Then addressing Mary Ellen, he said, "What's this? What's this now?"

Mary Ellen half turned from him, her hand held to her brow, muttering, "I ... I had to chastise her."

"By calling her a bastard?" His voice came from deep in his throat. "Come on. What's this? I've never heard that word spoken in this house afore."

When no one answered, his manner changing and his voice rising to a yell, he demanded, "Speak out one of you. *What is this?* I'll get to know in the end." He now went towards Maggie who, her head against the back of the settle, was bobbing as if on wires, and he cried at her, "What have you done, girl? What have you done to cause this narration?" As she did not speak, he turned around and his gaze came to rest on Kate. She had not removed her riding clothes, not even her scarf from her bonnet, and he looked her over before saying, "Well?"

As Kate went to speak, Mary Ellen came to his side, saying quickly, "Maggie cheeked Kate, that was all. She cheeked her, uncalled for. Yes, uncalled for."

He turned and stared into Mary Ellen's face but said nothing. Then looking at Kate again, he repeated the word, "Well?"

Kate now looked Hal steadily in the eyes as she said, "Maggie had news concerning Ben and me which she thought you should all know, particularly you."

When she paused, he said, "Aye. Well let's hear it."

Kate bowed her head before lifting it again, and once more looking him straight in the face she said, "Before I give you my news, I want you to know that ... that I love him very much, and therefore what I have done was to ease you pain, for I would not have you troubled for the world."

"Get on with it, lass." His voice was low.

And so she said, "Ben is ... is not whom he appears to be, not just Benedict Hamilton, he ... he is the son of—" Now she could not look him in the face and her head drooped before she managed to mutter, "Mary Bannaman."

As they all steeled themselves for his great burst of anger and his voice roaring through the house, they were amazed when he turned and, looking from one to the other, he nodded at them before going to the table and sitting down in the chair that Mary Ellen had vacated. Then putting out his hand, he moved aside a rolling-pin and a tin pastry shaper, and where they had been he laid his hand flat and his fingers tapped the floured board before he said and in a quiet tone, "I knew it. Right from the beginning I knew there was something, but I couldn't put me finger on it. But I knew it." He turned his head now and looked up at Mary Ellen. "Something about him. Not his voice, no. It was the way he stood. And his eyes. Aye, his eyes, those big black-looking eyes." Now he switched his gaze to Kate and lifted his hand from the board and moved it up and down as if weighing something in the palm before he said, "It was that that got your dad when he first saw her, those eyes." His hand flat on the table again, he looked at it and, more to himself, he muttered, "'Twas funny, but all along I knew, deep inside there was a warnin'."

"Dad." He turned his gaze back to Kate and, his voice changing now but still not harsh or loud, he asked, "How long have you known this?"

"From the time he b... b... bought the house."

"And you kept mum knowing how I felt?"

"Only because I ... I didn't want you to be hurt."

"*Didn't want me to be hurt?*" He was on his feet, and now his manner was recognizable to all of them, for his voice was deafening and his face ablaze with fury. It was as if the feeling had been injected into him like a knife into the rump of a horse. And very like that animal now, he reared. His two arms going above his head, his fist clenched, he cried, "Didn't want me to be hurt? Knowing what he did to me and mine and your grandfather an' all."

Although Kate had taken a step backwards, she now stood her ground and her voice was loud as she answered him, "He's done nothing to you. If you want to know he went through as much suffering at her hands as you did. Aye, and more, because it was prolonged, it went on for years. If you'd only listened to him as I have."

"Listen to him? Listen, lass, if I as much as set eyes on him, I won't be able to keep me hands off him. He's come in this house an' sat at my table, he's brought evil back into me life...."

"Don't you dare say that!" She was crying at him now, her whole body trembling. "If there is any evil, it isn't in him, it's what you've fostered all over the years."

The effect of her words on Hal brought Mary Ellen in between them, and now turning her back on Kate, she pleaded with him, saying, "She's upset, she's upset. Try to understand. Let's go in the other room and talk this...."

Without looking at her he thrust her aside, but not roughly. His gaze on Kate once more, he said, "Fostered evil, have I? The feeling that I've borne you all these years is evil, is it? That one—" He thumbed towards the settle where Maggie sat, her sobs having subsided, her eyes wide and in them a fear of the consequences of her action, and he said, "That one was right to be jealous. They were all right to be jealous. Everyone your mother has borne through me had a right to be jealous because you, in a way, were me first-born. I brought you into the world. I saved both you and your mother from dying. I loved you as I've never loved any of me own. Why? I've asked meself that hundreds of times, why, when I didn't sperm you. And now you stand there and tell me I'm full of evil."

"I didn't mean that." Now the tears were running down her cheeks. "Not like that, you know I didn't. You're twisting my words. I meant that you harboured the evil that was done to you. I don't deny that. Ben doesn't deny that. He's tried to erase it from his mind, that's why he came over here. He knew nothing about it until his grandmother told him. 'Twas the happiest day of his life when his mother died. 'Twas. 'Twas. If you'd only listen."

"Shut up, Kate."

She bowed her head deeply on her chest, and now John went to her and put his arm around her shoulders, but when he attempted to lead her to a chair she remained stiff, and she almost sprang from his hold when Hal, turning from her, sat down by the table again and said with finality, "Well, that's that. You'll not marry him."

"*I will. I will. Oh, yes, I will.*"

He was on his feet again, growling from deep in his chest, "By God! you won't, unless you do it over my dead body."

"Well" – her head was up, her shoulders back – "I will say this to you, Dad, and I mean it every word: whether you are dead or alive, I will marry Ben."

They all gaped at her as she went on, "He is for me and I for him. We have known it from the beginning. If I don't have him, then life won't matter to me. For years I have been aware of my size and my plainness. You yourself brought it more to the fore than anyone else when you arranged my marriage with Harry Baker. But now I have found a man, a very, very presentable man, a highly intelligent man, and a gentleman to boot, who does not think I'm a big awkward lump, nor that I'm as plain as a pikestaff, as has been said. And so he is my future, my life. Where he goes, I'll be there too, even if it is to America."

They were all speechless, and for a moment there hung over the kitchen a silence in which the only sound was the fire crackling and an occasional plup from the kettle on the hob as it spurted its boiling water onto the hot ash.

It was Hal who made the first move. Turning to the table he leant his two hands on the edge of it and, bending over, he said three words that caused Mary Ellen's body to shake: "We shall see," sounded so simple. But it wasn't the words, it was the tone in which they were said that was so ominous. She had heard that tone before many years ago, but it sounded as if it had been yesterday. It was the tone that preceded the fight. He could bawl and shout, or he could speak quietly, but when he used that tone, it meant trouble. She went to him, saying, "Hal." But again he pressed her aside, and now he went from them all, up the kitchen and through the door at the far end.

But the door had hardly closed on him when once again she turned on Maggie, crying at her now under her breath, "You! you see what you've done? Do you see what you've done?"

"Let up, Mam." Tom was at her side. "She knows what she's done, and she's sorry, and she'll be sorry for a long time. Won't you, Maggie?" He looked down on his sister, and she bent her head and no one could see the reaction of his words on her face.

And now Kate spoke again. She had taken off her scarf and bonnet and they hung limply from her hand as she looked at Mary Ellen and said, "It would have come out in any case. 'Tis better in the open, no matter what the consequences. I don't think I could have lived with it, knowing we were deceiving him."

As she made to walk away, Annie spoke for the first time, saying, "The past should be allowed to bury the past. What happened was a lifetime ago, yet at the same time I can say he has a side, for I can still see his twisted body when they brought him home. A thing that is not easily pushed into the back of your mind. You've got a trial afore you, lass, and although you say you've already made up your mind, who knows but time and thinking could change it."

Kate had turned towards Annie, and she now said, "Don't lay any stock on that, Annie. Come tomorrow, I'm going to him, married or not."

"*Oh my God!*" The words were a mere murmur from Mary Ellen, but they all heard them. Then their attention was turned from Kate as she went from the kitchen, to Florrie who, of a sudden, let out a cry then, turning to the wall, buried her face in the crook of her arm, and as her two brothers went to comfort her, Mary Ellen stood with her hands tightly pressed against the nape of her neck and her eyes directed onto the bowed head of Maggie. But she wasn't at this moment thinking of Maggie alone, she was thinking of them all for she knew in a way this was the end of the closeness of the family, a closeness she had imagined woud go on till the day she died.

14

Kate awoke to a white snow-muffled world. The room was icy cold. She lit the bedside candle; then pulling on a dressing-gown, she went to the window. There, to her dismay, she saw that the snow was banked up on the window-sill against the bottom pane. And when rubbing an upper pane, she could see it was still coming down thick and heavy, she thought, anxiously, if I don't get along there early the road will be blocked, if it's not already.

She had spent most of last evening packing her belongings. She had not gone down to the evening meal, and when Mary Ellen had brought her some food up on a tray, she thanked her but said she wasn't hungry. And Mary Ellen, sitting down on the edge of the bed, had looked sadly at her and said, "Aw, lass, for this to happen." And she had answered simply, "I can't help it, Mam."

"No, no. I understand that." Mary Ellen had said. "Your head's not much good when your heart is touched. Yes, yes, I understand that, lass. But for you to pick on someone like him. Why, if you had taken up with a savage Red Indian, he would have put up with it. But a Bannaman, never! Never! Never in this world, because it's still with him. He still has nightmares about it. He wakes up struggling and gasping and muttering as if the gag was still in his mouth. Many's the night I've had to get up and wipe the sweat from his body. I've even had to change the sheets, so damp were they. No, lass, he would have stomached you havin' anybody but a Bannaman."

Even when she tried to tell her how Ben had suffered at the hands of his own mother, it had seemed to make little impression. And even when they had held each other closely before Mary Ellen left the room, Kate knew that her mother was as hurt by her action as was Hal, though her hurt lacked his furious anger and bitterness.

She looked at the clock. It was half-past seven. She had overslept. Her time for rising was six o'clock and no one had come to waken her, which bore a significance all its own: already she was outside the family. She looked around the room which had been her own for years. She would miss this. Even if she slept in a finer one in the future, she would still miss this room.

At the foot of the bed were now piled four cloth bags on top of three boxes. She had brought them from the attic last night, and she had packed the contents of her wedding chest and the clothes from her wardrobe into them.

She washed herself in the ice-cold water from the ewer on the washhand stand, then dressed, and lastly did her hair. She did not hurry. All her actions were measured as if she was stretching each one out to hold in her memory. Breakfast, she knew, would be over now, and just as she was thinking, with a touch of sadness, that no one had come to bid her to it there came a tap on the door, and when she called, "All right," Florrie entered, balancing a tray.

"I brought you a little breakfast, Kate."

"Thanks, Florrie, but I'm not hungry."

"Well . . . well, have a drink then." Florrie's voice was low and she did not look at Kate, but, placing the tray on a small table, she began to pour out the tea from a small china pot. Then, after a moment, she picked up the cup and, turning to Kate where she was sitting on the bottom of the bed, she held it out to her in a shaking hand, and when it wobbled Kate took it quickly from her, and, getting to her feet, she placed it back on the tray. And then they stood tightly enfolded. Florrie's head resting on Kate's shoulder, she cried as she muttered, "Oh, Kate. Kate. I can't bear it. I'll never be happy when you're gone."

"You will, you will, dear. Charles will see to that. And . . . and I may not be so far away."

"America."

"No, no. Not for some time anyway."

"I like him, he's nice. If only Dad. . . ."

"Yes, if only Dad, but it's no use. Nothing will alter Dad in that way. I've always known it."

"Dad loves you, Kate."

"Yes, I . . . I know that, and I love him, but I love Ben more. There now, come on, dry your eyes." She pressed Florrie upwards and they stared at each other. Both their faces were wet, and when Florrie turned and looked at the packages on the floor she shook her head, saying, "You're really going then?"

Kate answered nothing to this but said, "It's a bad morning," and Florrie answered, "Yes, it has been at it all night. It's nearly knee-high in the yard. And there's a wind, it's drifting."

It was after a short pause that Florrie asked quietly, "Are you going straight along to that house?"

And there was another pause before Kate, nodding, said, "Yes, Florrie, I'm going along to that house."

At this Florrie turned sadly away, saying, "Eat something," then the door closed quietly behind her.

Kate didn't eat anything, but she drank another cup of tea, then got into her outdoor things, right to her bonnet and scarf, and lastly she tucked up the band of her skirt three times, bringing the hem up to her calfs. This was, in case her father didn't let her have the loan of a horse, she would have to walk it. In any case, it would be heavy going for the horse, and she couldn't ask for the trap to take her baggage for that would never get through the lanes in this. So she would leave it till later, with the exception of the bag which held her night clothes. That would be all she would be able to manage.

So thinking, she picked up the bag and went downstairs.

She was trembling as she entered the kitchen but was relieved to see that there were only her mother and Annie present, and they both stared at her. Mary Ellen was the first to speak. "You can't go, lass," she said; "not in this."

"I've got to, Mam. There's no use waiting. As soon as it clears I'll send for my things."

Mary Ellen came and stood before her, her voice quiet now as she said, "Lass, don't you understand he'll never let you go to him."

"He can't stop me, Mam, unless he shoots me or him."

"Don't say that lightly, lass, because I wouldn't put that past him either, for you have no idea how that man feels about the Bannamans, and rightly I'd say, he's got a cause. And all right, all right" – she held up her hand – "I know it's a pity that the sins of the fathers ... and the mothers are visited on the children, but 'tis true, as is also, what's bred in the bone comes out in the blood."

"You an' all, Mam?"

"I can't help it, lass, because I've seen more than you."

When Kate sighed, Mary Ellen, with a break in her voice, said, "Don't you know you're breakin' up this family, lass? What followed after Peg and Walter went will be nothing to what'll happen after you go to that fellow." As she spoke, the kitchen door opened and there was a sound of banging of feet against the wall before John came into the room. Pulling off his cap, he dusted himself down, then wiped the snowflakes from his face before looking at Kate and saying quietly, "You'll have to hold your hand a minute, Kate."

It was Mary Ellen who asked, "What d'you mean, she's got to hold her hand?"

"He's gone. Dad's gone out."

"*What!*" They all three stared at him, and he said quietly, "Now there's nothing more that can be done just yet." And looking at Kate directly, he added, "He gave me a message for you, Kate. He said, to stay put until he came back."

"How did he go?" Mary Ellen's hands were gripped tightly together now, and he answered her, "On horseback of course, how else?"

"You know what I mean. Did he take anything with him? A ... a ...?"

"No, Mam, he didn't take a gun."

"Are you sure?"

"Yes, Mam. I went and I saw to that. They're all there."

Slowly now, Mary Ellen sat down on a chair near the table, and Annie tapped her twice on the shoulder before looking at John and saying, "You'd like a cup?"

"Yes, please, Annie. Yes, please. It's bitter out." Then he turned to

Kate as she was pulling on her gloves and he said, "Now, now. He left that message precisely for you. You are to stay until. . . ."

"I'm not staying, John. If he's gone along there, only God knows what will happen when they meet."

"Well, I should think that Ben could hold his own if it comes to blows."

"Ben would never raise his hand to him."

"Not perhaps with the first blow, but there's few of us who can turn the other cheek. Now the only thing we can do is to sit tight and wait. He should be back within three hours even if the going's hard. That's giving him time to have his say as well."

"That's if he can get through at all."

He looked towards Annie now, saying, "Aye, you're right, Annie. I shouldn't be surprised if he turns round and comes back. So as I said, have patience." He was looking directly at Kate again. "But one way or the other he'll have his say, and after that it'll be up to you, Kate. You know what you want to do."

"I know what I want to do now, John."

"Aye. Aye, you do, Kate." He turned from her and went slowly out. And they all three noticed that he hadn't drunk his tea.

In the yard, John hurried across to the cow byres and as he thrust the door open the tallow candles stuck on the wooden shelf splattered, and he banged the door closed and lay against it for a moment, looking towards his brother who had stopped brushing the swill into the central gutter.

"Well?" Tom said, and he answered, "I told her, but she'll go, reason or none. But what I'm worried about at the moment is him. God knows what will happen when they meet up."

"Do you think you should go after him?"

"I'd given it a thought, but I don't know exactly where he'd be making for if. . . ."

"Well, there's only one place and that's the farm. That's if he gets there. He'll never attempt to go up into the hills. It would be useless."

"Aye, aye." John nodded. "But in the mood he's in, he'll see nothing as useless until he confronts him."

"Well, I can't imagine Ben being up in that hut in this. His own sense would bring him down to the farm, especially now that he knows he can hide behind his name no longer. Eeh! Our Maggie's caused something, hasn't she?"

"Oh, I don't know. It was bound to come out sooner or later, and I think Ben wanted it that way an' all. He's a decent fellow, Tom."

"Aye, I think along of you, he's a decent enough fellow, but then we're seeing him through a different pane of glass. We didn't have to go through what Dad had to go through. And that kind of thing helps your memory to last out."

John sighed now and said, "Aye well, there's nothing more we can do

378

for the moment. So let's get on with it. Somebody has to do it. But at this minute I wish I was miles away."

Hal had brought the horse to the outskirts of the farm with very little trouble, for the wind in many places had swept the track bare and there were only the usual potholes now filled with snow to contend with. Once he had to get off his horse and drag it through a drift; but over the years this had frequently happened.

Having dismounted again, he stood at the farm gate looking towards the yard. It was a smooth white mat which, he thought, pointed out plainly that the man he was seeking hadn't made a move outside the house as yet. He forced open the gate against the barrier of snow, led the horse in, then tied it with the reins to the central post of the gate, and as he did so the animal threw up its head in answer to a muffled neigh coming from the direction of the stables.

After saying, "Steady there. Steady there," he patted the animal's neck, then walked slowly towards the front of the house. And as he did so the memories of the past came flooding back to him, and it was as if it were only yesterday he was looking at Mary Bannaman hurrying back to the trap, then returning with the gun in her hand. And the bitterness deepened in him knowing that her son was in there, no doubt awaiting Kate's coming. Well, he would wait a long time, because he would sooner see her dead than being touched by a Bannaman in any way. And no matter how firm she had been in saying she would go to him, in the long run he had faith in her common sense and loyalty and her particular affection for himself.

There was an iron bell-pull to the side of the door and after he had dragged it downwards he stood listening to the muffled rattle beyond. But when it brought no response in the form of the man he was seeking, he took his fist and banged it hard on the panel. When still there was no response, he turned from the door and made his way round the side of the house. And as he entered the courtyard the muscles of his stomach seemed to go into knots, for his eyes were drawn to the door of the barn, the place wherein, as he put it to himself, he had suffered a crucifixion.

When he reached the back door he banged on this and when there was still no response, he put his hand to the latch in order to rattle it. But when surprisingly the door opened slowly under his grip, he stood back from it for a moment before, thrusting out his arm, he pushed it wide, then stepped inside.

He was in the kitchen. His eyes immediately went to the fireplace where the grey ash told him that there had been no one near that for some hours. Slowly he walked up the kitchen, his eyes darting from left to right as if expecting at any moment someone to spring out on him.

And when he reached the far door he opened his mouth and yelled, "If you're in here, show yourself." The thought entered his mind for a moment that the fellow was afraid to meet him. Yet, he dismissed that.

When he entered the hall he stood gazing about him. It was devoid of furniture, but he could see it had been freshly decorated. Even so, he remembered it as it once was, and also the situation of the room where he and others had confronted Bannaman himself. He did not go towards that door but stood at the foot of the stairs, yelling again, "Are you up there? Show yourself!"

Having thrust open the door of the sitting-room he then had to force himself to enter, and again his eyes went to the fireplace that showed the remains of a dead fire. But drawn up at right angles to it was a couch and on it, folded neatly, were three rugs. The room also held several pieces of furniture in the form of bureaux and bookcases and small tables. These were the pieces that were supposed to be stored here.

Strangely he did not turn about and leave the room but backed down it, again as if expecting some form to spring on him. But once in the hall, he hurried through it and into the kitchen, and out into the yard. And there he stood blinking against the snowflakes that were coming down more thickly now.

Where was he? Up in that hut skulking? Again his mind rejected the supposition. But there was one thing certain, he hadn't gone into any of the towns or else his horse wouldn't be over there neighing its head off.

He went towards the stables now and opened the half-door from where the sound was coming, and when the animal thrust its head at him, he pushed it to the side, saying, "Let up. Let up." He could see that it had hay, but the water bucket was almost empty, suggesting it hadn't been seen to since yesterday.

He closed the door on the thrusting head, then walked towards where his own horse was tethered. He did not mount up but went to the gate and looked towards the hills. If the snow kept up at this rate nobody would get up there for a day or so and nobody would get down either. Should he wait? And if he did, would Kate stay put? He was laying no stock on what she had said last night about her going to him even should he himself be dead or alive. They had both said things in the heat of the moment, yet he had meant every word he himself had said. By God! Yes, he had. And thinking this, he made a decision.

Swinging about, he untied the horse and led it back into the yard and to the stable next to the occupied one, and inside he tied it to a manger post in which there was some straw. And saying now, "Rest easy. I won't be long," he went out and closed the door, ignoring the sound of the animal kicking at the stanchion.

He knew where the shepherd's hut was and he knew the way to it; in fact, he knew every inch of these hills, that was in his younger days and when they weren't snow-covered.

He hadn't got very far when a bout of coughing brought him to a standstill and with his back to the driving snow. He told himself now he had to be careful. There was only one good thing: the further he went up the clearer the track would be in parts, for the wind was sweeping the snow from the hillside. But time and again the swirling of the snow like flour from the corn-mill almost blinded him.

When at last he could make out in the distance the smudge of the cottage, he stood for a moment, his back again to the wind, his hands clutching the top of his coat as if to stop his chest from heaving. He felt spent, but turning, he pushed on towards the cottage.

He was still some distance from it when he stopped and, wiping the snow from his eyelashes and face, he screwed up his eyes and peered through the swirling white mass at the man he had come in search of and who, as yet, was unaware of him, for he was pulling on a short rope, at the end of which was a goat.

It was when the goat decided to stop the tug of war and to come quietly that Ben almost fell on to his back in the snow, and as he twisted around he could just make out the outline of the huddled form standing some yards away. For a moment he imagined it was Kate; then when he straightened up and saw who it was, his grip on the rope slackened, and the goat taking advantage of this, scampered away towards the field, not knowing that the gate was closed and that it would have to make a long detour back to its shelter.

Ben watched the animal disappearing before, turning and hunching forward, he again looked towards Hal and called, "Come in!" then made towards the door of the cottage. And Hal's voice came back to him, crying, "I'm as near to you as is safe, for you that is."

"Mr Roystan, please!" Ben was shouting now. "I want you to listen to me." And Hal's voice was as loud but checked by his gasping breath as he cried, "Listen to you? I know all I want to know about you, young man. . . . And . . . and I've just come to tell you somethin' . . . and you'd better take heed. . . . You keep away from my Kate, 'cos if you don't, the next time we come face to face I . . . I won't come empty-handed. I mean that. I've always said I would swing for one of the Bannamans if I ever came across them . . . and I'd be quite willing to . . . to do that rather than let you put a finger on her, more than you have done up to now. . . . So, the best advice I can give you, is to get back onto a boat an' . . . an' get back to your homeland an' forget you ever came here."

"Have you had your say?"

Hal was slightly nonplussed by the seeming calmness of the reply, and he blustered more loudly than ever: "Yes, I've had me say, all that needs to be said, and from what little you know of me you'll have guessed I'm a man of me word. An' . . . an' I promise you, you won't live to tell the tale if you come . . . come near her again."

"What about her?"

"She'll do as she's told."

"Not if I know Kate, she won't. And you can't chain her up as much as you would like to. Drive me too far, Mr Roystan, and I'll take Kate out of this country under your very nose."

"By God!" The words were ground out through Hal's teeth, and Ben could just make out the older man's hand roughly wiping the snow from his face before he cried again, "It's a damn good job I made meself come empty-handed, 'cos it wouldn't have been buckshot I would have filled you with, but ... but a bullet at this minute. Now I've told you." The hand was stretched out towards him. "That's me final word. Take heed of it." And at this he turned about and began to stagger back the way he had come. And he was on the point of exhaustion as he leant against part of a drystone wall in an effort to get his breath. And as he stood gasping, he knew this business wasn't finished, not by a long chalk, for he was up against someone who was as determined as himself.

When he straightened up he saw the dark blur of the goat jumping through the snow just ahead of him, and in a way it was clearing the path for him, so, stumbling on, he followed it. Goats, he knew, were notoriously sure-footed and it could likely make out the track better than he could, for now the snow was falling and swirling so thickly that he could hardly see more than a few yards ahead.

The goat was making for its hut, which was its home and from which its master had dragged it a short while ago. It was used to the man who fed it, and milked it, and talked to it, but even he she butted whenever the occasion presented itself. Her irritation mounted when, reaching the gate that led into the bottom of the field where the hut was situated, she found it barred, and so it was natural that she should turn on the figure that was looming out of the snow and to lower her head and charge it.

Ben stood in the middle of the little room and looked about him. He knew it was the last time he would see it. The fire had smouldered low, but there was a pile of logs to the side of it. There was some food left in the cupboard and blankets on the single wooden platform bed. The door he would leave unlocked just in case some helpless traveller should be stranded this way. That was how he had found the place when he was stranded, although it wasn't as comfortable then as it was now.

He had put his books and papers into a canvas bag, and these he had slung across his shoulder, leaving his arms free to catch that dratted goat. He knew where it would have made for, but it wouldn't be able to get in for he had locked the gate. He had become fond of Biddy. She had supplied him with milk and acted as an audience to his mutterings many a time. But going on last year's experience he knew that if the weather kept like this the hills would become inaccessible, and without food or water she could easily die.

After his visitor had departed he had sat at the table and his anger had been equal to that of the man he had hoped to make his father-in-law. Of one thing he was certain, and that was Hal Roystan meant every word he had said and was capable of taking a gun to him. Well, that being so, he would have to show him that he, too, equally meant every word he said. And if he were to find it impossible to spirit Kate away from the house, then he would call in the law. The English always put themselves over as being a people that liked fair play. So, he would ask the law to come to his aid. But with or without it, he meant to have Kate. He had at times wondered why she had come to mean so much to him, and had asked himself if one of the reasons was that she was connected with the family that had suffered at his mother's and his grandfather's hands; and, too, if it was a form of erasing inherited guilt. But the answer was always no: whomsoever Kate had belonged to it would have been the same, for there was a deep affinity between them; she warmed him; she made him feel whole; besides which she was intelligent and humorous.

He planned in his mind now to go to the house and await her coming, and if she didn't appear within the next two or three days he would then enlist the help of Charles. If this failed, then he would let the law take over.

He went out and closed the door behind him, pressing the sneck down hard. He did not, however, make his way towards the track but along by the side of the cottage and towards the gate that led into the field, it being a short cut to the hut. In parts the snow came up to the top of his gaiters and got deeper as the field sloped steeply downwards.

Making his way to the gate that he had closed only an hour or so before, he was surprised to see that Biddy wasn't on the other side of it waiting impatiently to be let into her home.

Having forced the gate open, he peered along by the wall and made out the small dark form of her standing there. Ploughing now towards her, he again felt surprise when she didn't come at him head down with annoyance. And then a yard or so from her he came to a dead stop and stared in open-mouthed amazement at a boot sticking up out of the snow, and another near it but turned inwards. He bent down quickly and saw the form half-buried in a drift. The head was clear but pressed against the wall and was blood-covered.

"Oh God!" Throwing the bag of books from his shoulders, he bent down and, putting his arm around the still form, dragged it out of the shallow ditch and onto the comparatively firmer ground of the track. The head was bare and he could see the cut on the temple. The blood had congealed on it and had stained the grey hair around the ear and brow.

In the name of God! what was he to do? Was he dead? No, no; the chest was heaving. He'd have to get him into shelter. But where? The goat's hut? Even his nose wrinkled at the thought, but better that than out here until he could get help.

He got behind Hal now and eased up his shoulders by putting his own arms under Hal's oxters, and began to drag him towards the gate, the goat slowly following of its own accord now.

It was as he pulled him sideways through the small aperture the gate afforded that Hal let out a cry that was something between a groan and a scream. Ben stopped and, laying him down, bent over him, saying, "What is it? Where are you hurt?"

But there was no answer. The eyes were closed. The face was as it was before.

He was gasping hard himself when, at last, he pulled the limp form into the small, smelling, dark straw-covered hut, and when he had him stretched out he slumped down for a moment to recover his own breath, only to lift his head sharply as Biddy made her appearance in the open door. And now he cried, "Get away! Stay there!" Then turning his attention to the man who had, just a short while ago, threatened to kill him, he asked himself what he was to do now. One thing was certain, he couldn't stay here; they'd both freeze to death. He'd have to bring him round in some way or another. This in his mind, he began to slap gently the rough prickly cheek, saying, "Mr Roystan, come along. Mr Roystan."

When he had almost given up hope of this having any effect, Hal groaned, a long deep groan; then his lids slowly opening, he looked up to the wooden roof not five feet above his head, and he muttered something unintelligible before his eyes took in the face to the side of him. His mouth fell open; then he gasped, "Bloody goat!"

Ben looked from him to where the goat was still standing at the open door; then he almost wanted to laugh as Hal's voice came again, saying, "Butted ... me."

The goat had butted him into the ditch. But it was no laughing matter; if he hadn't come down that way, the great Mr Roystan could have died in the snow. His thoughts were cynical at the moment as they suggested that that would have been a solution.

"Are you in pain? Can you sit up?" he asked, attempting to put his arm around the older man's shoulders. But Hal shrank from his touch and made a sound like an angry animal; then in attempting to rise he let out another long groan that touched on a yell, and after gasping for a moment, he muttered, "Me ... me leg's broke."

Instantly now, Ben unbuttoned Hal's long coat. The corduroy breeches below showed no distortion, but the top boot on his right foot was lying at an angle, and when he touched it, and only gently, Hal again cried out.

"Your ankle's broken."

"Me ankle?"

"Yes."

"Not me leg?"

"No."

"Bloody goat!"

"How does your head feel?"

"I don't know. Thick." His voice was a mutter now, and he closed his eyes. "I'm spinnin' a bit," he said. Opening his eyes again and looking up into Ben's face he added, "What you goin' to do with me? Leave me here? It would be a way out, wouldn't it? Eh?"

"Don't talk stupid." Ben's tone held disdain.

"*What?*"

"You heard me. I've got to get you up to the cottage." And he could not help but add, "Get you fit enough again to use that gun."

"Aye, well" – the head moved slowly – "don't think this changes anything. I mean what I said. There's nothin' altered."

"As you say, there's nothing altered."

Hal now lowered his lids. His head was spinning; he felt rotten, real bad. He forced himself to look up again, saying now, "You could get down the hills, get help."

"Not until I get you up out of this. It will take a couple of hours before help comes; you would be stiff by then."

Aye, he was right, he would be at that.

He shivered visibly now and Ben said flatly, "Are you feeling cold?"

"A bit."

"Well, we'd better try and make a move."

Hal made no protest when Ben buttoned up his coat again. But when his body was racked with a fit of coughing and he shivered now from head to foot, and Ben took off his own greatcoat and put it around him, he clumsily thrust it aside, muttering between gasps, "I ... I don't ... want ... that."

Ben said nothing, but he kept the coat tight around Hal's shoulders for some minutes. Then when the shivering did not ease he said roughly, "Now look here. You've got to make an effort and get onto your feet ... or foot. It isn't all that far to the cottage. The worst part is the incline just outside the door here."

Hal stared up through the murky light into the thin face and into eyes that looked black and hard, and he thought: Make an effort, he said, Who did he think he was talking to? He'd show him.

As he pulled himself up into a sitting position his head spun, then his body seemed ripped apart by a flame of pain. He would have lain down quickly again but the fellow's knee was pressed between his shoulders, and now he felt his arms go around him, pushing him upwards.

God Almighty! He couldn't bear this. He was back in the loft again. His bones were snapping; the ropes were cutting into his flesh; the gag was stopping his breathing. And it was all through one of the hated Bannamans. Them buggers. Them evil buggers.

"Now hop. Grip my shoulder. Bend your back until we get through the door. There, that's it. We're in the open. Come on, come on. You can't lie down here."

The fellow was yelling at him. By God! nobody was going to yell at him, especially that bloke.

"Look, just hop. Put all your weight on me and hop."

The voice sounded to Hal now as if it were coming from a great distance, like an echo over the hills. He saw the white field before him, the rise that the fellow had talked about. It got higher and higher, and when he had hopped three times it came on him and felled him to the ground.

Oh my God! Ben drew in a long icy draught of air. This was a situation. How was he to get him up that slope? Drag him as he had done before? But that had been on the level. He certainly couldn't carry him. He was a dead weight to drag, but drag was the only thing he could do.

It took a full fifteen minutes to inch him up the slope. Time and again, he slipped and found himself flat on his back, his legs to each side of Hal's shoulders as if they were on a sleigh.

He did not know how long it was before he finally dragged the unconscious body through the gate and towards the door of the cottage. And when at last he managed to pull Hal into the room he fell down beside him and lay exhausted for some time.

Slowly rising to his feet now, he again put his frozen arms underneath the still form and pulled it towards the mat in front of the fireplace. Then taking the bellows that he had never expected to handle again, he blew up the dying embers, put on more wood, filled a pan of water from a bucket and placed it in the heart of the fire. Only then did he kneel down beside Hal and, patting his cheek again, say, "Come on. Come on. You're all right now." But when there was no response, he unbuttoned his topcoat and gently eased it off him. Then taking the blankets from the bed, he covered him up; and lastly he placed a pillow under his head. It was as he did this that Hal groaned and slowly opened his eyes. Then a fit of coughing dragged him into consciousness and, turning his head, he looked to where the fire was now blazing and he sighed and muttered something. And Ben, bending over him, said, "What did you say?"

"They've come ... help?"

"No."

"No?" His eyes opened wider. "How ... did ... I get ... here?"

"On the back of the goat, of course." Ben's voice was cynical, and Hal, looking up at him, thought, Oh no, not that. Not to have to be thankful to him for anything. Anyway, he couldn't have got him up that slope on his own – he remembered the slope – but he was here. God Almighty! Things were taking a turn that he didn't want, and he was going to have nothing to do with it. Nothing was altered.

It was some minutes later when Ben, holding a hot drink in front of Hal, said, "Can you sit up to drink this?" and he answered, "What is it?"

"Tea."

"Tea?"

"Yes, tea. I've lived quite a civilized life up here."

As Hal went to raise himself on his elbow, his head swam again, and the movement of his leg caused him to hold his breath and to grit his teeth. And when Ben said, "I should look at the foot," he made no protest, but, taking the mug, he drank the scalding liquid, then lay back again.

Gently now Ben undid the gaiter, then as gently as he could he pulled out the laces of the boot. But it was when, gripping the upper shin bone tightly with one hand, he went to ease the boot off the foot with his other hand that Hal let out a long scream and his hands clawed up handfuls of the mat to each side of him.

The boot off, Ben looked down in dismay at the point of bone piercing the stocking. Then glancing to where Hal was lying, his eyes screwed tightly shut, he added, "It's a bad break."

"What you intend doin'?"

What did he intend doing? Well, yes, what did he intend doing? The only thing he could do was to go down and get help, but that would have to wait until he thawed out himself, for he, too, was now shivering. The room, in spite of the fire blazing, appeared cold. But he wasn't afraid of catching cold; he couldn't remember having a real bad cold in his life.

He looked at his watch. It was half-past one. The light would be gone by four o'clock, and with all the candle lanterns in the county it would be madness for any rescue party to attempt the hills after dark. That left only two and a half hours at the most to get down and get back. It couldn't be done. In ordinary weather, yes, but not under these conditions. Anyway, there was still hope that quite shortly someone would appear on the hills, because surely the boys would have come out by now, thinking perhaps that their father had met up with him and likely had carried out his threat and had killed him without the aid of a gun.

"Are you going down?"

"I . . . I don't think it's any use. They wouldn't get back up here before dark. It looks as if we might have to make a night of it."

"She'll be worried. Mary Ellen."

"She'll not be the only one."

Before he could answer, Hal was overcome by a fit of shivering, and Ben asked, "Are you still cold?"

His teeth chattering, Hal nodded; then after a moment he asked, "Don't have a drop of the hard, whisky or anything?"

"No. I'm sorry. I finished it off last night. Will you have another cup of tea?"

"Aye, aye."

"How's the pain?"

"Bearable, as long as I don't move. . . . Why don't you make an effort and go down? I'll be all right. And they . . . they're used to the hills, they'll make it."

"Yes, they might make it up, but never down, not carrying you, not in this. It's coming down thicker than ever."

There followed a silence until Hal said, "What if we're snowed up here for days? It's happened afore. We could starve to death then."

"Not quite. There's some stale bread in the cupboard, and dried herring, and the end of a smoked ham, and I could always manage to bring Biddy up. She mightn't be a pleasant house-mate, but her milk would be welcome."

There followed another silence, then Hal, his voice almost inaudible now, said, "Life's funny, the tricks it plays on you. You know, if I'd had me gun with me earlier on, I likely would have shot you."

"I have no doubt of it."

"You're a cool customer, aren't you?"

"I don't see myself in that light, anything but."

"'Tis pity you are who you are, because I won't change me mind about you. Don't think this'll make any difference. Don't get that into your head."

"No, I won't get that into my head. I know how you feel about the whole situation, but I would like you to know how I feel about it too. Under the circumstances of this morning, there was no hope that you would ever listen to me, but now you've got no other choice, and I mean to tell you my side of it."

"'Twill be a waste of time."

"I'll chance that."

Before he drew up a chair, Ben went to the bed and took the remaining rug from it and put it round his own shoulders. He felt cold to the marrow and he was finding it an effort to stop his own teeth from chattering. But now, sitting close to the hearth, he looked into the fire before he said, "You don't know what hate is. Comparing your feeling for the Bannamans with mine for my mother is like comparing plaster with a slab of granite."

And slowly now, his eyes directed towards the burning and mushing wood, he told Hal of his life, as he had Kate. And he ended with the words, "The only excuse I have for her is that she was insane."

It was some time before Hal spoke; then quietly he said, "Aye, she was. But what you've got to remember, lad, is that you're part of her."

Ben turned and looked at the man lying prone to his side and, his voice low, he said, "I'm well aware of that, always have been, but I'm also aware that I'm my father's son, and he was one of the best men alive, as was my grandfather. And I can also say my grandmother, her mother, is a good woman. She knew nothing of what her daughter had done until her son told her. My uncle was a partner in the barn affair, as my grandmother called it when she related the story to me, but, as she said, he was a weak man and easily led. He had inherited none of his father's strength and little of his evil; it was my mother who became a replica of the man who killed your father. You, I may say, carry the scars of the Bannamans in your mind; I carry them both physically and mentally, for like a slave I bear the marks of a whip on my back, and not a simple horsewhip, but a thonged one. So there you are, that's my side of it."

The light was fading. Ben rose stiffly to his feet and, taking the tallow candle from out of a brass candlestick on the narrow shelf of the mantelpiece, he lit it at the fire. Then replacing it in the stick, he took it to the table and as he stood for a moment staring at it, Hal said, "Well, I'm sorry for you, lad, but you see, in me mind, you're still her son. Good, bad, or indifferent, you're still her son. And although I mightn't take a gun to you in the future, I'll still do everything in me power to stop you and Kate coming together, because I couldn't bear the thought. Funny, but I just couldn't bear the thought of her going to anybody that had any connections with a Bannaman. You won't understand that."

"Yes, I do." Ben's voice was quiet and he turned and looked at Hal and added, "All being said and done, it leaves us both in the same mind: you determined that I shan't have Kate, and I determined that I shall. Whatever happens, I shall."

"We'll see, lad. We'll see. Let's get out of this first, then we'll see."

15

The kitchen was crowded. Mary Ellen stood with her back to the fire, her hands joined tightly at her waist, and gazed at the numerous men standing awkwardly sipping at mugs of mulled ale. Men from different walks of life had been coming and going all day since noon. This was after John and Tom had gone over to the Bannamans' house and found the two horses in the stables. From there, they had climbed the hills to Ben's cottage, but found no one. They had been hardly able to see a hand before them; the snow, being powder dry, was whirling like low clouds over the hills. The only live thing they had seen between the swirling drifts of snow was a glimpse of a goat that had come out of its hut at the bottom of the field. It was after this that they had set the alarm.

The only lead they had as to where Hal might have gone had been from Jamie Pollock. But that had turned out to be a wild-goose chase, and as the men said, nobody should have taken any notice of what Jamie said, him being wrong in the head.

The manager from the mine said, "I'll have a group out come dawn, Mrs Roystan. Who knows, he could have taken shelter somewhere." As far as he and the others helping in the search knew, they were looking for only one man. It was Farmer Dickinson who said, "Funny, he should be makin' for Bannaman's place. Was he going to have a word with young Mr Hamilton, him that's taking it over?"

"Aye, yes, just a word," John answered, nodding at the man.

But Farmer Dickinson's curiosity was aroused: "Wouldn't have thought Hal had much time for anybody who took that place. Funny. 'Tis funny," he said.

"Would you like some more beer?" Florrie was proferring the jug towards Farmer Dickinson. And he, smiling at her, said, "No, lass, thank you very much; I want to keep straight legs to get me home, and that's strong stuff, that is. Good an' all." He jerked his chin at her. And Florrie turned to another man, saying, "Mr Robson?" and he answered, "Yes, just a drop. It gets down to your toes, that does."

Moving from the fireplace towards the table, Mary Ellen now said quietly, "Thank you very much, one and all. I'll . . . I'll be glad to see you in the mornin'."

Buttoning up their coats and pulling their caps tight on to their heads, the men now said their goodbyes, one after the other promising to be back at first light. And then she was left with her family.

"Come on, lass." Annie was gently guiding her towards the settle, saying, "Sit yourself down; you can do no good standing about. It wouldn't surprise me if he didn't come stumbling in that door at any minute."

"Oh, Annie, Annie." Mary Ellen closed her eyes, then murmured, "What in the name of God could have happened to them?" Then looking at Annie again, she said, "Where's Kate?"

"She's all right. She's all right. I've got her soaking her feet in her room. She was wet to the skin. And the best thing you can do is to go and lie down for an hour or two."

"Don't be silly, Annie; I'll never sleep again till I know what's happened to him . . . to *them*." She now looked towards Maggie who was placing a kettle on the hob and, leaning forward, she cried at her, "I hope you realize, girl, that this is all your fault. If your father's dead you'll have it on your conscience till the day you die. And. . . ."

"Mam. Mam" – John was standing over her – " 'Tis no good taking that line. It would have come out somehow, some time or other. It had to happen."

Mary Ellen looked up at him and asked pityingly now, "But where could they have got to? They must both be together, their horses being in the stables. What in the name of God! could have happened to them?"

"I don't know, no more than you do, except one thing, if there was any violence it would come from Father's side not Ben's."

"What a thing to say."

"Well, 'tis true, Mam, isn't it? Because let's face it, when he's aroused he's like a bull charging straight ahead."

"Shut up! John."

"I'm only trying to point out to you that he would come to no harm through Ben."

"Well, if it's any news to you, I'm worried an' all, and at bottom about the same thing that's worrying you, and that is, what he might have done to Ben. Oh God!" She put her two hands to her head and gripped her hair. "To think our family should come to this. Things were going too well for us, too smoothly. It seems as if there's a curse on us an' still connected with them Bannamans." And when no one made any attempt to be more enlightening she turned about and, leaning her forearm on the mantelpiece, dropped her head onto it, and in her own fashion she began to pray.

At first light the men were again in the yard. There were ten of them altogether and they said there were more to follow. They paired off in two's, planning to keep within hailing distance of each other in case they should come across what they were looking for. They spread out fanwise, John and Tom plumping once again for the road that led to the Bannamans' farm, feeling that at least Ben might turn up.

Terry and Gabriel were left to see to the cattle, while Annie and Florrie took it upon themselves to see to the hens and pigs.

It had stopped snowing sometime in the night, and now a thaw had set in and a weak sun was shining. Inside the house Maggie was seeing to the fires, and Kate and Mary Ellen were alone in the kitchen. They were both bleary-eyed as they had sat up all night, just dozing now and again. Neither of them had eaten anything, but they had drunk numerous cups of tea. And now Mary Ellen, brewing once again, turned from the hob at the sound of Kate's sharp tone as she said, "I can't just stay here, Mam; I've got to go out looking."

"There are plenty doing that, lass. Look how you came in last night. We don't want you bad."

"I won't take bad, but I've got to go out." She turned away and hurried from the kitchen, leaving Mary Ellen standing, asking herself once again just where it would end.

Five minutes later, when Kate returned to the kitchen, Mary Ellen gave her but a swift glance for there was a sudden commotion in the yard. She ran to the door, to see John and Tom and two of the searchers running towards the harness-room. Quickly, she went out into the yard, shouting, "What is it? What is it?"

"Be with you in a minute." John had turned from the harness-room door. He was talking rapidly to the men. Then he ran to her and, taking her by the arm, almost dragged her back into the kitchen. And there was a smile on his face as he looked from her to Kate, then back to her again, saying, "He's all right ... both of them. Ben made his way down the hills. We met him on the road. He's a bit exhausted. He was coming for a stretcher, a canvas one; he says a door's no good, too slippery up there."

"Why a stretcher? Why a stretcher?" Mary Ellen was clutching him.

"'Tis all right. 'Tis all right, Mam," John said, catching hold of his mother's hand. "He's had a blow on the head and his ankle's broken, but he's...."

"Who did that?"

"I don't know. I don't know. But he's alive and he's all right, Ben says."

"Ben. How is Ben?"

John looked at Kate and paused before he answered, "All right, Kate, but, naturally, tired. He must have had a time of it up there."

"I'll ... I'll go along with you."

"No, no." He now patted her shoulder. "You'd only be in the way. You'll be needed here. Anyway you'll have to get the bed ready, the warming-pan going and plenty of hot bricks."

"How long are you likely to be?"

He paused a moment thinking, then said, "Two hours I should say will see us down. Now there! Cheer up, they're all right." He looked from one to the other, and Mary Ellen said, "Thanks be to God." But

Kate didn't speak, for the wave of relief that was passing through her made her feel faint, and in case she should do something silly she turned quickly about and hurried out of the kitchen. And when she reached her own room she dropped onto her knees by the side of the bed and said deeply and profoundly, "Thank you. Thank you." She wasn't given to praying, she hadn't been brought up to pray. The only member of the family, she thought, who said a nightly prayer was Florrie. But she herself over the past twenty-four hours had made up for her lapse of years; every step she had taken through the snow yesterday had been accompanied by a beseeching prayer, especially while she was trying to reach the cottage and being sick at the thought of what she might find there. The only reason why she hadn't succeeded in getting that far was that she had met the boys coming down and they had found it empty and, as they had said, "Everything left tidy."

Slowly she rose from her knees and got out of her outdoor things before going downstairs again to await the return of her father and Ben, for surely they would bring Ben back with them.

Two and a half hours later when the almost exhausted men carried the canvas sling into the kitchen, Ben wasn't among those accompanying them.

When they laid Hal gently down on the mat before the fire Mary Ellen dropped on to her knees by his side and, touching the only exposed part of him besides his eyes, which was his cheek-bone, she said, "Oh, my dear, my dear." And at this he brought his hands from underneath the blanket that covered him and, gripping hers, he said, "'Tis all right, lass, 'tis all right. Get me to bed and warm, and I'll be as fit as a fiddle in no time."

Looking down into his face now, she saw that it was haggard and grey; then getting to her feet, she looked at her two sons and at the other two men who had helped to carry him the last part of the journey, and she said, "Would you take him up?"

At this, willing voices from others around said, "We'll do it, missis, they've done their stint." And the man laughed as they picked up the four poles that were threaded through the canvas sheet, and, Mary Ellen leading the way, they followed her out of the room. And as the door closed on them a strange thing happened, strange at least to John and Tom and the rest of the men who were crowded in the kitchen, for Annie, big Annie as she was known, buckled at the knees and fell in a dead faint down by the side of the table.

"Well, did you ever see anything like that?"

"Lift her up onto the settle."

"Get some burnt paper, lass."

"Well! I never thought Annie was one for fainting."

Kate rolled up a wad of paper, and lit it at the fire, then nipped it out before going to the settle and waving it backward and forward under Annie's nose, the while thinking, No, no one would imagine any one as big as Annie fainting; big people were supposed to be tough and didn't do silly things like that. They weren't to know that Annie loved her father almost as much as her mother did, perhaps equally, or more so, because her life had been frustrated. No one had ever put this into actual words except that time when her mother had said, "Annie's always been very fond of your father," and she had laughingly added, "Funny, but I think she had hopes in that quarter at one time."

Yes, it was funny, to everybody but Annie.

"There you are, lass. Come on, come on. Now what made you go and do that?" The man patted Annie's cheek.

Annie slowly opened her eyes, wetted her lips, and looked at Kate, and Kate, now taking her by the arm, heaved her up, saying, "Come and lie down for a while and I'll bring you a cup of tea." And with this she led her through the men and out into the hall and to the sitting-room, and there, pressing her down into the couch, she lifted her feet up, arranged a cushion at her head, then, bending over her, said, "You stay put there."

"It was a daft thing to do."

"We're all daft at the moment, Annie. I'll get you a cup of tea."

As Kate went to move away, Annie gripped her wrist and, staring up into her face, she said, "Whatever happens, go to him, lass. Don't let your life be wasted, because you'll never meet another like him around these quarters, you won't. As for your dad, he's had his life, or most of it. So follow your heart, lass."

"I will, Annie. I intend to do so, no matter what happens."

They looked at each other for a moment longer, then Kate went from the room.

The men had left the kitchen, but Florrie and Maggie were hurrying up the room carrying hot bricks wrapped in blankets. There was only Tom left. He was standing before the fire, one hand holding a mug of tea, the other held out to the blaze.

Going to him, she asked quietly, "Where's Ben?"

"He . . . he went off to the farm."

"How was he?"

"Tired, I would say."

"What had happened up there?"

"I don't know. He didn't say. He wasn't for talking much. But he had attended to Dad, got his boot off, cut off the sock and things. It's a bad break. He must have gone through it."

"You don't know what happened?"

"No."

"If they were in the cottage, why didn't you find them before?"

"Because they weren't there." His voice had an impatient ring to it.

As she said, "I'm sorry," the far door opened and Florrie came running into the room, saying, "Where's Annie? Mam wants her."

"Annie's not well. She's resting in the sitting-room."

"Well then, you had better come up, Kate. Maggie's no good, and he's yelling out, and ... and I'm sorry, but I can't bear to look at his foot."

Kate hurried from the room now and up the stairs and into her mother's bedroom. Hal was propped up in bed, covered all over except for his right foot, which was turned to the side and looked twice its size. But the swollen flesh hadn't covered the ominous piece of bone sticking up through the skin. Her mother was saying, "The doctor should be here any minute. The mine manager was sending in a man to Haydon Bridge. They've got the road cleared that far for the carts." She turned and glanced at Kate, saying, "Where's Annie?"

"She's ... she's not well. She in the sitting-room."

"Not well?" Mary Ellen made an impatient movement with her head for a moment; then said, "Well, you come and help me get your father changed."

"Leave me be, woman! I ... I can't stand much more of this. Get me some whisky."

Mary Ellen now looked across the bed to where Maggie was standing wringing her hands and she said, "Go and bring the bottle from the sideboard. Quick now."

As Maggie scurried from the room Kate moved up the side of the bed and looked down on to the haggard face, but she said nothing; nor did Hal, but he put out his hand and took hers and held tightly on to it.

And he retained his hold for the next twenty minutes or so. Mary Ellen had had to push a chair up near the bed so that Kate could sit down and they had exchanged glances but said nothing. Even when Maggie had returned with the whisky and Mary Ellen had poured a stiff measure into a glass, still he did not release his hold on Kate's hand, but took the glass from his wife with his left hand and swallowed the spirit almost in one gulp. It was only when the doctor entered the room that Kate rose and, pulling her hand from his grasp, stepped aside.

"Well now, what have you been up to?" Doctor Brunton had been a friend to Mary Ellen from the day when he took her to the prison to visit Roddy Greenbank, and he had attended each of her confinements over the years. He knew all about this family, particularly about its head, who was answering him now in characteristic fashion, saying, "Well, if you open your eyes you'll see what I've been up to."

The doctor bent over the foot and muttered something; then looking at Mary Ellen, he said, "When he does things, he always attempts to do them thoroughly. You know that, don't you, Mary Ellen?"

"I ... I do indeed, Doctor." She smiled wanly at him.

He had been divested of his greatcoat downstairs; now he unbuttoned his jacket and slowly took it off, saying the while, "Get John and Tom up here, will you? And then I'll want some hot water and two pieces of wood, about two foot long and three inches wide, and a shorter piece, and some strips of linen . . . and whisky, of course." He turned his head in Hal's direction, adding, "That's right, isn't it? You'd like to be washed inside and out with whisky?"

"Get on with it."

He looked at Mary Ellen again and smiled. Then unloosening the cuffs of his white shirt and rolling them back, he moved up the side of the bed and, bending over Hal, said, "Let's have a look at your face." Turning it gently to the side, he added, "You're lucky there, it's just below skin-deep. It'll want a stitch or two. Got a headache?"

"What d'you think?"

"I think you're a very lucky man to have been brought down the hill when you were. Another day and I mightn't have been able to do much with that." He thumbed towards the foot. "And I'm telling you –" His voice had lost its bantering tone, but he returned to it a minute later in greeting Tom and John entering the room saying to them, "Hello, there. Your father would like you to hang on to him time I straighten out this foot of his. By the way" – he turned and looked at Hal again – "how did you come to do it, and your head?"

When Hal did not answer immediately, Mary Ellen, Kate, and the two men looked at him apprehensively, waiting for the answer which would be in the nature of, "I got it in a fight." But when he said, somewhat reluctantly, "I was bumped by a bloody goat," their faces stretched, and they looked at each other in disbelief. Then as Kate covered her eyes, for she had a vision of Biddy carrying out her greeting to an intruder, the boys spluttered, but Mary Ellen burst into a high laugh touching on hysteria which ended abruptly as the doctor said, "There now, there now." And the tears spurted from her eyes and ran down her face.

Purposely ignoring her crying and the fact that the boys and the doctor were comforting her, Hal bawled, "Will you stop your patting session and get on with it?"

And they got on with it.

They gave him another stiff dose of whisky. Then John, kneeling on one side of the bed, held his father's arm, and Tom, standing at the other side, braced himself against the headpost as he aimed to keep his father steady as he writhed and groaned and his teeth brought the blood from his lower lip. Then after giving one high piercing yell, Hal was silent, and the doctor, glancing up towards him, said, "That's good. Now Kate, keep that foot still. And Mary Ellen, hand me that blue bottle from the table."

As he poured the liquid from the bottle over the jagged flesh, he said, "Let's hope that stops any further infection." Then taking a needle and thread from a case that had been laid on the bed to the side of the board on which the foot rested, he began to sew the flesh he'd had to cut in order to set the splintered bone. This done, he now bound the ankle tightly with the straps of linen. Then placing the smallest piece of wood against the bandaged sole of the foot, he secured this in position in the same way. After which he set the two thin slats of wood down each side of the leg and once again he began winding the torn sheeting round them till the foot and leg were held firmly in place.

Looking up to where the boys were still holding the inert arms, he said, "'Tis done. He'll be all right now. What I want next is a kind of cage to keep the bedclothes off the leg. Do you think you can knock something up?"

"Oh, yes, yes, Doctor." John spoke, but both nodded at him, and when John added, "You don't want us any more?" the doctor said, "No. He's all right now, except for his temper." He pulled a slight face. "And you can expect that to be touchy for a few days. Now let me see to that cut before he comes round." . . .

When Hal eventually came round, there was no show of temper, but he lay limp and exhausted, which filled Mary Ellen with concern, for she knew all about reactions to shock and exposure. Only last year a shepherd had died after lying on the hillsides all night after a fall. They had found him the next day, still alive, but within two days he was gone. . . .

It was in the middle of the afternoon when Kate, unable to stand the waiting any longer, said to Mary Ellen, "Mam, I'm . . . I'm going to slip along to see how he is. He . . . he was out there, too, you know."

"Lass, please, you can't go the day. You'd never get back in the light, and the roads are a bog now. Wait till the morrow. Anyway, he needs you." She jerked her head upwards. "He's more content when you're there. Do this for me." She put out her hand and gripped Kate's arm. "Don't leave him the day."

She knew she was going against every fibre of her being when she said, "All right. But I'll go tomorrow. Understand, Mam? I'll go tomorrow."

"All right, lass, all right."

Hal had a restless night. At one point he became feverish, but by morning the fever had left him and he lay limp and definitely in pain.

They had taken their turns at sitting up with him during the night and it was five o'clock in the morning when Kate had taken off her clothes and got into bed; so weary was she that it was five hours later when she awoke.

Getting into her dressing-gown, she went hurriedly across the landing and, as she neared the bedroom door, Mary Ellen came out, saying, "Oh, there you are, lass. Had a good sleep?"

"I'm sorry. I . . . I didn't intend to sleep till this time. How is he?"

"He's a bit washed out, very tired, but the fever's gone. That worried me, but he'll pick up now. He's asking for you." She paused, then said, "Be kind to him, Kate, patient like."

Kate said nothing but went into the room and towards the bed.

"Hello, Dad. How do you feel?"

"Not too bad, lass. Better than yesterday at this time, Oh aye—" his chin nobbled as he repeated, "better than yesterday at this time. Won't forget that in a hurry. Sit down, lass."

She sat down, and he took hold of her hand and, turning his head on the pillow, he stared at her as he said, "Has been an experience this. Me own fault I suppose, going out like a bull at the gap. But I had to do what I thought best and, I'm sorry to say this, lass, I haven't changed me mind. But ... aw, don't pull your hand away. Let me have me say, and 'tis this. He's a good enough fellow in his own way, aye, I'll give him that, and he told me a thing or two about himself and I believe him. But underneath, lass, he's still a Bannaman. And you know me thoughts in that quarter."

"Yes, I do, Dad. But you also know mine, don't you?"

"Aye, that's the pity of it, that's the pity of it. But being who I am I can't change. I can say at this moment. I wish I. . . ." His words were cut off by the door being thrust open and Mary Ellen stood there, saying, "Kate, can ... can I have a word with you for a minute?"

As Kate withdrew her hand from his, his old manner asserting itself, he cried, "Can't you come in and have a word with her. What is it? What's up?"

"I'll ... I'll be with you in a minute." Mary Ellen was nodding at him. Then as Kate passed her she closed the door and said, "Charles is downstairs. He ... he called in at the farm. Now lass, don't get agitated –" she put her hand on Kate's arm – "but he found Ben in a bad way, practically delirious, he said. He must have lain down in his wet clothes as soon as he got in yesterday. There was no fire in the place, nothing. He says he'll have to have the doctor, but that he can't stay there. He proposes to take him up to his place. But as you know he's only got the cowman's wife to see to his needs and her youngest, and neither of them's very bright. So ... so he says, you" – she swallowed – "you should come along with them and see to him, although I don't know how you're going to manage there as he's only got three bedrooms, and. . . . Wait a minute, lass! Wait a minute!"

But Kate was already running from her across the landing and into her room. And she went to follow her as Hal's voice again came from the bedroom, crying, "D'you hear me? D'you hear me, Mary Ellen? Tell me what's up?" And so, thrusting the door open, she went in and she couldn't keep the impatience from her tone as she said, "All right, I'll tell you what's up. Charles is downstairs. He's found Ben in a state, in a high fever. Lying in the cold house. He must have just dropped once he got in and has lain there since. He's taking him home to his place, but Kate will have to go with him to see to him."

He remained silent, staring at her, then he muttered, "Can't be, he

398

must be as strong as a horse to be still alive after what he did . . . an' going to Charles's? No place there for him. . . ."

"Stop agitating yourself. You've got to face up to it; she's going to look after him. You've got everybody in this house to look after you, he's got nobody. By what Charles says, it's serious. I mean, he's in a serious state."

"Where's Charles?"

"Downstairs."

"Fetch him up."

"What?"

"Woman!" – he closed his eyes – "don't aggravate me. Fetch him up."

Gritting her teeth, she went out and none too quietly.

Charles came up, and when he stood by the bedside, Hal said, "What's this I hear? He's bad?"

"Yes, very poorly I should say."

"Very poorly?"

"Oh, yes, yes. I'm . . . well I must admit, I'm worried. I passed one of the Robsons on the road, they were making for Haydon Bridge. I gave them a message for the doctor." Hal looked past him now towards Kate who was coming into the room dragging her coat. Following her came John, and he, seeming to ignore his father, addressed Charles, saying, "Tom's got the cart ready, and Annie's put some blankets on. Is there anything else you think you'll want?"

"No" – Charles had turned towards him – "not that I can think of at the moment."

"What's this? What's this?" Hal moved restlessly and went to pull himself further up on the pillows, but stopped and screwed his face up against the pain. And when Mary Ellen went to his side, saying, "Now don't frash yourself,' he thrust his arm out at her, saying, "Let me get a word in, woman." Then looking at Charles he said slowly, "It goes against the grain for me to admit this openly, but I owe that fellow me life. If he hadn't come across me after that damned goat hit me I wouldn't be here now. And how he got me from that shed up to the cottage will always remain a mystery, because the last I remember was him dragging me towards that snow-covered bank that looked as high as all the hills in Alston put together. So no matter what I think of him otherwise, I owe him something, and the only way I can repay it is by seeing that he's attended to now. So—" he drew in a long shuddering breath before ending, "bring him here."

"Here?" The word was small, and he turned on Mary Ellen, saying quietly, "You're not deaf, lass. That's what I said, here."

"Well, if you say so, Mr Roystan." There was a note of relief in Charles's tone, and he turned and looked at John, and John said, "Aye, well let's get going, the quicker the better."

As they hurried from the room, Kate went to follow them, but stopped for a moment and looked back towards the bed. She did not smile at the man lying there, but their glances met and held for a moment; then she was running across the landing and down the stairs, and as she passed through the kitchen, she cried to Annie, "We're bringing Ben here." And Annie replied calmly, "Good. Good, lass. Could be the beginning of the end."

It wasn't until sometime later, when she rushed through the cold house and into the sitting-room and saw the huddled still figure lying on the couch in the icy cold room that Annie's words struck her as ominous, "Could be the beginning of the end".

16

It was thirty-six hours since they carried Ben upstairs and placed him in Kate's bed, and for most of the time Kate had remained by his side. It was she who, with the help of Annie, had taken off his clothes and bathed his burning body. It was she who constantly mopped the sweat from his running face, and quite often quietened his gabbling with her voice. Between times he would recognize her and his dried throat would croak her name and his cracked lips move in an effort to say more, but always the heaving of his chest cut off his words, and she would stroke his face saying, "'Tis all right, my love, 'tis all right. I'm here. I shan't leave you. Never, never."

The doctor had made the hazardous journey again today, and it was hazardous for the slushed snow had now turned to ice and the roads were more treacherous than ever. He came out of the bedroom and stood on the landing looking at Mary Ellen, and when he made no immediate comment on his second patient she said, "What d'you think, doctor?" As an answer to this, he moved his head in a small despairing movement, then said, "I don't know . . . at least I do, but I don't want to voice it. The infection is congesting his chest. Yesterday his heart beat was strong, but today it has changed. The next twenty-four hours should give us the answer, but" – he drew in a long breath – "I'm sorry to say it's out of my hands now. I can't hold out much hope. In such circumstances I could say, he has youth on his side, but that would be a platitude now. I . . . I think you must prepare Kate."

"Oh, dear God!" When she hung her head he put his hand on her shoulder, patting it and saying, "She's having a bad deal all round, that girl. Well, I can do nothing more at the moment. I'll be over first thing in the morning, that is if it is at all possible. It just wants to snow again on top of this ice and we're really in for it. Now don't worry, I'll see myself out. The girls will have a drink waiting for me."

She stood still watching him walking down the landing to the stairs and not until he had disappeared from her view did she move, and then slowly towards her own bedroom. Once inside, she walked as slowly up to the bed and, dropping down onto the seat beside it, she looked at Hal, and he at her, and when he opened with his usual word, "Well?" she answered with a break in her voice, "He . . . he says there's not much hope."

"*Go on.*" He went to hitch himself away from her, crying now, "That can't be. He's young and strong. I know that, he must be as strong as a horse."

"Well, he must have spent his strength because doctor says he can do no more, it's touch and go within the next twenty-four hours. Oh, Hal, what will she do?"

He turned his head from her and stared down the bed to the bump of wire that caged his foot. He was the one that should be dying. He was twice the fellow's age, and had an infection of the chest that had put paid to many a stronger man than himself. Aye, he was the one that should be going. And it would have happened if that fellow hadn't seen to him. "God Almighty!" He groaned the words aloud and then turned his head slowly and looked at Mary Ellen. And what she next said brought his teeth dragging over his lower lip. "I know one thing," she said, "that if she loses him, we'll lose her ... *you'll lose her*, for she'll never stay here. I don't know what she'll do, but she'll go. I know it in me heart she'll go. And anyway, if he was by some miracle to get better, there's still you and your mania that's bent on keeping them apart. She's got that in her mind, and he must have an' all, because as you've drummed into both of them, you're not the kind of man to change his mind. Are you?"

"Mary Ellen" – his voice was low and sad sounding – "you've never hit below the belt before, don't start now. I know what I am without you puttin' it in writin'."

When he turned his head right round onto his other shoulder, she swiftly put her hand onto his where his fingers were scratching at the eiderdown and she said, "I'm sorry, Hal. I'm sorry. But as I see it, either way she has little to hope for."

There remained a long silence between them; then, with his head still turned from her, he said, "Well, if it's any news to you, I know when I'm beat. So if hope in that direction will be of any help, you can pass it on to her."

"Oh, Hal." She lifted his hand and pressed it against her cheek, but he did not turn his head towards her, for she knew that he couldn't bear even her to witness his weakness.

She left him quickly now and, crossing the landing, she quietly entered Kate's room. Going to the other side of the single bed she saw that Ben was conscious and she bent over him, and he looked at her but could not speak, and now slowly and quietly she said, "You've got to get better, Ben. D'you hear me? You've got to get better. Hal sent you a message. He says, you saved his life, and he's got to repay you, so don't go and do the dirty on him. And he knows the only way he can repay you is to be willing to let Kate go to you. And he said to tell you that. And also –" Her imagination taking over, she added, "You can be married as soon as he can put his foot to the ground and walk to your wedding. Now d'you hear me?"

The dark sunken eyes showed her no sign that he had heard her. But Kate certainly had, and apparently the message had on her the opposite effect from that intended, for now, getting to her feet, she motioned her mother from the bed and outside onto the landing, and there she almost hissed at her, "Well! you take a message back to Dad and tell him he's too late, about a week too late. I know what the doctor said. He told me."

"Now look you here, Kate." Mary Ellen was gripping her daughter's arms. "Where there's life there's hope, and where there's dismay there's death. And you go back in there with your thoughts set on him going, and by God! he'll do just that. As I said, where there's life there's hope. Will him to keep alive. Look as if you are over the moon at the turn of events. And believe me, it is a turn in events, 'cos never did I expect to hear my man say what he said to me a few minutes gone. It was as if he was broken in spirit. Now, you get yourself back in that room there, girl, and tell that man of yours he's going to come through. Push it out of your head that he's not. Just keep telling him that he's got to. Come the night will be the testing time. But you've got till then to work on him." Her voice softening, she now said, "I know you're worn out, lass, but get him over the next twelve hours or so and, pray God, there'll be a turn for the better. Go on now." She pushed her gently back towards the door.

Kate went slowly back into the room; her face was still set, even grim. When she reached the bed she placed her lips against the side of his dry and panting mouth and, her voice trembling, she said, "'Tis going to be all right. It . . . it's right what Mam said." Then looking into his eyes, she asked, "Do you understand me, Ben? Do you hear what I'm saying? Dad is for us. We can be married, and . . . and from this house. Only you . . . you've got to get well. Do you hear me, Ben? You . . . you've got to get well. You've got to fight. You must, Ben."

When he coughed and brought up some phlegm, she wiped it from his mouth, then looked aghast at the streak of blood running through it.

The door opened and Florrie entered carrying a tray. And Kate, going quickly to her, took it from her, saying, "Tell Mam I want her."

A few minutes later when Mary Ellen entered the room, Kate showed her the piece of linen, and Mary Ellen, looking at it, paused a long moment before she said, "Oh, that's nothing. That comes through the straining from coughing. Your dad's always bringing up streaks of blood, has for years. That's nothing."

"You sure?"

"Yes, I'm sure. Now don't be silly. Drink up that hot milk, then we'll wash him down again and get him ready for the night, because it could be a long one."

It was two o'clock in the morning. The room was hot and quiet, except for Ben's laboured breathing. Gabriel was asleep in an easy chair to the side of the fireplace. Kate, weary and hardly able to keep her eyes open, had just replenished the four candlesticks which she placed two on the dressing-table and two on the mantelpiece, and she was about to take her seat once again by the bed when Ben flung his arm wide and, bringing his shoulders from the pillow, coughed up some phelgm, then cried out in a clearer tone than he had used before, "Kate! Kate!"

"I'm here, darling. I'm here." She put her arms about him in an endeavour to press him backwards, but when he began to struggle with her, she turned her head and cried, "Gabriel! Gabriel!" And Gabriel, coming out of sleep, ran to the other side of the bed and, gripping Ben's arms, he said, "There you are. There you are, old fellow. Lie down. Lie down."

Slowly they eased him back on to the pillow, but he still thrashed, and when his breathing became painfully fast and each breath sounded like a gasp, she said quickly to Gabriel, "Go and bring Mam."

When Mary Ellen came hurrying into the room, pulling a gown around her, she merely glanced at Ben before she said, "This is it. Bring the dish and towels."

For the next half-hour they alternately sponged Ben's face and neck and hands, and tried to stop him rising from the bed, and it seemed to them that he had been imbued with a last fatal bout of strength.

It was towards three o'clock when he became limp in their hands and lay still. And Kate let out a cry, "Oh, no! Oh, no! Ben! Don't go. Please! Please, don't go. Don't leave me, Ben. Don't leave me."

"There, there, lass, there. He's all right, he's all right. Look, he's still breathing. Give over."

"Don't be silly, Kate." Gabriel was pulling her from the bed now. "Look, it's as if he was asleep. Look, his chest's still moving. Stop it! Stop it!"

Stretching her head towards the bed, Kate saw only the closed lids and the long white face, and she wondered why Gabriel was telling her to stop it. Of a sudden she was shivering from head to foot, her teeth chattered and she looked at her mother and asked pitifully, "Is he? Is he?"

"He's all right, lass. It's over. He's passed it." The words seemed to convey that he was gone, and she pulled herself from Gabriel's arms and went to the bed, crying, "Ben! Ben!" Then when Ben slowly raised his lids and as slowly closed them again, she turned and staggered to the chair and, dropping into it, she began to cry. One hand across her eyes, the other straining across her open mouth, she endeavoured to dull the sound of her sobbing, and when Gabriel remonstrated with her, saying, "Quiet, Kate, you'll wake him," Mary Ellen turned to him, saying, "'Tis all right. Let her be. 'Twill do her good. They'll both sleep after this. Now go and wake our Maggie, she'll stay with me, it will be a kind of penance for her, because this one here is dropping on her feet." She now drew Kate's head towards her, saying, "There, there, lass, the travail is over. Pray God He'll show us some peace from now on."

17

Ben's recovery was slow. It was a full fortnight before he was able to sit up in the bed. That he had neared death, he knew only too well. He could recall the moment when it almost touched him. It had seemed to keep its distance for days, and had actually backed away once when a voice had come to him, saying that he had leave to marry Kate, that the stubborn bull-headed man had given his consent.

He lay now looking towards the door. They were all so kind to him in this house. He hadn't seen the master of it yet, but he received messages from him, which was strange, even laughable. The only other person he hadn't seen was Maggie. Maggie, he understood, was in everybody's black books, so Gabriel had said. Yet, in a way, he had a lot to thank Maggie for, for how other could he have got round that irascible man if she hadn't run home with the dire news of his true identity, and so almost causing them both to die. In no other way would he have melted. He must ask Kate to tell Maggie that he felt no bitterness towards her, as indeed he didn't. But now, what would the head of the house say when he heard the doctor's opinion of what should happen when he was fit to travel? Would there be more protests, more tirades? Yes, very likely, because to keep them within his orbit he had, without giving his blessing, consented to their living in the Bannamans' house, although, as Kate had said, they weren't to expect him visiting, ever; they would have to do the calling. Well, he didn't mind that in the least as long as he could carry out the desire in his mind to erase the evil from that place.

But now, if he were to follow doctor's orders, Kate would be taken out of her dad's orbit not only for some months to come, but for many winter months of each year.

Kate coming back into the room, he said to her, "You've been a long time."

"A long time?" She smiled at him. "I said goodbye to the doctor, had a word with Annie about your dinner and told her she's not to make you such luscious meals, and I washed my face and hands, spoke to Mother at the top of the stairs, and here I am."

"It's been nearly fifteen minutes."

"Oh, Ben." She sat down on the edge of the bed and he put his arms out to her, and she held him, and he murmured into her neck, "Italy or France, the very sound of it, or perhaps Switzerland." Then raising his head and looking into her eyes, he added, "How do you think he'll take this last blow?"

"I don't know. Doctor told Mother what he told us; I'll give her time to tell him and then I'll go and face the barrage. Yet somehow, I don't think there'll be much, he's changed. . . . What really happened up there? You never said."

"There was nothing much to tell. After Biddy did her work I found him, dragged him into the hut, then got him up to the cottage, and there we told each other what we thought in no polite language." He laughed gently now as he said, "I recall, when I went to wash the blood from his face he snatched the cloth so quickly from my hand it slapped him across the mouth. I remember I wanted to laugh, but thought better of it."

"You saved his life, and nearly lost your own. And you hold no bitterness against him although it has left you with this?" She patted his chest. "That's small payment to extract for you, Kate, and for his willingness that we should be together, because although somehow or other I would have taken you from under his nose, you would never have been really happy, knowing how you had hurt him, whereas now—" He laughed again as he said, "He will really want to shoot me when he knows I'm going to take you out of the country for months at a time."

"I don't think so." She bent forward and kissed him gently. Then holding his face between her hands she said, "You know, I'll never be able to understand the reason why you love me. Of all the women in the world you could have had, and yes" – she nodded at him – "I think you could have had any one you chose, you've got to come into these backwoods and find me, and tell me that you love me. I know it's a dream, and I'm going to wake up from it some day, because it can't be true, can it?"

"No, of course it isn't true that I love you and you love me, and that you are the only woman in the world for me, and always will be. No, of course it isn't true. And one day we'll wake up and find we were both dreaming. But until then, let's make believe, eh?" Now he put his lips on hers and held her close to him until there was a rattle on the sneck of the door, and they moved apart. And Mary Ellen came in, saying, "Well, now. Making plans?"

"Yes, sort of." Kate rose from the bed, then added, "Have you told him?" And Mary Ellen said, "Aye. Aye, I've told him."

"How did he take it?"

"Quietly, which, in a way I'm sorry to say, hurts me, because as you know it isn't like him to be baulked in any way and take it quietly. But go in and say your piece, and I'll sit on the bed here and ask this man of yours how it is he's come to alter my husband so; and whether it's for better or worse, I'm not sure, because I miss me bawling lad." She smiled sadly now; then with a wave of her hand she sent Kate from the room.

But Kate didn't make straight for her father's room, because there, coming from the top of the landing was Maggie. She was carrying a clean water bucket in one hand and a broom and duster in the other, and she cast her eyes downwards and made to pass Kate without a word, as she had done since the day she delivered her message in the kitchen. But now Kate put out her hand and drew her to a stop, saying quietly, "Let's forget about this, Maggie. 'Tis all over. I hold you no bitterness, and neither does Ben. Believe that."

Maggie's head drooping lower now, and her voice breaking, she said, "I'm sorry. I don't know why I did it. And . . . and I've gone through hell thinking he might have died." The tears were running down her cheeks now. Kate, putting her hand on her shoulder, said gently, "Well, he didn't, and everything's turned out all right. In fact, if you hadn't done what you did do, I doubt if Ben and I would have ever come together, not really, at least not happily like we shall now. So there, you see, good's come of it."

When Maggie shook her head from side to side, Kate said, "Believe me, everything's all right. Look, when Mam comes out, go in and have a word with him."

At this, Maggie ran from her, her body half bent, the pail jangling in her hand. And Kate looked after her sadly for a moment before turning and going in to Hal.

He was propped up in bed and there was a newspaper and a magnifying glass lying on the quilt as if he had been reading. But his hands now lay idle in front of him and he greeted her with, "If he doesn't soon take this damn wood off me foot, I'll never be able to move it again."

"I thought he was going to do something this morning?"

"Aye, he's let me toes free, that's about all. Have a look at them."

She pulled back the cover from the cage and looked at his bare toes sticking out from the bandage, and she said, "Can you move them?"

"Can I hell! He says I've got to practise. But I haven't got to touch them, or anybody else, like massage them, I've got to think I can move them and then move them. That's what he says. He's up the pole, that fellow."

She covered up the cage, then sat down by the side of him, and he looked at her and said, "Well?" And she answered him in the same vein, saying, "Well?"

He moved restlessly for a moment, then began to pick at the threads from a square of patchwork in the quilt before he said, "Came as another shock, that."

"What? That Ben has an infected lung? Or that we must spend part of the winter months in a warm climate if he wants to get entirely better?"

"Aye, well, both you could say. But why not go to some warm part in England?"

"There are no really warm parts in England, not in the winter."

"Oh aye, there are. They say Devon's warm."

"Well, it's a different warmth Ben needs, so doctor says, constant sun and no damp."

"Where d'you think of going then?"

"France, Italy, perhaps Switzerland, we don't know yet. You see it was just sprung on us today."

"Aye, just sprung on us. An' you say, France. You'll go to Paris likely, eh? And call on him?"

Her eyes widened and her whole face stretched. It was the last thing she had thought of when naming France, that she would ever go to Paris and call on her father. She said now somewhat vehemently, "Just like you to say that, isn't it? No, I won't go to Paris to see him. He means nothing to me. I've told you before, but you're so thick-headed and...."

"All right, all right. Don't take a pattern from your mother. I only thought you might."

"Well, I won't." Her voice dropped. "I can promise you that, Dad, I won't go near him. We won't even go anywhere near Paris. He took twenty-four years to come and see me, so I'm not going to break my neck in the next six to twelve months to go and see him. No" – she caught hold of his hand – "never worry on that score. You are my father, always have been, and always will be." She leant towards him now and he put his arms about her, and they held each other close. When she muttered, "I could never have been really happy without your consent, no matter what I'd said," he pressed her from him and, his eyelids blinking and his nose sniffing, he said, "Damned hazardous way I had to go about giving it to you, hadn't I? And when we're on, about the house, he still intends to set up there?"

"He would like to, Dad. He's got this feeling that somehow there he can erase the harm his mother and his grandfather did."

"That's a tall order, lass. You cannot raise the dead, or erase how they met their death. But still, if he's bent on it, I've got no say in the matter now, have I? The only thing is, as I told you, I can't see me visiting you."

"Well—" She pulled a face at him, and rising from the bed she said, "We'll only have to bring the children every Sunday to visit you. And to make sure we don't go back on our word, I'll go now and get him to sign a paper to that effect." She laughed aloud as she backed from the bed, and at the door she turned and gave him a little wave. It was an action she had been wont to do as a child when, from her mother's arms, she had watched him ride out of the yard. And when the door closed on her his chin dropped on to his chest and he muttered to himself, "Bring the children every Sunday afternoon. Children with Bannaman's blood in them. The sins of the fathers are visited upon the children even to the third and fourth generation."

PART FOUR

And Hatred Therewith

1

❧❧

The cows coming across the yard made a chorus of moos, all thirty-two voices seeming to be vying with each other. Mary Ellen considered the sound a mixture between a wail at their having been driven from the pasture to a pean of praise at the imminent relief of their low-flung swinging udders.

She glanced sideways from the table where she was kneading bread in a big brown earthenware bowl and as her gaze fell on the man following the herd she said, "Terry's walking worse than ever. He'll have to get off his feet for a time. Yet, how we'll manage I don't know." Then her eyes were drawn sharply towards her daughter who was standing near the dresser changing her apron, for she had just said, "He'll have to engage another hand."

"You know your dad doesn't like new hands about the place."

"Then he shouldn't go enlarging the stock, should he? We're lucky to have what good pasture we have got in this area, but it'll only feed so many."

Maggie had her hands behind her neck adjusting the straps of the white bib, and her head was bent forward as she ended, "And what'll happen if Willy decides to up and go?"

Mary Ellen stared at her daughter, the one, as she put it to herself, she had never been able to fathom. There she was, thirty-nine years old, a spinster seemingly self-chosen, for it wasn't for the want of chances that she hadn't married. She couldn't understand her. She was the best looking one in the family yet seemed to have the sourest nature. She had been a flirt and a bit of a flibbertigibbet right up until she was twenty-three. But from the time she had exposed Ben's relationship to the Bannamans she had changed. Of course, what she had done could have been the means of killing both Ben and her father and that must have preyed on her mind, for from then her ways had changed: instead of setting out to attract every man who came within yards of her, she avoided him. Under the circumstances you would have thought she would have been glad to have married and got away from the house and the unspoken censure of her father, but the reverse was the case. In fact, for months at a time she would never leave the farm, not even to go into the market on a Saturday. That was, until she reached her middle thirties.

She couldn't quite pinpoint when the second change occurred in her daughter except that it was at a time of upheaval all round. What caused it was that Gabriel, who had worked on the farm for years alongside his brother John and was then thirty years of age, had up, without notice, and told them he was going into Newcastle to live with Hugh and find work there in the glass factory all because he had become interested in glass objects, such as engraved goblets and the like that were being produced in the city.

Like much else that had happened in her life it wasn't understandable. So they had to take on a new man. And in this they had been lucky. Oh yes, very lucky. Willy Harding would be worth his weight in gold on any farm for he could turn his hand to anything. Well, was it from when he came that Maggie had changed? Sometimes this thought worried her but she would push it out of her mind. No, it was from the day Jimmy Broadbent from over Allendale way came to the house with the sole purpose of asking her to marry him. That day, there had been an explosion in this very kitchen, for Maggie had threatened to throw a pan of hot stew over him and scratch his eyes out. And she might have done so at that if John hadn't restrained her.

Jimmy's wife had been dead for six months. She had left seven children all under ten, the youngest fourteen months old. She had died trying to deliver her eighth. And it was common knowledge that Jimmy had just used her for breeding, for he sought his pleasure with his fancy woman, a widow who lived in a cottage over in the dale. Apparently, he had expected this lady to come and take charge of his household while he got on with his work, which was mostly horse dealing, but he had been disappointed. His proposal to Maggie was covert and couched in terms as if he were doing her a favour by presenting her with a ready-made family because she was so far gone in her spinsterhood that it was very unlikely that she would breed now.

That day it appeared to Mary Ellen that her daughter had been sleeping for years and had just woken up, for after staring into the man's grinning face in utter silence for a full minute, she had emitted a sound like a screech, crying, "You dirty pot-bellied whoring swine! You dare think I would come within a mile of you or your tribe?" And she had swung round, looking for something to grab at. There was the long black handle of the iron pan sticking out towards her from the hob and, gripping it with both hands, she lifted it up, still screaming, "Get out! Or you'll get this over you." Then, because the weight of it was so heavy, she did an unheard of thing, she dropped the sooty-bottomed pan on to the long white scrubbed table, then advanced round it on the hastily retreating man. And she would have pounced on him if she hadn't been prevented by John gripping her from behind, while at the same time yelling to Jimmy Broadbent, "Get yourself away, man! And don't come back."

It was on that day too, and for the first time, that she heard an amicable exchange between Maggie and her father, because when Hal had come in saying, "Jimmy Broadbent passed me on the road galloping as if the devil was after him. He didn't stop for a word. What's afoot?" she had told him, and at that he had sat down on the settle where Maggie had been sitting stiff and tight staring into the fire, and he had put his hand on her shoulder, saying, "My! lass, it was a pity you didn't swipe him. The insulting bugger, I'll spit in his eye the next time I see him. I was about to buy a couple of shires off him, now he can go to hell. You could have had your pick of the countryside. I know that."

Her father's unusual kindness towards her had resulted in her bursting into tears and rushing from the room. Anyway, it was after that that she did her hair in a different style, and started wearing pretty prints again, and would now often go into the market on a Saturday. Yet the change brought forth no more suitors. This apparently didn't seem to bother her. Yet at times Mary Ellen felt there must be something bothering her daughter for she would become edgy and go a whole day without opening her mouth.

Mary Ellen told herself again and again that Maggie was no company, and yet at the same time she didn't know what she would do without her, for she worked from early till late both inside the house and in the byres and the dairy where she did a great deal of the milking. She seemed to like the milking more than any other work on the farm, whereas at one time she had hated all outside work. She knew while she was there she talked to Willy. And it was this knowledge that made her say now, "Has he said anything about leaving?"

"No" – Maggie pulled her starched apron tight around her hips – "but with the windfall he got last week, he could start up on his own, couldn't he?" She turned and looked fully at her mother, and Mary Ellen said, "A hundred pounds won't go very far."

"I understand Dad started on very little more and ill-got at that."

"Maggie!" The name was a growl. "I've told you before never to mention that. It's gone, forgotten. You came on that knowledge because you've got ears like cuddy's lugs. What is it, girl? At times you seem bent on upsetting me."

"I'm sorry. I'm sorry." Maggie wagged her head, and Mary Ellen looked away towards the window again – she had heard the sound of a horse's hoofs from the stone yard – and she said stiffly, "That must be your dad back. Let's have no more of it." And she lifted up the great wad of dough and flopped it onto a floured board.

Her face tight, obliterating the good looks it normally still bore, Maggie now made towards the kitchen door, but it opened before she reached it and both she and her mother exclaimed simultaneously "Kate!" Then Mary Ellen added, "What's wrong?"

Kate, now a woman turned forty who seemed to have grown even taller and broader, looked first at her mother then at Maggie. And it was to Maggie she said, "Fraser – our young Frag. He's run off again."

"No! not again. I thought ... well, he had promised."

Kate nodded at Maggie now, saying as she moved past her, "As Mam is always quoting, promises are like piecrusts, made to be broken."

Maggie had turned back into the kitchen and, quietly, she said, "But he's been good for a year now."

"Ten months to be exact. This'll put the finish to Ben."

"How is Ben?" Mary Ellen was pouring some boiling water into a large brown teapot, and Kate answered briefly, "The same," as she sat down in the rocking-chair to the side of the fireplace. Then looking from one to the other, she demanded, "Why does he do it? That's what I'd like to know." And it was Maggie who answered her, saying harshly now, "He hates to be cooped up. He was born to roam."

"Born to roam!" Mary Ellen's voice broke in high now, crying, "He wants a horsewhip taken to him. He knows how he upsets everybody. How did you find out?" She looked at Kate.

"By a special delivery letter from the headmaster. He must have got out last night. His bed hadn't been slept in."

"It'll be the drovers again. They're down from Scotland. Hal was saying they're camped in a field just beyond Corbridge, fattening the stock up afore taking them into market. But how would he know where they were? Still, he's got the devil in him. Always had. He's the spawn of Satan. He should be. . . ."

"No! Mam. No, don't say that. He's not got the devil in him. He's. . . ."

"Aye, well, you tell me what he is. He's caused you heartache from the time he could walk. He thinks of nobody but himself."

"That isn't true."

"Oh, you'll defend him with your last breath. 'Tis natural I suppose. But he's been at this game since he was five. He was five, wasn't he" – she turned her head towards Maggie, bobbing it now – "when he first went after the drovers? And that old Scot who stunk to high heaven brought him back. Then a year after he did the same. And how many times after that has he joined one or other of them? He's a byword, he's become notorious. If I had my way, I'd let him go his way and join the roadsters and live like the animals they're drovin'. It might have been funny at first, prankish, but now here he is coming up sixteen and looking all the world eighteen or over. Well, something must be done finally with him. It's up to you, 'cos Ben's in no fit state to deal with him. . . . Aw, here's your dad."

As the sound of Hal's voice came from the yard, Kate rose to her feet, saying, "I'll be off."

"Now look." Her mother turned to her, muttering under her breath now, "Don't walk out the minute he comes in."

"Well, I won't be able to stand his rampaging. Anyway, you needn't tell him until I'm gone."

"Did you tell John?" Mary Ellen was looking towards the window again. And when Kate answered, "Yes," her mother said, "Well, your dad's talking to him now."

"Oh, my God!" Kate leaned against the side of the table and Maggie, looking at her with concern, said, "Don't worry. John will go after him. He usually does."

"John's got enough on his plate; he can hardly get through the work now." Mary Ellen bit on her lip, then turned her head away, saying, "Aw, lass, I'm sorry, but that lad's forever upsettin' me."

"Goodbye, Mam." Kate made for the door, and she had reached the yard before Hal turned from John and saw her. Coming swiftly towards her, he said, "That bugger at it again, I hear?"

And she retorted in a similar fashion, "Yes, you're right, you've heard, the bugger's at it again."

"Kate!" Whether it was the tone of her voice or the repeating of his words that brought his sharp reaction didn't matter. But he went on more quietly, "I was only saying."

"Yes, Dad, I know you were only saying. But he's my responsibility and Ben's, and we'll deal with him."

At this his manner reverted to natural and he cried at her departing back, "Aye, like hell you will. He'll make you sup sorrow, that one, afore he's finished." And he continued to stare after her until the sound of Mary Ellen's voice calling from the kitchen door, "Enough! Enough! Come away in," made him turn about.

Pushing past his wife, he threw his tall hat onto the settle and dragged off his coat and now threw this towards Maggie crying, "The buckle end of a belt, that's what he wants. That's what he should have been given from he could walk. The money that's been wasted on his schoolin'. I said all along, put him to work. Aye, even at the pit or the mill. That would have cured him. But no, no." He turned now on Mary Ellen, his finger stabbing towards her as he cried, "But one of these days, mark me, she'll remember my words, because there's a Bannaman in that 'un if I ever saw an inherited streak of rottenness in anybody. . . ."

"Hal, stop that! Now don't start that again. The lad's a rover and that's all there is about it."

"Rover be damned!" He now went to where Maggie had placed his coat on the back of a chair and, thrusting his hand into a side pocket, he brought out four letters, saying as he did so, "I met the postie at the end of the road. There's one for you." He took the top letter and threw it onto the table, saying, "It must be from the lads, but they're altering the handwriting I would say."

As Mary Ellen picked up the letter, Maggie, looking at her father, said, "Is John riding out?" and when he answered briefly, "Aye," she said, "In that case I'd better get over to the milking; Willy can't do it all himself."

"Willy!" Hal turned to Mary Ellen now, saying, "What's the latest, do you think, I heard in town the day? Old Picker Robson has been at Willy to go in with him. It's got round about his windfall. The cartin' business isn't as bright as it was since the railways came on the scene. Moreover, he's likely got his eye on Willy for his lass, her kicking thirty an' hope gone. Anyway, I squashed that one flat. I. . . ."

"What did you say? You're going to raise his wages to keep him here?"

He swung round on Maggie now, crying, "Don't you be saucy. He's well paid to begin with, and he's got a cottage on his own."

"They give dogs kennels."

Hal's mouth opened wide, and his eyebrows seemed to rush up to the deeply grizzled hair sprouting from the top of his brow.

"Your tongue, miss, will get you a slap across the mouth one of these days. You're not too old for that."

"I wouldn't try it." Maggie walked calmly to the back of the door and lifted from it a head shawl which she put on and tied in a knot under her chin before turning once again and looking at her father, saying, "There's one thing certain in this life: you go out of it the way you came in; you can't even take your bank-book with you."

As the door opened, Mary Ellen sprang round the table and caught Hal's arm, saying, "Leave over. Leave over." And when the door closed on her daughter she added, "She's in one of her moods the day."

"But did you hear what she said?"

"Yes, I heard what she said and she's right in a way; and another way an' all, 'cos I think you should raise Willy's wages. A shilling a week won't hurt you and it might save you pounds in the end, for you'll never get another like him. And, as I told you last week, Terry won't last much longer."

He pulled away from her and walked to the window, saying, "All this, because that one puts me in me place. Be damned! if I will."

"Well, you might be damned if you won't. Anyway, sit yourself down. I'll pour you out a cup of tea an' then see to the bread, it's rising beyond itself."

"See what the lads say first." He pointed to the letter on the corner of the table, and she picked it up and looked at the envelope, saying, "It isn't from the lads this. It isn't their writing."

"No, I thought it wasn't. Well, open it up, woman, and see who it is from."

She picked up a knife from the table and split the envelope and took out the single sheet of notepaper. Then, after scanning a few lines, she raised her eyes and looked at him, and something in her expression made him cry, "What is it, woman? What is it?"

At this she resumed her reading; then, the letter held slightly away from her, she went and sat on the settle, and from there she gazed up at him as she said softly, "It's from Roddy."

"Roddy? Roddy Greenbank?"

"Which other Roddy do we know?"

"What does he want?"

"He wants to come and see me . . . us."

"*Why?* He's been a long time thinkin' about it, hasn't he? Must be all of sixteen or seventeen years gone since he was here. He never came to his own daughter's weddin'. And what did he send her? A picture. And

416

what was it about? The flamin' Smelt Mills. He had painted her a picture of the Smelt Mills."

"He sent her fifty pounds an' all. Remember that."

"Fifty pounds. Aye, and what was that an' all? Poor return for her being kept for years."

"*Hal!*" She sprang to her feet, and he wagged his hand at her, saying, "You know what I mean. You know what I mean. Don't twist me words. But tell us what he wants to come here for?"

"He" – she looked at the letter again – "he says he's got something to ask of me. He's . . . he's not well. Well, read it yourself." She thrust the letter towards him. But he hesitated before taking it from her and when he did he held the end of it between his finger and thumb as if in some way it might infect him. After a moment he handed it back to her, saying, "He could be here the morrow by that."

"Aye, yes." She nodded at him.

His chin thrust out, he said, "Aye well, aren't you gona fly round the house gettin' it spruced up? If I remember, the last time his majesty proposed to visit us you had the place turned upside down; non-stop work for twenty-four hours."

Her face took on a quiet, even sad expression, and her voice was low as she answered, "A lot of water has passed under the bridge since then, Hal. Then, I had wanted him to see how well you had done, and what a fine family we had. Well, now he knows. There will be no trumpets blown for him this time, I can assure you. If you keep your temper and show a little dignity, that'll be all that is required to impress him, and prove to him he's not the only one who's got on in the world."

She had expected him to come back at her, likely about the word dignity, but he must have thought better of it for when she rose to pour out his tea, he sat down, saying half to himself, "I wonder what he's after now? He wants something or else he wouldn't be comin' here."

"Yes, I think you're right." She handed him the cup of tea, adding, "But we'll only have to wait and see, won't we?"

"Aye, yes we will." He looked up at her. "He'll see his grandchildren for the first time and the boyo. I wonder what he'll make of him? Will he recognize him as a copy of the man who killed his father, do you think?"

"Hal! Hal! Don't rake that up, for God's sake. Whatever happens the morrow, don't rake that up. There's enough trouble, and right here an' all, because I'll tell you what's worrying me more than anything at this moment, and that is that Willy ups and goes."

Over in the cow byres Maggie was putting that very question to Willy himself and not in a very roundabout way. She had just come in from the

417

dairy with the two empty pails, and as she took the yoke from her shoulders, Willy Harding turned his head from one side to the other on the cow's belly and, glancing at her, said, "There'll only be two more, leave them, I'll see to them. And you know, I never see what good those wooden monstrosities do. Besides tearing the skin off your shoulders, they hump the spine through time an' all. I think it's just as easy to carry the buckets by hand."

"Oh, I don't mind them. I'm used to them, and I'll have to go on getting used to them if all rumours are true."

He lifted his face from the cow while his hands still kept working on its teats as he said, "What rumour is that?"

"That you've been given an offer to go in with Picker Robson."

"Huh! Oh, that." He was laughing now. She liked to hear him laugh. It started as a rumble in his chest and rose like the notes of a scale. It was like his voice, pleasing. He shook his head, saying, "It's funny what a few coppers will do."

"I don't call a hundred pounds a few coppers."

"No, perhaps not, but he never approached me afore the money was heard of."

"But others have, haven't they, without the money?"

"Oh aye, aye." He now stood up, pushed the stool back with one foot and, bending, drew out the pail from under the cow. Then patting its rump, he said, "You've done well today, girl. Look at that!" And he pointed down to the full pail. "As creamy and as thick as whitewash. You'll get some good butter there."

They were standing facing each other now. He was just a shade taller than her. His hair was fair to brown and had a wave on the top. His face was squarish: his eyes deep blue, round, and set in wide sockets; his nose was straight, inclining to largeness; his mouth too was large, the lips slightly shaped; but there was no jut to the chin, it lay flat and would have dismissed all aggressiveness and determination from the character except for the squareness of the jaw. His eyes narrowed and he peered at her in the dim light of the byres as she said, "Why do you stay then? You're not overpaid."

It was a moment before he spoke. "Why do you ask?" he said.

"Just that ... well" – she jerked her chin up – "you could get a better job than this with more money any day in the week."

"Perhaps I like it here, and ... and I'm not one for change." He smiled again. "This is only the second job I've had in me life, you know. I was about twenty-six years with Sir Reginald. It was a long time."

"Did you really start work when you were six? You once said you did."

"Oh yes, aye, anyway they said I did, because I howled me eyes out when me mother died. So her ladyship said the best cure was to give me something to do, so they put me to work with a miniature brush. I swept the yard and kept the hen crees clean, and her ladyship saw I went to half-day schooling too. That was up till I was eleven, by which time I had tried me hand at most things on the farm. Then her ladyship died and everything altered."

He now scraped his heavy boots on the edge of the brick channel that ran down the centre of the byre, and as if talking to himself he said, "'Tis strange how a woman can keep things going. Keep their heads above water, so to speak". He glanced now at Maggie, adding, "Sir Reginald was no farmer. He was but a distant relation of the old master, and had really been cut out for a teacher. Well, anything to do with books, 'cos he had been brought up in his father's bookshop in Cambridge. But when he came into the title everything changed, yet not his passion for books." His smile widened, then slid from his face as he said, "He seemed to lose interest even in life after the mistress went. Certainly, he left the reins in the wrong hands because he was rooked right, left, and centre. In my father's day, and when her ladyship was alive, there had been eight indoor servants and six working hands outside, not counting the steward. Not a big staff as estates go, but then it wasn't a big estate. But by the time I was sixteen there was only Betty Fowler left indoors, she was the cook, and her niece Emma, who was the housemaid. Most of the rooms were closed up. And outside there were only two men besides meself. But by the time I was twenty, that was down to one. And the stock had dwindled to practically nothing . . . well, about fifty sheep and half a dozen cows and a couple of horses and some arable fields. It kept you going. It was more than enough for the two of us, but we managed."

He was about to pick up the buckets when she said, "But I understood you spent a great deal of time with Sir Reginald."

He paused, his shoulders half bent, he turned his head towards her. "Yes, yes, that's true. He was lost for company. Well" – he smiled quietly – "not so much company, as someone to talk to, or talk at, which would be a better term. He was a natural teacher you see, and if he'd had his way, I would have spent half me time in the library. As it was, I used to go in there at nights." He straightened his back and looked down the byre as if seeing into the past. "It was a fine room, lined from floor to ceiling in black oak, and the shelves all spewin' books. And that's the correct word, spewin', they were all over the place. But I'm grateful to him. I'll be grateful all me days, for he opened a new world to me. And that chance isn't given to many farm lads. Oh no." His lips fell into a firm line and stayed there for a moment before he went on, his voice low, "He talked to you as if you were an equal, and he thought of you as an equal. He used to quote a man who died in the last century called Lord Chesterfield. Have you ever heard of him?" He cast his eyes sideways at her and she shook her head. "Well apparently. . . . Oh" – he stretched his neck out of his open-necked shirt – "I take that back, not apparently, because he was . . . he was a great man, as his books tell you. And Sir Reginald said that in his will Lord Chesterfield left his servants some money, saying, and these were his words" – he was nodding at her now –"'These men were my equals in nature, they were only my inferiors in fortune.' And Sir Reginald was like that an' all. He judged people for what they had in their minds, or what could be drawn out of their minds, not what they had in their pockets." Looking fully at her now he went on, "I don't mind sayin' this to you. I've never said it to anybody afore, but I looked upon him in the light of a father. And, I think, towards the end of his days, he saw me as the son he never had, and if he could have done anything more for me, he would have. But he did enough, he made me mind work, and in the right way: he showed me where true values lay." He paused again, and then said, "It was well he went when he did; I couldn't have borne it if he had been turfed out. But he was up over his head in debt, and had been for years. Huh! Dear Sir Reginald. Just think, in his last will, which he made when his mind was still clear" – he nodded at her – "he left me two thousand pounds in order that I could attend to my further education, and all the books I wished to take from his library."

He took in a long breath and let it out now before adding, "Well, it's common knowledge that when the bums moved in I wasn't allowed to take as much as a sheet of paper. But I already had a good store of my own books that he had given me over the years and all signed by him. It's taken over three years to settle his business, because the house remained unsold, but now all his debtors I understand are practically cleared, but my two thousand was reduced to one hundred pounds, for which I was grateful, though more so for the thought that generated it."

She stood staring at him. Her hands were joined tightly at her waist. There was a strong desire in her to let them loose and put them out towards him, to touch him, have him hold them. To check the madness she had to turn away, and at this he said, "I waste time."

She was round facing him again, saying rapidly, "Oh no, no. You've ... you've never wasted a minute in your life, I should imagine. I was only thinking, it ... it seems like an injustice that you weren't able to carry out what Sir Reginald wanted for you, an education."

"Oh" – he raised his eyebrows, his head to one side now – "there's part of me uppish enough to think that he saw to that himself: he gave me the chance to read and select what I wanted to read."

"You're lost here."

"Don't say that. I never feel lost where there's animals."

"You ... you'd be quite content to spend the rest of your life on a farm?"

"Yes." He inclined his head slowly towards her. "Yes. Did you hear what I said a little while ago about Sir Reginald putting my values straight for me? I know what I want."

"And is this all you want out of life, to work like this?"

He turned his head from her and looked at the bespattered white-washed wall, and it was some seconds before he turned to her again, and after a moment he said quietly, "No, it isn't all I want out of life. It's part of it, but certainly not all...."

"Willy." The byre door had opened and John was standing there.

"I'm off now. I don't suppose I'll find the rascal tonight as it'll be dark soon, but I might hear of him. I've finished next door. You'll see to the rest?"

"Yes, yes, I'll see to it." Then advancing two steps into the byres, John looked towards Maggie, saying, "If he should come to you to be cleaned up, don't take him into the house whatever time it is, because you know how Dad feels. You could take him along to Willy's. Could she, Willy?"

"Yes, yes, of course. Don't worry, if he turns up we'll see to him."

"Right then." John turned and went out.

Looking towards the door now, Maggie said quietly, "Hate's a deadly thing, isn't it? Eats its way through everything. Frag's been aware of hate since he could be aware of anything. It's made him like he is. Is it any wonder he makes for the drovers? They say he must be educated." She turned her head sharply now towards Willy, adding, "Education can be as harmful as it can be beneficial. You've got to be a very strong willed person to remain the same after education has been thumped into you."

At this she bent towards the full pails of milk, and when he said, "Leave them, I'll take them," she answered sharply, "No, I can manage. You'll have enough to see to." And lifting the pails, she walked erratically down the byres, and when he hurried before her and opened the door for her she did not look at him or thank him, and his head drooped for a moment before he turned back into the byres and, taking up a switch brush, attacked the muck in the channel.

It was around eight o'clock when John rode back into the yard. As he dismounted Maggie came to the kitchen door. She had a lantern in her hand and she held it high as she went towards him.

"Did you find out anything?" she said.

"Aye, and one thing certain, he's not with the drovers, nor has he been. There's one lot outside Hexham, and another beyond Corbridge. I spoke to them both."

"They could have been hiding him."

"No, no. They were decent fellows, and they both promised to send him packing if he turned up in the morning. Where are they?" He inclined his head towards the house, and Maggie replied, "In the office." She moved nearer to him. "What do you think? That man, Kate's father, is due to come tomorrow."

"What!"

"Mam had a letter from him."

"What for? Why does he want to come here now?"

"She said he didn't say. He's wanting to ask something of her, that's all I could get out of her. Dad's a bit up in the air."

"Aye, yes, I suppose he would be. There was a rumpus on his last visit as I recall, but that's many years ago. Well, well." He took the horse's bridle now and as he led it forward he remarked. "Who says nothing happens in the country." Then he asked, "Is Willy finished?"

"He was in the tack room a little while ago when I took him a bite." Her voice was curt, and she turned and went back into the house.

John was unsaddling the animal when Willy came in, saying, "You didn't find him then?"

"No. But I know one thing, Willy, that's the last time I go traipsing round after him. The way I see it, he's big enough now to know his own mind. If he wants to travel the road, I say let him, or put him to work on a job that will make him feel so damned tired all he'll want is bed. If I had him here I would see that was carried out all right.... You finished?"

"Aye, so leave him and I'll do him down."

"No. No. I've been sitting on me backside for the last three hours or more. I want to move, and you've had more than enough for one day, I should think. So get yourself along and put your feet up. Half-past four will be round afore you know where you are."

Willy did not stop to argue the point; turning about, he said, "Good-night, then."

"Good-night, Willy."

Out in the yard, Willy raised his eyes towards the sky. The moon was up, three-quarters of the yard was in deep shadow and in it stood the house. The only light showing through the darkness was from the kitchen window. He stood for a moment watching the figure passing backwards and forwards in the lamplight; then he turned away and walked the length of the yard, past the old barn, and the bigger newly built one with its store sheds attached, down by a drystone wall that bordered the vegetable garden, then turned to the left past the hen crees and through a gate into a small paddock at the far side of which stood his cottage.

The cottage consisted of two rooms and a loft, which at one time had housed a family of seven, and almost every time he entered it he wondered how they had fitted in, for the living room was but twelve feet square and the bedroom less than that. Over the past four years he had made the place comfortable and suited to his needs, although this entailed its becoming smaller still, for in the main room he had made racks for his books, and in the bedroom wall cupboards to hold his clothes. His furniture was simple, a small wooden square table, a single wooden chair, and one other with a high slatted back. To the left of the fireplace was a cupboard where he kept food for odd meals; and to the right of it, a rack that held kitchen utensils. Beyond this was a narrow door leading into a stone pantry. Outside the cottage stood two narrow rough stone erections. One was a coal-house, the other a bucket water-closet.

Before leaving the cottage in the morning, he always banked down his fire, then saw to it again at dinner time, and when he returned at night a blow with the bellows brought it into life again. But tonight he was some distance from the door when he saw a glow of firelight in the window, and he paused, then walked slowly forward.

Opening the door, he went in and looked at the figure sitting on the mat before the fire and, as if he had expected to find him there, he said, "Hello. See you've got it going for me."

Fraser Hamilton rose slowly to his feet. He was as tall as Willy, and in the firelight he could have been mistaken for a grown man. His hair was jet black and hung thickly about his ears. His eyes seemed to be of the same hue, their darkness emphasized by the paleness of his skin. His face was long and his mouth, in this light, appeared to be a slit in it. It was an unusual face, handsome, but not that of a youth. Often young boys of his age, if their features could be described as beautiful, would possess some quality appertaining to refinement, even when the spots of youth attacked the skin they emphasized rather than denied youth, but in Fraser's case his good looks gave off no such impression, for the rash on his chin was what one would expect to see on that of a grown man.

"Been at it again, now, have you?" Willy threw off his coat and went over to the cupboard on which stood a candlestick, and having lit the candle, brought it to the table before he spoke again. Looking the boy up and down, he said quietly, "By! you are in a mess. Where did you sleep last night?"

"In a haystack, after I fell in the mire."

"You askin' for your death?"

"Wouldn't matter."

"Don't talk rubbish. What brought it on this time?"

"This." The boy pointed to his chin. "I was growing hair. Bradshaw, the headmaster said, get it off. He gave me a brush and an old razor which was blunt. From then I got the spots. And then" – he put his hand to his hair – "he ordered that my hair be cut off, close-cropped."

"Why? Had it got dirty?"

"No. I was apparently paying too much attention to it, keeping it too clean. It happened to two other fellows. They looked like scarecrows. I wasn't havin' it."

"I can see your point."

"Willy" – the boy suddenly sat down on the high backed chair – "I'm not going back. If Father attempts to force me again through reason or any other damn thing, I'll take a ship. I won't need to be press-ganged."

"Don't be daft. You don't know what you're talkin' about. Whether you realize it or not, you've had it soft for years. That life would finish you."

"I'm not soft, Willy. I'm hard underneath. I'm hard. I've slept out in the open with the drovers for years. You know I have."

"Because most of them are decent fellows, lookin' after you and happin' you up. But you get on board one of those ships and you won't be happed up, I can tell you, but the skin'll be flayed off you. We had a crippled sailor came back on the estate a few years ago, he had hardly an inch of his skin that wasn't scarred and he was only discharged because he could no longer run or jump at the sound of a voice or the end of a whip. He'd only half a foot, and I won't tell you how he came by that. So get that idea out of your head. Anyway, get those things off and see if we can get them cleaned up. Have you had anything to eat?"

The boy nodded towards the cupboard, saying, "I took some of your bread and bacon."

"You're welcome. Well, let me get this pan on the fire and we'll have some hot gruel. But come on, strip off, the mud looks dry; I'll brush them down. But you can't go home like that."

When the boy took off his coat that had been buttoned to the neck, Willy gazed at him for a moment, saying, "You've got nothin' underneath. How's that?"

"I ... I was put in a detention room because of this." He tapped his head. "They always take away your small-clothes. There's not much warmth in serge. They call it cooling your capers."

"My God! And your father pays through the teeth for that. Surely there are better schools in Newcastle?"

"Yes, there are, but this one was chosen for its strong discipline, I understand."

"Brutality would be a better word. Come in here." Willy picked up the candle and led the way into the bedroom, and, setting it down on top of a chest, he opened the cupboard door and took from one of the shelves a shirt and woollen drawers and vest, saying, "Put them on."

But before getting into the clothes the boy handled them, saying, "'Tis fine wool."

"Yes, and so it should be, for these belonged to my old master. He saw me well supplied in this way over the years. There were cupboards full of such, lining the bedrooms. They had belonged to his relative who died. They must have both been about the same size and the only difference in stature between them and me was that their legs were slightly shorter. I've been well suited for years, inside and out."

"I used to wonder when I saw you dressed in the market, not like our herdsmen."

"So now you need wonder no longer." He looked at the boy, smiling now as he said, "They're a bit big, but they'll be warm. And here, put this lined waistcoat on. The nights are chilly and we've got a longish walk afore us."

"You're coming home with me?"

"Aye, in case you stray again."

"I'd rather stay here till the morning. I could sleep on the mat."

"You'll do no such thing. Your mother's half demented as usual. You're a thoughtless lad, you know."

"I'm not. I'm not really, but ... but I'm always being told what I must do and what I mustn't do."

"But you've been on the run since you were a nipper. You know you have."

Fraser turned away and went into the other room, saying, "I can't

424

help that. Something comes over me. I just must up and go. I . . . I want things to happen." He turned round now and faced Willy. "Can you understand that? I want things to happen."

"Adventures like?"

"Yes and no. I can't explain. I . . . well, there's only one thing I do know, I don't want to be like other people, all those around following their humdrum everyday existence. How do you stand it? You're well-read. Everybody says you're well-read. Superior in a way – Mother says that – so how do you stand it? I don't know how you can put up with this kind of life, working like a slave all day for my grandfather. And yet you go on. Why? Why?"

"Because it's my nature, I suppose: I like workin' with animals; I like the open air; I also like time to meself to read and think. Strangely, you have a lot of time to yourself when you deal with animals, time in which to think. It all depends upon how one's made, one's nature."

"Well, I'm not made like that, I suppose."

"You don't know, you've never given yourself a chance. Anyway, come on, let's get that mouthful of gruel and be on our way, because I want to get to bed sometime afore midnight."

"I can go by myself."

"You're not goin' by yourself, because what would you do when you got there, go and sleep in the barn until the morrow mornin'?" . . .

It was just a half-hour later when they left the cottage. The air was sharp and the moon bright, and they walked briskly, yet it was another good hour before Willy pulled the bell to the side of the door at Rooklands Farm. Fraser had wanted to go in by the kitchen way, but Willy had said, "And let the cook and maids know you are here afore your mother?"

When the door was opened, a maid stood there, the lamp held high in her hand, and she peered through the light for a moment a the two dark figures; then she let out a thin high squeal, crying, "Eeh! Master Fraser." And the boy, pushing past her, mimicked her: "Eeh! Annie Pollock."

It was as if his voice had thrust open two doors, one at each side of the hall, for Kate came hurrying from the dining-room, and the open drawing-room door showed Ben standing stiff and straight staring towards his son.

Kate said no word to the boy, but, going to him, she put her hand on his shoulder and steered him towards his father, while at the same time turning her head to Willy saying, "Come along in, Willy."

"Oh, I'll be on my way, Mrs Hamilton."

"Please." The word was a plea, and so, cap in hand, he followed her and the boy, and as Ben drew himself back to allow them to pass he said to Willy in a voice that was almost a growl, "Where did you find him?"

"I didn't. He found me," said Willy, and in a lower tone added, "He's all right. Tired, I think. He slept out all night. He wasn't with the drovers."

They both now moved up the long room to where the boy was

slumped into a big leather chair, and Willy was surprised but enlightened at what next took place, for Ben, confronting his son, demanded, "Get on your feet. You've been told before about sitting when your mother is standing." The boy hesitated for a moment, staring up into the thin white face above him until Kate, her hand again on his shoulder, pressed him back into the seat, and she herself sat down next to him, saying, "It's all right. It's all right. It isn't the time for courtesies."

"Every time is a time for courtesies. What is schooling for?"

"Yes, Father, what is schooling for?" The boy was sitting straight in the chair now, his dark features showing a look of venom as he cried, "It's for cropping your head. Giving you dirty razors." He dug his finger into his chin. "Stripping you naked, then putting you into your suit and thrusting you into a dead cold room for twenty-four hours. But you've got your suit on, so if a visitor should happen to see you being taken in or out, you're dressed. And it's also for a piece of leather with slit end which catches you across the back of the knees. Oh, you're protected by trousers, but it still makes you jump. It's for...."

"That's enough. You must have deserved it."

"I didn't deserve it, no more than the other fellows there. And for your information, Father, I'm not the only one that has run away. Two have done it this month, but their parents came and told the headmaster what they thought of him. But have my parents gone to see a headmaster, no matter what I've said? This is the third place you've put me in and each one worse than the other. Anything to get rid of me."

"Oh, Fraser, Fraser, don't say that. You know it isn't true."

He turned his furious gaze on his mother now, saying, "'Tis true. From I can first remember anything I remember that, being got rid of, left behind, time you went jaunting to France ... Switzerland."

"That was necessary for your father's health, Fraser, and you know it."

"I don't know it. I only know I saw more of Mrs Proctor and the maids than I ever did of you."

"It was necessary." Her voice was low now, patient sounding. "I couldn't have taken you with me...."

"No, no." He sprang to his feet. "You couldn't have taken me with you, but you took Rose, didn't you?"

"She was a girl and delicate. The air did her good."

"And dear Harry?" He was now looking at his father and he repeated, "Dear Harry who, as you said, Father, has never given you a day's worry since he was born, was he delicate too? He's as strong as a bull. He was four when you first took him abroad and there was no sign of any disease on him then, or...."

"Be quiet, boy!" The word disease seemed to have prodded Ben into life, for now he took two quick steps towards his son, crying, "Another word and I'll take the horsewhip to you myself."

"Ben! Ben!" Kate was standing between them. "Look, don't get excited, please, please." She turned her back on her son and gripped her

426

husband by the arms, pressing him away and into a chair, where he was seized with a bout of coughing that racked his whole body.

When Kate ran to a side-table and picked up a small silver tray on which was a bottle and a spoon, the boy got to his feet. His expression hadn't altered; the paroxysm of his father's coughing hadn't touched him at all. He looked towards Willy, and Willy with a slight motion of his head upwards indicated that he should leave the room. And this he did, but not quietly, for as the door banged behind him Kate, replacing the spoon on the tray, turned sharply and looked towards it. Then sighing, she let her gaze rest on Willy.

"I'm sorry, Willy. Sit down, will you, and have something to drink before you go?"

"If you don't mind, Mrs Hamilton, I'll be on me way."

She cast a glance at Ben who was now leaning back in his chair, his breath coming in short painful jerks. Then turning back to Willy, she said, "Do they know at home that he's back?"

"No, but I'll tell them."

He turned and made for the door. And she walked with him. In the hall he stopped and, looking at her, said, "He's had a pretty rough time at that school, I should say, Mrs Hamilton, from the bits he's let drop. It wasn't so much education that was pushed into them there, but fear. If I may speak, I wouldn't think about forcing him back, or to any other school. I . . . I think he wants to work. He's ready for it."

"Yes, yes, you're right, Willy, you're right. But——" Kate clasped her hands tightly now between her large breasts, and she looked towards the staircase as she said, "His father wanted to see him get on in the world, go to a university, take up science or law, he . . . he had great ideas for him." Then bringing her gaze back on Willy, she ended, "It was unfortunate we had to leave him when he was young, but you see, he . . . he was so boisterous. From he was a tiny baby he was so boisterous. He took up all one's time, and . . . and I hadn't that time to give him."

When Willy made no reply, and simply stared at her, she made an apologetic sound in her throat, then said, "Thank you, Willy, for seeing to him."

"That's all right. He's . . . he's not a bad boy, you know."

"No?" There seemed to be a question in the syllable; then more firmly she added, "No, of course he isn't, but he's got the sort of wanderlust on him. He doesn't take after either his father or me. I don't know whom he takes after." She smiled wanly, and he turned from her, saying, "Good-night, Mrs Hamilton," and she answered, "Good-night, Willy, and thank you again."

Out on the open road he repeated to himself, "I don't know who he takes after." That was a damn silly thing to say, because, if he'd heard it once since he had been connected with this family, he must have heard it a couple of dozen times from outsiders every time the boy went missing: "He's a true Bannaman, that one, following in his great-grandfather's footsteps." And the story of Dan Bannaman and his daughter, and the little fellow who hanged himself, which had become folklore around these parts, would once again be related.

Aye, it was silly for her to wonder who her son took after when his father was part Bannaman.

2

***

Mary Ellen stared at the man and the girl sitting opposite to her. After an hour and a half in their company she was still finding it difficult to say anything. She had been surprised at the change in her childhood play-mate when he had last come upon the scene seventeen years ago. But that change was nothing to what the intervening years had wrought on him. He was a little younger than Hal, just under two years, yet he could have been ten or twenty years older. His flesh at all points seemed to be pressing against his well cut clothes. His face was ruddy, the jowls heavy. There was no hair on the front of his head and the fringe covering the back and sides was pure white. In her mind, even till as late as this morning, she had seen a tall man, broad shoulders and straight. The breadth was still there, but the height was cut by the stoop of his shoulders.

Then this girl, this child, or whatever she was, who was his daughter, he said, she had never seen anyone like her, never in her life before. She was like someone you would see in a picture book. At a guess, she was a little over five feet, with form so slight as to be non-existent. Her fashionable dull red velvet coat and skirt did not suggest it was covering a body, however slight. And then the face . . . yes, it was the face that was the most amazing. The eyes were large and grey, and they had, she was discovering, the habit of staring at you without blinking while her expression changed from one moment to the next. When John had said one sentence in French, the only one he remembered from his school-days, the light in her eyes had been impish as she had answered him. And when the girl herself spoke in her mixed up English, the light would turn to merriment and would be accompanied by her laughter, which was more like a gurgle. It was only when she looked at her father that the light changed to a sober hue. And she noticed that when he spoke she gave him all her attention. But it was the girl's face as a whole that was startling: like her body, it was small; the skin, she could only liken to a piece of alabaster. And then the hair. What colour was her hair? Lemon-coloured, pale lemon-coloured, and it wasn't dressed like that of a fashionable young lady, which she evidently was, it was hanging loose, held only by a ribbon which was tied in a bow.

She was speaking now to Maggie who, like herself, had up till now seemed to be tongue-tied.

"Your cows make butter? I mean, you make . . . I mean you milk. . . .

429

Oh Papa—" She swung round at her father and spoke in rapid French, and he, looking at Maggie and smiling, said, "What Yvonne is trying to say is, do you milk the cows and make the butter yourself?" And Maggie, also laughing now, said softly, "Yes, I make the butter and milk the cows, at least some of them. John here" – she indicated John with her outspread hand – "he too helps with the milking."

"I have not yet been on a form."

Again there was laughter from Maggie and John; and now, her father, looking at her, said, "Farm not form . . . and I haven't before been on a farm, or, this is my first time on a farm. Comprends-tu?"

"Oui." There was more laughter. Then Hal, who all the while had been sitting to the side of Mary Ellen and, like her, had had little to say, spoke to John, saying, "Why don't you take the miss round the farm. And you, Maggie, show her how you make butter."

There was a slight pause before John and Maggie rose to their feet. They both realized they were being told to go and the reason why. Up till now the time had been taken up with the eating of light refreshments and small talk. But whatever the reason for this man's visit, it wasn't to indulge in small talk. And apparently their father, as usual, was anxious to get to the bottom of something he didn't understand. And, from the snatches of conversation at the breakfast table this morning, he certainly didn't understand the reason for his one-time friend's visit at this late stage in their lives.

When John tentatively held out his hand as he would do to a child, the girl sprang up and caught it. Then, her strange face alight, she turned and looked up at her father, saying, "Like Marie Antoinette, I go to learn milk."

"To be a milkmaid."

"Ah, oui." She nodded towards him, then allowed John to lead her from the room laughing.

Left to themselves now, Roddy Greenbank looked first at Mary Ellen, then at Hal, and his body slumped further into the big armchair before he said, "I know you are wondering what all this is about, and why the hell he's got to put in an appearance after all these years of apparent neglect, not even having any interest in his own daughter. Oh, I know what you're both thinking. Well, my answer is simple. I haven't long to go, a week, a month, three at the most." He made a sound like a mirthless laugh now as he added, "Perhaps one of old Kate's potions might have helped, I've thought about her a lot of late."

In the pause that followed, Mary Ellen and Hal glanced at each other, then looked at him again as he said, "My purpose in coming is to ask a great favour of you. And Hal, I know what your response will be immediately. Of all the bloody nerve! you'll say. And I can understand that perfectly. As for you, Mary Ellen, your reaction could be the same as Hal's, only put in a different way. It could be: You're got a nerve, Roddy Greenbank. By God! you have. Well, I don't know about a nerve, but a man does things out of desperation. I've searched my mind, going over all the so-called friends I've made in the past years. The only couple I could have trusted, besides yourselves, died last year within a month of each other. Well, I'll come to the point. . . . Will you take her under your care when I'm gone?"

He watched their faces. Simultaneously their jaws dropped and their eyes widened. He watched Hal's tongue move within the gap as if it was coiling round a word, suppressing it. He watched Mary Ellen put her hand up to her head and mutter, "You . . . you must be jokin'." And he made no reply to this, he just sat staring at them.

And Mary Ellen stared back at him. She knew it had been an inane reply to make, you must be joking, but how could she voice the words that were running round in her mind: the audacity, the bare-faced audacity, of all the damned impudence to turn up here after all this time. She jerked her head to the side as Hal spoke. His voice a rumble, he was saying, "A girl like that would never fit in here. You must know that. She smacks of the town. And there's bound to be some of your high up friends who would give her a home."

Roddy pulled himself upwards in the chair now and, his hands gripping the arms, he leant forward towards Hal, saying grimly, "Yes, they would come forward in their dozens, literally dozens, to give her a home, and she would be as safe with them as a virgin, which she is, in a brothel. There's a world out there, Hal, or up there as you yourself might put it, among the class that you know nothing of. Respectability is like thick cream on the top, but there's a pail full of whey beneath it and its rank. I know that nobody can teach you anything about life in the country, but there's another kind of life, Hal, a different kind of life."

"Your wife, where is she?"

He turned and looked at Mary Ellen, saying simply, "Dead these five years."

"What about her people? They would surely take her?"

Roddy wetted his full lips. "She wasn't my wife, Mary Ellen, my wife had no use for children. I had . . . I had a mistress. She was Yvonne's mother. She brought her up until she was seven and then I sent her to a convent school."

"Did you marry her after, the mother?" It seemed an odd question to ask, yet she wanted to know. And when he answered flatly, "No, of course not," she thought: You wouldn't. No, you wouldn't.

"Where is she now?"

"She's dead too. She died three years ago. From then I brought Yvonne to live with me."

"How old is she?" Mary Ellen waited for his answer. She saw him look down towards his knees before saying, "Sixteen."

'She looks younger."

"Yes." He nodded at her. "That's the trouble. Her whole appearance is deceptive. But she's not young in her mind. She's very bright, clever, accomplished in many ways. Except" – he forced a smile to his face – "in English. We speak mostly in our own language over there."

She noticed that he referred to French as his own language. "Does she still go to school?"

Again he hesitated, then said, "No, no, she . . . she left some time ago. Well?" He looked from one to the other. And they looked at each other and both shook their heads, and it was Mary Ellen who spoke, saying, "It's no good. I'm sorry, Roddy. As Hal here says, she's of the town. You should see that. And what's for a girl like that here? We have no social life, except among the family, and there'd be no men around here, among those we know, who would be suitable for the likes of her."

"She likes ordinary people and she doesn't care for the town. We had a cottage in the country and she was never happier than when she was there, and she's adaptable. And although she knows her own mind and would stand up for herself, she . . . she would be eaten alive if I were to leave her in Paris. There's many ways a girl like her can be ruined. You don't know." He shook his head. "Life here—" He now looked from one end of the room to the other, his expression encompassing the whole area as if they were on another planet, before he looked fully at Hal now, saying quietly, "We thought we knew life when we were lads, we thought we knew it all because we had witnessed murder, but I've learned since that even murder can be clean compared to some things."

Hal rose abruptly now as also did his voice as he said, "Well, there must be a lot of uncivilized and filthy buggers among your friends, that's all I can say, if there's not one of them she can go to."

Roddy's voice remained low in reply as he said, "I've told you, Hal, there are dozens and dozens I could let her go to and who would take her gladly, but men are men, even the best of them, and she's made that way she has an effect on people, especially on women, wives in particular. They see her as a menace."

"Already, at her age?"

He nodded towards Mary Ellen, repeating her words, "Already at her age. Yes, already. Yet, she's of the most loving and kind nature you would ever come across."

"My God!" Hal was walking up and down in his characteristic way now, talking as he strode, "'Tis like you to turn up and put us in this situation, one that we can't handle. I'm sorry. I am really, Roddy, that you find yourself in this fix, but" – he stopped – "about this business . . . well, the time you have. What's wrong with you?"

"A number of things." The answer came quietly. "But the heart mostly."

"Overeating, I suppose. Look at you."

"Yes, yes, that could be true. But eating can be a sort of compensation, compulsory compensation. You" – he turned his head from one to the other – "have been fortunate. You blame me for keeping my distance all these years. It isn't that I haven't thought of you and envied you, and I mean that, envied you. The worst thing that life did to me was to give me the power to draw. But for that, I'd have been here yet." He stared at Mary Ellen until her glance fell away. This did not go unnoticed by Hal, and, his voice louder now, he said, "Aye, well, you made your choice. You couldn't get away quick enough. Remember that, man. Anyway, your fame should be some compensation, 'cos your pictures sell they say. Oh—" He waved his hand now to the seated man, saying, "We may be in the back of beyond here, but Hugh and Gabriel are in the town and we get all the news, literary and otherwise from them. They went to see your last exhibition in the gallery. You were to come and open it, but you didn't turn up, did you?"

"I was ill. I only got as far as London."

"That was three years ago or more."

"Yes. I was told then I had only six months to go, but you see" – he shrugged his shoulders – "I'm still here. But a fortnight ago I had a London opinion and it seems to be final. Anyway—" He pulled himself slowly to his feet now, saying, "I see you don't feel you're able to help me in this, and I can understand. Yes, I can understand."

Mary Ellen too was on her feet and, looking at him, she said softly, "There's Kate, too, you know, Roddy. What would she think? Because no matter . . . well. . . ."

When she paused Hal put in roughly, "Go on. Go on, say it. I've got a skin like a hide, makes no difference to me. They'd be half-sisters. That's what you were going to say, wasn't it?" Then swinging round, he stared at Roddy, saying, "I'm sorry for you, that you've been given notice like this, but at the same time I've got to say this, you've got a real bloody nerve. You were born to be a disturber of the peace, d'you know that? All these years we sail along peacefully, or near so, and then you turn up like a hurricane and wreak havoc on. . . ."

"Hal! Hal, stop it! He knows the situation. He doesn't need to be reminded. Nor do I." Then looking at Roddy again, she said quietly, "I'm sorry, but it would be impossible in more ways than one. You can see that, surely?"

"Yes, yes, I understand, and . . . and I'm sorry I've disturbed you both, but . . . well. . . . Oh" – he shook his head – "there's no need for any more talking." He looked at his watch. "We should get a train from Haydon Bridge around four o'clock," he said. "We can just manage it if we leave now." A forced smile came on his face as he looked at Hal, saying, "Amazing isn't it, to be able to get a train from Haydon Bridge into Newcastle. Remember the carrier cart? I suppose you have the post delivered now too?"

"Oh, that's been delivered for years, and more bother than it's worth, I may say. At one time you could go to the office and pick up your letters, now they'll hardly give them to you at the end of the road. Must hand them in at the door. A lot of damned nonsense."

Mary Ellen now interrupted hesitantly, "I . . . I'll tell your daughter, and also Tom Briggs, that you're ready to go. . . . I bet you were surprised to see him still running his own trap?"

"Yes, yes, I was, Mary Ellen. He must be near eighty, but appears as spritely as ever."

She went out, leaving the two men together. And an embarrassed silence fell on them until Hal, his head bent and his words little above a mutter, said, "I'm sorry, Roddy. I am. I am, really. No matter what I've said, it's hard to face up to things near the end. I know that, I've experienced it a little of late an' all." He tapped his chest. "This doesn't get any better with the years, and I fear one of the bouts will finish me. So I know, too, a little how you feel. And . . . and about the lass. I . . . I wish I could do something, but . . . well, it's all been said, it would never work out. She would wither here, a lass like that. There's something about her, a sort of brightness that . . . that this life would dim."

"Yes, as you say, there's something about her, a sort of brightness. But I don't think this life would dim it, she would shine through it. Still, no more can be said." He held out his hand, saying, "Goodbye, Hal."

When Hal took the hand he was unable to speak for a moment, and when he did, all he could say was, "Aw, lad." Then they both turned and walked down the room towards the door. When they entered the hall, Mary Ellen, Maggie, and the girl were coming in from the kitchen and, going straight to her father, the girl looked up at him and spoke again in rapid French.

Roddy answered in the same tongue, and she stared at him before, turning and looking at Mary Ellen, she said, "I'm sad . . . sorry. It . . . it would have been good . . . nice."

Mary Ellen looked into the pale face. It did not look that of a girl any longer, but of some adult, a wise, understanding adult. It gave her a strange uneasy feeling.

"Viens, papa." And the girl gently took hold of her father's arm.

"Your hat," he said, and when she looked towards the table, Maggie quickly turned and brought the high-crowned velvet hat to her. And the girl thanked her in French, and put the bonnet on. Then again turning to her father, she took his arm; and like that they went out of the front door and on to the drive where the trap was waiting with John standing by it.

"Goodbye, John." Roddy held out his hand and John shook it, saying, "Goodbye, sir." Then he looked at the young girl who was looking up at him, and when she said, "Goodbye, Jean, and thank you. I much enjoyed the cows," he did not speak but, taking her elbow, he helped her up into the trap. And when Tom Briggs called, "Gee-up! there," and the horse went off at a sharp walk towards the gates, the girl turned and waved, and they all waved back.

No one spoke as now, instead of entering the house by the front door, it seemed natural for them to walk round the side, down the yard, and into the kitchen; and there John asked abruptly, "What did he want?"

Hal turned towards the fireplace and, bending forward, held his hands out to the blaze, while Mary Ellen stood by the table, her hands resting on it as she said, "He wanted us to take her. He's only got a short time. . . . He's bad, ill."

There was a long pause before John spoke, saying, his tone holding an incredible note, "And you wouldn't?"

"No. No, we couldn't." Mary Ellen's voice was high now. "There's Kate to think about. And ... and she wouldn't have fitted in here. Just look at her."

"I did. What makes you think she wouldn't have fitted in?"

"She's a town girl. She's ... well, convent bred, polished."

"She's a lonely girl." The words were flat, dull-sounding from Maggie's lips, and brought their attention to her. Even her father turned from the fireplace and stared at her as she added, "She's sort of lost."

"How, in the name of God, do you make that out, our Maggie?" Mary Ellen's head was bouncing now.

"I don't know how in the name of God I make it out. I only know what I feel about her, and I don't see why you couldn't have let her stay. She'd have brought a little lightness into this place, anyway."

"My God! Am I hearin' aright?" Her father was at the other side of the table now standing near Mary Ellen. "Is life so bloody dull here that it needs a light?"

"Yes, it is, if you want to know. It's dull. Dull. And if John here was speaking the truth, he would say the same. What life do we have anyway? A bachelor and an old maid as you've dubbed me yourself, Mam. And you can't say you haven't. That girl would have brought some lightness into our existence; talked about another way of life. She was bright, intelligent."

"God Almighty! I don't think I'm hearin' aright." Hal brought his hand across his mouth. "But, yes I am, because you've been cantankerous since the day you were born. You never kept to a pattern. You were determined to be different to other people. If you want a different way of life, you should have been married and had bairns. You had the chances. Who's to blame but yourself for your dull life, if that's how you see it? But it's too late now, so you'll just have to put up with it, an' us, won't you, madam?"

"Hal! Hal, stop it!" Mary Ellen had pushed him none too gently, and as he hitched up his coat around his shoulders and went to stamp from the room, he turned his head and spoke to John: "Are you in agreement with her?"

And John, looking straight back at him, said, "Partly, yes, and I think like she does, if the man's not long for the top you could have given the lass a home, at least for a time." And on that he turned about and went out, banging the door after him.

"Well, well, home truths are flying around the day. I never thought to live to see it. But Roddy Greenbank's visit has brought to me mind what I've been thinkin' quite a lot lately, I've outlived me time. In fact, I think we are both lucky we have had this long a span." He nodded towards Mary Ellen, then went on, "The lead should have killed me years ago, and high living him. Well, well, his number's been called, and who knows?" He let out a long-drawn sigh and now walked slowly up the room and into the hall. And Mary Ellen, flopping into a chair by the fire, turned and slanted her eyes towards Maggie, saying, "See what you've stirred up? As he said, you've always been cantankerous, always the stirrer."

Their glances were tightly mingled. Maggie had half turned away as if she was about to make for the back door, her lips were quivering slightly, and the mature beauty of her face was lost behind the tightened muscles. Then each word coated with bitterness, she said, "What do you expect from a bonded but unpaid servant?" And with that she went out, leaving Mary Ellen gaping.

It was about two hours later when Tom Briggs galloped his pony and trap back into the yard, calling as he did so, "Hey! there. Hey! there."

John had just returned from the field with the plough horses and was unharnessing them in the stable when he heard the man calling, and, going out, he was brought to a stop for a moment by the sight of Tom Briggs hurrying now towards the house, and cried, "What's up? What's wrong?"

"Everything, man. Everything, I would say. I've trailed all kinds of folks over the years in me trap an' nowt like this's happened afore."

"What, for God's sake?"

"Well, he fell over, just flat. Nearly fell out of the trap, and they took him into Peggy Bowen's cottage, and the lass had a job to hang on to him. She's in a state, I can tell you. 'Tis a good job we were near Peggy Bowen's. But we could hardly get him in, 'tis so cluttered. She has everything in there but her goats. Tell you the truth, she didn't want to let us in. It should happen that Mickie McGuire was passing at the time, off to set his traps no doubt. He'll get caught one of these days, he will. Anyway, he gave us a hand, and there we laid him on the mat. And then Mickie, who can move faster than any horse when he likes, cut over the field to Haydon Bridge an' fetched the doctor. Doctor Brunton was laid up with his leg again so his assistant came out, but he was too late, he was dead."

"*What did you say?*"

"I said, he was dead, the big fellow."

"Oh, my God!" John now turned and, yelling, "Mam! Dad!" rushed into the kitchen.

The sound of his yelling brought Maggie from the barn and she arrived at the house just as John was holding open the door for his mother to enter from the far end.

"What did you say?" Mary Ellen was staring at John.

"He's dead. That's what Tom Briggs has just come to tell us. He collapsed, and they took him into Peggy Bowen's cottage."

"Oh my God!" She turned back into the hall and called loudly, "Hal! Hal!"

And when he appeared from the office she said, "Come ... come and hear this. Roddy's dead, collapsed."

Hal stared from one to the other, then moved slowly past them into the kitchen. Tom Briggs was now standing beside Maggie, and as soon as he saw Hal, he blurted, "Lass's in a state. She had me come back here for one of you. She keeps rambling on in her foreign tongue."

"Get me hat and cape," Mary Ellen demanded of Maggie; then turning to Hal, she said "You should come an' all."

"Aye, yes." He sounded slightly dazed, but when John put in, "I'll go, Dad," his relief was obvious. "Aye, aye. You'd likely be more use than me," he said.

"I'll change me boots." John began to unlace his heavy working boots, and these off, he hurried up the kitchen and in the hall he met Maggie who stopped him and, gripping his arm, said, "Bring her back with you."

"I'll have to see ... Mam."

"She'll have no place else to go. They'll put him in the mortuary; you can't leave her in an inn by herself. Bring her back."

He stared at her in the gloom of the hall. Maggie had always appeared to him to be indifferent to other people's feelings, yet now she seemed set on having this girl in the house. He hadn't before fully realized her need for younger company, having imagined he was the only one who was chaffing at the bit. "I'll ... I'll see what I can do," he said.

A few minutes later both he and Mary Ellen mounted the trap, and Tom Briggs called, "Gee-up! there," and the pony went trotting out of the yard.

It took them forty minutes to reach Peggy Bowen's cottage, and Mary Ellen's reaction as she entered the room was to wrinkle her nose against the smell. Then she stopped still and looked at the bulk of the man stretched out on the floor, and her chest became constricted and her throat full.

Slowly she walked towards him. Her eyes were dry, but her sight seemed blurred. She let her gaze rest on the face, and this gradually came into focus. The puffiness had gone from it, the lines were smoothed out, there beneath the skin lay the Roddy Greenbank she remembered, the boy she had loved with a possessiveness that, with the years, grew almost into mania, and nothing had restrained her until he should possess her. But it was she who had possessed him. Even so, from his reluctance had come Kate. And now there he was, lying dead, a big bloated man. She became aware of John lifting the girl to her feet and of her looking up at him and muttering brokenly, "Mon père. Mon père. What I do without him? What I do?"

"'Tis all right. You're coming home with us."

At this the girl looked across at Mary Ellen and said, "Yes, but ... but my father?" Her hand waved slowly in the air like a benediction over the prostrate form, and it was as if she knew she had to endeavour to make

437

this woman understand, whereas the woman's son understood without explanation.

It was not Mary Ellen who answered her question but Peggy Bowen. "To the dead house, hospital," she said. "The sooner the better. Can't get stirred."

"No, no, not hospital." The girl turned and looked at John, and he looked at his mother and said quietly, "We should take him back home."

"Take him back now?" It was a bewildered question, and John answered, "Yes. There'll have to be arrangements made. He'll have to be buried. You and Dad ... well, you were his friends."

"Yes, but...." She seemed in a daze.

John now caught hold of Tom Briggs's arm and, drawing him through the door on to the rough grass, said, "Slip along, Tom, to Patterton's farm and ask them for a loan of a horse and flat cart. Tell them what's happened."

"Aye, all right. But who's goin' to stand the racket for all this?"

"I'll see you're paid."

"An' will I tell Patterton the same about the horse and cart?"

"Mr Patterton won't mind loaning the horse and cart." John's voice was sharp. "But to make it easier, you can tell him if you like, only get going."

John did not return to the cottage immediately, but he stood looking over the unkept ground to where four goats were tethered and hens were scratching and geese cackling. But he didn't see these, it was as if he were looking into a clear sky. There was a strange feeling within him, a feeling he seemed to be dragging back from past years, from the time when he was on the point of asking Nan Cody to be his wife, then changed his mind at the last minute. Yet what this feeling had to do with the dead man and the girl back in the cottage, he couldn't understand. There was no seeming connection. But what came over with the feeling, and strongly, was the knowledge that here he was, forty years old, and that life had passed him by.

3

Roddy Greenbank's return in such a dramatic way had stirred the memories of the older people. Many of them made a point of attending the funeral and, later, related the history to those who did not know the full details of the events that had taken place some forty years earlier. But the talk was centred mostly upon the daughter Roddy Greenbank had left behind him and who was the half-sister of Mrs Hamilton, who had been known as Kate Roystan, but who had really been fathered by the man who had dropped down dead on the road after visiting Mrs Roystan, for what purpose nobody seemed to have been able to find out, only that he had made his way from Haydon Bridge station and hired Tom Briggs's trap.

Another thing that set the tongues wagging was that the Roystan women had attended the funeral together with the young girl and Mrs Hamilton. And there was never such a contrasting pair as the half-sisters as they stood by the side of the grave, one as big as a house-end, the other such a slip of a thing the wind could have blown her away....

It was about the contrast between herself and her half-sister that Kate was speaking now to her mother. Mary Ellen was upstairs in her room resting, which was something she very rarely indulged in. But the past ten days had taken their toll on her, and she was now both physically and mentally exhausted. She hitched herself slowly up on the couch as Kate, who was sitting beside the window, said, "I still can't take it in about the relationship."

"Well, it's something you've got to accept, lass. She's your half-sister, and that's all there is to it."

"Well, nobody would believe it. And I can tell you this much, it came as a shock to her. Why didn't he tell her? She's not as innocent as all that. She knew her mother was his mistress, and, living in a place like Paris, she would know what life was all about. And the way she talks, even in her broken English, she's not without knowledge of lots of things."

"Don't be bitter against the lass. I'm not all that keen on her meself, 'cos she's foreign to me in more than nature somehow. She's not like anyone you would see in these parts."

"Well, you seem to be the only one in the family so far, Mam, who isn't taken with her. Even Dad has a smile and a word for her, and that's rare these days."

"Oh, it isn't only Dad, it's our Maggie and John. You would think

439

they'd got a new playmate. I'm amazed at our Maggie. She's like a clucking hen with her first chick."

There was a pause before Kate said, "Well, I can understand that. Our Maggie's frustrated. I say again and I've said it before, I can't understand her not marrying."

"Nor can I. But now she's got me worried. It's that Willy, and she's at that daft age."

"*Willy?*"

"Aye, Willy. Every opportunity she's talkin' to him, an' they laugh together. I've seen them."

"Well, you can't make anything out of that, Mam. *Willy?* Why, she's too high and mighty to stoop to anybody like Willy."

"Oh, I don't know. I've seen it happen afore. Women get desperate."

"But not for Willy. After all, he's a farmhand, and he may be a very good one, as Dad's always pointing out he's worth three of any of ours."

"Aye, and he's a bit different in other ways an' all in that he can read and write an' he studies books. At times I think he's got ideas about himself. All through coming under the protection of his old master. It's not a good thing to take people out of their class."

At this Kate got to her feet just in time to stop herself from saying, "You should say that to Dad sometime." Instead, she said, "We'll be over on Sunday as usual. You rest now." She put her hand out and stroked the hair back from Mary Ellen's forehead, and her mother, looking up at her, said, "How's things going with Fraser?"

"Oh" – Kate smiled – "I think we've struck the right note at last. No more schooling if he'll promise to learn the farming. He likes dealing with horses best, so Ben's put him in charge of the third stable with Pedro and Jasper there. They are both quiet animals. And he'll be under Dawson who's going to show him the ropes and take him into market for the sales and things. I'm sure this will work." But the smile slid from her face as she added, "It's got to. I can't have Ben worried any more. The winter's coming on and as we are not going away, he'll have to have at least peace of mind. Well, see you on Sunday, Mam."

"Goodbye, lass."

When the door closed on her daughter, Mary Ellen lay back, saying, "I can't have Ben worried any more." Always Ben. Although she herself held no bones for Fraser and, like Hal, she considered there was a broad bad streak in him, still, the lad mightn't have been as bad as he was if Kate had paid a little more attention to him and less to his father. But right from the very beginning when she first clapped eyes on the American – as in her mind she still thought of Ben – she had imagined the sun shone out of him. And yet, at one time if she remembered rightly, Kate's aim in life was just to have children. That's all she wanted, children.

Well, she closed her eyes, she was tired. She was almost as tired as Hal looked, and he did look tired these days. Deep inside she was worried about him. But she comforted herself with the thought that there hadn't been a winter for past years now but she had thought it would be his last, and he was still here. He had been lucky. He was the only one of his generation left alive in these parts, at least of those who had worked in the smelt mills. Some of them hadn't seen their mid-thirties, and those who had reached fifty were the exceptions. But here was Hal sixty-five. It was an amazing age, especially in his condition. But, as she often had said to herself, if will power had anything to do with it, he'd see a hundred.

On Sunday evening Fraser and Yvonne met for the first time. Kate introduced her son, saying, "This is Fraser, my eldest son," and she watched him stare unblinking at the young girl, his whole appearance so dark and hers so fair that she found herself thinking, "Night and day." Then quickly she went on to introduce Harry. Harry was thirteen years old and the image of his father with his ascetic countenance and pleasing smile.

Then Rose. Rose was plain, but not as plain as her mother had been at her age, nor as big.

The introductions over, it was Hal, his voice as usual drowning all the rest, saying, "Well, formalities over, let's eat." So they had all adjourned to the dining-room. And it could be said that the meal was quite merry, as John related their guest's faux pas. One that caused laughter was when he explained how awkward it was having an assistant who called the bull monsieur and the cows mesdemoiselles, when in her language the latter should really be madams, only for him to be corrected by Yvonne, saying, "Mesdames, Jean."

When Rose said, "My father speaks French and reads French books too," and glanced proudly towards Ben, the young girl, her face brightening, asked, "You do, monsieur?"

"I read at it, let's say. I haven't many French books."

"Have you read Flaubert?"

"Yes." Ben nodded towards her.

"*Madame Bovary?*"

Now Ben's eyes widened as he said, "You haven't read *Madame Bovary?*"

"Oui, monsieur. You surprise that I read her?"

"Well . . . er, yes I am." He pursed his lips while smiling. "I understand it caused a bit of a stir?"

"Oh, many books cause stir. Some are what you call stopped?"

"Banned."

"Oh" – her chin jerked upwards – "banned. But there are" – she paused – "what you say? channels to get them."

"I would have said, ways."

"Ways." She repeated, Then she turned her attention to Kate, saying, "You also, you read in French?"

"No, I'm afraid not," Kate's voice was flat. She was having difficulty in speaking to this girl. She doubted if she would ever feel at ease with her; she didn't think she would ever really like her. The nearest she had come to it was on the day after the funeral when the girl had cried for hours on end and they'd thought she'd make herself ill. Her mother had made her a cordial that had put her to sleep, and Mary Ellen's only comment on the crying spasm had been, "Well, it's about time. I thought she hadn't a tear in her. She's been too composed for her own good. I can't make her out."

She had said to her mother, "What does she mean to do? Stay on here?" And Mary Ellen had replied briefly, "That seems to be the position, but it's not one I like."

She now started slightly in surprise when Fraser's voice broke in saying, "Our French master was from Caen, in Normandy. We called him Bill."

"Oh?" Yvonne looked at the boy sitting opposite to her. She had been aware that he had been staring at her for most of the meal. His dark countenance, she thought, was not very appealing. She repeated, "Caen?" then added, "He was from the provinces."

"He spoke good French. He wouldn't let us speak English in his class." Fraser's voice had an aggressive note to it, and at this her eyebrows slightly raised, she spoke to him in French. The rest of the table was silent. Their eyes were on her, but their attention turned to Fraser for when he answered her, his reply coming hesitantly, but with force and in French, she answered him in English, for all to hear, and what she said was, "He has left you his accent."

The words and tone implied a snub which one would have expected from an adult, not from a sixteen-year-old fragile-looking slip of a girl who was now calmly splitting open the last plum on her plate and removing the stone, while the boy's face was showing a deepening red hue that spoke of temper.

It was Maggie who broke the silence: on a laugh, she said as she looked across at Fraser, "Accent or no accent, I'd give me eye teeth if I could speak any kind of French. All I remember from my school-days of French is, Içi on parle francais, and from German, because Miss Price was half German and she made us learn it, was the word umlaut."

"Umlaut?" Rose now took up the conversation. "What's umlaut mean, Auntie?"

"Don't ask me, I've forgotten." This brought forth laughter, but it was all slightly forced. And when the meal was ended, Kate's family, together with Hal and Mary Ellen, left the room and went into the sitting-room. Yvonne did not join them but stayed to help Maggie clear the table. Kate too stayed and it was when she went out carrying a tray of dishes that Maggie stopped Yvonne in the act of stacking the cups and saucers. Taking her gently by the arm, she looked into her face and said, "That wasn't very kind, Yvonne."

"You mean with the boy?"

"Yes, I mean with the boy. He meant to be friendly."

The girl turned her head away, then said quietly, "He spoke rude, and he stares all the time."

"Well" – Maggie gave a small laugh – "I'm sure you should be used to being stared at by now."

"Oh oui . . . yes, quite use, but his" – she moved her fingers over her face – "his countenance is black, dark, not like a boy's."

"No, you're right there, he doesn't look like a boy. Nevertheless, that's what he is, and he's been going through a rough time lately."

"This is he who ran from school?"

"Yes, this is he. I mean that is him. Oh" – she pushed the girl on the shoulder – "you get me as twisted as yourself."

"Oh, Mag . . . gie. You are my friend." Maggie's hand was clasped tight between the two pale long-fingered ones. "I am lost. I miss mon père, oh, so much . . . so much. We talked . . . lot of talk, and laughed. I have now only you and Jean. I must talk. . . ."

"Later, later." Maggie withdrew her hand as Kate entered the room, saying, "You should have help, Maggie. It's really ridiculous. Jessie Biggot would only be too willing, I'm sure, to come in and give a hand, part time."

"Jessie come in? Don't make me laugh. She didn't turn up for the washing last Monday. I had that to do an' all. She's on the bottle again."

"But she had joined the Methodists."

"That didn't last long. Anyway, I'd rather have her on the bottle because she became so pious for a time she'd hardly handle the men's long clothes.'

As she laughed out loud, Kate looked at her. Maggie seemed happier these days. Could it be Willy's influence? Or was it because of the girl? As her mother had said, she was acting like a clucking hen towards a chick. But that girl was no chick. Look how she had turned on Fraser. And Fraser had been taken with her, she could see that, for he had hardly opened his mouth since he had met her, and that was a sure sign of his interest. But oh my God! No, no. Because what was she in law? His aunt? Yes, she supposed so. What a situation. Well, she would see that the Sunday visits would be cut short after this, And the quicker the girl was persuaded to go back to her own country the better for all concerned. If only Maggie wasn't so taken with her. Why was it that whatever Maggie did always ended in trouble? She seemed born to create unrest.

When her son suddenly entered the room, she turned on him, saying sharply, "What do you want?"

"Grandad says I should help carry the trays."

"We are nearly finished."

He looked to where Yvonne had stacked the cups and saucers on a wooden tray and she was about to lift it up when he went to her and, taking it from her hands, he said, "Let me."

"Oh, merci." She smiled at him. And remembering what Maggie had said to her about this boy whilst chastising her about being rude to him, she endeavoured to be friendly, saying now, "I would likely have fallen them."

"You likely would." He was smiling back at her and what she thought now was, He could be nice. He is handsome.

She walked with him towards the door and here he did her the courtesy of pressing his back against it while still holding the tray and allowing her to go before him.

In the room the two women stood watching this; and when the door swung closed behind them, Maggie said, "She could be a good influence on him, and they're both about the same age." Then she was startled as Kate rounded on her and in a manner that she had never used before, for she had, in a way, been very careful to placate her. But now, her voice came almost as a growl, saying, "Don't be stupid, Maggie. Think of the relationship. Have you forgotten that? In a way she's his aunt."

Maggie made no reply, for yes, strangely, she had forgotten the relationship. Or had she closed her eyes to it, hoping for what? Well, what did she hope for? Anything that would keep here permanently the light that had come into this house, hoping that its warmth would soothe the desire that had been running riot in her of late, closing her mind to the fact that there was only one way this desire could be appeased.

She picked up the crumb-tray and brush and began to sweep the table-cloth, saying as she did so, "You take things too seriously, Kate. That girl would as soon think of Fraser in that way as—" She couldn't find a simile in her mind, and ended, "Oh, what does it matter?" Then she swept the bundle of crumbs on to the ornamental wooden shovel, before marching from the room.

Kate stood for a moment longer, and as she did so she provided the simile that Maggie had omitted by saying to herself, "As you would of Willy Harding."

It was half-past nine. The company had long since departed for home, and Hal and Mary Ellen had gone up to bed at nine o'clock. They very rarely retired later these days. John had just come in after doing the last round of the animals. He shivered as he took his coat off, saying, "By! it's nippy. If it wasn't just the beginning of November I would swear I smelt snow in the air."

Maggie turned, got up from the settle where she had been sitting sewing, and said, "Will I make some hot boily?"

"That would be nice." He looked towards where Yvonne was sitting in the rocking-chair to the right of the fireplace. The chair was motionless, as was her whole body. He went and bent towards her, saying, "I'll bet you've never had boily, have you?"

She looked up at him without making any movement and she didn't answer him, and, concerned, he said, "Are you all right?" And after a second she said, "Yes, Jean. Yes, I am all right."

"I think she's tired. She's had little to say all night." It was as if Maggie were talking about a small child, and her warm smile towards the girl emphasized this.

"No, I am not tired, Maggie, but I am full of thoughts."

"You have been thinking." Maggie placed a pan of milk on the hob as she corrected her, then looking at her again, she repeated, "You have been thinking?"

"Yes, I have been thinking, Maggie."

John drew a chair up to the fire and he held out his hands towards the blaze and stared into it as he said quietly, "Well, it's early days yet. We understand."

"No, no, you do not, not about my thinking, for it was not of my father. You know I got a letter yesterday ... well, three letters. One was from the ... how you say in law?"

"Solicitor?"

"Yes, yes, solicitor. There are, I understand, many affairs to settle. I should be there, in France, to ... to see them satisfied, but I am not ... not happy to go."

Maggie had been standing at the table cutting thick slices of bread into chunks. She now brought the pan from the fire and threw the bread into it, together with a large knob of butter, a spoonful of spice, a pinch of salt, and a scoopful of sugar, and she returned it to the hob before taking her seat again. And there she said, "Can you not just write to him?"

"No, I ... I do not think it good, satisfactory. There are documents to be signatured."

She now brought herself quickly to the edge of the chair and the folds of her black velvet skirt touched one of John's leggings. And her hand went out to him and covered his wrist where his hand was lying on his knee and, her voice eager, she looked into his face as she said, "I must tell you this, all, and you, ma chère." She extended her other hand out to Maggie, and Maggie moved towards the end of the settle but didn't reach out towards the extended hand, keeping her two hands joined in her lap.

Yvonne quickly withdrew her hand from John's wrist and looked down towards her swinging feet and she said, "You must help me with my English words as it is difficult for me to clear myself."

"Make yourself plain," Maggie interrupted gently. And at this John made an impatient movement, saying, "Leave her be. Go on." He looked at Yvonne, and now she began: "There is a house, my father's house. More so, it was his wife's house. She ... she it was who owned all.

Her husband . . . the first, was of money, and when she married my father she does all for him. She wants to make him famous, noted in the artist's world. Well—" She now bowed her head, then went on, slowly now, "There are many artists in Paris, very good, very good. My father, he was good in one way, drawing, but not so good with paint at all, not so good with portraiture. His wife, she pressed him hard. She paid for his exhibitions and the" – she now waved her hands – "pamphlets, programmers to spread his work. Artists are mostly poverty, I mean poor. They find difficulty in selling. My father too, but it did not matter so much because of the money. His wife had friends in London, and also in Rome. I think my father, he protest, but she was of strong mind, and in some ways I fear—" She now looked down and moved her head from side to side before she added, "He was not of strong character. Lovable, yes." She looked from one to the other now, waiting for their confirmation of the right term, but neither of them spoke, and so she went on: "She bought this house on the outskirts of Paris. It is a very nice house. She liked entertain. My mother told me of her. She not tolerate women, mostly men friends. She was very jealous for my father . . . of my father. She arranged all his life."

For the first time Maggie interrupted, saying now, "Did she know about your mother?"

"No, I do not think so or, as my father . . . hint? yes, hint, she would have changed her will. Well, she die and all her money and house, it is my father's, and" – she now lifted her shoulders and spread her hands wide – "it is mine. Unfortunate it is mine, and I must go back and see what they will do with it."

For the first time John spoke. Looking into her face, he said, "You will live there?"

"No, Jean, I do not wish I live there."

"But your home, your house?"

"It could be sold. It is a very nice house, not too big, eight sal . . . rooms. And up above" – she waved her hand above her head now – "all the top is studio for my father. That is another thing. I . . . I must see to his pictures. There is, what you call, an agent, that sell them when he could."

"When will you go?"

"I . . . I write back tomorrow and make arrangements. You see, I . . . it is not wise I travel alone. My father, he . . . he never left me. He never allow me travel alone."

"What will you do then?"

"There are two ladies in next house. One, Mademoiselle Marie, she teaches in the lycée. Mademoiselle Estelle, she remains at the house, cooking, and cleaning. They have little money. Father used to engage her to accompany me."

"You mean you could never go out alone?"

"No." Yvonne now smiled a knowing smile at Maggie as she shook her head. "It was not advisable. You understand?"

Maggie understood, then said, "'Tis coming to something when a child can't take a walk on her own. 'Tis a strange country."

"Not at all," John put in now; "there are times here in Newcastle when it wouldn't be safe for a woman of class to walk the streets by herself."

Looking at Maggie now, Yvonne said slowly, "I am not a child, Maggie, nor have been for some long time."

"What do you mean? I know you're sixteen, but you still look like a girl of fourteen."

"No, no, Maggie." The voice was strong now, the tone contradictory. "I must tell you. There has been a deception. It was my father's wish ... idea, my birthday is in January. I shall not be seventeen, I shall be nineteen years old. He thought, my father, that it was more possible for your mama to give protection in her home if I was a young girl, and it is unfortunate that I look so. So he said we will say sixteen. I was upset, but he advise it. He had a longing that I live in England. He had friends in London, but they were friends of his wife. We met but I was not sympathique with them. They do not accept me, so—"

She looked at John. His face was straight, his eyes narrowed, and her voice low now, she said, "You angry? It is a bad thing I do?" He shook his head but didn't speak. And now she added, "Will you tell your mama for me? I stand a little in fear ... awe of her."

"No, no." It was Maggie speaking again. "Better not. What do you say, John? Better not, at least for a time?"

Again he nodded but without looking at Maggie; he continued to stare into the eyes that, in the lamplight, seemed to encompass the whole face, and the sadness in them caught at his throat.

Maggie rising brought his gaze from the girl; she had gone to take the pan from the hob, and at the table she divided the contents into three bowls. When she handed John a bowl on a wooden platter, together with a spoon, he took it without a word. But he didn't begin to eat, not until Yvonne again said, "You are angry, shocked?"

"No, no," he answered. "No, not at all, only surprised."

"Yes" – she nodded her head – "surprised. I am unfortunate that I look so."

"*No, no.*" He was quick to contradict her. "No, you look all right." He gave her a weak smile. And when Maggie handed her the other bowl she gazed up at her, saying, "I would love to look like you, Maggie, beautiful and fresh."

"Beautiful? Don't be silly!" Maggie tossed her head. "Get on with that. See if you like it."

She herself now sat down on the settle and began to eat the boily, and there was silence for a moment or two, until Yvonne said, "Very nice. Very nice." Then Maggie said abruptly, "'Tis a wonder you're not married by now then, being as old as you are."

Gulping on a mouthful of the hot bread and milk, Yvonne made a small sound in her throat that resembled a laugh, then said, "Three times

I was prop ... osed. Three times, and serious, you know. Two were father's friends. He was vexed. One young man, an artist too, but he could not feed himself. He only ate when at our table, so poor." She smiled widely, but when John got up abruptly, she rose from the chair, saying, "You are annoyed all over? I am sorry."

"It's all right," he said; "I understand." And he emphasized his words by lifting his hand as if to touch her. Instead, he patted the air, then said, "Well, I'm off to bed. Good-night. And you, Maggie, good-night."

"Good-night, John."

After he had gone Yvonne stood looking towards the far door through which he had disappeared. The radius of the light from the lamp left half the kitchen in shadow, and she now walked into it, but there stopped and bowed her head and placed a hand over her face. And Maggie called to her, " 'Tis all right. Don't take on. I would get to bed. Things'll look different in the morning."

Standing in the shadow, Yvonne now said, "I would not hurt Jean. I have an affection for him." Then softly she added, "Good-night, Maggie," before walking slowly from the kitchen.

Maggie had not answered Yvonne's good-night, but she stood looking into the shadow of the room. She had an affection for John, she said, and he had for her, like herself she surmised, as the daughter he had never had. That was when they had imagined she was sixteen. But now they both realized they were no longer playing mother or father to a young girl who looked even younger than her sixteen years, for she had turned into a young woman ... who had been offered marriage three times.

She sighed deeply and, going to the dresser drawer, took out a rough linen cloth which she spread over two thirds of the wooden table, and on this she laid out the crockery for the breakfast. Then going over to the stone sink that was set below the window, she washed up the three bowls and spoons. And it was as she leant sideways to grip the handle of the pump in order to swill the sink that her fingers became tight on it, for there, out of the corner of her eyes, she imagined she saw a figure standing, that of a man. It wasn't until he moved into the dim radius of the light in the yard that she breathed freely, saying to herself, "Willy! What's he doing there?"

By the time she reached the door, he was standing outside it, and she said to him, "Something wrong?"

"No, nothing's wrong. I ... I hope I didn't give you a gliff."

"You did a bit. Being your half-day, I didn't expect you round in the yard."

"Oh, that makes no difference."

When she gave an audible shudder with the cold, he said, "I'm sorry. Go on in."

"No, no, I'm all right. Have you had a drink, anything hot?" She pulled the door wider. "Come in a minute."

He hesitated, then stepped into the light of the lamp, and she looked at

448

him for a moment without speaking. He always dressed smartly, not like a farmhand at all. Of course it was the old gentleman's clothes, and they certainly suited him. He had on an overcoat tonight that was made of Melton cloth. It was better than even the one her father had. She heard herself speaking her thoughts: "You look very smart," she said.

"Oh aye, yes, they skitted me down at the Boar's Head. Lord Cowhand, they called me."

When he smiled she asked tartly, "You weren't vexed?"

"No. Why should I be? Aren't I asking for it, going out dressed like this? I understand them."

She moved her head as if in perplexity, then said, "You're sure you won't have something hot? Have you had a meal today?"

"Yes. I had a good one in Hexham. I had my meal in a hotel, and the waiter said, 'What can I get you, sir?' Strange, isn't it? Then I walked round the Abbey. I like walking round the Abbey. It arouses memories in me. Strange memories. Memories of men without women down the ages. How did they manage without women? Some of them didn't I know. It was too hard for them. For others it would be easy. I had a few words with the Rector. We got on to that subject. He's a very wise man. He said he hadn't seen me there before. What was my work? And he didn't bat an eyelid when I said cowhand. Of course, he was the kind of man who wouldn't have batted an eyelid if I'd said I was the Archangel Gabriel." He put his head back and laughed, then brought his hand to his mouth to still the sound, saying, "I'm sorry." And after a moment's silence, during which they stared at each other, he said softly, "I feel very happy tonight, Maggie, and it isn't because I've gone over my alloted three mugs of ale. No, I keep to that. I'm happy because I came to a decision today, and it was just that, what I've said, your name, Maggie. Have you noticed that I've never called you Miss Maggie since shortly after I came here, because I never thought of you as Miss Maggie. But please" – he put his hand out towards her but didn't touch her – "don't be upset. I'm not going to say, don't be offended, because I don't think you would be. I know what I know and you know what you know. All I want to say now, Maggie, is that I know nothing can come of this. Oh, aye, my head's on me shoulders in that way, and 'tis a great pity, but I wanted you to know that there is someone who thinks of you and not just as a hand on the farm."

There had come into his voice now a bitter note and his face was straight as he said, "'Tis a shame. I've always felt how some people are taken for granted, and used, because they are of the family. I think about you a lot. You work from mornin' till night, and what is ahead of you? More work from mornin' till night."

He remained silent for a moment, then drew in a long breath that swelled his overcoat as he said, "I'll be away. Tomorrow things will be back to where they were. Yet not quite. We will meet and talk about passing items, but underneath you will know, and I will know what I've always known, that you are a beautiful woman, Maggie, and it is a shame unto God that you are not in a house of your own with a family of your own. Would, to the powers of law and class, that things could be different. Goodnight, Maggie."

She still did not open her mouth, but watched him turn and go out and draw the door closed softly behind him.

It was a full half-minute before she put her back to it, and pressed her hands flat against it to each side of her. Her head was touching it, her eyes looking upwards, her mouth open, as she gasped for breath. And when at last she pulled herself from its support, she staggered to the table, rested on it for a moment, then went to the settle and, dropping onto it, she brought her clenched hands up to each side of her face and as the tears spurted from her eyes she whispered aloud, "Oh! Willy. Willy."

4

The yard was full of people, their breaths forming almost a cloud in the
frosty air. The horse attached to the brake stamped on the cobbles as if
anxious to be away. Willy was helping Mademoiselle Estelle up the steep
steps at the back of the vehicle. Then stepping up himself, he put a rug
around her knees and another around her shoulders, while she kept
repeating, "Merci. Merci." Her long plain face looked grim as it had
done for the past two days. Apparently the sea crossing had been very
rough, and for most of the time since her arrival she had lain in bed. And
with what English she could speak she indicated that never again would
she come to this land.

John had placed the luggage under the high front seat. There were
only two cases, the rest had gone ahead yesterday. And now, both he and
Willy stood to the side of the brake looking to where Yvonne was saying
goodbye to Mary Ellen. The girl leant forward and kissed Mary Ellen on
both cheeks; then taking her hand, she said, "I cannot thank you so
much for your kindness to me." And to this Mary Ellen muttered, "It
was nothing, it was nothing. I hope you have a good journey." She did
not add, "Come back soon."

The farewell was different when Yvonne confronted Maggie, for they
put their arms around each other, and Maggie, with actual tears in her
eyes, said, "You'll come back, won't you?" And Yvonne said, "Yes,
Maggie. I will come back. Yes, I will come back."

"Well, come on. Not so much slavering." Hal's usual levelling tone
and voice drew them apart. And now Yvonne turned to him and held
out her hand, and he took it in both of his and, shaking it warmly, he
said, "It's been a pleasure havin' you, lass. You're welcome here any day
in the week. Let me tell you that."

"Oh." Spontaneously now she reached up and kissed him on both
sides of the face, much to his embarrassment, which he covered with
blustering laughter, saying, "Come on. Come on. Don't leave any of
your Frenchified ideas behind you. Get yourself up else you'll miss your
train an' that 'un up there" – his voice dropped – "who's come to protect
you, but to my mind 'tis the other way about, she'll die afore she leaves
the country. What d'you say?"

"Oui." She smiled, nodding her head. "She is willing to expire before
she gets on the boat. I pray the sea will be flat."

"Aye, me an' all. Well, away you go, lass." He pushed her towards

451

John, and he, taking her elbow, helped her up the steps. Then he himself took a seat beside her, and Willy, having mounted the front seat, called, "Get up there!" and the brake jerked forward, and they left the yard, Yvonne waving her hand to the three people standing grouped together, and they waved back.

When they passed through the gate and Yvonne could no longer see them, she sat back in the seat, but she did not speak or look at John. In fact, few words were exchanged on the road to Haydon Bridge except when Willy made some remark from his seat and turned his head towards them; or when John, leaning forward, would enquire of Mademoiselle Estelle if she was all right, to be answered in a spate of French, which Yvonne translated as: she found the journey very bumpy and that she would never reach home before she died.

And smiling, Yvonne added, "I am not looking toward the journey."

They had crossed the bridge and Willy was driving towards the station, when he turned his head sharply towards John and said, "There's Fraser ahead, shall I pull up?"

John glanced at his watch, answering, "Yes. We've got a bit of time. Better not pass him."

A few seconds later they stopped at the side of the road and Fraser, who had seen them, left the two men he was talking to and came slowly towards them. And John, leaning over the brake, said, "Yvonne's on her way."

The boy came round to the back of the brake and stood looking at Yvonne for a few seconds before he said, "You'll be glad to get back then?"

"No, no. I am not pleased to leave. No, no." Her head moved in small jerks. "I have been very happy here."

"Happy?" He laughed now, then turned his glance, first on John, then towards Willy, who had twisted round in his seat and was looking down on him. "Somebody's been happy around here. Isn't that strange, Willy? And you Uncle John?" He was again looking at John. "Isn't that strange to hear anybody's been happy around here?"

John stared at the boy. Then leaning forward, he asked quietly, "What are you doing here this time in the morning?"

"What am I doing here? I am about my father's business. Yes" – his head bobbed now – "I am about my father's business."

"Well then" – John's voice was grim – "if you're about your father's business, get about it and keep out of the inn. I'll have something to say to Swaffer when I come back."

"I haven't been in the inn. I've been with some friends." He jerked his head to where the two men were standing.

And to this John said, "If you're talking of Reilly and his mates, don't speak of them as friends. How did you get in?"

"On a horse. You know, a horse." He was grinning now. And John, straightening himself, said, "Well, don't get on that horse until Willy's coming back this way, and ride along of him. Now, I'm telling you. If you don't take heed to my words, don't expect any support from me in the future. You understand?"

"Yes, Uncle. Yes Uncle, I understand." The boy was not looking at him but towards Yvonne, and as he grinned at her John said, "Go on, Willy."

As the brake moved off, the boy, called, "You coming back, dear little Yvonne?"

She did not answer him or make any remark until a few minutes later when she alighted from the brake, and then she said, "He is young to drink so."

"He is that. But I'll put a stop to it. Has he been at it before?" The last part of the remark was addressed to Willy, and Willy answered, "No, I think this is something new. But he couldn't get better teachers than the Reillys. Beg, borrow, or steal for it, they would."

"See that he goes back with you, will you, Willy?"

"I'll do me best. But you know" – he paused while he slotted the horse's reins through an iron ring – "he's not a boy any longer, John. I think everybody's got to face up to that. In fact, to my way of thinking, he's never been a boy for years. He's got an old head on young shoulders."

"Be that as it may, tight at this time in the morning broods no good if he was twice as old as he is. Look, I'll manage the cases, and don't wait. You go back and see to him."

Willy nodded, then turning to Yvonne and holding out his hand, he said, "Goodbye, miss. 'Tis been a pleasure knowin' you."

"Goodbye, Willy. I likewise, it has been my pleasure. Pat Bessy for me, will you? Tell her to give plenty of milk."

"I'll do that."

He did not say goodbye to her companion because she had walked on ahead into the station, flexing the muscles of her arms as she went as if she had just been through some stiff exercise.

Five minutes later they were seated in the train on its way to New-castle. No one entered their compartment either in Hexham or Corbridge, and so they had ample opportunity for conversation. Yet again neither of them had much to say. Once or twice John spoke of the district through which they were passing, but Yvonne seemed to have little interest in it.

It was when, looking out of the window, he said, "We're running in now," that her hand came along the seat and gripped his, and she hitched herself closer to him. But she did not look at him, she had her eyes fixed on Mademoiselle Estelle who seemed to be dozing in the corner of the compartment, as she muttered, "Jean. Oh Jean, I do not want to go."

John was sitting, his back pressed tight against the wooden back of the seat. Her small hand gripping his was acting as a poker thrust into a damped down fire, the flame that had been smouldering was now being given air and was forcing its way through his body while a loud condemning voice was crying, Stop it! Check it! 'Tis madness.

Remember what you said yesterday. 'Twas a good thing she was going. Stick to that. Stick to that. Even so, he did not take his hand from hers until the companion showed signs of rousing, which he told himself had saved him from making a fool of himself.

But when, fifteen minutes later, she stood on the platform outside the carriage door of the London train, and the guard stood ready at the other end of the platform about to wave his green flag, she again caught hold of his hand and, looking up into his face, said, "Oh, Jean, mon cher, my dear, dear friend, I will miss you, so very much." And before he had time to answer, her hand had left his and she reached up both her arms and, standing on tiptoe, she kissed him, not on each cheek, but full on the mouth. Automatically his arms went about her and held her tightly to him. It would appear they were thrust apart only by the sound of the guard's whistle, and then his body seemed to have actually caught fire, for he put his arms out once again and lifted her bodily up the steps and into the train, then held onto her hands.

It was the porter who pressed him aside and banged the door closed. And there was her face looking down at him, a shadow behind the glass, a shadow all eyes that was telling him something he must not believe. As the train began to move slowly away, he walked by the side of the carriage, his eyes not leaving her until the train gathered speed, and the last glimpse he had of her was obliterated by steam.

The platform was empty even of porters when he turned about and made his way into the main hall and through the throng of people and out into the street. There he stood looking about him as if in a daze. Then slowly he left the station and walked until he came to a bar. And there he ordered a double whisky, something he had never done in his life before, because beer was his drink, and not a lot of that. Taking his glass, he sat down on a narrow form running alongside the walls and drank half of the spirit in one gulp. Then holding the glass between his two hands and, bending his back, he rested his elbows on his knees and sat gazing down into the yellow liquid. He could see her face in it, and that look in her eyes.

My God! For this to happen at his age, and she but a girl. No – his whole body moved in protest – she wasn't a girl. She was on nineteen and she could be what you called a woman of the world, no matter what she looked like. There was a fully grown woman in that delicate frame. . . . But still she was only nineteen and he was forty. He could be her father. Perhaps that's how she viewed him, as her father. What! with that look in her eye and that kiss. No. By God no! But he must pull himself together. What would happen when she came back? How could he pull himself together if he saw her every day. But would she come back? It would be better not. Oh, yes, better not, because they would never stand for that, them back home. And the people around. He would be a laughing stock; he wouldn't be able to live with it.

He drained his glass, took it to the counter, then walked out. But he didn't go straight back to the station, he spent another three hours walking around the town, mostly along the river-front watching the teeming life on the water: the loading and unloading of big ships, the scuttling of little ones, the tugs, the scullers. But wherever he looked he could still see her face and feel the imprint of her mouth on his.

When eventually he arrived at Haydon Bridge, it was dark, and Willy was outside the station with the trap. He knew that he would likely have met previous trains, but he made no apology. And all Willy said was, "She got off then?" And to this he answered, "Aye, she got off."

On the journey back Willy did not break the silence for he guessed what had happened to this man because it had happened to himself, and he saw as much hope for the one as there was for the other.

5

❧❧

On Christmas Eve a letter arrived from France. It was addressed to Maggie, and it was brief, saying mainly that the sea voyage had been very rough indeed and that Mademoiselle Estelle had become really ill. It went on to say that she was being made very busy with business, and ended that she thanked them all for their kindness to her, and she wished them a joyful Christmas.

Maggie read the letter out to them all in the kitchen. The men were having their eleven o'clock hot drink. No one made any comment. And she had hardly returned the sheet of paper to the envelope when the sound of a cart rumbling into the yard made Hal turn to the window, and there he exclaimed, "'Tis the carter. You ordered anything?" He looked over his shoulder towards Mary Ellen, and she said, "No. I've got all I want in this past week."

The man called across the yard, "Hello there, Mr Roystan. Got something for you."

Hal called back from the kitchen door, "Hello, Andy. Well, let's have it."

A moment later the man came into the kitchen and placed six packages on the table, all of different sizes.

"Where did these come from?" Mary Ellen asked as she stared at the neatly wrapped parcels.

"Different shops. I had me orders." He grinned broadly from one to the other. "Gather them up on Christmas Eve, that's what the letter said. And she paid well, she did that. Well, happy Christmas to you all."

"You'd like a drink?"

The man looked at Hal and said, "Aye, I wouldn't say no."

A bottle was brought and a drink poured out and the man raised his glass to them all, wishing them health, and wealth, and good crops. Then he went out, leaving them all looking at the table and the parcels.

It was Maggie who made the first move towards them. She looked down at an oblong shaped parcel and said, "That's addressed to you, Dad," and she handed it to him.

"And this is for you, Mam," she said. This was a soft package.

The biggest package on the table was a square box almost eighteen inches high, and she stared down at it as she said, "'Tis for me, this one." Then picking up another softish package she exclaimed in some surprise, "Willy! Willy! She didn't forget Willy, or Terry."

"How do you know they are from her?"

Maggie swung round on her mother, almost bawling now, "Who else would think of sending us presents like this, Mam, eh? Do you know anybody else?"

"The lads could have." Her mother's voice was as loud as hers now.

"Yes, they could have, but they don't. They never have done; they bring theirs, such as they are. Oh!" Impatiently she turned again to the table, but as she did so, John had put out his hand and picked up the last and smallest package.

They all stood watching him undoing the wrapping to disclose a three-inch-long flat black box. He stared at it for some seconds before opening it, then gazed down at the gold cravat pin shaped in the form of a whip, the top of the handle studded with four red stones. It was Maggie who, coming round to his side, said in a hushed voice now, "Eeh! she sent you that. We were looking at it in Monroe's the last time we were in Hexham. It . . . it was in the middle of a window on a velvet pad. 'Tis beautiful." She looked up into John's face, saying, "Isn't it beautiful?" But he did not utter a word until she said, "'Twas costly, very costly." Then he closed the lid and, turning to her, he said quietly, "Well, see what you've got."

She now quickly undid the wrapping to disclose a round box. Then, lifting the lid, she put in her hand and withdrew a broad pink satin ribbon, and as she hesitated to pull it upwards Hal exclaimed, "My! a band-box. Must be a hat."

When she lifted out a red velvet bonnet she stood gazing at it in amazement for a moment before she exclaimed, "'Tis the one we saw in Snells. I admired it and she said it was bonny, and it would suit her."

"Aye, likely it would have, but it looks too young for you."

Maggie's expression changed in a flash, and she glared at her mother for a moment as she said, "I'm not in me grave, Mam. I keep telling you."

"Try it on." John's voice came between them like a balm. But Maggie hesitated; she turned the bonnet round between her two hands while she gazed at it, and the muscles of her face moved, as if she were about to cry.

And now it was Hal who spoke, saying, "Well, go on then, woman. Put it where it belongs, on your head."

Slowly she pushed the stray strands of hair from about each ear with one hand, then she put the bonnet on, and again John's voice was quiet as he said, "It suits you." And when her father put in gruffly, "You could have picked worse. 'Tis your colour," she turned a grateful look on him. It was so seldom he approved of anything she did that even such a remark sounded like high commendation to her.

Now she confronted her mother with a firm, "Well?"

"'Tis all right. 'Tis better on than off. But a bonnet like that needs things to match it."

"Well, I'll have to see about getting them, won't I, Mam? Anyway" – she turned to her father now – "what have you got?"

457

He was already undoing the wrapping and when he disclosed a box of cigars, he laughed loudly, saying, "Why cigars, I've never smoked one in me life. My! a dozen of them. Eeh! now, would you believe that, to send me a box of cigars! Look." He held out the box towards Mary Ellen, and she said, "Aye, I can see what they are."

And as if aiming to hide his pleasure at the gift, he now cried at her, "Well, open your parcel, woman!" And when she did and disclosed a beautiful cashmere shawl which hung from her hands like a network of fine cobwebs, she blinked and said softly, "'Tis bonny."

"Aye, 'tis bonny," Hal repeated her words. And looking at John, he said, "'Tis amazing like, that one so young, a slip of a lass could be so thoughtful for each one of us, and Willy an' all." He nodded to the last parcel on the table. "She seemed but a bairn. . . ."

"She was no bairn."

"What?" Hal screwed up his face as he peered at his son. "What do you mean, she was no bairn?"

"Just what I say, she was no bairn. She wasn't sixteen as you were given to understand." He was now looking at his mother. "She's nineteen, or will be in a few days' time."

Hal and Mary Ellen exchanged a glance, then looked at John again, and it was Mary Ellen who asked now, "What are you sayin'? She was no nineteen, that one. Anyway, why should she lie about her age?"

"She didn't lie. It was him. He thought you would more likely give a home to a young lass than to a young woman."

"I don't believe it."

"Well, that's up to you, Mam."

Mary Ellen turned to Maggie. "You knew about this?" she asked.

"Yes, Mam, and he's right. But what difference does it make? She's still the same."

"It makes this much difference, I've been deceived. She should have told me if she'd told you."

"What chance did you give her, Mam? You hardly opened your mouth to her."

"Be that as it may, but there's one thing I do know, I'll not have her under this roof again."

"You mightn't have any choice." John was standing staring at her from across the table. His face had lost its colour, his mouth looked a grim line.

"What am I expected to make from that remark?" Mary Ellen's voice was low. And to this he answered, "You can make out of it whatever you like, only think on it." And at this he turned from the startled faces and marched up the kitchen and through the door into the hall, which was an unheard of thing to do, for he was still in his working boots.

There was a dead silence in the kitchen now and it wasn't broken until Maggie, picking up the two parcels from the table, pulled on her hooded cape and went out, leaving Mary Ellen and Hal looking at each other.

"What do you think he meant? He wouldn't, would he?" Mary Ellen said quietly but apprehensively. And Hal seemed to consider for a moment before he said quietly, "He could. It's been known afore."

"But she could be his daughter."

"Aye, but she isn't. And he doesn't look his age. But" – he put his hand out and gripped her shoulder – "don't worry, he's sensible, and he wouldn't make himself a laughing stock. He's made that way is John, he couldn't stand being ribbed, never could. So don't look so worried."

"Aren't you worried?"

It was some seconds before he answered when, turning from her, he said, "No, no. I know John. This place is his life, and it's his when I go, lock, stock, and barrel. He knows that. No, I'm not worried."

He buttoned up his coat, knotted a muffler round his neck, pulled on his cap and went out.

Alone now, Mary Ellen sat down in a chair by the side of the table and her fingers played a quick tattoo on the wood. My God! if that should happen, she wouldn't be able to stand it, not that girl, because every time she had looked at her she had been reminded of Roddy, and was transported back down the years to the time when she lay with him on the quarry top. 'Twas an odd thought, but it was as if she had given birth to the girl instead of Kate.

Oh, dear me. Her head wagged on her shoulders, now, and she looked around the kitchen. There along the delph rack were all the cold meats ready for the family coming. On the far table were the cakes and pies she had been baking for the last three days. She had been looking forward to this Christmas holiday because the lads would be here later today, and they always cheered the place up, although she was disappointed they were only staying for a couple of days. Apparently Gabriel had to get back to the glass works.

And then there was the big dinner the morrow with Kate and Ben, and the three children, and Tom and May and their Harry. Florrie and Charles didn't come to the Christmas dinner; they always went up to the manor for that, but they would be here for tea later on. She would have all her family round her, and they would eat and drink, and there would be laughter and news exchanged. And the children would have games, and Maggie would play the piano, and they would have a sing-song. . . . Maggie. She was another one that was causing her worry of late because somehow she was changed, for there were days when she appeared like a young lass again, her manner was almost gay. And there was that time she had heard her singing to herself while cleaning the rooms upstairs.

But her bright patches weren't as frequent as her sullen ones, when she didn't open her mouth for hours on end. And there was this other thing. Lately, she had been scrambling through the housework and spending much more of her time outside. She had felt the urge to talk to her and say, Don't make a fool of yourself, woman. Don't let yourself down. Have a bit of dignity. And she knew what her reception would be if she voiced anything like that.

But the worry over Maggie was nothing compared to this new bolt from the blue. Well, all she could do was to pray to God that that lass never set foot in this house again. And she would do that. . . . Yes, she would pray as she had never prayed in her life before. . . .

Maggie was in the barn. She was looking at Willy while he looked down on the white silk scarf lying across his hands, and he repeated, "'Tis a lovely thing." Then raising his eyes to her, he said, "And for her to think of me, remember me, and Terry with a pound of baccy. She had a lovely nature, and so young." He lifted his eyes to her, then added, "But as you say, not so young. And your bonnet, red velvet you say? I would like to see you in it."

"You shall. I'll put it on the next time I help to milk the cows." She checked the laugh that erupted from her by placing her hand tightly over her mouth, but he didn't check his, and amidst it, he exclaimed, "Why not! Why not! Only I don't think Bella would like it, 'cos she's only got a straw one. Remember the day I put the old straw hat on her in the field and they all gathered round as if admiring her, remember?"

She nodded at him. Her eyes were shining, her whole face seemed transformed. He stopped laughing and stood gazing at her. Then, lifting up the side of his smock, he thrust his hand into his breeches pocket; and now he was extending towards her a very small parcel.

The laughter slid from her face, leaving it soft; her eyes were wide as she looked down onto his rough hand, the parcel lying in his palm. Gently she picked it up. There was a single layer of paper around it and it wasn't tied. She unfolded it, then opened the box and gazed at the brooch made in the design of twined ivy leaves. The setting wasn't of gold, nor had it jewels like John's cravat pin, yet it was no cheap gimcrack.

"'Tisn't much. Not as I would like."

"Oh, Willy, 'tis beautiful." Her voice broke, "I . . . I have nothing for you."

"You have everything for me, Maggie, everything, and you know it." His words came on a whisper.

"Oh, Willy."

"'Tis all right. 'Tis all right. Don't upset yourself."

"I can't go on like this, Willy."

"There's no other way, is there?" It was a statement, also a question.

She bit tight on her lip, lowered her head, and now he pleaded, "Don't cry. For God's sake, Maggie, don't cry; 'twill be me undoing. Here, wipe your face on that." He held out the scarf that had been hanging over his wrist, and she protested, "No, no, not your scarf. I'm all right. Your new scarf indeed!" Her voice was reverting to normal, and to this he replied gallantly, "It would be of more value to me having touched your face."

She stared at him and again the tears came to her eyes, and abruptly she swung round and hurried down the barn and out of the door, and straight into John.

"What is it?" he asked, holding her by the arms, and she gulped in her

460

throat as she said, "'Tis nothing, nothing." He looked towards the barn door, and when he saw a spray of hay leaving a fork to land on the feed cart, he said softly, "Willy?" He looked at the paper and the box clutched in her hand held against the neck of her hood, and he said, "Aw, Maggie, Maggie. But 'tis no use for either of us. We're both in the same boat, aren't we? We've left it too late. Look, go into the tack-room and dry your face. We'll talk later."

He pushed her gently away; then he went into the barn where Willy was forking the hay, but he said nothing to him, he just picked up a fork and helped to fill the cart.

6

Towards the end of January two letters came from France: one was addressed to Maggie, and one to John. Maggie immediately read hers, but when Mary Ellen handed John his, he thrust it into his pocket, then stood listening to Maggie as she now read her letter out aloud to them.

"Ma chère Maggie,
The weather, it is bleak, but I am warm with business. I have had much business of late to attend. We have cleared my father's studio, most pictures have gone to the agent. It has been turned into apartments for an attendant . . . it is housekeeper I mean, is it not? My English is worse on paper than when I speak. The housekeeper has a husband who works. It is very convenient. The housekeeper, she attends me. Mademoiselle Estelle pretends illness. She is afraid I take another sea voyage. I think of you all very much, and I dream at night of the cows. There is much business to be done with the lawyers, but I hope to be soon free. Many friends call. People are kind. But I would wish I was with you. I send my warm greetings to your mother and father, and the family. To yourself, ma chère Maggie, I give my love.
                                                    In sincerity."

Maggie's voice trailed away, and she looked to where her father was sitting on the settle, then to where her mother was bending towards the fire holding a heavy iron pot in her hand in which was sizzling butter. She watched her whip it quickly up and onto a wooden stand on the table, then, pouring sugar into it, begin to stir the contents, and she said, "Well?" and Mary Ellen turned her head towards her and said, "Well what?"
"'Tis a nice letter."
"Yes, yes, 'tis a nice letter."
"What has she got to say to you, lad?"
John now looked at his father. Then on a sigh, he pulled the letter from his pocket, opened it, read it, then said briefly, "She's simply asking about the farm, and the weather." And with this he thrust the letter back into his pocket, picked up his cap from the corner of the table, pulled it well down over his ears, turned the collar of his coat up to meet it, then went out with his head bent against the piercing wind.

Back in the kitchen, Maggie went into the pantry, picked up her basket of household dusters and brushes and, it being Wednesday, began her work on the bedrooms.

She went into her own room first, but did not immediately get down on her hands and knees to brush the carpet; instead, she sat on the foot of her bed, her hand gripping the iron knob. She knew that John's letter had not contained questions about the farm, and she understood how he felt. They had become very close over the past weeks, saying little, but understanding each other's problem. There was a tension in the house that, as she put it to herself, you could cut with a knife. There was tension all round for that matter, and each member of the family was aware of it. Her mother had stated openly yesterday that nothing had been the same since that lass had come on the scene. And she had retorted to this, "Don't you mean, since your girlhood sweetheart put in his last appearance?" At this, they'd had high words. She knew she should keep her mouth shut, especially about her mother's past, but whenever she saw the blame apportioned in the wrong direction, she had to speak out.

Then Kate had arrived with her troubles. Apparently Fraser had come home the worse for drink from the market, and Ben had had one of his bad turns. She didn't want to, but she was being forced to agree with her father that there was a bad streak in Fraser. He seemed to gravitate towards the lowest of company. And yet there were times when he appeared a normal, nice enough lad.

Life was unfair when you came to think about it. There was that boy being given a chance of higher education. He still had time to make something of himself, but was already starting on the wrong road. And there was a man like Willy who had been working since he could toddle and had appreciated the chance he had been given to read and write and to inform himself. And she knew it to be a truth, that he was better informed than anyone on this homestead or round about for many a mile. Yet there he was, working almost every hour that God sent, for the most part of his life in a smock, with the title of cowhand. 'Twasn't fair, 'twasn't.

Twice of late she had almost burst into the sitting-room where her mam and dad had been comfortably ensconced in the evening, and cried at them, "I'm going to marry Willy. Do you hear? I'm going to marry Willy."

On the first occasion she was stopped only by the thought that he hadn't asked her to marry him, nor had he said that he loved her. It was only in gestures and looks and a few words of affection that she imagined he would want to marry her. There were men who didn't want to marry, who could get along without it, but who liked a woman about them, and a little romance on the side, nothing that would tie them. Was he like that? No. No. She had denied it in her mind. The second time she had been stopped in following her urge by the telling fact that he had not even tried to kiss her on the quiet. And it could have been done. There had been plenty of opportunity when they had been alone together. And oh, she had longed for him to put his arms about her and kiss her.

Lately, the nights were becoming unbearable. She walked the floor half the time. They had heard her from across the landing one night, and her mother had come over and she'd had to lie and say she had toothache; and her mother had gone downstairs and made her a mustard plaster, which she'd had to put on the supposedly offending tooth, only to spit it out when the door had closed on her, then dash to the ewer and gulp at the cold water.

What was she going to do? She couldn't go on much longer like this, she'd go mad. She should have married years ago. Yes, she knew that now. Yet there had never been the urge on her as there had been since she knew Willy. He had seemed to bring this thing alive within her, and oh, at times she wished he hadn't.... And strangely, her state of need had become worse since Yvonne had come into the house. Why was that?

John made for the tack-room, he would be warm in there and he would have a minute to himself to read her letter again. But when he opened the door, it was to see Terry sitting by the stove mending the harness.

"You want me, Master John? I just thought I'd warm me knees while seeing to this."

As he made to get up, John said, "Sit where you are, Terry. How are your feet the day?"

"Well, to tell the truth, Master John, I don't feel I've got any on. They're sort of numb. But 'tis funny, I can walk better on them when they're numb than when they're alive, so to speak. The ointment the missis gave me, I'm sure is helping, I'm sure of that, the new stuff she made up for me. It burns like blazes, but I don't mind that.... Want something, Master John?"

"No, no. I was just looking for a new bit. That one seems to be chafing old Noah." He walked to the far end of the room where the wall was covered with hanging braces and bits, bridles, and all accoutrements needed to dress a horse, and, selecting a bit, he went from the room, nodding towards Terry as he did so, saying, "Stay put. There's enough mending to keep you occupied for the next few hours. There's nothing spoiling so far."

"As you say, Master John, as you say. I'll do that. I'll do that."

John stood for a moment outside the door. What was it like to be in a subservient position like Terry back there, his body racked with pain most hours of the day, the result of years of toil spent working for them? He should be pensioned off, and with enough to keep him comfortable. By damn! he'd see the old man about it. There was Ozzie Taylor free for hiring. He was young and could be trained, and he was as strong as a bull. He'd tell his father the night and, storm or no storm, he'd have his way over this.

With a defiant movement he pulled the letter from his pocket now, and again read the few lines of writing on it. It did not begin, "Mon cher Jean", but started abruptly with,

Jean,
Why don't you write to me? You said you write to me. I am very lonely for a word from you. Do you not wish to hear from me again? Life here is not good. I miss you.

It was signed simply, Yvonne.

Slowly he placed the sheet back in the envelope and returned it to his pocket. As he went to walk across the yard, his father came towards him. He had just come out of the kitchen and had undoubtedly viewed him reading his letter, for now he said in a high breezy tone, "Well, what does she say that we haven't got to hear?" But he wasn't prepared for the answer he got.

"She says there's some very nice farms going in France that would suit me down to the ground, and she'll buy me one. That satisfy you?"

"What the hell's up with you? My God! I ask a civil question. . . . *Now you look here!*"

"No, *you look here*, Dad, and we'll forget about my letter and talk about this particular farm, eh? There's Terry over there, not able to stand on his feet. Now as I see it, he's ready for his pension. I know he's not that old, but there's not a day's work left in him, and he's given you his life since he was a lad. Ozzie Taylor's mother's wanting to place him. I promised her I'd see to it. There's the other cottage that could be done up. It'll want money spent on it, but I think you owe that to Terry."

"Well, I'll be buggered. Here's me, not dead yet, and a new boss taking over. Now let me tell you something, John." His father was digging him in the chest with his finger now, and when, with a swift movement, he pushed the hand away, Hal became silent and, his voice changing, he said, "Look, first tell me. What's brought this on? All right, all right, I know me duties. I know what I intend to do with Terry. I have for some time now. I don't need you to tell me. Another time you would have talked about this, not come laying the law down as if you were master of the place. And" – his voice was changing again – "don't you forget it, John, I'm still here. You're not in control yet."

"It might be news to you, Dad, that I never want to be." And on this he turned and marched away, leaving Hal gazing after him, his mouth agape, his mittened hand flat on the top of his cap. And now he went slowly back towards the kitchen door again, muttering, "What the hell's come over everybody? That's what I'd like to know."

*

The mood in the household changed in the middle of the afternoon when Charles rode into the yard. Having led his horse into an empty loose-box, he made swiftly for the kitchen door and, thrusting it open and seeing Maggie setting a tea-tray, he said, "Hello there, Maggie. Where's Mam?"

"She's in the sitting-room with Dad, coddling him again. He's had one of his coughing bouts."

He reached out a hand towards her, saying, "Come on. Come on in. I've got news."

As they went down the kitchen, the back door opened and John called, "Hello there, Charles, anything the matter?"

"Yes, yes, lots, John. Come in a minute. We're going into the sitting-room. I've got some news."

"Well, if your face is anything to go by, it must be good."

"'Tis that."

John pulled off his boots and in his stockinged feet hurried up the kitchen, through the hall, and into the sitting-room, to where his father was sitting before a roaring fire and his mother was standing looking towards Charles and saying, "You look as if you've lost a threepenny bit and found a sixpence, lad. What is it?"

Charles placed the high hat he had been holding in his hand on a side-table, unbuttoned the neck of his greatcoat, drew in a long breath, then let his gaze wander from one to the other before allowing it to rest on Mary Ellen, and he said slowly, "Florrie's going to have a child."

They all stared at him, no one saying a word. Charles and Florrie had been married fifteen years, and she hadn't shown a sign of falling.

Of a sudden there was a great hubbub. Hal was on his feet shaking Charles's hand and between coughs speaking unintelligibly, while Mary Ellen was saying, "Oh! this is great news. Oh! 'tis the best I've heard for many a long year."

John was smiling and his hand was on Charles's shoulder and he was saying, "I'm glad for you, man. I'm glad for you, and Florrie. Oh, she must be over the moon."

As yet Maggie said nothing, she just stood there. It was as if she had received a blow. Somehow the fact that Florrie, who was married, hadn't any children had, in a way, been a sort of comfort, in fact it had brought them close over the years, closer than they had ever been in their young days. Florrie was of a quiet, placid nature, yet her nerves had suffered badly because she had not been able to give Charles a child. And now, there she was at this age, carrying a child, and she almost as old as herself, there was only a year between them.

Hal had stopped coughing and his words were understandable as he croaked, "This calls for a celebration, a drink. What is it to be, lad, rum or whisky?"

"Oh, rum, Hal, rum. Although I shouldn't be taking any more. I made a big detour and called on Tom to tell him the news, then made

466

another one to tell Kate. And I've toasted the event in both places. Still, I've room for another rum."

"Aye, well, you have your rum, lad. It's me for the poker." He now bent and thrust the poker into the heart of a blazing fire. Then turning to Maggie, he said, "Draw up some beer, lass." And on this order she turned away, no one seeming to notice that she hadn't added her congratulations to the rest.

In the kitchen, she took down from the delph rack a large pewter jug. Then going into the cold meat store, she opened the door at the far end and descended the six steep steps into the cellar. And there she turned the tap of the hogshead that stood on a wooden cradle, and when the froth came to the top of the jug, she turned back the wooden peg. Then placing the jug on a rude wooden bench, she looked up to where a grating in the corner of the room let in some fading daylight. And then she said two words aloud, the meaning known only to herself, "That's it!" she said; then repeated them, "That's it!"

Back in the sitting-room that was full of chatter now, she filled the pewter mug from the jug and handed it to her father. He did not thank her, but immediately turned to the fire and, taking the red-hot poker, he thrust it into the middle of the mug, being careful not to let the hot iron touch the bottom. And when the sizzling stopped, he pushed the poker back into the fire. Then turning, he lifted the mug, saying, "Here's to a healthy son, lad."

"Oh, I don't mind son or daughter, either will please me."

"Oh, you want a son; we want some breeders in the family. Tom has only got one. It would appear that my lot are poor breeders. Four men and only one son among them."

It was noticeable that he didn't mention Kate's two sons. But Charles's three large rums in the last hour seemingly having loosened his usual cautious and tactful tongue, he said, "Oh, there's Kate's two, and both bright sparks, one a little brighter than the other if all the tales are true. Tom laughed his head off about what happened at the week-end."

"What did happen at the week-end?" Hal was smiling. But John's face became straight and Mary Ellen's full of concern. And Maggie, knowing what was coming, endeavoured to signal Charles from behind her father's chair. But Charles was too happy to notice and so he went on, "'Twas in the market on Saturday. Young Frag had apparently made the acquaintance of the Reillys and the four Smith lads. You know the ones from Allendale that work in the lead mines beyond. They're bits of hell raisers. No harm in them. But it was the day of the pays and they got the youngster blind and pushed him back on a barrow right into the yard."

"Couldn't be Frag, Charles" – Mary Ellen's voice was stiff – "they were all here on Sunday."

"Oh, well, he'd had plenty of time to sober up by then I suppose. Well, I must be off. Florrie wanted to come, but she's got a little cold on her and I wouldn't let her move." He turned now and for the first time addressed Maggie, saying, "Can you understand how I feel, Maggie?"

Her voice was quiet as she said, "Yes, Charles. I can, very well. Tell Florrie it's wonderful. Tell her I'll come over on Saturday."

"I will. I will, my dear. She's always pleased to see you. It gets a bit lonely out there for her sometimes. But now she'll never be lonely again. Oh!" He drew in a deep breath and buttoned up his coat before turning and picking up his hat; then going to where Hal was sitting in the chair, quiet now, he took his hand and said, "I'm pleased for myself and her, but I'm also pleased for you and all the family."

"That's as it should be, lad. That's as it should be. Bring her over soon."

"I will. I will. The first fine day I will. Goodbye, Mam." He had turned to Mary Ellen, and she took his hand and said, "Goodbye, Charles. I'll come over with Maggie on Saturday."

"I'll tell her. I'll tell her."

He went out accompanied by John, and they could hear his voice, as he crossed the hall, high with laughter.

But the door had hardly closed on them when Hal, bringing the poker from the fire, thrust it into a fresh mug of ale, saying as he did so, "That young bugger, brought home on a barrow by that tribe, the Smiths and the Reillys. God, could he get any lower? And there he was on Sunday, butter not melting in his mouth. 'Twasn't noticeable that he hardly said a word. No, he would be suffering from a thick head. But she made him come, or Ben did. I tell you, woman, something'll happen to that boy, as sure as I'm sitting here something'll happen to him. He's got a curse on him."

"Stop it! Stop it this minute! Never mind what he's got on him, what you've got on you is another cold, and if you don't want some days in bed you'll stay put the morrow." Then turning to Maggie, she said, "That was good news in a way – don't you think? – but not so good in others."

"Why not so good in others, Mam?"

"Well, at her age. She'll find it hard to pull through."

"Mrs Pratt, in the cottage over in the dip, they say she was forty-five when she had her last two years ago."

"Aye, but she'd had plenty of practice; eleven living and half-a-dozen dead, by all accounts. Firsts are dangerous in any case, I should know. That is when you're young, but at that age . . . well" – she sighed – "we'll just have to wait and see. . . . Had you got the tea-tray ready?"

"Yes."

"Well, bring it in."

Maggie went slowly from the room, slowly across the hall, and slowly down the kitchen, and she stood looking down at the heavily laden tray before lifting it and carrying it into the sitting-room. When she placed it on the table before her mother and was turning to go out, her mother said, "Aren't you going to stay and have a cup and a bite?"

"No, not on top of hot rum."

She returned to the kitchen and there, taking the jar that stood on the cupboard under the delph rack, she scooped out a spoonful of pork fat, put it into a small cup and, lifting aside her apron, she placed it in the pocket of her skirt. Then she went out of the kitchen again and quickly upstairs and made her way to the far end of the corridor. Here, she turned down a narrow passage, passed a side door that led to a store-room, and finally came to another door with two bolts, one top, and one bottom. They were both black iron, one showing slight rust spots from lack of use. Quickly she withdrew the bolts and rubbed fat in the slots, worked the bolts backwards and forwards two or three times until their passage made no sound, then wiped them clean, and returned to the kitchen. She emptied the remains of the fat into the slop bucket, washed out the cup and replaced it on the dresser. Then she went to the fireplace where, her arms outstretched, she gripped the brass rod underneath the mantelpiece and, drooping her head forward, she rested it on one arm, while her teeth clamped down tight on the sleeve of her dress as though she meant to bite through it.

Mary Ellen had been in bed this past hour. More mulled beer and hot rum during the evening had induced early sleep, and Hal's snores could be heard on the landing. John, too, had gone upstairs a while ago, for he too had drunk more than was usual for him.

Maggie took up the lamp and left the kitchen. When she reached the landing she placed it on a small oak table and turned down the wick to a mere glimmer, then went into her room.

After lighting her candle she took from the wardrobe a thick coat and a pair of overshoes, and, from a drawer, the biggest head-shawl she had.

Having put on the coat and shawl, and with the overshoes in her hand, she made quietly for the door which she had left slightly ajar; out on the landing she drew it after her but not closed. She then tiptoed over the polished boards to where a narrow rug ran down the middle, and on this she walked, being careful to avoid the part where a floor-board creaked. When she reached the door leading to the back stairs she withdrew the greased bolts. And now she was standing on a narrow wooden platform, the cold night frost cutting into her face like a razor. The sky was high and laden with stars, but there was no moon. She got quickly into her overshoes, then gripped the iron rail and went down the wooden stairs and so into the yard at the back of the house.

When one of the dogs growled she whispered quickly, "All right, Cass, all right, 'tis me. Lie down." And she went towards the kennel where the two dogs were housed. Cass was standing outside and she put her hand on his head and spoke to him again, then pushed him back into the warmth of the straw where his mate, Bessie, lay, too old now to bother about night noises.

In blackness, she groped her way along the back of the barn wall, but once clear of it the night seemed to become lighter. At one point there was a squeal and a scurry round her feet as she inadvertently walked into a chase. She wondered if she had saved the pursued or not, or whether that was its death cry? Nature was cruel. The whole world was cruel.

When she came in sight of the cottage there was no light in the window. He generally stayed up late reading, at least so he said. But she was looking on to the front of it; he might be in the back room and she wouldn't be able to see his candle-light from here.

She was within two feet of the door when she stopped and put her hand tightly over her mouth. Her hand was dead cold, her face was cold, she was shivering from head to toe. She was mad, this was awful. But what other solution was there? He couldn't come to her. Did he want to? She had to find out, even if she was shamed to death in the so doing. And if she was shamed, what then? Oh, God! God! She didn't know. Finish it perhaps. Aye, yes. And it wasn't the first time she'd thought of that. She couldn't go back, she couldn't. Her hand went out towards the door. She heard a distant cough and it seemed to smother her gentle tap. She waited, and when nothing happened she knocked again, harder this time. She heard movement in the room; then the door was pulled open, and there he stood, in a long flannel nightshirt, the brass candle-stick held head high, the flame guttering in the night air.

"In the name of God!" He thrust out his hand and pulled her into the room. Then closing the door quickly, he tugged her towards the banked-down fire. He said nothing more; nor did she speak until he had taken the glass from the lamp and lit the wick from the candle, replaced the glass, turned up the wick, then looked at her where she was standing visibly shivering. He did not say, "What is the matter? Why have you come?" but he took her hand and pressed her down into the wooden chair; then dropping onto his knees, he took up the bellows and blew vigorously on the fire.

The fire which had not been long banked down flared up and added its light to the room. Still on his knees, he now swung round and caught her cold hands. "Oh! Maggie," he said.

"I had to come." Each word was uttered on a tremor. "I . . . I had to know wh . . . wh . . . where I stood."

"Oh, my dear, my dear, dear Maggie." He now dropped his head onto her hands and pressed them over his face. Then looking up at her again, he said, "You know where you stand with me, always have done. I love you, you know that, you must know it, but what chance have I . . . I mean, what could I offer you? Even if I had dared to ask, a place not much bigger than this" – he rolled his head taking in the room – "and a smallholding somewhere, all pokey. You've been brought up ladylike."

At this her whole body moved in protest and she muttered, "Ladylike, Willy? Ladylike? Don't be silly, man. Since Kate and Florrie left I've had to work like three bonded women. Two outfits a year and a money present at Christmas and my birthday. Do you know how much I possess for all those years, Willy? Thirty-four pounds ... thirty-four pounds. A shilling a week maid would have gathered more. Oh! Ladylike. Willy? And me with me apron hardly ever off?" She now put her hands on his face and, her voice a whisper, she said, "I ... I love you. I know I'm older than you by five years and I'm a set woman ... I'll never be young again. As my mother is always hinting, I'm ready for my black bonnet and bead cape."

"Oh, Maggie, Maggie, be quiet. Don't talk so. You're beautiful, every bit of you, and for the last two years I've ached to do just this." And getting quickly to his feet, he pulled her upwards and into his arms, and kissed her. It was a gentle kiss at first and she lay against him quiet, even bewildered for a moment. Then, her arms about him, she returned his kiss, and, entwined, they stood swaying, she conscious of the heat of his body coming through his nightshirt.

When it was over, she did not withdraw from him but dropped her head onto his shoulder and let it stay there for a moment before he pressed her from him. He then quickly unknotted her head-shawl which had fallen onto her neck, undid her coat which he threw to one side, pressed her down into the chair again and took off her overshoes. His back bent, he lifted his head and his eyes on a level with hers, he asked quietly, "Will you marry me, Maggie?"

"Tomorrow, Willy."

"That's good enough for me."

She did not stay his hands as he unbuttoned her dress, but stood as a child might, quiet and docile, until he reached her bodice and last petticoat. Then he said softly, "Come, Maggie, the bed's still warm." And she went with him and lay down by his side in the narrow bed and knew for the first time in her forty years what it was to be loved.

471

7

The last week in February and the first week in March it snowed, thawed, and froze repeatedly, and it wasn't until a real thaw set in that communications were opened up again.

Mary Ellen hadn't seen Kate or any of the family during this period, so when Kate rode in through a drizzle of cold rain, she exclaimed loudly, "Oh, I am glad to see you, lass. It was as if all of you were dead. But you're wet through."

"No, only the top of me. But I thought I'd better come when the going was good, because all the signs show we're in for another bout."

"Don't say that."

"Anyway, how are you all?"

"Oh, same as usual I suppose. Get your things off, and I'll make a drink."

"I cannot stay long, Mam."

"Ben bad again?"

"No ... no, he's come through very well this winter, surprisingly well."

"The bairns all right?"

For answer, Kate said, "Harry's doing splendidly at school. You know, he was fourteen last Tuesday."

"Aye, I know, and I've got a present for him."

"Well, Ben was delighted by his school report. He passed everything with flying colours, and he's going into one of the best schools in Newcastle in the autumn, as a boarder ..."

"My! My! that will please Ben. But does the lad want to go?"

"Oh, yes. Oh, yes. He loves his books. He's like Ben in that way."

"Pity the other one hasn't a similar taste. Have you had any more trouble with him?"

"What do you mean?"

"Oh, you know what I mean. Being brought home drunk."

There was silence for a time, and Kate, from where she was now sitting at the end of the settle, looked at her mother's back as she bent over the fire, and after a moment she said, "Bad news travels fast."

"Oh, lass" – Mary Ellen turned her head towards her – "the whole countryside knew about it, and was laughing. Anything the Reillys or the Smiths get up to takes on headlines, you know that."

"He's not bad, Mam, only a bit wild."

"I'd like to think that, too, lass."

"Well, you can think it. And he's working well. He's taken to the farm work. He's as good as any hand, and Dawson says that an' all, and it's something for Dawson to praise a hand."

"Perhaps he knows which side his bread's buttered on."

"Oh, Mam. Mam."

"I'm sorry, lass. Anyway, let's change the subject."

"Yes, Mam, I agree with you there, once and for all, let's change the subject about Fraser. It's bad enough Dad feeling towards him the way he does without you going along that road too."

"I'm only thinking of you, lass, and Ben."

"Well, you needn't. We can manage our own affairs. Now, now, I'm not meaning that nasty, Mam, but just leave it, please. Anyway, where's Maggie?"

"Maggie." And now Mary Ellen's words came slowly: "Maggie was, at least the last time I saw her, supposed to be cleaning the sitting-room. But when I went in, there she sat warming her knees at the fire. What's come over her lately, I just don't know." Her voice dropped and, poking her head towards Kate, she went on, "I think it must be her time of life, you know." She nodded. "She was always moody, you know that. Could go without speaking for days. Well, she still has her moods, but not so often, and when she's not in them she chatters like a magpie. Well, I suppose, that's how it takes some people. You know how it is."

At this Kate laughed and said, "I don't yet, Mam, not yet."

"No? It hasn't happened?"

"Not that I'm aware of."

"Well, all I can say is you're lucky, because it can be a nasty time. Anyway, you'll have it to come."

"Thanks, Mam, thanks. It's something to look forward to." Kate rose, saying now, "I'll slip through and have a word with her."

"I've mashed the tea."

"I won't be a minute."

She was five minutes, and when she returned to the kitchen Mary Ellen greeted her with, "Well, what was she doing? Sitting on her backside again?"

"No, she was on her knees polishing the floor. But, as you remarked, Mam, she's changing. Funny, but. . . ."

"Funny, but what?"

"Well—" Kate put three spoonfuls of sugar into her mug of tea before she added, "It's a funny thing to say about our Maggie, but she seems happy. She looks pleasant, in fact like she used to look years ago. If that's the change on her I won't mind when it's my turn."

"Happy?" Mary Ellen pushed her head back into her shoulders as if in enquiry. But she didn't voice her next thoughts which were: Why should she be happy? What's making her happy? And she looked towards the slush-covered yard and gave herself the answer to her unspoken question with a loud, No! no! in her mind, emphasized with an Oh, no!

"Where's Dad?"

"He's gone round with John seeing what damage has been done to the bottom fields. If we have another bout of this, it's bound to put the ploughing back."

"Is John all right?"

Mary Ellen now took a seat opposite her daughter and, after sipping her tea, she said, "Kate, there's nobody in this house seems all right at the moment."

"What's wrong with John?" There was concern in Kate's voice, and Mary Ellen answered, "Nothing that anybody can put a finger on, but he's like a bear with a sore skull. He's had three letters in the last month from ... well, you know who."

"She writes to him?"

"Oh, aye, aye, and he must write back to her. I've never seen him give anything to the postie at this end; he's become secretive, and that's not John you know. I'm worried, Kate."

"What do you mean, you're worried?"

"Don't be silly, lass. I'm worried about him and her."

"John?" Now Kate's face was screwed up in disbelief, "John and that little piece? He could almost be her grandfather."

"He couldn't, Kate. She wasn't sixteen, she was nineteen."

"Nineteen?" Kate's voice was small. "Why did she say she was sixteen? Or just coming up seventeen?"

"It was your father, apparently, who thought it up, in case I wouldn't take her under my protection, if she was a young woman. That was the idea. But it strikes me that that one can take care of herself. She did from the beginning. She seemed to have an old head on young shoulders, although I couldn't understand what she said most of the time when she was talking that French gibberish."

"*John and her?* On no, Mam. John wouldn't."

"John would, lass, and that's what I'm afraid of. He's been acting funny lately, not himself. There's a pair of them, Maggie and him, both at the wrong age for this kind of thing to happen to them. Women go daft about this time, but men go clean barmy. I've seen it afore. Remember Jimmy Braithwaite? Forty-five he was. As solid as a rock, everyone thought. He had looked after his father and mother for years, and when they went what did he go and do? Marry a lass of twenty-two. You pass the place every time you come in here. She's got a squad around her, seven, and full with another. 'Tisn't decent. But it happens, you see, lass."

Kate was on her feet now, pulling on her gloves as she said, "I know it happens, Mam, but not John and her. Knowing the relationship, he wouldn't do it."

"I wouldn't put it past him, Kate. I wouldn't put it past him. But oh my God! To think of that lass in this house all the time, it would drive me mad. I couldn't put up with it, I just couldn't."

"What does Dad say?"

"Nothing, because he doesn't seem to notice anything. And anyway, he wouldn't mind her, I'm sure he wouldn't mind her. He seemed to cotton on to her, like most men do, an' he'd put up with anything rather than lose John. It's been a kind of secret fear with him that John, like Tom, would marry into a farm and go off. And where would we be then?"

Kate's voice had changed when she said, "He'd have to be like other people, Mam, and hire hands. It's been done, you know. You can't make use of your family all your lives. And both John and Maggie have got a life of their own to live. But, oh" – she shook her head – "not John and her, because I'm like you, Mam, I didn't like her. I wouldn't, would I? It's understandable."

Mary Ellen said nothing to this because it was understandable, and Kate said, "I must be off. We'll all be over as usual when the weather permits. Bye-bye, Mam."

"Bye-bye, lass." Mary Ellen opened the door for her and closed it quickly again to keep out the driving rain. Back in the middle of the kitchen, she stood drumming her fingers on the table in her usual way when worried. And the tattoo became louder as her mind moved from John to her daughter, and she said aloud, "I'll soon put a stop to that, if it is that."

During the next three weeks it was noticeable that Mary Ellen, who was to be seen almost daily visiting the byres, the barn, the stables, and the tack-room, presumably looking for Terry to see that he was all right, was on Maggie's own particular warpath. And Maggie wasn't blind to this, but she didn't think John had noticed anything, until one day when she was making for the barn, he passed her and out of the corner of his mouth he said, "Don't go in there. Mam's standing round the back."

She had stopped abruptly, turned and looked to where her brother was going into one of the stables. Then deliberately walking into the barn, she went to the far end where she knew Willy was and in a loud tone she said, "Go and give Terry a hand, will you? He's shifting the pigs. I'll see to that," while she gesticulated towards the far wall of the barn where the flaps let in the daylight, and he, taking her cue, said, "All right, I'll do that. But I told him to leave it. Sure you can manage?"

"Yes, thank you, Willy, I can manage. But I don't know how much longer." She made a face at him as he passed her. "I'm getting tired of being taken for the third farmhand. I'll be glad when young Ozzie starts. He'd have to go and twist his foot, wouldn't he?"

When Willy had gone, she did not take up the rake and pull the straw together, but, going to the end of the barn, she put her eye to a crack and saw her mother, bundled up to the eyes with clothes, making her way back into the yard.

A minute or two later, John came into the barn and they stood looking at each other until he said, "You want to be careful, Maggie."

"You know?"

"Couldn't help but. I'm a light sleeper, and I use that door sometimes."

She bowed her head as she muttered, "I don't care. It's my life, and . . . and I love him, and he, me. If she kicks up we'll go off."

"You can't do that, Maggie. She's alone as it is."

Her head bounced up as she demanded, "What's in the future for us then? A hole in the corner affair? He's worth marrying, John. He's a good man."

"I know that. I know that. Things are unfair. If it lay with me, but it doesn't, so. . . . Anyway, there'll be hell to pay if this comes out, you know there will. He could be ten times better than he is, but still Dad would send him packing. Huh! It's funny." He gave a short laugh. "People change out of all recognition. It must be age. I'll have to remember that. But he was as low as any cowman at one time, Dad."

"Yes, I know that, with not half the brains of Willy."

"Brains don't come into this, Maggie."

"How about you?"

"What do you mean, how about me?"

"You know what I mean. You know my position and I know yours."

"Well, there might be some hope for you, Maggie, but there's none for me."

"Don't say that, John. I . . . I'm not going to let them ruin my life." She put her hand out and gripped his arm. "We all need love. I found it and I'm going to hang onto it, come what may. And you should do the same."

"With some one I could have fathered?"

"Don't be daft." She shook his arm. "It happens every day, a young lass and an older man. And she's not a young lass inside. We both found out."

"Well, it's over, Maggie. There's no need to worry about me. In her last letter she said she would write no more."

"Have you answered her letters?"

"No."

"Oh, John. And she actually said that, she'd write no more?"

"Yes, she did. So that's one problem solved. But you look to yours. I don't know how things are going to work out for you, only be careful."

He nodded at her and as he turned from her she said, "Until I can be careful no longer."

He was looking at her again, staring into her face. "You're not? You haven't?"

"I'm not sure, but it doesn't matter. I hope I am. I long to be able to say I am."

"Oh, Maggie. Maggie."

"Don't worry about me, John. I'm happier than I've ever been in my life before. I'm living, for the first time I'm living. And if you were wise, you would too."

"We can't all be wise, Maggie. No, we can't." Now he turned from her and went out. And she, standing straight, put her hands on her stomach and looked down towards it, and, closing her eyes for a moment, she said, "Please God, let it be there."

8

It was the beginning of April when Maggie knew with absolute certainty that she was carrying a child. The monthly do's, as Mary Ellen referred to this quirk of nature, had always been erratic in Maggie's case, but for the past three days her condition had been confirmed when she awoke in the morning with a feeling of nausea and the reluctance to rise from her bed at half-past five.

It was four nights now since she had last visited Willy, and as yet he knew nothing about her condition. The uncertainty of it, together with a feeling of shyness, and also the fact that he might not receive her news in the same way as it was affecting herself, had stopped her from hinting at it during the spasmodic conversations they were able to indulge in during the day.

The reason she hadn't been to the cottage was not on account of the weather and the last heavy fall of snow, but the fact that her mother had taken to staying up late. It had been half-past ten when she had gone upstairs these past three nights, and it was an understood thing between her and Willy that he had not to expect her after eleven o'clock at night.

Anyway, she had made up her mind, if it was twelve o'clock tonight, she was going to see Willy.

It was a quarter to eleven when she left her room. Her mother had come upstairs rather earlier. John had been in his room this last hour. As she passed her parents' bedroom door, she heard her father's snoring end on a snort. She did not need a light to find the bolt. Her hand went immediately to it, but as she began to withdraw it, she gave a violent start when a light illuminated the passage, and there, coming out of the store-room, was her mother.

A lamp between them, they stared at each other, both their faces white with suppressed anger.

"Where do you think you're going?"

"Why ask the road you know?" Maggie's voice was a low hiss, and her mother's was equally low as she now said, "You're a slut, that's what you are, a slut. A cowman! You've got no shame."

Maggie was gulping in her throat now and she had to force the words through her teeth as she said, "Then I take after me mother, don't I? You should know all about it."

When Mary Ellen's hand came upwards, Maggie's voice rose as she cried, "You dare! Mam. Just you dare, and I'll walk out of here the morrow, and him with me. Think on that, him with me. Because not even three Ozzie Taylors and another one can make up for what Willy does. And inside the house you'd need a couple of maids. Aye, and you'd have to get your hand in more than you do now to keep things spruce as you want them. So be careful, Mam, don't attempt to hit me, because although I won't give you blow for blow, I'll hit you where it hurts most, your pockets, because you're as bad as Dad in that way. Now if you'll move aside I'll be on me way across to the cottage where I've been going this many a week."

"You bitch! You dirty bitch!"

"Be careful, Mam. I mightn't even wait for the blow. Just be careful. Remember what I said, I take after you."

"If ... if you go out that door, you won't get back."

"Well, I'll leave that to you. If I don't get back I stay in the cottage just long enough to get me things together, then we'll both go off. Think on it. I'll be gone about an hour, just think on it." With that she shot the bolt back none too quietly and went out, leaving the door wide behind her, knowing that her mother's infuriated gaze was on her.

She was shaking from head to foot when she reached the cottage. Willy jumped up from his seat beside the fire and came towards her. But as soon as he saw her face he said, "What is it, love? What is it?"

She fell against him, muttering incoherently.

When he raised her head sharply upwards, he demanded, "What happened? What happened?"

"She ... she caught me coming out, and ... and said things, called me names, and ... and I called them back. Oh, Willy, Willy."

He took off her coat and shawl and led her to a chair and, pulling another towards her, he sat by her side, holding her hands tightly, as he said, "Well, it would have had to come out sometime. Better now than later. I'll know where I stand and what I'm to do. I'll have a talk with the Rector on Sunday, although I want no church wedding. And neither do you. But he's a wise and kindly man, he'll direct me. And lass don't look so down. Look at me."

She raised her head and he smiled now as he said, "I haven't let the grass grow under me feet these past few weeks. I'd heard about a little place as soon as it came on the market. 'Tis over near Corbridge in the valley there, and the ground is lush. There's twenty acres and a good little house, three byres, two stables, and a loft. I never mentioned it afore because I didn't want to jump the gun, but now I can go ahead. The price will likely be around fifty or sixty pounds because the house has been let go. The old man's been on his own and past it for years. I hear he's going to live with his daughter. If I could get it for that, I have a little bit to start the stock, and I know who'd give me a helping hand if I asked him, and that's Mr Hamilton. He asked me a while ago why I didn't think of starting up on me own. Funny, it was shortly after that your dad gave me a shilling rise. I wondered if he had had anything to do about it."

"No, no." She shook her head. "That was John."

"Aye, of course, it would be. He's a good fellow, John. He's not happy, you know that, lass, don't you? He misses the little French lass. Funny, isn't it? Well, that's not the right word, you know what I mean."

"Willy."

"Yes, my love?" He now moved closer and put his arms about her.

"I ... I've got something to tell you."

"Aye, well, I'm listenin', and always will be, ready for your words."

She stared into his face while her eyes became moist, and the sight brought a fear to him. And now his hold tightened on her as she said, "You're not going to go back on me?"

She actually put her head back and laughed, saying, "Aw, Willy!" Then looking at him again, she said quietly, "I'm carrying."

"You're ... carrying? You mean?"

"Yes." She made a deep obeisance with her head, then found herself pulled roughly upwards. And now he was waltzing her round the narrow space between the fire, the chairs, and the small table. And when they fell against the table, he took her face between his hands and kissed her eyes, her nose, her cheeks. Then of a sudden, becoming still, his voice gentle, he said, "You happy, Maggie?"

"So happy, Willy, nothing matters, only you and me, and it." She patted her stomach. And he placed his hand on top of hers, and now, his voice serious, he said, "You're not afraid?"

"Afraid?" She pulled in her chin and screwed up her eyes and repeated, "Afraid?" And her voice firm, she said, "No, no, Willy. I am not afraid. I'm strong and healthy. I know it might be the wrong age, but I'll have your child if it's the last thing...."

His hand came tight across her mouth as he said, "Don't finish that. Don't say, if it's the last thing you do, because if it's the child or you, it's you. Always you. Know that, will you? Know that, lass. I want you. If we have a bairn, well and good. If we don't, still well and good, as long as I have you."

"Willy! Willy!" The tears were raining down her face now, and gently he held her while her crying mounted and he became concerned. But then taking her by the shoulders, he shook her gently, saying, "Look, lass, it's too soon for the waters to break." And at this she spluttered and her tears turned to laughter that rang through the cottage, and all she could say now was, "Oh! Willy, Willy. Willy, Willy."

An hour later when she mounted the back stairs she found the door open and, locking it, she quickly made her way to her room, and when she got into bed she took a pillow and, hugging it to her, she buried her face in it and went to sleep.

*

Mary Ellen was seething. She did not speak to Maggie the following morning, nor even look at her, but she was aware of her every movement, and she told herself that she couldn't stand this. Nothing, she imagined, could upset her more than she was at this moment. The thought of a daughter of hers lying with a cowman like Willy was nauseating, and for that daughter to say she was a pattern of herself had aroused an anger in her that was still raging. Her own mistake had occurred through one incident only; and then she had the excuse of having been a young lass with the fires of curiosity and need posing under the name of love. But in their Maggie's case, this dirty underhand business must have been going on for God knew how long.

It was towards dinner-time that she decided she would have to talk to someone, and the last person she could open her heart to about this thing was Hal. So she would go and tell Kate. She was forgetting that Kate had once visited a man week after week, going in all weathers into the hills, supposedly to exchange books with him. . . .

It was two o'clock in the afternoon, dressed in her second-best bonnet and a similar coat, that she mounted the trap and took the reins from John's hand, saying, "See your father gets his three o'clock tea, won't you?"

He did not say, "Maggie always sees to that, doesn't she?" because he had already guessed there was a storm raging between them. What he said was, "Enjoy your ride, but get back before it's dark if you can."

"Light or dark, the road's no stranger to me. You should know that."

She put her horse into a trot and he stood watching after her until she turned it out into the road before he moved away and went in search of Maggie. He found her crossing the hall from the direction of the sitting room. She had an empty coal bucket in one hand and a wood skip in the other. He turned with her and re-entered the kitchen. He had not taken his boots off and she looked down at his feet as she said, "You took a risk, didn't you?"

"She's gone."

"She could have popped back just to see what I was up to. I suppose you know all about it?"

"I know nothing. She hasn't opened her mouth to me. What is it, anyway?"

Maggie opened the kitchen door and put the bucket and the skip outside. Then closing the door again, she went to the sink and washed her hands, and as she dried them she turned and leant her buttocks against the stone, saying, "She caught me going down the back stairs last night to visit Willy."

He made no reply, just stared at her, and she went on, "It wasn't the first time and it won't be the last, as long as I'm here. We're going to find a place of our own. Has he said anything to you . . . Willy?"

"Yes. He said he's got his eye on a place. He's thinking of going and taking you with him."

"Surprised?"

"No, not at all."

"I mean that I should leave and go with him?"

"I said, no, not at all. Can I tell you something? I wish it was me."

"Oh, John." She threw down the towel and went to the table and, sitting down, she looked up at him. He now pulled a chair forward and he too sat down, and when she said, "Somehow, I couldn't imagine you being any place else but here, you love the farm," he broke in, "That shows, Maggie, how little you know of me. Where have I been in my life? How far have I been, I ask you? To Newcastle, aye. Durham, aye. Carlisle, yes. I would have loved to visit Edinburgh. And it's only a few years now since I stopped meself dreaming, knowing there was no purpose in it. But I used to long to go off, just walk out and go off. Do you know, I can understand young Frag. Oh, yes, I can understand him all right. There's something in one when you're young that makes you want to bolt for it, like a foal, you don't want to be tied. And in my case that urge went on till . . . oh" – he shook his head – "four or five years ago."

"Why didn't you do something about it then?"

"I nearly did. At one time I nearly did. Then Gabriel pipped me. It was when he decided to go and join Hugh. He had the feeling too. He said as much to me. 'What future,' he said, 'is there for me here? Dad won't let the reins go until he draws his last breath. And then there'll be you, John. And I'm not like Tom, I don't want to marry a farm.' That's what he said. And where did that leave me? Could I walk out then? Tom gone, Hugh gone, Gabriel gone, Kate gone, Florrie gone. What was there left? You, Maggie, for indoors, and me for outdoors. And although Terry was able to do a day's work then, things pile up on me. And remember the two hands we got one after the other but they wouldn't stick Dad? So, I ask you, could I get up and go? I made the best of it. This was my life, I thought; when Dad eventually goes, the farm will be mine, that'll be some compensation. When Willy came things were a lot easier. I began to feel settled. Well, I told myself, there was nothing else for it. Although in between times there was Betty Pringle and Mary Braithwaite. Did Mam welcome either of them? No. But it didn't matter very much. Until one day a man arrived here with a girl that I'd never seen the like of before in me life, except—" he turned his head away from her, as he quietly added, "sometimes at night in me dreams. But she was sixteen and I played father to her until she said she wasn't sixteen, she was on nineteen, and a young woman. And from then on in me mind I stopped playing father. And the comfort of even that was gone, until came the day when I said goodbye to her on the station."

He now put his elbows on the table and rested his head on his hands. And there was silence between them, and this lasted until Maggie said, "She liked you, John, more than liked you, and she kept on writing. Why don't you do something about it?"

"What could I do?" he asked her quietly now.

"Offer her a life here with Mam. Mam will be glad of anybody once I go, and she'll likely find her better company."

"No, no, she wouldn't, Maggie. Mam never took to her."

"No more than she took to the others, as you've just said yourself."

"This was different. Remember who she is. She's Kate's half-sister, she's the daughter of the man that Mam once loved. And what did he leave her with? A great big woman like Kate, a loving woman, but, nevertheless, an outsize of a woman. And what does he bring with him, expecting Mam to be sort of guardian to her, a small sylph-like creature, so beautiful it was painful for Mam to look on her. No. . . . Anyway, what are we talking about? My chapter's closed, Maggie, but yours is just opening. You get yourself away with Willy, and that'll mean Mam will be forced to have help in here. And I'll see that I have adequate help outside. By gum! I will that." He got to his feet now, then stopped and looked towards the door, saying, "What's that? Surely she hasn't come back already?"

He went quickly to the window, and Maggie followed him, and, their backs bent, they peered at Tom Briggs helping a green-coated figure down the back steps of his trap. As Maggie whispered, "Never!" John said, "It can't be!" Then straightening his back, he looked at Maggie and said, "God Almighty! And we've just been——" He motioned his hand back to the table. Then in the next moment he had sprung to the door and was out into the yard. But he didn't rush to her, he stood still as she came towards him. Her grey eyes wide, her lips apart, she walked forward and stood gazing up at him, then said, "Hello, Jean."

"Why . . . why didn't you say?"

"I . . . I didn't really know. It was on what you call, an impulse. . . . Hello, Maggie." She now turned from him and extended her hands towards Maggie who had come slowly out into the yard, and Maggie, gripping them, pulled her close and held her for a moment, saying, "Oh! Yvonne. I am glad to see you. Come in. Come in." And with one hand she led her into the kitchen as if she had never been in the room before, and there she said, "Take your things off. Give me your bonnet. You look cold."

"It . . . it has been a long journey."

John was standing behind her now as he asked, "You came on your own?"

She turned and looked up at him, saying, "Yes, yes. I travel all on my own, the whole way, all on my own, and people were very kind. It . . . it was surprising."

"I'll get you a drink. Come on, sit down, sit down by the fire." Maggie was bustling.

"Where do you want these put?"

John turned to the door where Tom Briggs was standing with a case in each hand, and he said, "Oh, just leave them down here."

"There's another two in the trap."

"Well . . . well, fetch them in."

When the man brought the other cases in, John walked with him out into the yard again and asked quietly, "How much?" And he said, "Oh, she's paid me, and rightly. She's a free-handed miss, I'll say that. Looks as if she's come to stay, doesn't it?" He glanced sideways at John, then said, "Your mam all right? I didn't see her. She's generally knocking about."

"She's gone visiting."

"Oh, aye. Well, I'll be off. An' I'll be pleased to take you to the station" – he nodded back towards the kitchen – "when she wants to go off. But as I said, lookin' at her baggage, it won't be the day or the morrow. So long then."

"So long."

John returned to the kitchen where Maggie was saying, "Will I get you something to eat?" And Yvonne answered, "No, thank you. I am in need of a drink only. I had a large meal in the hotel before I left Newcastle."

"When did you arrive there?"

She looked at John, saying, "Last night. And this morning I did shopping. It is very nice, the shops there. *They are very nice*, the shops there." She laughed gently now, saying, "My English is better, yes?"

"Oh, very much." Maggie nodded at her. "Yes, very much."

"I have been taking instruction from an English teacher. She taught in the lycée. Miss Marie introduce me to her."

Maggie looked at John, asking now, "Do you want a cup?" and when he shook his head, she said, "I'll ... I'll take one to Willy and Terry."

"Your mama ... mother, she is in?"

"No. She has gone visiting."

"Your father too?"

"He is in Allendale. He should be back shortly. Look, I won't be long." Maggie picked up the two cans of tea that she had just poured out and, nodding from one to the other, she hastily left the kitchen. And there they were, looking at each other.

Again Yvonne was the first to speak. However, she did not look at him but towards the fire as she said, "You are not pleased to see me?"

"*I am. I am.*" His reply had come quick and deep, and she turned towards him, her face bright, saying, "I had to come, Jean. You did not write me. But you were in my mind all the time."

He shook his head.

"Did you think of me?"

"Yes."

"You're pleased I come?"

When he hesitated she said quietly, "You are not. You are not."

"Yes, yes, I am." He went towards her. "But ... but it's impossible. I mean, you're so young. I ... I'm ... well, I'm old enough to be your father."

"Perhaps." She made a motion with her head while she stared up into his face, then repeated, "Perhaps, but I do not think of you as a father. I never did imagine you as my father, not ... not from the first time, I mean, when we first met, and I am unfortunate, as I once said, in looking so young. Inside I am not young. I have seen people, I mean, I know people, men especially. You are different."

"Oh, Yvonne, my dear." He caught hold of her hands. "We ... we must talk about this thing. There is so much ... so many obstacles."

"What obstacles?"

"Oh my God!" When he turned his head to the side and closed his eyes for a moment she said, "Why do you say mon Dieu! ... my God! You *are* sorry I come."

"No, no." He was shaking her hands up and down now. "Believe me, Yvonne, no, no. I'm ... I'm happy to see you, very happy to see you." His voice had sunk to a whisper. And when she said, "You thought of me?" he answered, "Always. Always, yes."

"Then there are no obstacles, just you and me."

He paused now before he said slowly, "There is my mother and my father, they need me here."

"Well" – her face brightened – "I stay with you here. What are obstacles? I stay with you here. I love the farm. I think of the cows too." She laughed now. "And I love Maggie, and ... and I hope I will get to know my half-sister better and cause her to like me. We should like each other, half-sisters. I have no other sister."

He wanted to close his eyes again and say, "Oh, my darling," when Maggie, making her presence known, cried as she opened the back door, "I told Willy and Terry you're here. They are very pleased. Well now, let's get these things up to your room and get you settled in. By that time, Mam" – she paused – "Mam will be back." And she did not add, "And if anything will, this will take her mind off me. By! yes, I'll say it will."

When John went to lift the cases, Yvonne said, "It is not all my luggage, it is presents. We will spend the evening dressing up."

"Dressing up?" Maggie questioned now, and Yvonne answered, "Yes, dressing up. You wait and see."

Hal was the first to arrive home. As he dismounted from his horse, John came out of the byres and went towards him, but before he could say anything, Hal exclaimed, "Daylight bloody robbers! That's what they are. They pick up the horses for practically nowt, feed them free on the fells, then charge the bloody earth for them. Trainin', they said, trainin'."

"Dad."

"Aye, what is it?"

"We've got a visitor."

485

"A visitor? Who, one of ours?"

"No, not one of ours. It's Yvonne. She's come back."

"No! Who brought her?"

"She came on her own."

"Never!"

"Yes."

They had been walking towards the door when Hal stopped and, looking at John through narrowed lids, he said, "Well ... well, for meself, I'll be quite pleased to see the lass, she was lively. But I don't know how your mother's gona take this. I suppose you know she didn't cotton on to her. Natural like, everything taken into consideration, don't you think?"

When John didn't answer, Hal, his voice brusque now, said, "Well, what did I say to you? 'Tis natural like your mother didn't cotton on to her, everything taken into consideration."

"Yes, I suppose you're right, but suppose she didn't come to see Mam."

They scrutinized each other for a moment, then Hal said quietly, "Well, I don't know what you're hinting at, lad, or perhaps I do, but I'd think twice on it. You don't want to make yourself a laughing-stock, do you?"

At that he turned and walked into the house leaving John, gritting his teeth, to go back into the byres; and there, taking his fist, he rammed it against one of the posts, cursing to himself as he did so. . . .

The dusk was falling as Mary Ellen reached home. She was very little happier than when she had left it. Kate's reaction to her news hadn't pleased her at all, for Kate, surprisingly, had reminded her in a tactful sort of way that Willy was in much the same position as Hal had been when she married him. And also that she didn't blame Maggie for grabbing at life. Mary Ellen was well aware that Kate was still as besotted with Ben after all these years as she had been when she married him, or before that. Kate had suggested that she knew how Maggie felt and that she had been deprived of life. When she had demanded, "And whose fault is that? She's had her chances, more than any other member in the family," Kate's answer was, "It's her nature I suppose. She's inclined to be contrary."

Contrary! Brazen was the word she would put to her now, not contrary.

There was no one in the yard when she drove in, and she yelled, "You! Willy." But it was Terry who appeared, saying, "I'll take her, missis."

"Where's everybody?"

"The boss and Master John are inside the house, I think. Willy is mending the fences down on the east side, least he was." He smiled widely at her, but did not mention that she had a visitor.

She marched into the kitchen, only to stop and gaze at the bare wooden table. It had been her rule of late to have the evening meal in the kitchen to save work, only using the dining-room at the week-ends, when the family visited. She looked towards the sink. There were a number of dirty teacups and mugs in there.

She was pulling at the strings of her bonnet as she entered the hall, and she was brought to a stop by the sound of laughter coming from the direction of the sitting-room, and she recognized her husband's high above the rest.

After pushing open the sitting-room door she was again brought to a standstill. The laughter slid from the faces turned towards her, and her eyes centred on the slip figure of the girl rising from the chair.

"Well, what d'you think?" Hal's voice greeted her overheartily. "Here she is, out of the blue. Surprise like, eh?"

"How do you do, madame?" Yvonne, her face unsmiling now, was looking at the woman who was returning her look whilst John was helping his mother off with her cloak.

Being forced to say something, Mary Ellen said, "Why didn't you let us know?"

"It was on the—" Yvonne paused "quick," she said and glanced towards Maggie, and Maggie, who was also on her feet and about to make for the door, said, "Spur of the moment."

"Yes, that is it." Yvonne nodded her head several times in Mary Ellen's direction, saying now, "I was bragging that my English was good, but I have a long way yet to travel."

Mary Ellen moved to the fire and, bending down, held out her hands to the blaze, and from there she asked, "Your house, how is it?"

"It is good. The painter men have finished. It is ... attractive ... comfortable. I have had some offers to sell it."

"Are you ... ?" Mary Ellen had turned from the fire and was chaffing her hands together now as if endeavouring to rub something off them.

"Oh, no, no." Then Yvonne paused as if she was thinking, before adding, "At least, not yet. I do not know." Then she asked quietly, "May I stay for a while?"

There was a significant pause before Mary Ellen said, "Yes, I suppose so, now that you're here." Then abruptly she walked from them, saying, "I could do with a cup of tea. Everybody else seems to have had one."

As she left the room John was on her heels, and he caught up with her in the middle of the hall and, taking her arm, he pulled her round to face him, saying, "Mam, she's travelled all the way from France on her own. You could have given her a civil greeting."

"What do you expect?"

"Well, what I expected was a little understanding. Mam, she's here, and she's here for a while, and what I'm going to say to you now is, she could be here for a long while, or there's an alternative."

She snapped her arm away from his hold, saying, "My God! that I should have lived to see this day. With one and another of you, my brain's going to be turned, and small wonder. You're mad, d'you know that? You'll be a laughing stock, ridiculed. You won't be able to hold your head up. Think on that afore you let your old man's fancy free."

He stood where she had left him, his chin now sunk on his chest. Let your old man's fancy free. Well, he wasn't old. Forty wasn't old, not for a man it wasn't. But she was right about the ridicule. Yes, she was right about that. If only Yvonne didn't look such a child, at first appearance at least. It would be hard for people to take in that she was nineteen, which meant in her twentieth year. But she was nineteen and she loved him, and he ... well, the feeling he had for her seemed to have no name, it went past love. He adored her, not only the way she looked, but the sound of her voice, her every movement, her thoughts, the warmth of her. Yes, yes, the warmth of her, and he couldn't do without that. Now he had felt it he couldn't do without it. Nothing mattered here any more. Nothing mattered to him but her, and he would have her. Mother, father, farm, ridicule, the lot, nothing would stop them from coming together.

It was turned ten o'clock when Mary Ellen and Hal went into their bedroom, and the door had hardly closed on them before Hal, in what was to him a whisper, said, "What's up with you, woman? Acting like a goat with its head down. You're not going to alter things. He's set on her, so you might as well make up your mind to it."

"Aw you! Make up my mind to what? My son and that chit of a girl? She can't speak our own language."

"She does pretty well, and better than most who've been brought up on it, I should say. If that's all you've got against her. . . ."

"It isn't. It isn't, and you know it. And one thing I'll tell you: I can't understand your attitude. You know who she belongs to, and you know her relationship to Kate, and yet you . . ."

"Aye, woman—" He was bending towards her, thrusting his face into hers, still whispering, "You don't need to stress that part of it. Aye, I know who she belongs to and I know who Kate belongs to. That's been bored into my mind since the day I saw your stomach full of her. But that's got nothing to do with this lass. She can't help it. And what I'm concerned about is our John. Now I'm tellin' you this, woman, you can come down too hard on a man where his feelings are concerned. And he's at the wrong age to be foiled. He's gone over the hills for the lass, you can see that, and you've got to accept it. The alternative is, he could up and go. Then where would we be? 'cos you can't rely on paid hands, even a fellow like Willy, as good as he is."

"Willy, as good as he is! Now I've got something to tell you, man. You're going to lose Willy afore you lose John."

"Lose Willy? He's goin', he said?"

"No, he didn't say, but your daughter said."

He stepped back from her and sat on the edge of the bed, then asked quietly, "What are you gettin' at?"

"Just that. Our Maggie's another one that's gone mad in her middle years. She's been carrying on with that fellow for weeks now."

"Our Maggie?"

"Our Maggie."

"And Willy?"

"And Willy."

"You're imagining things, woman."

"All right. Then I'm imagining an' all she's got a bairn in her belly."

He sprang up from the bed now, a purple hue spreading over his whiskered cheeks, and she stood nodding at him, saying, "She's been visiting him at nights for God knows how long. I caught her at it and threatened to send him packing. And she threatened me an' all. Our Maggie threatened me." She pulled her lips tight inwards for a moment before adding, "And now she's sick in the morning and eating cheese like an Irish navvy."

"My God! Willy." He dropped down on the bed again; then caused her anger to flare and rise to almost a scream as he said, "I'll never get another one like him."

"Is that all you can say? They're leavin', both of them. And what am I left with?"

"Woman, keep your voice down, this is our bedroom. Up till now it's been private. Do you want the whole house to know what you're thinkin'?"

Slowly she turned from him and when her head dropped and her shoulders began to shake, he rose and put his arm about her, saying, "Well, let them go; there's never been a good but there's a better. But I can't believe it of our Maggie. And, lass, what you've got to try to do is to like Yvonne, because it could be she's going to be with us for a long time." As the tears rained from her eyes, her mind answered him, Never. Never.

Over in the cottage Maggie was saying, "She brought me a beautiful dress. I ... I could be married in it. It's lovely. It's blue silk and all ruched" – she traced her hand across her chest – "and has a full skirt, and lovely wide sleeves. Oh, it is beautiful. And she brought John a velvet waistcoat, very, very smart. And Dad a similar one. And then" – she paused – "there was Mam's dress. It was green velvet, plain but beautiful. And you know, she wouldn't put it on. She hardly thanked her for it. I felt so wild that I nearly went for her, but we haven't opened our mouths to each other. Poor John, he's going to have a fight on his hands. But more so I'm sorry for that lass, because if anything comes of it, and you can see how she feels about him, she's going to have one hell of a life with my mother."

"Well, lass, we won't be here to see it, because I think it's nearly certain about that place."

"No!"

"Aye," he nodded, smiling widely at her, "and I think I could have it lock, stock, and barrel, together with the hens, geese, and three pigs, and one of them in litter, for eight-five pounds. That would include the odds and ends of bits of furniture. But mind, what I saw of them, they are odds and ends; they've been battered by seven of a family for years. Well, the house is over two hundred years old, I think."

"Oh, Willy." She put her arms around him. "I can't wait. I just can't wait. It'll be like walking into heaven."

"Well, you'll have to go through a lot of muck afore you get to the gates 'cos I was up to me ankles in it in the yard."

They held each other, laughing, and rocked together. Then putting his arm around her waist, he led her towards the bedroom, saying, "There's no rush any more then, is there?" And for answer, she smiled at him and pressed her head against his shoulder.

9

A fortnight had passed and everyone of the household felt that they couldn't bear the tension enveloping them much longer. Mary Ellen pointedly never addressed Maggie, nor Maggie her. And when Mary Ellen had to answer a question put to her by Yvonne, she did so in an abrupt fashion, and nearly always avoided looking at her.

Outside, Hal shouted most of his orders and spaced them more thickly with curses. A week previous, Willy had given him notice, saying, "My bond is up at Midsummer. I'll stay on till then to see you fixed up." And Hal's answer to this was, "I should bloody well kick your backside out of the yard at this minute, because you're a sly, underhand snipe." But he was silenced when Willy came back at him, saying firmly, "I am neither sly, underhand, nor a snipe, Mr Roystan. I care for Maggie and she cares for me, and it's been that way for both of us since shortly after I came onto your farm. But we did nothing about it until recently. And all I'll say to you, Mr Roystan, is, we're both adult people and entitled to pass the rest of our lives together, just the same as you did with the missis." And when Hal, searching in his agitated mind for something to say, cried, "You know you'll be my bloody son-in-law?" Willy answered him, "These things happen. And they can be unfortunate for both sides." And with that he had left Hal fuming yet wishing at bottom that the fellow's status had been other than that of a cowman, because he had his head screwed on the right way....

This being Saturday, Willy and Maggie were accompanying him into the market. They were taking the cart in and he was going in on horseback.

After they had gone Mary Ellen went into the dairy. She couldn't stay in the kitchen with that lass doing her fancy cooking. Twice this week she had asked if she could bake some French dishes. The last stuff she made was a kind of stew, and the rest of them "oohed and aahed" about it. But for herself, it tasted of nothing but bay leaves. And the pudding that she made, fluffy stuff, nothing in it, a French name she gave it, sufflay or something. And then this morning she asked if she could make some pastry. So what could she say? But the one thing she needn't do was to watch her. The girl was getting on her nerves. She felt she couldn't stand much more.

She had been in the dairy over an hour. She had made up some butter and had turned the little cheeses on the slab, but now she wanted to start up a fresh cheese, and she went towards the two dishes standing on the stone bench against the far wall, and finding one empty she bit hard down on her lip. There were always two or three bowls of cream left on a Saturday to start another batch of cheese. That was Maggie's job. She mustn't have skimmed yesterday's milk, likely thrown the lot to the pigs as it was. Him and her must be getting their heads together to slack off because she had noticed patches of mud lying on the bottom of the yard when she came out a while ago. Another time Willy wouldn't have dreamed of going to the market without seeing that the yard was scrubbed clean. They'd had heavy rain for the past four days and the mud from the road was often swept in, but up till now it had never lain.

She opened the door and stood looking out. The sky was high and a deep blue with white scudding clouds racing across it. There was a fresh wind blowing, but the sun was warmish. Spring was in the air, but this was the first time she could remember that she had never welcomed it.

As she stood she saw John coming out of a loose-box accompanied by the girl. She was like his shadow, she never left him alone for a minute. What had happened to her pastry-making? Her face tightened as she saw John open the door of the tack-room and allow her to pass in.

My God! How was she to put up with this? She knew what would be happening in there besides their making plans. And making plans they were, she was sure of that.

Going swiftly across the yard, she went into the main cow-byre, at the end of which was an old door that at one time had given access to the tack-room. It had long since been barred up, because should it accidentally be left open, a cow was apt to stroll in there and wreak havoc before leaving by the other door.

Quietly now she hurried past the empty stalls. Then moving close to the door, she put her ear to the side of it.

Their voices came low, but quite clear to her, and the first words she heard made her squirm, for her son was saying, "Oh, my love." And this was followed by a silence in which she let her imagination run rife. Then the girl's voice came to her, saying, "I have enough money, my dear, dear, Jean, to buy you three farms.... All right. All right, my dear, as you tell me you can have enough money of your own, with your share, then let us go."

"Yvonne, I've tried to explain, I can't."

"You don't want to?"

"Oh, my God, yes I do. There's nothing I want more than to take your hand and run from here, onto a train, onto a boat, and ... and to your home. Nothing, nothing more. But ... but my parents ... you see, they are old, they depend upon me."

"Your Mama, she does not like me."

"That's only her way. She ... she's not a woman who can show her feelings."

"Oh, but yes, yes, Jean, she shows her feelings to me, I know."

"Oh, my dear, what can I do? What can I do? What can I say? Only this, I won't press you to stay, but I don't know how I'll live my days without you."

"You won't have to, my dear Jean, my loved one. If you cannot come with me, I stay with you. We will be married and I will put up with conditions for your sake. I will put up with anything for your sake, and it cannot last forever. I am young and you are young. Yes, yes, you are. You look young and in your heart you are younger, and ... and I will keep you young. I promise, I will keep you young."

In the silence that followed, Mary Ellen slowly turned her body around and her feet dragged as if they were weighed down as she moved up the byres and out into the yard. Crossing it once again, she returned to the dairy, and there, leaning with her hands flat on the cold slab, she thrust her head from one shoulder to the other, saying aloud, "I can't bear it. It shouldn't be happening to me, not at this stage of my life. Both my daughter and my son breaking their necks to leave us. What have we done? What have I done to deserve this? I wish I was dead. I do, I do. Before this had happened to me I wish I'd died.

It was close on five o'clock when Hal returned. Not finding Mary Ellen in the kitchen, he yelled, "Where are you? Where are you, woman?"

He burst into the sitting-room and found she wasn't there; he went into the office; then into the dining-room; and lastly upstairs into the bedroom; and when he saw her sitting by the window, he said, "What's up with you, woman? Why are you up here? And no tea set."

She rose to her feet, saying, "Oh, I thought our French visitor was seeing to that."

"Oh, for God's sake! forget about the French visitor. Leave the lass alone. There's something more on me mind at this minute than her. Do you know what I saw in Hexham the day? That young swine, as drunk as a noodle, or nearly so. He could keep his feet but that's about all he could do. And there he was, with the youngest Reilly. And that's not all, Reilly's lass was with him an' all. Now she's a known whore, that one. And what d'you think he did when he saw me? He grinned at me, then laughed as he shouted, 'Hello there, Grandfather.' I could have murdered him on the spot, My God! the times I've felt like it. If I'd been near enough to him the day, God knows what I might have done. But I'll do for him yet. I swear I will."

"Don't say such things, man, even if you don't mean them. The boy's wild, he'll grow out of it. Anyway, it isn't your business, it's Ben's and Kate's, and they're old enough to see to their own."

"There's wickedness in that fellow. It's in his face. He's all the Bannamans put together."

"Will you stop it! Listen to me: we've got more things to think about than Fraser's capers. Do you know that that one, our French visitor, is egging John on to leave and set up in France?"

"What's that?"

"You heard what I said."

"How did you come by this?"

"I overheard them ... I purposely overheard them. I made it me business to do so. I wanted to know where we stood, and now we know."

"John wouldn't leave here. He knows where his bread's buttered. The place will be his when we go, 'cos the others are all set well."

"Don't be silly, man. By all accounts, she's got enough money to buy three farms, she said so herself. And hasn't she a fine house in Paris?"

"Did he say he was going?" Hal's voice was quiet.

"No, he said he was staying. And she agreed to stay with him. But I'm telling you this, Hal, I can't put up with her. Don't you see" – her voice broke – "I can't put up with her."

"As I see it, she's not hard to get on with. Can't you try? Now that you're going to lose Maggie, you'll be alone. She could be a daughter to you."

"I don't want her as a daughter, Hal. As I see it, she's the daughter of a loose woman. Roddy Greenbank's mistress for years. And if she had him, how many others did she have? And this one could be a chip off the old block. Frenchwomen are like that. I've heard about them."

"Aw, lass, lass, give over. Look, if you want our John to stay, you've got to pay the price, and she's the price. We're losing Willy, and by God! I'm going to say it even if begrudgingly, we'll not get another like him, and I for one will miss him. And another thing I'll say when we're on, you'll not get another one like Maggie, for she's worked like two or three over the years."

"Who's fault was that? You've always baulked at paying for hands inside and out."

"Well, that's how you wanted it, didn't you? You didn't want any other women flitting round your house. Well, as it seems now, you haven't any choice. And another thing you've got to remember if John were to go, he'd take his share with him, and that would take a big slice out of everything. My God!" He turned about. "I was a fool for putting that in writing. I should have let him wait until I was gone." He let out a long-drawn-sigh and turned from her and went out, leaving her with her mouth agape and her hands on her hips. She had the feeling she wanted to scream, just stand and scream. He couldn't see her side of it. It didn't bother him how she felt about the French piece, all he was concerned about was keeping John here, and also his share of the money. He wasn't really concerned about Maggie going, only the loss of Willy. He was a selfish beast, utterly, utterly selfish. She had given her life to him, and what had she in return?

In her mind she was back in her early days hating the boy called Hal Roystan, wanting to hit out at him with something.

Her actions now could have been indeed those of the young girl she once was, because going to the wardrobe, she took down the dress that Yvonne had bought for her and, taking it off its hanger, threw it on the floor and kicked it here and there. Then she sat down on the foot of the bed and, gripping the rail, she shook it as if she would wrench the whole iron support of the bed apart.

10

It promised to be a perfect spring day. By eleven o'clock the sun was warm, and the stream was rising here and there from the wet fields. The burn was running swiftly over the pebble bottom, and Yvonne stood on the bank and looked down onto it. But she didn't seem to see it as she would have done if Jean had been by her side: then, she would have pointed out again as she had done last Sunday, the colours in the water, and laughed, and shaken his arm when he said, "It just looks clear to me. I might see it differently if I was coming back from a fair or a celebration, but that's about the only time." And they had laughed together.

It wasn't often they laughed together since her return, and she wondered now if this was what life would be like if she married him . . . when she married him. And the farmhouse would become her home. How could she put up with his mother's attitude towards her day after day? At one time she had hoped to love her as a mother, but now she knew that was an impossibility: the woman disliked her wholeheartedly, and did not hide her feelings on any occasion. As things were now she still had Maggie, but Maggie would soon be gone with her Willy, and what then? The thought turned her from the bank and she walked along the path following the twisting of the burn until she came to the stepping-stones. She had crossed them last Sunday with Jean's help and walked through the wood beyond, but this morning the water was almost lapping over the top of the stones, and they looked slippery.

She was standing, undecided whether to chance getting her feet wet, or to take the bridle-path that ran along the top of the bank behind her, when she heard the sound of horses' hooves in the distance, and there, within a matter of seconds, appeared Fraser and Harry on ponies.

Fraser pulled his animal to a skidding stop above her, and sat staring down at her for a moment, and she up at him. And when he dismounted, his brother did likewise, but Fraser passed the reins of his pony to him, saying, "Stay there." Then, walking sideways, he made his way down the steep bank until he was facing her.

"Out for a stroll?" His tone was conversational, and she answered, "Yes, I am what you call, taking the air." She smiled.

"All by yourself?"

Her smile faded slightly as she repeated his words, "All by myself."

"My . . . my Uncle John is taking a chance, isn't he?"

Her face puckered in enquiry, but she did not ask for an explanation, she knew by his tone that his words were meant to be offensive.

"Is it true what I hear, you are going to marry him?"

"It is true."

"Well, well, my auntie marrying my uncle, because you are my auntie, aren't you? Funny that, you being my auntie. You look no more than a kid."

"You are being ... offensive."

"What! Me being offensive by just stating a fact? You are, aren't you, you are my mother's half-sister? Your dad seemed to get about a bit even when he was here."

"You are purposely rude ... in ... solent, and you are not drunk now, but sober, and acting like a ... a...." She searched for an English word to express herself.

"Like a what? Go on, tell me what I'm acting like ... Auntie."

She drew herself up and went to turn round and retrace her steps, but he was standing in her way, and to get to the path behind him she would have to climb a little way up the slippery bank, and rather than risk this and fall, she made her way now towards the stepping-stones, and she had her foot extended towards the first one when he grabbed her hand, saying, "Let me help you across."

"Please leave my hand go."

He mimicked her, saying, "Please leave my hand go. And let you fall in, Auntie? Oh, no, I couldn't do that. Come on."

He was standing on the first stone himself now, and as he went to tug her forward, Harry's voice came from the top of the bank, shouting, "Frag! Frag, behave. Leave her be, Frag."

And now he called back to his brother, "I'm just going to help Auntie across the stones, can't you see?"

Yvonne was now pulling back and, using more strength than he gave her credit for, she tugged him from the stone. But now he was holding her by both arms and looking down into her face, saying, "What you frightened of, that I'll duck you?" Suddenly his teasing tone changed, and there was a deep threat in his voice as he growled, "And I have a mind, you know, to do just that. Get you in the middle and duck you, cool your capers, because you're a disturber. You know that? You're a disturber. Anybody who looks at you can see you're a disturber. You've upset my mother, and my grandmother. But not the men, oh no, not the men."

"Leave go, please. Please."

"When I'm ready."

She turned her head and looked up the bank shouting now, "Harry! Harry! Go fetch Jean. Please! Please! Fetch...."

"Fetch John? You dirty French slut."

Now gripping her shoulders, he shook her with such force that her head wobbled and she let out a high scream, and then another and another.

She wasn't aware that Harry was about to mount the pony when he was stopped by a figure coming round the bend of the burn, and he shouted now down to Fraser. "It's Grandfather. It's Grandfather."

But Fraser was too intent now in holding this girl who had disturbed him from the first time he had seen her. With his arms about her struggling body now, the scent and softness of her was affecting him more strongly than any drink he had yet taken. And he only came to himself when she was wrenched from his hold and he was knocked staggering back by a blow from his grandfather's forearm. He stood panting now watching the girl clinging to Hal and sobbing loudly, until Hal's voice yelled at him, "You young bugger you! I'll flay you alive for this."

On hearing his grandfather's rough voice, the mist of his young passion was swept away and he cried back at him, "You try it on and see who'll come off best," at which Hal ground his teeth and, turning his head, shouted up the bank, "Harry! Come down here and take this lass back home."

"Yes, Grandfather. Yes, Grandfather." The boy hooked the reins of the ponies to the stump of a tree; then as he came down the bank, Fraser yelled at him, "He's not your grandfather. He's no relation to you or me. He's nothing, nothing but an old money-grabbing bully. Your grandfather was her father." He thrust out his finger in Yvonne's direction. "This one's nothing to us. Never was, and never will be. So—" He now leant forward and glared his hatred at Hal as he ended, "So Mr Roystan, don't you come the heavy hand with me."

For a moment, Hal became still, and, seemingly gently, he pushed Yvonne from him towards Harry. Then he took two slow steps forward before he jumped. The action could have been that of a young athletic man, and such was the force behind it that it bore both himself and Fraser to the ground and into the edge of the water. The boy was strong and was the first to recover from the impact, and he used his feet and his fists on the older man. Kicking and punching, he tried to free himself from Hal's grip, but Hal's superior weight rolled them over and further into the water. And now he was on top of the boy with his hands gripping his throat. And what happened next caused Yvonne to scream before she turned her face away and clutched at Harry who was standing frozen with terror as he watched the man, whom he had always called grandfather, shake his brother up and down, then finally bring his head crashing onto the stepping-stone.

There was no sound of a struggle coming from the water. Harry stared towards his brother who lay sprawled out, his head to the side: then he watched his grandfather crawl on to the bank, turn on to his back and grab at his chest; then he too lay still.

The boy didn't move. It was as if he had become rivetted to the spot. It was Yvonne who turned and looked at the two prostrate figures, and she whimpered, "Oh mon Dieu! Mon Dieu! Oh, mon Dieu!" Then, pushing Harry, she gasped, "Fetch them, someone, fetch, quick!" And at this he seemed to come alive and, scrambing up the bank, he mounted a pony and galloped away.

Yvonne remained where she was for a full minute before she moved towards the old man. She did not kneel by him, but, standing, she looked down on him. His eyes were open, and his chest was heaving. Then she looked towards the boy. The water covering the stone was running in rivulets of red, but his face showed ashen white against his black hair. She did not attempt to go near him, in fact, she couldn't. There was a great weakness coming over her and as she stood there she prayed to die so she could blot the sight from her mind; and it appeared her prayer was answered, for she fainted.

The men coming out of chapel, some miners taking their well-earned rest on a Sunday morning, the farmers and the hands from two farms, all gathered at the spot. Some carried the body of the dead boy back to his parents' home, and others carried the live, but paralysed, body of the man known as his grandfather back to the farm. And the whole countryside was agog, for the boy's brother had become hysterical and blurted out what had actually happened, repeating it and repeating it until the doctor had calmed him down with laudanum.

11

❧

It was Thursday. There had been incessant comings and goings up till today, but today the house was quiet, for today the boy was being buried.

Monday had brought Hugh and Gabriel from Newcastle. They had stayed until this morning. Meanwhile Hugh had dealt with the constables and the police inspector who had come to deal with the case of a man who had killed a boy known as his grandson. But as Hugh and the doctor pointed out to them, the man was totally paralysed, being now utterly deprived of speech and movement; the only sign that he was still alive was that he breathed and that his eyes remained open, although they did not focus.

Tom had come but not his wife. Charles and Florrie had come, but they had not stayed for there was nothing they could do, at least not in this house. At Kate's it was different, they were needed there, for as Florrie said, Kate and Ben were utterly distracted.

There had been visits from neighbours who were more acquaintances than friends and whose purpose in calling was not so much to offer sympathy as to satisfy their curiosity. But today, the only ones in the house were its normal inhabitants. Mary Ellen spent most of her time in the bedroom; Maggie ran the house as usual and saw to Yvonne, who was still in some state of shock, being weighed down by a great sense of guilt at having brought about this tragedy.

One thing was in the minds of four of them this morning, particularly in that of Mary Ellen, and it was that they were burying the boy this day.

She was sitting by the side of the bed she and Hal had shared for the past forty-odd years. She had washed him as she had done each day since they had laid him down. She had changed the soiled drawsheet, a task that had to be seen to two or three times in the day. She had combed his hair and laid his hands on top of the counterpane. And now she talked to him, which was also part of the pattern she had set herself. "There," she said, "do you feel comfortable? That's better." She leant over and stroked a grey wisp from his forehead, then she added, "I'll shave you this afternoon. No ... I won't get John to do it" – it was as if he had spoken to her – "I'll do it myself."

"Hal." She raised herself on the chair and bent over him until she was looking into his wide eyes, and, her voice soft and quivering now, she said, "Do you think you could give me a sign, blink or something, if you understand what I'm sayin'? Could you try? Try, lad, try."

She waited for a response, and when none came she sat back in the chair, then went on talking, her voice low, the words tumbling over each other now: "I want you to know I don't blame you. I don't blame you for what happened. It was her. She must have encouraged the lad, and nobody's blaming you." Oh what a lie she knew that to be. "You did what anyone else would do, it was an accident. Don't blame yourself. And you'll soon be better, you will. You will." That was another lie, he'd never be better. The doctor said yesterday he could go tomorrow or not till next month, or even next year. She prayed it would be next year for she couldn't bear to lose him, he was her life, he had given her so much, all he had promised her on that day so far gone in the past: a family, a big house and servants.... No he hadn't given her the last, she'd never had servants, she'd had to work from dawn till dusk all her days. There had been Annie, but Annie wasn't a servant. And yet her family had all been servants in one way or another. But they hadn't minded ... or had they? She didn't know, not really. There was one thing certain, for as long as Hal lived she would be a servant to him. Oh, and gladly.

She turned her head towards the door. She thought she heard voices, loud voices. Yes, there they were. It was Maggie's voice and someone else's. She had just got to her feet when the door burst open and there stood, Ben. Beside him were Kate and Maggie. She rushed at him, crying, "No! Ben. No! Get out."

With a slow movement of his arm he thrust her aside, and she stumbled back against the wardrobe, her hand across her mouth, and watched him go to the foot of the bed and stare down at the inert figure, crying as he did so, "*You did it, didn't you? You did it at last*. You've been waiting to do it for years. You wanted to kill me. You've always been sorry you didn't, but now you've purged yourself of your hate. You've killed someone with Bannaman blood in him, and you meant to do it. For years you've been leading up to it, just waiting your opportunity. As the boy said, you were nothing to him. And ... and do you hear? you're nothing to my wife either. *Do you hear that?*"

"*Leave be! Get out!*" Mary Ellen was gripping his arm now, but he took no notice of her. It wasn't until Kate said, quietly, "Come away, Ben, come away, it's finished, entirely." Only then did he wrench his agonized staring gaze from the man in the bed.

When they were out on the landing Mary Ellen, pulling the door behind her, caught hold of Kate's arm, saying, "Wait a minute, lass." And at this Kate paused and let Ben go on, and, looking at her mother, she said, "Well, what is it?" And Mary Ellen muttered brokenly, "You could have stopped this, you know. You could have stopped this."

"I didn't want to stop it, Mam. He had a right to come and say what he did, and I agree with him. It's ended, finished, finally finished. That man in there, who was supposed to love me, and I once thought I loved him, but I daren't put a voice to the feeling I now have for him, he killed my son, battered him to death. And what might prove to be even worse he could make me lose my second son in a more agonizing way, for he's almost turned his brain. A boy who had a most promising future." She swallowed deeply, then said quietly, "He's ruined our family. And from now on, as Ben said, he's nothing to me. And I'll say this, Mam, I'll never darken these doors again."

"*Kate! Kate! Leave be.*"

Kate now turned and looked at Maggie, and, her voice still quiet, she said, "Yes, I'll leave be, Maggie, just one last word and to you. Get out, you've been a slave long enough." And with this she went down the stairs.

Maggie now turned to where her mother was leaning against the wall, her hand held over her eyes, and she said, gently, "Come and sit down." At this Mary Ellen shook her head and, turning blindly, stumbled back into the bedroom and closed the door.

Maggie, stood for a second looking at the closed door, then nodding to herself, she repeated Kate's words. Yes, she would get out, but she couldn't go straightaway. As she had said to Willy last night, they would have to stay for a little while till things settled down and Yvonne got into the swing of things. But God help that girl, for only He could.

Slowly she turned and went down the stairs, asking herself now what she meant by settled down, and the answer she got was, when her father died. She felt no sorrow at the thought. She had never cared for him because he had never cared for her. It had always been Kate, Kate. Now Kate spurned him, and justifiably, for had he not killed her son? But then he'd had to take revenge on a Bannaman to give purpose to his life, for as far back as she could remember she had been aware of the hate in him. And yet it had only risen to the surface when Kate met Ben, and she herself had disclosed his identity. So in a way she wasn't guiltless. But hadn't she always been aware of this? Oh yes, and it had soured her life. Well, enough was enough, from now on her life would be sweet. Once she got away from this house she would, in a way, be born again. Along with her child, she would be born again.

12

They talked about young Fraser Hamilton's funeral for weeks. There hadn't been anything like it seen around the countryside, some said, since the old duke had died years ago.

When the cortège had left the house it had been joined on the road by men from every walk of life: Men from the mine, men from the smelt mills. Farmers and dignitaries from Allendale, Haydon Bridge, Bardon Mill, Haltwhistle and Hexham waited in their coaches at the crossroads; and no one raised his eyebrows when the cortège was joined by the two Reilly men and the four Smith brothers from Allendale. And when an old drover and his son, cleaned up for the occasion, joined them at the cemetery gates, folks said: "There you are. He was liked by high and low. Of course he was a bit wild, but aren't all lads at that age? But there was no bad in him. In fact, recalling his pranks of early years only went to make him more lovable. Yes, of course he was brought home drunk, but that was devilment on the part of the Smith lads, the youngster would never have done it on his own. And he was settling down to work on the farm.

So the consensus of opinion was, it was a damn shame his life had been cut off as it had. And look what it had done to his father and mother. Broke them up completely. And there wasn't a more respected man round about than his father. Although he was an American, who still retained his Southern drawl, he had settled into the local ways and was known to be a generous employer. That was more than could be said for a lot of the farmers around and particularly for his supposed father-in-law.

Old Hal Roystan had had a seizure, else he would be along the line this minute, because it had been murder, plain and simple, murder. The young brother kept saying that. Of course there was another witness, but she denied having seen anything of the fight, as she had fainted. But that wasn't what the boy said about her. Of course she wouldn't speak against the old man, 'cos wasn't she going to marry the son.... Now there was a scandal for you, if ever there was one. A man forty years old marrying a bit lass like that. She was supposed to be nineteen. Nineteen, they could say that again. Seventeen would be more like the mark, and if that. And she was a foreigner. It had leaked out through Terry Briggs that she didn't get on very well with the missis either. Well, that was understandable wasn't it? Anyway, there was one thing sure now, they'd have to engage another hand or two on the farm, and likely the same inside an' all, for hadn't the daughter Maggie gone off the rails an' all. Now there was something. They said she'd got a bellyful through the cowman, him that dressed like his betters. But a bellyful, and at her age! By! The things that were happening on that farm. Anyway it just showed you, put a devil on horseback and he'd ride to hell. And what did he find when he got there? Just that he had to pay for his ride, and by God! Hal Roystan was being made to pay through the teeth for his. But odd, now wasn't it, that he should be going the same way that Bannaman went, paralysed, and deaf and dumb into the bargain, when he himself had helped to bring Bannaman to that state. Life was funny, they'd say. By! yes.

"You wish that I should go away?"

"No, no." As John pulled her to him and held her close and muttered vehemently, "Never. Never," he knew that what she proposed would help solve the problem of the house, yet he couldn't now let her go. Life had become grim, and how long it would go on he didn't know. Each day as he helped to turn his father from one side to the other and saw his mother's agonized face, he could see no end to the problem.

It was now five weeks since they had carried his father home, and still there was no change in him one way or the other, so he reckoned this pattern of life could go on year after year, and without the solace of this beautiful loving being in his arms he didn't know how he could stand it, nor, should she stay, what the strain would do to her. And this he said.

"I never want you to leave me, you know that, but can you stand this way of living? My mother shows no sign of changing. Life could become unbearable for you."

She looked up at him without speaking for a moment, and then she said, "As long as I have you, I will bear it. If I return to France I shall be alone, so ... so very much alone."

"Not for long." He shook his head. "You would marry."

He had not expected anything like her reply, for she said, "Yes, yes, I could. Most Frenchwomen, they want to marry, and I would likely, yes, yes, I would likely, but ... but it would be a convenience not a love."

He looked at her in silence. This is what people could not see in her, the adult, she looked so young, so girlish. And for this very reason he hadn't been into the town with her yet; in fact, he hadn't been into the town since before the funeral. Willy and Maggie had been doing the selling. My God! What would the place be like when they went? And that would be soon. Well, one thing he knew he must do before he was left on his own, and that was to face his mother and tell her he was going to see the parson about the banns.

He heard Maggie's step outside the kitchen door and, pressing

Yvonne from him, he went to the other side of the table, and as Maggie entered the room he was saying, "What are you going to make for us the day?"

And Yvonne answered, "Maggie is to show me pastry, the kind she uses for her pies." He looked towards Maggie, then asked her quietly, "Is Mam still up there?"

"No. She was in the office the last time I saw her."

As he turned to go up the kitchen, she said, "Your boots." And he, looking down at them, replied, "They're dry."

"That won't make any difference."

"They're staying on, Maggie."

She said nothing to this, but now asked, "You haven't forgotten that Willy and I are going over Corbridge way this afternoon?" And he paused for a moment, looking back at her before saying, "No, I haven't forgotten, Maggie."

He pushed open the door of the office and saw his mother sitting behind the desk at which his father had sat for years, and where he himself had never sat.

"May I have a word with you?" he said.

"Aye, yes." She looked up from an open ledger, saying, "They didn't do bad on Saturday. Surprising how the prices go up and down. Sit down, John; don't tower over me." Then she went on without pause, "Your dad thought of ploughing the east slope this year. He said it could be done. Joe Hodgson lives higher up than us and. . . ."

"Mam." He stopped her stalling. "I don't want to talk of Joe Hodgson's doings, or what Dad intended to do, I want to talk about me and my life ahead here. I'll come straight to the point. I'm seeing the parson on Sunday with regard to the banns. I'm marrying Yvonne, Mam, no matter what you or anybody else thinks. If I can't marry her here, then" – he paused and turned his gaze to the side now – "I'll marry her someplace else."

He watched her close the ledger, push it to one side, then draw a letter towards her, unfold it, and spread the corners out with her fingers before saying further, "You know what you're doing to me, Mam. You're checkering me life. I've never known any real happiness until I met her. From then I've sort of come alive; I know there's something else besides a fourteen-hour day grind. At least there's something for me at the end of it, not just the unhealthy prospect of waiting for Dad dying so I can take over, and, as things were, that could have been years ahead. But even as they are now, his toughness could keep him going for God knows how long."

"John! for you to talk like that."

"Mam, face up to facts. For God's sake! face up to facts."

She pulled herself up from the chair and, leaning her hands on the desk, she bent towards him and hissed, "I am. I'm the one that's facing up to facts, and the fact is you're expecting me to spend the rest of *my* life with that bit of a lass who reminds me every time me eyes rest on her, not only from where she springs, but for what she's brought on this house."

"She's brought nothing on this house, Mam." His voice was loud now. "Whatever has come about, Dad is responsible for. As Kate said, he's been wanting to do something to a Bannaman for years. He was baulked in doing it to Ben. Ben saved his life or else God knows what might have happened. In the face of that he had to change his tune. But from that lad was born, from the very first sight of his black hair and dark eyes, Dad loathed him, because he saw the Bannaman man, whoever he was, and his daughter, the woman who was supposed to torture him."

"*No suppose about it.*" She was yelling at him now. "She did, and tried to murder him in the process."

"Well, he got his own back, didn't he? He murdered a young lad. And now he's paying the price."

With a thud she dropped back into the chair, saying, quietly now, "Is that how you see your father?"

And as quietly he answered, "Yes, Mam, that's how I see my father. Because I've recognized for years that, latent in him, was a deep hatred, a feeling of revenge. His blustering couldn't cover it up. But now all this is in the past, it's beside the point. It's the future I'm putting to you, Mam, my future and Yvonne's. For marry we will, and if you don't change your attitude towards her and accept her into the household, then your life is going to be as miserable as you yourself make it. I've thought things out. I'll have a couple of rooms built on the west side and take in two of the bedrooms from the end up above. That'll give us a place of our own and you won't have to see her more than you need. And you'll need help in the house. I've already thought about that. There's the Conway twins. One won't stay without the other. Well, you'll need two lasses here to train up. They're sixteen and hard-working. Maggie had a word with them some time ago. They are more than willing to leave their place in Hexham. They don't like it, they want to be in the open air again, to be brought up in the wilds, so to speak. So there you are, there's the plan as I see it for the future."

"*In the name of God!*" Mary Ellen turned her head slowly to the side and looked down the room, and as if addressing someone at the far end, she said, "That it should come to this. Me lifetime's work should come to this. I've got to be told who's coming into me house. I've been given an ultimatum. It's a good job me mind's still clear and I still have the reins in me hand, else I'll be put into the workhouse." She now turned and looked fully at John, ending, "I can't believe it. I can't believe all this is happening to me. I just can't." Her voice broke; then on a high note that was almost like a thin scream, she said, "Get out! Get out of me sight. Go! Go on, go on."

And he went out and stood in the hall, his hand to his head. And when Maggie saw him standing like this she went up to him, saying gently, "Rough?"

He brought his hand slowly down over his face as if attempting to pull down a shutter, but he didn't speak, he just made a helpless motion and turned from her.

Maggie stood looking towards the office door as she thought, Thank God, in a little while it'll be all over. We'll clinch it this afternoon. Then once I've broken in the two lasses, I'll be gone. We'll be gone. And she wondered if she should go and remind her mother that she was going out this afternoon, but decided to leave it for a while, she'd just had a do with John. She'd talk to her when she took her father's tray up. . . .

It was two hours later when she went upstairs carrying the bowl of beef tea. As he could only swallow liquids this was his main form of nourishment. She knew she would find her mother sitting at the bedside talking to him. It was weird. She herself didn't believe he understood a word that was said to him, but her mother was convinced that he was aware of everything. The doctor had said it could be so or it couldn't be so; there was no way of telling unless he made some sign.

Outside the door, she heard the mumble of her mother's voice, and when she opened it she was saying, "This is one thing I won't be able to stand, Hal. I won't. I won't."

She turned as Maggie put the tray on the table to her side, and when, her voice low, Maggie said, "Remember, Mam, I'm going out this afternoon over to the place. It's the settling day. I'm going to get ready now," Mary Ellen said nothing, she just watched her daughter go from the room after having calmly told her she was going out of her life, was leaving her, leaving her with that chit downstairs. *Oh, no, no, no. No!* The last word was like a scream in her head and she jumped up from her chair and rushed to the door, to see Maggie going into her room, and she burst in on her, crying, "Maggie! Maggie!" Then came to a dead stop, and Maggie, her mouth agape, said, "What is it, Mam? What is it? Dad?"

Mary Ellen shook her head. Her lips opening and shutting, her breath now coming in great gasps, she cried, "Maggie. Maggie don't leave me. For God's sake! don't leave me." And with that and tears spurting from her eyes, she threw her arms around her daughter and clung to her crying, "Lass! Lass! For God's sake! have pity on me and don't leave me!"

Maggie could never remember her mother putting her arms around her. Whenever her hand had touched her it had been in the form of a push, and she had never forgotten the blows she received the day she had brought the news of Ben's relationship to the Bannamans. And now here she was being held by her and she was listening to her pleading through tearing sobs, "Lass! Lass! I'll do anything, anything you say, only don't go. Let him go. Let him go to France with her, only you stay with me. And Willy. Yes, and Willy."

Slowly Maggie raised her arms and put one hand on her mother's hair, saying, "There now, quiet yourself, Mam. Come and sit down. Come and sit down." And as she did so she thought of Annie, because two days before she had dropped down dead in the kitchen she had said those very words to her. She had had a row with her mother and when Mary Ellen had stormed out of the kitchen, Annie had put her arms around her shoulders and led her to the settle, and she had added, "Aw lass, aw lass, I know how you feel, in a way we are both in the same boat." It was as if she was linking them in spinsterhood.

When they were both sitting side by side on the bed, Maggie lifted up her mother's apron and rubbed it round her face, saying, "There now, there now. Stop it; you'll make yourself ill." Never before had she seen her mother cry, not in this fashion anyway. When Peg and Walter went all those years ago, she had wept, but not like this. And now she found her hands gripped, her mother was holding them tight against her chest, begging, "You won't, will you, Maggie? You won't?"

"Mam" – Maggie's voice was quiet – "Willy's already paid some money down and we're settling the rest this afternoon. It's all cut and dried."

She watched her mother now bow her head, then toss it from side to side as she said, "It doesn't matter. It doesn't matter about the money. Buy it, buy it, then sell it, only don't . . . don't go. For God's sake! girl, don't go. Who have I got left but you? The others don't give a damn. There's Hugh and Gabriel can't get back to that town quick enough; Tom's living his own life very much so; as for Florrie and Charles, they moved into another world. Oh, they're polite and attentive when they come, I know, but they're moving now higher up, at least she is, he's taking her there. And John. Oh John. I'd never have thought it, not of John, but if I want him to stay I've got to take her. And . . . and Maggie, Maggie, I can't. You know what I'd do if I was left alone with her? I'd finish off Hal. I would, I would, then take meself along with him. There's herbs and things."

"Shut up, Mam. Don't say such things."

"I am saying them, Maggie. I am saying them."

"But Mam, there's not only myself now, there's Willy, and where Willy goes, I go."

"I'll see Willy. He's . . . he's got a sure job here."

At this Maggie pulled herself from her mother's hold and along the bed and, her tone and her expression altering, she said, "Oh no, Mam, Willy doesn't just want a job. Willy's got the chance this day of starting his own farm, the same as you and Dad started years ago. Willy's worth something more than a cowman's position, or even that of foreman. Willy wants his own place, and so do I, Mam." She pushed her face forward now towards her mother. "Do you know, I've had nothing in me life. Do you know that, Mam? I've been an unpaid servant in this house. I . . . I haven't even had the compensation of affection."

"Aw, lass."

"Don't say it, Mam, don't make any excuses now, not at this late day. We're facing up to things at this minute, so let's stick to the truth. It was

Kate, Kate, Kate for years, and Florrie. Oh, yes, your dear sweet Florrie. And your sons, wonderful, wonderful sons. But Maggie? Oh, Maggie was a thorn in the flesh. Maggie had a sharp tongue which got bitter over the years. And why, Mam? because I . . . I was never loved. Strange, but there's always one in a family that's never loved, and I happen to be that one. Yes, I was the best looker and the best chatterer, the best entertainer for the company, but I was without love. Now I've found it, Mam, such as I've never imagined. It seems that I'm being paid for all the empty years in that way. Do you know how much money I have, Mam, for all the work I've put in this house for you? Thirty-six pounds, eight shillings. The rest of me wealth consists of a bit of jewellery, not worth much, and some clothes. So, Mam, when I leave here, I'm not losing anything, am I?"

"Maggie! Maggie! For God's sake, don't talk like that. I . . . I'll give what you want."

" 'Tisn't what I want, Mam, it's what Willy needs, what Willy expects out of life, what he's willing to work for. He wants a place of his own."

"He can have a place of his own, lass. I'll see to it. I'll see to it. I promise you. He can run the place and hire hands. I'll leave it strictly to him, I promise you."

When Maggie didn't answer but stared at her, she whimpered, "Maggie, Maggie, please, think on it. Ask him, ask Willy to come and see me."

As Maggie rose from the bed, her mother caught at her hand, beseeching, "Please."

"I'll have to see what he says, Mam."

"Tell him to come and see me, lass. He . . . he can make his own terms. He can, he can."

Maggie looked down onto the swimming face. The pale eyes were blurred with tears, they were running unheeded from her chin. This was her mother as she had never seen her before. This was her mother who needed her . . . simply because she hadn't anybody else. Nevertheless, she needed her, and because she hadn't anybody else she needed her with more strength, with more longing than if she had had the others around her. And she knew in this moment she couldn't leave her. She had said Willy could state his terms, and by God, yes, he would, and she would lay the terms out for him to state.

She nodded now, "I'll be back, Mam, shortly."

Out of the room, she ran down the landing, down the stairs, across the hall, out into the yard, calling, "Willy! Willy!"

Willy did not appear, but John came from a loose-box leading a big shire, and she called to him, "Have you seen Willy?"

"He was ploughing the low bent a while ago. He should be finished now."

She made to run down the yard in the direction of the fields, when she stopped and, scampering back to him, she caught hold of his arm and shook it as she said, "You can be free. You can go to France. You and Yvonne, you can be free."

"What? What are you saying?"

"I'll tell you when I get back." With this she picked up her skirt and tore down the yard, round the hay-stacks, round by the hen crees, climbed a five-barred gate, ran round the perimeter of two fields where the cows were grazing. Then she saw Willy handling the two shires up the plough. He had just reached the corner of the field on the last furrow when her cry came to him, and he pulled the horses to a stop with a "Whoa! there" and a "Stay!" and went to meet her, saying, "What is it? What is it, lass? Why you running like that? You shouldn't."

And now to his open-mouthed astonishment, she gabbled at him, "Which would you rather have, Willy? Morton House or this place?" And she flung her two arms wide.

"What's the matter, lass? What's the matter with you? What do you mean?"

Gabbling again, she told him what had transpired between her and her mother, and now, her voice slowing, she said, "She needs me. I've never thought to see her like that, pleading almost on her knees. But . . . but it's up to you, Willy, it's up to you."

He turned and looked at the two shires and the land about him, and he said slowly, "Has she said this'll be . . . ours?"

"As much, but—" Her voice now taking on a hard tone she added, "Whatever she says, I won't let it rest there. Oh, no, no. People can change once they think they've got you. Whatever happens everything will go in writing to the last detail."

"Aw, lass, lass." As he thrust out his arms, she flung hers about him and they held tightly, and he muttered on half a laugh, "Have you told her about next Saturday?"

"No, not yet. One thing at a time. But she won't mind that now. Well, well" – she laughed into his face – "I don't want me name up altogether, I'll have to marry the man, won't I?"

"You know something, Maggie?"

"No, Willy."

"You're a wonderful woman."

"You know something, Willy?"

"No. What, Maggie?"

"You're a wonderful man, and how I love you is past description."

After they had kissed, long and hard, he looked round him with a laugh and said, "I wonder if ever this has happened in a ploughed field afore?"

"I wonder. Anyway, bring them back" – she nodded towards the horses – "and tidy up. Then come in, and we'll talk."

*

"You're going to stay then, Willy? Oh thank you, thank you. I'm grateful, and you'll—" She was about to go on when Maggie interrupted, "There's conditions, Mam, and they've got to be settled."

"Yes, lass, yes. What kind of conditions?"

"John's going with Yvonne to France, isn't he?"

Mary Ellen sighed, then said, "Yes, yes, I've told him, the road's open if he wants to take it that way."

"Well, then, as I see it, Tom's well set, so is Hugh, and Gabriel." She did not mention Kate. "None of them have any real claim on this place because none of them has ever worked for it, except Gabriel for a few years. So, as I see it, if we have to come here for the rest of our lives, the farm should come to me . . . us, when anything happens to you. But I hope that's many, many a long year ahead. But in the meantime, I'd want it stated that we have a share with yourself in the place, and . . . and I'd want it in writing."

"*In writing, lass?*" Mary Ellen's face was screwed up as if in surprise.

"Yes, in writing, Mam, legally, so there'd be no mistake, no changing of minds on either of our parts. We couldn't walk out, no more than you could change your mind, if it's in writing."

Mary Ellen looked from one to the other and there returned to her eyes a spark that had been in the young girl's face, and the woman's, a spark that signalled determination to hang on to what was hers. But as quickly as it had come, it faded, and, bowing her head, she said, "Just as you say, lass. Just as you say."

There was an impulse in Maggie to rush forward and put her arms about this woman who was now acting like a stranger, so soft was her manner, and say, It doesn't matter. It doesn't matter, Mam. We'll take each other's word for it. But she was wise enough to know that characters didn't change entirely, they were only shaped temporarily by the circumstances, and that her mother could one day rise from this apathy. Perhaps when her life's partner had gone, and she had to fill her mind with something else, perhaps then, her dominant nature would rise once more, for she could never imagine her mother remaining the beaten creature she was now. So there had to be a safeguard.

Her mother now looked at Willy and said, "Yes, perhaps, it's just as well, as Maggie says. Perhaps you could have a talk with Hugh."

"No, Mam, not Hugh. It's better not to have anyone in the family deciding on what's to be done. That Mr Brown Dad deals with, he could see to it."

"All right, Maggie, all right."

"Mrs Roystan."

"Yes, Willy?"

"I must tell you straight and be open about it, I'd been looking forward to having me own place, but now that things have turned out the way they have, I can promise you I will give you of my best. Sharers, partners, or no, I'll try to make up to you for those you have lost."

Mary Ellen swallowed deeply; the tears came into her eyes again and she said, "Thank you, Willy. You were always a capable and likeable fellow. Thank you. But ... but there's one thing more besides your outside work, there is—" She now turned her eyes on Maggie, saying, "your dad. I need help to turn him every day."

"Oh, don't worry, Mrs Roystan about that, I'd be only too pleased to assist you in any way I can inside or outside. And now I don't know whether Maggie has told you, but we are to be married next Saturday in the registry office in Newcastle."

"Oh." Mary Ellen looked from one to the other, then said, "Well, yes, yes, I understand."

"But we won't be gone all that long, just the morning." He glanced at Maggie and she nodded at her mother, repeating, "Just the morning. Would you like a cup of tea, Mam?" And after a pause Mary Ellen said, "Yes. Yes, lass, I think I would, and a drop of something in it. I wouldn't say no, lass, I wouldn't say no."

As they both made to go out of the room, Mary Ellen said, "About the little place you were after, what do you intend to do?"

It was Willy who turned and said, "Oh, we'll have to stand the loss. I'll tell them this afternoon."

"I wouldn't do that; I would take it and put someone in. Land and property is good round Corbridge."

Willy said nothing, only made a motion with his head, and when they were both out in the hall, Willy stopped and said, "Now would you believe that? Would you believe that?"

Maggie nodded at him slowly. Yes, she would believe that. She had been right to insist on everything legal like; her mother was far from being finished. Oh yes, she was far from being finished.

In the kitchen, John and Yvonne were waiting for them, and Maggie said immediately, "'Tis all right. It's fixed."

"It is all right for you?" There was a shadow of the old brightness in Yvonne's face, and Maggie nodded as John said, "She agreed to it being legalized?"

"Yes, John, yes." Then she laughed and looked towards Willy, saying, "She did, didn't she, without a murmur? Yet, being Mother, not quite. Anyway, you two" – she held out her hands, one to each of them – "you're free now. Like us, you can start a life together. It's come late in the day for both of us." She looked at John. "But there's a saying, you know: You should never pluck a herb before it is fully ripe."

At this John put his arms around her, and she about him, and they clung together for a moment. And she thought: How strange, I've had to wait, too, until I'm forty before my brother embraces me.

Quietly now, she turned from him and went towards Willy and, taking his waiting hand, she gripped it. She would have all the embraces she needed in life from now on. And when her child was born, be it male or female, she would see that it was cuddled and held as a baby, and that never in its life would it be starved for affection. So whatever it did in life, good, bad, or indifferent, could not be laid at the door of a starved life. Moreover, she would teach it not to hate.